Séfer haḤinnuch סֵפֶר הַחִנּוּךְ

THE BOOK OF [MITZVAH] EDUCATION

סֵפֶר הַחִנּוּךְ

כנראה מאת רבנו פנחס
(אחיו של רבנו אהרן) הלוי
איש ברצלונה

מהדורה מנוקדת, מבוססת על
ההוצאה הראשונה (ונציה רפ״ג)
בהשוואה עם ארבעה כתבי־יד עתיקים,
עם תרגום והערות באנגלית, מאת
אלחנן וֶנגרוֹב

כרך שני: ספר ויקרא, חלק ראשון

הוצאת ספרים פלדהיים
ירושלים / ניו יורק / תשד״ם

Séfer haḤinnuch

THE BOOK OF [MITZVAH] EDUCATION

evidently by Rabbi Pinḥas
(brother of Rabbi Aaron) haLévi
of Barcelona

the Hebrew text (with *n'kudoth*)
based on the first edition (Venice 1523)
compared with four old manuscripts,
with a translation and notes, by
Charles Wengrov

VOLUME II: LEVITICUS, PART 1

FELDHEIM PUBLISHERS
Jerusalem / New York / 5744 (1984)

הוצאת ספרים פלדהיים בע"מ
ירושלים

First published 1984
ISBN 0-87306-296-5
(The set: ISBN 0-87306-145-4)

Philipp Feldheim Inc.
200 Airport Executive Park
Spring Valley, NY 10977

96 East Broadway
New York, NY 10002

Feldheim Publishers Ltd
POB 6525 / Jerusalem, Israel

Printed in Israel

מכתב ברכה

ממרן הגאון ר' מרדכי גיפטר שליט"א

YESHVAT TELSHE
Kiryat Telshe Stone
Jerusalem

Rabbi Mordechai Gifter
President

ישיבת טלז
קרית טלז-סטון
ירושלים

הרב מרדכי גיפטר
ראש הישיבה

ב"ה

יקירי מאד נעלה ר' ישראל נ"י, שלום וברכה נצח!

לשמחה רבה היא לי הבשורה שהנך עומד להוציא לאור את ספר החינוך באנגלית.
החינוך הרי הוא מיסודי הספר החשוב לתרי"ג מצוות ה', לפי פשוטם השקול, יעזה לכך
שמאירות ומשכילות העוסק במעשה עצמה בתוספות בקביעות ההלכה שבכל מצוה,
ובזה נעשה החינוך ז"ל הפוסק והגדול בדבר.
ואחד מטעמי המצוות שבדרש החינוך ז"ל בכל מצוה - אשר דבר לא בעוני ספרי ההלכה -
ודרך שימוש להם דבר שטעמי המצוות לפי פשטות הכתובים - וכמבואר שנאמר
ספרי ביאור הבאור - והדרש של רבותינו הראשונים ז"ל הלבוש הכתובים
מחשבים עמוקות הדבר והמעון בטעם המצוות, וכמה פעמים הטעם
משמש להבנת גדר ההלכה. והדברים מעוררים לב ונפש שמן יהא הלב
המצוה המצוה, ושרה עומדת אשר רק היא מצוה בפרטיה, אשר קדושתם
מלאה מורשת התורה הקדושה - כמבואר בס' "נפש החיים" - כי כל מצוה
ונהרה אור, שכל מצוה נקבעת בקדושה מאותו אור ה' הצפון בתורה.
נקבעין הקפדות של החינוך בהקדמתו מעוררים לב ונפש
~~[illegible]~~ בדרך של תורה שבמצוה, למען יהא המעיין מושך
התורה לקיום מצותיה.
ואסמוך ידי שבאמת המחשבה שהוא בתרגום נאמן לרוח
החינוך והדברים יהא לפני עיני ר"ה שיבדקו הדברים לנקודת
כל שמצוה. ויהא השמים יזה פרי ברכה לבל ילה הבאמת לבש
ה' אשר השפה האנגלית קרובה להם, ומעוררו בזה להתקרב
לדברים גם המקרים.
ויזכה ה' לברך את המעשה. באהבה,
שרפי

contents — תוכן הענינים

List of abbreviations, etc.

§	numbered section or *mitzvah*
ad loc.	*ad locum*, at the place
b.	*ben*, the son of
cf.	*confer*, compare
col.	column
Deut.	the Book of Deuteronomy (*d'varim*)
ed.	edition of; edited by; editor
e.g.	*exempli gratia*, for example
et al.	*et alii*, and others (i.e. people)
etc.	*et cetera*, and others
et seq.	*et sequentes*, and the following
Ex., Exod.	the Book of Exodus (*sh'moth)*
ff.	and pages following
Gen.	the Book of Genesis (*b'réshith*)
Guide	Rambam (R. Moshe b. Maimon, Maimonides), *Guide of the Perplexed* (*Moreh N'vuchim*)
ibid.	*ibidem*, at the (same) place
idem	the same (person)
i.e.	*id est*, that is
l.	line
Lev.	the Book of Leviticus (*va-yikra*)
loc. cit.	*loco citato*, in the place cited
MdRSbY	*Midrash d'Rabbi Shimon b. Yoḥai* (ed. Epstein-Melamed)
MH	R. Joseph Babad, *Minḥath Ḥinnuch* (commentary on the *Ḥinnuch*)
MhG	*Midrash haGadol*, anthology of Midrash, etc. compiled in Yemen, 14th century
MS (plural, MSS)	*manuscriptum*, manuscript (plural, *manuscripta*, manuscripts)
MT	Rambam (R. Moshe b. Maimon, Maimonides), *Mishneh Torah* (also known as *Yad Ḥazakah*)
MY	R. Yitzḥak *ha-kohén* Aronovsky, *Minḥath Yitzḥak* (commentary on the *Ḥinnuch*)
n.s.	new series
Num.	the Book of Numbers (*ba-midbar*)
op. cit.	*opera citato*, in the work cited
o.s.	old series
p. / pp.	page / pages
q.v.	*quod vide*, which see
R.	Rabbi, Rabbénu, Rav
ShM	Rambam (Maimonides), *Séfer haMitzvoth*
sic	so, thus (i.e. something that looks peculiar is so in the source cited)
s.v.	*sub verbo*, *sub voce*, under the word (or words)
TB	*Talmud Bavli*, Babylonian Talmud
TJ	*Talmud Yerushalmi*, Jerusalem Talmud
viz.	*videlicet*, namely

Translator's Preface

THE ATTRIBUTION OF AUTHORSHIP

The translator's preface to the first volume began by noting that among the writers of well-known Torah literature in the Middle Ages, the author of *Séfer haḤinnuch* had the fairly rare distinction of being anonymous. It may now be assumed, at least tentatively, that this distinction has been taken from him, by evidence given in a scholarly article (in Hebrew) that appeared in Elul 5740 (September 1980): "The author of *Séfer haḤinnuch*," by Rabbi Yisrael Ta-Shma.[1]

Until the appearance of the article, the situation was as I outlined it in my previous preface. On the blank first page of an early manuscript of the work, dated 5093 (1333), it was written (apparently later), "I have heard that the author of this work was R. Aaron of blessed memory." On the title-page of the first printed edition, Venice 5283 (1523), we find a notation by the editor: "*Séfer haḤinnuch*, which R. Aaron of blessed memory composed." The editor, however, indicated no source for his notation.[2] In 5309 (1549), in a work that in the main chronicles Torah sages and scholars through the centuries, R. Aaron haLévi of Barcelona is duly listed; whereupon the author adds: "and I say that perhaps it is he who composed *Séfer haḤinnuch*."[3] In a later work of the same nature, written in 5437 (1677), there is no expression of doubt. The author states of R. Aaron haLévi, "he was a great rabbi, and he composed works of commentary on the Talmud, and also produced *Séfer haḤinnuch*..."[4]

It was a natural, perhaps inevitable, assumption to make. As I noted, toward the end of his Preface our author identifies himself as "a Jew of the house [tribe] of Lévi, of Barcelona"; and this R. Aaron was the most prominent Talmudic scholar generally known who fit the description.

1. מחברו האמיתי של ספר "החינוך", מאת י. תא־שמע in *Kiryat Sefer* 55:4, Elul 5740 (September 1980), pp. 787–790. The article was called to my attention by my good friend Prof. David Tamar. I have been further helped by a short paper on the subject (unpublished) written by Rabbi David Metzger, a research scholar in Jerusalem, at the suggestion of my publisher. Rabbi Metzger (a friend and colleague) placed his work at my disposal, for which I am grateful.

2. S. H. Kook, *'Iyyunim uMeḥkarim*, II, Jerusalem 5723 (1963), p. 316.

3. R. G'dalyah ibn Yaḥya, *Shalsheleth haKabbalah*; in the edition of Jerusalem 5722 (1962) it is on p. 129.

4. R. David Conforte, *Koré haDoroth*; in the Berlin 5606 (1846) edition it is on p. 22b.

Moreover (as I noted), in the second edition of the *Ḥinnuch*, Venice 5360 (1600), at the beginning of the second paragraph of §95 a marginal note points out that after the phrase "my brethren the Levites" the third word which follows is the name Aaron (in reference to the *kohen gadol*, the "high priest"); "in this," states the marginal note, "there is a hint that the author's name was Aaron...and that he was a Levite or a *kohen*; כ״ש." On the title-page, however, it is merely stated, "Composed in times of yore by a Levite of Barcelona whose name was widely known." Evidently the assertion on the title-page of the first edition, supposedly confirmed by the marginal note recorded above, was not yet "widely known" or not yet accepted. In fact, the abbreviation at the end of the note (given above) was astutely "decoded" by one researcher as *kén shama'ti*, "so I heard":[5] At that time the ascription of the work to R. Aaron haLévi was, if you will, in the early stages of rumor and hearsay. It evidently gained currency and acceptance, however, for it eventually appeared in such halachic works as *Séder Eliyahu* (by R. Elijah Alfandari), *Sifthé Kohen* ("the *shach*"), and *P'ri M'gadim.*[6] In these works it was merely stated in passing, as something known. No evidence was ever offered to substantiate the claim. Yet for many the ascription thus acquired an authority (as though it were a statement of *halachah*) that virtually put it beyond question. From 5559 (1799) onward his name appears regularly in every edition of *Séfer haḤinnuch* as the author, until present times.[7] In the major Jewish libraries of the world, the work is likewise so catalogued, but with the added qualification, "ascribed to" (or מיוחס לו).

DOUBT AND REFUTATION

The first to cast doubt on the assumption was the noted master of *halachah* and *kabbalah*, R. Ḥayyim Yosef David Azulai (popularly known as *Ḥida*, the acronym of his name). In his pioneering work of rabbinic bibliography, *Shém haG'dolim*, which he published in 5534 (1774: part I) and 5546 (1786: part II), he writes in part I, letter *'alef*, §132, s.v. *Rab-*

5. S. H. Kook, *op. cit.* p. 319.

6. **(a)** R. Elijah Alfandari (5430?/1670?–5477/1717; *av beth din* in Constantinople), *Séder Eliyahu Rabbah v'Zuta* (Constantinople 5479/1719), p. 67a. **(b)** R. Shabb'thai b. Meir haKohen (5381/1621–5422/1662; recognized *posék* in Lithuania), *Sifthé Kohen*, commentary on the *Shulḥan 'Aruch*: on *Yoreh Dé'ah* — §25, 1 (2); §70, 6 (33); §157, 1 (9); on *Ḥoshen Mishpat* — §33, 2 (1), 4 lines from the end. **(c)** R. Yosef b. Meir Teomim (c. 5487/1727–5552/1792; East European halachic authority), *P'ri M'gadim*, two supercommentaries on the *Shulḥan 'Aruch*: Preface to *Mishb'tzoth Zahav* (commentary on *Turé Zahav*) on *'Oraḥ Ḥayyim*, directly after the subheading גם אלה דברי המחבר נר״ו.

7. S. H. Kook, *op. cit.* p. 317.

bénu Aharon haLévi: "There is a statement current among rabbinic scholars, to be found in their written works, that R. Aaron haLévi composed *Séfer haḤinnuch*. So wrote R. Elijah Alfandari in *Séder Eliyahu*, fol. 67; and so [is it stated] in *Séfer haḤinnuch* itself, in a note in a printed edition, at the beginning of *sidrah t'rumah*.[8] This may be doubted somewhat, however, for by and large, when he [the anonymous author] mentions Ramban [the *rav muvhak*, main Torah instructor, of R. Aaron haLévi] he writes *zichrono livrachah* (of blessed memory), whereas many times he writes, 'from the teaching of my master instructor, may God preserve him.' This too I would adduce: that we find several times that the view of R. Aaron haLévi contradicts what is written in *Séfer haḤinnuch*." In part II of *Shém haG'dolim*, letter *ḥeth*, § 80, s.v. *Ḥinnuch*, he states, "It was written in *P'ri M'gadim* [on *Shulḥan 'Aruch*] *'Oraḥ Ḥayyim*, in the section titled *Mishb'tzoth Zahav*, in the Preface, that R. Aaron haLévi composed it; and so wrote a number of *aḥaronim* (later authorities); but in *Shém haG'dolim* part I ... I expressed doubt about it."

Now, regarding Ramban and *Séfer haḤinnuch*, in *Shém haG'dolim* part I, after the passage cited above, R. Ḥayyim Yosef David Azulai continues, "Know, however, that in *mitzvah* § 326 [§ 330 in our edition] toward the end, it appears that it was in the year 5017 (1257) [that the author wrote it], and Ramban migrated to the holy city of Jerusalem in the year 5027 (1267); yet he writes of him *zichrono livrachah*, as noted. Perhaps it is a scribal error." In other words, whether or not Ramban was our author's master teacher, the addition of the phrase "of blessed memory" after his name is a patent difficulty: for if our author wrote the *Ḥinnuch* in 5017 (1257) as he states, Ramban was very much alive then.

This question was taken up in my previous preface (vol. 1, p. xiv). I noted there that on the evidence of the early manuscripts, the date of 5017 must be accepted as accurate, and we must assume that in the author's original draft he put a suitable encomium after Ramban's name wherever it appeared, to wish him long life and/or Heaven's protection; then it must have been changed by later copyists of the manuscript work, when Ramban was no longer among the living. The key point about Ramban, however, is that whatever our author may have added after his name, nowhere does he refer to him in any way as his *rav muvhak*, his main, decisive instructor in Torah. Contrastingly, when our author mentions his master teacher, he invariably leaves him unnamed; and the views he cites in the name of his master teacher are not always in accord

8. This is the marginal note in the edition of Venice 5360 (1600), mentioned in the previous paragraph.

with the views of Ramban.[9] Yet Ramban was the *rav muvhak* of R. Aaron haLévi, whom R. Aaron accepted as his authority. How can it then be contended that R. Aaron wrote *Séfer haḤinnuch*?

More compelling, however, is R. Ḥayyim Yosef David Azulai's second point. In 5368 (1608) a volume of *halachah* by R. Sh'lomo ibn 'Adreth (Rashba) titled *Torath haBa-yith ha'Aruch* was printed in Venice. Subtitled (in several editions) *dinim ha-tz'richim l'béth ha'adam* (necessary laws for a person's home),[10] the work was (and always has been subsequently) printed together with *Bedek haBa-yith* by R. Aaron haLévi: a compilation of *hassagoth* (criticisms, refutations, differing views) in opposition to Rashba. (The two were contemporaries, both living in the city of Barcelona.) Thus a considerable number of R. Aaron's views and rulings in *halachah* came to be known. And scholars began to notice instances where *Séfer haḤinnuch* agrees with Rashba and differs with R. Aaron haLévi.

The first, apparently, to note such an instance was the scholar and sage R. Ḥayyim ibn 'Attar;[11] and on the basis of this, in a work on the 613 *mitzvoth* published in 5564 (1804) one learned rabbi declared that in his opinion R. Aaron was not the author of the *Ḥinnuch*.[12] At about the same time, R. Ephraim Zalman Margolioth (author of *Mattéh Ephraim* on the laws of Rosh haShanah and Yom Kippur) noted another difference in *halachah* between the *Ḥinnuch* and R. Aaron haLévi, and he wrote: "Now, from this it will be clear to you that the author of *Séfer haḤinnuch* is not R. Aaron haLévi of blessed memory, as many have thought... On the contrary, I have shown from several instances that the author of *Séfer haḤinnuch* was one of the disciples of Rashba."[13]

In writing his great commentary on our author's work, titled *Minḥath Ḥinnuch*, R. Yosef Babad took note of several other such instances of disagreement. Focusing on the problem in his scholarly monograph, David Rosin added an appendix listing five such instances, and seven more, in which *Séfer haḤinnuch* differs from views of R. Aaron found in other sources, principally in the Talmudic commentaries of R. Aaron's

9. So notes Rabbi Yisrael Ta-Shma in his article, p. 787.

10. In bibliographies the work is described as דיני איסור והיתר ונדה "laws of the forbidden and the permitted, and the menstrually defiled."

11. R. Ḥayyim ibn 'Attar (5456/1696–5503/1743), *P'ri To'ar*, commentary on *Shulḥan 'Aruch Yoreh Dé'ah*, printed together with *P'ri Ḥadash* by R. Ḥizkiyah da Silva, in *Péroth Ginosar*, Amsterdam 5502 (1742): §61, 23 (34).

12. R. Noaḥ Ḥayyim Tz'vi Berlin, *Ma'yan haḤochmah*, Rödelheim 5564 (1804), p. 117b, s.v. *'od*.

13. R. Ephraim Zalman Margolioth (5520/1760–5588/1828), *Béth Ephraim*, Lvov 5570 (1810): *kuntres ha-r'a'yoth*, §39, 3 (116a).

disciple R. Yom Tov b. Abraham Ishbili (i.e. of Seville), known as Ritba.[14] In his study of the subject, Rabbi Charles B. Chavel lists nine further instances of disagreement between *Séfer haḤinnuch* and *Bedek haBayith.*[15] To cap it all, in 5719 (1959) R. Yosef Kafeḥ published from manuscript the responsa of Ritba, the disciple of R. Aaron haLévi. There he found two rulings of R. Aaron given, with which, again, *Séfer haḤinnuch* differs.[16]

There is thus a considerable body of evidence to oppose the assertion that he was its author. Yet the question remains: Who did write *Séfer haḤinnuch?*

EVIDENCE FOR IDENTIFICATION

With the publication of other writings of R. Aaron haLévi, the solution to the problem began to emerge. Strangely enough, it was to be R. Aaron himself who would give our author's identity away. Yet as fate would have it, the evidence remained unrecognized or unappreciated (or perhaps unaccepted) until the present.

In Mainz, 5634 (1874), R. Simḥah and R. Nathan Bamberger published (from manuscript) a work of R. Aaron's titled *P'kudath haL'vi-im*: his commentary to the compendium of R. Isaac 'Alfasi (Rif) covering the Talmud tractates *B'rachoth* and *Ta'anith.* In the section on *B'rachoth* (edited by R. Simḥah Bamberger), on pp. 95–96 (misnumbered 93–94), we read:

"ורב׳ אחא ז״ל מפריש[17] that the reason for [the precept of] the bird's

14. R. Yosef Babad (5560/1800–5634/1874; rabbi in Tarnopol), *Minḥath Ḥinnuch*, Lemberg 5629 (1869): e.g. part II, 7b top; 52b toward the end of §147 (noted in R. Chavel, ed. *Séfer haḤinnuch*, p. 800). David Rosin, *Ein Compendium der jüdischen Gesetzeskunde* (Jahresbericht des jüdisch-theologischen Seminars), Breslau 1871 (also offprint): Appendix 5, pp. 131–134. His first numbered instance is the one recorded by R. Ephraim Zalman Margolioth (see note 13). His eleventh numbered instance is the one noted by R. Elijah Alfandari, which was mentioned by R. Ḥayyim Yosef David Azulai in his *Shém haG'dolim* (see five paragraphs above, and note 6). Before the eleven numbered instances he presents yet one more, relating to the order of the Passover *séder* given by our author in §21.

15. R. Chavel, ed. *Séfer haḤinnuch*, pp. 401–403.

16. R. Yosef Kafeḥ, ed. *R. Yom Tov b. Abraham Ishbili (Ritba): Responsa, published from manuscript*, Jerusalem 5719 (1959): Introduction, p. 16. The second instance is cited also by R. Chavel in *Séfer haHashlamah l'Minḥath Ḥinnuch*, New York 5712 (1952), p. 133; and by R. Kalman Kahane in an appendix to his edition of *Séfer haZikkaron* by Ritba, Jerusalem 5716 (1956). The relevant ruling of R. Aaron, with which the *Ḥinnuch* differs, was known to them from other sources.

17. The meaning of these words will be considered below.

nest[18] is to compel [belief that] the nature of the Lord's watchful care over other species, apart from man, is over the species [in general] — in other words, over the endurance of the species, but not of their individual members — except for the human being alone: as it is stated of him, *For His eyes are on (all) the ways of a man, and all his steps does He see* (Job 34:21). And perhaps this is [the sense of] what is written in the account of Creation regarding the formation of the animals, beasts and birds, 'after their kind,' 'after their kind' (Genesis 1:21, 24, 25): meaning, for the continuation of the existence of the species. And this is the reason for [the precept of] 'it [an animal] and its young,' forbidding their ritual slaying in one day (Leviticus 22:28). For some of the precepts are to make us know true concepts: as the subject of the Sabbath [attests] to the wholly new creation of the world [it was not eternally in existence]; and the reason for a railing [around a roof] (Deuteronomy 22:8) is to have us know that it is right and proper for a person to be safeguarded from accidents, and afterward he can reflect that he did what he could do and what it was in his power to do, after which the matter is in the sphere of power of his Creator... So too, some of the precepts are to proclaim and [make us] know of the fulfillment of true [Divine] promises: such as the matter of the 'covenant of salt' (Leviticus 2:13), since it is known that salt keeps things from spoiling, and so too the covenant of our God (be He exalted) is to be for us [the means of] the survival of the soul to [enjoy] good... to give us hope and an aftermath in this world and the world-to-come. For a similar purpose there is the prohibition of the *gid ha-nasheh*, the sinew of the thigh-vein (Genesis 32:33) to make us know the promise to [the people] descended from the loins of Jacob, that they shall not perish in the exile, though they suffer tribulations. Therefore he [Jacob's adversary] touched the hollow of his thigh, making him limp, but could not prevail against him to destroy him; and he was the celestial prince of Esau. *The sun* of healing *shone for him* [Jacob], adumbrating the Messiah, *as he passed through Penuel* (Genesis 32:32)..."

R. Aaron haLévi presents reasons, purposes, lessons to be learned from six *mitzvoth*; and as R. Simḥah Bamberger (the editor of *P'kudath haL'vi-im* on the section of *B'rachoth*) points out in his notes to this

18. I.e. that if we find by chance a nest with a mother-bird and its young, we may take the fledglings but must send the mother-bird away to its freedom (Deuteronomy 22:6–7). The passage relates to a teaching in the Mishnah (*B'rachoth* v 3; TB 33b): "If one says in his prayer 'To a bird's nest do Thy mercies reach' . . . he is silenced." Hence this precept does not mean that His merciful care extends to an individual bird; and from this the cited passage ensues.

passage, all are to be found in *Séfer haḤinnuch.*[19] Indeed, similarities between the parallel passages in the two sources, in both ideas and phrasing, are often striking. R. Aaron haLévi, however, gives the whole passage not in his own name but in the name of a certain *Rabbénu Aḥa*; and the question arises: Who is he?

At first glance we might read R. Aaron's introductory words as *Rabbénu Aḥa... miParis.* From the context, however, it is obvious that the last word is a verb; and in his preface to a reprint edition of *P'kudath haL'vi-im* (New York 5717/1957), Rabbi Moses Y. Blau notes in passing (p. 5, note 2) that מפריש is merely an error for מפרש, "explains" or "interprets." As for R. Aḥa, in his notes R. Simḥah Bamberger refers the reader to "the preface"; but the volume has two: one (the original) by R. Aaron haLévi, and one added by Rabbi Bamberger.

In his preface, explaining why he wrote the work, R. Aaron writes that Talmudic study is generally very difficult for many; "therefore the hand of my brother R. Joshua the Levite, son of my master, brother and teacher, R. Pinḥas haLévi of blessed memory, was upon me. He... poured out his entreaty before me to explain for him the *halachoth* of R. Isaac 'Alfasi of blessed memory, which are like a small Talmud."

R. Aaron refers to both R. Joshua and R. Pinḥas as "my brother"; yet R. Joshua is R. Pinḥas's son! The answer to this is quite simple, however: The first "my brother" is a title of honor that a fond uncle accorded his nephew. R. Pinḥas, whom he also he calls his master and his teacher, and who was no longer alive at the time he was writing, was evidently R. Aaron's older brother.

In directing the reader to "the preface," however, R. Simḥah Bamberger was referring not to this but to his own words in his introductory pages: "It seems to my humble mind that in writing ... *Rabbénu Aḥa of blessed memory*, this great scholar meant his brother R. Pinḥas, who was mentioned by him" (p. 6, note 11). In other words, רבי׳ אחא is to be understood as a disguise for something like רבי, אחי "my teacher, my brother," whom R. Aaron identified in his preface.

For this interpretation of *Rabbénu Aḥa* there are, actually, two confirmations by *rishonim* (early Torah scholars).

R. Aaron haKohen of Lunel is known to have been roughly contemporary with R. Aaron haLévi of Barcelona.[20] In his *'Orḥoth Ḥayyim*, a

19. Respectively: the precept about the bird's nest, §545; the precept not to slay an animal and its young the same day, §294; about the Sabbath, §§31–32; about putting a railing at the edges of one's roof, §546; about the "covenant of salt" (not to bring any offering to the altar unsalted), §119; about the sinew of the thigh-vein, §3.

20. By the Hebrew calendar, he lived in the first century of the sixth millennium

compilation of halachic rulings and laws by early authorities, which he evidently wrote some time after R. Aaron HaLévi's death, we find this: "Now, R. Aaron haLévi of blessed memory wrote in the name of R. Pinḥas haLévi of blessed memory that the reason for [the precept of] the bird's nest is to firmly establish that the watchful care of the blessed Lord over other species is general for the species, not individual; but for the human being alone it is individual, as it is stated, *His eyes are on (all) the ways of a man* (Job 34:21). The reason for [the precept of] 'it and its young' is to make us know this [same] concept. And [thus] many precepts are to make known true conceptions regarding [their particular] subject: the Sabbath, about the creation of the world as a new [previously non-existent] entity; and the reason for [the precept of] the railing is to have us know that it is right and proper for a person to beware of chance, accidental happenings, so that afterward he can reflect that he has done what lay in his power to do, after which the matter lies in the domain of his Creator..."[21]

Thus, according to a contemporary source, the passage in *P'kudath haL'vi-im* about the reasons or purposes of certain *mitzvoth* derived not from "Rabbénu Aḥa" but from a Torah scholar named R. Pinḥas haLévi. The only way to make sense of this is to accept R. Simḥah Bamberger's explanation that by "Rabbénu Aḥa" R. Aaron meant *rabbénu 'aḥi*, "our master teacher, my brother," whom he named in his preface as R. Pinḥas haLévi.

Now for the second confirmation: In 5646 (1886) a volume was printed in Jerusalem under the title of *'Ohel Mo'éd, part 1*, the author's name being given as R. Sh'mu'el b. M'shullam Yerondi (=Gerondi, "of Gerona"). Apart from a number of citations by R. Yosef Caro in his commentary *Béth Yoséf* on the *Tur* (somewhere about 5310/1550),[22] and

(somewhere between 1260 and 1340). R. Aaron haLévi's life ended in 5090 (1330).

21. R. Aaron haKohen of Lunel, *'Orḥoth Ḥayyim*, II, Berlin 5662 (1902), p. 439, toward the bottom of the page. Though he is known as R. Aaron haKohen of Lunel, from internal evidence in *'Orḥoth Ḥayyim* it seems more likely that he lived in Narbonne; but both Lunel and Narbonne are in southern France, not too far from R. Aaron haLévi's city of Barcelona in northeast Spain. Moreover, in 5066 (1306) R. Aaron haKohen was among those who were expelled from France by Philip IV, and he eventually settled in Majorca. Thus, most likely, he passed through the region of Aragon in northeast Spain, which includes Barcelona. Hence he may well have identified "Rabbénu Aḥa" as R. Pinḥas haLévi from current local or regional knowledge that he had.

22. As attested by R. Ḥayyim Yosef David Azulai in his *Shém haG'dolim*, II, letter *'alef*, § 36; e.g. in *Béth Yoséf* to *Tur 'Oraḥ Ḥayyim* §70: par. 2, s.v. *kathuv* (noted by L. Grünhut in *Jewish Quarterly Review*, o.s. XI, 1898, p. 345).

one citation almost a century later,[23] the work and its author are virtually unknown. However, the appellation *Yerondi* after his name indicates that he came from Gerona, where Ramban and his disciple Rabbénu Yonah lived; and Gerona and Barcelona (the city of R. Aaron haLévi) are both in the region of Aragon in northeast Spain. From a manuscript copy of *'Ohel Mo'éd* we learn that its author was born in 5095 (1335), and he wrote (or completed) it in 5156 (1396).[24] As R. Aaron haLévi's life ended in 5090 (1330), *'Ohel Mo'éd* was thus written less than a century after *P'kudath haL'vi-im*, and in the same general region of Torah study.

On page 56a of *'Ohel Mo'éd* we find: "And R. Aaron haLévi wrote in the name of his brother the wise scholar R. Pinḥas haLévi that the reason for [the precept of] the bird's nest is to firmly establish that the watchful care of the blessed Lord is general for a species and not individual—for [all] other species except the human, over which it is individual, as it is written, *His eyes are on (all) the ways of a man*. And many *mitzvoth* are to make known His true thought: [for example] in regard to the Sabbath, the creation of the world as a new [previously non-existent] entity."[25]

23. R. Ḥizkiyah da Silva (5419/1659–5455/1695), apparently in his *P'ri To'ar* (see above, note 11). The passage was cited from there by R. Yeḥezkel Landau in his *Noda biYhudah*, II, *Yoreh Dé'ah*, 29 (L. Grünhut, *loc. cit.*, and see note 5 there).

24. Sh'mu'el Wiener, *K'hillath Mosheh*, Petrograd 5643 (1893)–5678 (1918), p. 39, § 324. This reference and the one to Grünhut (in note 22, above) are given in R. Menaḥem M. Kasher and Jacob Mandelbaum, *Sarei haElef*, 2nd edition, p. 365, §6; 1909, however, should be corrected to 1898.

Grünhut writes (*loc. cit.* p. 345) that on p. 36a of *'Ohel Mo'éd* there is a *tofes ha-get*, an example of a bill of divorcement (to be followed as a model), and the date it bears is 5080 (1319); and Grünhut takes this to indicate when *'Ohel Mo'éd* was written. The evidence adduced by Wiener, however, is direct: statements by the author in a manuscript copy of the work. His dates for the work and for the author's birth must therefore be accepted, and we can only postulate that the author copied the *tofes ha-get* from an earlier source, which dated from the year 5080.

25. In his preface to the reprint edition of *P'kudath haL'vi-im* (New York 5717/1957, p. 5), Rabbi Moses Y. Blau cites this passage, and in a note (2) he points out that since R. Aaron haLévi wrote it in *P'kudath haL'vi-im* in the name of "Rabbénu Aḥa," we may assume that by this name R. Aaron always meant his brother R. Pinḥas (e.g. "Rabbénu Aḥa" occurs again in *P'kudath haL'vi-im* on *B'rachoth*, on p. 147; see note 34 there). Then Rabbi Blau continues: In R. Aaron's novellae (*ḥiddushim*) on Talmud tractate *K'thuboth*, several times we find passages accredited to מ״א נ״ר; we may accordingly understand this as *mori 'aḥi, natréh raḥamana*, "my teacher, my brother, may the Merciful One guard him"; i.e. there too R. Aaron meant his brother R. Pinḥas. (If we postulate that R. Aaron's puzzling reference here—puzzling because no scholar of that time named R. Aḥa is known otherwise—means his brother, we may assume the same there.) From this Rabbi Blau concludes further that R. Aaron wrote his work on *K'thuboth* while his brother was alive, and *P'kudath haL'vi-im* after his brother had departed this life (since both after his

What doubt can now remain that in citing from "Rabbénu Aḥa" the reasons, purposes or lessons to be learned from six *mitzvoth*, R. Aaron haLévi meant his brother R. Pinḥas? And for five *mitzvoth* out of the six we find these ideas expressed only in *Séfer haḤinnuch* and in *P'kudath haL'vi-im*[26]; and in *P'kudath haL'vi-im* they are given in the name of R. Aaron's brother—who fits our author's description of himself, as a Levite of the city of Barcelona![27]

It may be argued that the author of the *Ḥinnuch* was a third scholar, who simply took the ideas about the five precepts from *P'kudath haL'vi-im* and incorporated them in his work.[28] Alternatively, it may be contended that there is sufficient difference between *Séfer haḤinnuch* and *P'kudath haL'vi-im* in the expression of these ideas to warrant the contention that R. Aaron was quoting not from the *Ḥinnuch* but from a commentary by his brother on the tractate *B'rachoth* (lost to us); and from this our unknown author took them for use in the *Ḥinnuch*.[29] Both these theories, however, would thus postulate that there were three

brother's name in his preface and after "Rabbénu Aḥa" within the volume he adds "of blessed memory").

By comparing R. Aaron's writings on *K'thuboth* (Jerusalem 5716/1956, reset from the first edition, Prague 5483/1723) with the *ḥiddushim* on *K'thuboth* by Ritba (R. Yom Tov b. Abraham ibn Ishbili; ed. R. Moshe Goldstein, Jerusalem 5742/1982), Rabbi Blau's decipherment of מ״א can be confirmed: An explanation given by R. Aaron (col. 94b) in the name of מ״א נ״ר is cited by Ritba (his disciple) as מ״ר (=מפי רבינו) בשם ה״ר פנחס הלוי אחיו "from the words of our master teacher in the name of R. Pinḥas haLévi, his brother" (col. 671). Similarly, something else given by R. Aaron (col. 29b) in the name of מ״א נר״ו is cited in *Shittah M'kubetzeth* on *K'thuboth ad loc.* as from his brother. In two instances R. Aaron himself identifies what he has written as from מורי אחי נ״ר, leaving no doubt about the matter: col. 98a–99a (cited by Ritba, col. 707, as from "our master teacher in the name of R. Pinḥas haLévi, his brother"); and col. 105a (cited likewise by Ritba, col. 754). (This information was gathered for me by my son Naḥum.)

It is interesting that in all the instances where R. Aaron cites R. Pinḥas, he does not mention his brother's name; whether by abbreviation or explicitly, he writes only "my brother." It might be tentatively suggested that this may well reflect the nature of a man who chose to remain anonymous in writing a major work on the 613 *mitzvoth* of the Torah: for it is quite possible that R. Aaron did not name him in his citations (even after his brother had passed away, when he added ז״ל "of blessed memory" in mentioning him) because he knew (perhaps) that his brother's wish had been to remain self-effacing.

26. The exception is the point about the Sabbath, that by keeping the commandment to observe it as a holy day of rest we affirm the transcending truth of Scripture's account of the Creation, that the world was brought into being *ex nihilo*, "out of nothing." This thought was expressed earlier by Rambam (*Guide*, II 19) and by Ramban (*Commentary on the Torah*, on Deuteronomy 5:15; Hebrew ed. Chavel, II p. 367).

27. It is known that R. Aaron lived there, and he describes R. Pinḥas as his Torah instructor as well as his brother; hence they must have lived at least in the same city.

28. So Rabbi Chavel, ed. *Séfer haḤinnuch*, p. 804.

29. So Rabbi David Metzger (see above, note 1) would suggest.

scholars in Barcelona from the tribe of Lévi (R. Aaron, R. Pinḥas, and our still unknown author of the *Ḥinnuch*); whereas our theory assumes that there were only two. As this is a lesser assumption, it must be given preference in our present state of knowledge. If we may borrow a sentence from the *Ḥinnuch* itself, which our author sometimes put after positing some purpose or reason for a precept, "Until we hear something better than this, let us hold fast to this."[30]

One further prime piece of evidence for our author's identity remains to be given—again by R. Aaron haLévi himself. In 5735 (1975) his commentary on the Talmud tractate *Ḥullin* was published (from manuscript) in Jerusalem. On p. 99 there is an explanation of the teaching in the Talmud (*Ḥullin* 62a) that if a bird has the one sign (or characteristic) that it is not predatory, it is "clean" (i.e. of a kosher, permissible kind). As Rabbi Yisrael Ta-Shma has noted, this particular explanation of the Talmudic teaching, which R. Aaron haLévi gives, is to be found in full (although worded differently) in *Séfer haḤinnuch*, § 157.[31] And at the end of the paragraph R. Aaron writes, "This explanation of the halachic teaching comes originally from רבי׳ אחי ז״ל."

Here we have רבינו אחא again, but with a change in one letter that patently puts an end to all speculation or doubt about its meaning. In this version he is finally, unambiguously, "our Torah teacher, my brother, of blessed memory."

EVIDENCE OVERLOOKED OR UNACCEPTED

As indicated above, two scholars in the past took note of the passage in *P'kudath haL'vi-im* that gives, in the name of "Rabbénu Aḥa," reasons or lessons to be learned from six precepts, which are also found in *Séfer haḤinnuch*. As fate would have it, the second of the two, working within the past few decades, was evidently unaware that perhaps a century before, the first scholar had postulated that "Rabbénu Aḥa" was R. Aaron haLévi's brother. So Rabbi Charles B. Chavel took "Rabbénu Aḥa" to be an actual *rishon*, and for him the author of the *Ḥinnuch* remained an

30. So e.g. in § 100; similarly in §§ 72, 89 and 124.

31. In this instance, our author himself has enabled us to understand why R. Aaron chose to follow his explanation of the Talmudic dictum. At the conclusion of the explanation in the *Ḥinnuch* our author adds, "We have written this rule according to the view of certain authorities, since many interpretations were given in explanation of these matters concerning fowl." In other words, while various ways of understanding the teaching had been promulgated (and very likely were current), our author accepted this approach as clear and correct. And R. Aaron follows it in his commentary.

unknown sage who had drawn on *P'kudath haLvi-im* for at least five of the six reasons or lessons.

The earlier scholar, Rabbi Simḥah Bamberger, stated that he believed "Rabbénu Aḥa" to be R. Aaron's brother R. Pinḥas, but he drew no conclusions from this about the author of the *Ḥinnuch*. It might therefore be argued that he pondered the possibility that R. Pinḥas was the anonymous author, and decided not to accept it, probably because he considered the thesis not sufficiently proven.[29] And, it may be contended further, if he considered the identification too uncertain to put down in writing, why should we be more bold?

In answer to this it should be pointed out that R. Simḥah Bamberger could only state that it seemed to him that by "Rabbénu Aḥa" R. Aaron haLévi meant his brother. He might well hesitate then to posit a theory about the authorship of the *Ḥinnuch* on the basis of a supposition. We have three pieces of confirmation about the identity of "Rabbénu Aḥa," and the basic content of a further passage in the *Ḥinnuch* which R. Aaron clearly gives in the name of his brother.

Rabbi Moses Y. Blau represents a more difficult problem. He knew and accepted R. Simḥah Bamberger's surmise about "Rabbénu Aḥa," and he cited the passage in *'Ohel Mo'éd* which confirms it (see note 25, above). Why did *he* not suggest that from the passage in *P'kudath haL'vi-im* we may at least suspect that R. Pinḥas ha Lévi was the author of the *Ḥinnuch*?

Those who knew him, however, can attest that Rabbi Blau was a fine Talmudic scholar who dedicated his years to editing and publishing the writings of *rishonim* from early manuscripts. It was a task which took up all his time and interest, as he received no institutional backing. If the thought occurred to him that the evidence pointed to R. Pinḥas haLévi as the author of the *Ḥinnuch*, he could well have put the thought aside as beyond the range of his proper interest, or something to leave for others to suggest in print.

However it may be, Tradition teaches that "everything depends on fortune, even [the fate of] the Torah scroll in the Temple."[32] It was left only to these last few years for the existing evidence to be gathered and evaluated, and for the conclusion to be drawn that R. Pinḥas haLévi of Barcelona, the older brother of the well-known R. Aaron, may indeed be taken to be the author of *Séfer haḤinnuch*.

32. I.e. fortune determines even when that *séfer Torah* will be taken out of its ark to be read aloud to the congregation gathered for prayer: *Zohar* III 134a; *Tikkuné Zohar* 69 and 70.

A RAY OF LIGHT ON THE SON

As Rabbi Ta-Shma indicates further, once we accept that R. Pinḥas haLévi wrote *Séfer haḤinnuch*, we may also know the name of his son for whom he wrote this work—whom he often addresses directly, in the second person. For in his preface to *P'kudath haL'vi-im* (as noted above) R. Aaron haLévi mentions a son of his brother named R. Joshua.

The anonymous lad in *Séfer haḤinnuch* probably has a unique fame in the Torah literature of the Middle Ages, as the only son for whom a classic volume was written. And if he was indeed this R. Joshua, we can surmise something more about him. That passage in the preface to *P'kudath haL'vi-im* seems to suggest that in a time long before printing, when written works for the education of a young, growing Talmud scholar were quite certainly few and far between, this young scholar, presumably having benefited from his father's *Séfer haḤinnuch*, went on to ask his uncle R. Aaron to write another volume for him, to help him understand the work of R. Isaac 'Alfasi (Rif).

We may thus go on to conjecture that he fulfilled the verse in the Book of Proverbs (23:15), *My son, if your heart is wise, my heart too will rejoice.*

ACKNOWLEDGMENTS

My thanks are again due the *béth ha-s'farim ha-le'umi* in Jerusalem, without whose facilities and gracious staff my work on these volumes could not have been done, nor this preface written.

Rabbi Yaakov Schatz has placed me in his debt once more by carefully checking the translation and notes in volumes 2 and 3, as in the first volume. It need hardly be added that many corrections and emendations resulted from his labors. As a rule, too, the longer (explanatory) notes owe their origin to him. He alerted me to matters requiring attention, and generally those notes are the result of my study and research which ensued. Hence the responsibility for their content is of course mine.

Among my associates at Feldheim Publishers, all have been helpful in one way or another in the formidable task of readying volumes 2 and 3 for publication—particularly Yosef Katzburg in setting and reading the Hebrew text.

In the years that volumes 2 and 3 were in preparation, Heaven saw fit to give me both great happiness and tragedy; and if I came through both in fairly good order, it was only with the unexpected help of kind friends. When the Almighty said הבן יקיר לי אפרים He must certainly have meant the words to apply also to a most unusual brother-in-law, and his wife, because חסד ה׳ מלאה הארץ. Mr and Mrs Allan Resis of Chicago have left me most grateful by their unusual generosity to mutual family. At a time of stark, inexpressible need, Mr Yaakov Feldheim came to my aid in a way far beyond anything imaginable in the relationship of a publisher to a member of his staff. And there were those whose generous kindness at a difficult time took me by surprise: (listed alphabetically) Rabbi William Fierverker, Rabbi Sidney Greenwald, Meilech Laufer, Dr Sholom Singer, Rabbi Shubert Spero, and Joseph Wassner. If there are others who should be mentioned, I fail to do so only from a lack of awareness or memory, and for this I ask their forgiveness. May Heaven reward them all.

One last word, if I may: As this preface draws to a close, so does *shiv'ah* (the seven days of mourning) for Rabbi Menaḥem M. Kasher, by any standard one of the great Torah scholars of our time. His major achievement is of course *Torah Shelémah*; 37 of its projected 50 volumes stand today on the shelves of every important Jewish library in the world. For over 30 years I was privileged to serve him a variety of ways: I was his English secretary; for almost all of the nine volumes of *Torah Shelémah* that appeared in English (*Encyclopedia of Biblical Interpretation*, to the end of *sidrah yithro*) I served as technical editor, preparing them for printing and seeing them through the press. If space allowed, far more could be told about his unsuspected range of activities and my bit of a share in them; but let this suffice.

If ever I was in doubt about his relationship to me, Heaven made it clear: He passed away on the Jewish calendar date of my father's death. There was much that I learned from him, directly and indirectly. God willing, when I observe my father's *yortzeit*, perhaps I will be able to continue to be linked with him by observing his as well.

Blessed be his memory.

Charles Wengrov

Jerusalem, Kislev 5744 (November 1983)

Séfer haḤinnuch סֵפֶר הַחִנּוּךְ

THE BOOK OF [MITZVAH] EDUCATION

ספר ויקרא

סדרות ויקרא – אחרי מות

LEVITICUS

SIDROTH VAYIKRA—AḤARÉ MOTH

סֵפֶר וַיִּקְרָא

וַיִּקְרָא

יֵשׁ בָּהּ אַחַת־עֶשְׂרֵה מִצְווֹת עֲשֵׂה וְחָמֵשׁ מִצְווֹת לֹא־תַעֲשֶׂה

[מִצְוַת מַעֲשֵׂה הָעוֹלָה]

קטו לַעֲשׂוֹת הָעוֹלָה כְּמִשְׁפָּטָהּ, שֶׁנֶּאֱמַר: אִם עוֹלָה קָרְבָּנוֹ וְגוֹמֵר, כְּמוֹ שֶׁכָּתוּב בַּפָּרָשָׁה.

מִשָּׁרְשֵׁי הַמִּצְוָה, מַה שֶּׁכָּתַבְתִּי בְּמִצְוַת הַבַּיִת עַל עִנְיַן הַקָּרְבָּנוֹת, סֵדֶר וְיִקְחוּ לִי [תְּרוּמָה].

מִדִּינֵי הַמִּצְוָה, מַה שֶּׁאָמְרוּ זִכְרוֹנָם לִבְרָכָה בְּמַעֲשֵׂה הָעוֹלָה, שֶׁהָיְתָה נַעֲשֵׂית כֵּן: שׁוֹחֲטִין אֶת הַבְּהֵמָה בָּעֲזָרָה, וְהַשְּׁחִיטָה כְּשֵׁרָה אֲפִלּוּ בְזָרִים, וּמִקַּבָּלַת הַדָּם וָאֵילָךְ מִצְוַת כְּהֻנָּה, וְזוֹרֵק הַכֹּהֵן הַדָּם וּמַפְשִׁיט אוֹתָהּ וּמְנַתְּחָהּ אֵבָרִים שְׁלֵמִים, דִּכְתִיב "לִנְתָחֶיהָ", וּפֵרְשׁוּ זִכְרוֹנָם לִבְרָכָה: וְלֹא נְתָחֶיהָ לִנְתָחִים. וּכְשֶׁמְּנַתֵּחַ מֵסִיר גִּיד הַנָּשֶׁה מִן הַיָּרֵךְ וּמַקְטִיר כָּל הַנְּתָחִים עַל־גַּבֵּי הַמִּזְבֵּחַ.

וְצֶמֶר שֶׁבְּרָאשֵׁי כְבָשִׂים וְשֵׂעָר שֶׁבִּזְקַן הַתְּיָשִׁים, וְהָעֲצָמוֹת וְהַגִּידִים וְהַקַּרְנַיִם וְהַטְּלָפַיִם, בִּזְמַן שֶׁהֵם מְחֻבָּרִים מַקְטִירִים הַכֹּל, שֶׁנֶּאֱמַר: וְהִקְטִיר הַכֹּהֵן אֶת הַכֹּל; פֵּרְשׁוּ לֹא יַעֲלוּ, שֶׁנֶּאֱמַר: וְעָשִׂיתָ עוֹלֹתֶיךָ הַבָּשָׂר וְהַדָּם.

וְסֵדֶר הַנִּתּוּחַ כֵּיצַד הָיָה, וַהֲדָחַת בְּנֵי הַמֵּעַיִם כֵּיצַד, וּבְכַמָּה בְנֵי־אָדָם מוֹלִיכִין אֶת הָאֵבָרִים לַמִּזְבֵּחַ, שֶׁאָמְרוּ זִכְרוֹנָם לִבְרָכָה כִּי הַכֶּבֶשׂ בְּשִׁשָּׁה, וְהַשּׁוֹר בְּאַרְבָּעָה

§115

1. Literally, to do, or make.
2. I.e. at its north side; Leviticus 1:11.
3. TB B'rachoth 31b, etc.
4. Leviticus 1:5–6.
5. Sifra on the verse; TB Ḥullin 11a.
6. *Ibid.* 90b.
7. Leviticus 1:9.
8. But not any separate part of the animal which was neither flesh nor blood: Sifre, Deuteronomy §78.
9. Mishnah, Tamid iii.
10. TB Yoma 25a, 26b.

LEVITICUS

sidrah va-yikra

(Leviticus 1–5)

It contains eleven positive and five negative precepts.

115 [THE PRECEPT OF THE SACRIFICE OF THE 'OLAH] to process[1] the *'olah* (burnt-offering) according to its law—for it is stated, *If his offering be an* 'olah (*burnt-offering*), etc. (Leviticus 1:3)—as it is written in the *sidrah.*

At the root of the precept lies the purpose that I wrote in the precept of [building] the Temple, in regard to the animal offerings, in *sidrah t'rumah* (§95).

Among the laws of the precept, there is what the Sages of blessed memory said about the sacrifice of the *'olah*, that it would be done so: The animal would be ritually slain in the Temple forecourt;[2] the ritual slaying (*sheḥittah*) is acceptable even if done by outsiders [ordinary Israelites], but from the collection of the blood onward, it is a religious duty of the *kohanim.*[3] A *kohen* would sprinkle the blood [on the altar], skin it, and cut it up into whole limbs[4]—for it is written, [*he shall cut it*] *into its pieces* (Leviticus 1:6), and our Sages of blessed memory taught:[5] but not its pieces into pieces. As he cut it up, [the *kohen*] would remove the sinew of the thigh-vein from the thigh,[6] and burn all the pieces on the altar.[7]

As to the wool on the heads of sheep, the hair of goats' beards, the bones, tendons, horns and hooves, as long as they were attached, all would be burnt; for it is stated, *and the* kohen *shall burn the whole* (Leviticus 1:9). If they became separated, though, they were not to go up [on the altar]: for it is stated, *and you shall offer your* 'olah *sacrifices, the flesh and the blood*[8] (Deuteronomy 12:27).

Then there is the order of the cutting-up, how it was [done];[9] how the washing of the entrails was done; and by how many people the limbs and parts were taken to the altar—for our Sages of blessed memory taught[10] that a sheep [was taken] by six, and an ox by

וְעֶשְׂרִים בְּעוֹלוֹת צִבּוּר, וְעוֹלוֹת יָחִיד בְּפָחוֹת; וְעִנְיַן עוֹלַת הָעוֹף כֵּיצַד נַעֲשֵׂית; וְיֶתֶר פְּרָטֶיהָ, מְבֹאָרִים בִּזְבָחִים.

וְנוֹהֶגֶת בִּזְמַן הַבַּיִת בִּזְכָרֵי כְהֻנָּה. וְכֹהֵן שֶׁעָבַר וְלֹא עֲשָׂאָהּ כַּסֵּדֶר הַזֶּה בִּטֵּל עֲשֵׂה.

[מִצְוַת קָרְבַּן מִנְחָה]

קטז לַעֲשׂוֹת מְלֶאכֶת הַמִּנְחָה עַל הָעִנְיָן הַנִּזְכָּר בַּתּוֹרָה בְּפָרָשִׁיּוֹתֶיהָ, שֶׁנֶּאֱמַר: וְנֶפֶשׁ כִּי תַקְרִיב קָרְבַּן מִנְחָה, וּכְתִיב: וְאִם מִנְחָה עַל הַמַּחֲבַת, וּכְתִיב עוֹד: וְאִם מִנְחַת מַרְחֶשֶׁת.

וְעִנְיַן הַמְּנָחוֹת הוּא קָרְבָּן הַבָּא מִמִּינֵי הַקְּמָחִים וְלֹא מִבַּעֲלֵי־חַיִּים. וּכְבָר כָּתַבְתִּי לְמַעְלָה, כִּי הַקָּרְבָּן בְּבַעֲלֵי־חַיִּים הוּא בֶּאֱמֶת דִּמְיוֹן חָזָק אֵצֶל הָאָדָם לְהַכְנִיעַ וּלְהַשְׁפִּיל הַנֶּפֶשׁ הַמִּתְאַוָּה וְהַחוֹטֵאת, כְּמוֹ שֶׁהוּא רוֹאֶה שֶׁבַּעַל חָיוּת כְּמוֹתוֹ, אֶלָּא שֶׁאֵין בּוֹ שֵׂכֶל, נִשְׂרָף וְכָלֶה; וּכְמוֹ־כֵן הַנֶּפֶשׁ הַחוֹטֵאת מִצַּד חֻלְשַׁת הַשֵּׂכֶל תִּכְלֶה וְתֹאבַד גַּם־כֵּן אִם תַּתְמִיד בִּפְעֻלּוֹת בַּהֲמִיּוֹת, שֶׁהֵן הַחֲטָאִים, כִּי הַחֵטְא לֹא יָבֹא רַק מִשֹּׁרֶשׁ בַּהֲמִי.

וְהַקָּרְבָּן בְּמַה שֶּׁהוּא שֶׁאֵינוֹ בַעַל־חַיִּים, אַף־עַל־פִּי שֶׁהוּא בָא גַּם־כֵּן לְהַכְנָעַת הַיֵּצֶר, שֶׁיִּרְאֶה הָאָדָם כִּי בִּשְׁבִיל חֶטְאוֹ נִצְטָרֵךְ לִשְׂרֹף מָמוֹנוֹ וּלְכַלּוֹתוֹ, בֶּאֱמֶת אֵין דִּמְיוֹנוֹ חָזָק כְּמוֹ בְּבַעֲלֵי הַחַיִּים. וּמִן הַדּוֹמֶה לְפִי הַפְּשָׁט, כִּי עַל־כֵּן יִקָּרֵא מִנְחָה מִפְּנֵי שֶׁעִנְיָנָהּ מְעַט מִקָּרְבַּן בַּעַל־חַיִּים כְּמוֹ שֶׁמִּנְחוֹת בְּנֵי־אָדָם יִהְיוּ בְמוּעָט בְּרֹב הַפְּעָמִים; וְעוֹד מִפְּנֵי שֶׁהַרְבֵּה מֵהֶן בָּאוֹת נְדָבָה, וּמַה שֶּׁאֵינוֹ בְחִיּוּב אֵצֶל בְּנֵי־אָדָם יִקָּרְאוּ מִנְחָה.

וְאֵלּוּ הֵן כָּל מִינֵי הַמְּנָחוֹת שֶׁהָיוּ מַקְרִיבִין בִּזְמַן הַבַּיִת הַבָּאוֹת בִּפְנֵי עַצְמָן, כְּלוֹמַר שֶׁאֵינָן בָּאוֹת לְמִנְחַת נְסָכִים, רְצוֹנִי לוֹמַר בִּגְרִירַת קָרְבָּן אַחֵר: שָׁלֹשׁ

11. I.e. even by one *koheṇ; ibid.* 26b and Rashi.

§116 1. Cf. TB Sotah 3a: A man does not commit a sin unless he is possessed by a spirit of folly.

twenty-four, when [they were sacrificed as] *'olah* offerings of the community; but the *'olah* offerings of an individual [were taken] by a smaller number.[11] Then there is the subject of a fowl as an *'olah*, and its further details, which are clarified in the tractate *Z'vaḥim* (64b).

It applies when the Temple is in existence, for the male *kohanim*. If a *kohen* violated it and did not offer it up in this proper order, he would disobey a positive precept.

[THE PRECEPT OF THE MINḤAH OFFERING]

116 to perform the work of a *minḥah*, a meal-offering in the way that is mentioned in the Torah, in its various sections; as it is stated, *And when anyone brings a meal-offering* (Leviticus 2:1); and it is written, *if your offering is a meal-offering baked on a griddle* (*ibid.* 5); and it is written further, *if your offering is a meal-offering cooked in a pan* (*ibid.* 7).

In substance, a *minḥah* is an offering from the species of flour and not from living creatures. I have written earlier, above (§95), that an offering of a living creature is truly [intended to show] a strong semblance to the human being, in order to subdue and abase the craving and sinning spirit. Even as he sees that a living creature like himself, except that it lacks intelligence, is burnt and utterly consumed, just so will a person who sins on account of the mind's weakness[1] be consumed and equally perish if he will persist in beastly activities, i.e. sins. For sin derives from nothing but a beastly, animal root.

On the other hand, when an offering is not a living creature, although it also comes to subdue the [evil] inclination, for the man will see that on account of his sin, a chattel of his has to be burned and consumed, in truth the conception of the parallel is not as strong as it is with living creatures. And it would seem, according to the plain meaning, that for this reason it was called *minḥah* (a meal-offering) —literally, a gift—as in substance and significance it is less than an animal offering, just as the gifts of human beings are often of small things. Moreover, many of them would come as voluntary offerings, and whatever is not obligatory among human beings, they would call *minḥah*, a gift.

Now, these are all the kinds of meal-offerings that would be brought at the time of the Temple, which came [to be offered up] by themselves. In other words, they did not come as a *minḥah* with libations of wine, i.e. as an adjunct of another offering. There are

מְנָחוֹת הֵן שֶׁהֵן בָּאוֹת בִּשְׁבִיל כָּל הַצִּבּוּר, וְהֵן עֹמֶר בְּפֶסַח, שְׁתֵּי הַלֶּחֶם בַּעֲצֶרֶת, לֶחֶם הַפָּנִים בְּכָל שַׁבָּת; וּשְׁלָשְׁתָּן נִקְרָאוֹת מִנְחָה; וְתֵשַׁע שֶׁל יָחִיד, וְאֵלּוּ הֵן: א. מִנְחַת חוֹטֵא, וְהִיא הַמִּנְחָה שֶׁיַּקְרִיב הֶעָנִי כְּשֶׁיִּתְחַיֵּב חַטָּאת וְלֹא תַגִּיעַ יָדוֹ. ב. מִנְחַת סוֹטָה, וְהִיא מִנְחַת הַקְּנָאוֹת הַכְּתוּבָה בְּפָרָשַׁת נָשֹׂא. ג. הַמִּנְחָה שֶׁיַּקְרִיב כָּל כֹּהֵן כְּשֶׁיִּכָּנֵס לַעֲבוֹדָה, שֶׁמַּקְרִיב אוֹתָהּ בְּיָדוֹ, וְהִיא הַנִּקְרֵאת מִנְחַת חִנּוּךְ. ד. הַמִּנְחָה שֶׁמַּקְרִיב כֹּהֵן גָּדוֹל בְּכָל יוֹם, וְהִיא נִקְרֵאת מִנְחַת חֲבִתִּין. ה. מִנְחַת הַסֹּלֶת, וְהִיא בָּאָה בְּנֶדֶר וּנְדָבָה. ו. מִנְחַת הַמַּחֲבַת, וְהִיא בָּאָה בְּנֶדֶר וּנְדָבָה. ז. מִנְחַת הַמַּרְחֶשֶׁת, וְהִיא בָּאָה בְּנֶדֶר וּנְדָבָה. ח. מִנְחַת מַאֲפֵה תַנּוּר וְהִיא חַלּוֹת, וְהִיא בָּאָה בְּנֶדֶר וּנְדָבָה. ט. מִנְחַת מַאֲפֵה תַנּוּר וְהִיא רְקִיקִין, וּבָאָה בְּנֶדֶר וּנְדָבָה.

מְנָחוֹת אֵלּוּ, מֵהֶן סֹלֶת חִטִּים וּמֵהֶן שְׂעוֹרִים, מֵהֶן נֶאֱכָלוֹת לַכֹּהֲנִים חוּץ מִן הַקְּמִיצָה, וּמֵהֶן שֶׁהֵן נִשְׂרָפוֹת כֻּלָּן. וְאַחַת מֵהֶן חָמֵץ, וְהִיא שְׁתֵּי הַלֶּחֶם שֶׁמְּבִיאִין בְּיוֹם עֲצֶרֶת, שֶׁגַּם הֵן נִקְרָאִין מִנְחָה, וְאֵינָן קְרֵבִין לְגַבֵּי מִזְבֵּחַ; וְעַל שְׁתֵּי הַלֶּחֶם אֵלּוּ נֶאֱמַר בַּתּוֹרָה כְּשֶׁאֲסָרָהּ דֶּרֶךְ כְּלָל "כָּל הַמִּנְחָה אֲשֶׁר תַּקְרִיבוּ לַיי לֹא תֵעָשֶׂה חָמֵץ": פָּרַט בְּאֵלּוּ וְהוֹצִיאָם מִן הַכְּלָל, וַעֲלֵיהֶם נֶאֱמַר שָׁם "קָרְבַּן רֵאשִׁית תַּקְרִיבוּ אוֹתָם לַיי", כְּלוֹמַר בְּאֵלּוּ לֹא אֲסַרְתִּי לָכֶם הֶחָמֵץ; וּמִכָּל־מָקוֹם אֶל הַמִּזְבֵּחַ לֹא הָיוּ עוֹלִין מִכֵּיוָן שֶׁהָיָה בָּהֶן חָמֵץ, וּכְמוֹ שֶׁנֶּאֱמַר בָּהֶן: וְאֶל הַמִּזְבֵּחַ לֹא יַעֲלוּ לְרֵיחַ נִיחוֹחַ.

כָּל הַשְּׁאָר הָיוּ מַצָּה. וְסֵדֶר הֲבָאָתָן כָּךְ הִיא: אָדָם מֵבִיא סֹלֶת מִתּוֹךְ בֵּיתוֹ בִּכְלִי

2. Sifra, *va-yikra, parashah* 13, 4 refers to it as the *minḥah* of the ʻ*omer*.
3. Leviticus 23:15 and TB M'naḥoth 46a refer to them as a *minḥah*.
4. Called a *minḥah* in Sifra, *va-yikra, parashah* 12, 1, and TB M'naḥoth 57a.
5. So MT *hilchoth ma'aséh ha-korbanoth* xii 3.
6. Leviticus 5:11.
7. Leviticus 6:13.
8. *Ibid.* 15.
9. Leviticus 2:1–3.
10. *Ibid.* 5–6.
11. *Ibid.* 7–9.
12. *Ibid.* 4.
13. So MT *hilchoth ma'aséh ha-korbanoth* xii 4.
14. Those of barley were the ʻ*omer* and the *minḥah* of the *sotah*.
15. I.e. every *minḥah* brought by a *kohen* (Leviticus 6:15).

three *minḥah* offerings which are brought in behalf of the entire community: they are the *'omer* (sheaf-offering) on Passover,[2] the two loaves of bread on *Shavu'oth*,[3] and the showbread every Sabbath;[4] all three are each called *minḥah* (meal-offering).[5] And there are nine by an individual; these are: (1) The *minḥah* of a sinner. This is the meal-offering which a poor man is to bring when he becomes obligated to bring a *ḥattath* (sin-offering) and he has not the means [to bring an animal offering].[6] (2) The *minḥah* of a *sotah*, a woman suspected of adultery, which is the *meal-offering of jealousy* (Numbers 5:15) written in *sidrah naso*. (3) The *minḥah* that every *kohen* was to offer up when he entered the [Temple] service, which he would bring in his hand; this is what was called "the meal-offering of initiation."[7] (4) The *minḥah* that the *kohen gadol* would offer up every day, which was called "a meal-offering from the griddle."[8] (5) The meal-offering of fine flour,[9] which came [was brought] as either a vowed or voluntary offering. (6) The meal-offering from the griddle,[10] which came as either a vowed or a voluntary offering. (7) The pan-cooked meal-offering,[11] which came as either a vowed or voluntary offering. (8) The oven-baked meal-offering in the form of cakes:[12] and this [too] came by a vow or voluntarily. (9) The oven-baked meal-offering in the form of wafers,[12] which [equally] came by a vow or voluntarily.[13]

Some of these meal-offerings were of fine wheat flour, and some of barely.[14] Some were eaten by the *kohanim*, except for the handful [from the offering that was burned on the altar], and some were burned [there] entirely.[15] One of them was *ḥamétz*, leavened bread—i.e. the two loaves brought on the day of *Shavu'oth*; these too were called *minḥah*,[3] although they would not be offered up on the altar. As regards these two loaves, when the Torah gave the general injunction, *No meal-offering which you bring to the Lord shall be made with leaven* (Leviticus 2:11), it was quite specific about them, to exclude them from the general rule. For it is stated about them there, *As an offering of first-fruits you may bring them to the Lord* (*ibid.* 12): In other words, "For these I did not forbid you *ḥamétz* (leaven)"; nevertheless, they were not to go up on the altar, since there was *ḥamétz* in them—as it is stated about them, *but on the altar they shall not come up for a pleasing savor* (*ibid.*).

Every other one was of *matzah;* and this was the order of bringing them: A man would bring fine flour from his house in a vessel of

כֶּסֶף אוֹ זָהָב אוֹ שֶׁל מַתֶּכֶת וּמוֹלִיכָהּ אֵצֶל הַכֹּהֵן, וְהַכֹּהֵן מוֹלִיכָהּ אֵצֶל הַמִּזְבֵּחַ, וְקוֹמֵץ מִמֶּנָּה הַכֹּהֵן בְּרָאשֵׁי אֶצְבְּעוֹתָיו, וּמַקְטִיר הַקֹּמֶץ כֻּלּוֹ בַּמִּזְבֵּחַ, וְהַשְּׁאָר נֶאֱכָל לַכֹּהֲנִים. זֶהוּ סֵדֶר הַנֶּאֱכָלוֹת וְסֵדֶר הַנִּשְׂרָפוֹת, וְהַמְּלָאכוֹת שֶׁנַּעֲשׂוֹת בַּמְּנָחוֹת עַל־יְדֵי זָרִים וְהַנַּעֲשׂוֹת בָּהֶן עַל־יְדֵי כֹהֲנִים; וְיֶתֶר פְּרָטֶיהָ, מְבֹאָרִין בַּמַּסֶּכְתָּא הַבְּנוּיָה עַל זֶה, וְהִיא מַסֶּכֶת מְנָחוֹת.

וְנוֹהֶגֶת עֲשִׂיַּת הַמְּנָחוֹת בִּזְמַן הַבַּיִת בִּזְכְרֵי כְהֻנָּה. וְכֹהֵן שֶׁעָבַר וְשִׁנָּה מַעֲשֵׂה הַמִּנְחָה הַמְּפֹרָשׁ בָּהּ, בִּטֵּל עֲשֵׂה.

[שֶׁלֹּא לְהַקְרִיב שְׂאוֹר אוֹ דְבַשׁ]

קיז שֶׁלֹּא לְהַקְרִיב שְׂאוֹר וּדְבַשׁ עַל גַּבֵּי הַמִּזְבֵּחַ, שֶׁנֶּאֱמַר: כִּי כָל שְׂאֹר וְכָל דְּבַשׁ לֹא תַקְטִירוּ מִמֶּנּוּ אִשֶּׁה לַיי. וְנִכְפְּלָה הַמְּנִיעָה בְּרֹאשׁ הַפָּסוּק, שֶׁנֶּאֱמַר: כָּל הַמִּנְחָה אֲשֶׁר תַּקְרִיבוּ לַיי לֹא תֵעָשֶׂה חָמֵץ. וְהַדְּבַשׁ הוּא שֵׁם כּוֹלֵל לַדְּבַשׁ הַיָּדוּעַ, וְכֵן דְּבַשׁ תְּמָרִים שֶׁהוּא סְתָם הַדְּבַשׁ שֶׁל תּוֹרָה, וְכֵן מֹהַל הַיּוֹצֵא מִן הַפֵּרוֹת הַמְּתוּקִין. וּבִכְלַל "לֹא תַקְטִירוּ" הוּא גַּם־כֵּן שֶׁלֹּא לָתֵת מִמֶּנּוּ בְּפִטּוּם הַקְּטֹרֶת, וּכְמוֹ שֶׁהַפַּטָּמִים אוֹמְרִים: יָפֶה הָיָה הַדְּבַשׁ לַקְּטֹרֶת אֶלָּא שֶׁאֲסָרַתּוּ הַתּוֹרָה.

שָׁרְשֵׁי מִצְוָה זוֹ נַעֲלָמִים מְאֹד לִמְצֹא אֲפִלּוּ רֶמֶז קָטָן מֵהֶן. וְאוּלָם מִפְּנֵי שֶׁכְּבָר הוֹדַעְתִּי בְּפֶתַח דְּבָרַי שֶׁכַּוָּנָתִי בְּאֵלּוּ הַטְּעָמִים שֶׁאֲנִי כוֹתֵב לְהַרְגִּיל הַנְּעָרִים וּלְהַטְעִים לָהֶם בִּתְחִלַּת בּוֹאָם לִשְׁמֹעַ דִּבְרֵי סֵפֶר, כִּי יֵשׁ לְדִבְרֵי הַתּוֹרָה טְעָמִים וְתוֹעֲלוֹת, וִיקַבְּלוּם עַל דֶּרֶךְ הַהֶרְגֵּל שֶׁלָּהֶם וּכְפִי חֻלְשַׁת שִׂכְלָם, וְאַל יִהְיוּ לָהֶם הַמִּצְווֹת בִּתְחִלָּה כְּדִבְרֵי הַסֵּפֶר הֶחָתוּם, פֶּן יִבְעֲטוּ בָהֶם מִתּוֹךְ כָּךְ בְּנַעֲרוּתָם וְיַנִּיחוּם לְעוֹלָם וְיֵלְכוּ בַהֶבֶל — עַל־כֵּן אֶכְתֹּב בָּהֶם כָּל אֲשֶׁר יַעֲלֶה בִּתְחִלַּת

16. To touch it to the southwest corner of the altar (MT *ibid.* xiii 12, per Leviticus 6:7).

17. TB Sotah 14b.

§117 1. I.e. in regard to leaven; ShM negative precept §98.

2. So Rashi on the verse, based on TB Sh'vu'oth 12b.

3. In TJ Yoma iv 5 we read: "The apothecaries of Jerusalem used to say: If a bit of honey were put into it, the entire world would not be able to withstand it" — so exquisite would the scent of the holy incense be. The thought is similarly found in Sifra, *va-yikra, parashah* 12, 4.

silver, gold or metal, and take it up to the *kohen;* and the *kohen* would take it up to the altar.[16] The *kohen* would then gather a handful with the tips of his fingers and burn the entire handful on the altar, and the rest would be eaten by the *kohanim.* This is the procedure for those that were eaten.[17] The procedure for those that were [wholly] burnt, the tasks that might be done with the meal-offerings by outsiders [non-*kohanim*] and those that were to be done by *kohanim*, and the rest of its details, are explained in the tractate built about this subject, i.e. the Talmud tractate *M'naḥoth.*

The presentation of *minḥah* offerings is done when the Temple is extant, by male *kohanim.* If a *kohen* transgressed and changed the procedure of a *minḥah* that was set down explicitly for it, he would [thus] disobey a positive precept.

[THE PROHIBITION AGAINST OFFERING UP LEAVEN OR HONEY]

117 not to offer up leaven (yeast) or honey on the altar: as it is stated, *for of no leaven and of no honey shall you burn any as an offering by fire to the Lord* (Leviticus 2:11). The injunction was repeated at the beginning of the verse,[1] for it is stated, *No meal-offering which you bring to the Lord shall be made with leaven* (*ibid.*). Now, "honey" is a general name for the known [usual kind of] honey, as well as honey from dates, which is the general "honey" [mentioned] in the Torah, and also the juice that runs from [all] sweet fruits.[2] And the admonition not to burn it includes a ban not to put any of it into the compounding of the incense; as the apothecaries used to say, honey would be fine (excellent) for the incense, but the Torah forbade it.[3]

The root reasons for this precept are too hidden to find even a small hint of them. However, I conveyed before, at the beginning of my words, that my intention in these reasons [for the precepts] that I write, is to educate the young and make them realize, as they begin to learn sacred written texts, that the words of the Torah have reasons and purposes, and let them accept them in their way of learning, according to the limitations of their intelligence. The precepts should not be for them, at the beginning, like *the words of a sealed book* (Isaiah 29:11), lest they rebel against them as a result in their youth, and then leave them forever and go off to worthless vanity. Therefore I will write about them whatever comes to mind at first thought; and let

הַמַּחֲשָׁבָה, וְאַל יִתְפֹּשׂ עָלַי תּוֹפֵשׂ בְּשׁוּם דָּבָר אַחֲרֵי יֵדַע הַכַּוָּנָה.

וְאֹמַר כִּי עִנְיְנֵי הַקָּרְבָּן כֻּלָּם לְעוֹרֵר מַחֲשֶׁבֶת הַמַּקְרִיב, וּלְפִי הַמַּעֲשֶׂה הַהוּא יִקַּח דִּמְיוֹנוֹתָיו בְּנַפְשׁוֹ, הַכֹּל כַּאֲשֶׁר כָּתַבְנוּ כְּבָר; וְעַל־כֵּן בְּהַרְחִיק הֶחָמֵץ, שֶׁהוּא נַעֲשֶׂה בִשְׁהִיָּה גְדוֹלָה, מִקָּרְבָּנוֹ, יִקַּח דִּמְיוֹן לִקְנוֹת מִדַּת הַזְּרִיזוּת וְהַקַּלּוּת וְהַמְּהִירוּת בְּמַעֲשֵׂי הַשֵּׁם בָּרוּךְ הוּא, וּכְמוֹ שֶׁאָמְרוּ זִכְרוֹנָם לִבְרָכָה: הֱוֵי קַל כַּנֶּשֶׁר וְרָץ כַּצְּבִי (וְגִבּוֹר כַּאֲרִי) לַעֲשׂוֹת וְכוּלֵי. וְנִתְחַיֵּב הָעִנְיָן בְּמִנְחַת הַיְּחִידִים יוֹתֵר מִמִּנְחַת הַצִּבּוּר לְפִי שֶׁהַיֵּאוּשׁ וְהָעַצְלָה נִמְצָא בְיָחִיד יוֹתֵר, כִּי הָרַבִּים יַזְהִירוּ זֶה אֶת זֶה; וְלָכֵן לֹא תַקְפִּיד הַתּוֹרָה עַל זֶה בְּמִנְחַת הַצִּבּוּר הַבָּאָה מִזְּמַן לִזְמַן, כְּגוֹן שְׁתֵּי הַלֶּחֶם שֶׁל עֲצֶרֶת. אֲבָל בְּלֶחֶם הַפָּנִים אַף־עַל־פִּי שֶׁהוּא נִקְרָא גַּם־כֵּן מִנְחַת צִבּוּר, מֵחֲמַת שֶׁהִיא מִנְחָה תְּמִידִית בְּכָל שַׁבָּת וְשַׁבָּת, תַּקְפִּיד הַתּוֹרָה בָּהּ, וְנִצְטַוִּינוּ גַּם־כֵּן בָּהּ שֶׁתִּהְיֶה מַצָּה.

וּבְעִנְיַן הַרְחָקַת הַדְּבַשׁ נֹאמַר אֶל הַיְלָדִים רַכִּים כְּדֵי לְיַסְּרָם, שֶׁהוּא סִבָּה לַדִּמְיוֹן שֶׁיְּמַעֵט הָאָדָם מִלִּרְדֹּף אַחַר הַמַּאֲכָלִים הַמְּתוּקִים לְחִכּוֹ, כְּמִנְהַג הַזּוֹלְלִים וְהַסּוֹבְאִים, יִמָּשְׁכוּ לְעוֹלָם אַחַר כָּל מָתוֹק, וְלֹא יִתֵּן לִבּוֹ כִּי־אִם אֶל הַמַּאֲכָלִים הַמּוֹעִילִים לְגוּפוֹ וּצְרִיכִים לְמִחְיָתוֹ וְשׁוֹמְרִים בְּרִיאוּת אֵבָרָיו. וְלָזֶה רָאוּי לְכָל בַּעַל־שֵׂכֶל לְכַוֵּן בִּמְזוֹנוֹ וּשְׁתִיָּתוֹ, לֹא לְכַוָּנַת הֲנָאַת מִשּׁוּשׁ הַגָּרוֹן. וְלוּ חָכְמוּ בְנֵי־אָדָם יַשְׂכִּילוּ זֹאת, כִּי כָּל עִנְיַן חוּשׁ הַמִּשּׁוּשׁ חֶרְפָּה הִיא לָהֶם, כָּל־שֶׁכֵּן שֶׁאֵין רָאוּי לָהֶם לְכַוֵּן אֵלָיו וְלֵהָנוֹת בּוֹ, רַק הַצָּרִיךְ אֶל הַטֶּבַע בְּהֶכְרֵחַ. וּמֵאַנְשֵׁי הַחָכְמָה כָּתְבוּ: חוּשׁ הַמִּשּׁוּשׁ אֲשֶׁר הוּא חֶרְפָּה לָנוּ.

וְעוֹד שָׁמַעְתִּי טַעַם בְּאִסּוּר שְׂאוֹר וּדְבַשׁ: לְפִי שֶׁהַשְּׂאוֹר מַגְבִּיהַּ עַצְמוֹ, וְכֵן הַדְּבַשׁ מַעֲלֶה רְתִיחָתוֹ הַרְבֵּה, וְלָכֵן נִתְרַחֲקוּ, לִרְמֹז כִּי תוֹעֲבַת יי כָּל גְּבַהּ לֵב. וְעוֹד

4. Mishnah, 'Avoth v 20.
5. Expression based on MT *hilchoth dé'oth* iii 2.
6. Cited by Rambam, *Guide* II 36, in the name of Aristotle.

no questioner seize upon me [with objections] after he knows the purpose.

Now, I say that everything to do with an offering is in order to bestir the thought of the person who brings it; in accord with that deed he will acquire his conceptions in his soul—all as we have written earlier (§95). Therefore, by keeping *ḥamétz*, which is made in a long interval of time, far removed from his offering, a person will attain the idea of acquiring the quality of alertness, lightness and swiftness in the activity of the Eternal Lord, blessed is He. As our Sages of blessed memory said,[4] be light as an eagle, swift as a deer, and strong as a lion, to do the will of your Father in heaven. The lesson is more essential in the meal-offering of an individual than in the *minḥah* of the community, for despondency and lethargy are rather found in an individual, since [in] a community, one will alert another. Hence the Torah was not insistent about it for a *minḥah* of the community that was brought from time to time, such as the two loaves on *Shavu'oth*. With the showbread, however, even though it is also called a *minḥah* of the community, because it was a continual regular offering every Sabbath the Torah was insistent about it, and we were commanded about it too that it should be of *matzah*.

Now, concerning the rejection of honey, we would say to the tender children in order to discipline them, that it is to influence one's concepts so that a person will minimize his striving after foods that are sweet to his taste, in the way that gluttons and guzzlers are always drawn after everything sweet. Thus let him set his heart only on foods that are beneficial to his body and necessary to his sustenance, and that maintain the health of his limbs.[5] Hence it is fitting for every intelligent human being to set his intention in his food and drink not toward the purpose of the tactile sensations of his throat. If people *were but wise, they would understand this* (Deuteronomy 32:29)—that the entire matter of the tactile sense is shameful for them. Then all the more certainly is it not fitting for them to aim for it and to take pleasure in it, but only what nature makes absolutely necessary. It was some of the men of wisdom who wrote that the tactile sense is something shameful for us.[6]

I heard another reason, too, for the ban on leaven and honey: because leaven raises itself ["puffs itself up"], and honey similarly rises greatly when it is boiling. Hence they were rejected, to imply that *an abomination to the Lord is every one that is high, proud in heart*

רָאִיתִי בְּפֵרוּשׁ הָרַמְבָּ״ן זִכְרוֹנוֹ לִבְרָכָה שֶׁכָּתַב כֵּן, וְזֶה לְשׁוֹנוֹ: וּבַעֲבוּר שֶׁהַקָּרְבָּנוֹת לִרְצוֹן הַשֵּׁם הַנִּכְבָּד, לֹא יוּבְאוּ מִן הַדְּבָרִים אֲשֶׁר לָהֶם הַיָּד הַחֲזָקָה לְשַׁנּוֹת הַטְּבָעִים, וְכֵן לֹא יָבוֹאוּ מִן הַדְּבָרִים הַמְּתוּקִים לְגַמְרֵי, כְּמוֹ הַדְּבַשׁ, רַק מִן הַמְּזוּגִים, כַּאֲשֶׁר אָמְרוּ זִכְרוֹנָם לִבְרָכָה בִּבְרִיאַת הָעוֹלָם: שִׁתֵּף מִדַּת רַחֲמִים בְּמִדַּת הַדִּין וּבְרָאוֹ, עַד כָּאן.

דִּינֵי הַמִּצְוָה, כְּגוֹן מַה שֶּׁאָמְרוּ זִכְרוֹנָם לִבְרָכָה שֶׁכָּל הַמְּנָחוֹת הַקְּרֵבוֹת לְגַבֵּי הַמִּזְבֵּחַ בָּאוֹת מַצָּה, כְּמוֹ שֶׁאָמַרְנוּ; וְכֵן שְׁיָרֵי הַמְּנָחוֹת שֶׁאוֹכְלִין הַכֹּהֲנִים, אַף־עַל־פִּי שֶׁהֵן מֻתָּרִין לֶאֱכֹל אוֹתָן בְּכָל מַאֲכָל וּבִדְבַשׁ, אֵין אוֹכְלִין אוֹתָן חָמֵץ, שֶׁנֶּאֱמַר: לֹא תֵאָפֶה חָמֵץ חֶלְקָם, וְיֵשׁ בְּמַשְׁמָע אֲפִלּוּ חֶלְקָם לֹא יַחֲמִיצוּ. וְאִם הֶחֱמִיץ שְׁיָרֶיהָ לוֹקֶה, וְלוֹקִין עַל כָּל עֲשִׂיָּה וַעֲשִׂיָּה שֶׁבָּהּ. כֵּיצַד, לָשָׁהּ חָמֵץ אוֹ עֲרָכָהּ חָמֵץ אוֹ קְטָפָהּ חָמֵץ אוֹ אֲפָאָהּ חָמֵץ, לוֹקֶה, שֶׁנֶּאֱמַר: לֹא תֵעָשֶׂה חָמֵץ, וְנֶאֱמַר: לֹא תֵאָפֶה חָמֵץ, לְחַיֵּב עַל מַעֲשֶׂה יְחִידִי שֶׁבַּעֲשִׂיָּתָהּ חָמֵץ מַלְקוֹת.

וְאֵין לוֹתְתִין חִטִּים שֶׁל מְנָחוֹת, שֶׁמָּא יַחֲמִיצוּ; וְאַף־עַל־פִּי־כֵן אָמְרוּ זִכְרוֹנָם לִבְרָכָה שֶׁהַמְּנָחוֹת הַנֶּאֱפוֹת הָיוּ נִלּוֹשׁוֹת בְּפוֹשְׁרִין, וּמְשַׁמְּרִין אוֹתָן שֶׁלֹּא יַחֲמִיצוּ, שֶׁהַכֹּהֲנִים זְרִיזִין הֵן; וּשְׂאוֹר וּדְבַשׁ אִסּוּרָן בְּכָל־שֶׁהוּא, שֶׁנֶּאֱמַר: לֹא תַקְטִירוּ מִמֶּנּוּ, כְּלוֹמַר אֲפִלּוּ כָּל־שֶׁהוּא; וְאֵינוֹ חַיָּב אֶלָּא־אִם־כֵּן הִקְטִירָן עִם הַקָּרְבָּן אוֹ לְשֵׁם הַקָּרְבָּן; וְאֶחָד הַמַּקְטִיר עַצְמָן אוֹ תַעֲרֹבְתָּן לוֹקֶה, אֲבָל הִקְטִירָן בִּפְנֵי עַצְמָן לְשֵׁם עֵצִים פָּטוּר, שֶׁנֶּאֱמַר: וְאֶל הַמִּזְבֵּחַ לֹא יַעֲלוּ לְרֵיחַ נִיחוֹחַ, לְרֵיחַ נִיחוֹחַ אִי אַתָּה מַעֲלֶה אֲבָל אַתָּה מַעֲלֶה לְשֵׁם עֵצִים; וְיֶתֶר פְּרָטֶיהָ, מְבֹאָרִין בְּמַסֶּכֶת מְנָחוֹת.

7. To Leviticus 23:17.

8. Literally, mixed.

9. B'réshith Rabbah 12, end.

10. TB M'naḥoth 52b.

11. I.e. of those which were not wholly burnt on the altar (see §116, note 25) they ate everything but the handful removed for burning.

12. *Ibid.* 55a.

13. MT *hilchoth ma'aséh ha-korbanoth* xii 15.

14. TB P'saḥim 36a.

15. Even though this could make the dough become leavened more readily; M'naḥoth 55a.

16. Sifra on the verse; TB M'naḥoth 58a (MT *hilchoth 'issuré ha-mizbé-aḥ* v 1).

17. MT *ibid.* (implied by the Hebrew verb in the phrase, *you shall not burn of it,* and in Sifra).

18. Literally, as wood; TB Z'vaḥim 77b (and see Rashi, 77a, s.v. *l'ré-aḥ*).

(Proverbs 16:5). Moreover, I saw in the commentary of Ramban of blessed memory[7] that he wrote thus. This is his phrasing: Because the offerings are for the good will of the honored Eternal Lord, those things which have a strong power to change states of nature are not to be brought; and so also should utterly sweet things, like honey, not be brought; but only tempered, balanced[8] substances—as the Sages of blessed memory said,[9] in the creation of the world, He joined the quality of mercy with the quality of justice.

The laws of the precept are, for example, what the Sages of blessed memory said, that all meal-offerings which were offered up on the altar were to be brought of *matzah*,[10] as we stated. So too the remainders of meal-offerings which the *kohanim* ate:[11] even though they were allowed to eat them with every food, and with honey, they would not eat them as *ḥamétz*—for it is stated, *It shall not be baked with leaven; as their portion* [*have I given it*, etc.] (Leviticus 6:10), which would imply that even their portion they should not make into *ḥamétz*.[12] If someone made *ḥamétz* of its remainders, he would be given whiplashes. And one is thus whipped for any single action with it:[12] How so?—if he kneaded it as *ḥamétz*, shaped it into a loaf of *ḥamétz*, basted it with water [making it] *ḥamétz*, or baked it as *ḥamétz*, he is given whiplashes—for it is stated, *shall not be made with leaven* (Leviticus 2:11), and again, *It shall not be baked with leaven* (*ibid.* 6:10), to impose punishment for every individual action: thus, for making it *ḥamétz*, there is a penalty of whiplashes.[13]

Then [we have these laws]: The wheat of meal-offerings is not to be wet before grinding, for fear that it will become leavened.[14] Nevertheless, our Sages of blessed memory taught that meal-offerings that were baked were kneaded with lukewarm water,[15] and they were watched that they should not become leavened—because the *kohanim* were quick. As for leaven (yeast) and honey, their ban is on the slightest amount: for it is stated, *you shall not burn of it* (Leviticus 2:11), even the least bit.[16] But guilt is not incurred unless they are burnt with an offering or as an offering.[17] Whether they themselves are burned or a mixture containing them, the punishment of whiplashes is given.[16] However, if they are burned by themselves as fuel,[18] there is no guilt; for it is stated, *but on the altar they shall not come up for a pleasing savor* (*ibid.* 12): for a pleasing savor you shall not bring them up, but you may bring them up for fuel. The rest of its details are explained in the Talmud tractate *M'naḥoth*.

הָרַמְבָּ"ם זִכְרוֹנוֹ לִבְרָכָה חָשַׁב אִסּוּר שְׂאוֹר וּדְבַשׁ לְלָאו אֶחָד, כְּלוֹמַר שֶׁאִם הִקְרִיב שְׂאוֹר וּדְבַשׁ שְׁנֵיהֶם יַחַד אֵינוֹ לוֹקֶה אֶלָּא אַחַת, וְכֵן אִם הִקְרִיב כָּל אֶחָד בִּפְנֵי עַצְמוֹ לוֹקֶה עַל כָּל אֶחָד מַלְקוּת אַחַת. וְנָתַן טַעַם לִדְבָרָיו, שֶׁזֶּהוּ לָאו שֶׁבִּכְלָלוֹת, וּבְלָאו שֶׁבִּכְלָלוֹת כָּזֶה לוֹקִין מַלְקוּת אַחַת עַל שְׁנֵי דְבָרִים.

וְהָרַב רַבֵּנוּ מֹשֶׁה בַּר נַחְמָן זִכְרוֹנוֹ לִבְרָכָה חָלַק עָלָיו לַחְשֹׁב שְׂאוֹר וּדְבַשׁ שְׁנֵי לָאוִין, וְאָמַר שֶׁאֵינוֹ רוֹאֶה כָּאן לָאו שֶׁבִּכְלָלוֹת, שֶׁהֲרֵי בְּחָמֵץ מְיֻחָד לָאוֵהּ בְּפֵרוּשׁ, שֶׁנֶּאֱמַר: לֹא תֵאָפֶה חָמֵץ, וְאִם כֵּן לָאו דִּדְבַשׁ אַף־עַל־גַּב דְּאִכָּא שְׂאוֹר בַּהֲדֵיהּ יֵשׁ לָנוּ לוֹמַר: הַדְּבַשׁ נִדְרֹשׁ אוֹתוֹ לְחוּדֵיהּ, וְנִמְצָא לָאו בְּכָל אֶחָד. וְיֶתֶר רְאָיוֹתֵיהֶם בְּסִפְרָם.

וְנוֹהֶגֶת בִּזְמַן הַבַּיִת בִּכֹהֲנִים, כִּי לָהֶם הָעֲבוֹדָה.

[שֶׁלֹּא לְהַקְרִיב קָרְבָּן בְּלֹא מֶלַח]

קיח שֶׁלֹּא לְהַשְׁבִּית מֶלַח מֵעַל הַקָּרְבָּן אוֹ הַמִּנְחָה, כְּלוֹמַר שֶׁלֹּא יַקְרִיבוּ הַכֹּהֲנִים שׁוּם קָרְבָּן אוֹ שׁוּם מִנְחָה אֶלָּא־אִם־כֵּן יָשִׂימוּ בָהֶן מֶלַח, שֶׁנֶּאֱמַר: וְלֹא תַשְׁבִּית מֶלַח בְּרִית אֱלֹהֶיךָ מֵעַל מִנְחָתֶךָ; וְכָתוּב גַּם־כֵּן: עַל כָּל קָרְבָּנְךָ תַּקְרִיב מֶלַח.

מִשָּׁרְשֵׁי הַמִּצְוָה, כָּתַבְתִּי לְמַעְלָה בְּרֹאשׁ הַסֵּדֶר. דִּינֵי הַמִּצְוָה, אָמְרוּ זִכְרוֹנָם לִבְרָכָה שֶׁמִּצְוָה לִמְלֹחַ הַבָּשָׂר יָפֶה, כְּעֵין מוֹלֵחַ בָּשָׂר לְצָלִי, שֶׁמּוֹלְחוֹ מִשְּׁנֵי צְדָדָיו; וּבְדִיעֲבַד אֲפִלּוּ מָלַח כָּל שֶׁהוּא כָּשֵׁר; וְשֶׁהַמֶּלַח שֶׁמּוֹלְחִין בּוֹ הַקָּרְבָּנוֹת הוּא מִשֶּׁל צִבּוּר, כְּמוֹ הָעֵצִים; וְאֵין הַיָּחִיד מֵבִיא מֶלַח אוֹ עֵצִים לְקָרְבָּנוֹת; וְכָל זֶה מֵהַגְדָּלַת הַבַּיִת, דִּבְמְקוֹם עֲשִׁירוּת לֵיכָּא עֲנִיּוּת.

19. ShM negative precept §98.
20. Applying to more than one subject.
21. In his commentary to ShM *ibid.*

§118 1. MT *hilchoth 'issuré ha-mizbé-aḥ* v 11, based on his reading in TB M'naḥoth 21a (see *Kessef Mishneh*).
2. TB M'naḥoth 21b (MT *ibid.* 13).
3. A Talmudic dictum (TB Shabbath 102b); i.e. if someone brought his own salt, it would seem as if the Temple were too poor to provide it.

Rambam of blessed memory reckoned the prohibition on leaven and honey as one negative precept.[19] In other words, if a person offered up both leaven and honey together, he receives a whipping only once; but equally, if he offered up each by itself, he is punished for each with one whipping. And he gave a reason for his words—that this is a general, omnibus negative precept,[20] and for violating a general, omnibus prohibition, a person is punished with one whipping for two things.

Ramban of blessed memory, however,[21] differed with him, reckoning leaven and honey as two negative precepts; and he stated that he does not see here any general, omnibus negative precept, since about *ḥamétz* a specific prohibition is given explicitly, as it is stated, *It shall not be baked with leaven* (Leviticus 6:10). Hence about the prohibition of honey, even though leaven is [mentioned] there with it, we have the right to say that we will interpret it to apply to honey alone. Consequently, there is a negative precept about each. The rest of their proofs are in their volume.

It applies when the Temple is extant, for the *kohanim*, since the Temple service [was entrusted] to them.

118 [NOT TO OFFER UP ANY SACRIFICE WITHOUT SALT] not to withhold salt from any animal offering or meal-offering; in other words, the *kohanim* are not to offer up any animal sacrifice or meal-offering unless they put salt in them—for it is stated, *and you shall not let the salt of the covenant of your God be lacking from your meal-offering* (Leviticus 2:13); and it is written, furthermore, *with all your offerings you shall offer salt* (*ibid.*).

What lies at the root of the precept, I have written below, in the next precept (§119).

As for the laws of the precept, our Sages of blessed memory taught that it was a religious obligation to salt the meat well, as one would in salting meat for roasting, where it is salted on both sides;[1] after the fact, however, if it was done, even if it was just salted at all, in any way, it is acceptable.[1] The salt used for the offerings came from the public funds, like the wood [for the altar fire]; and an individual was not to bring salt or wood for offerings[2]—all this for the magnification of the glory of the Temple: for in a place of wealth there is no penury.[3]

וּבִשְׁלֹשָׁה מְקוֹמוֹת הָיוּ נוֹתְנִין הַמֶּלַח: בְּלִשְׁכַּת הַמֶּלַח וְעַל־גַּבֵּי הַכֶּבֶשׁ וּבְרֹאשׁוֹ שֶׁל מִזְבֵּחַ. בְּלִשְׁכַּת הַמֶּלַח הָיוּ מוֹלְחִין [עוֹרוֹת הַקֳּדָשִׁים, וְעַל־גַּבֵּי הַכֶּבֶשׁ הָיוּ מוֹלְחִין] הָאֵבָרִים, וּבְרֹאשׁוֹ שֶׁל מִזְבֵּחַ מוֹלְחִין הַקֹּמֶץ וְהַלְּבוֹנָה וְהַמְּנָחוֹת הַנִּשְׂרָפוֹת וְעוֹלַת הָעוֹף; וְיֶתֶר פְּרָטֶיהָ, מְבֹאָרִין בְּפֶרֶק שְׁבִיעִי מִזְּבָחִים.

וְנוֹהֶגֶת בִּזְמַן הַבַּיִת בִּזְכָרֵי כְהֻנָּה, כִּי לָהֶם לְהַשְׁלִים צָרְכֵי הַקָּרְבָּן. וְכֹהֵן הָעוֹבֵר עָלֶיהָ וְהִקְרִיב קָרְבָּן אוֹ מִנְחָה בְּלֹא מֶלַח כְּלָל, בִּטֵּל עֲשֵׂה, וְגַם עוֹבֵר עַל לָאו זֶה וְלוֹקֶה, שֶׁהֲרֵי מַעֲשֶׂה יֵשׁ כָּאן כְּשֶׁהוּא מַקְרִיב הַבָּשָׂר הַתָּפֵל שֶׁהֻזְהַר עָלָיו שֶׁלֹּא לְהַקְרִיבוֹ בְלֹא מֶלַח.

[מִצְוַת מְלִיחַת הַקָּרְבָּן]

קיט לְהַקְרִיב מֶלַח עַל כָּל הַקָּרְבָּנוֹת, כְּלוֹמַר שֶׁיִּתֵּן מֶלַח בִּבְשַׂר הַקָּרְבָּן וְכֵן בְּקֶמַח הַמְּנָחוֹת, שֶׁנֶּאֱמַר: עַל כָּל קָרְבָּנְךָ תַּקְרִיב מֶלַח. כְּבָר אָמַרְנוּ בְּמִצְוַת בִּנְיַן הַבַּיִת, כִּי מִשָּׁרְשֵׁי מִצְוַת הַקָּרְבָּן לְהַכְשִׁיר וּלְהֵישִׁיר נֶפֶשׁ הַמַּקְרִיב אוֹתוֹ, וְעַל־כֵּן לְעוֹרֵר נַפְשׁוֹ שֶׁל מַקְרִיב נִצְטַוָּה בְּהַקְרָבַת דְּבָרִים הַטּוֹבִים וְהָעֲרֵבִים וְהַחֲבִיבִים עָלָיו, וּכְמוֹ שֶׁכָּתַבְנוּ לְמַעְלָה. וְהַמֶּלַח בּוֹ גַּם־כֵּן מֵהַשֹּׁרֶשׁ הַזֶּה, כְּדֵי שֶׁתִּהְיֶה אוֹתָהּ פְּעֻלָּה שְׁלֵמָה, לֹא תֶחְסַר לְפִי הַנְהָגַת הָאָדָם דָּבָר, כִּי אָז יִתְעוֹרֵר לִבּוֹ אֵלָיו יוֹתֵר, כִּי כָל דָּבָר מִבְּלִי מֶלַח לֹא יֶעֱרַב לְאִישׁ לֹא טַעֲמוֹ וְלֹא אַף רֵיחוֹ. וּמִלְּבַד זֶה יֵשׁ בַּמֶּלַח עִנְיָן אַחֵר רוֹמֵז, כִּי הַמֶּלַח מְקַיֵּם כָּל דָּבָר וּמַצִּיל עַל הַהֶפְסֵד וְהָרִקָּבוֹן, וְכֵן בְּמַעֲשֵׂה הַקָּרְבָּן יִנָּצֵל הָאָדָם מִן הַהֶפְסֵד, וְתִשָּׁמֵר נַפְשׁוֹ וְתִשָּׁאֵר קַיֶּמֶת לָעַד.

מִדִּינֵי הַמִּצְוָה, מַה שֶּׁאָמְרוּ זִכְרוֹנָם לִבְרָכָה כִּי כָל הַקָּרְבָּנוֹת נִמְלָחִין קֹדֶם

4. That were to be burned entirely on the altar. The bracketed addition is based on TB M'naḥoth 21b and MT *ibid.* It was evidently present in the original, and omitted by an early scribe as an oversight between two identical phrases (*Mishneh l'Melech*).

§119 1. Since early times, salt has been used as a preservative for food. On the first reason cf. Ramban to Leviticus 2:11.

The salt was applied at three locations: in the "*lishkah* (chamber) of salt," on the ramp [leading to the altar], and at the head of the altar. In the "*lishkah* of salt" they would salt [the skins of holy sacrifices;[4] on the ramp they would salt] the limbs; and at the head of the altar they would salt the handful [taken from a meal-offering], the frankincense [that came with it], meal-offerings that were burned [entirely], and fowl sacrificed as *'olah* (a burnt-offering). The rest of its details are explained in the seventh chapter of the Talmud tractate *Z'vaḥim*.

It applies when the Temple is in existence, for male *kohanim*, as it is for them to complete the needs of an offering. If a *kohen* transgressed it and offered up an animal sacrifice or a meal-offering without salt at all, he would [thus] disobey a positive precept (§119), and also violate this negative precept; and hence he should receive whiplashes—for there is clearly a physical action here [involved in the transgression], when he offers up the unsalted meat which he was adjured not to offer without salt.

119 [THE PRECEPT OF SALTING ALL OFFERINGS]

to offer up salt on all the offerings: i.e. that one should put salt on the meat of an animal sacrifice, and so too on the flour of meal-offerings—as it is stated, *with all your offerings you shall offer salt* (Leviticus 2:13). We said earlier, at the precept of building the Temple (§95), that at the root of the religious duty of the offering lies the purpose of making the spirit of the person who brings it worthy and upright; and therefore, to arouse the spirit of the person offering it, he was commanded to bring good, savory things, which are beloved to him, as we wrote above. The salt in it is also for this root reason—so that this act will be complete, lacking nothing according to the norms of human behavior in the matter: then his heart will be the more aroused by it. For anything without salt will not be pleasing to a man, neither in its taste nor even in its aroma. And apart from this, there is another matter implicit in salt: Salt makes everything endure and prevents spoilage and rot.[1] So too with the act of the offering, a man is saved from becoming spoiled; his spirit will be protected and it will remain in existence forever.

Among the laws of the precept there is what the Sages of blessed memory taught, that all offerings were salted before they went [were brought] up to the altar; and you would find nothing brought to

שֶׁיַּעֲלוּ לַמִּזְבֵּחַ, וְאֵין לְךָ דָּבָר שֶׁקָּרֵב לַמִּזְבֵּחַ בְּלֹא מֶלַח חוּץ מִן הַנְּסָכִים וְהַדָּם וְהָעֵצִים, וְדָבָר זֶה קַבָּלָה וְאֵין לוֹ מִקְרָא; וְאִם עָבַר וְהִקְרִיב בְּלֹא מֶלַח, הַקָּרְבָּן כָּשֵׁר וְנִרְצָה, חוּץ מִן הַמִּנְחָה שֶׁהַמֶּלַח מְעַכְּבָה, שֶׁנֶּאֱמַר בָּהּ בְּפֵרוּשׁ: וְלֹא תַשְׁבִּית מֶלַח בְּרִית אֱלֹהֶיךָ מֵעַל מִנְחָתֶךָ; וְיֶתֶר פְּרָטֶיהָ, מְבֹאָרִים בְּסִפְרָא וּבִמְקוֹמוֹת מִמְּנָחוֹת.

וְנוֹהֶגֶת בִּזְמַן הַבַּיִת בִּזְכָרֵי כְהֻנָּה. וְעוֹבֵר עַל זֶה וְהִקְרִיב מִנְחָה אוֹ קָרְבָּן בְּלֹא מֶלַח כְּלָל, בִּטֵּל עֲשֵׂה, וְעוֹד שֶׁהוּא עוֹבֵר עַל לָאו, דִּכְתִיב: וְלֹא תַשְׁבִּית מֶלַח וְגוֹמֵר.

[מִצְוַת קָרְבַּן בֵּית־דִּין אִם טָעוּ בְּהוֹרָאָה]

קכ שֶׁיַּקְרִיבוּ סַנְהֶדְרֵי גְדוֹלָה קָרְבָּן אִם טָעוּ וְהוֹרוּ שֶׁלֹּא כַהֲלָכָה בַּעֲבֵרוֹת חֲמוּרוֹת שֶׁחַיָּבִין עֲלֵיהֶן כָּרֵת, וְעָשׂוּ הַקָּהָל אוֹ רֻבָּן עַל פִּיהֶן, שֶׁנֶּאֱמַר: וְאִם כָּל עֲדַת יִשְׂרָאֵל יִשְׁגּוּ וְנֶעְלַם דָּבָר מֵעֵינֵי הַקָּהָל, וְגוֹמֵר.

כְּבָר כָּתַבְתִּי לְמַעְלָה כִּי מְכֻוָּנוֹת הַקָּרְבָּן לְהַכְנָעַת נֶפֶשׁ הַמִּתְאַוָּה וּלְהַגְדָּלַת נֶפֶשׁ הַשִּׂכְלִית, וְעַל־כֵּן בְּהַגִּיעַ אֶל הַגְּדוֹלִים טָעוּת בְּדָבָר, יָדוּעַ כִּי בְחֻלְשַׁת הַשֵּׂכֶל אֵרַע לָהֶם וּרְאוּיִים לְחַזְּקוֹ עַל־כָּל־פָּנִים; וְעַל־כֵּן יָבוֹאוּ אֶל הַבַּיִת אֲשֶׁר שֶׁפַע הַשֵּׂכֶל עָלָיו וְיַעֲשׂוּ מַעֲשֵׂה הַקָּרְבָּן (וישובו) [וְיָשִׁיבוּ] אֶל לִבָּם בְּכֹחַ הַפְּעֻלָּה גְּרִיעוּת הַנֶּפֶשׁ הַבַּהֲמִית הַטּוֹעָה וַחֲשִׁיבוּת הַשִּׂכְלִית הַמְיֻשֶּׁרֶת וְהַזַּכָּה, וּמִתּוֹךְ מַחֲשֶׁבֶת טָהֳרָה זוֹ יַשְׁגִּיחוּ וְיַשְׂכִּילוּ בְּכָל הוֹרָאוֹתָם לְעוֹלָם.

מִדִּינֵי הַמִּצְוָה, מַה שֶּׁאָמְרוּ זִכְרוֹנָם לִבְרָכָה שֶׁיֵּשׁ טָעוּת בְּהוֹרָאוֹת בֵּית־דִּין

2. So MT *hilchoth 'issuré ha-mizbé-aḥ* v 11, based on TB M'naḥoth 20a.
3. MT *ibid.* 12, based on the verse (see *Kessef Mishneh*).

§120 1. I.e. of seventy-one justices, whose place of meeting was at the Temple Mount.
2. Sifra on the verse (*parashah* 4, 2); TB Horayoth 3a, 4b, 5a, 8a.

the altar without salt except libations of wine, blood, and wood. This matter is [known by] the Oral Tradition; there is no Scriptural verse for it.[2] If someone transgressed and brought an offering without salt, however, the offering would be fit and acceptable—except for the *minḥah* (meal-offering), which salt can prevent [from being acceptable, by its absence]: for it is stated about this explicitly, *and you shall not let the salt of the covenant with your God be lacking from your meal-offering* (Leviticus 2:13).[3] The rest of its details are explained in the Midrash *Sifra* and in certain places in the tractate *M'naḥoth*.

It is in effect when the Temple is extant, for male *kohanim*. If one transgressed this and offered up a *minḥah* or an animal sacrifice without any salt at all, he would thus disobey a positive precept; moreover, he would [thus] violate a negative precept (§118)—for it is written, *and you shall not let the salt . . . be lacking*, etc.

[THE OFFERING OF THE HIGH COURT IF IT ERRED IN A RULING]

120 that the great *sanhedrin* (supreme court)[1] should bring an offering if they [the justices] erred and gave a ruling not in accord with *halachah* (the normative law) in regard to serious sins punishable by *karéth* [Divine severance of existence], whereupon the community or its greater part acted on their word—for it is stated, *And if the whole congregation of Israel shall sin unwittingly, the thing being hid from the eyes of the assembly*, etc. (Leviticus 4:13).[2]

I have previously written, above (§95), that one of the purposes of an offering is to subdue the appetitive, desiring spirit and amplify the spirit of intelligence. Therefore, when an error in something occurs among the great [Torah scholars], it is evident that this happened to them on account of a failing in intelligence, and it is fitting to strengthen it under all circumstances. For this reason they are to come to the Temple, over which a Divine flow of intelligence is bountifully immanent, and there they are to present the sacrifice of an offering, thus repairing in their heart, through the force of this activity, the defect of the erring animalistic spirit and the eminence of the intelligent spirit, [now] rectified and clear. With the aid of this pure thought they will take watchful care and be wise in all their rulings forever.

Among the laws of the precept there is what the Sages of blessed memory said, that there is an error in rulings by the *beth din* [supreme court] for which the *beth din* is duty-bound to bring an offering and [the

שֶׁהַבֵּית־דִּין חַיָּבִין לְהָבִיא הַקָּרְבָּן וְלֹא עַל הָעוֹשֶׂה עַל פִּיהֶם, וְיֵשׁ שֶׁהָעוֹשֶׂה חַיָּב וְלֹא הֵם. וְאֵלּוּ מִן הַתְּנָאִים הַצְּרִיכִים בַּדָּבָר שֶׁיִּהְיוּ בֵית־דִּין חַיָּבִין וְלֹא הָעוֹשִׂים עַל פִּיהֶם: שֶׁיִּהְיוּ הַמּוֹרִים שֶׁל שִׁבְעִים וְאֶחָד, וְיִהְיֶה רֹאשׁ הַיְשִׁיבָה עִמָּהֶם בְּשָׁעָה שֶׁהוֹרוּ, וְיִהְיוּ כֻּלָּם רְאוּיִין לְהוֹרָאָה, שֶׁנֶּאֱמַר: אִם מֵעֵינֵי הָעֵדָה, עַד שֶׁיִּהְיוּ לָהֶם לְעֵינַיִם, כְּלוֹמַר רְאוּיִין לְהוֹרָאָה, וְיִטְעוּ רֻבָּם בְּדָבָר זֶה שֶׁהוֹרוּ בוֹ, וְיוֹרוּ בְּפֵרוּשׁ, שֶׁיֹּאמְרוּ לָעָם: מֻתָּרִין אַתֶּם לַעֲשׂוֹת, וְיַעֲשׂוּ כָּל הַקָּהָל אוֹ רֻבָּם עַל פִּיהֶם, וְיִהְיוּ הָעוֹשִׂין שׁוֹגְגִין עַל פִּיהֶן וּמְדַמִּין שֶׁהַדָּבָר שֶׁהוֹרוּ בֵית־דִּין כַּדָּת הוֹרוּ, וְלֹא שֶׁיָּדְעוּ אוֹתָן עוֹשִׂין שֶׁטָּעוּ וְעָשׂוּ אַף־עַל־פִּי־כֵן; וְעוֹד שֶׁיּוֹרוּ לְבַטֵּל מִקְצָת מִצְוָה וּלְקַיֵּם קְצָתָהּ, אֲבָל לֹא לַעֲקֹר כָּל מִצְוָה אַחַת, שֶׁנֶּאֱמַר "וְנֶעְלַם דָּבָר" וְלֹא כָל הַגּוּף; וְזֶהוּ גְּזֵרַת הַכָּתוּב; (וְאֶפְשָׁר כִּי טַעַם הָעִנְיָן שֶׁשִּׁגְגַת עֲקִירַת כָּל גּוּף הַמִּצְוָה אֵין לָחוּשׁ שֶׁלֹּא תִתְגַּלֶּה בִמְהֵרָה).

וּכְשֶׁיִּוָּדַע לָהֶם הַחַטָּאת, שֶׁיֵּדְעוּ גּוּפוֹ שֶׁל דָּבָר שֶׁהוֹרוּ בוֹ בִשְׁגָגָה וְלֹא שֶׁיִּסְתַּפְּקוּ עַל אֵי זֶה דָבָר אֵרְעָה לָהֶם הַשְּׁגָגָה, וְאַף־עַל־פִּי שֶׁיָּדְעוּ כִּי בְוַדַּאי שָׁגְגוּ בְאַחַת, וְאַף שֶׁהוֹדִיעוּם הַחוֹטְאִים וְאָמְרוּ לָהֶם בְּזוֹ שְׁגַגְתֶּם, כֵּיוָן שֶׁהֵם אֵינָם זוֹכְרִים אוֹתוֹ דָבָר בְּכִוּוּן פְּטוּרִין, שֶׁנֶּאֱמַר: וְנוֹדְעָה הַחַטָּאת, כְּלוֹמַר לָהֶם וְלֹא שֶׁיּוֹדִיעוּם אֲחֵרִים.

כָּל אֵלֶּה הַתְּנָאִים צְרִיכִין לִהְיוֹת בַּדָּבָר שֶׁיִּתְחַיְּבוּ הַבֵּית־דִּין בְּקָרְבָּן וְלֹא הָעוֹשִׂים עַל פִּיהֶם. (וְאָמְרֵי שֶׁיִּתְחַיְּבוּ הַבֵּית־דִּין קָרְבָּן, רוֹצֶה לוֹמַר שֶׁיָּבִיאוּ קָרְבָּן שִׁבְטֵי יִשְׂרָאֵל כְּנֶגְדָּם, כְּמוֹ שֶׁמְּבֹאָר בְּהוֹרָיוֹת. וְאִם בְּהוֹרָאַת עֲבוֹדָה זָרָה שָׁגְגוּ,

3. TB Horayoth 4b.

4. MT *hilchoth sh'gagoth* xiii 1 (see *Lehem Mishneh*).

5. TB Horayoth 3b.

6. *Ibid.* 2a.

7. MT *hilchoth sh'gagoth* xii 2, xiii 6, from TB Horayoth 4b.

8. E.g. "If you carry something from one domain to another, you are guilty of violating the Sabbath, for Scripture states, *let no man go out of his place* (Exodus 16:29); but it is permissible to throw it there" (MT *ibid.* xiv 2, from TB *ibid.* 4a).

9. And so we must accept it, even if we see no reason for it. (The earliest Hebrew edition has "this is the text of Scripture"—*girsath* in place of *g'zérath*. This, however, is not found in the oldest manuscripts of the work. It would therefore seem to be a scribal error in the manuscript from which the earliest edition was printed. It is regrettable that in such instances ed. Chavel followed the first printed edition blindly, without consulting the extant old manuscripts.)

10. This sentence is not in the oldest manuscripts, and is thus evidently a later marginal note by someone, that was incorporated into the text. Nor need too much weight be given it, since the law, as the author notes, is a decree of Scripture—and hence not for any apparent reason.

11. MT *ibid.* xiv 4, based on TB Horayoth 5a.

obligation] is not on anyone who acted on their word; and there is [an error] where the one who acted [on the ruling] is obligated, and not they [the justices]; and what conditions are necessary in the matter so that the *beth din* should be obligated and not those who acted on their word: that those who give the ruling should be [of the *beth din*] of seventy-one [justices], and the head of the academy should be with them when they give the ruling; and that all should be fit to render rulings in religious law.[3] For it is stated, *then it shall be, if [hidden] from the eyes of the congregation, it was done unwittingly* (Numbers 15:24): [the guilt does not fall on the *beth din*] until they are "eyes" for them, i.e. fit to render rulings,[4] and a majority of them err in this matter on which they gave the decision.[5] Moreover, they must rule explicitly, saying to the people, "You are permitted to do [this]"; and then all or most of the community acts on their word.[6] Those who act on their word must do so unwittingly, believing that in the matter where the *beth din* ruled, they gave a correct decision; and not that those acting in the matter should know that [the justices] erred but they go ahead nonetheless.[7] Furthermore, [the justices] must rule to nullify part of a *mitzvah* (religious duty) and fulfill part of it,[8] but not to uproot an entire single *mitzvah*—for it is stated, *a thing being hid* (Leviticus 4:13), and not the entire body [of the precept];[5] this is a decree of Scripture.[9] (Perhaps the reason for the matter is that when the entire body of a precept is uprooted unwittingly, there is no need to fear that it will not be quickly revealed.)[10]

Moreover, when the sin becomes known to them [the justices], they must know the actual matter in which they unwittingly ruled in error, and not be in doubt about what matter it was where they made the mistake, even though they know for certain that they erred unintentionally in something. Even if the sinners informed them and said, "In this you made the error," since they do not remember the matter precisely, they are free of the obligation. For it is stated, *when the sin becomes known* (Leviticus 4:14)—i.e., to them [of themselves] and not that others should make them know it.[11]

All these conditions must exist in the matter in order for the *beth din* to become duty-bound to bring an offering, and not those who act on their word. (Then it was said that the *beth din* becomes obligated to bring an offering, which is to say that the tribes of Israel should bring the offering in apposition to them [in their behalf], as explained in the Talmud tractate *Horayoth* (5b).[12] If they erred in a

מְבִיאִים שְׁנֵים־עָשָׂר שְׁבָטִים שְׁנֵים־עָשָׂר פָּרִים לְעוֹלָה וּשְׁנֵים־עָשָׂר שְׂעִירִים לְחַטָּאת; וְאִם בְּהוֹרָאַת שְׁאָר כְּרֵתוֹת שֶׁחַיָּבִים עַל שִׁגְגָתָם חַטָּאת, מְבִיאִים שְׁנֵים־עָשָׂר פָּרִים.)

וְאִם חִסֵּר אֶחָד, הָעוֹשֶׂה עַל פִּיהֶם חַיָּב חַטָּאת קְבוּעָה, וְהֵן פְּטוּרִין (שֶׁלֹּא חִיְּבָה הַתּוֹרָה בֵּית־דִּין בְּקָרְבָּן זֶה אֶלָּא כְּשֶׁהֵם בִּשְׁלֵמוּתָם, לְפִי שֶׁיֵּשׁ בָּזֶה הוֹרָאָה לְחַטֵּאת כָּל הָעָם שֶׁיִּשְׁגּוּ רָאשֵׁיהֶם וְהֵם בִּשְׁלֵמוּתָם).

וְיֶתֶר רִבֵּי הַצְּדָדִין שֶׁהַיָּחִיד חַיָּב וְהֵם פְּטוּרִין, אוֹ הֵם חַיָּבִין וְהוּא פָּטוּר, וְחִלּוּק הַקָּרְבָּנוֹת שֶׁבֵּינֵיהֶם — כְּגוֹן מַה שֶּׁאָמְרוּ זִכְרוֹנָם לִבְרָכָה: כָּל הַמִּצְוֹת שֶׁבַּתּוֹרָה שֶׁחַיָּבִין עַל זְדוֹנָן כָּרֵת וְעַל שִׁגְגָתָן חַטָּאת, הַיָּחִיד מֵבִיא כִּשְׂבָּה אוֹ שְׂעִירָה, וְהַנָּשִׂיא שָׂעִיר, וְכֹהֵן מָשִׁיחַ וּבֵית־דִּין מְבִיאִין פָּר; וְהוּא הַכֹּהֵן הַגָּדוֹל שֶׁנִּמְשַׁח בְּשֶׁמֶן הַמִּשְׁחָה — וְיֶתֶר פְּרָטֶיהָ, מְבֹאָרִין בְּמַסֶּכֶת הוֹרָיוֹת, וּבִמְקוֹמוֹת מִזְּבָחִים. וְנוֹהֶגֶת בִּזְמַן הַבַּיִת שֶׁיֵּשׁ לָנוּ סַנְהֶדְרֵי גְדוֹלָה.

[מִצְוַת קָרְבַּן חַטָּאת לְיָחִיד שֶׁשָּׁגַג בְּמִצְוַת לֹא־תַעֲשֶׂה שֶׁחַיָּבִין עָלֶיהָ כָּרֵת]

קכא שֶׁיַּקְרִיב כָּל שׁוֹגֵג בְּחֵטְא מֵהַחֲטָאִים הַגְּדוֹלִים הַיְדוּעִים קָרְבַּן חַטָּאת, שֶׁנֶּאֱמַר: וְאִם נֶפֶשׁ אַחַת תֶּחֱטָא בִשְׁגָגָה מֵעַם הָאָרֶץ, וְגוֹמֵר. וְזֹאת הִיא הַנִּקְרֵאת חַטָּאת קְבוּעָה, כְּלוֹמַר שֶׁהִיא לְעוֹלָם קָרְבָּן בְּהֵמָה וְלֹא יַעֲלֶה וְיֵרֵד לְפִי עֹשֶׁר הַמַּקְרִיב וְעָנְיוֹ. וְהַחֲטָאִים שֶׁיִּתְחַיְּבוּ עֲלֵיהֶם חַטָּאת הֵם לְעוֹלָם אוֹתָן שֶׁחַיָּבִין עַל זְדוֹנָן כָּרֵת. וּבִתְנַאי שֶׁתִּהְיֶה מִצְוַת לֹא־תַעֲשֶׂה וְיִהְיֶה בָהּ מַעֲשֶׂה.

12. View of R. Judah, which Rambam follows (MT *hilchoth sh'gagoth* xii 1; see *Kessef Mishneh*).

13. TB Horayoth 9a (MT *ibid.*). The section in parentheses, from "Then it was said," is found only in the first Hebrew edition. It is likewise absent in the oldest manuscripts. It would therefore seem to be a marginal addition by a later scholar that found its way into the first Hebrew printing.

14. This part of the sentence, in parentheses, is found only in the first Hebrew edition. See note 13, which applies here as well.

15. TB Horayoth 9a.

16. *Ibid.* 11b.

§121 1. TB Yevamoth 9a, etc.

2. TB Makkoth 13b, K'rithoth 2a. Paragraph based on ShM positive precept §69.

ruling about idolatry, the twelve tribes would bring twelve bullocks, each as an '*olah*, and twelve goats, each as a *ḥattath*. If it was in a ruling about another matter involving *karéth* [Divine severance of existence], where a *ḥattath* has to be brought for transgressing it inadvertently, they bring [only] twelve bullocks.)[13]

However, if any one [of these conditions] is lacking, whoever acts on their word is obligated to bring a standard unvarying *ḥattath*, but they [the justices] are free of obligation. (For the Torah required the *beth din* to bring this offering only when they [the conditions] exist in their entirety:)[14] because such is the ruling about a misdeed of the whole people where their heads erred inadvertently, when they [the conditions, are present] in their entirety.

There are many other instances in which the individual [who followed the mistaken ruling] is required [to bring an offering] and they [the justices] have no obligation, or they have the duty and he is free of it. And there is the difference in offerings between them—for example, what the Sages of blessed memory said:[15] Over all precepts in the Torah for whose deliberate violation *karéth* is given and for whose unintentional violation a *ḥattath* (sin-offering) is brought—an individual brings a female sheep or goat, a prince (head of a tribe) brings a male goat, and an anointed *kohen* and a *beth din* bring a bullock. This means the *kohen gadol* who was anointed with the anointing oil.[16] [These] and other details are explained in the Talmud tractate *Horayoth*, and in certain places in *Z'vahim*. It is in force at the time the Temple is extant, when we have a great *sanhedrin* (supreme court).

[THE PRECEPT OF A ḤATTATH FOR CERTAIN UNINTENTIONAL SINNERS]

121 that anyone who trangresses inadvertently one of the great (serious) known sins is to bring a *ḥattath* (sin-offering)—for it is stated, *And if any one of the common people sins inadvertently*, etc. (Leviticus 4:27). This is what is called a standard unvarying *ḥattath;* in other words, it must always be an animal offering, and it is not to be of greater or lesser value according to the wealth of the person offering it, or his poverty. The sins for which there is a duty to bring a *ḥattath* are always those which, if done deliberately, would bring a penalty of *karéth* [Divine severance of existence][1]—and this provided that it is [in every case] a negative precept whose violation involves some physical action.[2]

כְּבָר אָמַרְנוּ כִּי מִשָּׁרְשֵׁי הַקָּרְבָּן לְהַשְׁפִּיל הַנֶּפֶשׁ הַחוֹטֵאת, כַּחַטָּאת כָּאָשָׁם תּוֹרָה אַחַת לָהֶם, אֵינֶנִּי צָרִיךְ לְהַחֲזִירוֹ עַל כָּל אֶחָד וְאֶחָד.

מִדִּינֵי הַמִּצְוָה, כְּגוֹן מַה שֶּׁאָמְרוּ זִכְרוֹנָם לִבְרָכָה שֶׁאֵין חִיּוּב הַשּׁוֹגֵג לְהָבִיא חַטָּאת אֶלָּא עַל עֲבֵרָה שֶׁחַיָּבִין עַל זְדוֹנָהּ כָּרֵת; וְיֵשׁ בַּתּוֹרָה שְׁלֹשָׁה חֲטָאִים שֶׁאַף־עַל־פִּי שֶׁיֵּשׁ בִּזְדוֹנָן כָּרֵת אֵין בְּשִׁגְגָתָן חַטָּאת, וְאֵלּוּ הֵן: מְגַדֵּף וּמְבַטֵּל מִילָה וְחָדֵל מֵעֲשׂוֹת הַפֶּסַח, וְנָתְנוּ טַעַם בְּכָל אֶחָד, וּמְפֹרָשׁ בִּמְקוֹמוֹ. כָּל שְׁאָר הָעֲבֵרוֹת שֶׁזְּדוֹנָן כָּרֵת, שִׁגְגָתָן חַטָּאת קְבוּעָה, חוּץ מִטָּמֵא שֶׁאָכַל אֶת הַקֹּדֶשׁ וְטָמֵא שֶׁנִּכְנַס לַמִּקְדָּשׁ, שֶׁאַף־עַל־פִּי שֶׁזְּדוֹנָן כָּרֵת אֵין מְבִיאִין חַטָּאת קְבוּעָה אֶלָּא קָרְבָּן עוֹלֶה וְיוֹרֵד, שֶׁהוּא עוֹף אוֹ קֶמַח, כְּמוֹ שֶׁמְּפֹרָשׁ בַּכָּתוּב.

נִמְצֵאתָ לָמֵד שֶׁכָּל הָעֲבֵרוֹת שֶׁבַּתּוֹרָה שֶׁהַיָּחִיד מֵבִיא עַל שִׁגְגָתָן חַטָּאת קְבוּעָה שָׁלֹשׁ וְאַרְבָּעִים הֵם, צֵא וַחֲשֹׁב, כִּי כֵן תִּמְצָאֵם, וְרֻבָּם בָּעֲרָיוֹת. וְכֵן מֵעִנְיָן זֶה מַה שֶּׁפֵּרְשׁוּ זִכְרוֹנָם לִבְרָכָה שֶׁאֵין חִיּוּב הַקָּרְבָּן עַד שֶׁיְּהֵא שׁוֹגֵג מִתְּחִלָּה וְעַד סוֹף; וְחִלּוּקֵי הַיְּדִיעוֹת שֶׁאֶפְשָׁר שֶׁיִּהְיוּ לְשׁוֹגֵג בְּשִׁגְגָתוֹ רַבּוֹת; וְיֶתֶר רִבֵּי פְּרָטֶיהָ, מְבֹאָרִים בְּהוֹרָיוֹת וּכְרֵתוֹת, וּבִמְקוֹמוֹת מִשַּׁבָּת וּשְׁבוּעוֹת וּזְבָחִים.

וְנוֹהֶגֶת בִּזְמַן הַבַּיִת בִּזְכָרִים וּנְקֵבוֹת. וְעוֹבֵר עָלֶיהָ וְלֹא הִקְרִיב חַטָּאת עַל שִׁגְגָתוֹ, בִּטֵּל עֲשֵׂה.

3. I.e. the reason and purpose behind all offerings is the same.

4. Blasphemy involves no physical action; and circumcision and the Passover offering are positive precepts.

5. Listed in MT *hilchoth sh'gagoth* i 4 (cf. TB K'rithoth 2a, 3b).

6. But not if, for example, he began doing the sin unaware that it was forbidden, became aware in the middle, and continued the misdeed deliberately; TB Shabbath 102a.

7. E.g. in doing some task on the Sabbath, he may not be aware that this is a forbidden labor, or that the day is the Sabbath.

We have stated earlier (§95) that at the root of an offering lies the purpose to humble the sinful spirit. *As the* ḥattath, *so the* 'asham (*guilt-offering*): *there is one law for them* (Leviticus 7:7).[3] I do not need to repeat it about every one.

Among the laws of the precept, there is, for example, what the Sages of blessed memory said, that the obligation of the unintentional sinner to bring a *ḥattath* (sin-offering) is only for a transgression which if done intentionally brings the punishment of *karéth*. There are, however, three sins in the Torah which, even though there is *karéth* for committing them deliberately, no *ḥattath* need be brought if they are done unintentionally; these are [the sins of] a blasphemer (§70), one who deliberately and irrevocably ignores the precept of circumcision (§2), and one who refrains from bringing the Passover offering (§5). The Sages gave a reason for each one,[4] which is explained in its place. All other transgressions which are punishable by *karéth* if done deliberately, require a standard unvarying *ḥattath* if done inadvertently—except for a ritually unclean person who ate something sacred or entered the Sanctuary: Even though the punishment for doing these sins deliberately is *karéth*, [in these instances] a standard *ḥattath* is not brought, but rather an offering of greater or lesser value, which is fowl or flour, as explained in Scripture (Leviticus 5:6–13).

Consequently, you can learn that all the transgressions in the Torah for which an individual brings a standard unvarying *ḥattath* if he does any inadvertently, are forty-three [in number].[5] Go and make the reckoning, and thus will you find them, most of them in the subject of forbidden marital relationships.

Pertaining to this there is, too, what the Sages of blessed memory explained, that there is no obligation of an offering unless it was unintentional from the beginning to the end.[6] The knowledge or awareness which an inadvertent sinner may have while transgressing unintentionally, may be of many different kinds.[7] The rest of its manifold details are explained in the tractates *Horayoth* and *K'rithoth*, and in certain places in *Shabbath*, *Sh'vu'oth* and *Z'vaḥim*.

It is in force when the Temple is extant, for both man and woman. If a person violated it and did not bring a *ḥattath* for his inadvertent sin, he would [thus] disobey a positive precept.

[מִצְוַת עֵדוּת]

קכב לְהַגִּיד הָעֵדוּת בִּפְנֵי הַדַּיָּנִין בְּכָל מַה שֶׁנֵּדָעֵהוּ, בֵּין שֶׁיִּתְחַיֵּב בָּעֵדוּת מִיתָה אוֹ מָמוֹן הַמּוּעָד עָלָיו, אוֹ שֶׁיִּהְיֶה הַצָּלָתוֹ בְּמָמוֹנוֹ אוֹ בְנַפְשׁוֹ, שֶׁנֶּאֱמַר: וְהוּא עֵד אוֹ רָאָה אוֹ יָדָע אִם לֹא יַגִּיד וְנָשָׂא עֲוֹנוֹ; בְּכָל עִנְיָן חוֹבָה עָלֵינוּ לְהַגִּיד הָעֵדוּת לִפְנֵי הַבֵּית־דִּין.

וְאוּלָם חִלּוּק יֵשׁ בֵּין דִּינֵי מָמוֹנוֹת לְדִינֵי נְפָשׁוֹת וּשְׁאָר אִסּוּרִין שֶׁבַּתּוֹרָה, שֶׁבְּדִינֵי מָמוֹנוֹת אֵין אָדָם חַיָּב לְהָעִיד עֲלֵיהֶם מֵעַצְמוֹ אֶלָּא־אִם־כֵּן יִתְבָּעֶנּוּ בַּעַל הַדָּבָר אוֹ בַעַל־דִּין; וּבְדִינֵי נְפָשׁוֹת וּבְעֵדוּת שְׁאָר אִסּוּרִין שֶׁבַּתּוֹרָה, כְּגוֹן שֶׁרָאָה אֶחָד שֶׁעָבַר עַל אִסּוּר, וְכֵן בְּעֵדוּת נְפָשׁוֹת, כְּגוֹן שֶׁרָאָה מִי שֶׁהָרַג חֲבֵרוֹ, אוֹ בְעֵדוּת מַכּוֹת שֶׁהִכָּה הָאֶחָד אֶת חֲבֵרוֹ, בְּכָל זֶה חַיָּב אָדָם לָבֹא מֵעַצְמוֹ וּלְהַגִּיד הָעֵדוּת לִפְנֵי הַבֵּית־דִּין, כְּדֵי לְבַעֵר הָרַע וּלְהַפְרִישׁ בְּנֵי־אָדָם מֵאִסּוּר.

מִשָּׁרְשֵׁי הַמִּצְוָה, לְפִי שֶׁיֵּשׁ בְּמִצְוָה זוֹ תּוֹעֶלֶת גְּדוֹלָה לִבְנֵי־אָדָם, אֵין צָרִיךְ לְהַאֲרִיךְ בָּהֶם, כִּי יְדוּעִים הַדְּבָרִים לְכָל רוֹאֵי הַשֶּׁמֶשׁ.

דִּינֵי הַמִּצְוָה, כְּגוֹן הַחִלּוּקִים שֶׁגִּלּוּ לָנוּ חֲכָמִים זִכְרוֹנָם לִבְרָכָה שֶׁהֵם בְּמִצְוָה זוֹ בֵּין אִישׁ לְאִישׁ, שֶׁלֹּא כָל אָדָם חַיָּב לָבוֹא לִפְנֵי בֵית־דִּין לְהָעִיד לָהֶם; שֶׁאִם הָיָה הָעֵד חָכָם גָּדוֹל וְהַבֵּית־דִּין פָּחוּת מִמֶּנּוּ שֶׁיֵּשׁ לוֹ לְהִמָּנַע אִם יִרְצֶה מִלְּהָעִיד לִפְנֵיהֶם, שֶׁעֲשֵׂה שֶׁל כְּבוֹד תּוֹרָה דּוֹחֶה עֲשֵׂה דְעֵדוּת; וְכֵן כֹּהֵן גָּדוֹל אֵינוֹ חַיָּב לְהָעִיד אֶלָּא עֵדוּת שֶׁהִיא לְמֶלֶךְ בִּלְבַד; וּמַלְכֵי יִשְׂרָאֵל לֹא מְעִידִין עַל אֲחֵרִים וְלֹא אֲחֵרִים עֲלֵיהֶם, מִשּׁוּם מַעֲשֶׂה שֶׁהָיָה, כְּמוֹ שֶׁבָּא בְּסַנְהֶדְרִין פֶּרֶק כֹּהֵן גָּדוֹל; אֲבָל מַלְכֵי בֵית דָּוִד מְעִידִין וּמְעִידִין עֲלֵיהֶם, וְדָנִין אוֹתָם.

§122 1. So ShM positive precept §178; MT *hilchoth 'éduth* i 1. Cf. TB Bava Kamma 55b–56a, P'saḥim 113b.

2. MT *ibid.* based on TB Sh'vu'oth 31b. (The reading **או בית דין** in ed. Chavel, etc. derives from a misunderstanding of the abbreviation ב״ד, found in two of the oldest manuscripts.)

3. See MT *ibid.* 1–2, and R. Ashér to TB Makkoth i §11.

4. TB Sh'vu'oth 36b.

5. MT *ibid.* 3 (see *Leḥem Mishneh*).

6. A servant of King Yannai killed someone. Simeon b. Shattaḥ (the king's brother-in-law) summoned his colleagues to sit as a *beth din*, to try him, and he called on King Yannai to be present, as Torah law required. The king came and sat. When Simeon bade him stand, as Torah law demanded, the king refused unless Simeon's colleagues confirmed the law. They, however, did not dare support Simeon, out of fear of the king. Simeon b. Shattaḥ then invoked Heaven's vengeance upon them, and they died.

7. TB Sanhedrin 19a.

122 [THE OBLIGATION TO BEAR WITNESS IN COURT] to give testimony before judges about all that we know, whether a person will be sentenced through the testimony to death or to payment of goods and possessions that is imposed on him, or whether someone will thus be spared his goods and possessions or his life. For it is stated, *and he is a witness, whether he has seen or known [the matter]—if he will not tell, he shall bear his iniquity* (Leviticus 5:1): in any matter of guilt or obligation, it is for us to give our testimony before the court.[1]

There is, however, a difference between civil cases, involving goods and possessions, and capital cases [which try a person for his life] and other prohibitions of the Torah: In civil cases, a man is not duty-bound to testify about them of his own accord, but only if a party to the dispute or a litigant summons him [to appear].[2] But in capital cases, or with testimony concerning other prohibitions in the Torah—for example, if a person saw someone transgressing a prohibition, and likewise about testimony on a capital crime, for instance, if he saw who it was that killed his fellow-man, or in regard to testimony about physical attack, where one struck his fellow—in all this [all such cases] a man is duty-bound to come of his own accord and give his testimony before the *beth din*, in order to eradicate the evil and separate people from everything forbidden.[3]

At the root of the precept lies the fact that there is a great benefit for people in this commandment. There is no need to dwell on this; for these matters are evident to all who see the sun.

The laws of the precept are, for example, the differences that the Sages of blessed memory revealed to us, which exist for this precept between one man and another: For not every person is duty-bound to come before a *beth din* to testify to them [the judges]. If the witness is a great scholar and the *beth din* is below him [in rank], if he wishes he may refrain from testifying before them: for the positive precept of honor for the Torah thrusts aside the positive precept to bear witness.[4] Similarly, a *kohen gadol* is not required to give any testimony except for a king alone.[5] And the kings of Israel would not bear witness about others, nor others about them, because of an incident that occurred,[6] as recounted in the second chapter of the tractate *Sanhedrin* (19a). However, the kings of the House of David do testify, and others bear witness about them, and they are judged.[7]

We need not forbear to accept testimony on account of affection

וְאֵין נִמְנָעִין מִלְּקַבֵּל עֵדוּת בִּשְׁבִיל אַהֲבָה וְשִׂנְאָה, כִּי שְׁאֵרִית יִשְׂרָאֵל לֹא יַעֲשׂוּ עַוְלָה בְעֵדוּתָם; אֲבָל לְעִנְיַן הַדִּין אֵינוֹ כֵן, שֶׁאֵין דָּנִין הָאוֹהֵב וְהַשּׂוֹנֵא, מִפְּנֵי שֶׁהַשּׂוֹנֵא אֵין רוֹאֶה זְכוּת וְלֹא הָאוֹהֵב חוֹבָה.

וְכָתַב הָרַמְבָּ"ם זִכְרוֹנוֹ לִבְרָכָה שֶׁעִקַּר עֵדוּת שֶׁל תּוֹרָה הוּא מִפִּי הָעֵדִים וְלֹא מִפִּי כְתָבָם, שֶׁנֶּאֱמַר "עַל פִּי" וְגוֹמֵר, אֶלָּא שֶׁחֲכָמִים, מִפְּנֵי תִקּוּן הָעוֹלָם שֶׁיִּמְצְאוּ בְנֵי־אָדָם לִלְווֹת, תִּקְּנוּ שֶׁנֶּחְתַּךְ הַדִּין בְּמָמוֹן עַל־פִּי עֵדִים שֶׁבִּשְׁטָר כְּמוֹ מִפִּיהֶם.

וְהָרַמְבָּ"ן זִכְרוֹנוֹ לִבְרָכָה הִקְשָׁה עָלָיו בְּסֵפֶר הַמִּצְווֹת הַרְבֵּה עַל זֶה, וְיֶאֱרַךְ הָעִנְיָן אִם בָּאתִי לִכְתֹּב כֻּלּוֹ. וּכְלַל הַדָּבָר, כִּי הָרַמְבָּ"ן זִכְרוֹנוֹ לִבְרָכָה סוֹבֵר שֶׁעֵדוּת שְׁטָר דְּאוֹרַיְתָא הוּא, דִּכְתִיב: וְכָתוֹב בַּסֵּפֶר וְחָתוֹם.

וּמִדִּינֵי הַמִּצְוָה גַּם־כֵּן מַה שֶּׁאָמְרוּ זִכְרוֹנָם לִבְרָכָה שֶׁכָּל אָדָם שֶׁהִגִּיד עֵדוּתוֹ בִּפְנֵי בֵית־דִּין וַחֲקָרוּהוּ כִּרְצוֹנָם אֵין יָכוֹל לַחֲזֹר וְלִסְתֹּר דָּבָר מִכָּל מַה שֶּׁהִגִּיד בִּפְנֵיהֶם וְלוֹמַר שֶׁמָּטְעָה אוֹ שׁוֹגֵג הָיָה, אוֹ שֶׁנִּזְכַּר אַחַר־כָּךְ שֶׁאֵין הַדָּבָר כְּמוֹ שֶׁהֵעִיד; וַאֲפִלּוּ נָתַן טַעַם לִדְבָרָיו אֵין שׁוֹמְעִין לוֹ. וְכָל עֵדוּת שֶׁבִּשְׁטָר הֲרֵי הוּא כְעֵדוּת שֶׁחֲקָרוּהוּ בֵית־דִּין כִּרְצוֹנָם, וְשׁוּב אֵין הָעֵדִים יְכוֹלִים לַחֲזֹר בָּהֶם בְּשׁוּם דָּבָר שֶׁבַּשְּׁטָר.

וְדָנִין עַל פִּי הַחֲתוּמִין בְּכָל דָּבָר הַכָּתוּב בִּשְׁטָר, וְהוּא שֶׁנִּהְיֶה בְרִיאִים שֶׁאוֹתָם הַחֲתוּמִים הֵם שֶׁחֲתָמוּהוּ אוֹתוֹ שְׁטָר וְלֹא זִיְּפָם מְזַיֵּף. וְזֹאת הַחֲקִירָה יֵשׁ לָנוּ לַעֲשׂוֹתָהּ עַל פִּי אֲנָשִׁים שֶׁיַּכִּירוּ אוֹתָן חֲתִימוֹת שֶׁהֵן כְּתִיבַת אוֹתָב הָאֲנָשִׁים הַחֲתוּמִים, וּצְרִיכִין אָנוּ שְׁנֵי עֵדִים שֶׁיַּכִּירוּ שְׁתֵּי הַחֲתִימוֹת, כָּל אֶחָד מֵהֶם יַכִּירוּ שְׁנֵי הָעֵדִים. וְכֵן אִם שְׁנַיִם מִן הַדַּיָּנִים בְּעַצְמָם מַכִּירִין אוֹתָם, דַּי לָנוּ בְכָךְ, אוֹ אִם

8. I.e. if a witness is a good friend or an enemy of one of the litigants or of the person on trial.

9. TB Sanhedrin 27b, 29a. A witness merely reports what happened in his presence, and we do not assume he will lie; but a justice must use thought, reasoning and judgment, which can be colored by strong emotion (*Me'irath 'Enayim, Shulḥan 'Aruch Ḥoshen Mishpat* §33, 1).

10. MT *hilchoth 'éduth* iii 4.

11. Literally, on account of the rectification of the world.

12. Otherwise, if a borrower refused to pay, the lender could collect at court only if he produced the witnesses to the loan or the note. Since they might die or leave the country, people would refuse to lend anyone money in the first place.

13. I.e. in his commentary on ShM root principle 2, toward the end.

14. TB K'thuboth 18b, etc.

15. *Ibid.* 21a, etc.

or hate,[8] because *the remnant of Israel shall not do iniquity* (Zephaniah 3:13) in their testimony. In regard to rendering judgment, though, it is not so: one is not to judge a friend or an enemy, because an enemy will see nothing favorable [about a person], and a friend, nothing unfavorable.[9]

Now, Rambam of blessed memory wrote[10] that the main form of testimony [meant] in the Torah is from the mouths of the witnesses, and not from their written depositions: for it is stated [literally] *By the mouth of* [*two witnesses*, etc.] (Deuteronomy 17:6). It is only that for the sake of proper community life,[11] so that people should find it possible to borrow, the Sages made it a rule that we should render judgment in civil cases on the basis of witnesses [signed] on a deed or promissory note just as [we would] by their spoken word.[12]

However, Ramban of blessed memory refuted him greatly about this in the *Book of Precepts;*[13] the theme would run on at great length if I came to write it all. The crux of the matter is that Ramban of blessed memory holds that the [written] witnessing of a deed or promissory note is valid by Torah law: for it is written, *and it shall be written in a deed and sealed* (Jeremiah 32:44).

Among the laws of the precept there is, too, what the Sages of blessed memory taught,[14] that if any man gave his testimony before the *beth din* and they [the judges] examined him as they wished, he cannot retract and contradict anything out of all that he related before them and say that he was mistaken or he unintentionally lied, or that he remembered afterward that the matter was not as he had testified. Even if he gives a reason for his assertion, he is not heeded. And all attestation in a legal document (a deed or note) is like the testimony of witnesses whom [the judges of] the *beth din* have examined as they wished, so that the witnesses can no longer retract anything in the note.[14]

Thus cases are decided according to [the written attestation by those] who are signed, in regard to everything written in the legal document—but this if we are certain that those who are signed [to it] are the ones who put their signatures to the document, and some forger did not counterfeit them. We are to make this investigation by means of people who recognize the signatures, that they are the writing of the people who are signed to it. We need two witnesses who will recognize the two signatures: each of them should know both witnesses [to the note].[15] So also if two of the judges themselves

הַחֲתוּמִים בְּעַצְמָם לְפָנֵינוּ וְיָעִיד כָּל אֶחָד עַל חֲתִימָתוֹ דַּי בְּכָךְ; אֲבָל הָאֶחָד אֵינוֹ יָכוֹל לְהָעִיד עַל כְּתִיבָתוֹ וְעַל כְּתִיבַת חֲבֵרוֹ. וְכֵן אִם כְּתַב יָדָם יוֹצֵא מִמָּקוֹם אַחֵר לְפָנֵינוּ מְקַיְּמִין מִמֶּנּוּ.

וּמְפֹרָשׁ בַּגְּמָרָא שֶׁאֵין מְקַיְּמִין שְׁטָר מִשְּׁטָר אֶלָּא מִשְּׁנֵי שְׁטָרוֹת שֶׁל שְׁתֵּי שָׂדוֹת שֶׁאֲכָלוּם בַּעֲלֵיהֶן שָׁלֹשׁ שָׁנִים אֲכִילָה גְלוּיָה בְּלֹא שׁוּם יִרְאָה וָפַחַד מִן תְּבִיעַת בְּעָלִים, אוֹ מִשְּׁנֵי שְׁטָרוֹת שֶׁל כְּתֻבּוֹת, וְהוּא שֶׁיָּצְאוּ מִתַּחַת יְדֵי אַחֵר לֹא מִתַּחַת יְדֵי זֶה הָרוֹצֶה בַּקִּיּוּם, דְּחַיְשִׁינָן שֶׁמָּא הַכֹּל זַיֵּף; וְכֵן מִשְּׁטָר אֶחָד שֶׁקָּרָא עָלָיו עַרְעָר וְהֻחְזַק בְּבֵית־דִּין.

וּמַה שֶּׁאָמְרוּ זִכְרוֹנָם לִבְרָכָה גַּם־כֵּן שֶׁבְּעֵדוּת שֶׁל חֲתִימָה נֶאֱמָן קָרוֹב לְהָעִיד עַל כְּתִיבַת קְרוֹבוֹ שֶׁהוּא מַכִּירָהּ, וּמִצְטָרֵף עִם אַחֵר לְקַיֵּם הַשְּׁטָר, וְשֶׁבְּעֵדוּת זוֹ נֶאֱמָן אָדָם בְּגָדְלוֹ לְהָעִיד וְלוֹמַר: כְּשֶׁהָיִיתִי קָטָן רָאִיתִי כְּתַב אָבִי אוֹ אָחִי, וּמַכִּירָהּ אֲנִי עַכְשָׁיו שֶׁהִיא אוֹתָהּ שֶׁרָאִיתִי.

וּמַה שֶּׁאָמְרוּ שֶׁעֲשָׂרָה בְרִיּוֹת פְּסוּלוֹת לְעֵדוּת מִן הַתּוֹרָה, וּכְמוֹ שֶׁכָּתַבְנוּ לְמַעְלָה בְּמִצְוַת "אַל תָּשֶׁת רָשָׁע עֵד" [סי' ע"ה]; וְכֵן מִי שֶׁאֵינוֹ בְּמִקְרָא וְלֹא בְמִשְׁנָה וְלֹא בְדֶרֶךְ־אֶרֶץ שֶׁהוּא פָּסוּל מִדִּבְרֵיהֶם, שֶׁחֲזָקָה עָלָיו שֶׁהוּא רָשָׁע, וַהֲרֵי כְּתִיב: אַל תָּשֶׁת רָשָׁע עֵד. אֲבָל אִם יֵשׁ בּוֹ דֶרֶךְ־אֶרֶץ וְעוֹסֵק בִּקְצָת מִצְווֹת מְקַבְּלִין עֵדוּתוֹ אַף־עַל־פִּי שֶׁהוּא עַם־הָאָרֶץ. נִמְצֵאתָ אוֹמֵר כָּל תַּלְמִיד־חָכָם בְּחֶזְקַת כָּשֵׁר עַד שֶׁיִּפָּסֵל, וְעַם־הָאָרֶץ בְּחֶזְקַת פָּסוּל עַד שֶׁיֻּחְזַק עִמָּנוּ לְטוֹב. וְכֵן אֲנָשִׁים הַבְּזוּיִים בְּיוֹתֵר פְּסוּלִין מִדִּבְרֵיהֶם, כְּגוֹן הָאוֹכְלִים בַּשּׁוּק בִּפְנֵי הַכֹּל וְהַהוֹלְכִים עֲרוּמִים

16. *Ibid.* 21b.

17. *Ibid.* 20b.

18. *Ibid.* 21a.

19. *Ibid.* 20a (MT *hilchoth 'éduth* vi 3).

19a. Literally, "if they emerged under the hands of another, not under the hands of," etc.

20. *Ibid.* 28a.

21. See there, note 7.

22. The Hebrew is a shortened version of Exodus 23:1, which is interpreted to mean this (§75); TB Kiddushin 40b; MT *hilchoth 'éduth* xi 1.

23. MT *ibid.* 2.

24. *Ibid.* 5, from TB Kiddushin 40b.

recognize them, it is enough for us;[16] or if the signatories themselves are before us, and each attests to his signature, it is enough.[17] But one of them cannot testify on both his handwriting and that of his fellow.[18] Likewise, if their handwriting appears before us from another source, it can be validated from that.

Moreover, it is explained in the Talmud[19] that one promissory note or deed cannot be confirmed from another, but only through two deeds concerning two fields whose possessors have openly enjoyed their benefits for three years without any fear or anxiety about claims of ownership, or through two marriage contracts—but this if they were produced by[19a] another, not by the one who wants confirmation [of the document]—for then we fear that all may be counterfeit. So too [can it be confirmed] from one document whose validity was challenged and it was then validated in the *beth din*.[19]

Then there is what the Sages of blessed memory said, further, that in testimony regarding a signature [of a witness to a document] a near relative is believed if he bears witness about the handwriting of his kin, that he recognizes it; and he is counted with another [witness to the signature] to confirm the document.[20] And [there is the law] that in this testimony a man is believed in his adulthood if he bears witness and says, "When I was a youngster I saw the writing of my father (or, my brother) and I recognize it now that this is [the same as] the one that I saw."[20]

There is, likewise, what the Sages said, that ten kinds of human being are disqualified by Torah law from bearing witness—as we wrote above, in the precept, "Do not set a wicked person as a witness" (§75).[21] So also, a person who is versed neither in Scripture nor in the Mishnah, nor is he in good relations with society, is disqualified by a ruling of the Sages: for it may be assumed about him that he is wicked, and it is written, "Do not set a wicked person as a witness."[22] But if he is in good relations with society, and involves himself with some religious duties, his testimony is accepted, even if he is an ignoramus.[23] Consequently, you could say that every Torah scholar is held to be acceptable until he becomes disqualified; and an ignoramus is held to be disqualified until he becomes confirmed for us as good enough. So too, people who are very degraded are disqualified by the ruling of the Sages: for example, those who eat in the marketplace (street) in the presence of everyone, and those who go unclothed in the marketplace (street).[24] Included in the category of the degraded are those who

בַּשּׁוּק, וּמִכְּלַל הַבְּזוּיִים הָאוֹכְלִים צְדָקָה שֶׁל גּוֹיִים בְּפַרְהֶסְיָא. וְיֶתֶר פְּרָטֶיהָ, מְבֹאָרִים בְּסַנְהֶדְרִין וּשְׁבוּעוֹת.

.וְנוֹהֶגֶת בְּכָל מָקוֹם וּבְכָל זְמַן בִּזְכָרִים אֲבָל לֹא בְנָשִׁים, שֶׁאֵין הַנָּשִׁים בְּתוֹרַת עֵדוּת, לְקַלּוּת דַּעְתָּן. וְעוֹבֵר עָלֶיהָ וְלֹא הֵעִיד בְּדִינֵי מָמוֹנוֹת כְּשֶׁתְּבָעוּהוּ לְעֵדוּת בַּעַל־דָּבָר אוֹ בַעַל־דִּין, אוֹ בְדִינֵי נְפָשׁוֹת וּמַכּוֹת וּבְאִסּוּרִין שֶׁל תּוֹרָה מֵעַצְמוֹ, בִּטֵּל עֲשֵׂה וְעָנְשׁוֹ גָּדוֹל מְאֹד, כִּי בְכֹחַ הָעֵדוּת יִתְקַיְּמוּ הַיִּשּׁוּבִים, עַל־כֵּן נִכְתַּב בּוֹ: אִם לֹא יַגִּיד וְנָשָׂא עֲוֹנוֹ. וְאִם תִּהְיֶה הָעֵדוּת אֲשֶׁר כָּבַשׁ עֵדוּת מָמוֹן וְכִחֵשׁ בָּהּ הָעֵד וְנִשְׁבַּע עָלֶיהָ, כְּלוֹמַר שֶׁנִּשְׁבַּע שֶׁאֵינוֹ יוֹדֵעַ לוֹ עֵדוּת, חַיָּב לְהָבִיא קָרְבָּן עוֹלֶה וְיוֹרֵד, וּבַתְּנָאִים הַיְּדוּעִים בָּעִנְיָן, כְּמוֹ שֶׁמְּפֹרָשׁ בִּמְקוֹמוֹ בִּשְׁבוּעוֹת. וְהוּא אֶחָד מִשְּׁלֹשָׁה קָרְבָּנוֹת הַבָּאִין בֵּין עַל שׁוֹגֵג בֵּין עַל מֵזִיד.

[מִצְוַת קָרְבָּן עוֹלֶה וְיוֹרֵד]

קכג לְהַקְרִיב קָרְבָּן עוֹלֶה וְיוֹרֵד עַל חֲטָאִים מְיֻחָדִים, וְהֵם טֻמְאַת מִקְדָּשׁ, כְּלוֹמַר אָדָם שֶׁהוּא טָמֵא בְּאַב הַטֻּמְאָה וְנִכְנַס לַמִּקְדָּשׁ בִּשְׁגָגָה, וְטֻמְאַת קָדָשָׁיו גַּם־כֵּן שֶׁהוּא טָמֵא וְאָכַל בְּשַׂר קֹדֶשׁ בִּשְׁגָגָה, וּשְׁבוּעַת בִּטּוּי, כְּלוֹמַר שֶׁנִּשְׁבַּע לַשֶּׁקֶר עַל דָּבָר לַעֲשׂוֹת אוֹ שֶׁלֹּא לַעֲשׂוֹת, וּשְׁאָר צִדְדֵי שְׁבוּעַת בִּטּוּי הַיְּדוּעִים, וְעוֹבֵר עָלֶיהָ בִּשְׁגָגָה, וְכֵן שְׁבוּעַת הָעֵדוּת, כְּלוֹמַר שֶׁנִּשְׁבַּע לַחֲבֵרוֹ שֶׁאֵינוֹ יוֹדֵעַ לוֹ עֵדוּת, בֵּין בְּשׁוֹגֵג בֵּין בְּמֵזִיד.

עַל אֵלּוּ הַחֲטָאִים חַיָּב אָדָם לְהָבִיא קָרְבָּן עוֹלֶה וְיוֹרֵד, כְּלוֹמַר לְפִי עָשְׁרוֹ וְעָנְיוֹ שֶׁל אָדָם, כְּמוֹ שֶׁמְּפֹרָשׁ בַּכָּתוּב, שֶׁנֶּאֱמַר "וְנֶפֶשׁ כִּי תֶחֱטָא וְשָׁמְעָה קוֹל אָלָה", כְּלוֹמַר קוֹל שְׁבוּעָה שֶׁהִשְׁבִּיעָהוּ אִם יוֹדֵעַ עֵדוּת, "אִם לֹא יַגִּיד וְנָשָׂא עֲוֹנוֹ", וְסוֹף

25. MT *ibid.* from TB Sanhedrin 26b.
26. See the parenthesis in note 2, which applies also here.
27. Mishnah, K'rithoth ii 2 (TB 9a) lists four, but evidently our author reckons two of the instances, both involving oaths, as one (MY).

§123 1. Literally, an offering that ascends and descends.

publicly benefit from the charity of heathens.[25] The rest of its details are explained in the Talmud tractates *Sanhedrin* and *Sh'vu'oth*.

It is in effect in every place, at every time, for men but not for women, as women are not eligible to give testimony, on account of the lightness of their minds [lack of firmness]. If someone violated this and did not bear witness in a civil case when a disputing party or a litigant[26] summoned him to testify, or of his own accord in a case of a capital crime, a physical attack, or where the prohibitions of the Torah are involved, he would thus disobey a positive precept, and his punishment would be very great, for by virtue of testimony, human settlements endure. For this reason it was written about it, *if he does not speak, he shall bear his iniquity* (Leviticus 5:1). If the testimony that he suppressed was evidence in a civil case over goods and possessions, and he swore about it—in other words, he swore that he knew of no evidence to give—he would be obligated to bring an offering of greater or lesser value, under the known conditions [that apply] in the matter, as it is explained in its place in the tractate *Sh'vu'oth* (30a). This is one of three offerings[27] that are brought whether the misdeed was unintentional or deliberate.

[THE PRECEPT OF THE OFFERING OF GREATER OR LESSER VALUE]

123 to bring an offering of greater or lesser value[1] for certain particular sins, which are: Defilement of the Sanctuary; in other words, a man has contracted a major ritual uncleanness and entered the Sanctuary inadvertently; also defilement of its types of holiness, where he is ritually unclean and he eats holy meat inadvertently. An oath of expression, which means that a person swore falsely about something to do or not to do; and the other known ways (types) of an oath of expression; and he transgressed this unintentionally. So too the vow over testimony, i.e. that one swears [falsely] to his fellow that he knows nothing to testify for him—whether inadvertently or deliberately.

For these sins a person is obligated to bring an offering of greater or lesser value, i.e. according to the wealth or poverty of a person, as stated explicitly in Scripture. For it is asserted, *And if anyone sins in that he hears a voice of adjuration* (Leviticus 5:1)—i.e. the voice of an oath, because they made him swear if he knew anything to testify; *if he will not speak, he will bear his iniquity* (*ibid.*); and the end of the

הָעִנְיָן "וְהֵבִיא אֶת אֲשָׁמוֹ", וְלֹא נֶאֱמַר שָׁם "וְנֶעְלַם מִמֶּנּוּ", לְלַמֵּד שֶׁחַיָּב בְּקָרְבָּן בֵּין שׁוֹגֵג בֵּין מֵזִיד.

וּכְתִיב בְּטֻמְאַת מִקְדָּשׁ וְקָדָשָׁיו: אוֹ נֶפֶשׁ אֲשֶׁר תִּגַּע בְּכָל דָּבָר טָמֵא וְגוֹמֵר, וְנֶעְלַם מִמֶּנּוּ וְגוֹמֵר, וְנֶאֱמַר עַל הַכֹּל בְּסוֹף הָעִנְיָן: וְהֵבִיא אֶת אֲשָׁמוֹ. וְלֹא בָא בַכָּתוּב מְפֹרָשׁ שֶׁחִיּוּב הַטָּמֵא שֶׁנֶּאֱמַר שָׁם יִהְיֶה בְּהִכָּנְסוֹ בַמִּקְדָּשׁ אוֹ בְאָכְלוֹ בְשַׂר קֹדֶשׁ, אֶלָּא מִפִּי הַשְּׁמוּעָה שֶׁמָּעְנוּ שֶׁהוּא מְדַבֵּר עַל זֶה; וְאַף־עַל־פִּי שֶׁהַדָּבָר מִפִּי הַקַּבָּלָה, מָצָאנוּ בְּפֵרוּשׁ בְּמָקוֹם אַחֵר חִיּוּב כָּרֵת לַטָּמֵא שֶׁאָכַל קֹדֶשׁ אוֹ נִכְנַס לַמִּקְדָּשׁ, שֶׁנֶּאֱמַר: וְהַנֶּפֶשׁ אֲשֶׁר תֹּאכַל בָּשָׂר מִזֶּבַח הַשְּׁלָמִים אֲשֶׁר לַיי וְטֻמְאָתוֹ עָלָיו וְנִכְרְתָה (וְגוֹמֵר), וְכָתוּב אַחֵר אוֹמֵר בְּטָמֵא שֶׁנִּכְנַס לַמִּקְדָּשׁ: כִּי אֶת מִקְדַּשׁ יי טִמֵּא וְנִכְרְתָה, וְאַחַר שֶׁנִּכְתַּב כָּרֵת בִּזְדוֹנָן יֵשׁ קָרְבָּן בְּשִׁגְגָתָן, עִם הַכְּלָל שֶׁלָּנוּ שֶׁכָּל שֶׁבִּזְדוֹנוֹ כָּרֵת יֵשׁ בְּשִׁגְגָתוֹ חַטָּאת. וּכְתִיב בִּשְׁבוּעַת בִּטּוּי: אוֹ נֶפֶשׁ כִּי תִשָּׁבַע לְבַטֵּא בִשְׂפָתַיִם וְגוֹמֵר, וְנֶעְלַם מִמֶּנּוּ וְגוֹמֵר, וְהֵבִיא אֶת אֲשָׁמוֹ. וּמִנַּיִן שֶׁהַחִיּוּב בָּהּ בְּקָרְבָּן עוֹלֶה וְיוֹרֵד, שֶׁכָּתוּב שָׁם בַּפָּרָשָׁה: וְאִם לֹא תַשִּׂיג יָדוֹ וְגוֹמֵר.

מִשָּׁרְשֵׁי הַמִּצְוָה, כְּבָר אָמַרְנוּ כִּי עִנְיַן הַקָּרְבָּן לְהַזְכִּיר וּלְהָשִׁיב הַחוֹטֵא אֶל לִבּוֹ בְּכֹחַ הַפְּעֻלָּה כִּי הֵרַע מַעֲשָׂיו, וְשֶׁיְּבַקֵּשׁ מְחִילָה לָאֵל עַל הֶעָשׂוּי, וְיִזָּהֵר עַל הֶעָתִיד. וּמֵחָכְמָתוֹ בָּרוּךְ הוּא וּבִידִיעָתוֹ קַלּוּת שֵׂכֶל בְּנֵי אִישׁ וּמִעוּט הֲבָנָתָם וְדַלּוּת כֹּחָם הֵקֵל עֲלֵיהֶם הַכַּפָּרָה בַחֲטָאִים הָאֵלֶּה הַנִּזְכָּרִים לִהְיוֹתָם כְּפִי עֹשֶׁר בְּנֵי־אָדָם וְעָנְיָם,

2. TB Sh'vu'oth 6b.

matter is: *he shall bring his* 'asham *(guilt-offering)* (*ibid.* 6). It is not stated there, "and this was hidden from him," which indicates that he is obligated to bring a sacrifice whether he sinned unwittingly or deliberately.

Now, it is written about defilement of the Sanctuary and its sacred objects, *or if anyone touches any unclean thing . . . and it is hidden from him*, etc. (*ibid.* 2); then it is stated about everything at the end of the matter, *he shall bring his* 'asham *(guilt-offering)* (*ibid.* 6). It is not told in Scripture explicitly that this obligation of the ritually unclean person stated there should take effect when he enters the Sanctuary or eats sacred meat; but we have learned through the Oral Tradition that it means this.[2] And while this matter is by the word of the Oral Tradition, we find elsewhere quite explicitly a penalty of *karéth* [Divine severance of existence] for a ritually unclean person who [deliberately] enters the Sanctuary or eats sacred meat: for it is stated, *But the soul that eats of the flesh of the sacrifice of peace-offerings, that pertain to the Lord, while his uncleanness is upon him, that soul shall be cut off*, etc. (Leviticus 7:20); and another verse states about a ritually unclean person who enters the Sanctuary, *that soul shall be cut off . . . since he has defiled the Sanctuary of the Lord* (Numbers 19:20); and since *karéth* is written [as the punishment] if they are done deliberately, there should be a [*ḥattath*] offering when they are done unintentionally, by our rule that whatever merits *karéth* if done intentionally, a *ḥattath* (sin-offering) is due if it is done inadvertently. Then it is written about an oath of expression, *or if anyone swears clearly with his lips . . . and it is hidden from him . . . then he shall bring his* 'asham *(guilt-offering)* (Leviticus 5:4,6). How do we know that the obligation incurred for it is an offering of greater or lesser value?—because it is written there, in that section of Scripture, *But if he does not have the means*, etc. (*ibid.* 11).

As to the root purpose of the precept, we have stated earlier that the theme of an offering is to remind a person who sinned, and make him ponder in his heart, through the effect of this act, that he has made his deeds evil, and hence he should implore God's forgiveness for what was done, and take care about the future. In His wisdom (blessed is He), knowing as He does the lightness of human intelligence, the paucity of people's understanding, and the meagerness of their strength, He lightened for them the achievement of atonement for these aforementioned sins, that it should be according to the wealth of people, or their poverty. For their moral failings happen easily

לְפִי שֶׁכִּשְׁלוֹנָם קָרוֹב אֵצֶל בְּנֵי־אָדָם, שֶׁאֵין סָפֵק כִּי חֵטְא הַלָּשׁוֹן קָרוֹב וּתְמִידִי יוֹתֵר מֵחֵטְא הַמַּעֲשֶׂה; וְזֶה יַסְפִּיק לְךָ עַל הַשְּׁבוּעוֹת.

גַּם עַל עִנְיַן טֻמְאַת מִקְדָּשׁ וְקָדָשָׁיו יָדוּעַ שֶׁהַכִּשָּׁלוֹן מָצוּי בּוֹ, שֶׁעִנְיַן הַטָּהֳרָה קָשֶׁה מְאֹד עַל כָּל אָדָם לְשָׁמְרוֹ, עַד שֶׁיֵּשׁ לוֹ לָאָדָם הַטָּהוֹר לְהִזָּהֵר מֵהִתְקָרֵב אֵצֶל בְּנֵי־אָדָם מֵחֲשַׁשׁ הַטֻּמְאָה; וְיֶאֱרַךְ הָעִנְיָן אִם בָּאתִי לִכְתֹּב מִכַּמָּה צְדָדִין הַכִּשְׁלוֹנוֹת הַמְּצוּיִין בּוֹ, וְאוּלָם יָדוּעַ הוּא לְכָל מֵבִין.

וּמִן הַשֹּׁרֶשׁ הַזֶּה שֶׁאָמַרְנוּ, שֶׁהַכִּשָּׁלוֹן קָרוֹב בְּעִנְיָנִים אֵלֶּה, הֵקַל לָהֶם עוֹד בִּשְׁבוּעַת הָעֵדוּת לִהְיוֹתָם מְבִיאִים כַּפָּרָה בֵּין עַל שׁוֹגֵג אוֹ מֵזִיד, לְפִי שֶׁעִנְיַן הָעֵדוּת הוּא תְמִידִי בְּיוֹתֵר וְיֵצֶר לֵב הָאָדָם רַע, וְתוֹלִין הַשֶּׁקֶר בְּשִׁכְחָה וְלֹא יְכַוְּנוּ עֵדוּתָם; גַּם יֵשׁ מִן הַבְּרִיּוֹת שֶׁאֵין מַשְׁגִּיחִין כָּל־כָּךְ בָּרָעָה הַגְּדוֹלָה שֶׁעוֹשִׂין בְּהַטָּיַת כִּוּוּן הָעֵדוּת, אַחַר שֶׁבִּידֵיהֶם לֹא יִגְזְלוּ וְלֹא יַחְמְסוּ; אַף־עַל־פִּי שֶׁבְּסִבָּתָם אָדָם עָשׁוּק וְרָצוּץ, לֹא יִתְּנוּ לֵב עַל זֶה. וְעַל כֵּן מֵהַתְמָדַת הָעִנְיָן וְקַלּוּתוֹ בְּעֵינֵי הֲמוֹן הָעָם, הָיָה מֵחֲסָדָיו בָּרוּךְ הוּא לִהְיוֹת בּוֹ כַּפָּרָה בֵּין עַל שׁוֹגֵג בֵּין מֵזִיד.

וְאוּלָם הַמֵּבִין בִּבְנֵי־אָדָם יוֹדֵעַ כִּי כָל אֲשֶׁר יַרְחִיקֶנּוּ הָאֵל מִמֶּנּוּ, אַף־עַל־פִּי שֶׁנִּתַּק הַדָּבָר לְכַפָּרָה, רָאוּי לָנוּ לְהַרְחִיקוֹ תַּכְלִית הָרִחוּק. וְהָעִנְיָן הוּא כְּאִלּוּ יוֹדִיעַ הָאֵל בָּרוּךְ הוּא אֶל בְּנֵי־אָדָם: דָּבָר פְּלוֹנִי אֵין רְצוֹנִי שֶׁתַּעֲשׂוּ אוֹתוֹ בְּשׁוּם פָּנִים, וְאוּלָם הַנִּכְשָׁל מִכֶּם וְיַעֲבֹר עָלֶיהָ יַעֲשֶׂה תְּשׁוּבָה בְּכָל כֹּחוֹ וְיִגְדֹּר עַצְמוֹ בְּהַרְבֵּה גְּדָרִים וְיָבִיא קָרְבָּן לִקְבֹּעַ הַדָּבָר בְּלִבּוֹ, שֶׁלֹּא יִכָּשֵׁל בּוֹ עוֹד. וּמִכָּל־מָקוֹם לֹא נִצַּל הָאִישׁ הַהוּא שֶׁלֹּא עָבַר עַל מִצְוַת בּוֹרְאוֹ.

מִדִּינֵי הַמִּצְוָה, שֶׁכָּל אֶחָד מֵאַרְבָּעָה חֲטָאִים אֵלֶּה מְחַיֵּב עוֹשֵׂהוּ לְהָבִיא כִּשְׂבָּה אוֹ שְׂעִירָה, כְּדִין חַטָּאת קְבוּעָה הַיָּדוּעַ, וְאֵינוֹ נִפְטָר בְּעוֹף אוֹ בְקֶמַח אֶלָּא־אִם־כֵּן

with people: there can be no doubt that sin of the tongue is a more likely and frequent occurrence than sin of action. So this should be enough for you [to explain] about oaths.

In regard to defilement of the Sanctuary and its holy things also, it is known that blundering is usual. The matter of ritual purity is very hard for everyone to keep, so much so that a ritually clean person has to beware of coming close to people, out of fear of defilement. The subject would grow inordinately long if I proceeded to write in how many ways pitfalls are usual occurrences in this; but the matter is known [evident] to every understanding person.

Now, for this root reason that we have stated, that pitfalls are likely in these matters, He made it easy for them also about an oath in regard to bearing witness, that they should bring [an offering for] atonement whether the sin was inadvertent or deliberate. For occasions of bearing witness happen with very great constancy, and the inclination of the heart of man is evil; thus people can attribute a lie to forgetfulness and will not be accurate in their testimony. There are also some human beings who are not so very concerned or aware of the great evil they do by distorting the accuracy of testimony, since they do not commit robbery or extortion with their own hands.

Even though a man is wronged and broken because of them, they pay this no heed. Therefore, on account of the persistence of the matter and its insignificance in the eyes of the common people, it was a facet of His kindness (blessed is He) that there should be atonement for it whether it was done inadvertently or deliberately.

Yet the understanding man among people knows that whatever God puts at a distance from us, even though He has arranged atonement for the matter, it is fitting for us to remove it to an utmost distance. In substance, it is as though God (blessed is He) informed people, "As to that matter, it is not My desire that you should do it in any way whatever. However, if one of you stumbles and commits that misdeed, let him repent with all his strength and fence himself about with many fences [protective restraints], and let him bring an offering, to set the matter firmly in his heart, so that he will not stumble in it again." And in any event, that man is not saved from the fact that he disobeyed the commandment of his Creator.

Among the laws of the precept there is: that every one of these four sins obligates the one who commits it to bring a female sheep or goat, by the known law of the standard unvarying *ḥattath*, and he

הוּא עָנִי. וְאִם הוּא עָנִי וְהֵבִיא כִּשְׂבָּה אוֹ שְׂעִירָה לֹא יָצָא יְדֵי חוֹבָתוֹ, וְהַטַּעַם לְפִי שֶׁאַחַר שֶׁהָאֵל בָּרוּךְ הוּא רִחֵם עָלָיו וּפְטָרוֹ בְּכָךְ אֵינוֹ בְּדִין שֶׁיִּדְחַק עַצְמוֹ לְהָבִיא בְּיוֹתֵר [מִ]מַּה שֶּׁתַּשִּׂיג יָדוֹ. וּבָזֶה יִקְנֶה כָּל מֵבִין עֵצָה לְבִלְתִּי עֲשׂוֹת הוֹצָאוֹת בְּיֶתֶר מִן הָרָאוּי לוֹ לְפִי מָמוֹנוֹ, לְמַעַן כִּי בוֹ סִבָּה לִגְזֹל אֶת הַבְּרִיּוֹת כְּשֶׁמְּבַקֵּשׁ לְמוֹדוֹ וְאֵינוֹ מוֹצֵא.

וְאָמְרוּ גַם־כֵּן שֶׁמִּי שֶׁהָיָה עָשִׁיר וְהִפְרִישׁ מָעוֹת לִקַּח בָּהֶם כִּשְׂבָּה אוֹ שְׂעִירָה וְהֶעֱנִי וְצָרִיךְ לַמָּעוֹת, יִקַּח שְׁנֵי תוֹרִים אוֹ שְׁנֵי בְנֵי יוֹנָה וְיֹאמַר "הֲרֵי הַמָּעוֹת הַלָּלוּ מְחֻלָּלִין עַל עוֹפוֹת אֵלּוּ", וְאַחַר־כָּךְ יֵהָנֶה בְּכָל הַמָּעוֹת. וְכֵן אִם הִפְרִישׁ מָעוֹת לְעוֹפוֹת וְהֶעֱנִי וְצָרִיךְ לָהֶם, מְחַלְּלָן עַל עֲשִׂ־ירִית הָאֵיפָה קֶמַח, וְנֶהֱנֶה בָהֶן. וְכֵן עָנִי שֶׁהִפְרִישׁ מָעוֹת לַעֲשִׂירִית הָאֵיפָה וְהֶעֱשִׁיר, מוֹסִיף עֲלֵיהֶן וּמֵבִיא כִּשְׂבָּה אוֹ שְׂעִירָה. וְעָשִׁיר נִקְרָא לְעִנְיָן זֶה כָּל זְמַן שֶׁיֵּשׁ לוֹ.

וְחִיּוּב קָרְבָּנוֹת אֵלֶּה דַּוְקָא בְּשׁוֹגֵג, וּבִשְׁבוּעַת הָעֵדוּת אֲפִלּוּ בְּמֵזִיד, אֲבָל בְּאָנוּס אֵין בּוֹ חִיּוּב קָרְבָּן בְּאֶחָד מֵהֶם, שֶׁכָּל אָנוּס הַתּוֹרָה פְּטָרַתּוּ מִכָּל חִיּוּב.

וְהַצְּדָדִין שֶׁהֵן בִּשְׁבוּעוֹת שֶׁהָאָדָם נִקְרָא אָנוּס בָּהֶן וּפָטוּר, אוֹ שׁוֹגֵג וְחַיָּב; וְהַצְּדָדִין שֶׁאֵין מִתְחַיֵּב אֶלָּא קָרְבָּן אֶחָד אֲפִלּוּ עַל כַּמָּה שְׁבוּעוֹת אוֹ קָרְבָּן אֶחָד עַל כָּל שְׁבוּעָה וּשְׁבוּעָה.

וְכֵן בְּעִנְיַן קָרְבַּן טֻמְאַת מִקְדָּשׁ וְטֻמְאַת קָדָשָׁיו, הַצְּדָדִין שֶׁיֵּשׁ בָּהֶן לְחִיּוּב וְלִפְטוּר: צַד הַחִיּוּב יִהְיֶה בְּשֶׁיֵּשׁ לוֹ לַחוֹטֵא יְדִיעַת הַטֻּמְאָה וְהֶקְדֵּשׁ אוֹ מִקְדָּשׁ תְּחִלָּה וְכֵן בַּסּוֹף וְהֶעְלֵם בֵּינְתַיִם. כֵּיצַד, נִטְמָא וְיָדַע שֶׁנִּטְמָא וּבָא לְיָדוֹ בְּשַׂר קֹדֶשׁ

3. This is evident from Scripture: Leviticus 5:7, 11.

4. As *Mishneh l'Melech* notes, this is a novel view; MT *hilchoth sh'gagoth* x 13 rules otherwise, on the basis of Mishnah, N'ga'im xiv 12; see MY.

5. I.e. of money, to which he has grown accustomed.

6. TB K'rithoth 27b.

7. The amount needed for the meal-offering (Leviticus 5:11); an *'éphah* is 24,883 cubic centimeters according to one view, 43,000 cubic centimeters according to another.

8. I.e. he must bring the offering he can afford at the time.

9. So TB Sh'vu'oth 31b.

10. Or if he was the victim of an accident; the Hebrew term *'anuss* has this sense also (in either case he acted without choice).

11. A Talmudic dictum: TB Bava Kamma 25b; cf. also P'saḥim 71b.

12. TB Sh'vu'oth 31b, 33b.

does not acquit himself [of his obligation] with a fowl or flour unless he is poor;[3] and [conversely] if he is poor and has brought a female sheep or goat, he has not fulfilled his obligation.[4] The reason is that since God (blessed is He) had pity on him and let him go free of his obligation with this, it is not right that he should strain himself to bring more than he can afford. From this every understanding person can learn the wise lesson not to have expenditures more than are suitable for him according to his [level of] possessions: for in this lies a cause to rob people, when he will seek his habitual amount[5] and not find it.

Our Sages taught also[6] that if someone was wealthy and he set aside money to buy a female sheep or goat with it, and then he became poor and needed the money, he should buy two turtledoves or two young pigeons, and say, "This money is made non-holy in exchange for these birds"; and afterward he may derive benefit from all the money. So too, if he set aside money for fowl and he became poor and in need of it: he should make it non-holy in exchange for a tenth of an *'éphah* of flour,[7] and he may have the benefit of it. Similarly, if a poor man set aside money for the tenth of an *'éphah* and he became wealthy, he should add to it and bring a female sheep or goat. One is called wealthy in this respect as long as he has the means.[8]

The duty to bring these offerings is only for the unintentional sinner, and over an oath about testimony, even for an intentional sinner;[9] but if someone was forced to it,[10] he has no obligation to bring an offering in any of these matters. For whoever is forced[10] [to sin], the Torah absolves him of all guilt and obligation.[11]

[Then there are the laws of] which circumstances there are regarding oaths whereby a man is called forced (compelled) and is thus free of obligation, or [is called] an inadvertent sinner so that he bears the obligation; those circumstances in which a person would be obligated to bring no more than one offering even for several oaths, or one offering for each and every oath.[12]

So too, regarding the offering for defilement of the Sanctuary and defilement of its holy things, [there are the laws about] the circumstances which impose the obligation or leave one free of it: There will be obligation when the sinner has knowledge of his ritual uncleanness and [the holiness of] the sacred things or the Sanctuary at the start, and likewise at the end, but forgetfulness, lack of awareness in between. How so? A man became defiled, and he knew he was

וְיוֹדֵעַ שֶׁהוּא בְשַׂר קֹדֶשׁ, אוֹ בָא לִכָּנֵס לַמִּקְדָּשׁ וְיוֹדֵעַ שֶׁהוּא מִקְדָּשׁ, שֶׁעַכְשָׁיו יֵשׁ לוֹ יְדִיעָה מִן הַטֻּמְאָה וּמִן הַקֹּדֶשׁ בַּתְּחִלָּה, וְאַחַר־כָּךְ יֵשׁ לוֹ הַעֲלָמָה, שֶׁשָּׁכַח טֻמְאָתוֹ וְחָשַׁב שֶׁהוּא טָהוֹר, וְכֵן נַמִּי שֶׁנֶּעֶלְמוּ מִמֶּנּוּ הַקֹּדֶשׁ אוֹ הַמִּקְדָּשׁ וַחֲשָׁבָם לְחֻלִּין וְאָכַל מִן הַקֹּדֶשׁ אוֹ נִכְנַס לַמִּקְדָּשׁ, שֶׁזֶּהוּ הֶעְלֵם בֵּינְתַיִם, וְאַחַר־כָּךְ נוֹדַע לוֹ שֶׁטָּמֵא הָיָה אוֹ שֶׁבְּשַׂר קֹדֶשׁ אוֹ מִקְדָּשׁ הָיוּ, שֶׁזֶּהוּ יְדִיעָה בַסּוֹף, בְּעִנְיָן זֶה מֵבִיא קָרְבָּן; וְעַל זֶה אָמְרוּ רַבּוֹתֵינוּ זִכְרוֹנָם לִבְרָכָה: יְדִיעָה בַתְּחִלָּה וּבַסּוֹף וְהֶעְלֵם בֵּינְתַיִם.

וְצַד הַפְּטוּר הוּא כְּשֶׁנִּטְמָא וְלֹא יָדַע שֶׁנִּטְמָא, וְנִכְנַס לַמִּקְדָּשׁ אוֹ אָכַל בְּשַׂר קֹדֶשׁ, וְאַחַר־כָּךְ נוֹדַע לוֹ שֶׁנִּטְמָא, בְּעִנְיָן זֶה הוּא פָּטוּר מִקָּרְבָּן.

וְדִין זֶה אֵינוֹ כִּשְׁאָר חַיָּבֵי כְרֵתוֹת שֶׁבַּתּוֹרָה, שֶׁבִּשְׁאָר הַכְּרֵתוֹת מִכֵּיוָן שֶׁיָּדַע בַּסּוֹף אַף־עַל־פִּי שֶׁבַּתְּחִלָּה לֹא יָדַע חַיָּב בְּקָרְבָּן; וְהַכָּתוּב מַכְרִיעַ בְּכָאן לָדוּן כֵּן, דִּכְתִיב בְּטֻמְאַת מִקְדָּשׁ וְקָדָשָׁיו "וְנֶעְלַם מִמֶּנּוּ", מִכְּלַל שֶׁהָיְתָה לוֹ שְׁעַת יְדִיעָה בַּתְּחִלָּה, וְנֶאֱמַר אַחַר־כֵּן "וְהוּא יָדַע", הָא לָמַדְתָּ שֶׁצָּרִיךְ יְדִיעָה בַתְּחִלָּה וִידִיעָה בַסּוֹף וְהֶעְלֵם בֵּינְתַיִם.

אֲבָל בִּשְׁאָר חַיָּבֵי כְרֵתוֹת כְּתִיב: בַּעֲשׂוֹתָהּ אַחַת מִמִּצְוֹת יי אֲשֶׁר לֹא תֵעָשֶׂינָה וְאָשֵׁם אוֹ הוֹדַע אֵלָיו חַטָּאתוֹ, כְּלוֹמַר מִכֵּיוָן שֶׁיָּדַע בַּסּוֹף אַף־עַל־פִּי שֶׁלֹּא יָדַע בַּתְּחִלָּה, שֶׁהֲרֵי אֵין כָּתוּב שָׁם "וְנֶעְלַם" שֶׁנִּלְמַד מִמֶּנּוּ יְדִיעָה בַתְּחִלָּה.

וּמֵעִנְיַן הַמִּצְוָה גַם־כֵּן מַה שֶּׁאָמְרוּ זִכְרוֹנָם לִבְרָכָה שֶׁמִּי שֶׁיֵּשׁ לוֹ יְדִיעָה

13. *Ibid.* 2a.
14. The last three paragraphs are based on TB Sh'vu'oth 14a.
15. *Ibid.* 14b.

ritually unclean; sacred meat came into his possession, and he knew it was sacred meat; or he came to enter the Sanctuary and he knew it was the Sanctuary; thus, now, he had knowledge of the ritual uncleanness and of the sacredness, at the start. But afterward he had a loss of awareness: he forget that he was defiled and thought he was ritually clean; and so too if he lost his awareness of the holy object or the Sanctuary and thought them non-holy; and thus he ate of the holy food or entered the Sanctuary. This is the forgetfulness in between. After that it became known to him [he became aware again] that he was ritually unclean or that these were sacred meat and the Sanctuary—this being the awareness at the end. In such a situation he brings an offering. About this our Sages of blessed memory said [in description],[13] "knowledge at the beginning and end, and forgetfulness in between."

The situation in which a person is free of obligation is where he became defiled and did not know he was defiled, and so he entered the Sanctuary or ate the sacred meat; and afterward it became known to him that he had been defiled [at the time]. In such a situation he need bring no offering.

This law does not hold for other [unwitting] sins in the Torah punishable by *karéth* [Divine severance of existence, if done deliberately]. For other sins that involve *karéth*, as long as a person knew at the end [that he had sinned] even if at the beginning he did not know, he has the duty to bring an offering. But the Writ determines here to apply the law so: For it is written about the defilement of the Sanctuary and its sacred things, *and it became hidden from him* (Leviticus 5:2); from this it follows that he had a period of awareness at the beginning; and it is stated afterward, *when he knows of it* (*ibid.* 3). Hence you have learned that [for an offering to be required] there must be knowledge at the beginning, knowledge at the end, and loss of awareness in the meantime.[14]

However, about other sins involving the punishment of *karéth*, it is written, *in his doing any of the things which the Lord has commanded not to be done, and he is guilty, if his sin becomes known to him* (Leviticus 4:27–28). In other words, as long as he knows at the end, even if he did not know at the beginning—for it is not written there, "and it became hidden from him," that we should learn from it [the requirement of] awareness at the beginning.[15]

In the subject-matter of the precept there is also what the Sages of blessed memory taught,[13] that if someone had knowledge [aware-

בַּתְּחִלָּה וְלֹא בַּסּוֹף שֶׁאֵין יָכוֹל לְהָבִיא כַּפָּרָה, כְּמוֹ שֶׁאָמְרוּ שֶׁשָּׂעִיר שֶׁל יוֹם הַכִּפּוּרִים הַנַּעֲשֶׂה בִּפְנִים וְיוֹם הַכִּפּוּרִים בְּעַצְמוֹ תּוֹלִין עַד שֶׁיִּוָּדַע לוֹ וְיָבִיא קָרְבַּן כַּפָּרָתוֹ.

וְשֶׁאֵין לוֹ יְדִיעָה בַּתְּחִלָּה אֲבָל יֵשׁ לוֹ יְדִיעָה בַּסּוֹף, שֶׁאָמַרְנוּ שֶׁאֵינוֹ מֵבִיא קָרְבָּן לְעוֹלָם, שָׂעִיר הַנַּעֲשֶׂה בַּחוּץ וְיוֹם הַכִּפּוּרִים מְכַפְּרִין עָלָיו; וְעַל שֶׁאֵין בּוֹ יְדִיעָה לֹא תְחִלָּה וְלֹא סוֹף, שְׂעִירֵי הָרְגָלִים וּשְׂעִירֵי רָאשֵׁי חֳדָשִׁים מְכַפְּרִין עָלָיו; וְעַל זְדוֹן טֻמְאַת מִקְדָּשׁ וְקָדָשָׁיו, פַּר כֹּהֵן גָּדוֹל שֶׁל יוֹם הַכִּפּוּרִים מְכַפֵּר אִם הַמֵּזִיד מִן הַכֹּהֲנִים, וְאִם הָיָה מִיִּשְׂרָאֵל דַּם שָׂעִיר הַנַּעֲשֶׂה בִּפְנִים וְיוֹם הַכִּפּוּרִים מְכַפְּרִין, שֶׁנֶּאֱמַר: וְכִפֶּר עַל הַקֹּדֶשׁ מִטֻּמְאֹת בְּנֵי יִשְׂרָאֵל.

וּמַה שֶּׁאָמְרוּ זִכְרוֹנָם לִבְרָכָה כִּי בְּאַרְבָּעָה חֲטָאִים אֵלֶּה הַכֹּל שָׁוִין בָּהֶן בְּקָרְבָּן, מֶלֶךְ וְכֹהֵן מָשִׁיחַ וְהֶדְיוֹט, שֶׁאֵין חִלּוּק בֵּינֵיהֶם בְּקָרְבָּנָם, אֶלָּא בַּמִּצְוָה שֶׁחַיָּבִין עַל שִׁגְגָתָן חַטָּאת קְבוּעָה; אֲבָל בְּאֵלּוּ שֶׁחִיּוּבָן עוֹלֶה וְיוֹרֵד, הַכֹּל שָׁוִין בָּהֶן; וְיֶתֶר פְּרָטֶיהָ, מְבֹאָרִים בִּכְרֵתוֹת וּשְׁבוּעוֹת.

וְנוֹהֶגֶת בִּזְמַן הַבַּיִת בִּזְכָרִים וּנְקֵבוֹת, חוּץ מִקָּרְבַּן שְׁבוּעַת הָעֵדוּת, שֶׁאֵינוֹ נוֹהֵג בִּנְקֵבוֹת, שֶׁאֵינָן בְּתוֹרַת עֵדוּת, כְּמוֹ שֶׁכָּתַבְנוּ לְמַעְלָה. וְעוֹבֵר עָלֶיהָ וְלֹא הִקְרִיב קָרְבָּנוֹ עַל אַחַת מֵאֵלֶּה, בִּטֵּל עֲשֵׂה.

[שֶׁלֹּא לְהַבְדִּיל הָרֹאשׁ בְּחַטַּאת הָעוֹף]

קכד שֶׁלֹּא יַפְרִיד הַכֹּהֵן מִן הָעוֹף הַבָּא לְקָרְבָּן, וְהוּא הַנִּקְרָא חַטַּאת הָעוֹף, הָרֹאשׁ מִן הַגּוּף כְּשֶׁיִּמְלֹק אוֹתוֹ, שֶׁנֶּאֱמַר: וּמָלַק אֶת רֹאשׁוֹ מִמּוּל עָרְפּוֹ וְלֹא

16. I.e. its blood was sprinkled there.
17. So that he is not judged and punished for it.
18. I.e. its blood was sprinkled only on the outer, copper altar.
19. TB Horayoth 9a; MT *hilchoth sh'gagoth* x 7.

ness of the situation] at the start but not at the end, and thus cannot bring any atonement-offering—as they said,[13] the goat of the Day of Atonement which was sacrificed within [the holy chambers of the Sanctuary][16] and the Day of Atonement itself keep the matter in abeyance[17] until it becomes known to him, and then he brings the offering for its atonement.

Now, when he has no awareness at the start but is aware at the end, in which case, we said, he can never bring an offering—the goat sacrificed outside [the holy chambers][18] and the Day of Atonement atone for him. And for one who has no awareness either at the beginning or at the end, the goats offered up on the pilgrimage festivals and new-month days brought atonement. As for deliberate, intentional defilement of the Sanctuary and its sacred things, the bullock of the *kohen gadol* on the Day of Atonement atoned for it if the willful sinner was of the *kohanim*; if he was an ordinary Israelite, the blood of the goat sacrificed within [the holy chambers] and the Day of Atonement atoned for him—for it is stated, *And he shall make atonement for the holy place because of the uncleannesses of the Israelites* (Leviticus 16:16).[13]

There is, further, what the Sages of blessed memory taught,[19] that in respect of these four sins, all are equal in regard to the offering: king, anointed *kohen* [*gadol*] and commoner. There is no difference among them concerning their offerings, except over a precept for whose unintentional transgression a standard unvarying *ḥattath* (sin-offering) must be brought; however, for those which require an offering of greater or lesser value, all are equal in it. [These] and other details are explained in the Talmud tractates *K'rithoth* and *Sh'vu'oth*.

It applies when the Temple is extant, for both man and woman, except for the offering over an oath about testimony, which does not apply to women, since they are not accepted as witnesses, as we wrote above (§122). If someone transgressed it and did not bring his offering for one of these [sins], he would thus disobey a positive precept.

[NOT TO SEPARATE THE HEAD OF A BIRD BROUGHT AS A ḤATTATH]

124 that the *kohen* should not sunder from a fowl brought as an offering, which is called "a *ḥattath* (sin-offering) of fowl," the head from the body when he cuts it with the fingernail—for it is stated, *u-malak, and he shall sever its head from against its nape, but shall not divide it asunder* (Leviticus 5:8). The sense of the verb *(malak)* is that

יַבְדִּיל, וּפֵרוּשׁ מְלִיקָה הוּא שֶׁנּוֹעֵץ הַכֹּהֵן צִפָּרְנָיו מִמּוּל עָרְפּוֹ, דְּהַיְינוּ הָעֶצֶם הַנִּקְרָא עֶצֶם דְּמַפְרֶקֶת, וְחוֹתֵךְ הָעֶצֶם בְּצִפָּרְנוֹ עַד שֶׁמַּגִּיעַ לַסִּימָנִין, וְחוֹתֵךְ גַּם הַסִּימָנִין בְּצִפָּרְנוֹ, אוֹ רֻבּוֹ שֶׁל אֶחָד מֵהֶן; וְזֹאת הִיא שְׁחִיטָתוֹ שֶׁל חַטַּאת הָעוֹף; וְצָרִיךְ שֶׁיְּכַוֵּן הַכֹּהֵן שֶׁלֹּא יַחְתֹּךְ הַכֹּל לְגַמְרֵי עַד שֶׁיְּהֵא נִפְרָד הָרֹאשׁ מִן הַגּוּף; וְעַל זֶה נֶאֱמַר "לֹא יַבְדִּיל".

כְּבָר אָמַרְנוּ בְּמִצְוַת בִּנְיַן הַבַּיִת שֶׁאֵין בָּנוּ יְכֹלֶת וְגַם לֹא לַאֲשֶׁר קָטְנוֹ עָבָה מִמָּתְנֵינוּ, לִמְצֹא טַעֲנָה גַּם עַל צַד הַפְּשָׁט בְּפְרָטֵי הַקָּרְבָּנוֹת; וְדַי לָנוּ לִמְלַאכְתֵּנוּ זֹאת לְהוֹדִיעַ בְּעִנְיַן הַקָּרְבָּנוֹת דֶּרֶךְ כְּלָל קְצָת טַעַם עַל צַד הַפְּשָׁט; וּכְבָר כָּתַבְתִּי לְמַעְלָה מַה שֶּׁיָּדַעְתִּי וְשָׁמַעְתִּי. וְעִנְיַן הַמְּלִיקָה וְהָאַזְהָרָה שֶׁלֹּא יַבְדִּיל, גַּם זֶה מִפְּרָטֵי הַקָּרְבָּן הוּא. וְאַף אָמְנָה, אֲשֶׁר לֹא יָחוּשׁ לְהוֹצִיא כָּל רוּחוֹ יוּכַל לְהָשִׁיב כִּי אוּלַי בִּדְבַר הַמְּלִיקָה הַנַּעֲשֵׂית בְּיַד הַכֹּהֵן בְּחַטַּאת הָעוֹף, שֶׁהוּא קָרְבָּן שֶׁל עָנִי, רֶמֶז שֶׁיְּמַהֵר כָּל אָדָם בְּתַכְלִית הַמְּהִירוּת צָרְכּוֹ שֶׁל עָנִי; וְעַל־כֵּן אֵינוֹ צָרִיךְ קָרְבָּנוֹ שְׁחִיטָה, שֶׁלֹּא יִצְטָרֵךְ הַכֹּהֵן לְחַזֵּר אַחַר הַסַּכִּין וּלְבָדְקוֹ, וְיִתְבַּטֵּל הֶעָנִי שָׁם מִמְּלַאכְתּוֹ בֵּינְתַיִם. גַּם לְהַפְלִיג הַמְּהִירוּת אָמַר שֶׁיַּתְחִיל מִמּוּל עָרְפּוֹ, כִּי הוּא הַמּוּכָן אֶל יָדוֹ, וְלֹא יִצְטָרֵךְ לַהֲפֹךְ הַצַּוָּאר אֶל צַד הַסִּימָנִין.

וְעוֹד יֵשׁ רֶמֶז בְּעִנְיַן הַמְּלִיקָה, שֶׁהִיא מִמּוּל הָעֹרֶף בְּתוֹרִים וּבְנֵי יוֹנָה, שֶׁנִּמְשְׁלוּ יִשְׂרָאֵל בָּהֶם, שֶׁלֹּא נִהְיֶה קְשֵׁי עֹרֶף. וְעִנְיַן אִסּוּר הַבְדָּלַת הָרֹאשׁ מִן הַגּוּף דָּבָר רָאוּי הוּא לְהִדּוּר הַקָּרְבָּן, כִּי בֶּאֱמֶת כְּשֶׁרֹאשׁ הָעוֹף דָּבֵק עִמּוֹ הוּא יוֹתֵר מְהֻדָּר, וְרָאוּי לָנוּ לְהַדֵּר קָרְבָּנוֹ שֶׁל עָנִי בְּכָל כֹּחֵנוּ; דַּי לוֹ בַּעֲנִיּוּתוֹ, אֵין לָנוּ לְהוֹסִיף בְּדַלּוּתוֹ לִפְחֹת תֹּאַר קָרְבָּנוֹ.

§124 1. TB Z'vaḥim 64b–65b.

2. So MT *hilchoth ma'aséh ha-korbanoth* vii 6; this differs with Rashi on the verse cited and in TB Ḥullin 21b, s.v. *v'éno mavdil.*

3. Expression derived from I Kings 12:10 (indicating vast superiority).

4. See §104, note 3.

5. Expression based on Proverbs 29:11.

6. E.g. in TB B'rachoth 53b, Gittin 45a, Sanhedrin 95a, etc.

7. The Hebrew biblical idiom for this term means literally, hard of nape.

8. It would demean it to offer it up in small separate pieces.

the *kohen* digs his fingernail in at the nape, i.e. [at] what is called the neck-bone; he cuts the bone with his fingernail until he reaches the windpipe and gullet.[1] He cuts these organs also with his fingernail,[2] or [at least] the greater part of one of them. This is the ritual slaying of a *ḥattath* of fowl. And the *kohen* must concentrate that he should not cut everything completely until the head will be separated from the body; for this reason it was stated, *but he shall not divide it asunder.*

We stated earlier, in the precept of building the Temple (§95), that we have not the ability, nor would someone whose little finger is thicker than our hips,[3] to find a contendable reason, even by way of the plain meaning, about the details of the offerings.[4] For us it is enough, for this task of ours, to convey about the subject of the offerings, in a general way, some bit of reason in accord with the ordinary meaning; and I have already written above what I have known and heard. Then as for the subject of *m'likah* (partial severing of the bird's head) and the admonition not to separate it completely, this too is among the details of the offering.

In truth, though, one who does not mind expending all his spirit[5] [in search of a meaning] could rejoin that perhaps in the matter of *m'likah*, done by the hand of the *kohen* on the *ḥattath* (sin-offering) of the fowl, which is the offering of the poor, there is an intimation that every man should rush with the utmost swiftness [to supply] a poor man's need. For this reason, his offering does not require the usual ritual slaughter, so that the *kohen* should not need to go look for the knife and to examine it, while the poor man must be idled from his work in the meantime. In addition, to increase the speed, He said that he should start against its nape, since that is ready to his hand, and he will not need to turn its neck to [expose] the side of the gullet and windpipe.

There is another thought intimated in the matter of the partial severance of the bird's head, that was done at the nape with turtle-doves and young pigeons, to which the people Israel were likened[6]—that we should not be stiff-necked![7] As for the ban on separating the head completely from the body, it is something worthwhile for the distinction of the offering. For indeed, when the bird's head is attached to it, it has more eminence;[8] and it is fitting for us to make the offering of a poor man distinguished with all our might. It is enough for him that he is poor; we need not add to his impoverishment by diminishing the appearance of his offering.

All this [arises] from the basic tenet which we established at the

וְכָל זֶה מִן הַיְסוֹד אֲשֶׁר בָּנִינוּ תְּחִלָּה, כִּי מִשָּׁרְשֵׁי הַקָּרְבָּנוֹת לִקְנוֹת בְּנַפְשֵׁנוּ מִדּוֹת טוֹבוֹת וּמְעֻלּוֹת, וּלְהַכְשִׁיר פְּעֻלּוֹתֵינוּ בְּכֹחַ הַדִּמְיוֹנוֹת שֶׁאֲנַחְנוּ עֲסוּקִים בָּהֶן, כִּי מֵהְיוֹת הָאָדָם בַּעַל חֹמֶר לֹא יְצַיֵּר וְיִקְבַּע הַדְּבָרִים צִיּוּר חָזָק בְּנַפְשׁוֹ כִּי־אִם עַל יְדֵי הַפְּעֻלּוֹת. וְעַד שָׁמְעֵנוּ טַעַם אַחֵר נַחֲזִיק בָּזֶה.

מִדִּינֵי הַמִּצְוָה, מַה שֶּׁאָמְרוּ זִכְרוֹנָם לִבְרָכָה: כֵּיצַד אוֹחֵז הַכֹּהֵן חַטַּאת הָעוֹף בִּשְׁעַת מְלִיקָה, אוֹחֵז שְׁתֵּי רַגְלֵי הָעוֹף בֵּין שְׁתֵּי אֶצְבְּעוֹתָיו, וּשְׁתֵּי גַּפֶּיהָ בֵּין שְׁתֵּי אֶצְבְּעוֹתָיו, וּמוֹתֵחַ צַוָּארָהּ אֶל רֹחַב שְׁתֵּי אֶצְבְּעוֹתָיו, וּמוֹלְקוֹ; וְזוֹ מֵעֲבוֹדוֹת קָשׁוֹת שֶׁבַּמִּקְדָּשׁ. וְאִם שִׁנָּה וְאָחַז מִכָּל מָקוֹם כְּשֵׁרָה.

וְכָל הַמָּקוֹם מִן הַמִּזְבֵּחַ כָּשֵׁר לִמְלִיקָה; פֵּרוּשׁ, גַּם זֶה נֶאֱמַר שֶׁהוּא לְמַהֵר עִנְיָנוֹ שֶׁל עָנִי, וּלְפִיכָךְ אֵין לוֹ מָקוֹם מְיֻחָד; וְיֶתֶר פְּרָטֶיהָ, מְבֹאָרִים בִּזְבָחִים.

וְנוֹהֶגֶת בִּזְמַן הַבַּיִת בִּכְהֻנִּים וּבְכָל אָדָם, שֶׁכָּל מִי שֶׁהִבְדִּיל בְּחַטַּאת הָעוֹף לוֹקֶה.

[שֶׁלֹּא לִתֵּן שֶׁמֶן זַיִת בְּמִנְחַת חוֹטֵא]

קכה שֶׁלֹּא יָשִׂים הַכֹּהֵן שֶׁמֶן בְּמִנְחַת חוֹטֵא עָנִי, שֶׁנֶּאֱמַר: לֹא יָשִׂים עָלֶיהָ שֶׁמֶן, וְאַף־עַל־פִּי שֶׁבִּשְׁאָר מְנָחוֹת הָיוּ נוֹתְנִין שֶׁמֶן. וּמִפְּנֵי־כֵן אָמַרְתִּי חוֹטֵא עָנִי, כִּי חוֹטֵא עָשִׁיר אֵינוֹ מֵבִיא מִנְחַת קֶמַח לְעוֹלָם, כִּי־אִם קָרְבַּן בְּהֵמָה, כְּמוֹ שֶׁמְּפֹרָשׁ בַּתּוֹרָה.

מִשָּׁרְשֵׁי הַמִּצְוָה, לְפִי שֶׁהַשֶּׁמֶן רֶמֶז לְמַעֲלָה וְלִגְדֻלָּה, שֶׁאִם אַתָּה מְעָרְבוֹ בְּכָל מַשְׁקִין הוּא צָף עַל כֻּלָּן; וְהוּא דָּבָר חָשׁוּב מְאֹד, וְיָדוּעַ הוּא חֲשִׁיבוּת שֶׁמֶן הַטּוֹב; וְלָכֵן יִמְשְׁחוּ בוֹ הַמִּתְחַנְּכִים לְמַעֲלַת מַלְכוּת אוֹ כְהֻנָּה; עַל־כֵּן אֵין רָאוּי לָתֵת מִמֶּנּוּ בְּמִנְחַת הַחוֹטֵא, הַצָּרִיךְ לְהֵרָאוֹת בְּעַצְמוֹ דְאָגָה וּשְׁפְלוּת עַל שֶׁבָּא דְבַר עֲבֵרָה לְיָדוֹ.

9. TB Z'vaḥim 64b.
10. MT *hilchoth ma'aséh ha-korbanoth* vii 8 (see MY).
11. TB Z'vaḥim 63a (and see Rashi, 63b, s.v. *bakol*).

§125 1. So Rambam, *Guide* III 46; cf. TB Sotah 15a and M'naḥoth 6a: Said R. Simeon: It would be justice for the meal-offering of a sinner to require oil and frankincense, so that a sinner should not gain an advantage. Then for what reason does it not require them?—so that his offering should have no distinction.

start, that at the root of the offerings lies the purpose that we should acquire in our soul good and noble qualities, and make our actions worthy through the force of the conceptions with which we [thus] become occupied. For since man is a physical being, he cannot perceive and establish matters with a strong conception in his soul except through activities. Until we hear any other reason, let us hold to this.

Among the laws of the precept are what the Sages of blessed memory said:[9] How does the *kohen* hold the *ḥattath* (sin-offering) of fowl at the time of the partial severance?—he holds the two feet of the bird between two fingers of his, and its two wings between two fingers of his, and he draws its neck toward the width of his two fingers, and partially severs its head. It was among the difficult tasks in the Sanctuary. But if he acted differently and held it in any which way, it is acceptable.[10]

Every place at the altar was fit and acceptable for the partial severance.[11] In explanation of this too, we would say that it is in order to hasten the affair of a poor man; for this reason it did not have a particular place [for carrying it out]. The rest of its details are explained in the Talmud tractate *Z'vaḥim.*

It is in effect when the Temple is extant, for *kohanim* and every man—for whoever severed completely the head of a *ḥattath* (sin-offering) of fowl would be given whiplashes.

[NOT TO PUT OLIVE OIL IN AN UNINTENTIONAL SINNER'S MEAL-OFFERING]

125 that the *kohen* should not put oil into the *minḥah* (meal-offering) of a penurious sinner—for it is stated, *he shall put no oil on it* (Leviticus 5:11)—even though they would put oil in other meal-offerings. Now, for this reason I said a penurious sinner: because a wealthy sinner would never bring a *minḥah* (meal-offering) of flour but only an animal offering, as it is stated directly in the Torah.

At the root of the precept lies the reason that oil connotes excellence and greatness: for if you mix it with any and all liquids, it floats above them all. It is something very valuable, and the great value of good oil is known. Therefore they would anoint with it those who were initiated into the high position of kingship or as *kohen gadol.* For this reason it is not seemly to put any of it into the meal-offering of a sinner, who needs to manifest worry and humility because a matter of sin happened to him.[1]

וְעוֹד נֹאמַר שֶׁהוּא לְחֶמְלַת הֶעָנִי, שֶׁלֹּא לְהַטְרִיחוֹ יוֹתֵר מִדַּי לְהָבִיא שֶׁמֶן, כִּי הַשֵּׁם בָּרוּךְ הוּא לֹא יַטְרִיחַ בְּרִיָּה. וּמִפְּנֵי־כֵן גַּם־כֵּן לֹא חִיְּבוֹ רַק בִּמְעַט קֶמַח, שֶׁאִי־אֶפְשָׁר לְשׁוּם אָדָם אֲפִלּוּ בְּדַלֵּי דַלּוֹת בְּלֹא מְעַט קֶמַח. וְזֶה יַסְפִּיק לָנוּ גַּם עַל הַלְּבוֹנָה.

מִדִּינֵי הַמִּצְוָה, מַה שֶּׁפֵּרְשׁוּ זִכְרוֹנָם לִבְרָכָה, שֶׁמִּנְחַת חוֹטֵא הָיְתָה עִשָּׂרוֹן אֶחָד, לֹא פָּחוֹת וְלֹא יוֹתֵר. וְכָל הַמְּנָחוֹת הַקְּרֵבוֹת לְגַבֵּי מִזְבֵּחַ טְעוּנוֹת שֶׁמֶן וּלְבוֹנָה, וְלוֹג שֶׁמֶן לְכָל עִשָּׂרוֹן, וְקֹמֶץ לְבוֹנָה לְכָל מִנְחָה, בֵּין שֶׁהָיְתָה עִשָּׂרוֹן אֶחָד אוֹ אֲפִלּוּ שִׁשִּׁים עִשָּׂרוֹן; אֲבָל יוֹתֵר מִשִּׁשִּׁים אֵין מְבִיאִין בְּמִנְחָה אַחַת, חוּץ מִמִּנְחַת קְנָאוֹת וּמִנְחַת חוֹטֵא, שֶׁאֵין בָּהֶן שֶׁמֶן וּלְבוֹנָה, שֶׁנֶּאֱמַר; לֹא יָשִׂים עָלֶיהָ שֶׁמֶן וְלֹא יִתֵּן עָלֶיהָ לְבוֹנָה; וְיֶתֶר פְּרָטֶיהָ, מְבֹאָרִין בִּמְנָחוֹת.

וְנוֹהֶגֶת בִּזְמַן הַבַּיִת בְּזִכְרֵי כְהֻנָּה, כִּי לָהֶם הָעֲבוֹדָה. וְכֹהֵן הָעוֹבֵר עָלֶיהָ וְנָתַן שֶׁמֶן בְּמִנְחָה זוֹ שֶׁל חוֹטֵא עָנִי, לוֹקֶה.

[שֶׁלֹּא לִתֵּן לְבוֹנָה בְּמִנְחַת חוֹטֵא]

קכו שֶׁלֹּא לָתֵת לְבוֹנָה בְּמִנְחָה זוֹ שֶׁאָמַרְנוּ, שֶׁל חוֹטֵא עָנִי, שֶׁנֶּאֱמַר: וְלֹא יִתֵּן עָלֶיהָ לְבוֹנָה; וּלְשׁוֹן הַמִּשְׁנָה: וְחַיָּב עַל הַשֶּׁמֶן בִּפְנֵי עַצְמוֹ וְעַל הַלְּבוֹנָה בִּפְנֵי עַצְמָהּ — לְפִי שֶׁהֵן שְׁנֵי לָאוִין בְּלִי סָפֵק. כָּל עִנְיַן הַלְּבוֹנָה כְּעִנְיַן הַשֶּׁמֶן שֶׁכָּתַבְנוּ, אֵין לְהַאֲרִיךְ בּוֹ.

[מִצְוַת תּוֹסֶפֶת חֹמֶשׁ לְאוֹכֵל מִן הַתְּרוּמָה אוֹ מוֹעֵל בָּהּ]

קכז לְשַׁלֵּם כָּל הַנֶּהֱנֶה מִן הַהֶקְדֵּשׁ (אֶחָד קָדְשֵׁי מִזְבֵּחַ וְאֶחָד קָדְשֵׁי הַבַּיִת, וְאַף

2. Cf. Va-yikra Rabbah 27, 6: Said the Holy One, blessed is He: Ten pure [kosher] animals did I transmit to you, three in your domain and seven not in your domain. . . . Did I perhaps burden you to go about in the mountains and become wearied in the hills to bring an offering of a hart, deer or roebuck, which are not in your domain? I said [to bring] of none but those that are in your domain and in your manger.

3. TB M'naḥoth 76b (MT *hilchoth ma'aséh ha-korbanoth* xii 5).

4. TB M'naḥoth 59a, 88a (*ibid.* 6); see §31, note 2.

5. TB M'naḥoth 103b.

6. *Ibid.* 59a.

§126 1. TB M'naḥoth 59b.

Moreover, we would say that it is out of compassion for the impoverished man, not to trouble him inordinately to bring oil: for the Eternal Lord, blessed is He, will not overburden a human being.[2] For this reason, too, He required no more than a little flour from him—since it is impossible that any man, even of the utmost poverty, would be without a bit of flour. And this reason will suffice us [to explain] also about frankincense [which was equally omitted].

Among the laws of the precept there is what the Sages of blessed memory explained: that in the meal-offering there was one *'issaron* [tenth of an *'éphah* of flour], not less and not more.[3] All meal-offerings that were offered up on the altar required oil and frankincense: a *log* of oil for every *'issaron* [of flour], and a handful of frankincense for every *minḥah* (meal-offering), whether it was one *'issaron* or even sixty;[4] however, of more than sixty [times one *'issaron* of flour] one meal-offering was not to be brought.[5] This rule applies generally, except for a meal-offering of jealousy (§366) and the *minḥah* of a sinner,[6] as it is stated, *he shall put no oil on it, and shall put no frankincense on it* (Leviticus 5:11). The rest of its details are explained in the tractate *M'naḥoth*.

It is in force when the Temple is in existence, for the male *kohanim*, since the Temple service [was entrusted] to them. If a *kohen* transgressed it and put oil into this meal-offering, of an indigent sinner, he would receive whiplashes.

[TO PUT NO FRANKINCENSE IN AN UNINTENTIONAL SINNER'S MEAL-OFFERING]

126 not to put frankincense on this meal-offering that we have mentioned, of the penurious sinner—for it is stated, *and he shall not put put frankincense on it* (Leviticus 5:11). In the language of the Mishnah,[1] "One is punishable for the oil by itself, and for the frankincense by itself"—because they are two [separate] negative precepts, without any doubt. The theme of the frankincense is wholly like the theme of the oil, which we have written. There is no need to continue on about it.

[TO ADD A FIFTH OF THE VALUE IN PAYING FOR HALLOWED FOOD THAT WAS EATEN]

127 that if anyone derives benefit from something sacred (whether it is something holy from the altar or from the Sanctuary, and so too

בְּחֶרְמֵי כֹהֲנִים, וְכֵן בְּקָדָשִׁים קַלִּים), אוֹ אוֹכֵל קֹדֶשׁ בִּשְׁגָגָה, כְּלוֹמַר הַתְּרוּמָה, כָּל מַה שֶּׁאָכַל אוֹ נֶהֱנָה מִמֶּנּוּ, בְּתוֹסֶפֶת חֹמֶשׁ, וְיָבִיא קָרְבָּן עַל שִׁגְגָתוֹ אַיִל בִּשְׁנֵי סְלָעִים אוֹ יוֹתֵר; וְהוּא הַנִּקְרָא אֲשַׁם מְעִילוֹת, וְהוּא אֶחָד מֵחָמֵשׁ אֲשָׁמוֹת וַדָּאוֹת הַיְּדוּעִים — שֶׁנֶּאֱמַר: נֶפֶשׁ כִּי תִמְעֹל מַעַל וְגוֹמֵר, וְהֵבִיא אֶת אֲשָׁמוֹ וְגוֹמֵר, וְנֶאֱמַר: וְאֵת אֲשֶׁר חָטָא מִן הַקֹּדֶשׁ יְשַׁלֵּם וְאֶת חֲמִישִׁתוֹ יוֹסֵף עָלָיו.

מִשָּׁרְשֵׁי הַמִּצְוָה, לָתֵת אֵימָה וְיִרְאָה עַל כָּל אָדָם מֵהִתְקָרֵב בְּעִנְיְנֵי הַקֹּדֶשׁ, וּכְבָר כָּתַבְנוּ לְמַעְלָה תּוֹעֶלֶת הַיִּרְאָה וְהַהַגְדָּלָה בַּקֹּדֶשׁ אֶל בְּנֵי־אָדָם.

מִדִּינֵי הַמִּצְוָה, מַה שֶּׁאָמְרוּ רַבּוֹתֵינוּ זִכְרוֹנָם לִבְרָכָה שֶׁהַמּוֹעֵל אַחַר הַמּוֹעֵל, אִם הָרִאשׁוֹן בִּשְׁגָגָה הָאַחֲרוֹן פָּטוּר, לְפִי שֶׁכְּבָר נִתְחַלֵּל הַהֶקְדֵּשׁ, אַחַר שֶׁהָרִאשׁוֹן נִתְחַיֵּב בְּתַשְׁלוּמִין וּבְקָרְבָּן; וְאִם הָרִאשׁוֹן בְּמֵזִיד, שֶׁאֵינוֹ בְּתוֹרַת קָרְבָּן, הָאַחֲרוֹן בְּתוֹרַת מְעִילָה; וְאֵין מוֹעֵל אַחַר מוֹעֵל בַּמֻּקְדָּשִׁין אֶלָּא בִּבְהֵמָה וּכְלֵי שָׁרֵת בִּלְבָד; וְהַנּוֹטֵל פְּרוּטָה מִן הַהֶקְדֵּשׁ עַל מְנָת שֶׁהִיא שֶׁלּוֹ לֹא מָעַל עַד שֶׁיּוֹצִיאֶנָּה בַּחֲפָצָיו; נְתָנָהּ לַחֲבֵרוֹ, הוּא מָעַל וַחֲבֵרוֹ לֹא מָעַל, שֶׁאֵין מוֹעֵל אַחַר מוֹעֵל אֶלָּא בִּבְהֵמָה וְכֵלִים, כְּמוֹ שֶׁאָמַרְנוּ.

וְדִינֵי הַמְּעִילָה, בֵּין בְּקָדְשֵׁי מִזְבֵּחַ בֵּין בְּקָדְשֵׁי בֶּדֶק הַבַּיִת, וְשִׁעוּר מְעִילָה בְּשָׁוֶה פְרוּטָה; דְּבָרִים שֶׁהֻתְּרוּ בַּאֲכִילָה מִן הַקָּרְבָּנוֹת, כְּגוֹן בְּשַׂר חַטָּאת וְאָשָׁם, אַחַר זְרִיקַת דָּמָן, אוֹ שְׁתֵּי הַלֶּחֶם אַחַר זְרִיקַת דַּם שְׁנֵי הַכְּבָשִׂים, אֵין בָּהֶן מְעִילָה;

§127 1. The words in parentheses are not in the old manuscripts. They are evidently a later marginal note that was incorporated.

2. The paragraph is based on ShM positive precept §118.

3. TB Kiddushin 54b.

4. I.e. with the same sacred object or food.

5. TB Me'ilah 19b.

6. For until then it retains its holiness; *ibid.* 20a.

7. By giving it to the other; *ibid.*

8. *Ibid.* 13a, 15a, etc.

9. For less than that, no monetary compensation is required; *ibid.* 18a (see §58, note 7).

even banned devoted things of the *kohanim* and offerings of lesser holiness)[1] or if he eats holy food inadvertently, i.e. *t'rumah*—for whatever he ate or used for his benefit, he must pay with the addition of one fifth [its value], and he is to bring an offering for his inadvertent sin: a ram worth two *s'la'im* or more, which is called *'asham me'iloth* (a guilt-offering for breach of holiness); it is one of five *'asham* (guilt) offerings for certain, known sins. For it is stated, *If anyone commits a breach of holiness . . . he shall bring his* 'asham *(guilt-offering)*, etc. (Leviticus 5:15); and it is stated, *and for what he has done amiss he shall make restitution, and shall add to it a fifth of it*, etc. (*ibid.* 16).[2]

At the root of the precept lies the purpose of imposing on every person an awe and fear of coming close in matters of holiness. We have previously written, above (§§95, 101, etc.) the benefit derived from reverent fear and the grandeur of holiness for human beings.

Among the laws of the precept there is what our Sages of blessed memory taught,[3] that if one commits a breach of holiness after another has done so,[4] if the first one acted unintentionally, the later one is free of guilt, because the holiness already became profaned, since the first one became obligated to make payment and bring an offering. If, however, the first one acted deliberately, so that the issue of an offering does not arise for him, then the later one bears the onus of a breach of holiness.

One cannot make a breach of holiness with consecrated objects after another has done so, except with an animal or a utensil of Temple service alone.[5] If someone takes a *p'rutah* (small coin) of consecrated money with the intention that it should be his, he does not make a breach of holiness until he spends it for his desires.[6] If he gave it to his fellow, then he made the breach[7] and his fellow did not: for one cannot infringe on holiness after another has done so except over a [consecrated] animal or utensils, as we stated.

The laws of breach of holiness apply both to sacred entities of the altar and sacred goods for the repair and maintenance of the Temple.[8] The [minimal] value in profanation [that must be compensated] is a *p'rutah*'s worth.[9] With those parts of offerings that were permitted to be eaten—for example, the flesh of a *ḥattath* (sin-offering) and *'asham* (guilt-offering) after their blood was sprinkled [on the altar]; or the two loaves [offered on *Shavu'oth*] after the blood of the two sheep [brought with them] was sprinkled—there could be no breach of holiness, even if an outsider [a non-*kohen*] ate of these or anything

אֲפִלּוּ אָכַל הַזָּר מֵאֵלּוּ וְכַיּוֹצֵא בָאֵלּוּ, הוֹאִיל וְהֵן מֻתָּרִין לְמִקְצָת בְּנֵי־אָדָם לֵהָנוֹת בָּהֶן כָּל הַנֶּהֱנֶה מֵהֶן לֹא מָעַל; וַאֲפִלּוּ נִפְסְלוּ וְנֶאֶסְרוּ בַּאֲכִילָה, הוֹאִיל וְהָיְתָה לָהֶם שְׁעַת הֶתֵּר אֵין חַיָּבִין עֲלֵיהֶן מְעִילָה.

נִסְתַּפֵּק לוֹ אִם מָעַל אוֹ לֹא מָעַל, פָּטוּר מִתַּשְׁלוּמִין וְקָרְבָּן; וְתַשְׁלוּמֵי הַקֶּרֶן וַהֲבָאַת הַקָּרְבָּן מְעַכְּבִין הַכַּפָּרָה, וְלֹא הַחֹמֶשׁ, שֶׁנֶּאֱמַר: בְּאֵיל הָאָשָׁם וְנִסְלַח לוֹ, אַיִל וְאָשָׁם מְעַכְּבִין וְאֵין הַחֹמֶשׁ מְעַכֵּב; וְאַחַר שֶׁהוֹסִיף הַמּוֹסִיף הַחֹמֶשׁ, אִם נֶהֱנָה בַחֹמֶשׁ אַחַר־כָּךְ מוֹסִיף חֹמֶשׁ עַל חֹמֶשׁ, דִּכְתְחִלַּת הֶקְדֵּשׁ הוּא חָשׁוּב; וְהַחֹמֶשׁ הוּא אֶחָד מֵאַרְבָּעָה עַל הַקֶּרֶן, עַד שֶׁיְּהֵא הוּא וְחֻמְשׁוֹ חֲמִשָּׁה; וְיֶתֶר פְּרָטֶיהָ, מְבֹאָרִין בִּמְעִילָה וּבִתְמוּרָה.

וְנוֹהֶגֶת בִּזְמַן הַבַּיִת בִּזְכָרִים וּנְקֵבוֹת. וְעוֹבֵר עָלֶיהָ וְאָכַל אוֹ נֶהֱנָה בַּעֲשִׂיַּת מַעֲשֶׂה מִן הַהֶקְדֵּשׁ בְּשָׁוֶה פְרוּטָה בְּמֵזִיד, לוֹקֶה וּמְשַׁלֵּם מַה שֶּׁחִסֵּר מִן הַהֶקְדֵּשׁ הַקֶּרֶן לְבַד, כִּי הַמֵּזִיד אֵינוֹ בְתוֹסֶפֶת חֹמֶשׁ. וְאַזְהָרָה שֶׁל מְעִילָה לְהַלְקוֹתוֹ מִדִּכְתִיב: לֹא תוּכַל לֶאֱכֹל בִּשְׁעָרֶיךָ, וּכְמוֹ שֶׁנִּכְתֹּב בְּעֶזְרַת הַשֵּׁם בְּסֵדֶר רְאֵה בְּסִימָן (ת״ס) [תמ״ז]. מָעַל בִּשְׁגָגָה, מְשַׁלֵּם מַה שֶּׁנֶּהֱנָה וּמוֹסִיף חֹמֶשׁ וּמֵבִיא קָרְבָּן, כְּמוֹ שֶׁכָּתַבְנוּ.

[מִצְוַת קָרְבַּן אָשָׁם תָּלוּי]

קכח לְהַקְרִיב קָרְבָּן מִי שֶׁנִּסְתַּפֵּק לוֹ אִם חָטָא בְחֵטְא מֵהַחֲטָאִים הַגְּדוֹלִים שֶׁאָדָם מִתְחַיֵּב בַּעֲשׂוֹתוֹ אוֹתָם בְּזָדוֹן כָּרֵת וּבִשְׁגָגָה חַטָּאת קְבוּעָה, וְיִתְחַדֵּשׁ עָלָיו הַסָּפֵק בְּעִנְיָן זֶה, כְּגוֹן שֶׁתֹּאמַר עַל דֶּרֶךְ מָשָׁל שֶׁהָיוּ לְפָנָיו שְׁתֵּי חֲתִיכוֹת, אַחַת

10. *Ibid.* 2a.

11. TB K’rithoth 22a; MT *hilchoth me‘ilah* i 5.

12. The term *’asham* is now evidently interpreted as denoting this (in the sense of "guilt," since the withheld principal is the basic source of his iniquity) although its plain meaning is "guilt-offering"; TB Bava Kamma 111a.

13. Having become consecrated when he gave it; TB Bava M’tzi‘a 54b.

14. I.e. it is a fifth of the principal-plus-itself, since it will become part of the principal, as it were; hence a fourth of the principal; *ibid.* 54a.

15. MT *hilchoth me‘ilah* i 3.

§128 1. So TB K’rithoth 25a.

similar. Since they were permissible for some people [the *kohanim*] to have benefit from them, then whoever benefited from them would not breach holiness. Even if they became disqualified and forbidden to eat, since there was a period when they were permissible, there is no guilt for breach of holiness with them.[10]

If a doubt arose for someone, whether he had made a breach of holiness or not, he would have no obligation of payment and an offering.[11] [Failure] to pay the principal or bring the offering would withhold atonement, but not [payment of] the fifth: for it is stated, *with the ram of the* 'asham, *and he shall be forgiven* (Leviticus 5:16): the ram and the principal[12] withhold atonement [if they are withheld], but the fifth does not prevent it. After the one who had to add the fifth did so, if he had any benefit from the fifth later on, he would add on a fifth of the fifth: for it is considered as an original object of holiness.[13] The fifth is [actually] a fourth part of the principal, so that it and its "fifth" are five parts.[14] The rest of its details are clarified in the tractates *Me'ilah* and *T'murah*.

It is in force when the Temple is extant, for both man and woman. If a person transgressed it and ate something sacred or benefited by doing some activity with it in an amount worth a *p'rutah*—if it was deliberate, he would receive whiplashes and pay only the principal for what he made lacking in the sacred object; for the intentional sinner is not required to add a fifth.[15] The admonition about breach of holiness [which is the basis] for giving him whiplashes, derives from the verse, *You may not eat within your gates the tithe of your grain* (Deuteronomy 12:17), as we will write with the Eternal Lord's help in *sidrah r'éh*, in §447. If he made a breach of holiness unintentionally, he would make recompense for what he benefited, adding a fifth, and would bring an offering, as we have written.

[THE PRECEPT OF 'ASHAM TALUY, AN OFFERING FOR DOUBTFUL GUILT]

128 that a person should bring an offering if a doubt has arisen for him whether he committed some one of the great sins for which a man becomes punishable by *karéth* [Divine severance of existence] if he does them deliberately, and is obligated to bring a standard unvarying *ḥattath* (sin-offering) if he did them unintentionally.[1] The doubt could arise for him, for instance, in this way, which can be given as an illustration: There were two pieces of animal fat before him, one

חֵלֶב וְאַחַת שׁוּמָן כָּשֵׁר, וְאָכַל אַחַת מֵהֶן וְנֶאֶבְדָה הָאַחֶרֶת, וְדוֹאֵג בְּנַפְשׁוֹ שֶׁאֵינוֹ יוֹדֵעַ אִם שֶׁל חֵלֶב אָכַל אוֹ שֶׁל שׁוּמָן.

זֶה הַקָּרְבָּן הַבָּא עַל הַסָּפֵק הַזֶּה, נִקְרָא אָשָׁם תָּלוּי. וּמִלַּת תָּלוּי נֶאֶמְרָה עַל כָּל דָּבָר שֶׁרָאוּי לָבוֹא אַחֲרָיו עִנְיָן שֶׁיִּגָּלֶה בוֹ מַה שֶּׁלֹּא נוֹדַע בּוֹ מִקֹּדֶם, כְּגוֹן שֶׁאִם יִוָּדַע אֶל הַחוֹטֵא שֶׁחֵלֶב אָכַל, הֲרֵי נִגְלָה לוֹ שֶׁהָרִאשׁוֹן לֹא הִשְׁלִים לוֹ, וְצָרִיךְ לְהָבִיא קָרְבָּן אַחֵר, הַנִּקְרָא חַטָּאת קְבוּעָה, לְתַשְׁלוּם כַּפָּרָתוֹ; וְאִם יִוָּדַע אֵלָיו שֶׁהַהֶתֵּר אָכַל, הֲרֵי נִגְלָה לוֹ שֶׁהָרִאשׁוֹן הִסְפִּיק לוֹ, וְאֵינוֹ צָרִיךְ עוֹד לְקָרְבָּן אַחֵר אַחֲרָיו; זֶהוּ פֵּרוּשׁ תְּלִיָּתוֹ.

וְצִוּוּי קָרְבָּן זֶה מִדִּכְתִיב "וְאִם נֶפֶשׁ כִּי תֶחֱטָא וְעָשְׂתָה אַחַת מִכָּל מִצְוֹת יי אֲשֶׁר לֹא תֵעָשֶׂינָה וְלֹא יָדַע וְאָשֵׁם וְנָשָׂא עֲוֹנוֹ, וְהֵבִיא אַיִל תָּמִים מִן הַצֹּאן בְּעֶרְכְּךָ לְאָשָׁם אֶל הַכֹּהֵן, וְכִפֶּר עָלָיו הַכֹּהֵן עַל שִׁגְגָתוֹ אֲשֶׁר שָׁגָג וְהוּא לֹא יָדַע", כְּלוֹמַר עַל הֱיוֹתוֹ לֹא יָדַע אִם שָׁגַג אוֹ לֹא שָׁגַג; וְזֶה הָעִנְיָן יִקְרְאוּ אוֹתוֹ חֲכָמִים "לֹא הוֹדַע".

מִשָּׁרְשֵׁי הַמִּצְוָה, שֶׁיִּהְיֶה הָאָדָם זָהִיר וִירֵא חֵטְא וִיעַיֵּן בְּכָל מַעֲשָׂיו עִיּוּן טוֹב, לְבַל יִכָּשֵׁל בִּדְבַר עֲבֵרָה; וְעַל־כֵּן הִצְרִיכַתּוּ הַתּוֹרָה לְהָבִיא קָרְבָּן כְּשֶׁלֹּא נִזְהַר יָפֶה בְּמַעֲשָׂיו עַד כְּדֵי שֶׁלֹּא יִוָּלֵד עָלָיו סָפֵק זֶה. וְהָרְאָיָה שֶׁאֵינֶנּוּ בָּא רַק לְכַפֵּר עַל עַצְלוּתוֹ בְּכָךְ, שֶׁהֲרֵי אֵינוֹ מִשְׁתָּרֵשׁ אֵלָיו לְכַפֵּר עַל הַחֵטְא כְּלָל, שֶׁכְּשֶׁיִּוָּדַע אֵלָיו הַחֵטְא, מִיָּד צָרִיךְ לְקָרְבָּן שָׁלֵם, כְּמוֹ שֶׁהָיָה חַיָּב אִם לֹא הִקְרִיב הָרִאשׁוֹן.

מִדִּינֵי הַמִּצְוָה, מַה שֶּׁאָמְרוּ זִכְרוֹנָם לִבְרָכָה שֶׁאֵין חִיּוּב קָרְבָּן זֶה לְעוֹלָם עַד שֶׁיְּהֵא שָׁם אִסּוּר קָבוּעַ, כְּגוֹן שֶׁהָיוּ לְפָנָיו שְׁתֵּי חֲתִיכוֹת וּבְוַדַּאי אַחַת מֵהֶן חֵלֶב,

2. *Ibid.* 17b.

3. *Ibid.* 26b. (Thus it is the validity or effectiveness of the *'asham* which remains "in suspension"—uncertain.)

4. From the beginning to here is based on ShM positive precept §70.

5. TB K'rithoth 18a.

forbidden and the other permissible; he ate one of them, and the other was lost; and so he worries in his soul, as he does not know if he ate the forbidden or the permissible fat.[2]

This offering, brought over a matter of doubt, is called *'asham taluy*, "a guilt-offering of suspension." The term *taluy* (literally, "suspended") refers to every matter where it is quite possible that something will occur afterward to reveal what was not known about it previously: for example, if it will become known to that sinner that it was the forbidden fat he ate, he thus discovers that the first [offering] was no rectification for him, and he needs to bring another offering, called a standard unvarying *ḥattath*, for the completion of his atonement.[3] And should he find out that he ate the permissible piece, he thus discovers that the first was enough for him, and he does not need another offering, in addition, after it. This is the sense in which it is "in suspension."

The offering is ordained in these verses: *And if anyone sins and does any of the things which the Lord has commanded not to be done, though he does not know it, yet he is guilty and shall bear his iniquity. And he shall bring an unblemished ram out of the flock, by valuation, for a guilt-offering, to the* kohen; *and the* kohen *shall make atonement for him for his error which he committed, though he did not know* (Leviticus 5:17–18)—in other words, for his state of not knowing if he sinned inadvertently or not. This matter is what the Sages call "not made known."[4]

At the root of the precept lies the reason that a man should be careful and fearful of sin, and should regard all his deeds with great scrutiny, so that he should not come to grief through a matter of transgression. Therefore the Torah required him to bring an offering when in his actions he was not properly careful enough that this doubt should not arise [for him]. The proof that it comes for no other purpose but to atone for his indolence lies in the fact that it does not have for him the permanent effect of atoning for the sin at all: When the sin becomes known to him, he immediately needs a whole [new] offering, as he would have been obligated [to bring] if he had not offered up the first one.

Among the laws of the precept there is what the Sages of blessed memory said,[5] that the obligation of this offering never prevails unless there is a fixed [definite] prohibition there [involved in the matter]: for instance, if there were two pieces [of food] before one, and one of them was forbidden fat for certain—for then there is a

שֶׁהֲרֵי יֵשׁ כָּאן אִסּוּר קָבוּעַ, וְאָכַל אַחַת מֵהֶן; וְכֵן נַמִּי אִם אָכַל בְּוַדַּאי חֵלֶב אֲבָל הוּא מְסֻפָּק אִם הָיָה כְּזַיִת שָׁלֵם אוֹ לֹא, גַּם זֶה הוּא אִסּוּר קָבוּעַ.

אֲבָל הָיְתָה לְפָנָיו חֲתִיכָה אַחַת וְסָפֵק אִם הָיָה חֵלֶב אוֹ שׁוּמָן, וַאֲכָלָהּ, פָּטוּר מִן הַקָּרְבָּן, שֶׁאֵין כָּאן אִסּוּר קָבוּעַ, דְּשֶׁמָּא אֵין כָּאן אִסּוּר כְּלָל. וּמִן הַטַּעַם הַזֶּה אָמְרוּ שֶׁהַבָּא עַל סָפֵק מְגֹרֶשֶׁת חַיָּב בְּקָרְבָּן, שֶׁהֲרֵי יֵשׁ כָּאן אִסּוּר קָבוּעַ, שֶׁנַּעֲמִידֶנָּה בִּקְבִיעוּתָהּ, שֶׁהָיְתָה נְשׂוּאָה; אֲבָל הַבָּא עַל סָפֵק מְקֻדֶּשֶׁת פָּטוּר מִן הַקָּרְבָּן, שֶׁאֵין כָּאן אִסּוּר קָבוּעַ, וַהֲרֵי זֶה כַּחֲתִיכָה אַחַת וְסָפֵק אִם הִיא חֵלֶב אוֹ שׁוּמָן, שֶׁפָּטוּר מִקָּרְבָּן כְּמוֹ שֶׁאָמַרְנוּ; וְיֶתֶר פְּרָטֶיהָ, מְבֹאָרִין בִּכְרֵתוֹת.

וְנוֹהֶגֶת בִּזְמַן הַבַּיִת בִּזְכָרִים וּנְקֵבוֹת. וְעוֹבֵר עָלֶיהָ וְלֹא הִקְרִיב קָרְבָּן זֶה אִם אֵרַע לוֹ סָפֵק הַמְחַיֵּב בּוֹ, בִּטֵּל עֲשֵׂה.

[מִצְוַת קָרְבַּן אָשָׁם וַדַּאי]

קכט לְהַקְרִיב קָרְבָּן עַל חֲטָאִים יְדוּעִים כְּמוֹ שֶׁנְּפָרֵשׁ אוֹתָם, וְזֶה הַקָּרְבָּן נִקְרָא אָשָׁם וַדַּאי, וְהוּא קָרְבָּן שֶׁל אַיִל שֶׁצָּרִיךְ לִהְיוֹת שָׁוֶה שְׁתֵּי סְלָעִים. וְיֵשׁ מִן הַחֲטָאִים אֵלּוּ שֶׁקָּרְבָּן זֶה בָּא עֲלֵיהֶן בֵּין חָטָא בָהֶן בְּשׁוֹגֵג בֵּין בְּמֵזִיד, וְיֵשׁ שֶׁאֵינוֹ בָא אֶלָּא בְשׁוֹגֵג דַּוְקָא וְלֹא בְמֵזִיד.

וְאֶחָד מֵחֲטָאִים אֵלֶּה הוּא מִי שֶׁיֵּשׁ בְּיָדוֹ מָמוֹן יִשְׂרָאֵל מִשָּׁוֶה פְרוּטָה וָמַעְלָה שֶׁלֹּא כַדִּין, כְּגוֹן שֶׁגְּזָלוֹ אוֹ גְנָבוֹ, אוֹ נִשְׁאַר בְּיָדוֹ מִפִּקָּדוֹן שֶׁהָפְקַד לוֹ, אוֹ נִשְׁאַר בְּיָדוֹ מֵחֲמַת הַלְוָאָה אוֹ שֻׁתָּפוּת. כְּלָלוֹ שֶׁל דָּבָר, כָּל שֶׁאִלּוּ הוֹדָה לוֹ יִהְיֶה חַיָּב לְשַׁלֵּם בְּדִין, וּתְבָעוֹ מִמֶּנּוּ הַנִּגְזָל אוֹ הֶעָשׁוּק אוֹ יוֹרְשׁוֹ אוֹ הַבָּא מִכֹּחָם, וְכָפַר בּוֹ

6. *Ibid.* 17a.

7. There is doubt if she was properly divorced.

8. It is certain that she was married; it is not certain if she was divorced; hence there is no reason to assume that she has lost her married status, and the matter concerns a clear and definite prohibition (if the problem hinged on a doubt if she was validly married, no *'asham* would be required); MT *hilchoth sh'gagoth* viii 3, based on TB K'thuboth 22b.

§129 1. I.e. where there is certainty that the misdeed was committed, as opposed to *'asham talu-y*, "a guilt-offering of suspension" (§128).

2. TB K'rithoth 22b.

3. A *p'rutah* was established as the smallest value requiring compensation. See also §58, note 7.

fixed [definite] prohibition here—and he ate one of them. So too if he ate forbidden fat for certain, but he is in doubt whether he ate the whole amount of an olive or not;[6] this too involves a fixed prohibition.

However, if one piece [of fat] was lying before him, and there was doubt if it was forbidden or permissible fat, and he ate it, he is free of obligation to bring an offering: for there is no fixed [definite] prohibition here, since there is perhaps no prohibition at all [involved] here. For this reason, too, the Sages taught that if someone was conjugally intimate with a woman who was doubtfully divorced,[7] he is required to bring an offering: for there is a fixed [definite] prohibition [involved] here, since we give her her fixed, established status, of being married.[8] But if someone is intimate with a woman who was doubtfully married, he is free of any need to bring an offering: for there is no fixed prohibition here; it is like [the case of] the one piece [of fat] where there is doubt if it was forbidden or permissible fat, where one has no obligation of an offering, as we stated. The rest of its details are explained in the Talmud tractate *K'rithoth*.

It applies when the Temple is in existence, for both man and woman. If a person transgressed it and did not bring this offering when a doubt occurred for him which obligated him to bring it, he would thus disobey a positive precept.

[THE PRECEPT OF 'ASHAM VADDAI, AN OFFERING FOR DEFINITE GUILT]

129 to bring an offering for certain sins, as we will explain them. This offering is called *'asham vaddai*, "a guilt-offering of certainty";[1] and it is an offering of a ram which must be worth two *s'la'im*.[2] There are some among these sins for which an offering is brought whether they were committed unintentionally or deliberately, and there are some for which it is brought only if they were done specifically without intention, but not if they were deliberate.

One of these sins is [in a case where] someone has in his possession the goods of an Israelite, from a *prutah*'s worth[3] and up, illegally: for instance, if he robbed him or stole from him, or it remained with him having been entrusted to him for safekeeping, or it remained with him as a result of a loan or a partnership (joint ownership). In short: in every case where, if he admitted it to him [the other man] he would be duty-bound to pay under the law, and the robbed or exploited man, or his heir or legal representative, sues him for it, whereupon

וְנִשְׁבַּע עָלָיו לַשֶּׁקֶר, וְהָיָה כִּי יָשׁוּב וְנִחַם עַל חֶטְאוֹ וְיָשִׁיב הֶחָמָס אֲשֶׁר בְּכַפָּיו, חַיָּב לְהָבִיא קָרְבָּן זֶה שֶׁאָמַרְנוּ עַל חַטָּאתוֹ, מִלְּבַד הַחֹמֶשׁ שֶׁחַיָּב לְהוֹסִיף עַל הַקֶּרֶן וּלְתִתּוֹ לַנִּגְזָל; שֶׁנֶּאֱמַר: נֶפֶשׁ כִּי תֶחֱטָא וּמָעֲלָה מַעַל בַּיי וְכִחֵשׁ בַּעֲמִיתוֹ וְגוֹמֵר, וְאָמַר רַבִּי עֲקִיבָא: מַה תַּלְמוּד לוֹמַר "מַעַל בַּיי", לְפִי שֶׁכָּל הַלּוֹוֶה וְהַמַּלְוֶה אֵינוֹ עוֹשֶׂה אֶלָּא בְעֵדִים, וּכְשֶׁהוּא מְכַחֵשׁ אֵינוֹ מְכַחֵשׁ אֶלָּא בְעֵדִים; אֲבָל הַמַּלְוֶה שֶׁלֹּא בְעֵדִים וּמְכַחֵשׁ בּוֹ [מְכַחֵשׁ בַּ]שְּׁלִישִׁי שֶׁבֵּינֵיהֶם, שְׁכִינָה; לְכָךְ נֶאֱמַר: וּמָעֲלָה מַעַל בַּיי וְכִחֵשׁ בַּעֲמִיתוֹ וְגוֹמֵר.

וּכְתִיב בַּתְרֵיהּ "וְהָיָה כִּי יֶחֱטָא וְאָשֵׁם", כְּלוֹמַר שֶׁיַּעֲשֶׂה תְּשׁוּבָה שֶׁיַּחֲזִיק עַצְמוֹ בְּאָשֵׁם, "וְהֵשִׁיב אֶת הַגְּזֵלָה" וְגוֹמֵר, "וְשִׁלַּם אוֹתוֹ בְּרֹאשׁוֹ וַחֲמִשִׁתָיו יֹסֵף עָלָיו" וְגוֹמֵר, "וְאֶת אֲשָׁמוֹ יָבִיא לַיי אַיִל" וְגוֹמֵר; וְזֶהוּ נִקְרָא אֲשַׁם גְּזֵלוֹת, וְזֶה מִן הַבָּאִים בֵּין עַל שׁוֹגֵג בֵּין עַל מֵזִיד.

וּבְזֹאת הַפָּרָשָׁה לֹא נִזְכַּר מִן הָאֲשָׁמוֹת כִּי־אִם זֶה שֶׁאָמַרְנוּ, אֲבָל בַּפָּרָשָׁה שֶׁל מַעְלָה הַזְכַּר אָשָׁם אַחֵר שֶׁהוּא מִמִּין זֶה שֶׁנִּקְרָא גַּם־כֵּן אָשָׁם וַדַּאי, וְהוּא אֲשַׁם מְעִילוֹת, כְּלוֹמַר מִי שֶׁמָּעַל וְנֶהֱנָה מִן הַהֶקְדֵּשׁוֹת. וּלְפִיכָךְ נוֹפֵל בּוֹ לְשׁוֹן מְעִילָה לְפִי שֶׁהוּא דָּבָר רַע מְאֹד, וּכְעֵין מְסִירָה, מִי שֶׁפּוֹשֵׁט יָדוֹ לֵהָנוֹת בְּמָמוֹן שָׁמַיִם. וְזֶה הָאָשָׁם אֵינוֹ בָא כִּי אִם עַל הַשּׁוֹגֵג, וּכְמוֹ שֶׁכָּתַבְנוּ לְמַעְלָה בִּמְקוֹמוֹ.

וְעוֹד חִיְּבָה הַתּוֹרָה גַּם־כֵּן קָרְבָּן זֶה שֶׁל אָשָׁם וַדַּאי, וְהוּא אַיִל מִשְׁתֵּי סְלָעִים, לְנָזִיר שֶׁנִּטְמָא, וּכְמוֹ שֶׁנִּכְתֹּב בְּעֶזְרַת הַשֵּׁם בְּסֵדֶר נָשֹׂא [סי' שע"ז], וְזֶה גַּם־כֵּן יִהְיֶה בֵּין נִטְמָא בְמֵזִיד אוֹ בְשׁוֹגֵג.

וְעוֹד חִיְּבָה הַתּוֹרָה גַּם־כֵּן בְּקָרְבָּן זֶה לִמְצֹרָע כְּשֶׁיִּטְהַר מִצָּרַעְתּוֹ, וּכְמוֹ שֶׁנִּכְתֹּב

4. In Sifra, *va-yikra*, end (*perek* 22, 4).

5. TB K'rithoth 9a.

6. So Sifra, *va-yikra, parashah* 11, 8.

7. This is inaccurate (probably a scribal error, in unconscious repetition of the offering described at the beginning); Numbers 6:12 requires the offering to be a *sheep* up to a year old (MH, MY).

8. So TB K'rithoth 9a.

he denies it and swears falsely about it—when he turns penitent and has remorse for his sin, and he gives back the wrongful gain which is in his hands, he is duty-bound to bring this offering that we have mentioned, over his sin—this apart from the fifth which he must add on to the principal and give to the robbed man. For it is stated, *If anyone sins and commits a breach of faith against the Lord, and deals falsely with his neighbor*, etc. (Leviticus 5:21); and R. Akiva said:[4] Why is it stated, "and commits a breach of faith against the Lord"?—because every borrower and lender acts only with witnesses, and when he is false in denial, he is false only in denial [of the testimony] of the witnesses. But when someone lends money without witnesses and the other denies it [afterward], the third party between them is the *shechinah* (Divine Presence). Therefore it is stated, "and commits a breach of faith against the Lord and deals falsely with his neighbor," etc.

Now, it is written after this, *then it shall be, if he has sinned and is guilty*—in other words, if he repents and holds himself guilty—*he shall restore what he took by robbery . . . he shall restore it in full, and a fifth he shall add to it . . . And his guilt-offering shall he bring to the Lord, a ram*, etc. (Leviticus 5:23–25). This is what is called *'asham g'zéloth*, "a guilt-offering for robberies"; and it is one of those brought whether the sin was inadvertent or intentional.[5]

Now, in this section of Scripture, none of the guilt-offerings but this, which we have discussed, is mentioned. But in the section above (*ibid.* 15–16) another *'asham* is mentioned which is of this kind, as it is also called "a guilt-offering of certainty": That is *'asham me'iloth*, "a guilt-offering for breaches of holiness"—i.e. [to be brought by] one who committed a breach of holiness and derived benefit from sacred things. For this reason the term *me'ilah* (treachery) fits it, because it is something very evil, akin to informing treacherously [against someone, denoting] one who puts out his hand to benefit from the property of Heaven. That guilt-offering is due only if the sin was unintentional,[6] as we wrote above, in its place (§127).

In addition, the Torah also imposed the obligation of this offering of *'asham vaddai*, which is a ram worth two *s'la'im*,[7] on a Nazirite who became ritually unclean, as we will write, with the Eternal Lord's help, in *sidrah naso* (§377). That too would be [due] whether he became unclean intentionally or inadvertently.[8]

Furthermore, the Torah gave the duty of this offering also to a *m'tzora* when he becomes purified [cured] of his *tzara'ath*, as we will

בְּעֶזְרַת הַשֵּׁם בְּסֵדֶר "זֹאת תִּהְיֶה תּוֹרַת הַמְּצֹרָע" [סי׳ קע"ו]; וְאֵין לְפָרֵשׁ בָּזֶה שׁוֹגֵג וּמֵזִיד, שֶׁאֵין נוֹפֵל כָּאן עִנְיַן שְׁגָגָה וְזָדוֹן.

וְעוֹד חִיְּבָה תוֹרָה גַּם־כֵּן בְּקָרְבָּן זֶה מִי שֶׁבָּא עַל שִׁפְחָה חֲרוּפָה, וּכְמוֹ שֶׁכָּתוּב בְּסֵדֶר "קְדֹשִׁים תִּהְיוּ", שֶׁנֶּאֱמַר: וְאִישׁ כִּי יִשְׁכַּב אֶת אִשָּׁה וְגוֹמֵר, וְהִיא שִׁפְחָה נֶחֱרֶפֶת לְאִישׁ וְהָפְדֵּה לֹא נִפְדָּתָה וְגוֹמֵר, בִּקֹּרֶת תִּהְיֶה וְגוֹמֵר, וְהֵבִיא אֶת אֲשָׁמוֹ וְכוּלֵּי, אֵיל אָשָׁם; וְזֶה מִן הַבָּאִים בֵּין עַל שׁוֹגֵג בֵּין עַל מֵזִיד. נִמְצְאוּ בֵּין כֻּלָּן הָאֲשָׁמוֹת וַדָּאוֹת חֲמִשָּׁה, וְכֵן מָנוּ אוֹתָן חֲכָמִים זִכְרוֹנָם לִבְרָכָה בַּמִּשְׁנָה, שֶׁאָמְרוּ: אֵלּוּ הֵן אֲשָׁמוֹת: א. אֲשַׁם גְּזֵלוֹת, ב. אֲשַׁם מְעִילוֹת, ג. אֲשַׁם שִׁפְחָה חֲרוּפָה, ד. אֲשַׁם נָזִיר, ה. אֲשַׁם מְצֹרָע. וְאָשָׁם תָּלוּי הַנִּמְנֶה שָׁם, שְׁמוֹ עָלָיו שֶׁאֵינוֹ מִמִּין הָאֲשָׁמוֹת וַדָּאוֹת.

וּמֵאֵלּוּ הַחֲמִשָּׁה, שְׁלֹשָׁה מֵהֶן בָּאִין בֵּין עַל שׁוֹגֵג אוֹ מֵזִיד, וְהֵן אֲשַׁם גְּזֵלוֹת, אֲשַׁם שִׁפְחָה חֲרוּפָה, אֲשַׁם נָזִיר; וְאֶחָד מֵהֶן אֵינוֹ בָא אֶלָּא עַל שׁוֹגֵג וְלֹא עַל מֵזִיד, וְהוּא אֲשַׁם מְעִילוֹת; וְהַחֲמִישִׁי, שֶׁהוּא אֲשַׁם מְצֹרָע, אֵין נוֹפֵל בּוֹ לְשׁוֹן שְׁגָגָה וְזָדוֹן, כְּמוֹ שֶׁאָמַרְנוּ.

וְשִׁפְחָה חֲרוּפָה, הוֹאִיל וְאָתָא לְיָדָן נֵימָא בָּהּ מִילְּתָא, וְאַף־עַל־פִּי שֶׁאֵינוֹ בַּסֵּדֶר הַזֶּה; לְפִי שֶׁאֵינָהּ מֵחֶשְׁבּוֹן הַמִּצְווֹת אֵין לִי מָקוֹם לְדַבֵּר בָּהּ כִּי־אִם כָּאן.

פֵּרוּשׁ חֲרוּפָה, מְיֻעֶדֶת, כְּלוֹמַר מְקֻדֶּשֶׁת; וְאָמְרוּ בַּגְּמָרָא בְּרֵישׁ פֶּרֶק רִאשׁוֹן בְּקִדּוּשִׁין, שֶׁכֵּן בִּיהוּדָה קוֹרִין לַאֲרוּסָה חֲרוּפָה. וּבְשִׁפְחָה כְּנַעֲנִית הַכָּתוּב מְדַבֵּר שֶׁהִיא חֶצְיָהּ שִׁפְחָה וְחֶצְיָהּ בַּת־חוֹרִין, וְזֶהוּ שֶׁכָּתוּב בָּהּ "וְהָפְדֵּה לֹא נִפְדָּתָה", כְּלוֹמַר פְּדוּיָה וְאֵינָהּ פְּדוּיָה; וּכְגוֹן שֶׁפָּרְעָה לַאֲדוֹנֶיהָ חֲצִי דָמֶיהָ וְנִתְקַדְּשָׁה

9. TB Z'vaḥim 54b.
10. See § 35, note 8.
11. So TB K'rithoth 11a.

write, with the Eternal Lord's help, in *sidrah m'tzora* (§176). About this we need not elucidate whether it is for an inadvertent or willful sinner, as the concepts of unwitting and deliberate sin do not apply here.

Moreover, the Torah also required this offering of a person who was conjugally intimate with a bespoken maidservant, as it is written in *sidrah k'doshim*: for it is stated, *And if a man lies carnally with a woman who is a maidservant designated for a man and not at all redeemed . . . an inquiry shall be held . . . and he shall bring his guilt-offering . . . the ram of the guilt-offering* (Leviticus 19:20–21). This is one of those brought whether the sin was unwitting or willful.[8]

Thus the offerings of *'asham vaddai* (a guilt-offering of certainty) are found, in all, to be five; and so the Sages of blessed memory listed them in the Mishnah,[9] saying: These are the guilt-offerings: 1. *'asham g'zéloth* (a guilt-offering for robberies); 2. *'asham me'iloth* (a guilt-offering for breaches of holiness); 3. the guilt-offering for the bespoken maidservant; 4. the *'asham* of the Nazirite; 5. the *'asham* of the *m'tzora*. As for *'asham taluy* (a guilt-offering of suspension) which is listed there, its name [attests] about it that it is not of the same kind as the *'asham vaddai* (guilt-offering of certainty).

Among these five, three of them are brought for both an inadvertent and a deliberate sin; these are *'asham g'zéloth* (a guilt-offering for robberies), the guilt-offering of the bespoken maidservant, and the *'asham* of the Nazirite. One of them is due only for an unintentional sin, but not for a willful one: this is *'asham me'iloth* (a guilt-offering for breaches of holiness). As for the fifth, which is the *'asham* of the *m'tzora*, the terms "unintentional and deliberate sin" do not apply to it, as we have stated.

Now, regarding the guilt-offering of the bespoken maidservant, since the subject has arisen, let us say a word about it. Even though it is not in this *sidrah* [of Scripture], there is no proper place for me to speak about it except here.

The word *ḥarufah* (bespoken) means designated, i.e., betrothed or plighted in marriage;[10] it was stated in the Talmud, at the beginning of the first chapter of the tractate *Kiddushin* (6a), that so a betrothed woman is called, *ḥarufah*, in Judea. Scripture deals there with a heathen maidservant who is half slave and half free;[11] and this is why it written of her [literally] *and redeemed she was not redeemed* (Leviticus 19:20)—i.e. she was redeemed [into freedom] and not redeemed: for instance, if

לְיִשְׂרָאֵל אַחֵר, בְּזוֹ נֶאֱמַר שֶׁאִם בָּא עָלֶיהָ אָדָם אַחֵר בֵּין בְּשׁוֹגֵג בֵּין בְּמֵזִיד שֶׁחַיָּב לְהָבִיא קָרְבָּן זֶה שֶׁהוּא נִקְרָא אָשָׁם, וְהוּא אַיִל שָׁוֶה מִשְּׁתֵּי סְלָעִים וּלְמַעְלָה.

וּמִפְּנֵי זֶה מַסְפִּיק קָרְבַּן כַּפָּרָה לְמִי שֶׁבָּא עָלֶיהָ, לְפִי שֶׁאֵין קִדּוּשֶׁיהָ קִדּוּשִׁין גְּמוּרִים כְּמוֹ אִם הָיְתָה בַּת־חוֹרִין, שֶׁאִלּוּ בְּבַת־חוֹרִין מְקֻדֶּשֶׁת, חִיּוּב מִיתָה יֵשׁ לְמִי שֶׁבָּא עָלֶיהָ, אֲבָל בְּזוֹ אֵין קִדּוּשֶׁיהָ גְּמוּרִין מֵחֲמַת חֲצִי שִׁפְחוּת שֶׁבָּהּ עֲדַיִן, וּלְפִיכָךְ מַסְפִּיק קָרְבָּן לְכַפָּרָה אֶל הַנִּכְשָׁל בָּהּ.

גַּם הֵקֵלָּה הַתּוֹרָה בְּבִיאָתָהּ לִפְטֹר בְּקָרְבָּן גַּם הַמֵּזִיד, מַה שֶּׁאֵין דֶּרֶךְ בִּשְׁאָר זְדוֹנוֹת לְפָטְרָן בְּקָרְבָּן, לְפִי שֶׁהָאִשָּׁה הַשִּׁפְחָה, אַף־עַל־פִּי שֶׁחֶצְיָהּ פְּדוּיָה, קַלָּה הִיא בְּעֵינֵי כָל אָדָם, וְהַכִּשָּׁלוֹן קָרוֹב מְאֹד עָלֶיהָ, שֶׁאֵין לֵב הֶהָמוֹן חוֹשֵׁב בִּיאָתָהּ לְחֵטְא גָּדוֹל; וְעַל־כֵּן יוּסַר עֲווֹנָם וְחַטָּאָם יְכֻפַּר עִם הַקָּרְבָּן, וּכְעֵין מַה שֶּׁאָמְרוּ זִכְרוֹנָם לִבְרָכָה בְּעִנְיָנִים אֲחֵרִים אֶפְשָׁר לָנוּ לוֹמַר בָּזֶה: רַחֲמָנָא לִיבָּא בָּעֵי.

וּמִכָּל־מָקוֹם הַשִּׁפְחָה חַיֶּבֶת מַלְקוּת, שֶׁאֵין לוֹמַר בָּהּ שֶׁתִּהְיֶה קַלָּה בְּעֵינֶיהָ וְשֶׁמִּפְּנֵי־כֵן לֹא הִשְׁגִּיחָה בְּעַצְמָהּ לִזְנוּת. וּמִיהוּ גַּם הִיא לֹא תִתְחַיֵּב מַלְקוּת אֶלָּא כְּשֶׁנִּבְעֲלָה כְּדַרְכָּהּ, וְהִיא גְדוֹלָה וּמְזִידָה; וְעָלֶיהָ נֶאֱמַר "בִּקֹּרֶת תִּהְיֶה", כְּמוֹ שֶׁדָּרְשׁוּ זִכְרוֹנָם לִבְרָכָה, בִּקְרָאֵי תְהֵא, כְּלוֹמַר בְּמַלְקוּת. וְאָמְרוּ זִכְרוֹנָם לִבְרָכָה: הִיא לוֹקָה וְלֹא הוּא. וּמִפְּנֵי־כֵן הוֹצִיא הַכָּתוּב הַמַּלְקוּת בְּלָשׁוֹן זֶה שֶׁל קְרִיָּה, לְפִי שֶׁהָיוּ קוֹרְאִים עַל הַלּוֹקֶה פְּסוּקִים שֶׁל תּוֹכַחַת בְּעוֹד שֶׁהָיוּ מַלְקִין אוֹתוֹ, כְּדֵי שֶׁיִּשְׁמַע וְיִקַּח מוּסָר, וְהֵם "וְהִפְלָא יי" וְגוֹמֵר.

12. I.e. without knowing that she was forbidden to him.

13. I.e. He requires of people what is in accord with the capacities and limitations of the heart. The saying is found in TB Sanhedrin 106b, version of Rashi.

14. TB Makkoth 22b.

she repaid her master half her value and became betrothed (plighted in marriage) to another Israelite. About such a woman it is stated that if another man was conjugally intimate with her, [sinning] unwittingly[12] or willfully, he is duty-bound to bring this offering that is called *'asham*, which is a ram worth two *s'la'im*.

Now, for this reason an offering for atonement is enough for one who was intimate with her—because her betrothal is not a complete marriage bond, as it would be if she were a free woman. For with a betrothed free woman, there is a penalty of death for one who is intimate with her. But in this one's case her betrothal is not a complete marriage bond, on account of the half-servitude under which she still lives. Therefore an offering is enough for atonement for one who has come to grief with her.

The Torah was further lenient about intimacy with her, in acquitting the deliberate sinner too from guilt with an offering, although it is not the usual way with other intentional sinners to let them off with [the sacrifice of] an offering. For a maidservant, even if she is half redeemed, is lightly regarded by human beings, and moral blunder is very likely to happen with her, since the heart of the mass of people does not reckon conjugal intimacy with her as a great sin. Hence their iniquity is expunged and their sin atoned with the sacrifice of the offering. In keeping with what the Sages of blessed memory said in other matters, we can say about this, "The merciful God seeks the heart."[13]

The maidservant, however, incurs the punishment of whiplashes: for it cannot be said of her that she is lightly esteemed in her own eyes, and for this reason she was not careful about immorality. Even she, though, is not punishable by whiplashes unless the conjugal intimacy was in a natural way, and she was a grown woman who concurred deliberately.[11] Thus it is about her that Scripture states, *bikkoreth, an inquiry shall be held* (Leviticus 19:20); as our Sages of blessed memory interpreted it,[11] "it shall be *bik'ra'i*," i.e. with a whipping; and the Sages of blessed memory added: She is whipped, but he is not. For this reason Scripture conveyed the punishment of whiplashes by an expression of *k'ri'ah*, reading, because Scriptural verses of reproof were read over the person being whipped while he received the lashes, so that he should listen and take heed. These [verses] were *then the Lord will make your plagues extraordinary* (Deuteronomy 28:59), etc.[14]

At the root of the precept lies the aim that a man should not

מִשָּׁרְשֵׁי הַמִּצְוָה, לְבַל יַחֲשֹׁב אָדָם שֶׁאַף־עַל־פִּי שֶׁעִנְיַן אִסּוּר גְּזֵלַת הַמָּמוֹן נִתָּק לַעֲשֵׂה, שֶׁנֶּאֱמַר עָלָיו "וְהֵשִׁיב אֶת הַגְּזֵלָה", שֶׁיֵּלֵךְ כָּל אֶחָד וְיִגְזֹל מֵחֲבֵרוֹ מַה שֶּׁיִּרְצֶה וִידַמֶּה בִלְבָבוֹ לֵאמֹר לִכְשֶׁיִּהְיֶה לוֹ וְיָשִׁיב גְּזֵלָתוֹ, יְכֻפַּר עֲווֹנוֹ וְיִטְהַר מִמֶּנּוּ, וַהֲרֵי הוּא כְּאִלּוּ לֹא עֲשָׂאוֹ מֵעוֹלָם — וְיִהְיֶה זֶה פֶּתַח לְעוֹבְרֵי עֲבֵרָה — לָכֵן הוֹדִיעָה הַתּוֹרָה שֶׁאַף עִם הַהֲשָׁבָה בְּתוֹסֶפֶת חֹמֶשׁ צָרִיךְ הַקָּרְבָּן לְכַפָּרָה עַל שֶׁחָטָא. וּכְבָר כָּתַבְתִּי לְמַעְלָה בְּעִנְיָן זֶה כִּי מִכָּל־מָקוֹם לֹא נִצַּל זֶה שֶׁלֹּא עָבַר עַל רְצוֹן בּוֹרְאוֹ, וַחֲבַל עַל רֵישֵׁיהּ דַּעֲבַר עַל רַעֲוָא דְמָרֵיהּ שְׁמַיָּא וְלוּ יַקְרִיב כַּמָּה אִימְרִין שְׁמֵינִין לְעָלָתָא.

וְשָׁם כָּתַבְתִּי גַּם־כֵּן שֶׁהַקָּרְבָּן וְהַקֶּרֶן מְעַכְּבִין אֶת הַכַּפָּרָה וְאֵין הַחֹמֶשׁ מְעַכֵּב.

דִּינֵי הַמִּצְוָה, כְּגוֹן בְּאֵי זֶה עִנְיָן יִתְחַיֵּב בִּשְׁבוּעָה זוֹ שֶׁיִּהְיֶה חַיָּב עָלֶיהָ אָשָׁם זֶה, וּבְאֵי זֶה עִנְיָן יִהְיֶה פָּטוּר מִמֶּנָּה; וְעַל אֵי זֶה דֶרֶךְ יִתְחַיֵּב אֲשָׁמוֹת הַרְבֵּה כְּמִנְיַן חִיּוּב הַשְּׁבוּעוֹת וְעַל אֵי זֶה לֹא יִתְחַיֵּב אֶלָּא אָשָׁם אֶחָד; וְיֶתֶר פְּרָטֶיהָ, מְבֹאָרִים בִּכְרֵתוֹת וּבִשְׁבוּעוֹת.

וְנוֹהֶגֶת מִצְוַת חִיּוּב קָרְבָּן זֶה בִּזְמַן הַבַּיִת בִּזְכָרִים וּנְקֵבוֹת. וְעוֹבֵר עָלֶיהָ וְלֹא הִקְרִיבוֹ, אַף־עַל־פִּי שֶׁהֵשִׁיב גְּזֵלוֹ לֹא נִתְכַּפֵּר חֶטְאוֹ; וְאוּלָם יֵשׁ לְהַאֲמִין שֶׁאֵין עָנְשׁוֹ חָזָק כְּמוֹ שֶׁהָיָה אִלּוּ לֹא הֵשִׁיב הַמָּמוֹן. וְהַמָּשָׁל עַל זֶה, מִי שֶׁהִכָּה חֲבֵרוֹ וְנִתְחַיֵּב קְנָס לַמֶּלֶךְ, וְנִתְפַּיֵּס עִם הַמֻּכֶּה, וְלֹא נִשְׁאֲרָה עָלָיו רַק תְּבִיעַת הַמֶּלֶךְ.

[מִצְוַת הֲשָׁבַת גֶּזֶל]

קל שֶׁנִּצְטַוִּינוּ לְהָשִׁיב אֶת הַגְּזֵלָה בְּעֵין, כְּלוֹמַר שֶׁאִם הַדָּבָר מַמָּשׁ שֶׁגָּזַל הוּא

15. The original has "even though"; but the emendation is required by the context.
16. TB Sh'vu'oth 36b.

think that since[15] the matter of the ban on robbery is given to rectification by a positive precept—for it is stated about it, *he shall restore what he took by robbery* (Leviticus 5:23)—everyone can go and rob his fellow of whatever he wants, imagining in his heart that when he will have the means and will return what he took by force, his sin will be atoned and he will be cleansed of it; and then it will be as if he had never done it. This would be a doorway [of open invitation] to wrongdoers. Therefore the Torah let it be known that even with its return, with the addition of the fifth, he needs the offering to atone for the sin he did. I have written previously, above (§123), in this regard, that in any event, this man is not saved [as though] he had not disobeyed the will of his Creator. Woe upon his head that he has disobeyed the will of the God of heaven, even if he brings many fat sheep for *'olah* (burnt) offerings.

There (§123) I also wrote that the offering and the principal [of what he took by force] withhold atonement [if they are not given], but the fifth [to be added to the principal] does not withhold atonement [if not given].

The laws of the precept are, for instance, in what circumstances a man is required to take the oath which then obligates him to bring this *'asham* (guilt-offering), and in which circumstances he is free of the oath;[16] in which way he can become obligated to bring many guilt-offerings, as the number of required oaths [that he must take]; and in which way he incurs a duty to bring only one *'asham.*[16] [These] and other details are explained in the Talmud tractates *K'rithoth* and *Sh'vu'oth.*

The precept of the obligation of this offering is in effect when the Temple is extant, for both man and woman. If someone violated it and did not bring it, then even if he returned what he had taken by robbery, his sin would not be atoned. It can be believed, though, that his punishment would not be as great as it would be if he did not return the property. This is an analogy for it: Someone beat his fellow and was obligated to pay a fine to the king; he became reconciled with the beaten person, and only the claim of the king remained for him [to pay].

[THE PRECEPT OF RETURNING PROPERTY SEIZED IN ROBBERY]

130 that we were commanded to return intact property taken in robbery; in other words, if he has the actual object which he took by

אֶצְלוֹ וְלֹא נִשְׁתַּנָּה בִּרְשׁוּתוֹ, שֶׁחַיָּב לַהֲשִׁיבוֹ אֶל הַנִּגְזָל כְּמוֹת שֶׁהוּא, וְלֹא שֶׁיִּקָּחֶנּוּ לְעַצְמוֹ וְיִתֵּן דָּמָיו לַנִּגְזָל, שֶׁנֶּאֱמַר: וְהֵשִׁיב אֶת הַגְּזֵלָה אֲשֶׁר גָּזָל, וְאַמְרִינָן בְּקַמָּא פֶּרֶק הַגּוֹזֵל בַּתְרָא: תָּנוּ רַבָּנָן: "וְהֵשִׁיב אֶת הַגְּזֵלָה אֲשֶׁר גָּזָל", מַה תַּלְמוּד לוֹמַר: "אֲשֶׁר גָּזָל", יַחֲזִיר כְּעֵין שֶׁגָּזָל.

וְאִם נִשְׁתַּנֵּית הַגְּזֵלָה בִּרְשׁוּתוֹ שֶׁל גּוֹזֵל, חַיָּב לְהָשִׁיב דָּמֶיהָ וּפָטוּר בְּכָךְ, אַף־עַל־פִּי שֶׁלֹּא נִתְיָאֲשׁוּ הַבְּעָלִים מִמֶּנָּה.

וְאֵי זֶהוּ שִׁנּוּי הַפּוֹטֵר מֵהָשִׁיב אֶת הַגְּזֵלָה בְּעֵין, זֶה הַשִּׁנּוּי שֶׁאֵינוֹ יָכוֹל לַחֲזֹר אַחַר־כָּךְ הַדָּבָר לִבְרִיָּתוֹ, כְּגוֹן הַגּוֹזֵל עֵצִים וְשָׁפָן אוֹ קָצַץ מֵהֶן קְצָתָן אוֹ שֶׁחָפַר בְּתוֹכָן חֲפִירוֹת, וְכֵן הַגּוֹזֵל צֶמֶר וּצְבָעוֹ, אוֹ הַגּוֹזֵל מַטְוֶה וְעָשָׂה מִמֶּנּוּ בֶּגֶד, וְכָל כַּיּוֹצֵא בָזֶה; אֲבָל הַגּוֹזֵל לוּחוֹת עֵץ, אַף־עַל־פִּי שֶׁבָּנָה מֵהֶן תֵּבָה, אֵין זֶה שִׁנּוּי שֶׁאֵינוֹ חוֹזֵר לִבְרִיָּתוֹ, שֶׁהֲרֵי אֶפְשָׁר לְפָרֵק אוֹתָן וְהֵן חוֹזְרִין לוּחוֹת כְּמוֹ שֶׁהָיוּ, וּלְפִיכָךְ חַיָּב לְהַחֲזִיר אוֹתָן בְּעֵין; וְכֵן כָּל כַּיּוֹצֵא בָזֶה.

שֹׁרֶשׁ הַמִּצְוָה יָדוּעַ.

דִּינֶיהָ, כְּגוֹן מַה שֶּׁאָמְרוּ רַבּוֹתֵינוּ זִכְרוֹנָם לִבְרָכָה: כַּמָּה תִהְיֶה הַגְּזֵלָה שֶׁיִּתְחַיֵּב הַגּוֹזֵל לַהֲשִׁיבָהּ, כָּל גְּזֵלָה הַשָּׁוָה פְרוּטָה; אֲבָל פָּחוֹת מִכָּאן, אַף־עַל־פִּי שֶׁעָבַר עַל אִסּוּר תּוֹרָה אֵינָהּ בְּתוֹרַת הֶשָּׁבוֹן, וּכְמוֹ שֶׁנִּכְתַּב בַּאֲרֻכָּה עַל לָאו דְּלֹא תִגְזֹל [סי׳ רכ״ט], לְפִי שֶׁיִּשְׂרָאֵל, בְּנֵי אַבְרָהָם יִצְחָק וְיַעֲקֹב, נְדִיבִים בְּנֵי נְדִיבִים הֵם, וְיָדוּעַ הַדָּבָר שֶׁכָּל שֶׁהוּא פָּחוֹת מִשָּׁוֶה פְרוּטָה, אֲפִלּוּ עָנִי שֶׁבְּיִשְׂרָאֵל מִכֵּיוָן שֶׁנִּגְזַל מִמֶּנּוּ מוֹחֵל אוֹתוֹ וְאֵין חֶפְצוֹ אַחֲרָיו כְּלָל.

וּלְפִיכָךְ אָמְרוּ זִכְרוֹנָם לִבְרָכָה שֶׁהַגּוֹזֵל שָׁלֹשׁ אֲגֻדּוֹת שֶׁשָּׁווֹת בִּשְׁעַת גְּזֵלָה שָׁלֹשׁ פְּרוּטוֹת וְהוּזְלוּ בְּיַד הַגַּזְלָן וְעָמְדוּ עַל שְׁתֵּי פְרוּטוֹת, אַף־עַל־פִּי שֶׁהֶחֱזִיר הַשְּׁתַּיִם חַיָּב לְהַחֲזִיר הַשְּׁלִישִׁית, שֶׁאַחַר שְׁעַת גְּזֵלָה אָנוּ דָנִין, וּכְבָר הָיְתָה שָׁוָה פְרוּטָה בְּאוֹתָהּ שָׁעָה.

§130 1. TB Bava Kamma 66a.

2. *Ibid.* 93b, 96a, etc. The word וְשָׁפָן "and smoothed, or planed, them" (6 lines above) is the reading of the oldest manuscript. In the next oldest, the letter ר was added above the word between the ש and the פ, making it וּשְׂרָפָן, "and burned them"; and it so appears in the further manuscripts and printed editions — with no foundation in the halachic literature.

3. TB Sanhedrin 57a; see §129, note 3.

4. It is a Talmudic rule that whatever the minimal amount subject to a prohibition, half the amount is also forbidden by Torah law, even if it is not punishable (TB Yoma 73b).

5. TB Bava Kamma 105a.

force, and it did not become altered while with him, a person is duty-bound to return it to the robbed man as it is; he is not to take it for himself and give its value in money to the robbed man. For it is stated, *and he shall return the seized object which he took by robbery* (Leviticus 5:23); and it was stated in the tenth chapter of the Talmud tractate *Bava Kamma* (112a): Our Sages taught: *and he shall return the seized object which he took by robbery*—why does Scripture add "which he took by robbery"?—he is to return it just as he took it.

If the seized object became altered while in the robber's domain, he is required to return its monetary value, and he is quit of guilt with that, even if the owner did not give up hope for it.[1]

Now, what is an alteration that frees a person from the duty to return the seized object itself?—any change after which the object cannot revert to its original state: for instance, if someone seized logs and planed them, or chopped off part of them, or dug holes in them; so too if someone seized wool in robbery and dyed it, or seized spun yarn and made a garment of it; and so forth. But if someone seized wooden boards, even if he built a box with them, this is not an alteration from which it cannot revert to its original state: for here they can be taken apart, and they are boards once again, as they were. Therefore he is required to return them intact; and so anything similar.[2]

The root reason for the precept is known (evident).

Its laws are, for example, what our Sages of blessed memory said: How much should a seized object be worth for the robber to incur the duty to return it?—anything seized which is worth a *p'rutah*;[3] but if it was worth less, even though he violated a prohibition of the Torah,[4] it is not subject to the duty of restoration, as we will write at length about the negative precept, "do not commit robbery" (§229). This is because the Israelites (Jews) are the children of Abraham, Isaac and Jacob; they are generous children of generous forebears; and it is a known matter that whatever is less than a *p'rutah*'s worth, even a poor man in Jewry, once he has been robbed of it, forgives it and has no yearning after it at all.

Therefore our Sages of blessed memory taught[5] that if someone seized three bundles worth three *p'rutoth* at the time of the robbery, and they became cheaper while with the robber until their price stood at two *p'rutoth*, then even if he returned two, he is duty-bound to return the third [as well]: For we decide according to the time of the robbery, and it was previously worth a *p'rutah*, at that time.

גָּזַל שְׁתַּיִם שֶׁשָּׁוּוֹת פְּרוּטָה וְהֵשִׁיב אַחַת, גְּזֵלָה יֵשׁ כָּאן, הָשֵׁב גְּזֵלָה אֵין כָּאן.

וְדִינֵי יֵאוּשׁ וְשִׁנּוּי רְשׁוּת, רַבִּים; וּכְלַל הַדָּבָר כֵּן לְפִי הַנִּרְאֶה מִן הַגְּמָרָא, שֶׁכָּל זְמַן שֶׁהַגְּזֵלָה בְּיַד הַגַּזְלָן אוֹ אֲפִלּוּ בְּיַד בָּנָיו וְלֹא נִשְׁתַּנֵּית, אַף־עַל־פִּי שֶׁיָּדַעְנוּ בְּוַדַּאי שֶׁהַנִּגְזָל נִתְיָאֵשׁ מִמֶּנָּה — וְהוּא כְּמוֹ שֶׁאָמְרוּ בַּגְּמָרָא: כְּגוֹן דִּשְׁמָעוּהָ בְּנֵי־אָדָם שֶׁהָיָה אוֹמֵר "וַי לֵיהּ לְחֶסְרוֹנֵיהּ", כְּלוֹמַר שֶׁמַּסְכִּים בְּדַעְתּוֹ עַל אוֹתוֹ דָּבָר שֶׁכְּבָר נֶאֱבַד מִמֶּנּוּ וְאֵין דַּעְתּוֹ סוֹמֶכֶת שֶׁיִּרְאֶנּוּ עוֹד — אַף־עַל־פִּי־כֵן דִּין תּוֹרָה שֶׁחַיָּבִין לְהַחֲזִירָהּ לַנִּגְזָל כְּמוֹת שֶׁהִיא; אֲפִלּוּ הִשְׁבִּיחָה בְּיַד הַגַּזְלָן, הַשֶּׁבַח לַנִּגְזָל; וְזֶהוּ שֶׁכָּתוּב בַּתּוֹרָה: וְהֵשִׁיב אֶת הַגְּזֵלָה אֲשֶׁר גָּזָל, וּבָא הַפֵּרוּשׁ: אִם הִיא כְּמוֹ שֶׁגְּזָלָהּ, כְּלוֹמַר שֶׁלֹּא נִשְׁתַּנֵּית, יַחֲזִירֶנָּה כְּמוֹת שֶׁהִיא, וַאֲפִלּוּ הִשְׁבִּיחָה כַּמָּה.

אֲבָל חֲכָמִים תִּקְּנוּ מִפְּנֵי תַּקָּנַת הַשָּׁבִים שֶׁכָּל מַה שֶּׁהִשְׁבִּיחָה בְּיַד גַּזְלָן אַחַר יֵאוּשׁ הַבְּעָלִים יִהְיֶה שֶׁלּוֹ, וּכְשֶׁיָּבוֹא לְהַחֲזִירָהּ יַחֲשֹׁב עִם הַנִּגְזָל כַּמָּה הָיְתָה שָׁוָה בִּשְׁעַת הַגְּזֵלָה וְיָשִׁיב לוֹ הַנִּגְזָל דְּמֵי מַה שֶּׁהִשְׁבִּיחָה, וְיִקָּחֶנָּה. וְדָבָר זֶה יֵשׁ כֹּחַ בְּיַד חֲכָמִים לַעֲשׂוֹתוֹ, לְפִי שֶׁבְּכָל דָּבָר שֶׁבְּמָמוֹן הֵם יְכוֹלִין לַעֲשׂוֹת בּוֹ כְּחֶפְצָם, וַאֲפִלּוּ כְּנֶגֶד צִוּוּי הַתּוֹרָה, כְּמוֹ שֶׁיָּדוּעַ שֶׁהֶפְקֵר בֵּית־דִּין הֶפְקֵר.

וּלְפִיכָךְ גּוֹי שֶׁגָּזַל וְהִשְׁבִּיחַ בֵּין קֹדֶם יֵאוּשׁ אוֹ לְאַחַר יֵאוּשׁ, אוֹ יִשְׂרָאֵל גַּזְלָן שֶׁמָּכַר לְגוֹי וְהִשְׁבִּיחַ הַגּוֹי [הַשֶּׁבַח לַנִּגְזָל. מְכָרָהּ] לִפְנֵי יֵאוּשׁ, הַדִּין עִם הַשֵּׁנִי כְּמוֹ עִם הָרִאשׁוֹן בְּשָׁוֶה, שֶׁאֵין שִׁנּוּי רְשׁוּת עוֹשֶׂה קִנְיָן אֶלָּא אַחַר יֵאוּשׁ. אֲבָל אַחַר יֵאוּשׁ, בֵּין שֶׁהָיָה אוֹתוֹ יֵאוּשׁ אַחַר שֶׁבָּאָתָה הַגְּזֵלָה לְיַד לוֹקֵחַ אוֹ בְעוֹד שֶׁהָיְתָה

6. Because a *p'rutah*'s worth was taken.

7. Because he did not return half.

8. I.e. if the robber sold or gave it to someone else.

9. TB Bava M'tzi'a 23a.

10. TB Bava Kamma 111b.

11. *Ibid.* 67a.

12. That those wishing to repent should not feel, in despair, that repentance is beyond them; *ibid.* 94b.

13. I.e. they can deprive a man of the ownership of his property if there is just cause; TB Yevamoth 89b, Gittin 36b.

14. I.e. the Torah's law stands, as the Sages did not enact their regulation for benefit of non-Jews. The bracketed addition follows MY, who adds three Hebrew words at this point, without which the text is incomprehensible.

15. TB Bava Kamma 111b.

If someone seized two [bundles] worth a *p'rutah* and returned one, there is [a case of] robbery here,[6] but there is not the return of the seized goods.[7]

Then there are the many laws about the loss of hope [of the owner for the seized property], and the change of domain.[8] The rule of the matter is this, according to what we gather from the Talmud: As long as the seized property is in the domain of the robber, or even of his sons, and it did not become altered, then even if we know for certain that the robbed man gave up hope for it—i.e. as it was said in the Talmud:[9] for instance, if people heard him saying, "Woe to him for his loss!" which is to say that he accepts in his mind the fate of that object that it is already lost to him, and his mind does not reliably expect that he will ever see it again—nevertheless, the law of the Torah is that they are duty-bound to return it to the robbed man as it is.[10] Even if it improved in worth while with the robber, the increase in the value belongs to the robbed man. Hence it is written in the Torah, *he shall return the seized object which he took by robbery* (Leviticus 5:23); and the interpretation was given for it:[11] if it is as at the time he seized it, i.e. it was not altered, he is to return it as it is, even if it became quite improved in value.

However, the Sages enacted as a regulation for the benefit of the penitent,[12] that all its increase in worth while in the robber's domain, after the owner abandoned hope for it, should be his [the robber's]; and when he comes to give it back, he is to make a reckoning with the robbed man of how much it was worth at the time of the robbery, and the robbed man should give him the monetary value of its improvement and take it. This matter, the Sages have the power to effect, because in anything concerning goods and possessions they are able to do as they wish with them, even against an order of the Torah—as it is common knowledge that what the *beth din* declares ownerless, is ownerless.[13]

Consequently, if a heathen took something by robbery and it improved in worth, whether before or after the owner lost hope for it, or if it was a Jewish robber who sold it to a heathen and the heathen improved its value, [the increase in worth belongs to the robbed man.[14] If he sold it] before the owner's loss of hope, the law for the second is the same as it is for the first—because a change of domain effects a change of possession only after the owner loses hope for it.[15]

 After his loss of hope, though, whether that occurred after the seized

בְּיַד גַּזְלָן, כֵּיוָן שֶׁיֵּשׁ בִּגְזֵלָה זוֹ יֵאוּשׁ וְשִׁנּוּי רְשׁוּת קְנָאָהּ הַלּוֹקֵחַ לְגוּפָהּ שֶׁל גְּזֵלָה; וְאִם אוֹתוֹ גַזְלָן שֶׁמְּכָרָהּ לוֹ הוּא גַזְלָן שֶׁאֵינוֹ מְפֻרְסָם, תִּהְיֶה שֶׁלּוֹ לְגַמְרֵי וְאֵין חַיָּב לְהָשִׁיב כְּלוּם לַנִּגְזָל, אֶלָּא יֵלֵךְ לוֹ נִגְזָל וְיַעֲשֶׂה דִין עִם הַגַּזְלָן; וְאִם הוּא גַזְלָן מְפֻרְסָם, חַיָּב לְהָשִׁיב הַלּוֹקֵחַ דְּמֵי הַגְּזֵלָה לַנִּגְזָל וְהוּא יַעֲשֶׂה דִין עִם הַגַּזְלָן.

וְדִינֵי הַגְּזֵלָה, עַד הֵיכָן הוּא חַיָּב לִטְרֹחַ לַהֲשִׁיבָהּ אֶל בְּעָלֶיהָ, כְּמוֹ שֶׁאָמְרוּ רַבּוֹתֵינוּ זִכְרוֹנָם לִבְרָכָה: הַגּוֹזֵל חֲבֵרוֹ שָׁוֶה פְרוּטָה שֶׁחַיָּב לְהוֹלִיכָהּ אַחֲרָיו אֲפִלּוּ לְמָדַי, כְּלוֹמַר לְמָקוֹם רָחוֹק. וּכְדֵי לְהָקֵל טָרְחוֹ אִם הַהוֹצָאָה מְרֻבָּה, אָמְרוּ רַבּוֹתֵינוּ זִכְרוֹנָם לִבְרָכָה שֶׁיַּנִּיחֶנָּה בְּיַד בֵּית־דִּין וְיוֹדִיעֵם שֶׁאוֹתוֹ מָמוֹן הוּא שֶׁל פְּלוֹנִי וְהֵם יִתְּנוּהוּ לוֹ לִכְשֶׁיִּזְדַּמֵּן.

וְדִין גָּזַל קוֹרָה וּבְנָאָהּ בְּבִירָה מַה יְּהֵא עָלֶיהָ, וְדִין גָּזַל בְּיִשּׁוּב וְרָצָה לְהַחֲזִיר בַּמִּדְבָּר, וְדִין גָּזַל וְהִקְדִּישׁ, וְגָזַל טָלֶה וְנַעֲשָׂה אַיִל מַה דִּינוֹ; וְדִין שֶׁבַח הַבָּא מֵחֲמַת יֹקֶר, שֶׁאֵינוֹ מִן הַתַּקָּנָה אֶלָּא חוֹזֵר לַנִּגְזָל, שֶׁלֹּא תִקְּנוּ לַגַּזְלָן אֶת הַשֶּׁבַח אַחַר יֵאוּשׁ אֶלָּא כְּגוֹן שֶׁבַח גִּזּוֹת וּוְלָדוֹת, אֲבָל שֶׁבַח הַיֹּקֶר לֹא; וְדִין תּוֹקֵף עֶבֶד חֲבֵרוֹ וְעָשָׂה בּוֹ מְלָאכָה, וְדִין תּוֹקֵף סְפִינָתוֹ, וְדִין הַדָּר בַּחֲצַר חֲבֵרוֹ שֶׁלֹּא מִדַּעְתּוֹ; וְיֶתֶר פְּרָטֶיהָ, מְבֹאָרִין בַּפְּרָקִים הָאַחֲרוֹנִים מִן קַמָּא.

וְנוֹהֶגֶת בְּכָל מָקוֹם וּבְכָל זְמַן, בִּזְכָרִים וּנְקֵבוֹת. וְעוֹבֵר עָלֶיהָ וְגָזַל וְלֹא הֵשִׁיב, בִּטֵּל עֲשֵׂה זֶה, מִלְּבַד הַלָּאו שֶׁעָבַר בִּשְׁעַת גְּזֵלָה. וְאוֹי לוֹ לְמִי שֶׁבְּיָדוֹ לְתַקֵּן הַמְעֻוָּת וְאֵינוֹ מְתַקְּנוֹ טֶרֶם מוֹתוֹ.

16. *Ibid.* 115a.

17. *Ibid.* 103a.

18. I.e. whether the dwelling must be demolished so that the beam can be returned intact, since it was not altered; TB Gittin 55a.

19. TB Bava Kamma 118a.

20. TB Bava M'tzi'a 7a, etc.

21. Because he kept it long enough for the animal to mature; TB Bava Kamma 65b (MT *hilchoth g'zélah* ii 14).

22. *Ibid.* 65a (MT *ibid.* 16).

23. TB Bava Kamma 97a–b.

object came into the buyer's hand or while it was still with the robber, since both loss of hope and change of domain occurred for this seized object, the buyer gains possession of the object itself. And if that robber who sold it to him is not a notorious, well-known outlaw, it becomes his completely, and he need give the robbed man nothing in return. Instead, let the robbed man go and take the robber to trial. But if he is a notorious robber, the buyer is obligated to return the monetary value of the seized object to the robbed man, and *he* can take the robber to trial.[16]

Then there are the laws about the seized object—to what extent he [the robber] is required to trouble and toil in order to return it to its owner: As our Sages of blessed memory said,[17] if someone robs his fellow of a *p'rutah*'s worth, he has a duty to take it to him, following him even to Media—i.e. to a distant location [if necessary]. But in order to lighten his trouble if the expense is very great, our Sages of blessed memory ruled[17] that he may leave it with the *beth din*, informing them that this property belongs to so-and-so; and they will give it to him when he will happen to come.

There is, further, the law about a beam which [the robber] built into a dwelling: what should be done about it;[18] the law if someone committed the robbery in the settled (civilized) community and he wishes to return it in the wilderness;[19] the law if someone seized something by robbery and consecrated it;[20] and if someone seized a lamb and it became a ram,[21] what should his law be. And there is the law about improvement in value which came because of a rise in price, that this is not under the regulation of the Sages, but reverts to the robbed man: for they made the ruling to grant the robber only such improvement, after the owner abandons hope for it, as, for example, improvement in the wool [of a sheep] and its young [that are born to it]; but not the the improvement of a rise in price.[22]

There is, too, the law if someone seizes the servant of his fellow and puts him to work;[23] the law if someone seizes a boat;[23] and the law if a person resides in the courtyard of his fellow without his knowledge.[23] [These] and further details are explained in the last chapters of the tractate *Bava Kamma*.

It applies in every place and every time, for both man and woman. If someone violates it, committing robbery and not returning [what he has taken], he thus disobeys a positive precept, apart from the prohibition which he violates during the robbery. And woe to him

צַו אֶת אַהֲרֹן

יֵשׁ בָּהּ תֵּשַׁע מִצְוֹות עֲשֵׂה וְתֵשַׁע גַּם־כֵּן מִצְוֹות לֹא־תַעֲשֶׂה

[מִצְוַת הֲרָמַת הַדֶּשֶׁן]

קלא שֶׁיָּסִיר הַכֹּהֵן הַדֶּשֶׁן בְּכָל יוֹם וָיוֹם מֵעַל הַמִּזְבֵּחַ, וְזֶהוּ שֶׁנִּקְרָא תְּרוּמַת הַדֶּשֶׁן, שֶׁהָיְתָה נַעֲשֵׂית בְּכָל יוֹם, שֶׁנֶּאֱמַר: וְלָבַשׁ הַכֹּהֵן מִדּוֹ בַד וְגוֹמֵר, וְהֵרִים אֶת הַדֶּשֶׁן.

מִשָּׁרְשֵׁי מִצְוָה זוֹ, מַה שֶּׁכָּתַבְנוּ לְמַעְלָה, לְהַגְדִּיל כְּבוֹד הַבַּיִת וּלְהַדְּרוֹ בְּכָל יְכָלְתֵּנוּ, מִן הַטַּעַם שֶׁאָמַרְנוּ שָׁם; וְנוֹי הוּא לַמִּזְבֵּחַ לְפַנּוֹת הַדֶּשֶׁן מִמָּקוֹם שֶׁרָאוּי לְהַדְלִיק בּוֹ הָאֵשׁ; וְעוֹד שֶׁהָאֵשׁ דּוֹלֵק יָפֶה כְּשֶׁאֵין תַּחְתָּיו דֶּשֶׁן.

מִדִּינֵי הַמִּצְוָה, מַה שֶּׁאָמְרוּ זִכְרוֹנָם לִבְרָכָה, שֶׁהֲרָמַת הַדֶּשֶׁן הִיא עֲבוֹדָה מֵעֲבוֹדוֹת הַכְּהֻנָּה; וּבִגְדֵי הַכְּהֻנָּה שֶׁהָיוּ תוֹרְמִין בָּהֶן הַדֶּשֶׁן הָיוּ פְחוּתִין מִן הַכֵּלִים שֶׁמְּשַׁמֵּשׁ בָּהֶן שְׁאָר עֲבוֹדוֹת, שֶׁנֶּאֱמַר: וּפָשַׁט אֶת בְּגָדָיו וְלָבַשׁ בְּגָדִים אֲחֵרִים; וְאַף־עַל־פִּי שֶׁפָּסוּק זֶה נֶאֱמַר בְּהוֹצָאַת הַדֶּשֶׁן אֶל מִחוּץ לַמַּחֲנֶה, מִכָּל־מָקוֹם גַּם בִּתְרוּמַת הַדֶּשֶׁן, דְּהַיְנוּ כְּשֶׁמְּסַלֵּק אוֹתָהּ מֵעַל הַמִּזְבֵּחַ וּמוֹרִידָהּ לָרִצְפָּה שֶׁאֵצֶל הַמִּזְבֵּחַ, יֵשׁ לָנוּ לִלְמֹד גַּם־כֵּן שֶׁאֵין רָאוּי לַעֲשׂוֹת אוֹתָהּ מְלָאכָה בְּאוֹתָן בְּגָדִים שֶׁהוּא מְשַׁמֵּשׁ. וְנֶאֱמַר בָּזֶה עַל דֶּרֶךְ מָשָׁל: בְּגָדִים שֶׁבִּשֵּׁל בָּהֶן קְדֵרָה לְרַבּוֹ אַל יִמְזֹג בָּהֶן כּוֹס לְרַבּוֹ.

וְאֵימָתַי תּוֹרְמִין הַדֶּשֶׁן: בְּכָל יוֹם מִשֶּׁיַּעֲלֶה עַמּוּד הַשַּׁחַר, וּבַמּוֹעֲדִים מִשְּׁלִישׁ (האחרון) [הָאֶמְצָעִי] שֶׁל לַיְלָה, וּבְיוֹם הַכִּפּוּרִים מֵחֲצוֹת הַלַּיְלָה. וְכֵיצַד תּוֹרְמִין אוֹתָהּ: מִי שֶׁזָּכָה וּבָא גוֹרָלוֹ לַהֲסִירָהּ טוֹבֵל וְלוֹבֵשׁ בִּגְדֵי הֲרָמָה וּמְקַדֵּשׁ יָדָיו

24. Expression based on Ecclesiastes 1:15.

§131 1. TB Yoma 23b.

2. *Ibid.* 20a; MT *hilchoth t'midin* ii 11 (see *Lehem Mishneh*).

3. I.e. from the beginning of the middle third. The original has "the last third," but it is clear from the Talmud and MT that it must be a scribal error; TB Yoma 20a; MT *ibid.* (MH).

4. Because the entire service that day had to be done by the *kohen gadol* alone, they began this early; TB *ibid.*; MT *ibid.*

5. Originally, any *kohen* who wished could remove it; but once two raced to the altar, vying for the honor, and an accident happened. Since then, lots were cast each morning to choose the *kohen*; Mishnah, Yoma ii 1–2.

who has it in his power to straighten out what is crooked[24] and he does not set it aright before his death.

sidrah tzav

(Leviticus 6–8)

There are nine positive and also nine negative precepts in it.

[THE PRECEPT OF LIFTING OFF THE ASH FROM THE ALTAR]

131 that a *kohen* should remove the ashes every day from the altar. This is what was called *t'rumath ha-deshen* (the lifting off of the ash), which was done every day—as it is stated, *And the* kohen *shall put on his linen garment . . . and he shall take up the ashes* (Leviticus 6:3).

At the root of this precept lies the purpose that we have written above, to magnify the glory of the Temple and give it distinction with all our ability, for the reason we stated there. It is an embellishment for the altar to remove the ash from the place where it is proper to light the fire. Moreover, fire burns splendidly when there is no ash underneath it.

Among the laws of the precept there is what the Sages of blessed memory said,[1] that lifting off the ash was one of the tasks in the Temple service of the *kohanim*. The clothing of the *kohen* in which they would remove the ash was inferior to the garments in which other tasks were done: for it is stated, *Then he shall put off his garments and put on other garments* (Leviticus 6:4).[1] Although this verse was stated about taking the ashes out of the camp [beyond community limits], nevertheless we can learn from it also about lifting off the ash, i.e. when it is removed from the altar and lowered to the floor near the altar, that it is not fitting to do this work in those garments in which one serves. About this it was said, by way of analogy:[1] In the clothing in which he has cooked a pot of food for his master, one should not pour a cup of wine for his master.

When was the ash lifted off?—every day, when dawn came up;[2] on the festivals, from the middle third of the night;[3] on the Day of Atonement, from midnight.[4] How was it lifted off? The one who won and it fell to his lot to remove it[5] would undergo ritual immersion [in the *mikveh*], put on the clothing for the removal, and

וְרַגְלָיו, וְהָיוּ אוֹמְרִים לוֹ אֶחָיו הַכֹּהֲנִים "הִזָּהֵר שֶׁמָּא תִּגַּע בַּכְּלִי עַד שֶׁתְּקַדֵּשׁ יָדֶיךָ וְרַגְלֶיךָ", וְאַחַר כָּךְ לוֹקֵחַ הַמַּחְתָּה, וְשֶׁל כֶּסֶף הָיְתָה, נְכוֹנָה בַּמִּקְצוֹעוֹת בֵּין כֶּבֶשׁ לַמִּזְבֵּחַ בְּמַעֲרָבוֹ שֶׁל כֶּבֶשׁ, וְנוֹטֵל אֶת הַמַּחְתָּה וְעוֹלֶה לְרֹאשׁ הַמִּזְבֵּחַ, וּמְפַנֶּה אֶת הַגֶּחָלִים הֵילָךְ וְהֵילָךְ, וְחוֹתֶה מִן הַגֶּחָלִים שֶׁנִּתְאַכְּלוּ בְּלֵב הָאֵשׁ, וְיוֹרֵד לְמַטָּה לָאָרֶץ, וְהוֹפֵךְ פָּנָיו לְצָפוֹן וּמְהַלֵּךְ בָּאָרֶץ לְמִזְרַח הַכֶּבֶשׁ כְּמוֹ עֶשֶׂר אַמּוֹת כְּלַפֵּי הַצָּפוֹן, וְצוֹבֵר אֶת הַגֶּחָלִים שֶׁחָתָה עַל־גַּבֵּי הָרִצְפָּה רָחוֹק מִן הַכֶּבֶשׁ שְׁלֹשָׁה טְפָחִים, בִּמְקוֹם מוּרְאַת הָעוֹף וְדִשּׁוּן מִזְבֵּחַ הַפְּנִימִי וְהַמְּנוֹרָה. וַחֲתִיָּתָהּ זוֹ שֶׁחוֹתֶה בַּמַּחְתָּה וּמוֹרִיד לָרִצְפָּה אֵצֶל הַמִּזְבֵּחַ, הִיא הַמִּצְוָה שֶׁל כָּל יוֹם.

וְאַחַר שֶׁיָּרַד זֶה שֶׁתָּרַם, רָצִין אֶחָיו הַכֹּהֲנִים וּמְקַדְּשִׁין יְדֵיהֶם וְרַגְלֵיהֶם בִּמְהֵרָה, וְנוֹטְלִין אֶת הַמַּגְרֵפוֹת וְהַצִּנּוֹרוֹת וְעוֹלִין לְרֹאשׁ הַמִּזְבֵּחַ, וְגוֹרְפִין אֶת הַדֶּשֶׁן מִכָּל צִדֵּי הַמִּזְבֵּחַ, וְעוֹשִׂין מִמֶּנּוּ עֲרֵמָה עַל־גַּבֵּי תַּפּוּחַ, וְהוּא מָקוֹם מִן הַמִּזְבֵּחַ שֶׁנִּקְרָא כֵן; וּכְשֶׁאוֹתוֹ תַּפּוּחַ הָיָה גָדוֹל מוֹרִידִין מִמֶּנּוּ קְצָת לְמַטָּה בִּכְלִי גָדוֹל מַחֲזִיק לֶתֶךְ שֶׁנִּקְרָא פְּסַכְתֵּר, וְעוֹמֵד שָׁם עַד שֶׁמּוֹצִיאִין אוֹתוֹ כֻּלּוֹ מִחוּץ לַמַּחֲנֶה; וְיֶתֶר פְּרָטֶיהָ, בְּמַסֶּכֶת תָּמִיד וְיוֹמָא.

וְנוֹהֶגֶת בִּזְמַן הַבַּיִת בִּזְכְרֵי כְהֻנָּה. וְעוֹבֵר עָלֶיהָ וְלֹא הֵסִירָהּ כְּמִצְוָתָהּ, בִּטֵּל עֲשֵׂה.

[מִצְוַת הַדְלָקַת אֵשׁ עַל הַמִּזְבֵּחַ בְּכָל יוֹם]

קלב לְהַבְעִיר אֵשׁ עַל הַמִּזְבֵּחַ בְּכָל יוֹם תָּמִיד, שֶׁנֶּאֱמַר: אֵשׁ תָּמִיד תּוּקַד עַל הַמִּזְבֵּחַ; וּבָא הַפֵּרוּשׁ שֶׁל "תָּמִיד", כְּלוֹמַר לְהָשִׂים בּוֹ עֵצִים בַּבֹּקֶר וּבֵין הָעַרְבַּיִם; וּבְבֵאוּר אָמְרוּ זִכְרוֹנָם לִבְרָכָה: אַף־עַל־פִּי שֶׁהָאֵשׁ יוֹרֵד מִן הַשָּׁמַיִם, מִצְוָה לְהָבִיא מִן הַהֶדְיוֹט.

וְאַל יִקְשֶׁה עָלֶיךָ לֵאמֹר מַה הִיא מִצְוָה זוֹ, וַהֲלֹא עַל־כָּל־פָּנִים הָיָה לָהֶם

6. See Leviticus 1:16 that it was to be removed from fowl brought as offerings; it was always thrown onto this place.

7. I.e. the one in the holy chamber; the incense was burned on it.

8. Mishnah, Tamid i.

9. TB Yoma 20a.

10. The shovels to gather the remaining ash, the large forks to move aside the parts of offerings being burned.

11. I.e. a large, fairly constant heap; Mishnah, Tamid ii 1.

12. So Rabad, on MT *hilchoth t'midin* ii 7.

13. A *lethech* equals 124,416 cubic centimeters according to one view, 215,000 cubic centimeters according to another.

14. Mishnah, Tamid v 5.

15. It is inferred from Leviticus 4:12 that there was to be a place outside the camp (beyond the community limits) where the ash would ultimately be dumped.

sanctify his hands and feet [by rinsing them]; and his brother *kohanim* would tell him, "Beware lest you touch a holy object until you sanctify your hands and feet." After that he would take a censer, which was of silver, waiting in the corner between the ramp and the altar, at the western edge of the ramp. Taking the censer, he would go to the head of the altar, move the burning embers aside hither and thither, and gather of the burnt embers in the heart of the fire; he would then go down to the ground, turn his face northward, and walk on the ground to the east side of the ramp, about ten cubits to the north; and he would heap the embers that he had gathered on the floor, three handbreadths away from the ramp, at the place for the crop of a fowl[6] and the removal [piling] of the ash from the inner altar[7] and the *menorah* (lamp).[8] This gathering [of the ash] which was taken up in the censer and brought down to the floor near the altar was a religious duty every day.[9]

After this one who lifted it off came down, his brother *kohanim* would run and sanctify [rinse] their hands and feet quickly, take the shovels and forks,[10] go up to the head of the ramp, and shovel up the ash from all the sides of the altar, making a pile of it on the "apple,"[11] which was a place on the altar called so.[12] When that "apple" [pile] became large, some of it was taken down below in a great container that could hold a *lethech*,[13] which was called *p'sachter* (large pot).[14] It would stand there until it would all be taken outside the camp.[15] [These] and its further details are in the tractates *Tamid* and *Yoma*.

It is in effect when the Temple is extant, for the male *kohanim*. If someone violated it and did not remove it as its commandment [requires], he would thus disobey a positive precept.

132 [THE PRECEPT OF KINDLING THE FIRE ON THE ALTAR]

to burn fire on the altar every day, regularly: for it is stated, *Fire shall be kept burning on the altar continually* (Leviticus 6:6); and the interpretation of *tamid*, "continually," was given [in the Oral Tradition][1] that it signifies putting wood on it morning and evening. In elucidation, our Sages of blessed memory said:[2] Although fire would descend from heaven, it was a religious duty to bring of common [earthly fire].

Now, let this not be a difficulty for you, to ask, "What [sort of] precept is this? Surely they had to burn fire in any case, for the need

לְהַבְעִיר אֵשׁ לְצֹרֶךְ הַקָּרְבָּן שֶׁנִּתְחַיְּבוּ לְהַקְרִיב, וּבְלֹא אֵשׁ אִי אֶפְשָׁר. כִּי מִצְוָה זוֹ בִּפְנֵי עַצְמָהּ הִיא, כִּי מִלְּבַד אֵשׁ הַצָּרִיךְ לַקָּרְבָּן הָיוּ בּוֹעֲרִים אֵשׁ בַּמִּזְבֵּחַ לְמִצְוָה זוֹ, וּכְמוֹ שֶׁדָּרְשׁוּ זִכְרוֹנָם לִבְרָכָה שָׁלֹשׁ מַעֲרָכוֹת שֶׁל אֵשׁ מִן הַכְּתוּבִים, כְּמוֹ שֶׁנִּכְתֹּב בְּדִינִין שֶׁל מִצְוָה זוֹ.

מִשָּׁרְשֵׁי הַמִּצְוָה, הַקְדָּמָה: יָדוּעַ הַדָּבָר בֵּינֵינוּ וְאֵצֶל כָּל חָכָם כִּי נִסִּים גְּדוֹלִים אֲשֶׁר יַעֲשֶׂה הָאֵל אֶל בְּנֵי־אָדָם בְּטוּבוֹ הַגָּדוֹל, לְעוֹלָם יַעֲשֵׂם דֶּרֶךְ סֵתֶר, וְנִרְאִים הָעִנְיָנִים נַעֲשִׂים קְצָת כְּאִלּוּ הֵם בְּדַרְכֵי הַטֶּבַע מַמָּשׁ אוֹ בְּקָרוֹב לַטֶּבַע; כִּי גַּם בְּנֵס קְרִיעַת יַם־סוּף, שֶׁהָיָה נֵס מְפֻרְסָם, כָּתוּב שָׁם: וַיּוֹלֶךְ יי אֶת הַיָּם בְּרוּחַ קָדִים עַזָּה כָּל הַלַּיְלָה וַיָּשֶׂם אֶת הַיָּם לֶחָרָבָה וַיִּבָּקְעוּ הַמָּיִם; וְהַמַּשְׂכִּילִים יָבִינוּ כִּי עִנְיַן סֵתֶר זֶה לְמַעֲלַת הָאָדוֹן וְשִׁפְלוּת הַמְקַבֵּל.

וּמִזֶּה הָעִנְיָן צֻוֵּינוּ לְהַבְעִיר אֵשׁ בַּמִּזְבֵּחַ, אַף־עַל־פִּי שֶׁשָּׁם יוֹרֵד אֵשׁ מִן הַשָּׁמַיִם, כְּדֵי לְהַסְתִּיר הַנֵּס. לְפִי הַדּוֹמֶה שֶׁהָאֵשׁ הַיּוֹרֶדֶת לֹא הָיְתָה נִרְאֵית בִּירִידָתָהּ, מִן הַטַּעַם שֶׁאָמַרְנוּ, חוּץ מִיּוֹם שְׁמִינִי שֶׁל מִלּוּאִים, וְשֶׁל גִּדְעוֹן וּמָנוֹחַ, שֶׁהָיְתָה נִרְאֵית.

וַעֲדַיִן אָנוּ צְרִיכִין לוֹמַר מַהוּ עִנְיַן הַמִּצְוָה לְהַדְלִיק אֵשׁ עַל הַמִּזְבֵּחַ מִלְּבַד הָאֵשׁ הַצָּרִיךְ שָׁם לְקָרְבָּן. וְנֹאמַר עַל צַד הַפְּשָׁט שֶׁהוּא כְעִנְיַן מַה שֶּׁכָּתַבְנוּ בְּמִצְוַת לֶחֶם הַפָּנִים, שֶׁהָאָדָם מִתְבָּרֵךְ לְפִי מַעֲשָׂיו שֶׁהוּא עוֹסֵק בָּהֶם לִרְצוֹן בּוֹרְאוֹ, וְעַל זֶה הַדֶּרֶךְ אָמַרְנוּ שֶׁהַבְּרָכָה מְצוּיָה בְּכָל לֶחֶם חֹל מִתּוֹךְ עִסְקֵנוּ בְמִצְוָה בְּלֶחֶם קֹדֶשׁ, כְּאִלּוּ תֹאמַר עַל דֶּרֶךְ מָשָׁל שֶׁהַבְּרָכָה תִּתְפַּשֵּׁט בְּמִינָהּ. וּכְמוֹ־כֵן הוּא עֵסֶק הַמִּצְוָה בָּאֵשׁ בְּכָל יוֹם שֶׁיִּתְבָּרֵךְ הָאָדָם בְּעִנְיַן הָאֵשׁ שֶׁבּוֹ.

וּמַהוּ אֵשׁ זֶה, הוּא הַטֶּבַע שֶׁבָּאָדָם; כִּי מִן הָאַרְבָּעָה יְסוֹדוֹת שֶׁבָּאָדָם, הוּא אֵשׁ וְהוּא רֹאשׁ לְאַרְבַּעְתָּן, כִּי בוֹ יִתְחַזֵּק הָאָדָם וְיִתְנוֹעֵעַ וְיִפְעַל; וְעַל־כֵּן צְרִיכָה

§132 1. See TB Yoma 45b.

2. *Ibid.* 21b. (The first paragraph is based on ShM positive precept §29.)

3. *Ibid.* 45a.

4. So that it would seem the natural cause for the division of the sea (Ramban on the verse).

5. Whose open revelation cannot occur in this physical world.

6. Who would be overwhelmed by too open a revelation of His presence.

of the offerings which they were required to sacrifice, which could not be done without fire?" For this is a separate religious duty, by itself. Apart from fire needed for an offering, they would burn fire on the altar by this precept. As our Sages of blessed memory taught:[3] there were three piles of wood for fire, [as derived] from the verses [of Scripture]—as we shall write among the laws of this precept.

Regarding the root purpose of the precept, [let me begin with] a preface: It is a matter well known to us and to every man of wisdom that when God does major miracles for human beings in His great goodness, He always works them in a hidden way, and the matters seem done somewhat as though actually in natural ways or in ways close to the natural order. For even about the miracle of the division of the Red Sea, which was a renowned miracle, it is written, *the Lord drove the sea back by a strong east wind all the night,*[4] *and made the sea dry land, and the waters were divided* (Exodus 14:21). Those with intelligence will understand that this matter of hiddenness is on account of the exalted state of the Lord[5] and the lowly state of the recipient.[6]

For this reason He commanded us to burn fire on the altar, even though flame would descend there from heaven—in order to conceal the miracle. Evidently the fire that came down there was not perceived in its descent, for the reason we have stated, except on the eighth day of the inauguration [of the *mishkan*, the Tabernacle] (Leviticus 9:24), [the fire] of Gideon (Judges 6:21) and of Manoaḥ (*ibid.* 13:20), in which cases it was seen.

It remains necessary for us to convey what the significance of the religious duty was to kindle fire on the altar apart from the fire needed there for the offerings. We would say by way of the plain meaning that in substance it is akin to what we wrote about the precept of the showbread (§97)—that man is blessed according to his activities in which he engages for the good will of his Creator. By this approach we said that blessing would be manifest in all ordinary (non-holy) bread on account of our occupation with a *mitzvah* with the sacred bread—as you might say by way of analogy, the blessing spreads through its kind. Similarly, the occupation with the religous duty of fire every day was that man should be blessed in regard to the aspect of fire in him.

Now, what is this fire?—it is the [force of] nature in man. For out of the four elements in man, this [force] is fire, and it is the chief one of the four, since with it man is strengthened and can move and

הַבְּרָכָה בּוֹ יוֹתֵר. וְעִנְיַן הַבְּרָכָה הוּא שְׁלֵמוּת, כְּלוֹמַר דָּבָר שֶׁאֵין בּוֹ חִסָּרוֹן וְלֹא מוֹתָר, וְכֵן הָאֵשׁ שֶׁבָּאָדָם צָרִיךְ לִבְרָכָה זוֹ שֶׁיְּהֵא מִמֶּנּוּ בָּאָדָם מַה שֶּׁצָּרִיךְ אֵלָיו, לֹא פָּחוֹת כִּי יֶחֱלַשׁ כֹּחוֹ, וְלֹא יוֹתֵר כִּי יִשָּׂרֵף בּוֹ, כְּדֶרֶךְ בְּנֵי־אָדָם שֶׁמֵּתִים בְּתוֹסֶפֶת הָאֵשׁ בָּהֶם יוֹתֵר מִדַּי, וְהוּא הַקַּדַּחַת. וּבְנֵי אַהֲרֹן הוֹסִיפוּ בָאֵשׁ מִבְּלִי שֶׁנִּצְטַוּוּ, וְנוֹסַף גַּם בָּהֶם אֵשׁ וְנִשְׂרְפוּ, כִּי לְפִי פְּעֻלַּת בֶּן־אָדָם יָבֹא עָנְשׁוֹ אוֹ תָנוּחַ בִּרְכַּת יי בּוֹ.

מִדִּינֵי הַמִּצְוָה, מַה שֶּׁאָמְרוּ זִכְרוֹנָם לִבְרָכָה שֶׁאַף־עַל־פִּי שֶׁהָאֵשׁ יוֹרְדָה מִן הַשָּׁמַיִם מִצְוָה לְהָבִיא מִן הַהֶדְיוֹט, שֶׁנֶּאֱמַר: וְנָתְנוּ בְּנֵי אַהֲרֹן הַכֹּהֵן אֵשׁ וְגוֹמֵר. וּבַבֹּקֶר הָיוּ עוֹרְכִין עֵצִים וְעוֹשִׂים בְּרֹאשׁ הַמִּזְבֵּחַ מַעֲרָכָה גְדוֹלָה שֶׁל (אֵשׁ) [עֵצִים], שֶׁנֶּאֱמַר: וּבִעֵר עָלֶיהָ הַכֹּהֵן עֵצִים בַּבֹּקֶר בַּבֹּקֶר. וּמִלְּבַד הָעֵצִים הָעֲרוּכִים עַל הַמַּעֲרָכָה מִצְוָה עַל הַכֹּהֵן לַעֲלוֹת לַמִּזְבֵּחַ בִּשְׁנֵי גְזִירִין שֶׁל עֵץ, שֶׁנֶּאֱמַר "וּבִעֵר עָלֶיהָ הַכֹּהֵן עֵצִים", וּמִעוּט עֵצִים שְׁנַיִם; וְכֵן מוֹסִיפִים גַּם־כֵּן שְׁנֵי גְזִירִין עִם תָּמִיד שֶׁל בֵּין הָעַרְבַּיִם, וּמַעֲלִין אוֹתָם שְׁנֵי כֹהֲנִים, שֶׁנֶּאֱמַר "וְעָרְכוּ"; וְשֶׁל שַׁחַר, כֹּהֵן אֶחָד.

וְשָׁלֹשׁ מַעֲרָכוֹת שֶׁל אֵשׁ הָיוּ עוֹשִׂים בַּמִּזְבֵּחַ בְּכָל יוֹם: הָרִאשׁוֹנָה גְּדוֹלָה, שֶׁעָלֶיהָ מַקְרִיבִין הַתָּמִיד עִם שְׁאָר קָרְבָּנוֹת; שְׁנִיָּה בְּצִדָּהּ קְטַנָּה מִמֶּנָּה, שֶׁמִּמֶּנָּה לוֹקְחִין אֵשׁ בַּמַּחְתָּה לְהַקְטִיר קְטֹרֶת בְּכָל יוֹם; וּמַעֲרָכָה שְׁלִישִׁית אֵין עָלֶיהָ כְּלוּם, אֶלָּא לְקַיֵּם מִצְוַת הָאֵשׁ, שֶׁנֶּאֱמַר: אֵשׁ תָּמִיד תּוּקַד וְכוּלֵי. וּשְׁלֹשָׁה כְתוּבִים בָּעִנְיָן שֶׁהֵם מוֹרִים עַל שָׁלֹשׁ מַעֲרָכוֹת אֵלֶּה, כְּמוֹ שֶׁלָּמַדְנוּ מִפִּי הַשְּׁמוּעָה, שֶׁאָמְרוּ זִכְרוֹנָם לִבְרָכָה: "עַל מוֹקְדָה", זוֹ מַעֲרָכָה גְדוֹלָה; "וְאֵשׁ הַמִּזְבֵּחַ תּוּקַד בּוֹ", זֶה מַעֲרָכָה שְׁנִיָּה שֶׁל קְטֹרֶת; "וְהָאֵשׁ עַל הַמִּזְבֵּחַ תּוּקַד בּוֹ", זֶה מַעֲרָכָה שְׁלִישִׁית שֶׁל קִיּוּם הָאֵשׁ. וְיֶתֶר פְּרָטֶיהָ, מְבֹאָרִים בְּפֶרֶק ד׳ מִיּוֹמָא וְשֵׁנִי מִתָּמִיד.

7. Mishnah, Tamid ii 1.
8. As the injunction in Leviticus 6:5 is in the singular; TB Yoma 26b.
9. TB Yoma 43b.

function. Therefore blessing is most needed in it. The aim of a blessing is wholeness, i.e. something that has nothing missing and nothing superfluous. So the [element of] fire in man has need of this blessing, that there should be in a man the amount of it that he needs—not less: for his strength will be weakened; and not more: for then he will be burnt by it, in the way of people who die from an increase of fire in them beyond the norm, which is fever. The sons of Aaron added fire without being commanded (Leviticus 10:1); hence fire was added within them, and they were burnt (*ibid.* 2). For according to a person's activity will his punishment come, or the blessing of the Lord will rest upon him.

Among the laws of the precept, there is what the Sages of blessed memory said,[2] that although fire would descend from heaven, it is a religious duty to bring of common (non-holy) fire: for it is stated, *And the sons of Aaron the* kohen *shall put fire* [*on the altar*] etc. (Leviticus 1:7). In the morning they would arrange wood and place a great pile of wood at the head of the altar: for it is stated, *and the* kohen *shall burn wood on it every morning* (*ibid.* 6:5).[7] Apart from the wood arranged in a pile, it was a religious duty for the *kohen* to ascend to the altar with two wood logs [to burn]: for it is stated, *and the* kohen *shall burn wood on it* [the Hebrew for "wood" being in the plural] and the minimum plural of the wood is two. So too were two logs added with the daily *'olah* (burnt-offering) of the evening, which two *kohanim* would bring up: for it is written, [*the sons of Aaron . . .*] *shall put fire* [in the plural]; but [with the *'olah*] of the morning, only one *kohen* [brought the logs].[8]

Three piles of wood were set on the altar every day. The first was large, for on it the daily *'olah* (burnt-offering) was offered up, with other offerings. The second, by its side, was smaller: for from it fire would be taken in the censer for burning the incense every day. As for the third pile, nothing would go on it [to be burnt]; it was only to fulfill the precept of fire, as it is stated, *Fire shall be kept burning continuously*, etc. (Leviticus 6:6). There are three verses on the subject, which indicate these three piles, as we learned in the Oral Tradition. For the Sages of blessed memory said: *on its fire-wood* (*ibid.* 2)—this denotes the great pile; *and the fire of the altar shall be kept burning by it* (*ibid.*)—this signifies the second pile, for the incense; *And the fire on the altar shall be kept burning by it* (ibid. 5)—this denotes the third pile, for maintaining the fire.[9] [These] and the rest of its details are explained

וְנוֹהֶגֶת בִּזְמַן הַבַּיִת בְּזִכְרֵי כְהֻנָּה. וְאִם לֹא הִבְעִירוּ הַכֹּהֲנִים מַעֲרָכָה שְׁלִישִׁית בַּמִּזְבֵּחַ, בִּטְּלוּ מִצְוַת עֲשֵׂה זוֹ.

[שֶׁלֹּא לְכַבּוֹת אֵשׁ מֵעַל הַמִּזְבֵּחַ]

קלג שֶׁלֹּא לְכַבּוֹת אֵשׁ מֵעַל הַמִּזְבֵּחַ, שֶׁנֶּאֱמַר: אֵשׁ תָּמִיד תּוּקַד עַל הַמִּזְבֵּחַ לֹא תִכְבֶּה.

מִשָּׁרְשֵׁי מִצְוַת הָאֵשׁ כָּתַבְתִּי לְמַעְלָה בְּמִצְוַת עֲשֵׂה דְ״אֵשׁ תּוּקַד״ [סי׳ קל״ב], וְשֹׁרֶשׁ הַצַּוָּאָה בָּאֵשׁ לְהַבְעִירָהּ וְשֶׁלֹּא לְכַבּוֹתָהּ אֶחָד הוּא, אֵין צֹרֶךְ לְהַחֲזִירוֹ.

מִדִּינֵי הַמִּצְוָה, מַה שֶּׁאָמְרוּ זִכְרוֹנָם לִבְרָכָה שֶׁאֲפִלּוּ הוֹרִיד הָאֵשׁ מֵעַל הַמִּזְבֵּחַ וְכִבָּהוּ לוֹקֶה, אֲבָל אֵשׁ מַחְתָּה וְאֵשׁ מְנוֹרָה שֶׁהֱכִינָהּ בַּמִּזְבֵּחַ לְהַדְלִיק מִמֶּנָּה, אַף־עַל־פִּי שֶׁכִּבָּה אוֹתָהּ בְּרֹאשׁ הַמִּזְבֵּחַ פָּטוּר, שֶׁהֲרֵי נִתְּקָהּ מִן הַמִּזְבֵּחַ וְאֵין אֲנִי קוֹרֵא בוֹ אֵשׁ הַמִּזְבֵּחַ, וְלֹא הֻזְהַרְנוּ אֶלָּא עַל כִּבּוּי אֵשׁ הַמִּזְבֵּחַ, שֶׁנֶּאֱמַר: אֵשׁ תָּמִיד תּוּקַד עַל הַמִּזְבֵּחַ לֹא תִכְבֶּה, וְאָמְרוּ בְסִפְרָא: ״לֹא תִכְבֶּה״, מְלַמֵּד שֶׁכָּל הַמְכַבֶּה עוֹבֵר בְּלֹא־תַעֲשֶׂה; וְיֶתֶר פְּרָטֶיהָ, בְּפֶרֶק עֲשִׂירִי מִזְּבָחִים.

וְנוֹהֶגֶת בִּזְמַן הַבַּיִת בִּזְכָרִים וּנְקֵבוֹת, אֲפִלּוּ יִשְׂרְאֵלִים. וְעוֹבֵר עָלֶיהָ וְכִבָּה אֲפִלּוּ גַּחֶלֶת אַחַת מֵאֵשׁ הַמִּזְבֵּחַ, לוֹקֶה.

[מִצְוַת אֲכִילַת שְׁיָרֵי מְנָחוֹת]

קלד שֶׁנִּצְטַוּוּ הַכֹּהֲנִים לֶאֱכֹל שְׁיָרֵי מְנָחוֹת, כְּלוֹמַר אַחַר שֶׁהִפְרִישׁוּ מִמֶּנָּה מַה שֶּׁהָיוּ מַקְטִירִין בַּמִּזְבֵּחַ, שֶׁיֹּאכְלוּ הֵם כָּל הַשְּׁאָר, שֶׁנֶּאֱמַר: וְהַנּוֹתֶרֶת מִמֶּנָּה יֹאכְלוּ

10. Which, as mentioned above, was brought solely to fulfill this precept; for the first, large pile was for burning the parts of the offerings, and the second was to provide fire for the incense.

§133 1. TB Yoma 46b.

2. Literally, "and I do not read in it." The fire was significantly "detached" from the altar not in the physical sense (this would not affect guilt) but spiritually, by being dedicated to another *mitzvah*, so that it is no longer "altar fire."

3. *Ibid.* (MT *hilchoth t'midin* ii 6).

in chapter 4 of the Talmud tractate *Yoma* and chapter 2 of *Tamid*.

It applies when the Temple is in existence, for the male *kohanim*. If the *kohanim* did not kindle the third pile on the altar,[10] they would disobey this positive precept.

[NOT TO PUT OUT ANY FIRE ON THE ALTAR]

133 not to extinguish fire on the altar: for it is stated, *Fire shall be kept burning on the altar continuously; it shall not go out* (Leviticus 6:6).

The root reason behind the religious duty of the fire, I wrote above, about the positive precept that "fire shall be kept burning" (§132); and the root reason behind the command about kindling fire, and [the command] not to extinguish it, is one and the same; there is no need to repeat it.

Among the laws of the precept, there is what the Sages of blessed memory said,[1] that even if someone took the fire off the altar and [then] put it out, he is given whiplashes. As for the fire of the censer [for burning incense] or fire for [lighting] the *menorah* (lamp), which was prepared at the altar in order to kindle [other fire] from it, even if he extinguished it at the head of the altar, he is free of guilt: for here it was "detached" from the altar [permissibly] and it is not considered[2] altar fire; and we were adjured only about extinguishing fire of the altar[3]—for it is stated, *Fire shall be kept burning on the altar continuously; it shall not go out*; whence it was taught in the Midrash *Sifra*: "it shall not go out"—this teaches that whoever puts it out transgresses a negative precept. The rest of its details are in the tenth chapter of the Talmud tractate *Z'vaḥim*.

It applies when the Temple is extant, for both man and woman, even ordinary Israelites (non-*kohanim*). If someone violated it and put out even one burning ember from the altar fire, he would be given whiplashes.

[THE PRECEPT OF EATING THE REMAINDERS OF MEAL-OFFERINGS]

134 that the *kohanim* were commanded to eat the remnants of meal-offerings: in other words, after they separated from it what they would burn on the altar, they should eat all the rest. For it is stated, *And what is left of it, Aaron and his sons shall eat; it shall be eaten without leaven*, etc. (Leviticus 6:9). In the phrasing of the Midrash

אַהֲרֹן וּבָנָיו, מַצּוֹת תֵּאָכֵל וְגוֹמֵר; וּלְשׁוֹן סִפְרֵי, "מַצּוֹת תֵּאָכֵל" מִצְוָה, "יְבָמָהּ יָבֹא עָלֶיהָ" מִצְוָה, כְּלוֹמַר שֶׁשְּׁנֵיהֶם מִצְוַת עֲשֵׂה, לֹא רְשׁוּת.

מִשָּׁרְשֵׁי מִצְוָה זוֹ, כָּתַבְנוּ לְמַעְלָה בְּמִצְוַת "וְאָכְלוּ אֹתָם אֲשֶׁר כֻּפַּר בָּהֶם" בְּ"וְאַתָּה תְּצַוֶּה", עֲשֵׂה ג׳ [סי׳ ק"ב], שֶׁכָּבוֹד הוּא לַקָּרְבָּן שֶׁיֹּאכְלוּהוּ מְשָׁרְתֵי הַשֵּׁם בְּעַצְמָם וְלֹא שֶׁיִּתְּנוּהוּ לִפְחוּתִים לְאָכְלָם, וְכוּלֵי, כְּמוֹ שֶׁכָּתוּב שָׁם.

מִדִּינֵי הַמִּצְוָה, מַה שֶּׁאָמְרוּ זִכְרוֹנָם לִבְרָכָה שֶׁכָּל הַמְּנָחוֹת הַקְּרֵבוֹת לְגַבֵּי הַמִּזְבֵּחַ נִקְמָצוֹת, וּמַקְטִירִין הַקֹּמֶץ כֻּלּוֹ עַל־גַּבֵּי הַמִּזְבֵּחַ, וְהַשְּׁאָר נֶאֱכָל לַכֹּהֲנִים, חוּץ מִמִּנְחַת זִכְרֵי כְהֻנָּה, שֶׁאֵינָהּ נִקְמֶצֶת, שֶׁנֶּאֱמַר: וְכָל מִנְחַת כֹּהֵן כָּלִיל תִּהְיֶה לֹא תֵאָכֵל. נִמְצָא שֶׁמִּנְחַת חִנּוּךְ וַחֲבִתִּין, וְכֹהֵן שֶׁהֵבִיא מִנְחַת חוֹטֵא אוֹ מִנְחַת נְדָבָה, נִשְׂרָפוֹת עַל־גַּבֵּי הַמִּזְבֵּחַ וְלֹא נִקְמָצוֹת. הַכֹּהֶנֶת, מִנְחָתָהּ נִקְמֶצֶת וּשְׁיָרֶיהָ נֶאֱכָלִין, דְּכֹהֵן דַּוְקָא אַמְרִינָן וְלֹא כֹהֶנֶת; וְיֶתֶר פְּרָטֶיהָ, מְבֹאָרִים בִּמְנָחוֹת.

וְנוֹהֶגֶת בִּזְמַן הַבַּיִת בְּזִכְרֵי כְהֻנָּה, שֶׁנֶּאֱמַר: כָּל זָכָר בִּבְנֵי אַהֲרֹן יֹאכְלֶנָּה. עָבַר וְלֹא אֲכָלָהּ, בִּטֵּל עֲשֵׂה.

[שֶׁלֹּא לַעֲשׂוֹת שְׁיָרֵי מְנָחוֹת חָמֵץ]

קלה שֶׁלֹּא לְבַשֵּׁל שְׁיָרֵי מְנָחוֹת חָמֵץ, וְהוּא חֵלֶק הַמְּנָחוֹת אֲשֶׁר לַכֹּהֲנִים, שֶׁנֶּאֱמַר בְּמִנְחָה: לֹא תֵאָפֶה חָמֵץ חֶלְקָם נָתַתִּי אוֹתָהּ מֵאִשָּׁי, וְהוּא כְאִלּוּ אָמַר: חֶלְקָם, שֶׁהוּא שְׁיָרֵי הַמִּנְחָה, לֹא יֵאָפֶה חָמֵץ; וּבְפֵרוּשׁ אָמְרוּ זִכְרוֹנָם לִבְרָכָה בַּמִּשְׁנָה: וְחַיָּבִין עַל אֲפִיָּתָהּ חָמֵץ.

§134 1. The paragraph is based on ShM positive precept §88.

2. TB M'naḥoth 72b.

3. Hebrew, *kometz*—according to other sources, gathered only with the three middle fingers.

4. *Ibid.* 74b.

5. See above, §116.

6. Hence her meal-offering is treated like that of an Israelite; TB Sotah 23a.

§135 1. TB M'naḥoth 55a.

 Sifra, "it shall be eaten without leaven" is a commandment; "her husband's brother shall go in to her" (Deuteronomy 25:5) is a commandment. In other words, both are positive precepts, not voluntary matters.[1]

As to the root reason for this precept, we wrote above, in the precept, *they shall eat those things with which atonement was made* (Exodus 29:33), in *sidrah tetzavveh*—the third positive precept (§102)—that it is a distinction for an offering that the ministers of the Eternal Lord should eat it themselves, and not give it to lesser, inferior people to eat, and so forth—as it is written there.

Among the laws of the precept there is what the Sages of blessed memory said,[2] that of all meal-offerings brought to the altar, a handful[3] was taken off, and the handful was entirely burned on the altar, whereas the rest was eaten by the *kohanim*—except for a *minḥah* (meal-offering) of the male *kohanim*, from which a handful was not taken:[4] for it is stated, *every meal-offering of a* kohen *shall be wholly burned; it shall not be eaten* (Leviticus 6:16). Consequently, a *minḥah* of a *kohen*'s inauguration, or the one [by the *kohen gadol*] baked on a griddle,[5] or if a *kohen* brought a sinner's meal-offering or a voluntary *minḥah*—these were burned on the altar, and no handful was taken off. As for a female *kohen*, a handful is taken from her *minḥah*, and its remainder is eaten, for a male *kohen* was specifically mentioned, and not a woman.[6] The rest of its details are clarified in the Talmud tractate *M'naḥoth*.

It is in force when the Temple exists, for the male *kohanim*—for it is stated, *Every male among the children of Aaron may eat it* (Exodus 6:11). If someone transgressed it and did not eat it, he would thus disobey a positive precept.

[NOT TO MAKE THE REMAINDERS OF MEAL-OFFERINGS BECOME LEAVENED]

135 not to cook (prepare) the remnants of meal-offerings as *ḥamétz*—i.e. the part of meal-offerings which is [given] to the *kohanim*. For it is stated about the *minḥah* (meal-offering), *It shall not be baked with leaven; as their portion have I given it of My offerings by fire* (Leviticus 6:10)—and it is thus as though He had said, "their portion, i.e. the remnants of the meal-offerings, shall not be baked with leaven";[1] our Sages of blessed memory said explicitly in the Mishnah:[1] and one is punishable for baking it as *ḥamétz* (with leaven).

 Among the laws of the precept, there is, for example, what our

מִדִּינֵי הַמִּצְוָה, כְּגוֹן מַה שֶּׁאָמְרוּ זִכְרוֹנָם לִבְרָכָה שֶׁהַמְחַמֵּץ אַחַר הַמְחַמֵּץ חַיָּב, וְהַמְחַמֵּץ מִנְחָה פְּסוּלָה פָּטוּר, שֶׁנֶּאֱמַר: אֲשֶׁר תַּקְרִיבוּ לַיי לֹא תֵעָשֶׂה חָמֵץ, הַכְּשֵׁרָה לַשֵּׁם וְלֹא הַפְּסוּלָה; חִמְּצָהּ בְּרֹאשׁ הַמִּזְבֵּחַ אֵינוֹ לוֹקֶה, שֶׁנֶּאֱמַר: אֲשֶׁר תַּקְרִיבוּ לַיי לֹא תֵעָשֶׂה חָמֵץ, וְזוֹ כְּבָר קְרֵבָה; וְיֶתֶר פְּרָטֶיהָ, מְבֹאָרִים בְּפֶרֶק חֲמִישִׁי מִמְּנָחוֹת.

וְנוֹהֶגֶת מִצְוָה זוֹ בִזְמַן הַבַּיִת בִּזְכָרִים וּנְקֵבוֹת. אֲפִלּוּ עָבַר יִשְׂרָאֵל אֶחָד וַאֲפָאָהּ חָמֵץ חַיָּב מַלְקוֹת, וְאֵין צָרִיךְ לוֹמַר כֹּהֵן.

[מִצְוַת קָרְבַּן מִנְחָה שֶׁל כֹּהֵן גָּדוֹל בְּכָל יוֹם]

קלו שֶׁנִּצְטַוִּינוּ שֶׁיַּקְרִיב הַכֹּהֵן הַגָּדוֹל מִנְחָה בְּכָל יוֹם פַּעֲמַיִם, בַּבֹּקֶר וּבֵין הָעַרְבַּיִם, שֶׁנֶּאֱמַר: זֶה קָרְבַּן אַהֲרֹן וּבָנָיו אֲשֶׁר יַקְרִיבוּ לַיי וְכוּלֵי; וְהִיא הַנִּקְרֵאת חֲבִתֵּי כֹהֵן גָּדוֹל, וְנִקְרֵאת גַּם־כֵּן מִנְחַת כֹּהֵן מָשִׁיחַ.

מִשָּׁרְשֵׁי הַמִּצְוָה, לְפִי שֶׁהַכֹּהֵן הַגָּדוֹל הוּא הַשָּׁלִיחַ בֵּין יִשְׂרָאֵל לַאֲבִיהֶם שֶׁבַּשָּׁמַיִם, כְּלוֹמַר כִּי הוּא הַנּוֹשֵׂא תְּפִלָּה אֵלָיו בַּעֲדָם, וְעַל־יְדֵי תְפִלּוֹתָיו וּמַעֲשֵׂה קָרְבְּנוֹתָיו הֵם מִתְכַּפְּרִים, וְלָכֵן רָאוּי לְאִישׁ כָּזֶה לִהְיוֹת לוֹ קָרְבָּן מְיֻחָד תְּמִידִי כְּמוֹ תְמִידֵי הַצִּבּוּר; וּכְמוֹ שֶׁהַתְּמִידִין שְׁנַיִם לְיוֹם, נִתְחַיֵּב הוּא גַּם־כֵּן לְהַקְרִיב מִנְחָתוֹ פַּעֲמַיִם בַּיּוֹם.

וְכָל זֶה נִסְמָךְ אֶל הַטַּעַם שֶׁאָמַרְנוּ בְקָרְבָּן, כְּדֵי שֶׁיִּתְעוֹרְרוּ כָּל מַחְשְׁבוֹתָיו וְיָשִׂים דַּעְתּוֹ וְכַוָּנָתוֹ אֵצֶל הַשֵּׁם בָּרוּךְ הוּא, וּלְמַעַן זֹאת יוֹעִיל לוֹ וְלָהֶם; וְאֵין סָפֵק שֶׁאֵין דּוֹמָה הִתְעוֹרְרוּת הָאָדָם כְּשֶׁמַּקְרִיב קָרְבָּנוֹ הַמְיֻחָד לוֹ לִכְשֶׁהוּא מַקְרִיב

2. *Ibid.* 56b.
3. *Ibid.* 57a.
4. The handful removed for burning (Rashi).
5. In the Talmud (*ibid.*) this remains an unresolved question; hence a transgressor is not punished (MY).

§136

1. This echoes the statement of the elders to the *kohen gadol* when they prepared him for his Temple service on the Day of Atonement: "... you are our messenger and the messenger of the *beth din*" (Mishnah, Yoma i 5).
2. I.e. of the person bringing the offering.

Sages of blessed memory said,[2] that if someone makes it leavened after another made it leavened, he incurs punishment; but if someone adds leaven to a disqualified, unacceptable *minḥah*, he is free of punishment: for it is stated, *No meal-offering which you shall bring to the Lord shall be made with leaven* (Leviticus 2:11)—[i.e.] which is fit, acceptable to the Lord, but not one which is disqualified.[3] If one made it[4] leavened at the head of the altar, he is not given whiplashes: for it is stated, "which you shall bring to the Lord," and this was already brought.[5] The rest of its details are explained in chapter 5 of the Talmud tractate *M'naḥoth*.

This precept is in force when the Temple is extant, for both man and woman. Even if an Israelite (non-*kohen*) transgressed and baked it as *ḥametz* (with leaven), he would be punishable by whiplashes; and there is no need to add, a *kohen*.

[THE PRECEPT OF THE KOHEN GADOL'S DAILY MEAL-OFFERING]

136 that we were commanded that the *kohen gadol* should bring a *minḥah* (meal-offering) twice every day: in the morning and evening—for it is stated, *This is the offering of Aaron and his sons, which they shall offer to the Lord* (Leviticus 6:13). This is the one called "the griddle-cakes of the *kohen gadol*"; and it is also called "the *minḥah* of the anointed *kohen*."

As the root of the precept lies the reason that the *kohen gadol* is a "messenger" between the Israelites and their Father in heaven:[1] that is to say, he entreats Him in prayer in their behalf, and through his prayers and the service of his offerings they find atonement. It is therefore fitting that he should have a special continual offering, like the continual [daily burnt] offerings of the community. And just as those continual offerings were two a day, he was obligated likewise to offer up his *minḥah* twice a day.

Now, this is all based on the reason we have given about the offerings [in general: that it is] in order that all his thoughts[2] should be aroused and and he should set his mind and purpose toward the Eternal Lord, blessed is He. For this reason, it would be of benefit for him [the *kohen gadol*] and them [the Israelites]. Beyond any doubt, there can be no comparison between the arousal in a man when he brings an offering that is specifically for him, and [the arousal] when he brings an offering in which he [merely] has a share. This is something

קָרְבָּן שֶׁהוּא מִשְׁתַּתֵּף עִמּוֹ, וְזֶה דָּבָר יָדוּעַ וּמְנֻסֶּה בְּכָל אָדָם, כִּי לְמַה שֶּׁמְּיֻחָד לוֹ לְבַדּוֹ מִתְעוֹרֵר יוֹתֵר; אֵין לְהַאֲרִיךְ בָּזֶה.

מִדִּינֵי הַמִּצְוָה, מַה שֶּׁאָמְרוּ: כֵּיצַד עֲשִׂיַּת חֲבִתֵּי כֹהֵן גָּדוֹל, מֵבִיא עִשָּׂרוֹן שָׁלֵם שֶׁל קֶמַח שָׁלֵם, וְחוֹצֵהוּ בַחֲצִי עִשָּׂרוֹן שֶׁבַּמִּקְדָּשׁ — שֶׁאַף־עַל־פִּי שֶׁמִּנְחַת הָעִשָּׂרוֹן קְרֵבָה לַחֲצָאִין, כְּלוֹמַר חֶצְיָהּ בַּבֹּקֶר וְחֶצְיָהּ בָּעֶרֶב, אֵינָהּ מִתְקַדֶּשֶׁת לַחֲצָאִין, כְּלוֹמַר שֶׁכֻּלָּהּ מְבִיאָהּ בְּיַחַד — וּמֵבִיא עִמָּהּ שְׁלֹשָׁה לוֹגִין שֶׁמֶן, וּבוֹלֵל הַסֹּלֶת בַּשֶּׁמֶן וְחוֹלֵט אוֹתָהּ בְּרוֹתְחִין וְלָשׁ מִכָּל חֲצִי עִשָּׂרוֹן שֵׁשׁ חַלּוֹת; נִמְצָא שֶׁהֵם שְׁתֵּים־עֶשְׂרֵה חַלּוֹת, וְאַחַת אַחַת הָיוּ נַעֲשׂוֹת.

וְכֵיצַד עוֹשֶׂה: מְחַלֵּק הַשְּׁלֹשָׁה לוֹגִין בָּרְבִיעִית שֶׁבַּמִּקְדָּשׁ, רְבִיעִית לְכָל חַלָּה, וְאוֹפֶה הַחַלָּה מְעַט, וְאַחַר־כָּךְ קוֹלֶה אוֹתָהּ עַל הַמַּחֲבַת עִם הַשֶּׁמֶן שֶׁלָּהּ, וְאֵינוֹ מְבַשְּׁלָהּ הַרְבֵּה, וְאַחַר־כָּךְ חוֹלֵק כָּל חַלָּה לִשְׁתַּיִם כְּדֵי שֶׁיַּקְרִיב הַחֵצִי בַבֹּקֶר וְהַחֵצִי בָעֶרֶב; וְלוֹקֵחַ הַחֲצָאִין וְכוֹפֵל כָּל אֶחָד מֵהֶן לִשְׁנַיִם וּפוֹתֵת, עַד שֶׁתִּמָּצֵא כָּל פְּתִיתָה כְּפוּלָה לִשְׁנַיִם, וּמַקְרִיב הַחֲצָאִין עִם חֲצִי קֹמֶץ לְבוֹנָה בַּבֹּקֶר, וְהַחֵצִי הַנִּשְׁאָר עִם חֲצִי קֹמֶץ לְבוֹנָה בָּעֶרֶב, וְהִיא כָּלִיל לָאִשִּׁים.

וְנוֹהֶגֶת בִּזְמַן הַבַּיִת בְּכֹהֵן גָּדוֹל. וּמִנְחַת הַבֹּקֶר וְהָעֶרֶב מִצְוַת עֲשֵׂה אַחַת, וְאֵין חוֹלֵק בָּזֶה; כִּי גַם הָרַמְבַּ״ן זִכְרוֹנוֹ לִבְרָכָה, שֶׁמּוֹנֶה שְׁנֵי תְמִידִין שְׁתֵּי מִצְווֹת, מוֹדֶה בָּזֶה.

[שֶׁלֹּא לֶאֱכֹל מִנְחַת כֹּהֵן]

קלז שֶׁלֹּא לֶאֱכֹל מִמִּנְחַת כֹּהֵן, שֶׁנֶּאֱמַר: וְכָל מִנְחַת כֹּהֵן כָּלִיל תִּהְיֶה לֹא תֵאָכֵל. מִשָּׁרְשֵׁי הַמִּצְוָה, הַיְסוֹד שֶׁאָמַרְנוּ תְּחִלָּה, כִּי כַוָּנַת הַקָּרְבָּן לְעוֹרֵר לֵב הַמַּקְרִיב

3. An *'issaron* (literally, a tenth — i.e. of an *'éphah*) is 2,488 cubic centimeters in one view, and 4,300 cubic centimeters by another.

4. TB M'naḥoth 50b.

5. Since the consecration would not take effect on the half; afterward he could offer up one half the amount at a time; *ibid.* 8a.

6. *Ibid.* 51a.

7. *Ibid.* 72b.

8. Sifra, *tzav, perek* 4, 5.

9. TB M'naḥoth 76a, 94a. The paragraph is based on MT *hilchoth ma'aséh ha-korbanoth* xiii 2–3.

10. *Ibid.* 88b.

11. MT *ibid.* 3, based on his interpretation of R. Yosé's teaching in TB M'naḥoth 50b (*Kessef Mishneh*).

12. Derived from *ibid.* 87b.

13. *Ibid.* 75b.

14. *Ibid.* 50b, 59a. (About the handful, see §137, fourth paragraph.)

15. Leviticus 6:15. The paragraph is based on MT *ibid.* 3–4.

16. In his commentary on ShM, end, paragraph s.v. *v'attah 'im tavin.*

known and experienced by everyone—that by what is especially for him, alone, a person is stirred the more. There is no need to go on about it.

Among the laws of the precept, there is what the Sages of blessed memory said, on how the griddle-cakes were made: He would bring a whole *'issaron*[3] of whole flour, and divide it in two by the measure of the half-*'issaron* in the Sanctuary.[4] For though the meal-offering of an *'issaron* [of flour] was offered up by halves, i.e. half in the morning and half in the evening, it could not be consecrated by halves. In other words, he had to bring it all at once.[5] And he would bring with it three *log* of oil,[6] mix the fine flour with the oil,[7] scald it with boiling water,[8] and knead six loaves out of each half of the *'issaron*. Consequently, there were twelve loaves, which he would make one by one.[9]

What would he do? He would divide the three *log* [of oil] with the measure of the *r'vi'ith* in the Sanctuary—a *r'vi'ith* [one fourth of a *log*] for each loaf.[10] He would bake the loaf a bit, then roast it on a griddle with its oil, but not let it seethe very much.[11] Afterward he would divide each loaf in two, so that he could offer up the half in the morning and the half in the evening.[12] Then he would take the halves and bend each in two, and break it into pieces so that each piece should be found to be bent in two.[13] He would offer up the halves with half a handful of frankincense in the morning, and the remaining half [of the *minḥah*] with half a handful of frankincense in the evening.[14] And it was entirely burned as an offering on the fire [of the altar].[15]

This applies when the Temple is extant, for the *kohen gadol*. The meal-offering of the morning and that of the evening are both one positive precept; no one disagrees about this. For even Ramban of blessed memory, who counted the two daily *'olah* (burnt) offerings as two precepts,[16] concurs about this.[17]

[THAT THE MEAL-OFFERING OF A KOHEN SHOULD NOT BE EATEN]

137 not to eat of the *minḥah* (meal-offering) of a *kohen*: for it is stated, *And every meal-offering of a* kohen *shall be wholly burned; it shall not be eaten* (Leviticus 6:16).

At the root of the precept lies the fundamental concept that we stated at the beginning, that the purpose of an offering is to bestir

אוֹתוֹ, וְאִם יֹאכַל הַכֹּהֵן מִנְחָתוֹ לֹא יִתְעוֹרֵר לִבּוֹ עָלֶיהָ יָפֶה, שֶׁהִיא דוֹמָה בְעֵינָיו כְּאוֹפֶה פַּת לְצָרְכּוֹ וְאוֹכְלוֹ; וְאַף כִּי יֹאכְלוּ חֲבֵרָיו שֶׁלּוֹ וְהוּא שֶׁלָּהֶן יַעֲלֶה הַכֹּל לְחֶשְׁבּוֹן אֶחָד; לָכֵן צִוָּה שֶׁתִּהְיֶה כָלִיל, לֹא תֵאָכֵל לְשׁוּם אָדָם.

מִדִּינֵי הַמִּצְוָה, מַה שֶּׁאָמְרוּ זִכְרוֹנָם לִבְרָכָה: כָּל הַמְּנָחוֹת הַקְּרֵבוֹת לְגַבֵּי הַמִּזְבֵּחַ נִקְמָצוֹת, וּמַקְטִירִין הַקֹּמֶץ כֻּלּוֹ לְגַבֵּי הַמִּזְבֵּחַ וְהַשְּׁאָר נֶאֱכָל לַכֹּהֲנִים, חוּץ מִמִּנְחַת זִכְרֵי כְהֻנָּה, שֶׁאֵינָהּ נִקְמֶצֶת אֶלָּא מַקְטִירִין אוֹתָהּ כֻּלָּהּ, שֶׁנֶּאֱמַר: וְכָל מִנְחַת כֹּהֵן כָּלִיל תִּהְיֶה לֹא תֵאָכֵל; וְלָמַדְנוּ מֵעַתָּה שֶׁמִּנְחַת חִנּוּךְ וַחֲבִתִּין, וְכֹהֵן שֶׁהֵבִיא מִנְחַת חוֹטֵא אוֹ מִנְחַת נְדָבָה, כֻּלָּן נִשְׂרָפוֹת עַל־גַּבֵּי הַמִּזְבֵּחַ וְאֵינָן נִקְמָצוֹת, וּכְמוֹ שֶׁאָמַרְנוּ לְמַעְלָה בְּסֵדֶר זֶה עֲשֵׂה ג׳ [סי׳ קל״ד].

וְעִנְיַן הַקְּמִיצָה הוּא שֶׁנּוֹטֵל הַכֹּהֵן מִן הַקֶּמַח בְּקֻמְצוֹ, כְּלוֹמַר בְּרָאשֵׁי אֶצְבְּעוֹתָיו כְּדֶרֶךְ שֶׁקּוֹמֵץ כָּל אָדָם, שֶׁפּוֹשֵׁט פַּס יָדוֹ וְקוֹמֵץ בְּרָאשֵׁי אֶצְבְּעוֹתָיו, כְּלוֹמַר שֶׁאֶצְבְּעוֹתָיו דְּבֵקִים עִם הַכַּף וְאֵינָם מַחֲזִיקִים מִן הַקֶּמַח הַרְבֵּה. וְאִם הוֹסִיף בַּקֹּמֶץ, כְּגוֹן שֶׁהִרְחִיק אֶצְבְּעוֹתָיו וְקָמַץ, פָּסַל; וְיֶתֶר פְּרָטֵי הַמִּצְוָה, בִּמְנָחוֹת.

וְנוֹהֵג אִסּוּר אֲכִילַת מִנְחַת כֹּהֵן בִּזְכָרִים וּנְקֵבוֹת, בִּזְמַן הַבַּיִת. וְעוֹבֵר עַל זֶה וְאָכַל מִמֶּנָּה כַּזַּיִת, לוֹקֶה. וּלְשׁוֹן סִפְרָא: "כָּלִיל תִּהְיֶה לֹא תֵאָכֵל", כָּל שֶׁהוּא בְּכָלִיל תִּהְיֶה, לִתֵּן לֹא־תַעֲשֶׂה עַל אֲכִילָתוֹ.

[מִצְוַת מַעֲשֵׂה הַחַטָּאת]

קלח שֶׁנִּצְטַוִּינוּ שֶׁיַּעֲשׂוּ הַכֹּהֲנִים קָרְבַּן הַחַטָּאת עַל הָעִנְיָן הַנִּזְכָּר בַּכָּתוּב, אֵי זֶה חַטָּאת שֶׁיִּהְיֶה, שֶׁל בְּהֵמָה אוֹ עוֹף, שֶׁנֶּאֱמַר: זֹאת תּוֹרַת הַחַטָּאת וְגוֹמֵר.

כְּבָר אָמַרְנוּ לְמַעְלָה כִּי בִּפְרָטֵי הַקָּרְבָּנוֹת, כְּלוֹמַר בְּסֵדֶר שְׁחִיטָתָן, בְּאֵי זֶה

17. Since Scripture itself writes of it as "a continual meal-offering, half of it in the morning and half of it in the evening" (Leviticus 6:13).

§137 1. Similarly Rambam, *Guide* III 46, and Ramban to Leviticus 6:10.

1a. So MT *hilchoth ma'aséh ha-korbanoth* xii 9, based on TB M'naḥoth 72b, Leviticus 6:16.

2. At first sight this seems difficult: for whether the tips or the full fingers were to be used is an unresolved question in TB M'naḥoth 11a; and hence MT *ibid.* xiii 13 has "with his fingers onto the palm of his hand; if he gathered it with his fingertips . . . he should not burn it [on the altar]; but if he did burn it, it is acceptable." Therefore MH and MY postulate a scribal error here and read "with his fingers." This is not likely, though, since in §116, sixth paragraph, our author similarly writes, "The *koben* would then gather a handful with the tips of his fingers"; it is hardly plausible that a scribe would add the same word erroneously in two different instances.

In the sources, however, we find this phrase, "with the tips of his fingers" (or "with the heart of the one who brings it. Well, if a *kohen* eats his *minḥah*, his heart will not be properly aroused over it: It will seem to him as though he baked bread for his own need and ate it; and even if his colleagues eat of his [*minḥah*] and he [eats] of theirs, it will amount to the same thing. Therefore He commanded that it should be burned altogether, not eaten by any man.[1]

Among the laws of the precept, there is what the Sages of blessed memory taught: Of all meal-offerings brought to the altar, a handful is removed; the handful is burned entirely on the altar, and the rest is eaten by the *kohanim*—except for a meal-offering of male *kohanim*: a handful is not removed, but it is rather wholly burned; for it is stated, *every meal-offering of a kohen shall be wholly burned; it shall not be eaten*. Hence we learn that the *minḥah* of [a *kohen*'s] initiation and the griddle-cakes [of the *kohen gadol*], or if a *kohen* brought a "sinner's meal-offering" or a voluntary *minḥah*—all were burned on the altar, and a handful was not taken from them[1a]—as we stated above, in the third positive precept (§134) [of this *sidrah*].

As regards the handful, the *kohen* would take of the flour in his fist, i.e. with the tips of his fingers,[2] in the way that any man gathers a handful: he puts forth the palm of his hand and gathers it with the tips of his fingers; in other words, his fingers would cling to the palm and would not grasp very much of the flour. But if he added to the handful—for instance, if he spread his fingers apart and took a handful, he would make it unfit, disqualified.[3] The remaining details of the precept are explained in the Talmud tractate *M'naḥoth*.

This ban on eating the *minḥah* of a *kohen* applies to both man and woman, when the Temple is extant. If someone violated it and ate an olive's amount from it, he would receive whiplashes. In the words of Midrash *Sifra*: "it shall be wholly burnt; it shall not be eaten"—whatever is under an injunction to be wholly burnt,[4] a negative precept (prohibition) is thus placed on eating it.

138 [THE PRECEPT OF THE SACRIFICE OF THE ḤATTATH]

that we were commanded that the *kohanim* should sacrifice a *ḥattath* (sin-offering) in the way mentioned in the Writ, whatever *ḥattath* it may be, whether of a domestic beast or fowl—as it is stated, *This is the law of the sin-offering*, etc. (Leviticus 6:18).

We said earlier, above (§95) that about details of the offerings—

מָקוֹם, וְעִנְיַן הַקְרָבָתָן וְהַזָּאָתָן, וּמְקוֹם וּזְמַן אֲכִילָתָם אוֹ שְׂרֵפָתָן בִּקְצָת מֵהֶן, אֵין לָנוּ לְיַגֵּעַ מַחְשַׁבְתֵּנוּ אַחַר שָׁרְשֵׁי עִנְיָנִים אֵלֶּה, שֶׁאֵין לָהֶם חֵקֶר וְאֵין לָנוּ בַּשֵּׂכֶל הַקָּנוּי בָּזֶה קִנְיָן; אֶחָד מֵעִיר, חָכָם מְקֻבָּל, יִהְיֶה שֶׁיִּזְכֶּה לָדַעַת קְצָת רָאשֵׁי דְּבָרִים מִן הָעִנְיָן; וְדַי לָנוּ אַחֲרֵי כָתְבֵנוּ מַה שֶּׁעָלָה בְמַחְשַׁבְתֵּנוּ מִן הַטַּעַם עַל דֶּרֶךְ הַפְּשָׁט בְּקָרְבָּנוֹת דֶּרֶךְ כְּלָל. וּבָזֶה אֲנִי פוֹטֵר עַצְמִי בְּקָרְבַּן הַחַטָּאת וְכָל כַּיּוֹצֵא בוֹ מִכְּתֹב בָּהֶן שֹׁרֶשׁ כְּמִנְהָגִי בַּשְּׁאָר, כִּי בִכְלַל פְּרָטֵי הַקָּרְבָּן הֵם, שֶׁהַכְּלָל הוּא הַקְרָבַת הַקָּרְבָּן וְהַפְּרָטִים הֵם תּוֹרַת הַקְרָבָתוֹ כֵּיצַד.

וְהִנֵּה הָרַמְבָּ״ן זִכְרוֹנוֹ לִבְרָכָה לֹא יַחְשֹׁב תּוֹרַת הַחַטָּאת וְהָאָשָׁם וְהָעוֹלָה וְהַשְּׁלָמִים מֵחֶשְׁבּוֹן הַמִּצְוֹות, מִן הַיְסוֹד זֶה שֶׁאָמַרְתִּי, לְפִי שֶׁעִקַּר הַצִּוּוּי יָבֹא עַל חִיּוּב הַקְרָבַת הַקָּרְבָּן, וְסֵדֶר עֲשִׂיָּתוֹ אַחַר־כֵּן אֵינוֹ בְדִין שֶׁיֵּחָשֵׁב מִצְוָה בִּפְנֵי עַצְמָהּ, כִּי עַל־כָּל־פָּנִים יִצְטָרֵךְ הַכָּתוּב לְלַמֵּד אוֹתָנוּ מַעֲשֵׂה כָּל אֶחָד מֵהֶם, אַחַר שֶׁחִיְּבָנוּ בָהֶן.

וְזֶה לְשׁוֹנוֹ: כָּל מַעֲשֵׂה הַקָּרְבָּנוֹת מִצְוָה אַחַת, וְנִצְטַוּוּ כָּל זֶרַע אַהֲרֹן בַּעֲבוֹדָתָם, וְהִיא מִצְוַת עֲשֵׂה אַחַת, שֶׁנֶּאֱמַר: וַעֲבַדְתֶּם עֲבוֹדַת מַתָּנָה אֶתֵּן אֶת כְּהֻנַּתְכֶם, וּפֵרוּשׁוֹ, תַּעַבְדוּ בְּכָל עֲבוֹדַת הַכְּהֻנָּה, כִּי הִיא עֲבוֹדָה וּמַתָּנָה לִי וּמַתָּנָה לָכֶם, שֶׁיֵּשׁ לָכֶם בָּהּ שָׂכָר בַּאֲשֶׁר תִּקְחוּ מִשֻּׁלְחַן גָּבוֹהַּ יִתְבָּרֵךְ. עַד כָּאן.

וְעִם כָּל זֶה, מִדֶּרֶךְ חֶשְׁבּוֹן הָרַמְבָּ״ם זִכְרוֹנוֹ לִבְרָכָה, אֲשֶׁר תָּפַשְׂנוּ בַּמִּצְוֹות, לֹא נָטָה, וְהַדָּבָר אֲשֶׁר יִקְשֶׁה נִתְלֶה הַקֹּשִׁי בָּנוּ וְלֹא בוֹ, כִּי הוּא בֶאֱמֶת סִבָּתֵנוּ בְּעֵסֶק זֶה, וּמִיָּדוֹ זָכִינוּ לוֹ, יָנוּחַ הַצַּדִּיק עַל מִשְׁכָּבוֹ.

his fingertips") used in different contexts, with different meanings: In Mishnah, M'naḥoth i 2 we read, "If the handful was . . . too little, it is disqualified. . . . What is meant by 'too little'?—if he took the handful with his fingertips." Rashi and *Shittah M'kubetzeth* explain: if he bent his fingers in and took just a bit in them, without spreading them over his palm. Similarly in TB M'naḥoth 11a: "I might think it should be taken with the fingertips?—hence Scripture states, etc. Then how should it be done? He bends his three [middle] fingers onto the palm of his hand, and thus he takes the handful." As Rashi explains, "with the fingertips" has the same meaning here as in the Mishnah. (The commentary attributed to Rashba notes: It means that they [the fingers] do not reach the palm of his hand; i.e. he bends just his fingertips to the beginning of his palm and he takes no more than a bit of the flour, what his fingertips can hold until the beginning of his palm.) Then R. Papa queries: "If one took the handful with his fingertips, what is the law?" Here Rashi explains that it means if a *kohen* put his fingertips into the flour with his palm downward, and thus scooped up a handful. R. Papa queries further: "[If he took it] from below upwards, what is the law?" As Rashi explains, it means if a *kohen* put the back of his hand into the flour and thus plunged it further until he could gather a handful—with the tips of his fingers (see *tosafoth*). These queries of R. Papa are left unresolved.

Thus it is not the fingertips *per se* that disqualify a *minḥah* or leave it in doubt, but how the hand is used. The proper way, as the Mishnah states (and a *baraitha* affirms) is i.e. about the order of the ritual slaying, in which place and in what way they should be offered up and their blood sprinkled, and the place and time for eating them, or for burning some of them—we need not weary our mind [searching] after root reasons for these matters which cannot be probed; with our acquired intelligence we can acquire no purchase or grasp of understanding in them. There may be one in a city, a wise master of the mystic tradition, who will succeed in knowing some beginnings of reasons in this regard. It will be enough for us that we wrote what arose in our thoughts by way of a reason, along the lines of the plain meaning, about the offerings in general. And with this I acquit myself of my obligation, for the offering of the *ḥattath* and everything similar, to write a root reason for them as my custom is with the rest [of the precepts]. For these are included among the details of the offerings. The general, overall duty is bringing the offering; and the details are the instructions on presenting or sacrificing it—how [it was to be done].

Now, you see, Ramban of blessed memory[1] does not count the law of the *ḥattath* (sin-offering), of the *'asham* (guilt-offering), of the *'olah* (burnt-offering) and of the *sh'lamim* (peace-offering) in the reckoning of the [613] precepts—on account of this basic principle that I have stated. For the main commandment applies to the obligation of bringing the offering, and it is not justifiable that the order of its presentation or sacrifice afterward should be reckoned as a precept by itself. For in any event, Scripture would have to teach us the proper treatment of each one of them, since their duty was imposed on us.

These are his words: The entire treatment of the offerings is one commandment; all the descendants of Aaron were charged with their service; and it is one positive precept—as it is stated, *and you shall serve; as a service of gift I give you your status as* kohen (Numbers 18:7)—which means, "you shall serve in every task of a *kohen*, because it is [Divine] service, and a gift to you and a gift to Me—for you have reward from it, in that you take [your portion] from the table [altar] of the One on high, be He blessed."

Nevertheless, we shall not swerve from the way of reckoning of Rambam of blessed memory in the precepts, which we have firmly adopted. And if something is difficult, we will attribute the difficulty to ourselves,[2] not to him. For he, in truth, is our very reason for this occupation; on his account we arrived at it. May the righteous man rest in his repose.

מִדִּינֵי הַמִּצְוָה, מַה שֶּׁאָמְרוּ זִכְרוֹנָם לִבְרָכָה שֶׁהַחַטָּאוֹת בָּאִין מֵחֲמִשָּׁה מִינִים, מִכְּבָשִׂים וְעִזִּים וּבָקָר, בֵּין גְּדוֹלִים בֵּין קְטַנִּים; וּקְטַנּוֹת וּגְדוֹלוֹת שֶׁלָּהֶם נְפָרֵשׁ עִנְיָנָם בִּשְׁלָמִים בְּעֶזְרַת הַשֵּׁם; וּבָאִין גַּם־כֵּן בֵּין מִן הַזָּכָר אוֹ הַנְּקֵבָה; וּמִן הַתּוֹרִים אוֹ מִן בְּנֵי הַיּוֹנָה; וּכְבָר כָּתַבְנוּ לְמַעְלָה קְצָת דִּינִין בְּחַטַּאת הָעוֹף. וְיֵשׁ מִן הַחַטָּאוֹת שֶׁהָיוּ בָּאִין עַל הַצִּבּוּר כֻּלָּן, וְיֵשׁ שֶׁהֵן בָּאִין עַל הַיָּחִיד; וּמֵהֶן מִן הַצִּבּוּר וּמִן הַיָּחִיד שֶׁהָיוּ נִשְׂרָפוֹת כֻּלָּן עַל מִזְבֵּחַ הַחִיצוֹן, וּמֵהֶן שֶׁהָיוּ נֶאֱכָלוֹת כֻּלָּן חוּץ מִן הָאֵמוּרִין שֶׁבָּהֶן, שֶׁהָיוּ נִשְׂרָפִין עַל מִזְבֵּחַ הַחִיצוֹן — שֶׁאֵין עוֹשִׂין בִּפְנִימִי כָּל הַשָּׁנָה אֶלָּא הַקְּטֹרֶת, כְּמוֹ שֶׁאָמַרְנוּ לְמַעְלָה.

וְאֵלּוּ הֵן הָאֵמוּרִין שֶׁל שׁוֹר אוֹ שֶׁל עֵז: הַחֵלֶב שֶׁעַל הַקֶּרֶב, וּבִכְלָלוֹ חֵלֶב שֶׁעַל־גַּבֵּי הַקֵּבָה, וּשְׁתֵּי הַכְּלָיוֹת בַּחֵלֶב שֶׁעֲלֵיהֶם עִם הַחֵלֶב אֲשֶׁר עַל הַכְּסָלִים, וְיוֹתֶרֶת הַכָּבֵד הַנִּקְרָא פּוּלִיגַאר בְּלַעַז, וְנוֹטֵל מִן הַכָּבֵד מְעַט עִם הַיּוֹתֶרֶת.

וְהָאֵמוּרִין שֶׁל מִין כֶּבֶשׂ הֵם אֵלּוּ בְּעַצְמָן, וּמוֹסִיף עֲלֵיהֶן מִן הַכֶּבֶשׂ שֶׁנּוֹטְלִין מִמֶּנּוּ עוֹד הָאַלְיָה תְּמִימָה עִם חֻלְיוֹת שֶׁבַּשִּׁדְרָה עַד מְקוֹם הַכְּלָיוֹת, שֶׁנֶּאֱמַר: לְעֻמַּת הֶעָצֶה יְסִירֶנָּה, כְּלוֹמַר מִלְּעֻמַּת מְקוֹם הַכְּלָיוֹת, וְכִנּוּ הַמָּקוֹם הַהוּא כֵּן מִפְּנֵי שֶׁאָמְרוּ זִכְרוֹנָם לִבְרָכָה שֶׁהַכְּלָיוֹת יוֹעֲצוֹת.

וְכֵן מַה שֶּׁפֵּרְשׁוּ זִכְרוֹנָם לִבְרָכָה בְּמַעֲשֵׂה חַטָּאת הַנֶּאֱכֶלֶת בִּשְׁחִיטָה וּזְרִיקָה, וְיֶתֶר כָּל עִנְיָנָיו, וְכֵן בְּמַעֲשֵׂה הַחַטָּאת הַנִּשְׂרֶפֶת גַּם־כֵּן; וְאִם יַעֲשֶׂה בָהֶם שׁוּם מַעֲשֶׂה שֶׁל הֶפְסֵד מַה דִּינָם; וְיֶתֶר פְּרָטֶיהָ, כֻּלָּן בִּזְבָחִים.

וְנוֹהֶגֶת בִּזְמַן הַבַּיִת בִּזְכְרֵי כְהֻנָּה. וְכֹהֵן הָעוֹבֵר וְלֹא עָשָׂה הַחַטָּאת כַּמִּשְׁפָּט, בִּטֵּל עֲשֵׂה זֶה.

to "spread (or bend) the fingers onto the palm." Rashi (TB M'naḥoth 11a s.v. *kid'kamtzi 'inshi*) explains, "He puts the sides of his fingers into the flour and presses (or forces) the flour so that the flour goes into his hand." As Tif'ereth Yisra'el on the Mishnah understands it, it means the fingers are held rigidly bent over the palm and the flour is forced in sideways by the pressure of the hand (sideways) on the flour. Yet perhaps our author learned from his master teachers that it means that after the fingers and palm came into contact sideways with the flour (the palm neither up nor down) with the fingers *lightly* bent, the fingers would scoop or press a handful toward the palm. This would seem to accord with R. Papa's statement in the Talmud (*ibid.*), "It is obvious to me that 'a full handful' means in the way that people usually take a handful." Our author might then simply mean that the fingertips take the lead in enclosing the handful and holding it firm against the palm, and he would not be at variance with the Talmud or Rambam.

3. TB M'naḥoth 6a; MT *hilchoth ma'aséh ha-korbanoth* xiii 13.

4. I.e. even an *'olah*, an animal offering that was wholly burned, and the *'émurim* (fatty parts for burning on the altar) of any offering.

§138 1. In his commentary on ShM root principle 12.

Among the laws of the precept, there is what the Sages of blessed memory said, that the *ḥattath* (sin) offerings may be brought from five species of creatures: sheep, goats and cattle—both old and young; as to the terms "old" and "young" for them, we will explain their significance in connection with the *sh'lamim* (peace-offering; §141), with the Eternal Lord's help; and they are brought, in addition, from both the males and the females;[3] and [they may be] of turtledoves or of young pigeons. We have already written above (§124) some laws of a *ḥattath* of fowl. Now, there are some sin-offerings that came in behalf of the entire community, and some would come in behalf of an individual. Of them, both of those for the community and those for individuals, there were some which were entirely burned, [the *'émurim*, certain fatty parts, going] on the outer altar,[4] and there were those which were entirely eaten, except for their *'émurim*, which were burned on the outer altar. For on the inner altar nothing was offered up during the whole year except the incense, as we stated above (§104).

Now, these are the *'émurim* of an ox or a goat: the fat which is on the entrails, including the fat on the maw (stomach); the two kidneys with the fat on them, with the fat that is on the loins; the appendage of the liver called *pulegar* in the foreign tongue [Spanish]; and a bit of the liver was taken with the appendage.[5]

The *'émurim* of the species [called] sheep were these same parts; but with a sheep there was something additional: for the fat-tail, whole, was also taken from it, with vertebrae of the spinal column, till the place of the kidneys—for it is stated, *close by the* 'atzeh *shall he take it away* (Leviticus 3:9)—in other words, from opposite the place of the kidneys. That place was so named [*'atzeh*, = *'étzah*, counsel] because our Sages said[6] that the kidneys provide counsel.

Then there is, too, what our Sages of blessed memory explained about the treatment of a *ḥattath* that was eaten, regarding the ritual slaying and the sprinkling of the blood, and all its other matters; and so also the treatment of a *ḥattath* that was wholly burned, as well; and if one does any spoiling or damaging action with them, what is their law. [These] and the rest of its details are in the Talmud tractate *Z'vaḥim*.

It is in effect when the Temple exists, for the male *kohanim*. If a *kohen* transgressed and did not offer up a *ḥattath* lawfully, he would disobey this positive precept.

[שֶׁלֹּא לֶאֱכֹל מִבְּשַׂר חַטָּאוֹת הַנַּעֲשׂוֹת בִּפְנִים]

קלט שֶׁלֹּא יֹאכְלוּ הַכֹּהֲנִים מִבְּשַׂר הַחַטָּאוֹת הַנַּעֲשׂוֹת בִּפְנִים, כְּלוֹמַר מֵאוֹתָן חַטָּאוֹת שֶׁהָיוּ מַזִּין מִדָּמָן בַּמִּזְבֵּחַ הַפְּנִימִי שֶׁהָיָה בַּהֵיכָל, שֶׁנֶּאֱמַר: וְכָל חַטָּאת אֲשֶׁר יוּבָא מִדָּמָהּ אֶל אֹהֶל מוֹעֵד לְכַפֵּר בַּקֹּדֶשׁ לֹא תֵאָכֵל בָּאֵשׁ תִּשָּׂרֵף. וּלְשׁוֹן סִפְרֵי: ״בָּאֵשׁ תִּשָּׂרֵף״, כָּל שֶׁהוּא טָעוּן שְׂרֵפָה, לַעֲבֹר עָלָיו בְּלֹא־תַעֲשֶׂה עַל אֲכִילָתוֹ. וְכָל חַטָּאת שֶׁדָּמָן טָעוּן הַזָּיָה בִּפְנִים, כְּלוֹמַר בַּמִּזְבֵּחַ שֶׁהָיָה בַּהֵיכָל, הָיוּ נִשְׂרָפִין, יָדוּעַ הַדָּבָר וּמְפֹרָשׁ בַּכְּתוּבִים; וְכָל הַחַטָּאוֹת שֶׁלֹּא הָיוּ מַזִּין מִדָּמָן אֶלָּא בַּמִּזְבֵּחַ שֶׁבַּחוּץ הָיוּ נֶאֱכָלִין; וְעַל זֶה נֶאֱמַר מִקְרָא זֶה, שֶׁכָּל חַטָּאת שֶׁדִּינָהּ בִּשְׂרֵפָה לֹא יֹאכְלוּ מִמֶּנָּה. וּפְרָטֵי הַחַטָּאוֹת, אֵי זֶה מֵהֶן נִשְׂרָף וְאֵי זֶה נֶאֱכָל, מְפֹרָשׁ בַּכָּתוּב, וּמַה שֶּׁאֵינוֹ מְבֹאָר יָפֶה בַּמִּקְרָא פֵּרְשׁוּ לָנוּ חֲכָמֵינוּ זִכְרוֹנָם לִבְרָכָה בִּזְבָחִים.

כְּבָר אָמַרְנוּ כִּי בִפְרָטֵי הַקָּרְבָּנוֹת אֵין לָנוּ בָהֶם עֵסֶק, וְגַם זֶה מִפְּרָטֵיהֶם הוּא, אִם נֶאֱכָל אִם לֹא נֶאֱכָל.

מִדִּינֵי הַמִּצְוָה, מַה שֶּׁאָמְרוּ זִכְרוֹנָם לִבְרָכָה דְּמִכֵּיוָן שֶׁנִּכְנָס דַּם חַטָּאת הַנֶּאֱכֶלֶת בְּאֹהֶל מוֹעֵד, פָּסוּל; וְלָמְדוּ לוֹמַר כֵּן מִזֶּה הַמִּקְרָא שֶׁאָמַר: וְכָל חַטָּאת אֲשֶׁר יוּבָא מִדָּמָהּ וְגוֹמֵר, לֹא תֵאָכֵל. וְדַוְקָא שֶׁנִּכְנַס דֶּרֶךְ שַׁעַר הַהֵיכָל, כְּמוֹ שֶׁכָּתוּב ״יוּבָא״, כְּלוֹמַר דֶּרֶךְ בִּיאָה; אֲבָל אִם הִכְנִיסוֹ בַּפִּשְׁפֵּשׁ אוֹ דֶּרֶךְ חַלּוֹן אוֹ גַּג, אֵינוֹ נִפְסָל, דְּלָאו דֶּרֶךְ בִּיאָה הוּא.

וְהוּא הַדִּין לַחַטָּאוֹת הַנִּשְׂרָפוֹת שֶׁמַּזִּין דָּמָן בַּמִּזְבֵּחַ הַפְּנִימִי, שֶׁאִם הִכְנִיס דָּמָן לִפְנִים מִן הַפָּרֹכֶת, דְּזֶהוּ קֹדֶשׁ הַקֳּדָשִׁים, שֶׁפְּסוּלִין, שֶׁגַּם בָּהֶן אֲנִי קוֹרֵא: וְכָל

2. I.e. to our lack or failure in understanding.

3. So MT *hilchoth ma'aséh ha-korbanoth* i 9, based on verses of Scripture about the various kinds of sin-offerings in *sidrah va-yikra (Kessef Mishneh).*

4. The bracketed addition follows an emendation by MY to correct an obvious scribal oversight. These details of the laws can all be found in Scripture, e.g. Leviticus 4 and 6:17–23.

5. So Sifra, *va-yikra, parashah* 14, 8. The paragraph derives from MT *ibid.* 18 (see *Kessef Mishneh* on sources).

6. TB B'rachoth 61a.

§139 1. In the Sanctuary, which corresponded to the Tent of Meeting in the *mishkan* (Tabernacle), mentioned in the verse below.

2. Sifra, *tzav, perek* 5, 4; so too TB Makkoth 18b, etc.

3. TB Z'vaḥim 81b (MT *hilchoth p'sulé ha-mukdashin* ii 13).

4. *Ibid.* 82b. The verb *yuva* (brought) is from the same root as *bi'ah*, "coming," and hence denotes "made to enter" or "made to come in"—i.e. in the usual way that someone or something would enter.

5. Literally, "For in them too I read"; *ibid.* (MT *ibid.* 14).

[NOT TO EAT OF ANY ḤATTATH WHOSE BLOOD IS SPRINKLED WITHIN]

139 that the *kohanim* should not eat of the flesh of *ḥattath* (sin) offerings that are sacrificed within [the holy chamber][1]—i.e. of those sin-offerings of whose blood they would sprinkle on the inner altar which was in the *héchal*: For it is stated, *And any sin-offering from whose blood any is brought into the tent of meeting to make atonement in the holy place, shall not be eaten; it shall be burned with fire* (Leviticus 6:23). In the words of the Midrash *Sifra*:[2] "it shall be burned with fire"—whatever requires burning, this is to make it the transgression of a negative precept if it is eaten. Now, every *ḥattath* whose blood had to be sprinkled within, i.e. on the altar in the *héchal*, was burned: this is a known matter, being stated explicitly in Scripture (Leviticus 6:23). On the other hand, all sin-offerings whose blood was not sprinkled within, but only on the altar without, would be eaten. About this the [above] verse is stated—that any *ḥattath* for which the law is burning, is not to be eaten.

The details about the sin-offerings, which are to be burned and which eaten, are given distinctly in Scripture; and what is not clarified well in the Writ, our Sages of blessed memory explained to us in the Talmud tractate *Z'vaḥim*.

We stated previously that with the details of the offerings we can have no concern [to find reasons for them]. This too is among their details—whether we may eat [of their flesh] or not.

Among the laws of the precept, there is what the Sages of blessed memory said,[3] that once the blood of a *ḥattath* that is to be eaten entered the Tent of Meeting, it would become disqualified, unacceptable. They learned to rule so from this verse, which states, *And any sin-offering from whose blood any is brought . . . shall not be eaten*; but this is only if it entered [was taken in] by way of the entrance of the *héchal*—as it is written, "is brought," i.e. in the usual way of coming in. But if it was taken in through the small opening in the gate or by way of a window or the roof, it would not be disqualified, since this is not the proper way of bringing it.[4]

The same law holds for sin-offerings that were to be burned, whose blood was sprinkled on the inner altar—that if its blood was brought within [beyond] the curtain, where it is the holy of holies, it became disqualified, unacceptable. For to them too we apply the verse,[5] "And any *ḥattath* from whose blood any is brought within," since

חַטָּאת אֲשֶׁר יוּבָא מִדָּמָהּ פְּנִימָה, שֶׁמָּקוֹם זֶה פְּנִימָה לִמְקוֹמָן הוּא; וְיֶתֶר פְּרָטֶיהָ, בִּזְבָחִים.

וְנוֹהֵג אִסּוּר אֲכִילַת חַטָּאת פְּנִים בַּכֹּהֲנִים, וְהוּא הַדִּין לְכָל אָדָם, שֶׁדֶּרֶךְ כְּלָל נֶאֱמַר לֹא תֵאָכֵל. וְהָעוֹבֵר וְאָכַל מִמֶּנָּה כַּזַּיִת, לוֹקֶה.

[מִצְוַת מַעֲשֵׂה הָאָשָׁם]

קמ שֶׁנִּצְטַוִּינוּ שֶׁיַּעֲשׂוּ הַכֹּהֲנִים מְלֶאכֶת קָרְבַּן הָאָשָׁם עַל הָעִנְיָן הַנִּזְכָּר בַּכָּתוּב, שֶׁנֶּאֱמַר: וְזֹאת תּוֹרַת הָאָשָׁם וְגוֹמֵר, כְּמוֹ שֶׁכָּתוּב בַּפָּרָשָׁה.

הֲלֹא אָמַרְתִּי אֵלֶיךָ שֶׁאֵין לָנוּ לִכְתֹּב שֹׁרֶשׁ בִּמְלָאכוֹת אֵלּוּ, לְפִי שֶׁהֵן כְּעֵין פְּרָטֵי הַקָּרְבָּן, וְאֵין לְחַזֵּר אַחַר טַעֲמָן, כִּי סְתוּמִים הַדְּבָרִים וַחֲתוּמִים.

דִּינֵי הָאָשָׁם, זָכַרְנוּ קְצָתָם לְמַעְלָה בְּפָרָשַׁת וַיִּקְרָא עֲשֵׂה י׳ [סי׳ קכ״ט]. וַעֲדַיִן נוֹדִיעַ שֶׁהָאָשָׁם אֵינוֹ בָא לְעוֹלָם אֶלָּא מִזִּכְרֵי כְבָשִׂים בִּלְבַד; יֵשׁ אָשָׁם בָּא מִגְּדוֹלֵי הַמִּין, וְיֵשׁ מִן הַקְּטַנִּים; מַעֲשֵׂהוּ בִּשְׁחִיטָה וּזְרִיקָה וּמְלִיחָה וְהָאֵמוּרִין (והתנופה) [וְהָאֲכִילָה] בָּאֲשָׁמוֹת שָׁוֶה, חוּץ מֵאֲשַׁם מְצֹרָע, שֶׁיֵּשׁ שִׁנּוּי קְצָת בְּקַבָּלַת דָּמוֹ; וְיֶתֶר פְּרָטֵי הַמִּצְוָה, מְבֹאָרִין בִּזְבָחִים.

וְנוֹהֶגֶת בִּזְמַן הַבַּיִת בְּזִכְרֵי כְהֻנָּה. וְכֹהֵן הָעוֹבֵר עָלֶיהָ וְלֹא הִקְרִיב הָאָשָׁם כְּמִשְׁפָּטוֹ, בִּטֵּל עֲשֵׂה.

[מִצְוַת מַעֲשֵׂה זֶבַח הַשְּׁלָמִים]

קמא שֶׁנִּצְטַוִּינוּ שֶׁיַּעֲשׂוּ הַכֹּהֲנִים מַעֲשֵׂה קָרְבַּן הַשְּׁלָמִים כַּמִּשְׁפָּט הַכָּתוּב בַּפָּרָשָׁה, שֶׁנֶּאֱמַר: וְאִם זֶבַח שְׁלָמִים קָרְבָּנוֹ וְגוֹמֵר, וְאָמַר עוֹד לְהַשְׁלָמַת הַמְּלָאכָה: וְזֹאת תּוֹרַת זֶבַח הַשְּׁלָמִים... אִם עַל תּוֹדָה יַקְרִיבֶנּוּ. וּבְאַרְבָּעָה שֵׁמוֹת נִכְלָלִין

6. I.e. one whose blood was sprinkled on the inner altar.

§140 1. So MT *hilchoth ma'aséh ha-korbanoth* i 10 (from Scripture).

2. See above, §118.

3. The term *v'ha-t'nufah* (and lifting — them — up), found in the early manuscripts as well, is evidently an early scribal error, since only the *'asham* of a healed *m'tzora* was lifted up, while yet alive (MH, MY). The emendation is conjectural.

4. Mishnah, N'ga'im xiv 8.

this place is "within" [beyond] the proper place for them. The rest of its details are in the Talmud tractate *Z'vaḥim*.

The ban on eating an "inner" *ḥattath*[6] applies to *kohanim*, but the law holds equally for every man, as the words *shall not be eaten* were stated as a general rule. If someone violated it and ate the amount of an olive, he would receive whiplashes.

140 [THE PRECEPT OF THE SACRIFICE OF THE 'ASHAM]

that we were commanded that the *kohanim* should perform the task of an *'asham* (guilt) offering in the way mentioned in Scripture—as it is stated, *And this is the law of the guilt-offering*, etc. (Leviticus 7:1)—as it is written in the section of Scripture.

Now, I have told you firmly that it is not for us to write any root reason for these tasks, since they are akin to details of an offering. There is no point in seeking about after their reasons, as these matters are locked and sealed.

As to the laws of the *'asham*, we mentioned some of them above, in *sidrah va-yikra*, in the tenth positive precept (§129). It remains for us to convey that an *'asham* is never brought from any creatures but male sheep alone. There is an *'asham* that comes from the grown ones of the species, and some are brought from the young.[1] As regards the task of ritual slaying, sprinkling the blood, applying salt,[2] the *'émurim*, and eating [the flesh],[3] the law for all *'asham* offerings is the same—except for the *'asham* of a *m'tzora*, as there is a slight difference in the way its blood was collected.[4] [These] and other details of the precept are explained in the tractate *Z'vaḥim*.

It is in effect when the Temple is extant, for the male *kohanim*. If a *kohen* violated it and did not offer up an *'asham* in its proper way, he would thus disobey a positive precept.

141 [THE PRECEPT OF THE SACRIFICE OF SH'LAMIM]

that we were commanded that the *kohanim* should perform the task of a *sh'lamim* (peace) offering in the proper way that is written in the *sidrah*: for it is written, *And if his offering is a sacrifice of a peace-offering* (Leviticus 3:1); and it is stated further, for the completion of the task, *And this is the law of the sacrifice of the peace-offering . . . If he offers it for a thanks-giving* (*ibid.* 7:1–2). Under four names all types of

עִנְיְנֵי הַקָּרְבָּנוֹת כֻּלָּן, וְהֵם: עוֹלָה, חַטָּאת וְאָשָׁם וּשְׁלָמִים; שֶׁכָּל קָרְבָּן שֶׁיַּקְרִיבוּ צִבּוּר אוֹ יָחִיד, מֵאֶחָד מֵאֵלֶּה יִהְיֶה לְעוֹלָם.

כְּבָר כָּתַבְתִּי פַּעֲמַיִם שֶׁאֵין לִכְתֹּב שָׁרָשִׁים בְּאֵלּוּ הַמְּלָאכוֹת.

מִדִּינֵי הַמִּצְוָה, מַה שֶּׁאָמְרוּ זִכְרוֹנָם לִבְרָכָה שֶׁהַשְּׁלָמִים בָּאִין מִן הַכְּבָשִׂים וּמִן הָעִזִּים וּמִן הַבָּקָר, וּמִן הַזְּכָרִים וּמִן הַנְּקֵבוֹת, מִן הַגְּדוֹלִים וּמִן הַקְּטַנִּים; וְאֵין הָעוֹף בָּא שְׁלָמִים; וּקְטַנִּים נִקְרָאִים מִבֶּן שְׁמֹנַת יָמִים עַד שָׁנָה תְּמִימָה מִיּוֹם לְיוֹם. נִתְעַבְּרָה שָׁנָה נִתְעַבְּרָה לוֹ, כְּלוֹמַר וְיִהְיֶה קָטָן עַד תַּשְׁלוּם הָעִבּוּר. וְגָדוֹל נִקְרָא בַּבָּקָר מִשָּׁנָה עַד שָׁלֹשׁ שָׁנִים, וּבַצֹּאן מִשָּׁנָה עַד שְׁתֵּי שָׁנִים שְׁלֵמוֹת; יָתֵר עַל כֵּן הֲרֵי הוּא זָקֵן וְאֵין מַקְרִיבִין אוֹתוֹ.

וְאַרְבָּעָה מִינִין הֵם הַשְּׁלָמִים, הָאֶחָד שַׁלְמֵי צִבּוּר וְהַשְּׁלֹשָׁה שַׁלְמֵי יָחִיד. שַׁלְמֵי צִבּוּר נִקְרָאִין קָדְשֵׁי קָדָשִׁים, וְאֵין לַצִּבּוּר שְׁלָמִים כִּי־אִם קָרְבָּן אֶחָד, וְהוּא שְׁנֵי כְבָשִׂים הַבָּאִין עִם שְׁתֵּי הַלֶּחֶם בַּעֲצֶרֶת. אוֹתָן שְׁנֵי כְבָשִׂים הֵן הַנִּקְרָאִים זִבְחֵי שַׁלְמֵי צִבּוּר, וְנֶאֱכָלִין לַכֹּהֲנִים חוּץ מִן הָאֵמוּרִין, כַּחַטָּאת וְכָאָשָׁם. הַמְּלָאכוֹת שֶׁלָּהֶן, כְּגוֹן שְׁחִיטָה, זְרִיקָה, הֶפְשֵׁט וְנִתּוּחַ וּמְלִיחָה וְהַקְטָרַת אֵמוּרִין, מְפֹרָשׁ בִּמְנָחוֹת.

וְשַׁלְמֵי הַיָּחִיד נִקְרָאִים קָדָשִׁים קַלִּים, וּמְקוֹם שְׁחִיטָתָן וּמַעֲשֵׂה הַזְּרִיקָה וְהֶפְשֵׁט וְנִתּוּחַ וּתְנוּפָה וְהַפְרָשַׁת אֵמוּרִין, מְפֹרָשׁ בִּמְנָחוֹת; וְהַשְּׁלֹשָׁה מִינִין אֵלּוּ שֶׁל שַׁלְמֵי יָחִיד שָׁוִין הֵן בִּמְלָאכוֹת אֵלּוּ, אֲבָל יֵשׁ לְךָ לָדַעַת עִנְיַן הַחִלּוּק שֶׁבֵּינֵיהֶן בִּקְצָת עִנְיְנֵיהֶם דֶּרֶךְ כְּלָל.

דַּע כִּי מִשְּׁלֹשָׁה מִינִין שֶׁל שַׁלְמֵי יָחִיד, הָאֶחָד הוּא קָרְבַּן הַשְּׁלָמִים הַבָּא בְלֹא לֶחֶם עִמּוֹ, וְהֵם שַׁלְמֵי חֲגִיגָה וְשִׂמְחָה. וְאֵלּוּ הֵן הַנִּקְרָאִין שְׁלָמִים; וְהַשֵּׁנִי שְׁלָמִים

§141

1. The paragraph is based on ShM positive precept §66.
2. TB M'naḥoth 104b.
3. The Hebrew noun is both singular and plural.
4. I.e. from the eighth day of its life until the anniversary of the day of its birth.
5. See §4, note 3.
6. The paragraph is drawn from MT *hilchoth ma'aséh ha-korbanoth* i 11.
7. So MT *ibid.* ix 3.
8. Literally, "holy of holies"; TB Z'vaḥim 55a.
9. *Ibid.* 54b.
10. See above, §118.
11. See TB Z'vaḥim 54b, 103b, M'naḥoth 20a.
12. Literally, "light holinesses"; TB Z'vaḥim 55a, etc.
13. See Leviticus 23:20.
14. TB Z'vaḥim 55a, 103b, M'naḥoth 61a.

animal offerings are included: these are the *'olah* (burnt-offering), *ḥattath* (sin-offering), *'asham* (guilt-offering), and *sh'lamim*. For every offering that the community or an individual would ever bring, would always be one of these.[1]

I have written twice previously that root reasons cannot be written for these tasks.

Among the laws of the precept, there is what the Sages of blessed memory said,[2] that *sh'lamim*[3] were brought from sheep, goats and cattle, both male and female, grown animals and young; but fowl could not be brought as *sh'lamim*. Those between the ages of eight days and a whole year, from day to day,[4] are called young. If the year was intercalated,[5] it was intercalated for it [too]—i.e. it remains "young" until the intercalated year is completed. Among cattle an animal is called "grown" from one to three years of age; and among sheep, from one to two whole years. When one is more than that, it is old, and is not to be offered up.[6]

The *sh'lamim* are of four kinds: one, the *sh'lamim* of the community, and three, the *sh'lamim* of an individual.[7] The *sh'lamim* of the community is called a most holy offering.[8] The community had but one offering as a *sh'lamim*, which was the two sheep that were brought with the two loaves on *Shavu'oth*. Those two sheep were those called the sacrifices of the *sh'lamim* of the community. They were eaten by the *kohanim*, except for the *'émurim* (the parts burned on the altar), like a *ḥattath* and an *'asham*.[9] Their [various] tasks, such as the ritual slaying, sprinkling the blood, skinning it, cutting it into parts, applying salt,[10] and burning the *'émurim*, are explained in the Talmud tractate *M'naḥoth*.[11]

The *sh'lamim* of an individual are called offerings of lesser holiness.[12] The proper place for their ritual slaying, and the proper way of sprinkling the blood, skinning them, cutting them into pieces, lifting them up,[13] and separating the *'émurim*, are [all] explained in *M'naḥoth*.[14] Now, these three kinds of *sh'lamim* of an individual are alike in regard to these tasks. But you should know about the differences among them in certain respects, in a general way:

Know that of the three types of *sh'lamim* of an individual, one is an offering of *sh'lamim* that is brought without bread with it. These are the peace-offerings of festival celebration (§88) and occasions of joy (§488)—the which are called *sh'lamim*. The second is a peace-offering that comes with certain known loaves—which is brought

הַבָּאִים עִם הַלֶּחֶם הַיָּדוּעַ, וְהוּא הַבָּא בְּנֶדֶר אוֹ בִנְדָבָה, וְאֵלּוּ הַשְּׁלָמִים נִקְרָאִים תּוֹדָה, וְהַלֶּחֶם הַבָּא עִמּוֹ נִקְרָא לֶחֶם תּוֹדָה; וְהַמִּין הַשְּׁלִישִׁי שְׁלָמִים שֶׁמַּקְרִיב הַנָּזִיר בְּיוֹם מְלֹאת יְמֵי נִזְרוֹ, וְהֵן בָּאִין גַּם־כֵּן עִם לֶחֶם, וְאֵלּוּ הַשְּׁלָמִים נִקְרָאִים אֵיל נָזִיר.

וּבֵאֲרוּ זִכְרוֹנָם לִבְרָכָה שָׁם בַּגְּמָרָא, חָזֶה וָשׁוֹק מֵהֶן הַנֶּאֱכָלִין לַכֹּהֲנִים כַּמָּה שִׁעוּרָן, וְהַזְּרוֹעַ בְּשֵׁלָה מִן אֵיל נָזִיר הַנֶּאֱכָל לַכֹּהֲנִים מִלְּבַד חָזֶה וָשׁוֹק, גַּם־כֵּן כַּמָּה שִׁעוּרוֹ, וּבְאֵי זֶה מָקוֹם מִן הַבַּיִת מְבַשְּׁלִין אוֹתוֹ.

וְדִינֵי הַלֶּחֶם הַבָּא עִם שְׁנֵי מִינִין מִן הַשְּׁלָמִים, וְהֵן תּוֹדָה וְאֵיל נָזִיר, מִכַּמָּה עֶשְׂרוֹנִים הוּא, וְאֵי זֶה מֵהֶן בָּא חָמֵץ וְאֵי זֶה בָא מַצָּה לְבַד, וְהַבָּא חָמֵץ וּמַצָּה אֵיךְ יֵחָלֵק, וְכֵיצַד מְחַמְּצָן, וְחֶשְׁבּוֹן הַחַלּוֹת הַבָּאוֹת מַצָּה, כַּמָּה מֵהֶן מַאֲפֵה תַנּוּר וּרְקִיקִין וּמֻרְבָּכוֹת — הַכֹּל בִּזְבָחִים.

וְעִנְיַן אוֹתָן הַבָּאוֹת מַצָּה בְתוֹדָה הָיָה כֵן: מֵעֲשָׂרָה עֶשְׂרוֹנִים שֶׁל קֶמַח הָיוּ עוֹשִׂין שְׁלֹשִׁים חַלּוֹת; הָעֲשָׂרָה מֵהֶן הָיוּ נַעֲשׂוֹת מַאֲפֵה תַנּוּר, כְּלוֹמַר שֶׁלֹּא הָיָה נַעֲשֶׂה בָהֶן דָּבָר רַק שֶׁהָיוּ מְשִׂימִין בְּעִסָּתָן בִּשְׁעַת לִישָׁה שְׁמִינִית לוֹג שֶׁמֶן, שֶׁכֵּן הוּא הֲלָכָה לְמֹשֶׁה מִסִּינַי, וְאוֹפִין אוֹתָן; וְהָעֲשָׂרָה מֵהֶן נִקְרָאוֹת רְקִיקִין, וְאֵין חִלּוּק בֵּין הָעֲשָׂרָה שֶׁל רְקִיקִין לָעֲשָׂרָה שֶׁל מַאֲפֵה תַנּוּר אֶלָּא שֶׁבָּעֲשָׂרָה שֶׁל מַאֲפֵה תַנּוּר הָיוּ מְעָרְבִין בָּהֶן שְׁמִינִית לוֹג שֶׁל שֶׁמֶן בִּשְׁעַת לִישָׁה, וְהָעֲשָׂרָה שֶׁל רְקִיקִין הָיוּ מוֹשְׁחִין אוֹתָן בִּשְׁמִינִית הַלּוֹג שֶׁמֶן אַחַר אֲפִיָּתָן בַּתַּנּוּר; וְהָעֲשָׂרָה מֵהֶן הָיוּ מֻרְבָּכוֹת, וּפֵרוּשׁ רְבִיכָה הוּא שֶׁחוֹלְטִין הַחַלָּה בְמַיִם רוֹתְחִין וְאוֹפֶה אוֹתָהּ מְעַט, וְאַחַר־כָּךְ קוֹלֶה בְשֶׁמֶן כְּדֶרֶךְ שֶׁקּוֹלִין בְּנֵי־אָדָם הַסֻּפְגָּנִין בָּאִלְפָּס, וּמַרְבִּיךְ בְּשַׁמְנָן שֶׁל עֲשָׂרָה הָרְבוּכוֹת, כִּי הַשֶּׁמֶן שֶׁקָּלוּ בוֹ הָיָה רְבִיעִית לוֹג, כְּשִׁעוּר כָּל

15. I.e. one who vowed to be a *nazir* for a certain period, in which time he was not to become defiled, cut his hair, or take grapes or wine, etc. (Numbers 6).

16. The paragraph derives from MT *hilchoth ma'aséh ha-korbanoth* ix 5.

17. E.g. whether the thigh and shoulder were the right and left; TB Ḥullin 134b.

18. Mishnah, Middoth ii 5.

19. Plural of *'issaron*; see § 136, note 3.

20. I.e. how many of the loaves or cakes were to be *ḥametz* (leavened), and how many *matzah*.

21. See TB M'naḥoth 76b, 78a, 52b (Z'vaḥim in the text is evidently a scribal error for M'naḥoth).

by a vow or as a voluntary offering. These peace-offerings are called *todah*, "thanks-giving"; and the loaves brought with it are called the bread of thanks-giving. The third type is a peace-offering that a *nazir*[15] would bring on the day when the period of his naziriteship was completed; and these would also come with bread. These peace-offerings were called "the ram of the *nazir*."[16]

There in the Talmud, our Sages of blessed memory explained about the breast and thigh [taken] from them, which were eaten by the *kohanim* (Leviticus 7:34)—what they were exactly;[17] and the boiled shoulder from the *nazir*'s ram as well, which was eaten by the *kohanim* apart from the breast and thigh—exactly what it was,[17] and in what place in the Temple they would boil it.[18]

As to the laws of the bread brought with two kinds of peace-offerings, i.e. the *todah* (thanks-giving) and the ram of the *nazir*—out of how many *'esronim*[19] [of flour] they were made; which of them were brought leavened, and which were of *matzah* (unleavened bread) alone; and if they were to be brought of both leavened and unleavened bread, how they were to be divided up,[20] and how the leavening was done; then, out of the sum of loaves that were brought unleavened, how many of them were baked in the oven, baked as wafers, or made mixed with hot water and oil—all is [to be found] in the tractate *Z'vaḥim*.[21]

Now, the procedure for those that were brought as *matzah* with a *todah* (thanks-giving offering), was this: Out of ten *'esronim* of flour, thirty loaves would be made. Ten of them were made oven-baked; in other words, nothing was done with them but this: into their dough, during the kneading, an eighth of a *log* of oil would be put—as this was a law [given orally] to Moses at Sinai; and it was baked. Ten of them were called wafers. There was no difference between the ten wafers and the ten baked in the oven except this: in the ten that were oven-baked, an eighth of a *log* of oil was mixed during the kneading; the ten that were wafers were smeared with an eighth of a *log* of oil after they were baked in the oven. And ten of them were made with hot water and oil. This means that the loaf would be scalded with boiling water and baked a little; then it would be fried with oil, in the way that people fry [soft] dough-cakes in a stew-pot. Oil was used aplenty for the ten soft loaves: for the oil in which they were fried was a fourth of a *log*, requiring as much as all the oil used for the twenty [other] loaves. This measure of oil for the oil-soaked loaves

הַשֶּׁמֶן שֶׁל הָעֶשְׂרִים חַלּוֹת; וְגַם שִׁעוּר זֶה שֶׁל שֶׁמֶן הָרְבוּכוֹת הֲלָכָה לְמֹשֶׁה מִסִּינַי. וְזֶה שֶׁאָמַרְנוּ, הוּא פֵּרוּשׁ מֻרְבֶּכֶת בְּכָל מָקוֹם בַּתּוֹרָה.

וְשָׁם מִתְבָּאֵר כַּמָּה חֵלֶק יֵשׁ לַכֹּהֵן בַּחַלּוֹת, וְהַשְּׁאָר נֶאֱכָל לַבְּעָלִים; וְיֶתֶר כָּל פְּרָטֶיהָ, שָׁם בְּמַסֶּכֶת זְבָחִים.

וְנוֹהֶגֶת מִצְוַת הַשְּׁלָמִים בִּזְמַן הַבַּיִת בִּזְכְרֵי כְהֻנָּה, כִּי לָהֶם חִיּוּב הָעֲבוֹדָה. וְעוֹבֵר עָלֶיהָ וְשִׁנָּה אֶת סִדְרָן בִּצְדָדִין יְדוּעִין בַּגְּמָרָא, בִּטֵּל עֲשֵׂה, מִלְּבַד שֶׁיֵּשׁ צְדָדִין שֶׁהַקָּרְבָּן פָּסוּל.

[שֶׁלֹּא לְהוֹתִיר מִבְּשַׂר קָרְבַּן הַתּוֹדָה]

קמב שֶׁלֹּא לְהוֹתִיר שׁוּם דָּבָר מִקָּרְבַּן הַתּוֹדָה עַד הַבֹּקֶר, כְּלוֹמַר לְמָחֳרַת יוֹם זְבִיחָתוֹ, שֶׁנֶּאֱמַר בְּקָרְבַּן תּוֹדָה: לֹא יַנִּיחַ מִמֶּנּוּ עַד בֹּקֶר. וּמִמֶּנּוּ לָמַדְנוּ לִשְׁאָר קָדָשִׁים גַּם־כֵּן שֶׁכָּל מַה שֶׁיִּשָּׁאֵר מֵהֶם לְאַחַר זְמַן אֲכִילָתָן שֶׁהוּא נוֹתָר, וְחַיָּב לְשָׂרְפוֹ, לְפִי שֶׁהוּא נִתַּק לַעֲשֵׂה שֶׁיִּשְׂרְפֶנּוּ, כְּמוֹ שֶׁכָּתַבְנוּ לְמַעְלָה בְּסֵדֶר זֶה בְּמִצְוַת עֲשֵׂה ח׳ [סי׳ קמ״ג]. וְשָׁם כָּתַבְנוּ רֶמֶז מִשָּׁרָשָׁיו, וּקְצָת דִּינָיו, כְּמִנְהָגֵנוּ.

[מִצְוַת שְׂרֵפַת נוֹתַר הַקֳּדָשִׁים]

קמג שֶׁנִּצְטַוִּינוּ לִשְׂרֹף הַנּוֹתָר, וְהוּא בְּשַׂר הַקֳּדָשִׁים שֶׁנִּשְׁאַר אַחַר עֲבֹר זְמַן אֲכִילָתָן הַמֻּגְבָּל לָהֶן, שֶׁנֶּאֱמַר: וְהַנּוֹתָר מִבְּשַׂר הַזָּבַח בַּיּוֹם הַשְּׁלִישִׁי בָּאֵשׁ יִשָּׂרֵף; וְזֹאת הַשְּׂרֵפָה הִיא מִצְוַת עֲשֵׂה, שֶׁכֵּן אָמְרוּ בִמְכִלְתָּא גַּבֵּי פֶּסַח: ״וְלֹא תוֹתִירוּ מִמֶּנּוּ וְגוֹמֵר, וְהַנּוֹתָר ... בָּאֵשׁ תִּשְׂרֹפוּ״, בָּא הַכָּתוּב לִתֵּן עֲשֵׂה עַל לֹא־תַעֲשֶׂה — דְּמַשְׁמַע שֶׁמִּצְוַת שְׂרֵפַת נוֹתָר עֲשֵׂה הוּא.

וְדִין הַפִּגּוּל וְהַנּוֹתָר שָׁוֶה בָּזֶה, שֶׁיֵּשׁ מִצְוַת עֲשֵׂה גַּם־כֵּן בִּשְׂרֵפָתוֹ, שֶׁמָּצִינוּ

22. The paragraph is based on MT *hilchoth ma'aséh ha-korbanoth* ix 18–21 (sources given in *Kessef Mishneh*).
23. TB M'naḥoth 77b.

§142 1. From the beginning to here is based on ShM negative precept §120.
2. As noted previously, in the original work the positive precepts in each *sidrah* were arranged first, then the negative; hence this was "above." In our order of the later editions, following the verses of Scripture, it is below.

§143 1. The term is explained below, in §144.

 was also a law [given orally] to Moses at Sinai. And what we have stated is the meaning of the term *murbecheth* (oil-soaked) everywhere in the Torah.[22]

There [in the Talmud][23] it is explained what share the *kohen* receives from the loaves, the rest being eaten by the owner [who brought them]. All its other details are there, in the tractate *Z'vaḥim*.

The precept of *sh'lamim* is in effect when the Temple is extant, for the male *kohanim*, as they have the obligation of the Temple service. If one violated it and changed their procedure in certain known ways [described] in the Talmud, he would thus disobey a positive precept—this apart from the fact that there are certain procedures by which the offering becomes disqualified and unacceptable.

[NOT TO LET THE FLESH OF A TODAH BE LEFT OVER]

142 not to let anything of a *todah* (thanks-giving offering) remain until the morning, i.e. till the morrow of the day of its sacrifice—for it is stated regarding the thanks-giving offering, *he shall not leave any of it until the morning* (Leviticus 7:15). And from this we learn about other holy offerings as well, that whatever is left of them after the proper time for eating them is *nothar*, "remainder," and there is a duty to burn it, since it is given to correction by the positive precept to burn it,[1] as we have written (above) [below][2] in the eighth positive precept of this *sidrah* (§143). There we have also written an indication of its root reason and some of its laws, as our custom is.

[THE PRECEPT OF BURNING LEFTOVER REMNANTS OF SACRED OFFERINGS]

143 that we were commanded to burn *nothar*, which is the meat of holy offerings that remains after the allotted time for eating it has passed. For it is stated, *But that which remains of the flesh of the sacrifice on the third day shall be burned with fire* (Leviticus 7:17); and this burning is a positive precept, as it was taught in the Midrash *Mechilta* about the Passover offering: "*And you shall let nothing of it remain . . . but that which remains . . . you shall burn with fire* (Exodus 12:10): the Writ comes to add a positive precept onto the negative one"—which indicates that the duty of burning *nothar* is a positive precept.

The laws of *piggul* (an offering turned vile)[1] and *nothar* (leftover flesh) are the same in this respect, as there is also a positive precept

הַכָּתוּב מוֹצִיא הַפִּגּוּל בִּלְשׁוֹן נוֹתָר.

מִשָּׁרְשֵׁי הַמִּצְוָה, לְפִי שֶׁטֶּבַע כָּל בָּשָׂר לְהִפָּסֵד בִּשְׁהִיָּה וְלָבוֹא לִידֵי סִרְחוֹן, וְעַל־כֵּן, לְהַגְדָּלַת דְּבַר הַקָּרְבָּן, כְּמוֹ שֶׁאָמַרְנוּ לְמַעְלָה, נִצְטַוִּינוּ לְשָׂרְפוֹ מִיָּד וּלְבַעֲרוֹ מִן הָעוֹלָם, לְבַל יָקוּץ אָדָם בּוֹ וּבְרֵיחוֹ; וְתַכְלִית הַכִּלָּיוֹן הַגָּמוּר הוּא עַל־יְדֵי הָאֵשׁ, יוֹתֵר מִן הַפֵּרוּד וּזְרִיָּה לָרוּחַ אוֹ כָל דָּבָר אַחֵר. גַּם מִלְּבַד זֶה יֵשׁ בַּדָּבָר רֶמֶז אֶל הַבִּטָּחוֹן בַּשֵּׁם בָּרוּךְ הוּא, שֶׁלֹּא יְהֵא אָדָם חוֹנֵק עַצְמוֹ בְּמַאֲכָלוֹ יוֹתֵר מִדַּי לְהַצְנִיעוֹ לְיוֹם מָחָר, בִּרְאוֹתוֹ כִּי הָאֵל יְצַוֶּה לְכַלּוֹת בְּשַׂר קֹדֶשׁ מִשֶּׁעָבְרָה שְׁעָתוֹ כִּלָּיוֹן גָּמוּר וְלֹא רָצָה שֶׁיֵּהָנֶה בּוֹ בְּרִיָּה אַחַר־כֵּן, לֹא אָדָם וְלֹא בְהֵמָה.

מִדִּינֵי הַמִּצְוָה, מַה שֶּׁאָמְרוּ זִכְרוֹנָם לִבְרָכָה שֶׁבִּכְלַל הַנּוֹתָר וְהַפִּגּוּל שֶׁנִּשְׂרָפִין, הֵם כָּל פְּסוּלֵי הַמֻּקְדָּשִׁין, שֶׁכֻּלָּן נִשְׂרָפִין גַּם־כֵּן; וְקָרְבָּן שֶׁנִּפְסַל אוֹ נִתְפַּגֵּל בְּוַדַּאי, מִיָּד נִשְׂרָף, וְאִם סָפֵק, תְּעֻבַּר צוּרָתוֹ וְאַחַר־כָּךְ נִשְׂרָף; וְכָל בָּשָׂר הַנִּמְצָא בָעֲזָרָה אֵבָרִים, עוֹלוֹת — פֵּרוּשׁ, נָדִין אוֹתָן שֶׁהֵן עוֹלוֹת; וְאִם נִמְצָא חֲתִיכוֹת, חַטָּאוֹת, וְהַנִּמְצָא בִּירוּשָׁלַיִם, שְׁלָמִים; וְנַפְקָא מִנָּהּ לְעִנְיָן שֶׁאִם עָבַר אֶחָד וְאָכַל מֵהֶן, מֵבִיא עַל כָּל אֶחָד כַּפָּרָתוֹ כְּפִי חֲזָקָה זוֹ. וְעַל הַכֹּל אָמְרוּ זִכְרוֹנָם לִבְרָכָה: תְּעֻבַּר צוּרָתָן וְיֵצְאוּ לְבֵית הַשְּׂרֵפָה, שֶׁמָּא נוֹתָר הוּא.

וְאֵין שׂוֹרְפִין אֶת הַנּוֹתָר אֶלָּא בַּיּוֹם, שֶׁנֶּאֱמַר: בַּיּוֹם הַשְּׁלִישִׁי בָּאֵשׁ יִשָּׂרֵף; וְאַף־עַל־פִּי שֶׁהַשְּׁלָמִים אֲסוּרִין בַּאֲכִילָה מִתְּחִלַּת לֵיל שְׁלִישִׁי אֵין שׂוֹרְפִין אוֹתָם אֶלָּא בַּיּוֹם; וְיֶתֶר פְּרָטֶיהָ, מְבֹאָרִים בִּפְסָחִים וְסוֹף תְּמוּרָה.

וְנוֹהֶגֶת בִּזְמַן הַבַּיִת בְּזִכְרֵי כְהֻנָּה, כִּי לָהֶם הָעֲבוֹדָה. וְכֹהֵן שֶׁעָבַר וְלֹא שָׂרַף

2. In Sifra on Leviticus 7:18, TB Z'vaḥim 28a, etc. the Sages explain that the verse applies to one who thinks (intends) to eat it on the third day, who thus makes it *piggul*, although the verse speaks of its actually being eaten the third day, when it would be *nothar*. (The two paragraphs are based on ShM positive precept §91.)

3. Hence human beings should similarly not hoard food unduly, but should trust in Divine providence.

4. TB P'saḥim 82b.

5. I.e. it should be left until it is certainly *nothar*; otherwise one might be burning sacred meat without cause, which is a sinful treatment of it; MT *hilchoth p'sulé ha-mukdashin* xix 2.

6. Since an *'olah* was cut into whole limbs and parts (§115).

7. For in the Temple court only the *ḥattath* and *'asham* (guilt-offering) were eaten, and the law for both is identical.

8. As most meat eaten in Jerusalem was of *sh'lamim*; Mishnah, Sh'kalim vii 3.

9. In regard to burning them, it would make no difference of what they were. For eating a whole limb found in the Temple forecourt, assumed to be from an *'olah*, an *'asham me'ilah* (guilt-offering for breach of holiness) is brought. For eating pieces found there, assumed to be from a *ḥattath*, an *'olah* is brought. For eating pieces found in Jerusalem, assumed to be from *sh'lamim*, there is no penalty, unless by chance they were

 about burning that, since we find Scripture expressing the concept of *piggul* as *nothar* (Leviticus 7:18, 19:7).[2]

At the root of the precept lies the reason that it is in the nature of all meat to spoil on being left over, and to develop a stench. Hence, for the distinction of the concept of the offering—as we have stated above (§102)—we were commanded to burn it at once and so remove it from the world, that no man should be disgusted by it and its smell. Now, ultimate utter destruction is by fire, more so than by dividing into very small pieces and scattering in the wind or any other means. Then too, apart from that, there is an allusion in the matter to trust in the Eternal Lord, blessed is He: that a man should not restrict himself from his food in order to put it away until the next day—since he sees that God ordained to utterly destroy sacred meat once its time has passed; He did not wish any creature to have any benefit from it after that—neither a human being nor an animal.[3]

Among the laws of the precept, there is what our Sages of blessed memory said,[4] that included in the rule for *piggul* and *nothar*, that they should be burned, are all disqualified sacred offerings—that they should all be burned likewise. If an offering became unacceptable or *piggul* for certain, it was to be burned at once; if there was doubt, its original form [state] should be allowed to pass,[5] and then it was to be burned. If any flesh was found in the Temple forecourt [as whole] limbs, it was from *'olah* (burnt) offerings, which means that we judge them to be of *'olah* offerings;[6] if they were found in pieces, they would be of *ḥattath* (sin) offerings;[7] and what was found in Jerusalem would be *sh'lamim* (of peace-offerings).[8] It makes a practical difference in this regard: that if someone sinned and ate some of them, he would bring atonement for each according to this rule.[9] But about all, our Sages of blessed memory said: Let their form [state] pass by, and let them go out to the place of burning, for perhaps they were *nothar*.[10]

Sacred meat left past its time was to be burned only in the daytime, for it is stated, *on the third* day *shall be burned with fire* (Leviticus 7:17). Thus, even though *sh'lamim* are forbidden to be eaten from the start of the second night, they might be burned only during the day. The rest of its details are elucidated in the Talmud tractate *P'saḥim* and toward the end of *T'murah*.

It is in force when the Temple exists, for the male *kohanim*, as the Temple service is for them to carry out. If a *kohen* sinned and did

הַנּוֹתָר, בִּטֵּל עֲשֵׂה, וְעָבַר עַל לָאו דְּ"לֹא תוֹתִירוּ", אֲבָל אֵין לוֹקִין עַל לָאו זֶה, לְפִי שֶׁאֵין בּוֹ מַעֲשֶׂה.

[שֶׁלֹּא לֶאֱכֹל פִּגּוּל]

קמד שֶׁלֹּא לֶאֱכֹל הַפִּגּוּל; וּפִגּוּל הוּא קָרְבָּן שֶׁחָשַׁב עָלָיו הַכֹּהֵן הַמַּקְרִיב מַחֲשֶׁבֶת פְּסוּל בִּשְׁעַת זְבִיחָה אוֹ הַקְרָבָה; וּפְסוּל הַמַּחֲשָׁבָה הוּא, כְּגוֹן שֶׁהִסְכִּים בְּדַעְתּוֹ, בְּעֵת הַזְּבִיחָה אוֹ בְּעֵת הַהַקְרָבָה, שֶׁיֹּאכַל מֵאוֹתוֹ קָרְבָּן אַחַר זְמַן הַמְּגֻבָּל לַאֲכִילָתָן, אוֹ יַקְטִיר מִמֶּנּוּ מַה שֶּׁטָּעוּן הַקְטָרָה אַחַר זְמַן הַמְּגֻבָּל לְהַקְטָרָה, שֶׁאֲכִילַת הַמִּזְבֵּחַ וַאֲכִילַת אָדָם הַכֹּל נִשְׁמָע בִּלְשׁוֹן אֲכִילָה; וּבֵאֵר הַכָּתוּב שֶׁהָאוֹכֵל מִמֶּנּוּ שֶׁיִּשָּׂא עָוֹן, שֶׁנֶּאֱמַר: וְאִם הֵאָכֹל יֵאָכֵל וְגוֹמֵר, וְהַנֶּפֶשׁ הָאֹכֶלֶת מִמֶּנּוּ עֲוֹנָהּ תִּשָּׂא, וּנְשִׂיאוּת עָוֹן בְּכָאן הוּא כָּרֵת, כְּמוֹ שֶׁנִּלְמַד בַּגְּמָרָא בִּגְזֵרָה שָׁוָה.

וְאוּלָם אַזְהָרָתוֹ, כְּלוֹמַר הַלָּאו הַמְפֹרָשׁ עַל זֶה מִלְּבַד הָעֹנֶשׁ שֶׁנִּזְכָּר בְּכָאן, הוּא מַה שֶּׁכָּתוּב בְּמִלּוּאִים: לֹא יֵאָכֵל כִּי קֹדֶשׁ הוּא, וְאָמְרוּ זִכְרוֹנָם לִבְרָכָה שֶׁאוֹתוֹ הַכָּתוּב כּוֹלֵל בְּאַזְהָרָה כָּל מַה שֶּׁנִּפְסָד מִן הַקֳּדָשִׁים, וְאֵין רָאוּי לְאָכְלוֹ כְּמוֹ הַנּוֹתָר וְהַפִּגּוּל. וּכְמוֹ כֵן אָמְרוּ זִכְרוֹנָם לִבְרָכָה שֶׁנִּכְלְלוּ בְּאַזְהָרַת "לֹא תֹאכַל כָּל תּוֹעֵבָה", שֶׁדָּרְשׁוּ: כָּל שֶׁתִּעַבְתִּי לְךָ הוּא בְּבַל תֹּאכַל; וְכֵיוָן שֶׁכֵּן נֹאמַר שֶׁהָאֶחָד לְתוֹסֶפֶת לָאוִין, וְזֶה הַפָּסוּק שֶׁבְּכָאן יְדַבֵּר בְּעֹנֶשׁ הָאוֹכְלוֹ, שֶׁכֵּן בָּא לָנוּ הַפֵּרוּשׁ עָלָיו.

וְזֶה שֶׁאָמַר "וְאִם הֵאָכֹל יֵאָכֵל ... בַּיּוֹם הַשְּׁלִישִׁי", כְּלוֹמַר שֶׁחָשַׁב עָלָיו לְאָכְלוֹ

nothar: hence an *'olah* is brought, with the stipulation that if the eaten pieces were *nothar*, the *'olah* should atone; otherwise the *'olah* should be a good-will offering (MY).

10. MT *hilchoth p'sulé ha-mukdashin* xix 4.

§144 1. This is explained in the fourth paragraph. From the beginning to here is based on ShM negative precept §132. It should be noted that "offered up" in line 1 and line 3 of the paragraph has the specific technical meaning of the sprinkling of the blood on the altar.

2. TB P'saḥim 24a, etc.

3. TB 'Avodah Zarah 66a, Ḥullin 114b.

4. I.e. so that if a person commits the sin, he violates two negative precepts.

not burn *nothar* (leftover sacred meat), he would thus disobey a positive precept, and he would violate the negative precept, *you shall not let remain* (Leviticus 22:30). However, whiplashes are not given over this negative precept, since it involves no physical action [for its violation].

[THE PROHIBITION AGAINST PIGGUL, "VILE MEAT"]

144 not to eat *piggul*; *piggul* is an offering about which the *kohen* who attended to it entertained a disqualifying thought while it was ritually slain or offered up. It would be a disqualifying thought if, for example, he decided in his mind at the time of the ritual slaying, or while it was being offered up, that he would eat of that offering after the time allotted for eating it, or that what had to be burned of it, he would burn after the time allotted for burning it. For what the altar consumed [by fire] and what man consumes by eating would both be signified by the expression of "eating." And the Writ makes it clear that whoever ate of this would bear guilt for a sin: for it is stated, *And if any . . . shall be at all eaten . . . the soul that eats of it shall bear its iniquity* (Leviticus 7:18); and the bearing of iniquity here denotes *karéth* [Divine severance of existence], as we learn in the Talmud through a *g'zérah shavah* [identity of terms in two verses].[1]

However that may be, its admonition, i.e. the explicit forbiddance about it, apart from the punishment mentioned here, is a verse written in the Scriptural section on the initiation of the *kohanim*: *it shall not be eaten, because it is holy* (Exodus 29:34). And the Sages of blessed memory said[2] that this verse comprises an admonition about anything of the holy sacrifices that became disqualified and was not to be eaten, such as *nothar* (leftover meat) and *piggul*. Likewise, the Sages of blessed memory taught that these are included in the injunction, *You shall not eat any abominable thing* (Deuteronomy 14:3); for they interpreted: "Whatever I have declared abominable for you, is subject to the injunction, *You shall not eat*."[3] This being the case, we say that one [of these two verses] is for an additional prohibition,[4] while this [our original] verse speaks of the punishment of one who eats it, since such is the interpretation that has come down to us [in the Oral Tradition].

Now, when Scripture states, *And if any . . . shall be eaten at all on the third day* (Leviticus 7:18), it means that someone thought

בַּיּוֹם הַשְּׁלִישִׁי, שֶׁכֵּן דָּרְשׁוּ זִכְרוֹנָם לִבְרָכָה בָּזֶה הַפָּסוּק: וְאִם הֵאָכֹל יֵאָכֵל וְגוֹמֵר, פִּגּוּל הוּא, כֹּף אָזְנְךָ לִשְׁמֹעַ, בִּמְחַשֵּׁב עַל זִבְחוֹ שֶׁיֹּאכַל מִמֶּנּוּ בַּיּוֹם הַשְּׁלִישִׁי הַכָּתוּב מְדַבֵּר, שֶׁהוּא נִפְסָד בְּזֹאת הַמַּחֲשָׁבָה. וְהָאוֹכְלוֹ חַיָּב כָּרֵת, שֶׁנֶּאֱמַר בּוֹ: וְהַנֶּפֶשׁ הָאוֹכֶלֶת מִמֶּנּוּ עֲוֹנָהּ תִּשָּׂא, וְנֶאֱמַר בַּנּוֹתָר: וְאוֹכְלָיו עֲוֹנוֹ יִשָּׂא כִּי אֶת קֹדֶשׁ יי חִלֵּל וְנִכְרְתָה, וְגָמְרִינַן לֵיהּ בִּכְרֵתוֹת בִּגְזֵרָה שָׁוָה, שֶׁאָמְרוּ שָׁם: אַל תְּהִי גְזֵרָה שָׁוָה קַלָּה בְעֵינֶיךָ, שֶׁהֲרֵי פִּגּוּל אֶחָד מִגּוּפֵי תוֹרָה וְלֹא לִמְדוֹ הַכָּתוּב אֶלָּא בִגְזֵרָה שָׁוָה, דְּיָלִיף עָוֹן עָוֹן מִנּוֹתָר, מַה לְּהַלָּן כָּרֵת אַף כָּאן כָּרֵת.

מִשָּׁרְשֵׁי מִצְוָה זוֹ, הַיְסוֹד אֲשֶׁר בָּנִינוּ תְחִלָּה, שֶׁאָמַרְנוּ כִּי עִנְיְנֵי הַקָּרְבָּן לְהַכְשֵׁר מַחֲשָׁבוֹת בְּנֵי אִישׁ וּלְצַיֵּר בְּנַפְשָׁם מִתּוֹךְ הַפְּעֻלָּה שֶׁבֵּין יָדָם, רֹעַ הַחֵטְא וְטוּב דַּרְכֵי הַיֹּשֶׁר; עַל־כֵּן מֵהְיוֹת עִקַּר סִבָּתוֹ עַל דְּבַר הַמַּחֲשָׁבוֹת, הָיָה רָאוּי לְהִפָּסֵל בְּמַחֲשֶׁבֶת הַנְּטוּיָה בּוֹ מִן הַיֹּשֶׁר בְּכָל מַעֲשָׂיו. וְזֶה דָּבָר בָּרוּר קָרוֹב אֶל הַשֵּׂכֶל לַמּוֹדֶה עַל הָאֱמֶת.

מִדִּינֵי הַמִּצְוָה, מַה שֶּׁאָמְרוּ זִכְרוֹנָם לִבְרָכָה שֶׁאֵין חִיּוּב כָּרֵת אֶלָּא לָאוֹכֵל מִן הַקָּרְבָּן מִן הַחֵלֶק שֶׁיֵּשׁ בּוֹ לָאָדָם אוֹ לַמִּזְבֵּחַ מִמֶּנּוּ, אֲבָל מִן הַחֵלֶק מִמֶּנּוּ שֶׁמַּתִּיר הַקָּרְבָּן אֵין חַיָּבִין עָלָיו כָּרֵת מִשּׁוּם פִּגּוּל. כֵּיצַד, הָאוֹכֵל כַּזַּיִת מִן הַדָּם מִקָּרְבָּן שֶׁנִּתְפַּגֵּל, אֵין חַיָּב עָלָיו כָּרֵת מִשּׁוּם פִּגּוּל, שֶׁהֲרֵי הַדָּם הַחֵלֶק הַמַּתִּיר הַקָּרְבָּן הוּא, שֶׁאַחַר זְרִיקַת הַדָּם, הָאֵמוּרִין מֻתָּרִין לִקָּרֵב וְלֹא קֹדֶם לָכֵן; וּמִכָּל־מָקוֹם, אַף־עַל־פִּי שֶׁאֵין בּוֹ כָּרֵת, לוֹקִין עָלָיו; אֲבָל הָאוֹכֵל כַּזַּיִת מִן בְּשַׂר הַקָּרְבָּן אוֹ אֲפִלּוּ מִן הָאֵמוּרִין, חַיָּב כָּרֵת מִשּׁוּם פִּגּוּל, שֶׁהַדָּם הוּא הַמַּתִּיר הָאֵמוּרִין לַמִּזְבֵּחַ, וְאַחַר

5. TB Z'vaḥim 29a.

6. I.e. the phrase, "shall bear his iniquity."

7. TB Z'vaḥim 43a.

8. As for eating any part of a holy sacrifice that became disqualified; MT *hilchoth p'sulé ha-mukdashin* xviii 7.

9. TB Z'vaḥim 13b.

[planned] about it, to eat it on the third day. For so the Sages of blessed memory interpreted this verse:[5] "*And if any . . . shall be eaten at all . . . it shall be* piggul, *an abhorred thing* (*ibid.*)—bend your ear to hear: the verse speaks of one who thinks [has the intention] about his sacrifice that he will eat of it on the third day"—for it becomes "spoiled" [unacceptable] by this thought, and anyone who eats it incurs *karéth* [Divine severance of existence]; as it is stated about it, *the soul that eats of it shall bear its iniquity* (*ibid.*); and it is stated about *nothar, but every one who eats it shall bear his iniquity, because he has profaned a holy thing of the Lord; and that soul shall be cut off* (Leviticus 19:8). Thus we learn this in the tractate *K'rithoth* (5a) by a *g'zérah shavah* [from identical expressions in the two verses]; because it was said there, "Let a *g'zérah shavah* not be a trival matter in your eyes: for here *piggul* is one of the main rules in the Torah, and Scripture teaches about it only by a *g'zérah shavah*"—since we learn it from *nothar* by the occurrence of 'iniquity'[6] in both verses: "just as there the punishment is *karéth*, so is the punishment *karéth* here."

At the root of this precept lies the fundamental principle that we established at the beginning, when we said that the purpose of an offering was to make people's thoughts worthy and to form a conception in their soul, out of the activity of their hand, of the evil of sin and the goodness of upright, honest ways. Therefore, since its main reason concerns the thoughts, it is right that it should become disqualified by a thought about it that swerves from the upright, honest path in regard to any of its [required] tasks. This is something clear, easily understood by anyone who admits to the truth.

Among the laws of the precept, there is what the Sages of blessed memory said, that there is a punishment of *karéth* only for one who ate of the offering some of the part that a man or the altar was to receive; but if it was of that part which would make the offering permissible, no punishment of *karéth* would be incurred on account of *piggul*.[7] Thus, if someone ate an olive's amount of blood from an offering that turned into *piggul*, he is not punishable by *karéth* on account of *piggul*: for here the blood is the part which makes the offering permissible, since after the blood is sprinkled, it is permissible to offer up the *'émurim* [the parts for burning on the altar], but not before. However, although there is no *karéth* for it, whiplashes are given for it.[8] But if someone ate an olive's amount of the flesh of the offering, or even of the *'émurim*, he would be punishable by *karéth* on account of *piggul*:[9] for the blood

מַתִּיר רִאשׁוֹן אָנוּ הוֹלְכִין בְּדִין זֶה, לְחַיֵּב הָאוֹכֵל בְּכָל הַשְּׁאָר, וּלְפִיכָךְ חַיָּב הָאוֹכֵל אַף מִן הָאֵמוּרִין, וְאַף־עַל־פִּי שֶׁהֵן גַּם־כֵּן מַתִּירִין הַבָּשָׂר לָאָדָם אֵין בְּכָךְ כְּלוּם, שֶׁאַחַר הַדָּם שֶׁהוּא מַתִּיר רִאשׁוֹן אָנוּ הוֹלְכִים, כְּמוֹ שֶׁאָמַרְנוּ.

וְכֵן מִנְחָה שֶׁנִּתְפַּגְּלָה, הָאוֹכֵל כַּזַּיִת מִשְּׁיָרֶיהָ חַיָּב מִשּׁוּם פִּגּוּל; אֲבָל הָאוֹכֵל כַּזַּיִת מִן הַקֹּמֶץ שֶׁלָּהּ אוֹ מִן הַלְּבוֹנָה, שֶׁהֵן הַמַּתִּירִין, אֵין חַיָּבִין עָלָיו כָּרֵת, וּמִכָּל־מָקוֹם לוֹקֶה עֲלֵיהֶן, כְּמוֹ שֶׁאָמַרְנוּ.

וְאֵלּוּ הֵן הַדְּבָרִים שֶׁאֵין חַיָּבִין עֲלֵיהֶן מִשּׁוּם פִּגּוּל לְעוֹלָם: הַקֹּמֶץ וְהַלְּבוֹנָה וְהַדָּם, כְּמוֹ שֶׁאָמַרְנוּ; וְהַיַּיִן וּמְנָחוֹת הַנִּשְׂרָפוֹת כֻּלָּן, שֶׁהֲרֵי אֵין בָּהֶן קֹמֶץ לְהַתִּירָן, וְכָל שֶׁאֵין לוֹ מַתִּירִין חוּץ מִמֶּנּוּ אֵין חַיָּבִין מִשּׁוּם פִּגּוּל עָלָיו; וְלֹג שֶׁמֶן שֶׁל מְצֹרָע גַּם־כֵּן אֵין חַיָּבִין עָלָיו. וְאִם תֹּאמַר וַהֲלֹא דַּם הָאָשָׁם מַתִּירוֹ, הַתְּשׁוּבָה שֶׁאֵינוֹ תָלוּי בּוֹ, שֶׁהֲרֵי אָדָם מֵבִיא אֲשָׁמוֹ הַיּוֹם וְלֹג אַחַר כַּמָּה יָמִים.

וְכֵן מֵעִנְיַן הַמִּצְוָה מַה שֶּׁאָמְרוּ גַּם־כֵּן שֶׁהַמַּקְרִיב הַמְחַשֵּׁב מַחֲשֶׁבֶת פִּגּוּל עוֹבֵר בְּלָאו, שֶׁנֶּאֱמַר: לֹא יֵחָשֵׁב לוֹ, וּמִפִּי הַשְּׁמוּעָה לָמַדְנוּ שֶׁבִּכְלַל זֶה אַזְהָרָה לַמַּקְרִיב שֶׁלֹּא יְחַשֵּׁב מַחֲשֶׁבֶת פִּגּוּל; אֲבָל מִכָּל־מָקוֹם אֵינוֹ נֶחֱשָׁב מֵחֶשְׁבּוֹן שס"ה לָאוִין, לְפִי שֶׁהוּא כְּעֵין סְנִיפִין לְלָאו אַחֵר שֶׁהוּא נֶחֱשָׁב בְּלָאוִין; וְהוּא מַה שֶּׁכָּתוּב בְּסֵדֶר "אֱמֹר אֶל הַכֹּהֲנִים": כָּל מוּם לֹא יִהְיֶה בּוֹ, וְדָרְשׁוּ זִכְרוֹנָם לִבְרָכָה מִשָּׁם, לָאו לְמֵטִיל מוּם בְּקָדָשִׁים, וּכְמוֹ שֶׁנִּכְתֹּב בְּעֶזְרַת הַשֵּׁם; וְזֶה הָעִנְיָן גַּם־כֵּן שֶׁל מְחַשֵּׁב

10. See above, § 134.
11. Leviticus 14:10.
12. TB M'naḥoth 15b.
13. TB Z'vaḥim 29b.
14. TB B'choroth 33b.

permits the *'émurim* to [go up on] the altar, and after the first cause of permission [that makes the offering permissible] we apply this law, to impose punishment on one who eats of the rest. For this reason, if a person ate even of the *'émurim*, he would be guilty. Even though they likewise make the flesh permissible to human beings, this is of no matter, since we apply the rule in regard to the first cause of permission, as we have stated.

So too, if a *minḥah* (meal-offering) became *piggul* [abhorrent, on account of a disqualifying thought], if someone then ate an olive's amount from its remainder,[10] he would be punishable on account of *piggul*. But if he ate an olive's amount of its handful or of the frankincense [that were both to be burned on the altar], which are what would make it permissible, there would be no penalty of *karéth* for it. However, whiplashes would be given for it, as we stated.

Now, these are the things for which there would never be any punishment on account of *piggul*: the handful [of the *minḥah*], the frankincense, and the blood, as we said; the wine [of libations], and meal-offerings that were entirely burned, since they had no handful taken to make them permissible—and whatever has nothing to make it permissible apart from itself, there can be no guilt over it on account of *piggul*; likewise, over a *m'tzora*'s *log* of oil[11] there can be no punishment. You might ask, though, "But surely the blood of the *'asham* (guilt-offering) made it permissible?" The answer is that it did not depend on that; for you see, a man could bring his *'asham* today and the *log* [of oil] several days later.[12]

In the subject-matter of the precept there is, likewise, what the Sages said further, that if one brought an offering and entertained a thought of *piggul*, he would violate a negative precept: for it is stated, *lo yéḥashév lo*, "nor shall it be accounted to him" (Leviticus 7:18); and in the Oral Tradition we learned that in this there is implicit an admonition to a man who brings an offering that [*lo yaḥashov lo*], he should not entertain a thought of *piggul* [that makes his offering *piggul*].[13] But in any event, it is not counted in the list of the 365 negative precepts, because it is a sort of corollary to another prohibition, which *is* counted among the negative precepts. That is the one written in *sidrah 'emor, there shall be no blemish in it* (Leviticus 22:21); our Sages of blessed memory interpreted this[14] as a negative precept applying to one who blemishes (injures, disfigures) an animal consecrated for an offering—as we will write (§287) with the Eternal

פְּסוּל כְּעֵין הַמֵּטִיל מוּם הוּא נֶחֱשָׁב, וּלְפִיכָךְ לֹא חֲשַׁבְנוּהוּ מִן הַחֶשְׁבּוֹן; וּמִכָּל־מָקוֹם אֵינוֹ לוֹקֶה עַל זֶה, לְפִי שֶׁאֵין בּוֹ מַעֲשֶׂה אֶלָּא מַחֲשָׁבָה בִּלְבָד.

וְיֶתֶר דִּינֵי הַמַּחֲשָׁבוֹת, אֵי זוֹ מַחֲשָׁבָה פּוֹסֶלֶת, כְּגוֹן מַחֲשֶׁבֶת שִׁנּוּי הַשֵּׁם וּמַחֲשֶׁבֶת מָקוֹם וּמַחֲשֶׁבֶת זְמַן; וּבְאֵי זֶה קָרְבָּן וּבְאֵי זוֹ עֲבוֹדָה, כְּגוֹן שְׁחִיטָה זְרִיקָה קַבָּלָה הוֹלָכָה, וְכָל פְּרָטֵי דִּינֵי הַפִּגּוּל וְגַם נוֹתָר הַדּוֹמֶה לוֹ, מְבֹאָרִים בִּמְקוֹמוֹת רַבִּים מִסֵּדֶר קָדָשִׁים.

וְנוֹהֵג אִסּוּר אֲכִילַת הַפִּגּוּל בִּזְמַן הַבַּיִת בִּזְכָרִים וּנְקֵבוֹת, אֲפִלּוּ יִשְׂרְאֵלִים, שֶׁדֶּרֶךְ כְּלָל אֲסָרַתּוּ הַתּוֹרָה לַכֹּל, בֵּין כֹּהֵן בֵּין יִשְׂרָאֵל. וְעוֹבֵר עָלֶיהָ וְאָכַל כַּזַּיִת מִמֶּנּוּ בְּמֵזִיד, חַיָּב כָּרֵת; בְּשׁוֹגֵג מֵבִיא חַטָּאת קְבוּעָה. וּכְבָר פֵּרַשְׁנוּ פַּעֲמַיִם שֶׁקָּרְבָּן שֶׁאֵינוֹ עוֹלֶה וְיוֹרֵד לְפִי עֲנִיּוּת וְעֹשֶׁר נִקְרָא קָבוּעַ.

[שֶׁלֹּא לֶאֱכֹל בְּשַׂר קָדָשִׁים שֶׁנִּטְמָא]

קמה

שֶׁלֹּא לֶאֱכֹל בְּשַׂר הַקֳּדָשִׁים שֶׁנִּטְמָא, שֶׁנֶּאֱמַר: וְהַבָּשָׂר אֲשֶׁר יִגַּע בְּכָל טָמֵא לֹא יֵאָכֵל; וְהוּא הַדִּין אָדָם טָמֵא שֶׁאָסוּר לֶאֱכֹל בָּשָׂר טָהוֹר, וּכְמוֹ שֶׁנִּכְתֹּב בְּלָאו בִּפְנֵי עַצְמוֹ בְּעֶזְרַת הַשֵּׁם. וּבְפֶרֶק שֵׁנִי דִּפְסָחִים אָמְרוּ: טֻמְאַת הַגּוּף בְּכָרֵת, טֻמְאַת בָּשָׂר בְּלָאו.

מִשָּׁרְשֵׁי מִצְוָה זוֹ, מַה שֶּׁכָּתַבְנוּ לְמַעְלָה, שֶׁנִּצְטַוִּינוּ לְהַגְדִּיל עִנְיְנֵי הַקָּרְבָּן בְּכָל

15. E.g. to offer up as *sh'lamim* an animal consecrated as a *ḥattath*.
16. E.g. to eat the offering *where* it was forbidden.
17. E.g. to eat the offering *when* it was forbidden.
18. In §§ 108 and 121.

§145

1. If he ate sacred meat.
2. So that a transgressor who eats it is punished by whiplashes.

Lord's help. Well, this matter likewise, of someone who entertains a disqualifying thought, is considered akin to causing a blemish (a disfiguring injury); and it was therefore not counted in the reckoning. But in any case, one is not given whiplashes for it, as it involves no physical action [for its violation], but merely thought.

As to the remaining laws about thoughts [intentions]—which intent disqualifies [an offering], such as a thought about a change of its name,[15] a thought about the place,[16] or a thought about the time;[17] in which offering, and in which task—for example, the ritual slaying, sprinkling the blood, collecting it, taking it [to the altar]; and all the details of the laws of *piggul*, as well as *nothar*, which is similar to it [in law]—these are explained in many places in the order of *Kodashim* [in the Talmud].

The ban on eating *piggul* is in effect when the Temple is extant, for both man and woman, even Israelites (non-*kohanim*): for the Torah prohibited it as a general rule for everyone, both *kohen* and Israelite. If a person violated it and ate the amount of an olive from it—if it was deliberate, he would be punishable by *karéth* [Divine severance of existence]; if it was inadvertent, he would bring a standard unvarying *ḥattath* (sin-offering). We have previously explained twice[18] that an offering which is not to be of greater or lesser value according to [a person's] poverty or wealth is called standard ("fixed"), unvarying.

[THAT THE FLESH OF DEFILED HOLY OFFERINGS IS NOT TO BE EATEN]

145 not to eat the flesh of a holy offering that became defiled: for it is stated, *And the flesh that touches any unclean thing shall not be eaten* (Leviticus 7:19); so is it the law that a ritually unclean person is forbidden to eat ritually clean meat, as we will write in a separate precept (§167), with the Eternal Lord's help. Now, in the second chapter of the Talmud tractate *P'saḥim* (24b) it was taught: ritual uncleanness of a person's body incurs *karéth* [Divine severance of existence];[1] ritual uncleanness of meat [imposes a ban] by a negative precept.[2]

At the root of this precept lies what we wrote above, that we were commanded to make everything about an offering distinguished in every respect; and it is certainly a distinction for it not to eat it except in

עִנְיָן, וּבְוַדַּאי מִמַּעֲלָתוֹ שֶׁלֹּא לְאָכְלוֹ כִּי־אִם בְּטָהֳרָה וּבְגוּף נָקִי; וּבִדְבַר הַגְּדֻלָּתוֹ מַה תּוֹעֶלֶת לָנוּ בּוֹ כְּבָר כָּתַבְנוּ טַעֲמוֹ.

מִדִּינֵי הַמִּצְוָה, כְּגוֹן מַה שֶּׁאָמְרוּ זִכְרוֹנָם לִבְרָכָה שֶׁאָסוּר לְטַמֵּא הַקֳּדָשִׁים אוֹ לְסַבֵּב לָהֶם טֻמְאָה, אֲבָל הַמְטַמְּאָן אֵינוֹ לוֹקֶה, אֶלָּא טָהוֹר הָאוֹכְלָן טְמֵאִים הוּא שֶׁלּוֹקֶה, מִדִּכְתִיב: לֹא יֵאָכֵל. וְאַף־עַל־פִּי שֶׁכָּתוּב זֶה (במלואים) [בִּשְׁלָמִים], הוּא הַדִּין לִשְׁאָר הַקָּרְבָּנוֹת כֻּלָּן. וַאֲפִלּוּ הָאוֹכֵל כַּזַּיִת מִלְּבוֹנַת הַמִּנְחָה שֶׁנִּטְמֵאת אַחַר שֶׁנִּתְקַדְּשָׁה בִּכְלִי לוֹקֶה, שֶׁגַּם הִיא חֵלֶק מֵחֶלְקֵי הַקָּרְבָּן.

וְאֵין הַחִיּוּב אֶלָּא בְטֻמְאַת אַב הַטֻּמְאָה אוֹ וְלַד הַטֻּמְאָה שֶׁל תּוֹרָה, אֲבָל מִפְּנֵי טֻמְאָה שֶׁל דִּבְרֵיהֶם אֵינוֹ לוֹקֶה, אֲבָל מַכִּין אוֹתוֹ מַכַּת מַרְדּוּת. וְיֶתֶר רֵבֵי פְּרָטֶיהָ, בְּפֶרֶק שְׁלֹשָׁה־עָשָׂר מִזְּבָחִים.

וְנוֹהֶגֶת בִּזְמַן הַבַּיִת בִּזְכָרִים וּנְקֵבוֹת. וְעוֹבֵר עָלֶיהָ וְאָכַל כַּזַּיִת בְּמֵזִיד מִבְּשַׂר קֹדֶשׁ שֶׁנִּטְמָא, לוֹקֶה.

[מִצְוַת שְׂרֵפַת בְּשַׂר קֹדֶשׁ שֶׁנִּטְמָא]

קמו שֶׁנִּצְטַוִּינוּ לִשְׂרֹף קָדָשִׁים שֶׁנִּטְמְאוּ, שֶׁנֶּאֱמַר: וְהַבָּשָׂר אֲשֶׁר יִגַּע בְּכָל טָמֵא לֹא יֵאָכֵל בָּאֵשׁ יִשָּׂרֵף.

מִשָּׁרְשֵׁי הַמִּצְוָה, מַה שֶּׁכָּתַבְנוּ בְּנוֹתָר סָמוּךְ [סי׳ קמ״ג].

מִדִּינֵי הַמִּצְוָה, מַה שֶּׁאָמְרוּ זִכְרוֹנָם לִבְרָכָה שֶׁאִם נִטְמְאוּ בִּפְנִים שׂוֹרְפִין אוֹתָן בִּפְנִים, נִטְמְאוּ מִבַּחוּץ שׂוֹרְפִין אוֹתָן בַּחוּץ; וּבֵין שֶׁנִּטְמָא בְּאַב הַטֻּמְאָה אוֹ בִוְלַד הַטֻּמְאָה שׂוֹרְפִין אוֹתוֹ; וְנוֹתָר שֶׁל קָדָשִׁים קַלִּים שׂוֹרְפִין אוֹתוֹ הַבְּעָלִים בְּבָתֵּיהֶן; וְכָל עַצְמוֹת הַקֳּדָשִׁים שֶׁאֵין בָּהֶן מֹחַ אֵינָן טְעוּנִין שְׂרֵפָה, חוּץ מֵעַצְמוֹת הַפֶּסַח.

3. TB Makkoth 14b; MT *hilchoth p'sulé ha-mukdashin* xviii 12.

4. TB P'saḥim 35a; MT *ibid.*

5. Literally, "defilement by a father of uncleanness or a child of uncleanness"; see §159.

6. See §12, note 4.

§146 1. Mishnah, Sh'kalim viii 7; MT *hilchoth p'sulé ha-mukdashin* xix 6.

2. See §145, note 4, which applies here.

3. TB P'saḥim 81b; MT *ibid.* 7.

4. Cf. TB P'saḥim 83a; see MH.

ritual purity and with a clean body. As to why there is benefit in giving it eminence, we have written the reason previously (§103).

Among the laws of the precept, there is, for example, what the Sages of blessed memory taught, that it is forbidden to defile holy offerings or to cause them ritual uncleanness, but a person who defiled them would not receive whiplashes; it is only a ritually clean person who ate them when they were defiled, who would be given lashes—since it is written, "shall not be eaten."[3] Now, although this is written about *sh'lamim* (peace-offerings), the law is the same for all other offerings. Even if someone ate an olive's amount of the frankincense of a *minḥah* (meal-offering) that was defiled after it was consecrated in a vessel, he would be given whiplashes: for this is also one of the various parts of an offering.[4]

Punishment is incurred only if the defilement was by a primary type of ritual uncleanness or a derivative kind[5] of uncleanness by Torah law; but on account of ritual defilement by a ruling of the Sages, a person is not given whiplashes, although he is given "punishment for disobedience."[6] The rest of its very many details are in chapter 13 of the Talmud tractate *Z'vaḥim*.

It is in force when the Temple exists, for both man and woman. If someone violated it and deliberately ate an olive's amount of sacred meat that had become defiled, he would receive whiplashes.

[THE PRECEPT OF BURNING HALLOWED FLESH THAT BECAME DEFILED]

146 that we were commanded to burn holy sacrifices that became defiled: for it is stated, *And the flesh that touches any unclean thing shall not be eaten; it shall be burned with fire* (Leviticus 7:19).

At the root of the precept lies what we wrote recently about *nothar* (leftover sacred meat; §143).

Among the laws of the precept, there is what the Sages of blessed memory said:[1] that if they became defiled within [the Temple forecourt] they would be burned within; if they became defiled outside [the Temple forecourt] they would be burned outside. Whether they were defiled by a primary kind of ritual uncleanness or a derivative kind,[2] they would be burned. As for *nothar* (leftover sacred meat) of offerings of lesser holiness, the owners would burn it in their houses.[3] All bones from holy sacrifices which contained no marrow did not require burning, except the bones of a Passover sacrifice.[4] And this

וְהָעִנְיָן הַזֶּה יְחַזֵּק קְצָת טַעֲנָתֵנוּ בְּהֶפְסֵד הַבָּשָׂר שֶׁאָמַרְנוּ, וְעַל־כֵּן הָעֲצָמוֹת, שֶׁאֵינָם בָּאִים לִידֵי הֶפְסֵד, אֵינָם טְעוּנִין שְׂרֵפָה — חוּץ מֵעַצְמוֹת הַפֶּסַח: לְפִי שֶׁהֵן בְּאַזְהָרַת "וְעֶצֶם לֹא תִשְׁבְּרוּ בוֹ", תִּשָּׁאֵר מֵהֶם בָּרֹב מְעַט בָּשָׂר עָלָיו מִפְּנֵי אֵימַת הַשְּׁבִירָה, וּלְפִיכָךְ אָמְרוּ עֲלֵיהֶם דֶּרֶךְ כְּלָל בְּכֻלָּן, שֶׁיִּהְיוּ טְעוּנִין שְׂרֵפָה.

וְאֵלּוּ הֵן הַנִּשְׂרָפִין: בְּשַׂר קֹדֶשׁ שֶׁנִּטְמָא אוֹ נוֹתָר, אוֹ קָרְבָּן שֶׁנִּפְסָל, וְכֵן הַמִּנְחָה שֶׁנִּטְמֵאת אוֹ נִפְסְלָה אוֹ נוֹתְרָה, וְאָשָׁם תָּלוּי שֶׁנּוֹדַע לוֹ לְבְעָלָיו שֶׁלֹּא חָטָא (אחר) [קֹדֶם] שֶׁנִּזְרַק דָּמָן, וְחַטַּאת הָעוֹף הַבָּאָה עַל הַסָּפֵק, וּשְׂעַר נָזִיר טָהוֹר, וְהָעָרְלָה וְכִלְאֵי הַכֶּרֶם; וְדָבָר שֶׁאֵין דַּרְכּוֹ לְהִשָּׂרֵף, כְּגוֹן מַשְׁקִין שֶׁל עָרְלָה וְכִלְאֵי הַכֶּרֶם, הֲרֵי אֵלּוּ יִשָּׁפְכוּ. וְאַגַּב גְּרָרָא נִכְתֹּב הַנִּקְבָּרִין, וְאֵלּוּ הֵן: קָדָשִׁים שֶׁמֵּתוּ, בֵּין קָדְשֵׁי מִזְבֵּחַ בֵּין קָדְשֵׁי בֶדֶק הַבַּיִת; וְקָדָשִׁים שֶׁהִפִּילוּ, יִקָּבֵר הַנֵּפֶל; הִפִּילָה שִׁלְיָא, תִּקָּבֵר; וְשׁוֹר הַנִּסְקָל וְעֶגְלָה עֲרוּפָה וְצִפֳּרֵי מְצֹרָע וּשְׂעַר נָזִיר טָמֵא וּפֶטֶר חֲמוֹר וּבָשָׂר בְּחָלָב וְחֻלִּין שֶׁנִּשְׁחֲטוּ בָעֲזָרָה; וְיֶתֶר פְּרָטֵי הַמִּצְוָה, מְבֹאָרִים בִּפְסָחִים וְסוֹף תְּמוּרָה.

וְנוֹהֶגֶת שְׂרֵפַת הַקָּדָשִׁים שֶׁנִּטְמְאוּ בִּזְמַן הַבַּיִת, בְּכֹהֲנִים וּבְיִשְׂרְאֵלִים. כֵּיצַד, הַקָּדָשִׁים שֶׁטְּעוּנִין שְׂרֵפָה בַּמִּקְדָּשׁ, שְׂרֵפָתָן מֻטֶּלֶת עַל הַכֹּהֲנִים; וְהַנִּשְׂרָפִין בְּכָל הָעִיר, כְּגוֹן קָדָשִׁים קַלִּים, הַבְּעָלִים שׂוֹרְפִין אֶת חֶלְקָם אִם נִטְמָא אוֹ נוֹתָר, בְּבָתֵּיהֶם. וְהָעוֹבֵר עָלֶיהָ וְלֹא שָׂרַף בָּשָׂר טָמֵא אוֹ נוֹתָר שֶׁהוּא בְיָדוֹ, בִּטֵּל עֲשֵׂה זֶה.

5. *Ibid.* 82b.

6. TB Sotah 22b.

7. Brought by a person who was in doubt if he had sinned (§128).

8. The standard text has "after," but it is clear from TB K'rithoth 23b and MT (note 12) that this must have its origin in a scribal error. Interestingly enough, though, in the Rome 1480 edition of MT (facsimile edition, Jerusalem 1955) this passage (see note 12) likewise reads "after." In MT *ibid.* iv 19, Rambam gives the laws for dealing with an *'asham talu-y* whose owner learned the truth about his possible guilt (a) before it was ritually slain; (b) after that, but before the blood was sprinkled; (c) after the sprinkling. It might be conjectured that here Rambam was correspondingly specific and wrote originally אחר שנשחט קודם שנזרק דמו "after it was ritually slain, before its blood was sprinkled," and a copyist later omitted two Hebrew words (*shenish-ḥat, kodem*), giving rise to the error in the MT of Rome 1480 and in this work.

9. E.g. if there was doubt whether a woman delivered a true infant or fetus in still-birth or miscarriage; TB T'murah 34a (see R. 'Ovadyah Bertinoro to Mishnah, T'murah vii 6).

10. TB T'murah 34a; see Numbers 6:18.

11. TB *ibid.*

12. The paragraph is taken almost verbatim from MT *hilchoth p'sulé ha-mukdashin* xix 10.

matter somewhat strengthens our point about the spoilage of meat [when it is left too long] that we made (§143): For this reason, the bones, which cannot become spoiled, do not require burning—except for the bones of the Passover sacrifice: As they are subject to the injunction, *you shall not break a bone of it* (Exodus 12:46), mostly a bit of meat would be left on them, for fear of breaking them. Therefore it was ruled about them all, generally, that they require burning.

Now, these are the items to be burned: sacred meat that became defiled or was allowed to remain too long, or an animal offering that became disqualified, unacceptable;[5] so too a *minḥah* (meal-offering) that became defiled or disqualified, or was left over too long;[6] an *'asham taluy* ("guilt-offering of suspension")[7] whose owner found out, before[8] its blood was sprinkled, that he had not sinned; a *ḥattath* (sin-offering) of fowl brought over a matter of doubt;[9] the hair of a ritually pure *nazir;*[10] fruit of a tree's first three years and mixed crops raised in a vineyard;[11] and whatever is not for burning, such as liquids [juice] from the fruit of a tree's first three years and mixed crops raised in a vineyard, should be spilled out.[12]

Along with this, in its wake, let us write those items that were to be buried.[13] These were: consecrated animals that died, whether they were consecrated for the altar [as offerings] or for the maintenance of the Temple;[14] if consecrated animals miscarried, the stillborn young were to be buried; [even] if one delivered [only] a placenta, it was to be buried; an ox stoned to death;[15] a beheaded calf,[16] the birds of a *m'tzora*,[17] the hair of a defiled *nazir*,[18] a firstborn donkey,[19] meat [boiled] in milk, and non-holy animals that were ritually slain in the Temple forecourt.[20]

The remaining details of the precept are explained in the tractate *P'saḥim* and toward the end of *T'murah*. The burning of holy offerings that were defiled is in force when the Temple is extant, for both *kohanim* and Israelites (non-*kohanim*). How so? If holy offerings required burning at the Temple, the duty to burn them lay upon the *kohanim;* and of those to be burned throughout the city [of Jerusalem], such as offerings of lesser holiness, the owners would burn their share, if it became defiled or *nothar* (left too long), in their houses. If someone violated it and did not burn meat that was defiled or *nothar*, which was in his possession, he would [thus] disobey a positive precept.

[שֶׁלֹּא נֹאכַל חֵלֶב]

קמז שֶׁלֹּא נֹאכַל חֵלֶב בְּהֵמָה טְהוֹרָה, שֶׁנֶּאֱמַר: כָּל חֵלֶב שׁוֹר וְכֶשֶׂב וָעֵז לֹא תֹאכֵלוּ.

כְּבָר כָּתַבְתִּי בְּאִסּוּר טְרֵפָה בְּסֵדֶר מִשְׁפָּטִים [סי׳ ע״ג], כִּי מִהְיוֹת הַגּוּף כְּלִי לַנֶּפֶשׁ וּבוֹ תִּפְעַל כֹּשֶׁר פְּעֻלּוֹתֶיהָ, וּלְפִי זַכּוּתוֹ וְטוּב מִזְגּוֹ יָבִין דֶּרֶךְ הַנֶּפֶשׁ הַחֲכָמָה הַנְּתוּנָה בּוֹ, וְיַאֲמִין לַעֲצָתָהּ וְיֵלֵךְ אַחֲרֶיהָ, מִפְּנֵי זֶה צָרִיךְ הָאָדָם לְהִשְׁתַּדֵּל עַל־כָּל־פָּנִים בְּהַיְשָׁרַת גּוּפוֹ לְהַעֲמִידוֹ עַל יָשְׁרוֹ וּבָרְיוֹ וְכֹחוֹ. וְיָדוּעַ הַדָּבָר וּמְפֻרְסָם בֵּין בְּנֵי־אָדָם כִּי לְפִי הַמַּאֲכָלִים יִתְפַּעֵל הַגּוּף בִּבְרִיאוּת אוֹ בְחֹלִי, כִּי בְּשַׂר הַגּוּף הַזֶּה נִפְסָד בְּכָל יוֹם וָיוֹם, וּלְפִי הַמְּזוֹנוֹת הַטּוֹבִים יִתְהַוֶּה בּוֹ בָּשָׂר בָּרִיא וָטוֹב, וּלְפִי רֹעַ הַמַּאֲכָל יִתְהַוֶּה בְּהֵפֶךְ. וְעַל־כֵּן הָיָה מֵחַסְדֵי הָאֵל הַגְּדוֹלִים עָלֵינוּ, אֲנַחְנוּ עַמּוֹ אֲשֶׁר בָּחַר, לְהַרְחִיק מִמֶּנּוּ כָּל מַאֲכָל מַזִּיק אֶל הַגּוּף וּמוֹלִיד בּוֹ לֵיחוֹת רָעוֹת. וְזֶה הַכְּלָל שֶׁיֵּשׁ לִי לְפִי הַפְּשָׁט בְּכָל אִסּוּר הַמַּאֲכָלוֹת, כְּמוֹ שֶׁאָמַרְנוּ לְמַעְלָה. וְיָדוּעַ כִּי הַחֵלֶב דָּבֵק וּמוֹלִיד לֵיחוֹת רָעוֹת.

מִדִּינֵי הַמִּצְוָה, כְּגוֹן מַה שֶּׁפֵּרְשׁוּ לָנוּ זִכְרוֹנָם לִבְרָכָה שֶׁאֵין אִסּוּר חֵלֶב אֶלָּא בְּשָׁלֹשׁ בְּהֵמוֹת שֶׁבַּכָּתוּב, שׁוֹר וְכֶשֶׂב וָעֵז, וְאוֹתָן שָׁלֹשׁ בֵּין כְּשֵׁרוֹת אוֹ טְרֵפוֹת וּנְבֵלוֹת חַיָּב עַל חֶלְבָּן; אֲבָל שְׁאָר מִינֵי בְהֵמָה וְחַיָּה, בֵּין טְמֵאָה בֵּין טְהוֹרָה, חֶלְבָּהּ כִּבְשָׂרָהּ. וְכֵן עֵבָר הַנִּקְרָא שָׁלִיל, הַנִּמְצָא בִמְעֵי שָׁלֹשׁ בְּהֵמוֹת הַנִּזְכָּרוֹת, אֵין בּוֹ גַּם־כֵּן אִסּוּר חֵלֶב, וּלְפִיכָךְ אָמְרוּ: הַשּׁוֹחֵט אֶת הַבְּהֵמָה וּמָצָא בָהּ שָׁלִיל כָּל חֶלְבּוֹ מֻתָּר, וַאֲפִלּוּ מְצָאוֹ חַי, וְאִם שָׁלְמוּ לוֹ חֳדָשָׁיו וּמְצָאוֹ חַי, אַף־עַל־פִּי שֶׁלֹּא הִפְרִיס עַל־גַּבֵּי קַרְקַע וְאֵינוֹ טָעוּן שְׁחִיטָה, חֶלְבּוֹ אָסוּר, וְחַיָּבִין עָלָיו כָּרֵת, וַהֲרֵי דִּינוֹ כִּשְׁאָר הַבְּהֵמוֹת בְּעִנְיַן חֶלְבּוֹ. וּלְפִיכָךְ יֵשׁ לָנוּ לְהוֹצִיא מִמֶּנּוּ כָּל הַחוּטִין וְכָל הַקְּרוּמוֹת הָאֲסוּרִין.

זֶהוּ דַּעַת הָרַמְבַּ״ם זִכְרוֹנוֹ לִבְרָכָה בְּשָׁלִיל שֶׁכָּלוּ לוֹ חֳדָשָׁיו, שֶׁיֵּשׁ חִיּוּב כָּרֵת

13. There is no law to bury these, but as all benefit or use from them was forbidden, they had to be buried to let no one come to grief through them.

14. TB T'murah 32a.

15. See e.g. Exodus 21:28–32.

16. See Deuteronomy 21:3–4.

17. Of the two brought when he was healed, the one ritually slain; see Leviticus 14:4–5.

18. See Numbers 6:9.

19. That was not redeemed; see Exodus 13:13, and above, §23.

20. TB T'murah 33b.

§147 1. TB K'rithoth 4b.

2. Because the ritual slaying of the mother animal makes it entirely permissible.

[NOT TO 'EAT ḤÉLEV, FORBIDDEN ANIMAL FAT]

147 that we should not eat the forbidden fat of a pure [permissible] animal: as it says, *You shall eat no fat of ox or sheep or goat* (Leviticus 7:23).

Earlier I wrote, about the ban on *t'réfah* (a fatally injured animal) in *sidrah mishpatim* (§73) that the body is a vessel, an instrument for the spirit, with which it achieves the fulfillment of its functions. According to its merit and the good nature of its temperament, it can understand through the soul the wisdom inherent in it, have faith in its counsel and follow its direction. For this reason, a person must strive at all costs that his body should be in order, to achieve its proper state of health and strength. It is a matter of common, widespread knowledge among people that according to the food the body is affected, for health for for illness. For the flesh of this body wears away every single day, and by virtue of good food, strong, good flesh is formed in it, while by virtue of bad food, the opposite is formed. It was therefore of the great kindness of God toward us, His people whom He chose, to remove from us every food that is injurious to the body and engenders in it evil humors. This is the rule to which I hold, according to the plain meaning, in every ban imposed on food, as we stated above. And it is known that the forbidden fat clings and engenders evil humors.

Among the laws of the precept there is, for instance, what the Sages of blessed memory explained to us:[1] that the ban on the fat applies to none but the three animals in the verse: ox, sheep and goat. With those three, whether they are kosher (fit to eat), *t'réfah* (fatally injured) or *n'vélah* (died of itself), their fat brings punishment; but of other kinds of animal, domestic or wild, unclean (forbidden species) or pure (permitted species), the fat is like the meat [in law]. Similarly, if a fetus, called *shalil*, is found in the innards of [any of] the three animals mentioned above, neither is there a ban on fat for it.[2] It was therefore taught: If one ritually slays an animal and finds an embryo in it, all its fat is permissible, even if he finds it living.[3] But if its months of gestation were completed and he found it alive, even if it did not stand with its feet on the ground [giving a sign of its viability] and it does not require ritual slaying,[2] its fat is forbidden,[4] and there is the punishment of *karéth* for it. Hence, its law is like that of other animals in regard to its fat; therefore we have to remove from it all forbidden sinews and membranes.

Now, this is the view of Rambam of blessed memory about an embryo whose months of gestation were completed for it[5]—that its fat entails a penalty of *karéth*. But most of the authorities[6] differ about

בְּחֶלְבּוֹ; אֲבָל רַבֵּי הַמְפָרְשִׁים חוֹלְקִים בָּזֶה וְאָמְרוּ דְחֶלְבּוֹ מֻתָּר, וְדִבְרֵי הַגְּמָרָא מַכְרִיעוֹת כְּמוֹתָן, דְּהָא אַשְׁכְּחָן רַבִּי מֵאִיר וְרַבִּי יְהוּדָה דִּפְלִיגֵי בְּחֶלְבּוֹ, וְרַבִּי יְהוּדָה, דְּקַיְימָא לָן כְּוָתֵיהּ, הוּא דְּשָׁרֵי לֵיהּ.

וְעוֹד לִמְדוּנוּ זִכְרוֹנָם לִבְרָכָה בְּדִין שָׁלִיל, שֶׁאַרְבָּעָה סִימָנִין אַכְשַׁר בֵּיהּ רַחֲמָנָא, כְּלוֹמַר שֶׁאִם נִטְרְפָה אִמּוֹ שׁוֹחֲטָהּ וְהַשָּׁלִיל מֻתָּר, דְּלָאו יֶרֶךְ אִמּוֹ הוּא. וּמַה שֶּׁאָמְרוּ שָׁם שֶׁאִם הִפְרִיס עַל־גַּבֵּי קַרְקַע דְּבָעֵי שְׁחִיטָה, מִפְּנֵי מַרְאִית הָעַיִן לְבַד הוּא דְּבָעֵינָן לְמִשְׁחֲטֵיהּ, וּלְפִיכָךְ לֹא מַפְסִיל בִּשְׁהִיָּה וּדְרָסָה וּשְׁאָר מִינֵי טְרֵפוֹת.

וּשְׁלֹשָׁה חֲלָבִים הֵם בִּבְהֵמָה שֶׁהֵן בְּחִיּוּב כָּרֵת, שֶׁעַל הַקֶּרֶב וְשֶׁעַל הַכְּלָיוֹת וְשֶׁעַל הַכְּסָלִים, וּפֵרוּשׁ שְׁלָשְׁתָּן בְּבֵאוּר רָחָב בִּמְקוֹמוֹ בַּגְּמָרָא; וּבִכְלָל אָמְרוּ זִכְרוֹנָם לִבְרָכָה בְּחֻלִּין: חֵלֶב שֶׁהַבָּשָׂר חוֹפֶה אוֹתוֹ מֻתָּר, שֶׁ"עַל הַכְּסָלִים" אָמַר רַחֲמָנָא וְלֹא שֶׁבְּתוֹךְ הַכְּסָלִים.

וְעוֹד יֵשׁ בִּבְהֵמָה מִלְּבַד אֵלּוּ הַשְּׁלֹשָׁה, חוּטִין וּקְרוּמוֹת שֶׁאֲסוּרִין מִשּׁוּם חֵלֶב. וְאָמְרוּ זִכְרוֹנָם לִבְרָכָה שֶׁהַטַּבָּחִים הַבְּקִיאִין בְּנִקּוּר הַחֵלֶב נֶאֱמָנִין עַל הַדָּבָר כָּל זְמַן שֶׁלֹּא יָצְאוּ מֵחֶזְקַת בְּקִיאוּתָן וְכַשְׁרוּתָן.

וְחֵלֶב הַלֵּב וְחֵלֶב הַמֵּעַיִם, וְהֵן הַדַּקִּין הַמְלֻפָּפִין, מֻתָּרִין וַהֲרֵי הוּא כְשׁוּמָן, חוּץ מֵרֹאשׁ הַמֵּעַיִם הַסָּמוּךְ לַקֵּיבָה שֶׁהוּא תְּחִלַּת בְּנֵי־מֵעַיִם, שֶׁצָּרִיךְ הָאָדָם לִגְרֹר הַחֵלֶב שֶׁעָלָיו, וּמִמֶּנּוּ אָמְרוּ זִכְרוֹנָם לִבְרָכָה בַּגְּמָרָא: רֵישׁ מֵעַיָּא בְּאַמְּתָא בָּעְיָא גְרִירָא. וְיֵשׁ מִן הַגְּאוֹנִים שֶׁאָמְרוּ שֶׁזֶּה הַמְּעִי הוּא הַמְּעִי שֶׁיּוֹצֵא בוֹ הָרְעִי, שֶׁהוּא סוֹף הַמֵּעַיִם. וְיֶתֶר פְּרָטֵי הַמִּצְוָה וְכָל עִנְיָנֶיהָ, מְבֹאָרִים בְּפֶרֶק ז׳ מֵחֻלִּין.

וְנוֹהֶגֶת בְּכָל מָקוֹם וּבְכָל זְמַן, בִּזְכָרִים וּבִנְקֵבוֹת. וְעוֹבֵר עָלֶיהָ וְאָכַל כַּזַּיִת חֵלֶב, בְּמֵזִיד לוֹקֶה, בְּשׁוֹגֵג מֵבִיא חַטָּאת קְבוּעָה.

3. The ritual slaying of the animal makes the embryo also permissible to be eaten, as the embryo is considered part of it; TB Ḥullin 74a.

4. Because as regards the fat, it is a complete creature in its own right.

5. MT *hilchoth ma'achaloth 'asuroth* vii 3 (see *Maggid Mishneh*).

6. R. Isaac 'Alfasi, R. 'Ashér, R. Jacob b. 'Ashér (*Tur*; see *Shulḥan 'Aruch Yoreh Dé'ah* § 64).

7. TB Ḥullin 92b.

8. *Ibid.* 75a.

9. I.e. through the gullet and windpipe of the dam (mother) or the gullet and windpipe of the embryo. These two organs are cut, entirely or mostly, in the ritual slaying (*sheḥittah*) that makes an animal permissible to eat. The embryo in this case is a completely formed young animal found alive, just before birth, in the womb.

10. I.e. it is not considered a part of the dam, like a thigh, but an animal in its own right, which can become allowed to be eaten by its own ritual slaying — even though the

this and rule that its fat is permissible. And the words of the Talmud weigh in their favor: for we find that R. Meir and R. Judah differ about its fat,[7] and R. Judah, whose ruling is the one we follow, is the one who permits it.

Our Sages of blessed memory taught us further[8] about an embryo, that the merciful God let it become permissible through four organs.[9] In other words, if its dam (mother animal) became *t'réfah* (fatally injured), one can ritually slay it [the embryo] and the embryo is permissible, as it is not the "thigh" of its dam.[10] As to what they said there, that if it trod on the ground,[11] it requires ritual slaying, it is only for the sake of appearances that ritual slaying is demanded.[12] And therefore it it does not become unfit to eat if the knife tarried or pressed down,[13] or through other ways of becoming *t'réfah*.

Now, there are three quantities of forbidden fat in a domestic beast which entail the penalty of *karéth:* the one on the entrails, the one on the kidneys, and the one on the loins. The explanation of all three, with ample clarification, [will be found] in its place in the Talmud.[14] As a rule, the Sages of blessed memory said in the tractate *Ḥullin* (93a): fat which meat covers is permissible: for the merciful God said "over the loins" (Leviticus 3:4), and not "within the loins."

Moreover, apart from these three, there are sinews and membranes in the domestic beast which are forbidden by reason of fat. Further, the Sages of blessed memory said[15] that butchers who are expert in cleaning out the forbidden fat are trusted about the matter, as long as they do not lose their status as experts and worthy, honest men of piety.

The fat of the heart and the fat of the bowels, which are the small convoluted bowels, are permissible, being like *shuman*, permissible fat—except for the "head of the bowels" near the maw (stomach), which is the beginning of the entrails: for a man needs to scrape away the fat that is on it. About this the Sages of blessed memory said in the Talmud:[14] the beginning of the bowels, for the length of a cubit, needs to be scraped. But there are some *ge'onim* who said that this means the entrails from which the waste matter is evacuated, i.e. the end of the bowels.[16] The remaining details of the precept and all its ramifications are explained in chapter 7 of the Talmud tractate *Ḥullin*.

It is in force in every place, at every time, for both man and woman. If a person transgresses it and eats an olive's amount of forbidden fat deliberately, he is given whiplashes; if it was inadvertent, he is to bring a standard unvarying *ḥattath*.

[שֶׁלֹּא נֹאכַל דַּם בְּהֵמָה חַיָּה וָעוֹף]

קמח שֶׁלֹּא לֶאֱכֹל דַּם בְּהֵמָה חַיָּה וָעוֹף, שֶׁנֶּאֱמַר: וְכָל דָּם לֹא תֹאכְלוּ, וְנֶאֱמַר בְּמָקוֹם אַחֵר: לָעוֹף וְלַבְּהֵמָה, וְחַיָּה בִּכְלַל בְּהֵמָה. וְנִכְפְּלָה הַמְּנִיעָה בְּדָם בְּהַרְבֵּה מְקוֹמוֹת בַּתּוֹרָה.

כְּבָר כָּתַבְתִּי מַה שֶּׁאֲנִי חוֹשֵׁב עַל צַד הַפְּשָׁט בְּאִסּוּרֵי הַמַּאֲכָלוֹת בְּאַזְהָרַת טְרֵפָה וְחֵלֶב; וְאֶפְשָׁר לוֹמַר בַּדָּם עוֹד כִּי מִלְּבַד רֹעַ מִזְגּוֹ, שֶׁהוּא רַע הַמֶּזֶג, יִהְיֶה בַּאֲכִילָתוֹ קְצָת קִנְיָן בְּמִדַּת אַכְזָרִיּוּת, שֶׁיִּבְלַע הָאָדָם מִבַּעֲלֵי־הַחַיִּים שֶׁכְּמוֹתוֹ בַּגּוּף, אוֹתוֹ הַדָּבָר שֶׁבָּהֶם שֶׁהַחִיּוּת מַמָּשׁ תָּלוּי עָלָיו, וְנַפְשָׁם נִקְשֶׁרֶת בּוֹ. כִּי יָדוּעַ שֶׁיֵּשׁ לַבְּהֵמוֹת נֶפֶשׁ, יְכַנּוּהָ הַחֲכָמִים נֶפֶשׁ חִיּוּנִית, כְּלוֹמַר שֶׁאֵינָהּ שִׂכְלִית; גַּם נִרְאֶה אוֹתָם, שֶׁיֵּשׁ לְנַפְשָׁם בְּחִינָה לְהִשָּׁמֵר מִנְּפֹל בְּאַחַת הַפְּחָתִים וּבִקְצָת דְּבָרִים אֲחֵרִים.

וְהָרַמְבָּ״ן זִכְרוֹנוֹ לִבְרָכָה כָּתַב בְּטַעַם הַדָּם כִּי יָדוּעַ שֶׁהַנֶּאֱכָל יָשׁוּב בְּגוּף הָאוֹכֵל, וְאִם יֹאכַל אָדָם הַדָּם תִּהְיֶה עֹבִי וְגַסּוּת בְּנֶפֶשׁ הָאָדָם, כְּמוֹ שֶׁנֶּפֶשׁ הַבְּהֵמָה עָבָה וְגַסָּה. וְכָתַב עוֹד כְּעֵין זֶה שֶׁאָמַרְתִּי אֲנִי: אֵין רָאוּי שֶׁתֹּאכַל הַנֶּפֶשׁ אֶת הַנֶּפֶשׁ.

מִדִּינֵי הַמִּצְוָה, מַה שֶּׁאָמְרוּ זִכְרוֹנָם לִבְרָכָה שֶׁדַּם דָּגִים וַחֲגָבִים, שְׁקָצִים וּרְמָשִׂים, וְדַם הָאָדָם, אֵין חַיָּבִין עָלָיו מִשּׁוּם דָּם; וּלְפִיכָךְ אָמְרוּ שֶׁדַּם דָּגִים וַחֲגָבִים מֻתָּרִין, שֶׁמֻּתָּר לֶאֱכֹל דָּמָן וַאֲפִלּוּ כְּנָסוֹ בִּכְלִי, וְהוּא שֶׁיְּהֵא נִכָּר לַכֹּל שֶׁהוּא דַּם דָּגִים, וּכְמוֹ שֶׁאָמְרוּ בַּגְּמָרָא, שֶׁיִּהְיֶה בַּכְּלִי קְצָת מִקַּשְׂקְשֵׂי הַדָּג; אֲבָל דַּם הַדָּגִים הָאֲסוּרִין אָסוּר, לְפִי שֶׁהוּא כַּחֲלֵב בְּהֵמָה טְמֵאָה, שֶׁאָסוּר מִן הַכְּלָל שֶׁבְּיָדֵינוּ שֶׁמַּאֲכָל הַיּוֹצֵא מִן הַטָּמֵא טָמֵא, כְּמוֹ שֶׁמָּצִינוּ שֶׁאָסְרָה תּוֹרָה בֵּיצַת הַיַּעֲנָה, לְפִי שֶׁיּוֹצְאָה מִן הַטָּמֵא.

shehittah of the dam makes it permissible too, since the kosher slaying makes everything in the dam permissible.

11. As remarked above, standing firmly is a sign that the animal will survive; TB Ḥullin 75b.

12. So that people who might see it being eaten without proper ritual slaughter should not draw any wrong conclusions, unaware that it was taken alive from the womb of a properly prepared animal.

13. Which would ordinarily render an animal *t'réfah*, fatally injured before the completion of the ritual slaying. Here our author follows Rashba (evidently his master teacher), cited by *Maggid Mishneh* to MT *hilchoth ma'achaloth 'asuroth* v 14.

14. TB Ḥullin 93a.

15. *Ibid.* 89b.

16. MT *ibid.* vii 9.

[THAT WE SHOULD NOT EAT THE BLOOD OF ANY BEAST OR FOWL]

148 not to eat the blood of a domestic or wild animal, or a fowl:[1] for it is stated, *And you shall not eat any blood*—which is stated elsewhere, also[2]—*of fowl or of beast* (Leviticus 7:26); and a wild animal is included under "beast."[3] The prohibition of blood was repeated in many places in the Torah.

I have previously written what I think, by way of the plain meaning, about forbidden foods—in the injunctions about the *t'réfah* (a fatally injured animal; §73) and about forbidden fat (§147). Now, it can be further said about blood that apart from its evil nature—for it is evil in nature—through eating it there would be some slight acquisition of the quality of cruelty. For a man would swallow from living creatures that are physically like him, that element in them on which life actually depends, to which their souls are attached. For it is known that animals have a soul, which the men of wisdom designate as the vital soul[4]—in other words, it is not possessed of intelligence. Moreover, we can see in them that their soul has the capacity to guard against falling into any particular snare, and quite a few other such matters [of ability].

Ramban of blessed memory wrote[5] on the reason about blood that it is known that what is eaten is converted into the body.[6] Then if a man eats blood there will be coarseness and crassness in the man's soul, just as the soul of an animal is coarse and unrefined. And he wrote, further, something similar to what I have conveyed: It is not right that a soul should eat a soul.

Among the laws of the precept, there is what the Sages of blessed memory said:[7] that over the blood of fish, locusts, and abhorrent crawling creatures, as well as over human blood, there is no punishment on account of [the ban on] blood. They therefore ruled that the blood of fish and locusts is permitted: one is allowed to eat their blood even if it was collected in a vessel—but this [on condition] that it should be recognizable to all that it is fish blood; thus it was said in the Talmud[8] that there should be some scales of the fish in the vessel. However, the blood of forbidden fish is prohibited, because it is like unpermissible milk from an unclean (prohibited) kind of animal, which is forbidden by the rule we hold,[9] that food which emerges from an unclean creature is unclean—as we find [for instance] that the Torah forbade the egg of an ostrich, because it derives from an unclean (forbidden) creature.[10]

וְדַם הָאָדָם אֲסָרוּהוּ חֲכָמִים מִפְּנֵי מַרְאִית הָעַיִן, וּלְפִיכָךְ אָמְרוּ: דַּם שֶׁבֵּין הַשִּׁנַּיִם מוֹצְצוֹ וּבוֹלְעוֹ, וְשֶׁעַל הַפַּת גּוֹרְרוֹ מֵעָלָיו וְאוֹכֵל הַפַּת. (וְכֵן דַּם בֵּיצִים מֻתָּר, שֶׁאֵין אֲנִי קוֹרֵא בּוֹ דַּם עוֹף, וְלֹא מִין בָּשָׂר הוּא וַאֲפִלּוּ הִתְחִיל לְהִתְרַקֵּם, וְכֵן דַּעַת רַבּוֹתֵינוּ בַּעֲלֵי הַתּוֹסָפוֹת, וְכִדְמַשְׁמַע בִּפְשָׁטָא דִּבְרַיְתָא בִּכְרֵתוֹת. זֶהוּ דִּין תּוֹרָה.

אֲבָל חֲכָמִים אָסְרוּ בֵּיצָה שֶׁרִקְמָה, וְסָמְכוּ הַדָּבָר לִקְרָא דְשֶׁרֶץ הַשּׁוֹרֵץ, וְלָכֵן אָסְרוּ דַם בֵּיצִים מִשּׁוּם סָפֵק רִקּוּם, אֲבָל כָּל שֶׁאֵין בּוֹ סָפֵק רִקּוּם לֹא אֲסָרוּהוּ אֶלָּא מִשּׁוּם מַרְאִית הָעַיִן, וְלָכֵן דַּם בֵּיצִים הַנִּמְצָא בַּחֶלְבּוֹן זוֹרֵק הַדָּם וְאוֹכֵל הַשְּׁאָר, וְיֵשׁ מַחְמִירִין בְּנִמְצָא בַּקֶּשֶׁר וְחוּץ לַקֶּשֶׁר לֶאֱסֹר כָּל הַבֵּיצָה.)

וְהַדָּם הָאָסוּר מִן הַתּוֹרָה יֵשׁ שֶׁאִסּוּרוֹ בְּכָרֵת וְיֵשׁ מִמֶּנּוּ בְּלָאו: דַּם הַנֶּפֶשׁ הוּא בְּכָרֵת, שֶׁבְּמָקוֹם שֶׁבָּא בַּתּוֹרָה הַכָּרֵת בְּדָם, נֶאֱמַר שָׁם נֶפֶשׁ, שֶׁנֶּאֱמַר: כִּי נֶפֶשׁ הַבָּשָׂר בַּדָּם הוּא; וּמַה שֶׁאֵינוֹ דַּם הַנֶּפֶשׁ אֶלָּא דַּם הָאֵבָרִים אֵין אִסּוּרוֹ אֶלָּא בְּלָאו, שֶׁעָלָיו נֶאֱמַר סְתָם: וְכָל דָּם לֹא תֹאכְלוּ. וּלְפִיכָךְ בֵּאֲרוּ זִכְרוֹנָם לִבְרָכָה וְאָמְרוּ שֶׁחַיָּבִין כָּרֵת בְּדָם הַיּוֹצֵא בִּשְׁעַת שְׁחִיטָה וּנְחִירָה אוֹ הַתָּזַת הָרֹאשׁ, כָּל זְמַן שֶׁיֵּשׁ בּוֹ אַדְמִימוּת, וְכֵן בְּדָם הַכָּנוּס בְּתוֹךְ הַלֵּב, וְדַם הַקָּזָה כָּל זְמַן שֶׁמְּקַלֵּחַ וְיוֹצֵא, שֶׁגַּם הוּא דַּם הַנֶּפֶשׁ כְּשֶׁהוּא מְקַלֵּחַ, וּלְפִיכָךְ חַיָּבִין עָלָיו. וְדַוְקָא מְקַלֵּחַ, לְהוֹצִיא הַשּׁוֹתֵת בִּתְחִלַּת הַקָּזָה וּבְסוֹפָהּ, שֶׁאֵינוֹ דַּם הַנֶּפֶשׁ, שֶׁאֵין חַיָּבִין עָלָיו כָּרֵת.

וְכֵן דַּם הַתַּמְצִית, כְּלוֹמַר אוֹתוֹ הַדָּם שֶׁמִּתְמַצֶּה בִּשְׁעַת שְׁחִיטָה מְעַט מְעַט אַחַר שֶׁיָּצָא הַדָּם הַנּוֹבֵעַ; וְכֵן דַּם הָאֵבָרִים, כְּגוֹן דַּם הַטְּחוֹל וְדַם הַכְּלָיוֹת וְדַם

§148 1. So TB K'rithoth 20b.

2. Leviticus 3:16.

3. So TB Ḥullin 71a.

4. See Rambam, *Sh'monah P'rakim* ("the eight chapters"), 1; MT *hilchoth yesodé ha-torah* iv 8.

5. In his commentary, Leviticus 17:11.

6. Literally, returns into (i.e. becomes part of) the body.

7. TB K'rithoth 21a.

8. *Ibid.* 21b.

9. MT *hilchoth ma'achaloth 'asuroth* iii 1, from TB B'choroth 5b, etc.

10. So TB Ḥullin 64b: *and the daughter of the ostrich* (Leviticus 11:16, literal translation): but does an ostrich then have a daughter? It rather denotes the egg of an unclean (unpermitted) bird. (The paragraph is based on MT *hilchoth ma'achaloth 'asuroth* vi 1.)

11. Otherwise, since it resembles animal blood, it could give rise to the belief that blood is generally permissible.

12. TB K'rithoth 21b–22a. (This refers to an instance where a person's mouth is bleeding.)

As for human blood, the Sages banned it for appearance sake.[11] Therefore they said: If there is blood between the teeth, it may be sucked and swallowed; but if on bread, it is to be scraped off, and the bread may be eaten.[12] Likewise, blood of eggs is permissible: for it is not considered blood of fowl, nor is it a kind of meat, even if it began to develop embryonically. This is the view of our sages the scholars of *tosafoth*, and so it can be inferred from a *baraitha* in the tractate *K'rithoth* (22a). And this is the law of the Torah.

(The Sages, however, forbade an egg which has begun embryonic development, supporting the ruling by the verse, *all the swarming things that swarm upon the earth, you shall not eat* (Leviticus 11:42).[13] And therefore they banned blood of eggs, because of the possibility of embryonic development. But whatever is under no doubt of embryonic development, they forbade only on account of appearances. Hence, if blood is found in the albumen (the white of the egg), one may throw out the blood and eat the rest. Some are stringent if it is found both in the nexus and outside it, forbidding the entire egg.)[14]

As to the blood forbidden by Torah law, there is some banned under the penalty of *karéth* [Divine severance of existence], while some is banned only by an injunction. The lifeblood entails the punishment of *karéth*: for in the instance where *karéth* occurs [in Scripture] regarding blood, the term *nefesh* (soul, life) is mentioned: as it is stated, *For the* nefesh, *the life of the flesh is in the blood* (Leviticus 17:11). Whatever is not lifeblood but only the blood of the limbs, its ban is only by an injunction, for it is simply stated about it, *you shall eat no blood* (*ibid.* 7:26).[15] Therefore our Sages of blessed memory explained and said that *karéth* is incurred for blood that issues during ritual slaying, piercing or decapitation, as long as there is redness in it; and so too for blood gathered in the heart, and the result of bloodletting, as long as it continues to pour out. This too is lifeblood when it pours forth; and therefore there is penalty over it. But this means specifically when it pours out, to exclude what drips or flows lightly at the beginning of the bloodletting and at its end, which is not lifeblood: over this there is no punishment of *karéth*.[16]

So too the final oozing blood, which means that blood which is exuded at the time of the ritual slaying bit by bit after the welling blood has poured out. Similarly, the blood of the limbs and organs, such as the blood of the spleen and of the kidneys, blood in testes, and that which collects in the heart during the ritual slaying: there is no penalty of

שֶׁבַּבֵּיצִים, וְדָם הַמִּתְכַּנֵּס לַלֵּב בִּשְׁעַת שְׁחִיטָה, אֵין חַיָּבִין עָלָיו כָּרֵת אֶלָּא מַלְקוֹת — וְהוּא שֶׁיֹּאכַל מִמֶּנּוּ כַּזַּיִת.

דָּם הַבָּלוּעַ בִּשְׁאָר הַבָּשָׂר, שֶׁנִּקְרָא גַּם־כֵּן דַּם הָאֵבָרִים, כָּל זְמַן שֶׁלֹּא פֵּרַשׁ מֻתָּר לֶאֱכֹל הַבָּשָׂר עִם הַדָּם הַבָּלוּעַ לְתוֹכוֹ, שֶׁאוֹתוֹ דָם כְּבָשָׂר נֶחֱשָׁב לָנוּ כָּל זְמַן שֶׁלֹּא פֵּרַשׁ מִן הַבָּשָׂר; וּלְפִיכָךְ הִתִּירוּ זִכְרוֹנָם לִבְרָכָה לֶאֱכֹל בָּשָׂר חַי בְּלֹא מְלִיחָה כָּל זְמַן שֶׁהוּדַח יָפֶה שֶׁלֹּא יִהְיֶה עַל פָּנָיו דָּם בְּעַיִן; אֲבָל כָּל זְמַן שֶׁפֵּרַשׁ הַדָּם הַבָּלוּעַ בְּתוֹךְ הַבָּשָׂר וְיָצָא לַחוּץ, חַיָּבִין עָלָיו בְּלָאו כְּמוֹ בְדַם הָאֵבָרִים, שֶׁמָּנִינוּ לְמַעְלָה, שֶׁהֵן בְּלָאו.

וּלְפִיכָךְ הָרוֹצֶה לֶאֱכֹל בָּשָׂר מְבֻשָּׁל בִּקְדֵרָה, חִיְּבוּהוּ חֲכָמִים לְהוֹצִיא מִמֶּנּוּ הַדָּם שֶׁיִּהְיֶה פּוֹרֵשׁ מִתּוֹכוֹ וְיוֹצֵא לְתוֹךְ הַמָּרָק בַּבִּשּׁוּל; וְלֹא מָצְאוּ תַחְבּוּלָה לְהוֹצִיאוֹ כִּי־אִם בְּמֶלַח, שֶׁהוּא שׁוֹאֵב הַדָּם וּמְיַבְּשׁוֹ בְטֶבַע וְכֹחוֹ רַב וְנִכְנָס בַּבָּשָׂר; וַאֲפִלּוּ בַחֲתִיכָה עָבָה בְּיוֹתֵר יֵשׁ כֹּחַ בּוֹ לְהוֹצִיא הַדָּם מִתּוֹךְ הָעֳבִי; וְכֵן הַדָּבָר יָדוּעַ וּמְנֻסֶּה, שֶׁאִם יִמְלַח אָדָם חֲתִיכָה שֶׁל בָּשָׂר יָפֶה כְּשִׁעוּר שֶׁנָּתְנוּ חֲכָמִים לִמְלִיחָה, יִמָּצֵא טַעַם הַמֶּלַח בְּכָל הַבָּשָׂר, וַאֲפִלּוּ בַחֲתִיכָה גְדוֹלָה שֶׁל שׁוֹר הַפָּטוּם.

וְאַחַר שֶׁהַדָּבָר כֵּן בְּבֵרוּר וְנִרְאֶה לָעַיִן, מֻתָּר לָתֵת כָּל בָּשָׂר שֶׁנִּמְלַח כְּשִׁעוּרוֹ בִּקְדֵרָה, בֵּין שֶׁיִּהְיוּ הַמַּיִם רוֹתְחִין אוֹ פּוֹשְׁרִין וְצוֹנְנִין, לְפִי שֶׁאָנוּ רוֹאִין הַבָּשָׂר אַחַר מְלִיחָה כְּשִׁעוּר, לְכָל דָּבָר, כְּאִלּוּ נִתְמַצָּה מִמֶּנּוּ כָּל דָּם הָאָסוּר בּוֹ. וְאִם גַּם אַחַר מְלִיחָה אָנוּ רוֹאִין שֶׁיּוֹצֵא מִמֶּנּוּ מְעַט דָּם, אֵין לוֹ תוֹרַת דָּם אֶלָּא (כמיחל) [כְּמוֹהַל] אָדָם הוּא חָשׁוּב, וְעַל כַּיּוֹצֵא בוֹ נֶאֱמַר בַּגְּמָרָא: רַבִּי פְלוֹנִי קָרֵי לֵיהּ "חֲמַר בָּשָׂר" וּמַתִּירוֹ.

וְיֵשׁ בַּבְּהֵמָה קְצָת אֵבָרִים שֶׁל רִבּוּי דָּם שֶׁבָּהֶם נָהֲגוּ כָּל יִשְׂרָאֵל לְהוֹצִיא הַדָּם שֶׁבָּהֶם בְּכֹחַ הָאֵשׁ טֶרֶם שֶׁיְּבַשְּׁלוּם בִּקְדֵרָה, וְלֹא רָצוּ לִסְמֹךְ בָּהֶם בִּמְלִיחָה לְבָד, וְהֵם הַמֹּחַ וְהַכָּבֵד; צוֹלִין אוֹתָן מְעַט עַל הָאֵשׁ וְאַחַר־כָּךְ מְבַשְּׁלִין אוֹתָן, בֵּין שֶׁיִּרְצוּ לְבַשְּׁלָן בִּפְנֵי עַצְמָן אוֹ עִם בָּשָׂר אַחֵר; וּמִנְהָגָן שֶׁל יִשְׂרָאֵל תּוֹרָה הִיא. עָבַר וּבִשְּׁלָן בִּמְלִיחָה לְבַד עִם הַבָּשָׂר, הַכֹּל מֻתָּר, וּבִלְבַד שֶׁלֹּא יְכַוֵּן אָדָם לַעֲשׂוֹת כֵּן

13. TB Hullin 64a. I.e. although after full development it will be permissible as a chicken, now it is considered a "swarming creature."

14. So R. 'Ashér and Rashba, cited by Rama in *Shulḥan 'Aruch Yoreh Dé'ah* §66, 3. (This part in parentheses, from "Likewise, blood of eggs," is not in the oldest manuscripts. It is therefore very likely an incorporated later marginal addition.)

15. TB K'rithoth 22a.

16. MT *hilchoth ma'achaloth 'asuroth* vi 3, based on TB *ibid.*

17. MT *ibid.* 4.

18. Rabad to MT *ibid.* 12; so also Ramban and Rashba (*Maggid Mishneh*).

karéth over it, but only whiplashes—and this only if the amount of an olive is eaten.[17]

As for blood absorbed in the rest of the flesh, also called blood of the organs, as long as it has not separated out, the flesh may be eaten with the blood absorbed in it. For that blood is considered by us as meat [under the law] as long as it has not been separated from the flesh. For this reason the Sages of blessed memory permitted raw meat to be eaten without salting [to extract the blood], so long as it is washed well, so that no discernible whole blood remains on its surface.[18] However, at any time that the blood absorbed in the flesh leaves it and issues out, it entails punishment for violating a negative precept, like the blood of the organs that we listed above, which bears the ban of a negative precept.

Hence, if someone wants to eat meat cooked in a pot, the Sages obligated him to extract from it the blood that would separate out and go into the soup in the cooking. They found no other device to extract it but by salt, which naturally draws the blood and dries it; it has a great power and penetrates the meat. Even with an extremely thick piece, it has the power to extract the blood from the thickness. And so the matter is known and verified, that if a man will salt a piece of meat well, to the extent that the Sages ordained for salting, the taste of salt will be found throughout the meat, even in a huge piece from a fatted ox.

Well, since the matter is clearly, obviously so, one is allowed to put into a pot any meat that was salted properly,[19] whether the water [in it] is boiling, warm, or cold.[20] For after proper salting, we regard the meat in every respect as though all the forbidden blood in it has been extracted. Even if after the salting we see that a little blood issues from it, it is not blood under the law, but is considered as a red secretion. About something like this it is told in the Talmud, "Rabbi So-and-so[21] called it the wine of meat" and he ruled it permissible.

There are a few organs with amassed blood in an animal, for which all Jewry has adopted the practice to extract the blood in them by the force of fire before cooking them in a pot, not wanting to rely on salting alone for them. These are the brains and the liver. They are roasted a bit on the fire, and then they are cooked, whether the wish is to cook them by themselves or with other meat.[22] And the practice of Jewry is as a Torah rule. Yet if someone transgressed and cooked them with [other] meat after merely salting them, the whole may be eaten—pro-

לְכַתְּחִלָּה כְּדֵי שֶׁיָּשׁוּב הַדָּבָר עָלָיו בְּדִיעֲבַד אַחַר הַבִּשּׁוּל, שֶׁכָּל הָעוֹשֶׂה כֵן בְּאִסּוּרִין, אוֹסְרִין עָלָיו הַכֹּל כְּמוֹ בַתְּחִלָּה, וַאֲנִי קוֹרֵא עָלָיו: וּפוֹרֵץ גָּדֵר יִשְּׁכֶנּוּ נָחָשׁ.

וְסֵדֶר מְלִיחָה כָּךְ הִיא: מֵדִיחַ הַבָּשָׂר יָפֶה מִדָּם שֶׁעָלָיו, וְאַחַר־כָּךְ מַנִּיחַ עָלָיו מֶלַח בֵּינוֹנִי — לֹא עָבֶה בְּיוֹתֵר, כְּדֵי שֶׁיִּדְבַּק בּוֹ קְצָת, וְלֹא דַק בְּיוֹתֵר כְּדֵי שֶׁלֹּא יִדְבַּק בּוֹ יוֹתֵר מִדַּי — וּמַנִּיחוֹ בְּמִלְחוֹ כְּדֵי הִלּוּךְ מִיל; וַאֲפִלּוּ לִבְשַׂר שׁוֹר עָבֶה דַּי בְּכָךְ.

וְאַחַר שֶׁיַּעֲמֹד בְּמִלְחוֹ שִׁעוּר זֶה בִּמְקוֹם מִדְרוֹן שֶׁיּוּכַל הַדָּם לָזוּב יָפֶה, אוֹ בִּכְלִי מְנֻקָּב, לוֹקֵחַ הַבָּשָׂר בְּיָדוֹ וּמַגְבִּיהוֹ, וּמְנַפֵּץ הַמֶּלַח מֵעָלָיו, וְאַחַר־כָּךְ מְדִיחוֹ יָפֶה בְּמַיִם שֶׁבִּכְלִי פְּעָמִים שָׁלֹשׁ אוֹ יוֹתֵר, עַד שֶׁיּוּסַר הַמֶּלַח וְיִשָּׁאֲרוּ הַמַּיִם שֶׁמֵּדִיחַ הַבָּשָׂר בָּהֶם זַכִּים. וְאִם נִשְׁתַּהָה הַבָּשָׂר בְּמִלְחוֹ יוֹתֵר מִן הַשִּׁעוּר הָרָאוּי לִמְלִיחָה, אֵין חוֹשְׁשִׁין שֶׁמָּא חָזַר הַבָּשָׂר וּבָלַע מִדָּם שֶׁעַל פְּנֵי הַמֶּלַח, לְפִי שֶׁאָנוּ אוֹמְרִים שֶׁהַבָּשָׂר אַחַר שֶׁפָּלַט דָּמוֹ הָאָסוּר, פּוֹלֵט צִירוֹ, כְּלוֹמַר (מיחל) [מוֹהַל] הַבָּשָׂר, וְהוּא הַלַּחוּת שֶׁבַּבָּשָׂר, וְכָל זְמַן שֶׁיִּפְלֹט הַבָּשָׂר אוֹתוֹ הַצִּיר אֵין בְּטִבְעוֹ שֶׁיּוּכַל לִבְלֹעַ דָּם, לְפִי שֶׁהַדָּם חָלָק בְּטִבְעוֹ הַרְבֵּה וְאֵינוֹ נִבְלָע כִּי־אִם בְּמָתוּן, רְצוֹנִי לוֹמַר כָּל זְמַן שֶׁלֹּא יִפְלֹט שׁוּם דָּבָר, לֹא דָם וְלֹא צִיר.

וְכַמָּה יִהְיֶה שִׁהוּי זֶה שֶׁנַּחֲזִיק הַבָּשָׂר שֶׁיִּפְלֹט עֲדַיִן צִיר, אָמְרוּ הָרַבָּנִים יִשְׁמְרֵם הַשֵּׁם, שֶׁהוּא עַד י״ב שָׁעוֹת. נִשְׁתַּהָה יוֹתֵר מִכֵּן בְּמִלְחוֹ, אָסוּר לְאָכְלוֹ עַד שֶׁיִּקְלֹף פְּנֵי הַבָּשָׂר כֻּלּוֹ, וּמִיהוּ בִּקְלִיפָה סָגֵי, לְפִי שֶׁאָנוּ מַחֲזִיקִין מָלִיחַ כְּרוֹתֵחַ דִּצְלִי, וּבְאִסּוּר הַנּוֹגֵעַ בִּצְלִי קָיְמָא לָן דִּסְגֵי קְלִיפָה, בְּשֶׁאֵין שָׁם אִסּוּר מְפַעְפֵּעַ, וְדָם אֵינוֹ מְפַעְפֵּעַ.

וְאִם לֹא רָצָה לְקַלֵּף הַבָּשָׂר מֻתָּר לְאָכְלוֹ בִּצְלִי, שֶׁאַף־עַל־פִּי שֶׁאָנוּ אוֹמְרִים שֶׁאֵין כֹּחַ בַּמֶּלַח לְהוֹצִיא דָּם הַבָּא לַבָּשָׂר מִמָּקוֹם אַחֵר, כֹּחַ הָאֵשׁ חָזָק מִן הַמֶּלַח

19. Literally, as its measure.

20. Rabad to MT *ibid.* 10.

21. I.e. Rava; TB Ḥullin 112a.

22. See MT *ibid.* 7.

23. TB Ḥullin 23a.

24. About twenty minutes—but standard practice requires one hour (*Shulḥan 'Aruch Yoreh Dé'ah* §69, 6); MT *ibid.* 10.

25. So that the blood can run out through the holes; MT *ibid.* 11.

26. Rashba, *Torath haBa-yith* III 3, in the name of R. Yonah.

27. And in this case, since the salt extracted all the blood onto the surface and it now begins to flow back into the meat, it is in effect blood reaching the meat from another source.

vided that a man should not plan to do so from the start, so that the matter will turn out to be a *fait accompli* after the cooking. For if anyone acts like that concerning food that bears a ban, the whole is made forbidden for him as at the beginning, "before the fact," and this verse is applied to him: *whoever breaches a fence, may a serpent bite him* (Ecclesiastes 10:8).

Now, the order of salting is this: The meat is washed well of the blood on it,[23] and then salt of medium size is put on it: not too thick, so that it should stick to it somewhat, and not too thin, so that it should not adhere to it unduly. Then it is left with its salt for enough time to walk a *mil;*[24] even for a thick piece of ox meat, this is enough.

After it has remained with its salt this long, on a slanting surface, so that the blood can run down well, or in a perforated vessel,[25] one takes the meat with his hand and lifts it up, and scatters (shakes) the salt off it. Then he washes it well with water in a vessel, two or three times, or more, until the salt is removed and the water with which he washes the meat remains clear. If the meat remained with its salt beyond the measure of time proper for salting, we do not fear that perhaps the meat reabsorbed some of the blood that was on the surface of the salt. For we say that after discharging its forbidden blood, the meat discharges its juice, i.e. the secretion of the meat, which is the moisture in the meat; and as long as the meat exudes that juice, it is not in its natural power to absorb blood: because blood is very smooth in its composition, and can be absorbed only quite slowly, by which I mean only at the time that the meat is discharging nothing—neither blood nor juice.[26]

Now, how long is this interval during which we assume the meat to be yet exuding juice?—the Rabbis (the Eternal Lord preserve them) said[26] it is up to twelve hours. If it remained longer than that with its salt, it is forbidden to eat it until a thin layer is removed from the entire surface of the meat. This "peeling" is enough, though, for we hold salted meat to be as though boiling-hot through roasting; and for something forbidden that touches a roast, we have an established rule that "peeling" (removing a surface layer) is enough when there is nothing forbidden there that spreads easily throughout—and blood does not spread readily throughout.[26]

If one does not wish to "peel" the meat, it is permitted to eat it roasted. For although we say that salt does not have the force to extract blood which reaches it from another source,[27] the force of the fire is greater than that of the salt to draw it out. Therefore, if meat remained

לְהוֹצִיאוֹ; וּלְפִיכָךְ בָּשָׂר שֶׁנִּשְׁתַּהָה בְּמִלְחוֹ יוֹתֵר מִדַּי מֻתָּר לְאָכְלוֹ בִּצְלִי בְּלֹא קְלִיפָה; וּבִקְלִיפָה אֲפִלּוּ בִּקְדֵרָה, כְּמוֹ שֶׁאָמַרְנוּ.

וְיֶתֶר רִבֵּי דִינֵי מְלִיחָה, כְּגוֹן דָּגִים וְעוֹפוֹת שֶׁמְּלָחָן זֶה עִם זֶה, וְדָג טָהוֹר שֶׁמְּלָחוֹ עִם דָּג טָמֵא, וְכֵלִים שֶׁל חֶרֶס אוֹ שֶׁל עֵץ שֶׁמָּלְחוּ בָהֶן, מַה דִּינָם; וְהַמֶּלַח עַצְמוֹ שֶׁמָּלְחוּ בָהּ מַה דִּינָהּ; וְיֶתֶר רִבֵּי פְּרָטֵי הַמְּלִיחָה, מְבֹאָרִים בְּחֻלִּין פֶּרֶק כָּל הַבָּשָׂר, וּבְפֶרֶק חֲמִישִׁי מִכְּרֵתוֹת יִתְבָּאֵר גַּם־כֵּן דִּינֵי הַדָּם וְחִלּוּקֵי דַם הַנֶּפֶשׁ וְדַם הָאֵבָרִים.

וְנוֹהֶגֶת בְּכָל מָקוֹם וּבְכָל זְמַן, בִּזְכָרִים וּנְקֵבוֹת. וְעוֹבֵר עָלֶיהָ וְאָכַל כַּזַּיִת דַּם הַנֶּפֶשׁ בְּמֵזִיד, חַיָּב כָּרֵת; בְּשׁוֹגֵג, מֵבִיא חַטָּאת קְבוּעָה; וְאִם אָכַל כַּזַּיִת מִדַּם הָאֵבָרִים בְּמֵזִיד לוֹקֶה, בְּשׁוֹגֵג פָּטוּר.

וַיְהִי בַּיּוֹם הַשְּׁמִינִי

יֵשׁ בָּהּ שֵׁשׁ מִצְווֹת עֲשֵׂה וְאַחַת־עֶשְׂרֵה לֹא־תַעֲשֶׂה

[שֶׁלֹּא יִכָּנְסוּ הַכֹּהֲנִים לַמִּקְדָּשׁ מְגֻדְּלֵי שֵׂעָר]

קמט שֶׁלֹּא יִכָּנְסוּ הַכֹּהֲנִים לַמִּקְדָּשׁ מְגֻדְּלֵי שֵׂעָר, כְּמוֹ שֶׁיַּעֲשׂוּ הָאֲבֵלִים, כְּלוֹמַר שֶׁלֹּא יְגַדְּלוּ שַׂעֲרוֹתֵיהֶם, שֶׁנֶּאֱמַר: רָאשֵׁיכֶם אַל תִּפְרָעוּ, וְאָמַר הַתַּרְגּוּם: לָא תְרַבּוּן פְּרוּעַ, וִיחֶזְקֵאל הַנָּבִיא בֵּאֵר וְאָמַר: וּפֶרַע לֹא יְשַׁלֵּחוּ, וּכְמוֹ־כֵן נֶאֱמַר בִּמְצֹרָע: וְרֹאשׁוֹ יִהְיֶה פָרוּעַ; וְאָמְרוּ בְסִפְרָא, יְגַדֵּל פֶּרַע; וּלְשׁוֹן סִפְרָא עוֹד: "רָאשֵׁיכֶם אַל תִּפְרָעוּ", אַל תְּגַדְּלוּ פֶרַע.

וּכְבָר נִכְפְּלָה מְנִיעָה זוֹ בְּכֹהֵן גָּדוֹל וְאָמַר: אֶת רֹאשׁוֹ לֹא יִפְרָע; וְאוּלָם נִכְפְּלָה

28. I.e. whether they are fit for other uses with food.
29. I.e. whether it may be reused.
30. Explained in §121.

unduly long with its salt, it may be eaten roasted without "peeling" it; and if with "peeling" [if a surface layer is removed, it may be eaten] even [cooked] in a pot, as we said.

The rest of the many laws about salting—for instance, if fish and fowl were salted together; if a clean [permissible kind of] fish was salted with an unclean [forbidden kind of] fish; earthenware or wooden utensils that were used for salting—what their law is;[28] and the salt itself that was used for salting—what its law is[29]—[these] and the rest of the many details about salting are explained in chapter 8 of the tractate *Ḥullin*. In chapter 5 of *K'rithoth* the laws about blood are likewise clarified, including the differences [in law] between the lifeblood and the blood of the organs.

It is in force in every place and every time, for both man and woman. If a person violates it and eats an olive's amount of lifeblood—if it was deliberate, he must pay by *karéth* [Divine severance of existence]; if it was unintentional, he should bring a standard unvarying *ḥattath*.[30] If one eats an olive's amount of the blood of the organs—if it was intentional, he should be given whiplashes; if it was inadvertent, there is no penalty.

sidrah sh'mini

(Leviticus 9–11)

There are six positive and eleven negative precepts in it.

[THE KOHANIM MAY NOT ENTER THE HOLY TEMPLE WITH HAIR GROWN LONG]

149 that the *kohanim* should not enter the Sanctuary with overgrown hair, as mourners wear it; in other words, they should not grow their hair overly long—for it is stated, *Do not let your heads be overgrown* (Leviticus 10:6), and Onkelos rendered it, "Do not have a mass of *pera*, long wild growth." The prophet Ezekiel clarified it by saying, *and they shall not let their locks grow long* (Ezekiel 44:20); likewise it is stated about a *m'tzora*: *and his head shall be* paru'a, *wildly overgrown* (Leviticus 13:45), whereupon it was taught in the Midrash *Sifra:* he should raise *pera*—long, unshorn hair; and we read further in *Sifra: Do not let your heads be widly overgrown*—do not raise *pera*.

Now, this prohibition was repeated for the *kohen gadol*, with the

כְּדֵי שֶׁלֹּא נַחְשֹׁב מַה שֶּׁנֶּאֱמַר לְאֶלְעָזָר וְאִיתָמָר "רָאשֵׁיכֶם אַל תִּפְרָעוּ", שֶׁיִּהְיֶה מִצַּד הַמֵּת בִּלְבַד, וּכְשֶׁיַּעֲשׂוּ זֶה שֶׁלֹּא עַל צַד הָאֵבֶל שֶׁתַּחְשֹׁב שֶׁיִּהְיֶה מֻתָּר; עַל־כֵּן נִתְבָּאֵר בְּכֹהֵן גָּדוֹל שֶׁזֶּה בִּשְׁבִיל הָעֲבוֹדָה הוּא שֶׁיְּצַוֵּהוּ הַשֵּׁם לְהִסְתַּפֵּר.

מִשָּׁרְשֵׁי הַמִּצְוָה הוּא הַגְדָּלַת הַבַּיִת, וּכְמוֹ שֶׁאָמַרְנוּ לְמַעְלָה, שֶׁנִּצְטַוִּינוּ לְהַגְדִּילוֹ בְּכָל כֹּחֵנוּ, מִן הַטַּעַם שֶׁאָמַרְנוּ; וְעַל־כֵּן רָאוּי לָנוּ שֶׁלֹּא נָבוֹא שָׁם מְגֻדְּלֵי שֵׂעָר כְּדֶרֶךְ הָאֲבֵלִים, וּכְעִנְיַן מַה שֶּׁנֶּאֱמַר בִּמְגִלַּת אֶסְתֵּר: כִּי אֵין לָבוֹא אֶל שַׁעַר הַמֶּלֶךְ בִּלְבוּשׁ שָׂק; כְּלוֹמַר, אֵין רָאוּי לָבוֹא אֶל בֵּית הַשֵּׁם רַק דֶּרֶךְ שָׂשׂוֹן וְשִׂמְחָה וְתַעֲנוּג, לֹא דֶּרֶךְ אֵבֶל וְצַעַר.

וְכָל זֶה יְחַזֵּק הַיְסוֹד הַבָּנוּי בְּרֹאשׁ הַבִּנְיָן, כִּי כָל עִנְיְנֵי הַבַּיִת וּמַעֲשָׂיו לְחַזֵּק וּלְצַיֵּר בְּלֵב הָעוֹשִׂים מַעֲשֵׂה הַכֹּשֶׁר, וּלְהַרְחִיק מִלִּבָּם וּמַחְשְׁבוֹתָם כָּל כִּעוּר וְכָל חֵטְא. וְעַל־כֵּן בִּהְיוֹת כַּוָּנַת הַבַּיִת בָּזֶה, רָאוּי לָנוּ לָבוֹא שָׁם דֶּרֶךְ כָּבוֹד וְיִרְאָה וּגְדֻלָּה וְשִׂמְחָה, וּמִתּוֹךְ קְבִיעוּת מַחְשַׁבְתֵּנוּ עַל חֲשִׁיבוּת הַמָּקוֹם וְגָדְלוֹ וְתִפְאַרְתּוֹ וְהוֹדוֹ, יִתְרַכְּכוּ לְבָבֵינוּ שָׁם וְנִהְיֶה רְאוּיִים לְקַבָּלַת הַטּוֹב.

דִּינֵי הַמִּצְוָה, כְּגוֹן מַה שֶּׁאָמְרוּ זִכְרוֹנָם לִבְרָכָה שֶׁאִסּוּר גִּדּוּל פֶּרַע בְּכֹהֲנִים הֶדְיוֹטִים אֵינוֹ אֶלָּא בִּשְׁעַת בִּיאָה לַמִּקְדָּשׁ, אֲבָל כָּל זְמַן שֶׁאֵין כֹּהֵן הֶדְיוֹט נִכְנָס לַמִּקְדָּשׁ אֵינוֹ בְּאִסּוּר גִּדּוּל פֶּרַע כְּלָל; אֲבָל כֹּהֵן גָּדוֹל, לְפִי שֶׁהוּא תָּמִיד בַּמִּקְדָּשׁ אָסוּר בְּגִדּוּל פֶּרַע לְעוֹלָם, כְּאִלּוּ תֹאמַר, שֶׁאִם יִהְיֶה לוֹ דֶּרֶךְ אֹנֶס לַעֲמֹד חוּץ לַמִּקְדָּשׁ קְצָת יָמִים מִן הַחִיּוּב עָלָיו, אַף־עַל־פִּי־כֵן שֶׁלֹּא יְגַדֵּל פֶּרַע. וְכַמָּה הוּא גִּדּוּל פֶּרַע, שְׁלֹשִׁים יוֹם, כִּנְזִירוּת, שֶׁסְּתַם נְזִירוּת אֵינוֹ פָּחוֹת מִשְּׁלֹשִׁים יוֹם. וְיֶתֶר פְּרָטֶיהָ מְבֹאָרִים.

§149 1. I.e. we might think they were forbidden to do this only as a sign of mourning for their brothers Nadav and 'Avihu, whose lives had only just ended (Leviticus 10:1–2).

2. The first two paragraphs are based on ShM negative precept §163; see also Ramban there.

3. Literally, at the "beginning of the structure"; i.e. at the first mention of the precept about building the Sanctuary (§95).

4. As opposed to the *kohen gadol* (literally, the great *kohen*), the chief of the *kohanim*, who had special duties and special laws affecting him.

5. MT *hilchoth bi'ath ha-mikdash* i 10, based on TB Sanhedrin 22b.

6. If someone took a vow to be a *nazir* without specifying a length of time, it was for this period; during the time, he was forbidden to cut his hair—and Scripture refers to this as "growing the hair of his head as *pera*" (Numbers 6:5). Hence thirty days' growth is *pera*, which is forbidden to the *koben*; TB Sanhedrin 22b; Mo'ed Katan 19b.

words, *his head he shall not make overgrown* (Leviticus 21:10). In truth, it was repeated so that we should not think that when El'azar and Ithamar were told, "Do not let your heads be overgrown," it was only on account of the dead,[1] but if they would do this without regard to mourning, you might think it permissible. It was therefore made clear in connection with the *kohen gadol* that it is for the sake of the [Divine] service that the Eternal Lord would command him to have his hair cut.[2]

At the root of the precept lies the purpose of increasing the Temple's distinction. As we noted above, we were commanded to ennoble it with all our power, for the reason we have stated. It is therefore right for us that we should not enter there with overgrown hair, in the way of mourners. It is akin to what is stated in the Scroll of Esther: *for no one might enter the king's gate clothed with sackcloth* (Esther 4:2). In other words, it is proper to come to the House of the Eternal Lord only in a state of happiness, joy and delight, not in a state of mourning and grief.

All this supports the fundamental concept established at the beginning[3]—that everything to do with the Temple and its tasks [was intended] to confirm and impress in the heart of those who do them a state of worth and nobility, and to move far from their heart and thoughts every ugliness and sinfulness. Therefore, as this was the purpose of the Temple, it would be proper for us to come there in a mood of respect and reverent fear, dignity and joy, while fastening our thoughts on the importance of the place. Then its grandeur, splendor and majesty will soften our hearts there [making them receptive] and we will be worthy to receive good [reward].

As for the laws of the precept, there is, for example, what our Sages of blessed memory said: that the ban on growing *pera* (long hair) for ordinary *kohanim*[4] is only during entry into the Sanctuary; but as long as an ordinary *kohen* does not enter the Sanctuary, he is under no ban at all about growing *pera*. However, the *kohen gadol*, since he was constantly in the Sanctuary, was always forbidden to grow *pera*[5]—which is to say that if through some accident he was compelled to stay out of the Sanctuary for a few days, the prohibition remains for him, nevertheless, that he should not grow unduly long hair. How long does it take for *pera* to grow?—thirty days, like the period of naziriteship; for the general, unspecified period of naziriteship is not less than thirty days.[6] The rest of its details are explained.

It is in effect when the Temple is extant, for the male *kohanim*. If

וְנוֹהֶגֶת בִּזְמַן הַבַּיִת, בִּזְכְרֵי כְהֻנָּה. וְעוֹבֵר עָלֶיהָ וְנִכְנַס לַמִּקְדָּשׁ פְּרוּעַ רֹאשׁ, כְּלוֹמַר אַחַר שֶׁגִּדֵּל שַׂעֲרוֹ שְׁלֹשִׁים יוֹם, וְעָבַד שָׁם, חַיָּב מִיתָה בִּידֵי שָׁמַיִם, שֶׁנֶּאֱמַר: רָאשֵׁיכֶם אַל תִּפְרָעוּ... וְלֹא תָמוּתוּ — וְדִבְרֵי הַתּוֹרָה נוֹטְרִיקוֹן הֵם, כְּלוֹמַר הָא אִם יִפְרְעוּ רָאשֵׁיהֶם יָמוּתוּ; וּמִכָּל־מָקוֹם אֵין עֲבוֹדָתוֹ פְּסוּלָה. וּמִי שֶׁנִּכְנַס לְשָׁם וְלֹא עָבַד, הוּא בְאַזְהָרָה, כְּלוֹמַר שֶׁעָבַר עַל לָאו וְלוֹקֶה; אֲבָל אֵינוֹ בְמִיתָה אֶלָּא־אִם־כֵּן עָבַד, שֶׁכֵּן בָּא לָנוּ הַפֵּרוּשׁ.

וְהָרַמְבָּ״ן זִכְרוֹנוֹ לִבְרָכָה כָּתַב כִּי פְּרוּעַ הָרֹאשׁ שֶׁלֹּא יִכָּנֵס לַמִּקְדָּשׁ, מַעֲלָה הִיא מִדִּבְרֵיהֶם וְלֹא מִדְּאוֹרַיְתָא, וּ־רְאָיוֹתָיו בְּסִפְרוֹ; וְאָמַר שֶׁלֹּא בָא הַכָּתוּב לֶאֱסֹר אֶלָּא קְרִיבָה לַעֲבוֹדָה, וְהוּא בִכְלַל לָאו דְּבַעַל־מוּם שֶׁעָבַד. וְכָתַב עוֹד שֶׁאַף חֲכָמִים לֹא אָסְרוּ אֶלָּא הַמָּקוֹם הַנִּקְרָא בֵּין הָאוּלָם וְלַמִּזְבֵּחַ, אֲבָל כְּנֶגֶד הַמִּזְבֵּחַ עַצְמוֹ, שֶׁהוּא שְׁתַּיִם וּשְׁלֹשִׁים אַמָּה, כְּמוֹ שֶׁשָּׁנִינוּ, ״הַמִּזְבֵּחַ שְׁתַּיִם וּשְׁלֹשִׁים אַמָּה, בֵּין הָאוּלָם וְלַמִּזְבֵּחַ שְׁתַּיִם וְעֶשְׂרִים״, לֹא אָסְרוּ.

[שֶׁלֹּא יִכָּנְסוּ הַכֹּהֲנִים לַמִּקְדָּשׁ קְרוּעֵי בְגָדִים]

קנ שֶׁלֹּא יִכָּנְסוּ הַכֹּהֲנִים בַּמִּקְדָּשׁ קְרוּעֵי בְגָדִים, שֶׁנֶּאֱמַר: וּבִגְדֵיכֶם לֹא תִפְרֹמוּ, פֵּרוּשׁ, אַל תִּקְרְעוּ בִגְדֵיכֶם. וְנִכְפְּלָה מְנִיעָה זוֹ בְּכֹהֵן גָּדוֹל, שֶׁנֶּאֱמַר עָלָיו: וּבְגָדָיו לֹא יִפְרֹם; וְכָפַל הַמְּנִיעָה בוֹ מִפְּנֵי תוֹסֶפֶת דָּבָר שֶׁבּוֹ, שֶׁאֵינוֹ רַשַּׁאי לִקְרֹעַ עַל מֵת שֶׁיָּמוּת לוֹ, וַאֲפִלּוּ שֶׁלֹּא בִשְׁעַת עֲבוֹדָה. וְאָמְרוּ בְסִפְרָא: ״רֹאשׁוֹ לֹא יִפְרָע וּבְגָדָיו לֹא יִפְרֹם״, עַל מֵתוֹ, כְּדֶרֶךְ שֶׁבְּנֵי־אָדָם פּוֹרְעִין וּפוֹרְמִין עַל מֵתֵיהֶן; הָא כֵיצַד, כֹּהֵן גָּדוֹל פּוֹרֵם מִלְּמַטָּן וְהַהֶדְיוֹט מִלְּמַעְלָן.

7. TB Sanhedrin 22b; Ta'anith 17b.

8. MT *hilchoth bi'ath ha-mikdash* i 15; ShM negative precept §163 (on the source see Ramban on *ibid.*)

9. On ShM *ibid.*

10. So MY: i.e. just as that precept (§275) applies only to Temple service, so this. The literal meaning of the Hebrew, "included under," is inappropriate.

11. Mishnah, Tamid iii 1, 6.

§150 1. I.e. a close relative, over whom an ordinary person would make a tear in his clothing as a mark of grief.

2. So TB Horayoth 12b; the paragraph derives from ShM negative precept §164.

someone violated it and entered the Sanctuary with overgrown hair, i.e. after he let his hair grow thirty days, and served there, he would be punishable by death at Heaven's hands: for it is stated, *Do not let your heads be overgrown . . . that you should not die* (Leviticus 10:6); and the Torah's words are abbreviated (concise): it means that if they do let their heads become overgrown, they will die. However, his Temple service would not be disqualified.[7] If someone entered there and did not serve, this [was forbidden] by an admonition: in other words, he violated a negative precept, and would receive whiplashes; but he would not incur death [at Heaven's hands] unless he served [in the Temple]; for so the interpretation has come down to us [in the Oral Tradition].[8]

However, Ramban of blessed memory wrote[9] that [the restriction on] one with overgrown head not to enter the Sanctuary is a higher standard set by the Sages, and not by the Torah; and his proofs are in his work. He stated that the Writ came to forbid nothing more than drawing near to [do] the Temple service; it is similar to[10] the negative precept about a blemished (disfigured) *kohen* who did service (§275). He wrote further that the Sages in turn place a ban only on the area called "between the *'ulam* (entrance hall) and the altar"; but around the altar itself, which measured thirty-two cubits [on each side]—as we learned:[11] the altar was thirty-two cubits; between the *'ulam* and the altar, twenty-two—they imposed no ban.

[THE KOHANIM ARE NOT TO ENTER THE HOLY TEMPLE IN TORN CLOTHING]

150 that the *kohanim* should not enter the Sanctuary with torn clothes: for it is stated, *and do not rend your clothes* (Leviticus 10:6), which means, "do not tear your clothing." This prohibition was repeated for the *kohen gadol:* as it is stated about him, *and his clothes he shall not rend* (Leviticus 21:10). The forbiddance was repeated for him because of something additional in it: that he is not allowed to rend [a garment] over someone who dies[1] even outside the time of the Temple service. It was taught in the Midrash *Sifra:* "he shall not let his head become overgrown, and his clothes he shall not rend" (*ibid.*) over his dead [kin] in the way that people let their hair grow disheveled and tear their clothing over their dead. Then how?—the *kohen gadol* makes the tear below [in the bottom hem], and an ordinary *kohen* above [in the upper hem].[2]

מִשָּׁרְשֵׁי הַמִּצְוָה, כָּתוּב בִּפְרִיעַת הָרֹאשׁ, הַקּוֹדֵם לָזֶה. וְדִין פְּרוּעֵי רֹאשׁ וּקְרוּעֵי בְגָדִים שָׁוִים בְּכָל דִּינֵיהֶם.

מִדִּינֵי הַמִּצְוָה, מַה שֶּׁאָמְרוּ זִכְרוֹנָם לִבְרָכָה שֶׁחִיּוּב קְרִיעָה זוֹ הִיא שֶׁתִּהְיֶה כְּמוֹ קְרִיעָה שֶׁקּוֹרְעִין עַל הַמֵּתִים; וּמִן הַדּוֹמֶה שֶׁהוּא טֶפַח, שֶׁכֵּן אָמְרוּ בְּמוֹעֵד קָטָן שֶׁאֵין קְרִיעָה פְּחוּתָה מִטֶּפַח. וְיֶתֶר פְּרָטֶיהָ מְבֹאָרִים.

וְנוֹהֶגֶת בִּזְמַן הַבַּיִת בִּזְכְרֵי כְהֻנָּה. וְעוֹבֵר עָלֶיהָ וְנִכְנַס לַמִּקְדָּשׁ מִן הַמִּזְבֵּחַ וְלִפְנִים קְרוּעַ בְּגָדִים וְעָבַד, חַיָּב מִיתָה בִידֵי שָׁמַיִם; וְאִם לֹא עָבַד, הֲרֵי הוּא בְּאַזְהָרָה וְלוֹקֶה; וְזֶהוּ לְדַעַת הָרַמְבַּ"ם זִכְרוֹנוֹ לִבְרָכָה; אֲבָל לְדַעַת הָרַמְבַּ"ן זִכְרוֹנוֹ לִבְרָכָה אֵין מַלְקוֹת בְּנִכְנַס לַמִּקְדָּשׁ קְרוּעַ בְּגָדִים, שֶׁאֵין אִסּוּר הַכְּנִיסָה בְלֹא עֲבוֹדָה אֶלָּא מַעֲלָה מִדִּבְרֵיהֶם; אֲבָל אִם עָבַד וְהוּא קְרוּעַ בְּגָדִים לוֹקֶה, לְפִי מַה שֶּׁכָּתַב בְּשֵׁם בַּעַל הֲלָכוֹת.

[שֶׁלֹּא יֵצְאוּ הַכֹּהֲנִים מִן הַמִּקְדָּשׁ בִּשְׁעַת עֲבוֹדָה]

קנא שֶׁלֹּא יֵצְאוּ הַכֹּהֲנִים מִן הַמִּקְדָּשׁ בִּשְׁעַת עֲבוֹדָה, שֶׁנֶּאֱמַר: וּמִפֶּתַח אֹהֶל מוֹעֵד לֹא תֵצְאוּ פֶּן תָּמֻתוּ. וְנִכְפְּלָה מְנִיעָה זוֹ כְּמוֹ־כֵן בְּכֹהֵן גָּדוֹל, וְאָמַר: וּמִן הַמִּקְדָּשׁ לֹא יֵצֵא. וּלְשׁוֹן סִפְרָא: "וּמִפֶּתַח אֹהֶל מוֹעֵד", יָכוֹל בִּשְׁעַת עֲבוֹדָה וְשֶׁלֹּא בִשְׁעַת עֲבוֹדָה, תַּלְמוּד לוֹמַר: וּמִן הַמִּקְדָּשׁ לֹא יֵצֵא וְלֹא יְחַלֵּל, הֱוֵי אוֹמֵר בִּשְׁעַת עֲבוֹדָה; "כִּי שֶׁמֶן מִשְׁחַת יי עֲלֵיכֶם", אֵין לִי אֶלָּא אַהֲרֹן וּבָנָיו שֶׁנִּמְשְׁחוּ בְשֶׁמֶן הַמִּשְׁחָה שֶׁאִם יָצְאוּ בִשְׁעַת הָעֲבוֹדָה חַיָּבִים מִיתָה, מִנַּיִן לְכָל הַכֹּהֲנִים שֶׁבְּדוֹרוֹת, שֶׁנֶּאֱמַר: כִּי שֶׁמֶן מִשְׁחַת יי עֲלֵיכֶם.

3. MT *hilchoth bi'ath ha-mikdash* i 15, derived from Sifra cited above.
4. MT *ibid.*
5. In his commentary to ShM negative precept §163, end.

§151 1. When his leaving may cause profanation — of the service.
2. To sanctify you and all your descendants as *kohanim*. All future generations were thus sanctified by his anointment. Hence the precept applies to all.

What lies at the root of the precept has been written about letting the head become overgrown, which precedes this (§149). The cases of those with overgrown heads and those with torn clothes are alike in all their laws.

Among the laws of the precept, there is what our Sages of blessed memory said, that punishment for this tearing is incurred if it is like the rending done over the dead[3]—which evidently means a handbreadth: for so was it stated in the tractate *Mo'ed Katan* (22b), that a tear [in clothing, over the dead] is not to be less than a handbreadth. The rest of its details are explained.

It applies when the Temple is extant, for the male *kohanim*. If one violated it and went into the Sanctuary, beyond the altar, with torn clothing, and did service, he would deserve death at Heaven's hands; but if he did no [Temple] service, this involves [only] an injunction, and he would receive whiplashes. This is by the view of Rambam of blessed memory.[4] However, to the mind of Ramban of blessed memory,[5] the penalty of whiplashes does not apply to entering the Sanctuary in torn clothing: for the ban on entering without doing service is only a higher standard set by the Sages; but if he did service while in torn clothing, he would receive a whipping, according to what he wrote in the name of the author of *Halachoth G'doloth.*

[THE KOHANIM ARE NOT TO LEAVE THE TEMPLE DURING THEIR SACRED SERVICE]

151 that the *kohanim* should not go out of the Sanctuary during the service: for it is stated, *And from the door of the tent of meeting do not go out, lest you die* (Leviticus 10:7). This prohibition too was repeated for the *kohen gadol*, in the statement, *and from the sanctuary he shall not go out* (Leviticus 21:12). In the wording of the Midrash *Sifra*: "And from the door of the tent of meeting": I might think it means both during the [Temple] service and outside the time of the service; hence Scripture states, *and from the sanctuary he shall not go out, and he shall not profane* (*ibid.*)—i.e. during the service;[1] *for the anointing oil of the Lord is upon you* (Leviticus 10:7): hence I can know about none but Aaron and his sons, who were anointed with the anointing oil (Leviticus 8:30), that if they went out during the Temple service, they would be punishable by death. How can I know it about all *kohanim* through the generations?—because it is stated, "for the anointing oil of the Lord is upon you."[2]

וְכָתַב הַמַּעְתִּיק בְּשֵׁם הָרַמְבָּ״ם זִכְרוֹנוֹ לִבְרָכָה: דַּע שֶׁיֵּשׁ בְּכֹהֵן גָּדוֹל תּוֹסֶפֶת, שֶׁהוּא לֹא יֵלֵךְ אַחַר הַמִּטָּה, וְזֶהוּ נִגְלֶה בִּלְשׁוֹן הַכָּתוּב בְּאָמְרוֹ: וּמִן הַמִּקְדָּשׁ לֹא יֵצֵא. וְכָךְ נִתְבָּאֵר בְּפֶרֶק שֵׁנִי מִסַּנְהֶדְרִין, שֶׁהוּא אִם מֵת לוֹ מֵת אֵינוֹ יוֹצֵא אַחַר הַמִּטָּה, וְהֵבִיאוּ רְאָיָה עַל זֶה מֵאָמְרוֹ: וּמִן הַמִּקְדָּשׁ לֹא יֵצֵא.

וְלָמַדְנוּ מִזֶּה שֶׁמֻּתָּר לוֹ לַעֲבֹד בְּיוֹם שֶׁיָּמוּת לוֹ מֵת; וְכָךְ אָמְרוּ זִכְרוֹנָם לִבְרָכָה בְּמַסֶּכֶת סַנְהֶדְרִין: ״וּמִן הַמִּקְדָּשׁ לֹא יֵצֵא וְלֹא יְחַלֵּל״, הָא אַחֵר שֶׁעָבַד חִלֵּל — כְּלוֹמַר כֹּהֵן הֶדְיוֹט, שֶׁאֵין הָעֲבוֹדָה מֻתֶּרֶת לוֹ, וְהוּא אוֹנֵן, הוּא מֻזְהָר עַל זֶה, כְּלוֹמַר שֶׁלֹּא יַעֲבֹד אוֹנֵן; וְכָךְ נִתְבָּאֵר בְּסוֹף הוֹרָיוֹת זֶה הָעִקָּר, שֶׁכֹּהֵן הֶדְיוֹט אוֹנֵן לֹא יַעֲבֹד, וְכֹהֵן גָּדוֹל עוֹבֵד וְהוּא אוֹנֵן. הִנֵּה נִתְבָּאֵר לְךָ שֶׁאָמְרוֹ הִנֵּה ״וְלֹא יְחַלֵּל״ שָׂמוּהוּ שְׁלִילוּת לֹא מְנִיעָה, לוֹמַר שֶׁלֹּא תִהְיֶה עֲבוֹדָתוֹ חֻלִּין וְאַף־עַל־פִּי שֶׁהוּא אוֹנֵן.

וּמִן הַנִּרְאֶה מִדִּבְרֵי הָרַמְבָּ״ן זִכְרוֹנוֹ לִבְרָכָה כִּי הוּא סוֹבֵר כִּי ״לֹא יְחַלֵּל״ אֵינוֹ שְׁלִילוּת, אֲבָל הוּא מְנִיעָה. לְכֹהֵן גָּדוֹל שֶׁנִּצְטַוָּה שֶׁלֹּא יֵצֵא מִן הַמִּקְדָּשׁ מִפְּנֵי מֵתוֹ וְלֹא יְחַלֵּל עֲבוֹדַת הַשֵּׁם (יִתְבָּרֵךְ), כִּי חִלּוּל יִהְיֶה לָעֲבוֹדָה שֶׁיַּנִּחֶנָּה הַמְשָׁרֵת הַגָּדוֹל בִּשְׁבִיל שׁוּם דָּבָר בָּעוֹלָם; וְהוּא יְפָרֵשׁ כָּל עִנְיָן זֶה בְּדֶרֶךְ אַחֶרֶת, כְּמוֹ שֶׁכָּתַב בְּפֵרוּשׁ הַחֻמָּשׁ.

מִשָּׁרְשֵׁי הַמִּצְוָה, הַיְסוֹד הַבָּנוּי לָנוּ בְּהַגְדָּלַת הַבַּיִת וְהָעֲבוֹדוֹת הַנַּעֲשׂוֹת שָׁם, וְעַל־כֵּן רָאוּי עַל־כָּל־פָּנִים שֶׁלֹּא לָצֵאת וּלְהַנִּיחַ הָעֲבוֹדָה הַיְקָרָה בְּשׁוּם דָּבָר בָּעוֹלָם, כִּי בֶאֱמֶת אִם יַנִּיחוּהָ יִהְיֶה זִלְזוּל בָּהּ וְיִהְיוּ מַרְאִים בְּעַצְמָם שֶׁיִּהְיֶה

3. R. Abraham b. Ḥisdai, the first to translate ShM (an earlier version) from Arabic to Hebrew (but the translation has not survived).

4. ShM negative precept §165. (See also MT *hilchoth k'lé ha-mikdash* v 5, and *Kessef Mishneh*.)

5. The verse is now understood to convey that it is only the *kohen gadol* who does not cause profanation (desecration) if he stays on at the Sanctuary and continues ministering while he is an *'onén*; but should an ordinary *kohen* do so, it is profanation.

6. The citation from ShM negative precept §165 (on which the first paragraph of the section, too, is based) ends here.

6a. See his commentary, Leviticus 10:6.

7. Literally, the foundation built for us; see §95.

Now, the transcriber[3] wrote in the name of Rambam of blessed memory:[4] Know that there is an additional law for the *kohen gadol*—that he should not follow the coffin [at a funeral]; this is apparent in the expression of the verse, "and from the sanctuary he shall not go out" (Leviticus 21:12).

So is it explained in chapter 2 of the tractate *Sanhedrin* (18a), that if someone of his kin died, he was not to go out to follow the coffin; and confirmation was brought for this from the verse, "and from the sanctuary he shall not go out."

And we learn from this that it is permitted him to serve on the day that kin of his dies. As our Sages of blessed memory stated in the tractate *Sanhedrin* (84a): "and from the sanctuary he shall not go out, and he shall not profane"—hence if someone else did service, he *would* profane (cause desecration).[5] In other words, if an ordinary *kohen*, for whom [Temple] service is not permitted, was an *'onén* [in grief over dead kin before the burial], he is enjoined against this—which means that an *'onén* was not to do service. And so it is clarified at the end of tractate *Horayoth* (12b): "This is the main rule: that when an ordinary *kohen* is an *'onén*, he is not to do service; but a *kohen gadol* serves when he is an *'onén*." Thus it has been explained to you that Scripture's words here, "and he shall not profane," are given as a negative statement, not as a restriction; it is to convey that his Temple service will not be profane (non-holy) even if he is an *'onén*.[6]

However, it would appear from the words of Ramban of blessed memory[6a] that he holds that "he shall not profane" is not a negative statement but rather a restriction on the *kohen gadol*—that he was commanded not to leave the Sanctuary on account of his dead and [thus] he should not profane the service of the Eternal Lord (be He blessed); it would be a desecration of the service for this great minister to leave it because of anything whatever in the world. So he [Ramban] would explain this entire matter in a different way, as he wrote in his commentary on the Pentateuch (Leviticus 21:12).

At the root of the precept lies the foundation-concept firmly established[7] for us, about the magnification of the grandeur of the Temple and the tasks of service that were done there. It is therefore right, no matter what, not to go out and abandon the precious service for anything at all in the world. For truly, if it were left, that would be a degradation for it, as people would thus demonstrate that for them there is something greater than the service of the Eternal Lord, since it could

בָּעוֹלָם דָּבָר גָּדוֹל מֵעֲבוֹדַת הַשֵּׁם, אַחַר שֶׁתִּהְיֶה נִדְחֵית אֲפִלּוּ לְפִי שָׁעָה בִּשְׁבִיל שׁוּם דָּבָר אַחֵר; וְעַל־כֵּן הֻזְהֲרוּ עַל זֶה בְּמִיתָה.

דִּינֵי הַמִּצְוָה, כְּגוֹן מַה שֶּׁאָמְרוּ רַבּוֹתֵינוּ זִכְרוֹנָם לִבְרָכָה שֶׁכֹּהֵן הֶדְיוֹט אַף־עַל־פִּי שֶׁאֵינוֹ רַשַּׁאי לָצֵאת מִן הַמִּקְדָּשׁ בִּשְׁעַת עֲבוֹדָה, כְּמוֹ שֶׁנֶּאֱמַר: וּמִפֶּתַח אֹהֶל מוֹעֵד לֹא תֵצְאוּ פֶּן תָּמֻתוּ, מִכָּל־מָקוֹם אִם מֵת לוֹ מֵת שֶׁהוּא רָאוּי לְהִתְאַבֵּל עָלָיו, אֵינוֹ עוֹבֵד, לְפִי שֶׁהוּא אוֹנֵן, וְאוֹנֵן אָסוּר בַּעֲבוֹדָה; וְאַף־עַל־פִּי שֶׁאֵינוֹ עוֹבֵד, הֻזְהַר שֶׁלֹּא לָצֵאת מִשָּׁם עַד שֶׁתִּגָּמֵר הָעֲבוֹדָה שֶׁהָיָה הוּא עָסוּק בָּהּ, מִן הַטַּעַם שֶׁאָמַרְנוּ, לִכְבוֹד הַדָּבָר, שֶׁלֹּא יְהֵא דוֹמֶה כְּעוֹסֵק בְּדִבְרֵי עֲרַאי. וְיָתֵר עָלָיו כֹּהֵן גָּדוֹל שֶׁהוּא חַיָּב שֶׁלֹּא יֵצֵא מִן הַמִּקְדָּשׁ וְגַם שֶׁלֹּא לְהַנִּיחַ עֲבוֹדָתוֹ כְּלָל בִּשְׁבִיל אֲנִינוּת, שֶׁנֶּאֱמַר: וּמִן הַמִּקְדָּשׁ לֹא יֵצֵא וְלֹא יְחַלֵּל וְגוֹמֵר, וּבָא הַפֵּרוּשׁ בְּזֶה הַמִּקְרָא, כְּלוֹמַר שֶׁלֹּא יֵצֵא אֶלָּא יַעֲבֹד עֲבוֹדָתוֹ שֶׁהוּא עוֹסֵק בָּהּ, וְלֹא תְהֵא עֲבוֹדָתוֹ מְחֻלֶּלֶת בִּשְׁבִיל אֲנִינוּתוֹ; וְיֶתֶר פְּרָטֶיהָ, מְבֹאָרִים בִּזְבָחִים.

וְנוֹהֶגֶת בִּזְמַן הַבַּיִת בְּזִכְרֵי כְהֻנָּה. וְאִם עָבַר וְיָצָא בִּשְׁעַת עֲבוֹדָה, לוֹקֶה.

[שֶׁלֹּא לְהִכָּנֵס שָׁתוּי יַיִן בַּמִּקְדָּשׁ וְכֵן שֶׁלֹּא יוֹרֶה שָׁתוּי]

קנב שֶׁלֹּא לְהִכָּנֵס שָׁתוּי בַּמִּקְדָּשׁ, וְכֵן שֶׁלֹּא לְהוֹרוֹת, כְּלוֹמַר שֶׁלֹּא לָדוּן בְּדָבָר מִדִּינֵי הַתּוֹרָה, בְּעוֹד שֶׁיְּהֵא הָאָדָם שִׁכּוֹר, שֶׁנֶּאֱמַר: יַיִן וְשֵׁכָר אַל תֵּשְׁתְּ וְגוֹמֵר, בְּבֹאֲכֶם אֶל אֹהֶל מוֹעֵד. וּלְשׁוֹן הַתַּלְמוּד: שָׁתָה רְבִיעִית אַל יוֹרֶה. וּלְשׁוֹן סִפְרֵי: "יַיִן ... אַל תֵּשְׁתְּ", אֵין לִי אֶלָּא יַיִן, מִנַּיִן לְרַבּוֹת שְׁאָר הַמְּשַׁכְּרִים, תַּלְמוּד לוֹמַר: וְשֵׁכָר. אִם־כֵּן לָמָּה נֶאֱמַר יַיִן, עַל הַיַּיִן בְּמִיתָה וְעַל שְׁאָר הַמְּשַׁכְּרִין בְּלָאו.

וְשָׁם נֶאֱמַר: מִנַּיִן שֶׁאֵינוֹ חַיָּב אֶלָּא בִּשְׁעַת הָעֲבוֹדָה, תַּלְמוּד לוֹמַר: אַתָּה

8. I.e. by someone else (MY following *Kessef Mishneh* to source in note 9).
9. MT *hilchoth bi'ath ha-mikdash* ii 6 (see *Kessef Mishneh* for sources).

§152
1. TB 'Eruvin 64a.
2. Since the second, general term for all strong drink would include wine.

be thrust aside, if even for a while, for the sake of something else. For this reason they were adjured about it on pain of death.

The laws of the precept are, for instance, what our Sages of blessed memory said: that although an ordinary *kohen* was not permitted to leave the Sanctuary during the service, as it is stated, *and from the door of the tent of meeting do not go out, lest you die* (Leviticus 10:7), in any event if someone of his [kin] died for whom he should properly mourn, he was not to do service, since he was an *'onén* [in grief before the burial], and Temple service was forbidden to an *'onén*. But even though he was not to serve, he was adjured not to go out from there until the task of service in which he was engaged would be finished[8]—for the reason we have conveyed: for the honor of the matter, that he should not seem like a person engaged in something occasional. The *kohen gadol* bore a greater restraint than he did, in that he was duty-bound not to leave the Sanctuary and also not to abandon his service at all on account of being an *'onén:* for it is stated, *and from the sanctuary he shall not go out, and he shall not profane*, etc. (Leviticus 21:12); and the interpretation was given for this verse that it means to say he should not leave but rather do his task of service in which he is engaged, and his service will not be disqualified because he is an *'onén.*[9] The rest of its details are explained in the Talmud tractate *Z'vaḥim.*

It is in effect when the Temple is extant, for the male *kohanim*. If one transgressed and went out during service, he would be given whiplashes.

[AFTER DRINKING WINE A KOHEN SHOULD NOT ENTER THE SANCTUARY, AND NO ONE IS TO GIVE A RULING]

152 not to enter the Sanctuary while intoxicated, and so too not to render a ruling—i.e. that nothing of the laws of the Torah should be judged [by him] while a man is drunk: for it is stated, *Drink no wine nor strong drink . . . when you go into the tent of meeting* (Leviticus 10:9). In the language of the Talmud: If one drank a *r'vi'ith* [of wine] he should not give any ruling.[1] In the language of the Midrash *Sifra:* "Drink no wine . . ."—thus I know this about no more than wine; how do I learn to enlarge this to include all intoxicating beverages?—Scripture adds "and strong drink." In that case, why was wine stated?[2]—for wine the penalty is death; with other strong drink, a negative precept is transgressed.

It is stated there, further: How do we know that punishment is

וּבָנֶיךָ... וְלֹא תָמוּתוּ, אַתָּה וּבָנֶיךָ בְּמִיתָה, וְאֵין יִשְׂרָאֵל חַיָּבִין מִיתָה עַל הַהוֹרָאָה.

שֹׁרֶשׁ הַמִּצְוָה יָדוּעַ, שֶׁאֵין רָאוּי לְהִתְעַסֵּק בַּדְּבָרִים הַיְקָרִים בְּתַכְלִית הַיֹּקֶר כְּמוֹ עִנְיְנֵי הַמִּקְדָּשׁ וְדִבְרֵי הַתּוֹרָה רַק בְּעֵת שֶׁיִּהְיֶה הָאָדָם מְיֻשָּׁב בְּדַעְתּוֹ וּמְכֻוָּן בְּכָל מַעֲשָׂיו; אֵין לְהַאֲרִיךְ בִּדְבָרִים פְּשׁוּטִים.

מִדִּינֵי הַמִּצְוָה, מַה שֶּׁאָמְרוּ זִכְרוֹנָם לִבְרָכָה שֶׁכָּל כֹּהֵן הַכָּשֵׁר לַעֲבוֹדָה, אִם שָׁתָה יַיִן, הֲרֵי זֶה אָסוּר לוֹ לְהִכָּנֵס מִן הַמִּזְבֵּחַ וְלִפְנִים; וְאִם נִכְנַס וְעָבַד, עֲבוֹדָתוֹ פְּסוּלָה וְחַיָּב מִיתָה בִּידֵי שָׁמַיִם, שֶׁנֶּאֱמַר: וְלֹא תָמוּתוּ. וְכֵן אָסוּר לְכָל אָדָם, בֵּין כֹּהֵן בֵּין יִשְׂרָאֵל, לְהִכָּנֵס לַמִּקְדָּשׁ כֻּלּוֹ, מִתְּחִלַּת עֶזְרַת יִשְׂרָאֵל וְלִפְנִים, כְּשֶׁהוּא שָׁתוּי יַיִן אוֹ שִׁכּוֹר אוֹ פְרוּעַ רֹאשׁ דֶּרֶךְ נִוּוּל, כְּלוֹמַר שֶׁשַּׂעֲרוֹת רֹאשׁוֹ גְּדוֹלִים בְּיוֹתֵר, אוֹ קְרוּעַ בְּגָדִים; וְאַף־עַל־פִּי שֶׁאֵינוֹ בְּאַזְהָרָה, אִסּוּר יֵשׁ בַּדָּבָר, וְהָאִסּוּר אֵינוֹ אֶלָּא מִפְּנֵי כְבוֹד הַבַּיִת. וּלְפִיכָךְ יִשְׂרָאֵל מֻתָּר לִכָּנֵס שָׁם בְּשַׂעֲרוֹת רֹאשׁוֹ מְגֻדָּלוֹת יוֹתֵר מִשְּׁלֹשִׁים יוֹם, שֶׁאֵין זֶה נִוּוּל אֵצֶל בְּנֵי־אָדָם; וְאַף־עַל־פִּי שֶׁהַכֹּהֲנִים הֻזְהֲרוּ בָּזֶה לְגֹדֶל קְדֻשָּׁתָן וְקִרְבָתָן בְּבֵית הַקָּדוֹשׁ, שֶׁרָאוּי שֶׁלֹּא יְהֵא בָהֶם דָּבָר יָתֵר כְּלָל, רַק שֶׁיִּהְיוּ כֻלָּן יָפִים וּמוּם אֵין בָּם, אֵין שְׁאָר כָּל אָדָם בַּגֶּדֶר שֶׁלָּהֶם, רַק שֶׁלֹּא יִכָּנְסוּ שָׁם בִּשְׂעָרוֹת גְּדוֹלִים בְּיוֹתֵר, כְּמוֹ שֶׁאָמַרְנוּ.

וְשִׁעוּר הַיַּיִן שֶׁיִּשְׁתֶּה הָאָדָם וִיהֵא אָסוּר לִכָּנֵס לַמִּקְדָּשׁ אוֹ לְהוֹרוֹת, הוּא רְבִיעִית לֹג, שֶׁהוּא בֵּיצָה וּמֶחֱצָה, וְשֶׁיִּשְׁתֶּה אוֹתוֹ חַי וּבְבַת־אַחַת, וּבִתְנַאי שֶׁעָבְרוּ

3. The bracketed addition is according to ShM negative precept §73, from which the first two paragraphs are derived. It was obviously present in the original, and omitted by a scribe's oversight between two identical expressions.

4. Sifra, *sh'mini, perek* 1, 6.

5. TB Sanhedrin 22b (see § 149, sixth paragraph).

6. MT *hilchoth bi'ath ha-mikdash* i 17.

7. See § 149, note 6.

8. Expression based on Song of Songs 4:7.

9. TB K'rithoth 13b. ("One and a half eggs" means the amount of liquid that this volume would displace.)

incurred only at the time of the Temple service?—because Scripture states, [*you nor your sons with you, when you go into the tent of meeting, that you should not die* (Leviticus 10:9). I might think that Israelites (non-*kohanim*) should incur death for giving a ruling—while intoxicated?—Hence Scripture states][3] *you nor your sons . . . that you should not die:* you and your sons are under pain of death, but ordinary Israelites are not punishable by death for giving a ruling [at a time when they are not sober].

The root reason for the precept is known (evident): it is not proper to be occupied with matters of the utmost preciousness, such as the matters of the Sanctuary and the words of the Torah, at any other time but when a man is settled in his mind and concentrated in all his actions. There is no need to elaborate about plain, simple matters.

Among the laws of the precept, there is what the Sages of blessed memory said: that if any *kohen* who was fit and worthy for the Temple service drank wine, he was forbidden to go in beyond the altar;[4] if he entered and did service, his service would be disqualified, unacceptable, and he would be punishable by death at Heaven's hands—for it is stated, *that you should not die* (Leviticus 10:9).[5] It is likewise forbidden for every man, *kohen* or Israelite (non-*kohen*), to enter any part of the Sanctuary, from the beginning of the court of the Israelites and within, when he was drunk with wine or [otherwise] inebriated; with his head overgrown in a disheveled way—in other words, if the hair on his head was inordinately long; or with torn clothing.[6] Even though this is under no injunction [of Scripture], there is a ban on the matter, the ban being only for the sake of the honor of the Temple. Therefore an Israelite (non-*kohen*) is allowed to enter there with the hair of his head grown for more than thirty days, since this is not a state of dishevelment among ordinary people.[7] Even if the *kohanim* were adjured about this, on account of their great holiness and their close connection with the holy Temple, so that it is fitting that there should be nothing excessive about them but they should only be "all fair, with no flaw in them,"[8] other people are not in their category. Hence they should merely not enter there with excessively long hair, as we stated.

The measure of wine a man must drink in order to become forbidden to enter the Sanctuary or render a ruling, is a *r'vi'ith*, a fourth of a *log*, which is the amount of one and a half eggs—and this if he drinks it neat [unmixed] and all at once, and provided forty days passed since the wine was made.[9] If one of these [conditions] was lacking, he is

עַל הַיַּיִן אַרְבָּעִים יוֹם מִשֶּׁנַּעֲשָׂה. חָסֵר אַחַת מֵאֵלּוּ, פָּטוּר אֲבָל אָסוּר, וְאֵינוֹ מְחַלֵּל עֲבוֹדָה בְּכָךְ.

שָׁתָה יוֹתֵר מֵרְבִיעִית מִן הַיַּיִן, אַף־עַל־פִּי שֶׁהָיָה מָזוּג וְאַף־עַל־פִּי שֶׁהִפְסִיק וְשָׁתָה מְעַט מְעַט, חַיָּב מִיתָה וּפוֹסֵל הָעֲבוֹדָה. הָיָה שִׁכּוֹר מִשְּׁאָר הַמְשַׁכְּרִים, אָסוּר לְהִכָּנֵס לַמִּקְדָּשׁ; וְאִם נִכְנַס וְעָבַד וְהוּא שִׁכּוֹר מִשְּׁאָר הַמְשַׁכְּרִים, אֲפִלּוּ מִן הֶחָלָב אוֹ מִן הַדְּבֵלָה, הֲרֵי זֶה לוֹקֶה, וַעֲבוֹדָתוֹ כְשֵׁרָה, שֶׁאֵין חַיָּבִין מִיתָה אֶלָּא עַל הַיַּיִן בִּשְׁעַת הָעֲבוֹדָה, וְאֵין מִתְחַלֶּלֶת אֶלָּא בְשִׁכּוֹר מִן הַיַּיִן.

וּכְשֵׁם שֶׁאָסוּר לְכֹהֵן לָבוֹא לַמִּקְדָּשׁ מִפְּנֵי הַשִּׁכְרוּת כָּךְ אָסוּר לְכָל אָדָם, בֵּין כֹּהֵן בֵּין יִשְׂרָאֵל, לְהוֹרוֹת כְּשֶׁהוּא שָׁתוּי; אֲפִלּוּ שָׁתָה דְּבַשׁ תְּמָרִים אוֹ חָלָב וְנִתְבַּלְבְּלָה דַעְתּוֹ, אַל יוֹרֶה — שֶׁנֶּאֱמַר בְּפָרָשַׁת יַיִן וְשֵׁכָר אַל תֵּשְׁתְּ: וּלְהוֹרֹת אֶת בְּנֵי יִשְׂרָאֵל.

וְאִם הוֹרָה בְּדָבָר שֶׁהוּא מְפֹרָשׁ בַּתּוֹרָה עַד שֶׁיּוֹדִיעוּהוּ הַצְּדוֹקִין, מֻתָּר — כְּגוֹן שֶׁהוֹרָה שֶׁהַשֶּׁרֶץ טָמֵא וְהַדָּם אָסוּר וְכַיּוֹצֵא בָהֶן; וּמֻתָּר לְשִׁכּוֹר לִקְרוֹת בַּתּוֹרָה, וַאֲפִלּוּ הֲלָכוֹת וּמִדְרָשׁוֹת, וְהוּא שֶׁלֹּא יוֹרֶה. וְאִם הָיָה חָכָם קָבוּעַ לַהוֹרָאָה לֹא יְלַמֵּד, שֶׁלִּמּוּדוֹ הוֹרָאָה הִיא.

שָׁתָה כְּדֵי רְבִיעִית בִּלְבָד וְהָיָה בָהּ מַיִם כָּל שֶׁהוּא, אוֹ יָשַׁן מְעַט, אוֹ הָלַךְ כְּדֵי מִיל, כְּבָר עָבַר הַיַּיִן וּמֻתָּר לַעֲבֹד; אֲבָל אִם שָׁתָה יוֹתֵר מֵרְבִיעִית, אֲפִלּוּ מָזוּג, אִם יָשַׁן שֵׁנָה מְעַט אוֹ הָלַךְ בַּדֶּרֶךְ מוֹסִיפִין בְּשִׁכְרוּתוֹ, אֶלָּא יִשְׁהֶא לְפִי הַשִּׁכְרוּת עַד שֶׁלֹּא יִשָּׁאֵר מִשִּׁכְרוּתוֹ שׁוּם דָּבָר בָּעוֹלָם.

אַנְשֵׁי מִשְׁמָר מֻתָּרִין לִשְׁתּוֹת יַיִן בַּלֵּילוֹת אֲבָל לֹא בִימֵי שַׁבָּתָן; וַאֲפִלּוּ שְׁאָר בָּתֵּי־אָבוֹת שֶׁל מִשְׁמָר, שֶׁאֵין עֲבוֹדָתָן אוֹתוֹ הַיּוֹם, אֲסוּרִים, שֶׁמָּא תִּכְבַּד הָעֲבוֹדָה עַל אַנְשֵׁי בֵית־אָב שֶׁל אוֹתוֹ יוֹם וְיִצְטָרְכוּ לַאֲחֵרִים מֵאַנְשֵׁי מִשְׁמָרָן לְסַיְּעָן; וְאַנְשֵׁי

10. TB *ibid.* MT *ibid.* i 1.

11. MT *ibid.* 1–2.

12. TB K'thuboth 10b.

13. Like the later Karaites, they accepted only the Written Torah as authoritative.

14. TB K'rithoth 13b.

15. See § 80, note 8. For practical purposes, it means about twenty minutes.

16. MT *hilchoth bi'ath ha-mikdash* i 5, based on TB 'Eruvin 64b.

17. In the days of the Temple, the *kohanim* were divided into twenty-four groups, called watches; each watch served in its turn at the Sanctuary for a week.

18. Every watch (note 17) was further divided into seven subgroups, called "fathers' houses," each of which served one day of the week that was the watch's period of duty.

free of penalty, although it is forbidden. But he would not profane the Temple service by this.[10]

If someone drank more than a *r'vi'ith* of wine, then even if it was mixed [with water], and even if he paused and drank bit by bit, he would deserve death and make his service unacceptable. If he was drunk from other intoxicating beverages, he was forbidden to enter the Sanctuary; and if he entered and did service while unsober from other intoxicating beverages, even [if made] from milk or pressed figs, he would receive whiplashes, but his Temple service would be acceptable: for the death penalty would be incurred over nothing other than wine [causing inebriation] during the Temple service; and it is profaned by none but someone drunk from wine.[11]

Now, just as a *kohen* was forbidden to enter the Sanctuary on account of intoxication, so is any man, *kohen* or Israelite (non-*kohen*) forbidden to render a ruling while drunk. Even if he drank [fermented] date honey or milk and his mind became confused, he should not give a ruling:[12] for it is stated in this section of "Drink no wine nor strong drink": *and to teach the Israelites* (Leviticus 10:11).

If a person gave a ruling about something so explicit in the Torah that even the Sadducees[13] would declare it so, this is permissible: for example, if he ruled that a [dead] crawling creature is ritually unclean, or that blood is forbidden (§148), and so on.[14] It is permissible, too, for an intoxicated person to read aloud in the Torah, even normative laws and homiletic teachings—but this if he gives no ruling.[14] If he was a scholar permanently assigned to render rulings, he should not teach, for his teaching is [regarded with the authority of] legal decision.[14]

If someone drank solely the amount of a *r'vi'ith* and there was some bit of water in it, or if he slept a little or walked the amount of a *mil*[15] [afterward, then the effect of] the wine passed off, and he would be permitted to serve [in the Sanctuary]. But if he drank more than a *r'vi'ith*, even if it was mixed [with water], then he took a little nap or took a walk on the road, it would [only] add to his intoxication. He should rather wait according to the [degree of] intoxication, until nothing whatever remained of his drunkenness.[16]

The members of a watch[17] were permitted to drink wine at night, but not during the days of their week [of duty]. Even the other "fathers' houses" of the watch, whose turn of service was not on that day,[18] would be forbidden—in case the Temple service became too much for the members of the "father's house" of that day and they would need

מִשְׁמָר שֶׁל אוֹתוֹ יוֹם אֲסוּרִין לִשְׁתּוֹת בֵּין בַּיּוֹם בֵּין בַּלַּיְלָה, שֶׁמָּא יִשְׁתֶּה בַּלַּיְלָה וְיַשְׁכִּים לַעֲבוֹדָתוֹ וַעֲדַיִן לֹא סָר יֵינוֹ מֵעָלָיו.

כֹּהֵן שֶׁיּוֹדֵעַ מֵאֵי זֶה בֵּית־אָב הוּא, וְיוֹדֵעַ שֶׁבָּתֵּי אֲבוֹתָיו קְבוּעִים הֵם בַּעֲבוֹדַת הַיּוֹם, אָסוּר לוֹ לִשְׁתּוֹת כָּל אוֹתוֹ יוֹם. הָיָה יוֹדֵעַ מֵאֵי זֶה מִשְׁמָר הוּא וְאֵינוֹ מַכִּיר בֵּית־אָב שֶׁלּוֹ, אָסוּר לִשְׁתּוֹת כָּל אוֹתוֹ שַׁבָּת שֶׁמִּשְׁמַרְתּוֹ עוֹבְדִין בָּהּ. לֹא הָיָה מַכִּיר מִשְׁמַרְתּוֹ וְלֹא בֵּית אֲבוֹתָיו, הַדִּין נוֹתֵן שֶׁאָסוּר לִשְׁתּוֹת לְעוֹלָם, אֲבָל תַּקָּנָתוֹ קַלְקָלָתוֹ וַהֲרֵי הוּא מֻתָּר לִשְׁתּוֹת תָּמִיד, לְפִי שֶׁאֵינוֹ יָכוֹל לַעֲבֹד עַד שֶׁיִּקָּבַע בְּבֵית־אָב שֶׁלּוֹ וּבְמִשְׁמַרְתּוֹ.

וְנוֹהֵג אִסּוּר בִּיאַת מִקְדָּשׁ בְּשִׁכְרוּת בִּזְמַן הַבַּיִת, בִּזְכָרִים וּנְקֵבוֹת; וּמְנִיעַת הַהוֹרָאָה בְּכָל מָקוֹם וּבְכָל זְמַן בִּזְכָרִים, וְכֵן בְּאִשָּׁה חֲכָמָה הָרְאוּיָה לְהוֹרוֹת. וְכָל מִי שֶׁהוּא חָכָם גָּדוֹל שֶׁבְּנֵי־אָדָם סוֹמְכִין עַל הוֹרָאָתוֹ, אָסוּר לוֹ לִשְׁנוֹת לְתַלְמִידָיו וְהוּא שָׁתוּי, שֶׁהַלִּמּוּד שֶׁלּוֹ כְּמוֹ הוֹרָאָה הוּא, כְּמוֹ שֶׁאָמַרְנוּ.

וְעוֹבֵר עָלֶיהָ וְנִכְנַס שְׁתוּי יַיִן מִבֵּין הָאוּלָם וְלַמִּזְבֵּחַ וְלִפְנִים, חַיָּב מַלְקוֹת; וְאִם עָבַד עֲבוֹדָה חַיָּב מִיתָה בִּידֵי שָׁמַיִם; וְאִם שָׁתָה מִשְּׁאָר הַמְּשַׁכְּרִין וְעָבַד, חַיָּב מַלְקוֹת לְבַד, לֹא מִיתָה. וְכֵן כָּל מִי שֶׁהוֹרָה וְהוּא שָׁתוּי, בֵּין כֹּהֵן אוֹ יִשְׂרָאֵל, עָבַר עַל לָאו, בֵּין שָׁתוּי מִן הַיַּיִן אוֹ שָׁתוּי מִשְּׁאָר הַמְּשַׁכְּרִין. וְהָרַמְבַּ״ן זִכְרוֹנוֹ לִבְרָכָה כָּתַב כִּי מַעֲלָה הִיא מִדִּבְרֵיהֶם שֶׁלֹּא לְהִכָּנֵס לַמִּקְדָּשׁ שְׁתוּי יַיִן, וְאֵין מִן הַתּוֹרָה, אֶלָּא שֶׁלֹּא יַעֲבֹד שָׁתוּי.

[מִצְוַת בְּדִיקַת סִימָנֵי בְּהֵמָה וְחַיָּה]

קנג שֶׁנִּצְטַוִּינוּ לִבְדֹּק סִימָנֵי בְּהֵמָה וְחַיָּה כְּשֶׁנִּרְצֶה לֶאֱכֹל מֵהֶם, וְהֵם מַעֲלַת

19. MT *ibid.* 6, based on TB Ta'anith 15b, 17a.
20. In case the Sanctuary is rebuilt and he will be needed to serve there (Rashi, TB Ta'anith 17a, s.v. *'asur*). Here a concrete law was formulated out of the invincible Jewish faith that on any day the Messiah can come and the Sanctuary be instantly rebuilt with Divine aid.
21. TB K'rithoth 13b.
22. In his commentary to ShM negative precept §73.

others of the members of their watch to help them. The members of the watch for that day were forbidden to drink both during the day and the [preceding] night—for perhaps someone would drink at night and rise to his task of service, and the effects of his wine would not have worn off as yet.[19]

If a *kohen* knows of which "father's house" he is, and he knows that his "father's house" is assigned to the Temple service of this day, he is forbidden to drink the entire day.[20] If he knows of which watch he is, but does not recognize his "father's house," he is forbidden to drink that entire week in which his watch should be working. If he would recognize neither his watch nor his "father's house," the law would require that he should be forbidden forever to drink. But his remedy lies in his very state of abasement: you see, he is permitted to drink always, because he cannot serve [at the Temple] until he will be assigned his set place in his "father's house" and in his watch.[19]

The ban on entering the Sanctuary in a drunken state applies when the Temple is extant, for both man and woman; and the restriction on giving rulings applies in every place and every time, for men, and so too for a wise (learned) woman who is fit to render a ruling. Moreover, any man who is a great scholar on whose legal teaching people rely, is forbidden to teach his pupils while he is drunk: for his teaching is like giving decisions,[21] as we stated.

If someone violated it and entered, drunk with wine, further in than the area between the *'ulam* (entrance hall) and the altar, he would deserve whiplashes; and if he did any Temple service, he would deserve death at Heaven's hands. If he drank of other intoxicating beverages and did service, he would incur lashes alone, not death. Likewise, if anyone gave a ruling while drunk, whether a *kohen* or an Israelite, he would transgress a negative precept, whether he was drunk with wine or with any other of the intoxicating beverages.

Ramban of blessed memory wrote, however,[22] that it is [merely] a higher standard set by the Sages not to enter the Sanctuary drunk with wine; but by Torah law there is only the restriction that one should not serve [at the Temple] while drunk.

[TO EXAMINE THE SIGNS OF ANIMALS WHICH DETERMINE IF THEY ARE KOSHER]

153 that we were commanded to examine the [determining] marks
⟨147⟩ of a domestic or wild animal when we would wish to eat of them—

גֵּרָה וְשׁוֹסַעַת שֶׁסַע, שֶׁנֶּאֱמַר: זֹאת הַחַיָּה אֲשֶׁר תֹּאכְלוּ מִכָּל הַבְּהֵמָה אֲשֶׁר עַל הָאָרֶץ כֹּל מַפְרֶסֶת פַּרְסָה וְגוֹמֵר. וּלְשׁוֹן סִפְרָא: ״אוֹתָהּ תֹּאכֵלוּ״, אוֹתָהּ בַּאֲכִילָה וְאֵין בְּהֵמָה טְמֵאָה בַּאֲכִילָה — כְּלוֹמַר וְנִלְמַד מִזֶּה לָאו לִבְהֵמָה טְמֵאָה; וְלָאו כָּזֶה נִקְרָא לָאו הַבָּא מִכְּלַל עֲשֵׂה; וְנֶאֱמַר בְּמָקוֹם אַחֵר: וְהִבְדַּלְתֶּם בֵּין הַבְּהֵמָה הַטְּהוֹרָה לַטְּמֵאָה, וּכְתִיב עוֹד: לְהַבְדִּיל בֵּין הַטָּמֵא וּבֵין הַטָּהוֹר.

מִשָּׁרְשֵׁי מִצְוַת אִסּוּר הַמַּאֲכָלוֹת, כָּתַבְנוּ לְמַעְלָה בְּאַזְהָרַת טְרֵפָה וְחֵלֶב מַה שֶּׁיָּדַעְנוּ, וְהוּא הַשֹּׁרֶשׁ הַמַּסְפִּיק כְּפִי הַפְּשָׁט לְכֻלָּן. וְעִנְיַן הַצַּוָּאָה לִבְדֹּק סִימָנֵיהֶן הוֹלֵךְ אַחַר טַעַם אִסּוּרָן, שֶׁכָּל מַה שֶּׁבָּא לָנוּ אִסּוּר עָלָיו רָאוּי וּמְחֻיָּב עָלֵינוּ לְבָדְקוֹ יָפֶה.

וְהִנְנִי לֹא חָשַׂכְתִּי עֵטִי מִכְּתֹב דִּבְרֵי הָרַמְבָּ״ם זִכְרוֹנוֹ לִבְרָכָה בְּכָאן, שֶׁחָשַׁב הַמִּקְרָא הַזֶּה לְמִצְוַת עֲשֵׂה, מִפְּנֵי שֶׁיָּעַדְתִּי בְּרֹאשׁ דְּבָרַי לִכְתֹּב הַמִּצְווֹת עַל הַסֵּדֶר שֶׁחֲשָׁבָם הוּא — עִם הֱיוֹת לִבִּי נֶאֱחָז בְּעִנְיַן זֶה בִּסְבָרַת הָרַמְבָּ״ן זִכְרוֹנוֹ לִבְרָכָה, שֶׁכָּתַב שֶׁאֵין רָאוּי שֶׁנִּמְנֶה בְדִיקַת סִימָנֵי טָהֳרָה בִּבְהֵמוֹת מִצְוָה. כִּי בֶאֱמֶת אַחַר שֶׁאָסְרָה לָנוּ הַתּוֹרָה קְצָת הַבְּהֵמוֹת, עַל־כָּל־פָּנִים יִתְחַיֵּב לְהוֹדִיעֵנוּ סִימָנֵי הַטְּהוֹרוֹת לְהַפְרִישֵׁנוּ מִן הָאִסּוּר, וְאֵין זֶה רָאוּי כְּלָל לְהֵחָשֵׁב בְּחֶשְׁבּוֹן מִצְוָה. וְהוּא הַדִּין וְהוּא הַטַּעַם גַּם־כֵּן בִּבְדִיקַת עוֹפוֹת וְדָגִים וַחֲגָבִים, שֶׁיַּחְשֹׁב הָרַמְבָּ״ם זִכְרוֹנוֹ לִבְרָכָה לִשְׁלֹשָׁה, וְהָרַמְבָּ״ן זִכְרוֹנוֹ לִבְרָכָה לֹא יַחְשְׁבֵם.

מִדִּינֵי הַמִּצְוָה, שֶׁכָּל בְּהֵמָה וְחַיָּה שֶׁמַּעֲלַת גֵּרָה אֵין לָהּ שִׁנַּיִם בַּלֶּחִי הָעֶלְיוֹן; וְכָל בְּהֵמָה בָּעוֹלָם מַעֲלַת גֵּרָה, הִיא מַפְרֶסֶת פַּרְסָה, חוּץ מִן הַגָּמָל; וְכָל שֶׁמַּפְרֶסֶת פַּרְסָה הִיא מַעֲלַת גֵּרָה, חוּץ מִן הַחֲזִיר; וַעֲשָׂרָה מִינִין הֵן בֵּין בְּהֵמוֹת וְחַיּוֹת

§153
1. I.e. for all foods banned by the Torah.
2. Literally, in most of my words.
3. In his commentary to ShM root principle 6.
4. MT *hilchoth ma'achaloth 'asuroth* i 2, based on TB Ḥullin 59a. The added word "[kosher]" (four lines above) is per *Maggid Mishneh* to MT *ibid.* — for rabbits and hares chew their cud and have upper teeth (TB *ibid.*).

which are the chewing of the cud, and the cloven hoof; for it is stated, *These are the living things which you may eat among all the beasts that are on the earth: whatever parts the hoof*, etc. (Leviticus 11:2–3). In the language of the Midrash *Sifra:* "which you may eat" (*ibid.* 3)—*that* is for eating, but an unclean beast is not for eating. In other words, we thus infer from this a negative precept (injunction) about an unclean animal. An injunction of this kind is called a negative precept that derives from a positive one. It is stated elsewhere, too, *You shall therefore differentiate between the clean beast and the unclean* (Leviticus 20:25); and it is written further, *to differentiate between the unclean and the clean* (*ibid.* 11:47).

What lies at the root of a ban on certain food, we wrote above, about the injunction on a *t'réfah* (fatally injured animal; §73) and on forbidden fat (§147)—what we have known. This is a root reason that is enough, in accord with the plain meaning, for them all.[1] Now, the purpose of examining their determining marks follows from the reason for their forbiddance: whatever is the possible subject of a ban that we have been given, it is right and obligatory for us to inspect it well.

Now, here I have not withheld my pen from writing the words of Rambam of blessed memory about this, who reckoned this verse as a positive precept—for I resolved at the start of my work[2] to write the precepts in accord with the listing as he reckoned them—even though my heart is taken in this matter by the approach of Ramban of blessed memory, who wrote[3] that it is not right for us to list the examination for marks of cleanness [permission to eat them] in animals as a precept: For in truth, since the Torah prohibited some animals to us, He would be obliged in any event to inform us of the distinguishing marks of the clean [permitted] ones, in order to separate us from what is forbidden; and it is thus not fit at all to be counted as a precept in the reckoning. The same ruling and the same reason should hold equally for the examination of fowl and fish and locusts, which Rambam of blessed memory reckons as three [precepts], and Ramban of blessed memory does not count.

Some laws of the precept are: that every [kosher] domestic and wild animal which chews its cud has no teeth in the upper jaw; every domestic animal in the world that chews its cud has cloven hooves except the camel; and every one with cloven hooves chews its cud, except the pig.[4] There are ten species among domestic and wild animals that are permissible: the three known kinds of domestic animals, namely the

הַמֻּתָּרִין: שְׁלֹשָׁה מִינֵי בְהֵמוֹת הַיְּדוּעוֹת, וְהֵן שׁוֹר, כֶּבֶשׂ וְתַיִשׁ, וְשִׁבְעָה מִינֵי חַיָּה הַמְּפֹרָשִׁים בַּכָּתוּב: אַיָּל וּצְבִי וְגוֹמֵר.

וּכְמוֹ שֶׁאָנוּ צְרִיכִין לָדַעַת סִימָנֵי הַכַּשְׁרוּת לְהַבְדִּילָן מִן הַטְּמֵאוֹת, כְּמוֹ־כֵן אָנוּ צְרִיכִין לֵידַע אֵי זוֹ הִיא מִין בְּהֵמָה וְאֵי זוֹ מִין חַיָּה, מִצַּד הַחֵלֶב: שֶׁחֵלֶב בְּהֵמָה אָסוּר וְחֵלֶב חַיָּה מֻתָּר, כְּמוֹ שֶׁכָּתוּב בְּהַזְהָרַת הַחֵלֶב לְמַעְלָה; וְעוֹד שֶׁדַּם הַחַיָּה טָעוּן כִּסּוּי וְלֹא דַם הַבְּהֵמָה.

וְסִימָנֵי הַחַיָּה בַּמָּה הִיא חֲלוּקָה מִן הַבְּהֵמָה לֹא נֶאֱמַר בַּתּוֹרָה, אֲבָל מִפִּי הַשְּׁמוּעָה לָמַדְנוּ שֶׁהִיא נִכֶּרֶת בְּקַרְנֶיהָ, שֶׁקַּרְנֵי הַחַיָּה עֲשׂוּיוֹת כֵּן: כְּרוּכוֹת חֲדוּקוֹת הֲדוּרוֹת; כְּרוּכוֹת כְּקַרְנֵי הַשּׁוֹר, חֲדוּקוֹת כְּקַרְנֵי הָעֵז וְיִהְיֶה הַחֶדֶק מֻבְלָע בָּהֶן, וַהֲדוּרוֹת כְּקַרְנֵי הַצְּבִי; לְפִיכָךְ כָּל שֶׁאֵין לָהּ סִימָנִין אֵלּוּ בְּקַרְנֶיהָ, חַיָּב אָדָם לִנְהֹג אִסּוּר בְּחֶלְבָּהּ; וְהַמּוֹצֵא חַיָּה בְּלֹא קַרְנַיִם, שֶׁאֵין יָכוֹל לְבָדְקָהּ בְּקַרְנֶיהָ, אִם מַכִּירָהּ בְּצוּרָתָהּ יָפֶה, כְּגוֹן שֶׁהֻרְגַּל בָּהֶם, מֻתָּר לוֹ לִבְטֹחַ בְּהַכָּרָתוֹ, וְלֹא נֹאמַר שֶׁיִּהְיֶה צָרִיךְ לִבְדֹּק בְּקַרְנַיִם עַל־כָּל־פָּנִים. וְיֶתֶר פְּרָטֶיהָ, בְּחֻלִּין.

וְנוֹהֶגֶת בְּכָל מָקוֹם וּבְכָל זְמַן, בִּזְכָרִים וּנְקֵבוֹת. וְעוֹבֵר עָלֶיהָ וְלֹא בָדַק אֶלָּא שֶׁרָאָה בָהּ הַסִּימָן הָאֶחָד וְסָמַךְ עָלָיו וְאָכַל מִמֶּנָּה, אַף־עַל־פִּי שֶׁמָּצָא אַחַר־כֵּן שֶׁהֶתֵּר אָכַל, בִּטֵּל עֲשֵׂה זֶה שֶׁל בְּדִיקַת הַסִּימָנִין.

[שֶׁלֹּא לֶאֱכֹל בְּהֵמָה וְחַיָּה טְמֵאָה]

קנד שֶׁלֹּא לֶאֱכֹל בְּהֵמָה וְחַיָּה טְמֵאָה, שֶׁנֶּאֱמַר: אֶת זֶה לֹא תֹאכְלוּ מִמַּעֲלֵי הַגֵּרָה וּמִמַּפְרִסֵי הַפַּרְסָה, אֶת הַגָּמָל וְהַחֲזִיר וְהָאַרְנֶבֶת וְהַשָּׁפָן; וּמִינֵי שְׁאָר בְּהֵמָה טְמֵאָה לֹא בָא עֲלֵיהֶם לָאו בְּבֵאוּר, אֲבָל מִכֵּיוָן שֶׁאָמְרָה הַתּוֹרָה: כָּל בְּהֵמָה מַפְרֶסֶת פַּרְסָה... מַעֲלַת גֵּרָה בַּבְּהֵמָה אֹתָהּ תֹּאכֵלוּ, נֵדַע שֶׁכָּל מַה שֶׁאֵין בּוֹ שְׁנֵי

5. MT *ibid.* 8, based on TB Ḥullin 80a.

6. MT *ibid.* 9.

7. TB Ḥullin 59b.

8. MT *ibid.* 10. "Layered" means with one rough part or bit growing hard upon and about another (Rashi to TB Ḥullin 59b s.v. *k'ruchoth*, and Me'iri *ad loc.*); like scabs, layered like an onion (R. Moses Isserles in *Yoreh Dé'ah* §80 ¶ 1); "rough": with very close notches all about, ensconced in one another (*idem*); "rounded": and not broad (*idem*).

§154 1. Literally, the two marks together.

ox, sheep and goat; and seven kinds of wild beast, which are listed in Scripture: the hart, gazelle, etc. (Deuteronomy 14:5).[5]

Now, just as we need to know the distinguishing marks of the kosher kinds, to differentiate them from the unclean kinds, so do we need to know which is a domestic kind and which a wild species, in regard to *ḥélev*, the forbidden kind of fat: for this fat in a domestic animal is forbidden, while in a wild animal it is permitted—as we wrote about the injunction against this fat, above (§ 147). Moreover, the blood of a wild animal needs to be covered, but not the blood of a domestic beast.[6]

The distinguishing marks of the wild animal—in what way it differs from the domestic—are not stated in the Written Torah; but through the Oral Tradition we learned[7] that it can be recognized by its horns: For the horns of the wild beast are formed thus: layered, rough, rounded—layered like an ox's horns, rough like a goat's horns, the rough points being close, dovetailed in them, and rounded like the horns of a deer.[8] Therefore, if any animal does not have these characteristics in its horns, its *ḥélev* must be considered forbidden. If a person finds an animal without horns, so that he cannot examine it by its horns, if he recognizes its form well—for instance, if he is familiar with them—he is permitted to trust to his discernment; and we do not say that he must examine the horns under all circumstances. The rest of its [the precept's] details are in the tractate *Ḥullin*.

It remains in force in every place, at every time, for both man and woman. If a person violated it and made no examination, but merely saw one distinguishing mark and relied on that to eat of it—even if he should discover afterward that he ate permissible food, he would thus disobey this positive precept of examining the distinguishing marks.

[THE PROHIBITION AGAINST EATING ANY NON-KOSHER ANIMAL]

154 not to eat an unclean [kind of] domestic or wild animal: for it is stated, *these you shall not eat of those that chew the cud or part the hoof: the camel . . . the rock badger . . . the hare . . . and the swine* (Leviticus 11:4–7). About other kinds of unclean animals an injunction was not conveyed clearly; but since the Torah states, *Whatever parts the hoof . . . and chews the cud, among the beasts, that you may eat* (*ibid.* 3), we know that whatever does not have both of these two marks,[1] is forbidden to be eaten. This is an injunction (negative precept) which comes by

הַסִּימָנִין יַחַד הוּא נִמְנַע מִלְּאָכְלוֹ; וְזֶה לָאו הַבָּא מִכְּלַל עֲשֵׂה, וְהָעִקָּר: לָאו הַבָּא מִכְּלַל עֲשֵׂה — עֲשֵׂה, וְאֵין לוֹקִין עָלָיו.

וְאָמְנָם נֶאֶסְרוּ לָנוּ גַּם־כֵּן שְׁאָר בְּהֵמָה וְחַיָּה מִקַּל וָחֹמֶר, שֶׁאָנוּ אוֹמְרִים: הַחֲזִיר וְהַגָּמָל, שֶׁיֵּשׁ בָּהֶן סִימַן טָהֳרָה אֶחָד, אָנוּ לוֹקִין עָלָיו, קַל וָחֹמֶר שְׁאָר בְּהֵמָה וְחַיָּה שֶׁאֵין לָהֶן סִימַן טָהֳרָה כְּלָל, שֶׁלּוֹקִין עֲלֵיהֶן.

וּלְשׁוֹן סִפְרָא: "אֹתָהּ תֹּאכֵלוּ", אוֹתָהּ בַּאֲכִילָה וְאֵין בְּהֵמָה טְמֵאָה בַּאֲכִילָה. אֵין לִי אֶלָּא בַּעֲשֵׂה; בְּלֹא־תַעֲשֶׂה מִנַּיִן, תַּלְמוּד לוֹמַר: אֶת זֶה לֹא תֹאכְלוּ מִמַּעֲלֵי הַגֵּרָה וְגוֹמֵר. אֵין לִי אֶלָּא אֵלּוּ בִּלְבָד; שְׁאָר בְּהֵמָה טְמֵאָה מִנַּיִן, וְדִין הוּא, וּמַה אֵלּוּ שֶׁיֵּשׁ בָּהֶן סִימַן טָהֳרָה הֲרֵי הֵן בְּלֹא־תַעֲשֶׂה עַל אֲכִילָתָן, שְׁאָר בְּהֵמָה טְמֵאָה, שֶׁאֵין בָּהֶן סִימַן טָהֳרָה, אֵינוֹ דִין שֶׁיְּהֵא לֹא־תַעֲשֶׂה עַל אֲכִילָתָן. נִמְצָא הַגָּמָל וְהָאַרְנֶבֶת וְהַשָּׁפָן וְהַחֲזִיר מִן הַכָּתוּב, וּשְׁאָר בְּהֵמָה טְמֵאָה מִקַּל וָחֹמֶר.

וְאָמְנָם הוּא לְגַלּוּיֵי מִלְּתָא בְּעָלְמָא, כְּלוֹמַר שֶׁקַּל וָחֹמֶר כָּזֶה כְּעֵין מְבֹאָר בַּכָּתוּב הוּא, שֶׁאִם הִזְהִיר עַל אוֹתָן שֶׁיֵּשׁ בָּהֶן סִימָן אֶחָד שֶׁל טָהֳרָה, כָּל־שֶׁכֵּן עַל שֶׁאֵין לָהֶם סִימַן טָהֳרָה כְּלָל; וְלֹא שַׁיָּךְ בְּכָאן כְּלָל לוֹמַר אֵין עוֹנְשִׁין מִן הַדִּין; וּלְפִיכָךְ כָּל מִי שֶׁאָכַל כַּזַּיִת מִבְּהֵמָה טְמֵאָה מֵאֵי זֶה מִין שֶׁיִּהְיֶה, לוֹקֶה מִדְּאוֹרַיְתָא.

וּפֵרוּשׁ "מַפְרֶסֶת פַּרְסָה" הוּא שֶׁפַּרְסוֹתֶיהָ סְדוּקוֹת. וּפֵרוּשׁ "שֹׁסַעַת שֶׁסַע" לוֹמַר שֶׁתְּהֵא הַפַּרְסָה מֻבְדֶּלֶת לְגַמְרֵי מִלְּמַעְלָה וּמִלְּמַטָּה; אֲבָל אִם הָיְתָה סְדוּקָה לְמַטָּה וּמְחֻבֶּרֶת לְמַעְלָה אוֹ בְהֶפֶךְ, טְמֵאָה הִיא. וּפֵרוּשׁ "מַעֲלַת גֵּרָה" שֶׁמְּקִיאָה מִן הַמֵּעַיִם וּמְשִׁיבָה אוֹתוֹ לְפִיהָ לְכָתְשׁוֹ וּלְטָחְנוֹ הָדֵק.

מִשָּׁרְשֵׁי הַמִּצְוָה, מַה שֶּׁכָּתַבְנוּ בְּאַזְהָרַת טְרֵפָה בְּסֵדֶר מִשְׁפָּטִים [סי׳ ע״ג], כִּי יוֹדֵעַ אֱלֹהִים כִּי כָל הַמַּאֲכָלוֹת שֶׁהִרְחִיק מֵעַמּוֹ אֲשֶׁר בָּחַר יֵשׁ בָּהֶם נְזָקִים מְצוּיִּים

2. I.e. even though we thus learn from the Torah an injunction, not to do something, it has the force of a positive, not a negative precept; TB P'saḥim 41b, etc.

3. TB Sanhedrin 54a; i.e. this applies only to laws that are not readily obvious from Scripture, and would not be perceived without the argument of *kal va-ḥomer*. Then because they are only derived, no punishment is given for their violation. This, however, is considered obvious from Scripture.

4. The first three paragraphs are based on ShM negative precept §172.

5. Based on Rashi, Leviticus 11:3.

inference from a positive precept; and we have the principle: an injunction inferred from a positive precept is a positive precept,[2] and whiplashes are not given for it.

However, other kinds of domestic and wild animals were forbidden us by *kal va-ḥomer*, reasoning *a fortiori* (from the less to the more): For we say: if regarding the pig or the camel, which have [each] one mark of cleanness, whiplashes are given over it, how much more certain is it about other domestic and wild animals which have no mark of cleanness at all, that a whipping should be suffered for them.

In the language of the Midrash *Sifra*: "which you may eat"—*that* is for eating, but an unclean [kind of] animal is not for eating. Then I know only that this is [ordained] by a positive precept; how do I know it is by a negative precept [as well]?—Scripture states, *these you shall not eat of those that chew the cud*, etc. (Leviticus 11:3). Hence I know this only about these; how do I know it about other unclean animals?—it is only logical: If these, which have one mark of cleanness, bear a negative precept prohibiting eating them, is it not just that for other unclean animals, which have no mark of cleanness, there should be a negative precept banning their consumption? Consequently, the camel, rock badger and hare are [forbidden] by Scripture, and other unclean animals by *kal va-ḥomer*, a deduction *a fortiori*.

But actually, this is merely a way to convey the matter lucidly. In other words, a *kal va-ḥomer* like this is as if it were stated clearly in the Writ: for if it adjured [us] about those that have one mark of cleanness, all the more certainly did it do so about those with no distinguishing sign of cleanness at all. Hence here the rule would not apply that says, "Punishment is not given for something logically inferred [by *kal va-ḥomer*]."[3] So whoever eats the amount of an olive of an unclean beast, of whatever kind it might be, is given whiplashes by the Torah's law.[4]

The meaning of the term "parts the hoof" is that its hooves are split; the meaning of "and is cloven-footed" is to convey that the hoof is completely split, from top to bottom. But if it is split at the bottom and unified at the top, or vice versa, it [the animal] is unclean. The meaning of "chews the cud" is that it ejects food from the innards and returns it to its mouth in order to pound and grind it fine.[5]

At the root of the precept lies what we wrote about the injunction against a *t'réfah* (fatally injured animal) in *sidrah mishpatim* (§73): that God knows that in all foods which He removed from the people He chose, elements injurious to the body are found—our bodies being

לַגּוּפִים, אֲשֶׁר הֵם כֵּלִים לַנְּפָשׁוֹת לִפְעֹל בָּהֶם וּלְהִתְעַלּוֹת עַל יְדֵי מַעֲשֵׂיהֶם הַטּוֹבִים, וְעַל־כֵּן הִרְחִיקָנוּ מֵהֶם, לְמַעַן יִפְעֲלוּ הַנְּפָשׁוֹת פְּעֻלָּתָן וְלֹא יְנֻעֲלוּ בִּפְנֵיהֶם רֹעַ מֶזֶג הַגּוּפוֹת וְטִמְטוּם הַלְּבָבוֹת, וּכְמוֹ שֶׁכָּתַבְתִּי שָׁם.

מִדִּינֵי הַמִּצְוָה, מַה שֶּׁאָמְרוּ זִכְרוֹנָם לִבְרָכָה שֶׁלֹּא חָלַק הַכָּתוּב בִּבְהֵמָה וְחַיָּה טְמֵאָה בֵּין בְּשָׂרָהּ לְחֶלְבָּהּ, שֶׁהַכֹּל אָסוּר; וּבְשַׂר אָדָם, אַף־עַל־פִּי שֶׁנִּקְרָא הָאָדָם נֶפֶשׁ חַיָּה וְאֵינוֹ מַעֲלֶה גֵרָה וְשׁוֹסַע שֶׁסַע, אֵין בְּשָׂרוֹ בִּכְלַל אִסּוּר בְּהֵמָה טְמֵאָה לַעֲבֹר עָלָיו בְּלָאו; וּלְפִיכָךְ הָאוֹכֵל מִבְּשָׂרוֹ אוֹ שׁוֹתֶה מֵחֶלְבּוֹ, בֵּין חַי בֵּין מֵת, אֵין לוֹקִין עָלָיו; אֲבָל מִכָּל־מָקוֹם אָסוּר הוּא בַּעֲשֵׂה, שֶׁהֲרֵי מָנָה הַכָּתוּב שִׁבְעַת מִינֵי חַיָּה וְאָמַר בָּהֶן "זֹאת הַחַיָּה אֲשֶׁר תֹּאכְלוּ", מִכְּלָל, שֶׁכָּל שֶׁהוּא חוּץ מֵאֵלּוּ לֹא תֹאכְלוּ; וְלָאו הַבָּא מִכְּלַל עֲשֵׂה — עֲשֵׂה. זֶהוּ דַּעַת הָרַמְבָּ"ם זִכְרוֹנוֹ לִבְרָכָה.

אֲבָל הָרַמְבָּ"ן זִכְרוֹנוֹ לִבְרָכָה כָּתַב שֶׁבִּבְשַׂר הָאָדָם אֲפִלּוּ עֲשֵׂה אֵין בּוֹ, וְהֵבִיא רְאָיָה מַה שֶּׁאָמְרוּ זִכְרוֹנָם לִבְרָכָה: דַּם מְהַלְּכֵי שְׁתַּיִם וְחֶלְבָּם אֲפִלּוּ מִצְוַת פֵּרוּשׁ אֵין בּוֹ; וְכָתַב הוּא זִכְרוֹנוֹ לִבְרָכָה דְּהוּא הַדִּין לְבָשָׂר שֶׁמֻּתָּר כְּמוֹ הַדָּם, שֶׁאִם לֹא כֵן אֵיךְ יְהֵא מֻתָּר הַדָּם — וּכְמוֹ שֶׁאָמְרוּ זִכְרוֹנָם לִבְרָכָה: דָּם שֶׁל בֵּין הַשִּׁנַּיִם מוֹצְצוֹ וּבוֹלְעוֹ — וְהָא קַיְמָא לָן כָּל הַיּוֹצֵא מִן הַטָּמֵא טָמֵא; וּמִכָּל־מָקוֹם בְּשַׂר יִשְׂרָאֵל מֵת אָסוּר בַּהֲנָאָה. וְיֶתֶר רְאָיוֹתָיו בְּסִפְרוֹ.

וּשְׁאָר פְּרָטֵי הַמִּצְוָה מְבֹאָרִין בְּחֻלִּין פֶּרֶק ג׳ וּבִמְקוֹמוֹת אֲחֵרִים.

וְנוֹהֶגֶת בְּכָל מָקוֹם וּבְכָל זְמַן, בִּזְכָרִים וּנְקֵבוֹת. וְעוֹבֵר עָלֶיהָ וְאָכַל כַּזַּיִת מִכָּל בְּהֵמָה טְמֵאָה אוֹ שָׁתָה רְבִיעִית מֵחֶלְבָּהּ, בְּמֵזִיד לוֹקֶה; בְּשׁוֹגֵג פָּטוּר.

6. MT *hilchoth ma'achaloth 'asuroth* ii 2, based on TB Ḥullin 117a.

7. I.e. those fats which, in a kosher animal, are forbidden. Ed. Eshkol reads here and in the paragraph's first sentence, and consequently also in the last paragraph, *ḥalav* (milk, i.e. of the female) instead of *ḥélev*. This, however, is untenable (MH), as TB K'rithoth 22a rules it entirely permissible. The verb "drinks" is peculiar, too, as the usual verb with *ḥélev* in Talmudic literature is eating. It may have arisen from the error of a scribe who likewise misunderstood the noun as *ḥalav*.

8. MT *ibid.* 3.

9. In his commentary on Pentateuch, Leviticus 11:3.

10. TB K'rithoth 21b–22a.

vessels and instruments for the souls to work through them and to be ennobled through their good deeds. For this reason He removed us from them [the injurious food elements] so that the souls can do their functions, and no bad temperament of the body or stupor of the heart will shut the door before them—as I wrote there.

Among the laws of the precept, there is what the Sages of blessed memory said: that the Writ made no distinction in unclean domestic and wild beasts between the meat and *ḥélev*, the forbidden kind of fat—it is all forbidden.[6] As for human flesh, even though man was called *nefesh ḥayyah* (a living being; Genesis 2:7) [which could be rendered, literally, the soul of an undomesticated animal] and he does not chew his cud or have cloven hooves, his flesh is not included under the ban on unclean animals, to make eating it the transgression of a negative precept. Therefore, if someone eats of his [a human being's] flesh or drinks of his *ḥélev*,[7] while he is either alive or dead, no whiplashes are given for it. But in any event, it is forbidden by a positive precept: for Scripture listed seven kinds of *ḥayyah*, undomesticated animals, and it said of them, *These are the animals you may eat* (Deuteronomy 14:4); hence it follows that anything except these, you shall not eat; and an injunction derived from a positive statement is a positive precept.[2] This is the view of Rambam of blessed memory.[8]

However, Ramban of blessed memory[9] wrote that not even a positive precept applies to human flesh. And he cited as proof what the Sages of blessed memory said:[10] The blood of those who walk on two feet, and their milk—there is not even a religious duty to keep apart from them. Then he wrote (be his memory for a blessing) that the same holds for the flesh—it is as permissible as the blood. For if it were not so, how could the blood be permissible?—as our Sages of blessed memory taught:[10] blood that is between the teeth may be sucked and swallowed; and we have an established rule: whatever issues from something unclean is unclean. But in any event, it is forbidden to have any benefit from the flesh of a dead Israelite. The rest of his proofs are in his work.

The remaining details of the precept are elucidated in chapter 3 of the tractate *Ḥullin*, and elsewhere. It is in force in every place, at every time, for both man and woman. If someone transgressed it and ate an olive's amount of any unclean animal or drank a *r'vi'ith* of its *ḥélev*—if deliberately, willfully, he should receive whiplashes; if inadvertently, he is free of penalty.

[מִצְוַת בְּדִיקַת סִימָנֵי דָגִים]

קנה לִבְדֹּק בְּסִימָנֵי דָגִים, כְּלוֹמַר שֶׁהָרוֹצֶה לֶאֱכֹל מִן הַדָּגִים שֶׁיִּבְדֹּק תְּחִלָּה בָּהֶם יָפֶה הַסִּימָנִין שֶׁנָּתְנָה הַתּוֹרָה בָּהֶן, וְהֵן סְנַפִּיר וְקַשְׂקֶשֶׂת — שֶׁנֶּאֱמַר: אֶת זֶה תֹּאכְלוּ מִכֹּל אֲשֶׁר בַּמָּיִם וְגוֹמֵר.

כְּבָר כָּתַבְנוּ בַּמִּצְוָה הַקּוֹדֶמֶת לְזוֹ שֶׁהָרַמְבָּ״ן זִכְרוֹנוֹ לִבְרָכָה לֹא יַחֲשֹׁב בְּמִנְיַן הַמִּצְווֹת בְּדִיקַת סִימָנִין בַּמִּינִין שֶׁהִתִּירָה הַתּוֹרָה, וְכִי הָאֱמֶת אִתּוֹ בָּזֶה לְפִי הַנִּרְאֶה לָנוּ. וְאַף־עַל־פִּי שֶׁמָּצָאנוּ בַגְּמָרָא בְּפֵרוּשׁ בִּקְצָתָן ״זוֹ מִצְוַת עֲשֵׂה״, הַכַּוָּנָה בָעִנְיָן לְחַיֵּב בַּמִּינִין הַטְּמֵאִין בַּעֲשֵׂה וְלֹא־תַעֲשֶׂה, עִם הַכְּלָל הַיָּדוּעַ לָנוּ: לָאו הַבָּא מִכְּלַל עֲשֵׂה — עֲשֵׂה, וּכְמוֹ שֶׁנִּכְתֹּב גַּם־כֵּן בְּעֶזְרַת הַשֵּׁם בְּמִצְוַת הַלְוָאַת הַנָּכְרִי [סי׳ תקע״ג], שֶׁחֲשָׁבָהּ הָרַמְבָּ״ם זִכְרוֹנוֹ לִבְרָכָה לְמִצְוָה, וְלֹא בָא הַכָּתוּב לְפִי הַדּוֹמֶה רַק לְחַיֵּב בַּעֲשֵׂה וְלֹא־תַעֲשֶׂה בְּהַלְוָאַת יִשְׂרָאֵל בְּרִבִּית.

שֹׁרֶשׁ הַמִּצְוָה כְּתַבְתִּיו גַּם־כֵּן לְמַעְלָה בְּסִימָנֵי בְהֵמָה, וְהוּא כְּלָל לְאַרְבַּעַת הַמִּינִין.

מִדִּינֵי הַמִּצְוָה (כְּגוֹן מַה שֶּׁאָמְרוּ זִכְרוֹנָם לִבְרָכָה), שֶׁסְּנַפִּיר הוּא מַה שֶּׁבַּדָּג שֶׁהוּא לוֹ כְעֵין כְּנָפַיִם שֶׁפּוֹרֵחַ בָּהֶן, וְקַשְׂקֶשֶׂת הִיא אוֹתָהּ קְלִפָּה שֶׁעָלָיו, הַדְּבוּקָה בְּכָל גּוּפוֹ; וְאַף־עַל־פִּי שֶׁלֹּא נִמְצָא קַשְׂקֶשֶׂת כִּי־אִם בְּמִקְצָת גּוּפוֹ, וַאֲפִלּוּ אַחַת לְבַד, דַּיּוֹ וְכָשֵׁר; וְאָמְרוּ בְתוֹסֶפְתָּא: וְהוּא שֶׁתְּהֵא תַחַת לְחָיוֹ אוֹ תַחַת זְנָבוֹ אוֹ תַחַת סְנַפִּירָיו, אֲבָל בִּשְׁאָר גּוּפוֹ לֹא סָגֵי לָן בְּפָחוֹת מִשְּׁתַּיִם.

וְכָל שֶׁנִּמְצָא בוֹ קַשְׂקֶשֶׂת, וַאֲפִלּוּ אַחַת בַּמְּקוֹמוֹת הַנִּזְכָּרִים, אֵין צָרִיךְ לִבְדֹּק אִם יֵשׁ לוֹ סְנַפִּיר, כִּי בְּוַדַּאי יֵשׁ לוֹ; אֲבָל כְּשֶׁיִּמָּצֵא בוֹ סְנַפִּיר צָרִיךְ לִבְדֹּק אִם יֵשׁ בּוֹ קַשְׂקֶשֶׂת, כִּי יֵשׁ דָּגִים טְמֵאִים הַרְבֵּה שֶׁיֵּשׁ לָהֶם סְנַפִּיר.

וְכָל דָּג שֶׁבְּטִבְעוֹ יֵשׁ לוֹ קַשְׂקַשִּׂים אַף־עַל־פִּי שֶׁאֵין נַעֲשִׂין בּוֹ בְּעוֹדוֹ קָטָן עַד שֶׁיַּגְדִּיל, כְּגוֹן הַסּוּלְתָּנִית וְהָאַפְיָן, הֲרֵי זֶה מֻתָּר; וְכָל שֶׁיֵּשׁ בּוֹ קַשְׂקַשִּׂים בְּעוֹדוֹ בַיָּם

§155 1. As noted before, in the original version, in each *sidrah* the positive precepts were arranged before the negative; hence our §155 is §150 there, while our §153 is §149 there.

2. TB Ḥullin 66b.

3. I.e. to eat them is to violate both an explicit negative precept of Scripture and an injunction derived from a positive precept (Ramban, commentary on ShM root principle 4).

4. See §154, note 2.

5. TB Ḥullin 59a.

6. I.e. it moves through the water with them.

7. Sifra on Leviticus 11:9 (*sh'mini, parashah* 3, 5).

8. Tosefta, Ḥullin iii, beginning (see Ramban on TB Ḥullin 66a that this is the *halachah*, normative law).

9. TB Niddah 51b.

10. TB Ḥullin 66a.

[THE PRECEPT OF EXAMINING THE SIGNS OF FISH TO SEE IF THEY ARE KOSHER]

155 to examine the determining marks of fish: in other words, that if someone wishes to eat fish, he should first examine them well for the signs [that they are kosher] that the Torah gave for them, i.e., fins and scales—as it is stated, *These you may eat of all that are in the waters*, etc. (Leviticus 11:9).

We wrote earlier, in the precept preceding this (§153),[1] that Ramban of blessed memory does not count, in the reckoning of the precepts, the examination of determining marks in the [various] species that the Torah made permissible; and the truth lies with him, as it appears to us. Even though we find in the Talmud[2] explicitly about some of them, "This is a positive precept," the purpose of this statement is to impose punishment over unclean kinds of creatures for both a positive and a negative precept[3]—by the rule known to us: an injunction derived from a positive precept is a positive precept[4]—as we will write further, with the Eternal Lord's help, at the precept of lending to a Gentile (§573), which Rambam of blessed memory reckons as a precept, that the verse evidently came to impose punishment for [violating] a positive and a negative precept by lending to a Jew at interest.

As to the root reason for the precept, I wrote that also above, about the distinguishing marks of a beast (§153). That is a general point which holds for all four kinds [beasts, fish, fowl and grasshoppers].

Among the laws of the precept, there is, for instance, what the Sages of blessed memory taught:[5] that fins are what a fish has, which are like wings for it, as it "flies" with them;[6] and the scales are that "shell" on it which clings to its entire body; but even if scales are found only on part of the body—and even if but one [scale]—it is enough, and it is kosher.[7] It was taught in the Tosefta, though:[8] but this, provided it is under its cheek, under its tail, or under its fins; but on the rest of its body, less than two are not enough for us.

When scales—even [if only] one—are found in [any of] the above-mentioned places, there is no need to investigate if it has fins: for it certainly has.[9] However, if one finds a fin on it, he needs to investigate if it has scales; for there are many unclean [kinds of] fish which have fins.

Any fish which by its nature has scales, even if they do not form on it when it is young, until it is grown—for example, the *sultanith* and the bakefish—is permissible.[10] Any fish which has scales while in the

אַף־עַל־פִּי שֶׁהוּא מַשִּׁיר אוֹתָן כְּשֶׁעוֹלֶה מִן הַיָּם, כְּגוֹן אָקוֹנָס וְאַפּוּנָס בִּסְפַתְיָס אַפְּנַסְטִיָּס וַאֲטוּנָס הַנִּקְרָא בִּירֶט בְּלַעַז, הֲרֵי זֶה כָּשֵׁר, שֶׁלֹּא תַקְפִּיד הַתּוֹרָה רַק בְּמִין בַּעַל קַשְׂקֶשֶׂת וּסְנַפִּיר, כִּי הוּא הַנָּאוֹת אֶל טֶבַע בְּנֵי־אָדָם, וּמִן הַטַּעַם שֶׁכָּתַבְנוּ בְּאִסּוּר הַמַּאֲכָלוֹת לְפִי הַפְּשָׁט.

וְנוֹהֶגֶת בְּכָל מָקוֹם וּבְכָל זְמַן, בִּזְכָרִים וּבִנְקֵבוֹת. וְעוֹבֵר עָלֶיהָ וְלֹא בָדַק יָפֶה, כְּגוֹן שֶׁרָאָה סִימָן אֶחָד לְבַד בַּדָּג וְסָמַךְ עַל הָאַחֵר בְּלֹא בְדִיקָה, אַף־עַל־פִּי שֶׁנִּמְצָא אַחַר־כֵּן כָּשֵׁר, בִּטֵּל עֲשֵׂה זֶה.

[שֶׁלֹּא לֶאֱכֹל דָּג טָמֵא]

קנו שֶׁלֹּא לֶאֱכֹל דָּג טָמֵא, שֶׁנֶּאֱמַר: מִבְּשָׂרָם לֹא תֹאכֵלוּ וְאֶת נִבְלָתָם תְּשַׁקֵּצוּ.

וְסִימָנֵי דָּגִים כְּשֵׁרִים כְּתַבְנוּם לְמַעְלָה בְּמִצְוַת עֲשֵׂה ב׳ [סי׳ קנ״ב], שֶׁהִיא לִבְדֹּק בְּסִימָנֵי דָגִים, שֶׁחֲשַׁבְנוּ מִן הַמִּנְיָן לִכְבוֹד הָרַב רַבֵּנוּ מֹשֶׁה זִכְרוֹנוֹ לִבְרָכָה.

מִשָּׁרְשֵׁי הַמִּצְוָה, מַה שֶּׁכָּתַבְנוּ לְמַעְלָה בְּעִנְיַן אִסּוּר הַמַּאֲכָלוֹת, שֶׁהָאֵל בָּרוּךְ הוּא הִרְחִיק מֵעַמּוֹ כָּל מַה שֶּׁנֶּזֶק נִמְצָא בוֹ, הֵן בְּהֵמָה אוֹ עוֹף אוֹ דָגִים, מִן הַטַּעַם שֶׁאָמַרְנוּ שָׁם.

דִּינֵי הַמִּצְוָה כְּתַבְנוּם לְמַעְלָה גַּם־כֵּן, וְהֵם בְּחֻלִּין פֶּרֶק ג׳. וְנוֹהֶגֶת בְּכָל מָקוֹם וּבְכָל זְמַן, בִּזְכָרִים וּנְקֵבוֹת. וְעוֹבֵר עָלֶיהָ וְאָכַל כַּזַּיִת מִדָּג טָמֵא, בְּמֵזִיד לוֹקֶה; בְּשׁוֹגֵג פָּטוּר.

[שֶׁלֹּא לֶאֱכֹל עוֹף טָמֵא]

קנז שֶׁלֹּא לֶאֱכֹל עוֹף טָמֵא, שֶׁנֶּאֱמַר: וְאֶת אֵלֶּה תְּשַׁקְּצוּ מִן הָעוֹף לֹא יֵאָכְלוּ, וְגוֹמֵר.

מִשָּׁרְשֵׁי הַמִּצְוָה, מַה שֶּׁכָּתַבְנוּ בְּמַאֲכָלוֹת אֲסוּרוֹת.

מִדִּינֵי הַמִּצְוָה, מַה שֶּׁאָמְרוּ זִכְרוֹנָם לִבְרָכָה: סִימָנֵי בְהֵמָה וְחַיָּה נֶאֶמְרוּ מִן

11. *Ibid.* 67a–b.

§156 1. See the statement of our author in §153 (third paragraph) that he listed it as a precept only because he follows Rambam's reckoning of the precepts, but Ramban's thesis that it is not tenable to count it as a precept seems closer to the truth. Our author indicates now that this point applies here equally.

water, even if it sheds them at the time it leaves the water—for example, the *colias*, *pelamys*, *xiphias*, *athnias*, and the tunny-fish, called *biret* in the foreign language [Spanish]—is permissible.[11] For the Torah was insistent only about a kind with scales and fins, as this is suitable for the nature of man—for the reason we wrote about the ban on [certain] foods, according to the plain sense.

It is in effect in every place, at every time, for both man and woman. If a person transgressed it and did not investigate well—for instance, if he saw one determining mark alone on the fish, and he trusted that the other was there—then even if it was found afterward to have been kosher, he would thus disobey a positive precept.

[THE PROHIBITION AGAINST EATING NON-KOSHER SPECIES OF FISH]

156 not to eat an unclean [non-kosher kind of] fish: for it is stated, *of their flesh you shall not eat, and their carcasses you shall detest* (Leviticus 11:11).

The distinguishing marks of kosher fish, we wrote above, in the second positive precept (§155), which is to investigate the marks of fish—which we have counted in the reckoning in honor of R. Moses [Rambam] of blessed memory.[1]

At the root of the precept lies what we have written above (§§73, 147) in regard to the ban on certain foods—that God, blessed is He, removed from His people everything in which some harmful element is found, whether it is a beast, fowl or fish—for the reason we explained there.

The laws of the precept we also wrote above. They are in chapter 3 of the tractate *Ḥullin*. It applies in every place and every time, for both man and woman. If someone violated it and ate an olive's amount of an unclean fish—if deliberately, he would be given whiplashes; if inadvertently, he is free of penalty.

[THE PROHIBITION AGAINST EATING NON-KOSHER SPECIES OF FOWL]

157 not to eat an unclean [kind of] fowl, as it is written, *And these you shall abhor among the fowl; they shall not be eaten*, etc. (Leviticus 11:13).

At the root of the precept lies the point we have written about forbidden foods (§§73, 147).

Among the laws of the precept, there is what the Sages of blessed

הַתּוֹרָה, כְּלוֹמַר שֶׁהֵן מְפֹרָשִׁין בַּתּוֹרָה, וְהֵן פַּרְסָה חֲלוּקָה לְגַמְרֵי, כְּמוֹ הַשּׁוֹר וְהַכֶּבֶשׂ, וּמַעֲלֵה גֵרָה. וְסִימָנֵי הָעוֹף לֹא נֶאֶמְרוּ, לְפִי שֶׁהַתּוֹרָה פֵּרְשָׁה לָנוּ בְּשֵׁם, כָּל הַטְּמֵאִים שֶׁבָּעוֹלָם, וְכֵיוָן שֶׁכֵּן הוּא אֵין צֹרֶךְ לִכְתֹּב לָנוּ סִימָנֵיהֶן, כִּי כָל עוֹף הַנִּמְצָא בָעוֹלָם חוּץ מֵהֶם הוּא כָשֵׁר.

וּמִכָּל־מָקוֹם, מִפְּנֵי שֶׁכָּל אוֹתָן מִינִין שֶׁהוֹדִיעַתְנוּ הַתּוֹרָה אֵין כָּל אָדָם בָּקִי בָּהֶן, הוֹדִיעוּנוּ חֲכָמִים סִימָנִין בָּהֶן, כְּדֵי שֶׁיַּכִּיר אוֹתָן כָּל אָדָם וְיוּכַל לֶאֱכֹל מִן הָעוֹפוֹת אַף־עַל־פִּי שֶׁאֵינוֹ מַכִּיר אֲפִלּוּ אֶחָד מִכָּל הַמִּינִין הַטְּמֵאִים הַמְפֹרָשִׁים בַּכָּתוּב.

נִמְצָא לְפִי דְבָרֵינוּ שֶׁכָּל הַמַּכִּיר יָפֶה כָּל הַמְנוּיִין בַּתּוֹרָה, שֶׁהֵן כ״ד מִינִין, יָכוֹל לֶאֱכֹל מִכָּל עוֹף אַחֵר שֶׁיִּמְצָא, כֵּיוָן שֶׁאָמְרוּ שֶׁכָּל עוֹף שֶׁלֹּא נִזְכַּר בְּמִנְיַן הַטְּמֵאִים בַּתּוֹרָה, כָּשֵׁר; וּכְמוֹ שֶׁאָמְרוּ זִכְרוֹנָם לִבְרָכָה: גָּלוּי וְיָדוּעַ לִפְנֵי מִי שֶׁאָמַר וְהָיָה הָעוֹלָם שֶׁעוֹפוֹת טְהוֹרִין מְרֻבִּים עַל הַטְּמֵאִין, לְפִיכָךְ פֵּרַט הַטְּמֵאִים, כְּלוֹמַר פֵּרַט כָּל הַטְּמֵאִים שֶׁבָּעוֹלָם.

כֵּן הוּא הַפֵּרוּשׁ לְפִי דַעַת רֹב הָרַבָּנִים, כִּי כָל הַטְּמֵאִין שֶׁבָּעוֹלָם הֻזְכְּרוּ בַתּוֹרָה. וּמִי שֶׁאֵינוֹ מַכִּירָן, אָמְרוּ חֲכָמִים זִכְרוֹנָם לִבְרָכָה שֶׁאֵלּוּ סִימָנֵיהֶם: כָּל עוֹף הַדּוֹרֵס, בְּיָדוּעַ שֶׁהוּא מִמִּינֵי הַטְּמֵאִים שֶׁבַּתּוֹרָה; וּפֵרוּשׁ דּוֹרֵס, כְּלוֹמַר שֶׁנּוֹעֵץ הַצִּפָּרְנַיִם עַל עוֹף אַחֵר וּמֵטִיל בּוֹ אֶרֶס, כְּמִנְהַג הַנֵּץ וּשְׁאָר הָעוֹפוֹת שֶׁצָּדִין בָּהֶן בְּנֵי־אָדָם.

וְיֵשׁ שֶׁאֵינוֹ דוֹרֵס וְהוּא גַם־כֵּן מִמִּינֵי הַטְּמֵאִים. וְאָמְרוּ לָנוּ חֲכָמִים זִכְרוֹנָם לִבְרָכָה דֶּרֶךְ כְּלָל שֶׁכָּל שֶׁיֵּשׁ בְּגוּפוֹ ג׳ סִימָנִין אֵלּוּ, שֶׁיֵּשׁ לוֹ אֶצְבַּע יְתֵרָה, וְהוּא הָאֶצְבַּע הַגָּדוֹל שֶׁיּוֹצֵא יוֹתֵר מִשְּׁאָר הָאֶצְבָּעוֹת, וְזֶפֶק, הוּא מָקוֹם רָחָב בְּסוֹף הַוֵּשֶׁט שֶׁמְּקַבֵּץ הָעוֹף שָׁם הַמַּאֲכָל בִּתְחִלַּת הָאֲכִילָה, וְקֻרְקְבָן נִקְלָף, וְהוּא הַמָּקוֹם הַטּוֹחֵן בּוֹ הָעוֹף הַמַּאֲכָל, הַנִּקְרָא בְלַעַז וֶנְטְרַאי, וְיֵשׁ לוֹ עוֹר דַּק בְּתוֹךְ הַבָּשָׂר לְפָנִים, וְאוֹתוֹ הָעוֹר נִקְלָף מִמִּקְצָת הָעוֹפוֹת — מִכֵּיוָן שֶׁיֵּשׁ לוֹ לָעוֹף ג׳ סִימָנִין אֵלּוּ, בְּיָדוּעַ שֶׁאֵינוֹ מִמִּין הַטְּמֵאִים, וּמֻתָּר.

§157 1. TB Ḥullin 59a.

2. *Ibid.* 63b.

3. Literally, treads (*dorés*) — which our author goes on to explain.

4. With the passage of time all certainty about the precise meaning of birds named in the Talmud, etc. has vanished; and this is even more true for birds named in Scripture. Therefore the Hebrew names have been retained in this section, always followed by the standard English name, in parentheses, that is generally given as the equivalent. It is to be understood that the English names do not represent translations of certainty.

5. So Ramban to Leviticus 11:13; Rashi explains it to mean that the bird holds its food down with its talons while eating (TB *ibid.*); while R. Tam explains it as tearing flesh for food from living creatures (Ḥullin 61a, *tosafoth* s.v. *ha-dorés*).

memory said:[1] The distinguishing marks of the domestic and wild beast were stated by Scripture; in other words, they are explained in the Torah. They are: a completely split hoof, as in the ox and sheep, and the chewing of the cud. But the distinguishing marks of fowl were not stated—because the Torah specified for us by name all the unclean kinds in the world, and hence there was no need to write their determining marks for us, since any fowl found in the world except those is kosher.

Nevertheless, because not every man is familiar with all those kinds which the Torah named to us, the Sages informed us of signs for them, so that every man can recognize them and will be able to eat of the fowl even if he recognizes not even one of all the unclean kinds mentioned explicitly in the Writ.

Consequently, according to our words, whoever recognizes well all those listed in the Torah, which are twenty-four species, can eat of every other fowl that he finds, since it was taught that every fowl not mentioned in the list of the unclean ones in the Torah is kosher. As our Sages of blessed memory said:[2] It is revealed and known before the One who spoke and the world became, that the clean [kosher] fowl are more numerous [in kind] than the unclean; therefore He itemized the unclean ones; i.e. He itemized all the unclean kinds in the world.

This is the elucidation [of the subject] according to the view of most of the rabbinic authorities: that all the unclean kinds in the world were mentioned in the Torah. For one who could not recognize them, the Sages of blessed memory said[1] that these are its characteristics: If any bird is predatory,[3] it is known (certain) that it is one of the unclean kinds in the [listing in] the Torah. The meaning of being "predatory" (*dorés*) is that it digs its talons into another bird and casts a virulent substance into it, in the way of the *nétz* (hawk)[4] and other birds with which people hunt.[5]

Then there are those which are not predatory, yet are also among the unclean kinds. The Sages of blessed memory taught us,[6] as a general rule, that whichever has these three signs in its body: if it has an extra claw—meaning a large claw projecting beyond the other claws; a crop, which is a broad place at the end of the gullet where the bird collects food when it begins to eat; and a gizzard that can be peeled, this being the place where the bird grinds the food, called *ventrai*[6a] in the foreign tongue [Spanish]; it has a thin skin within the flesh, and that skin can be peeled away in some birds—when a fowl has these three

שְׁנֵי כְלָלִים אֵלּוּ שֶׁכָּלַלְנוּ, אֶחָד לְאִסּוּר וְאֶחָד לְהֶתֵּר, כָּל עוֹף שֶׁהֵן בּוֹ אֵין צָרִיךְ שׁוּם אָדָם לִשְׁאֹל עָלָיו לְבָקִי בָּעוֹפוֹת אֶלָּא יֶאֱסֹר הָאָסוּר וְיַתִּיר הַמֻּתָּר מִיָּד, שֶׁאֵין בָּזֶה פִּקְפּוּק.

וְנִמְצָא לְפִי כְלָל זֶה שֶׁאַרְבָּעָה סִימָנֵי טָהֳרָה הֵן בְּעוֹפוֹת, וְאֵלּוּ הֵן: אֵינוֹ דוֹרֵס וְאֶצְבַּע יְתֵרָה וְזֶפֶק וְקֻרְקְבָן נִקְלָף. וּכְבָר כָּלַלְנוּ שֶׁכָּל עוֹף שֶׁנִּמְצָא חָסֵר אֶחָד מֵהֶם וְהוּא הַמְיֻחָד שֶׁבָּהֶן, דְּהַיְנוּ אֵינוֹ דוֹרֵס, כְּלוֹמַר שֶׁיִּהְיֶה דוֹרֵס, שֶׁהוּא טָמֵא לְעוֹלָם וְאֵינוֹ צָרִיךְ לִבְדֹּק בּוֹ דָּבָר אַחֵר; וְאֵין צָרִיךְ לוֹמַר אִם חָסֵר מִכֻּלָּן, שֶׁאֵין בּוֹ אֲפִלּוּ אֶחָד מִסִּימָנֵי טָהֳרָה אֵלּוּ, שֶׁאָסוּר, שֶׁהֲרֵי אֲפִלּוּ מִן הָאֶחָד הַמְיֻחָד לְבַד יֵאָסֵר, כְּמוֹ שֶׁאָמַרְנוּ, כָּל־שֶׁכֵּן אִם חָסֵר מִכֻּלָּן. וְהַנֶּשֶׁר הוּא כֵּן, שֶׁאֵין בּוֹ אֶחָד מִכָּל סִימָנֵי טָהֳרָה.

נִמְצָא עוֹף חָסֵר מִן הַשְּׁנַיִם, כְּלוֹמַר שֶׁיִּהְיוּ בוֹ שְׁנֵי סִימָנֵי טָהֳרָה לְבַד וְיֶחְסְרוּ מִמֶּנּוּ הַשְּׁנַיִם הָאֲחֵרִים, וְהָאֶחָד מִן הַשְּׁנַיִם שֶׁל טָהֳרָה שֶׁיִּמָּצְאוּ בוֹ יִהְיֶה שֶׁאֵינוֹ דוֹרֵס, כָּל עוֹף שֶׁהוּא כֵן הוּא טָהוֹר לֶאֱכֹל לְכָל מִי שֶׁמַּכִּיר עוֹרֵב וְכָל מִין עוֹרֵב, לְפִי שֶׁאֵין בְּכָל מִין הַטְּמֵאִים שֶׁיִּהְיֶה כֵן כִּי־אִם עוֹרֵב וּמִינוֹ, שֶׁהוּא כֵן, שֶׁאֵינוֹ דוֹרֵס וְיֵשׁ לוֹ סִימָן אֶחָד בְּגוּפוֹ מִסִּימָנֵי הַטָּהֳרָה; וְסִימָן זֶה שֶׁל טָהֳרָה אֵינוֹ קָבוּעַ בְּכָל מִין הָעוֹרֵב, אֶלָּא יֵשׁ בְּמִין הָעוֹרֵב שֶׁיֵּשׁ לוֹ אֶצְבַּע יְתֵרָה וְאֵינוֹ דוֹרֵס, וְיֵשׁ שֶׁיֵּשׁ לוֹ זֶפֶק וְאֵינוֹ דוֹרֵס, וְיֵשׁ שֶׁקֻּרְקְבָנוֹ נִקְלָף וְאֵינוֹ דוֹרֵס. כְּלַל הַדָּבָר, כִּי בְמִינוֹ יִמָּצְאוּ שְׁנֵי הַסִּימָנִין אֵלּוּ שֶׁל טָהֳרָה וְלֹא בְמִין אַחֵר; כֵּן פֵּרְשׁוּ קְצָת מִן הַמְפָרְשִׁים. וְיֵשׁ שֶׁאָמְרוּ כִּי יֵשׁ לָעוֹרֵב שְׁנֵי סִימָנֵי טָהֳרָה בְגוּפוֹ מִלְּבַד שֶׁאֵינוֹ דוֹרֵס.

נִמְצָא עוֹף חָסֵר הַשְּׁלֹשָׁה סִימָנֵי טָהֳרָה וְלֹא יִשָּׁאֵר לוֹ כִּי־אִם הָאֶחָד הַמְיֻחָד, וְהוּא שֶׁאֵינוֹ דוֹרֵס, טָהוֹר לְעוֹלָם, לְפִי שֶׁאֵין בְּכָל הָעוֹפוֹת הַטְּמֵאִים שֶׁלֹּא יִהְיֶה

6. TB Ḥullin 62a.

6a. Or *vientre* (so David Rosin).

7. I.e. either one of the two rules.

8. This is how most early commentaries understand the Talmudic teaching about *dorés*, being predatory (Ḥullin 59a), that if a bird has this characteristic, it is a forbidden kind even if it should have the other three marks of cleanness (permissibility).

9. TB Ḥullin 61a.

10. I.e. if he can be certain that the fowl he has is not a member of the crow and raven families, as they are unclean (non-kosher); *ibid.* 62a, and *tosafoth* s.v. *mip'né*.

11. This can be inferred from TB Ḥullin 62a.

12. R. Moses b. R. Joseph, cited by R. Nissim to TB Ḥullin 21b.

signs, it is known (certain) that it is not one of the unclean kinds, but is permissible.

Concerning these two rules that we have given, one for prohibition and one for permission, when they[7] apply to any bird, a man need not ask an expert in fowl about it, but he can ban the forbidden and allow the permitted at once; because there are no doubts or qualms about this.

Consequently, according to this, there are four signs of cleanness in fowl [that they are kosher]. These are: not being predatory, and [having] an extra claw, a crop, and a gizzard that can be peeled. And we have previously given the rule that if any bird is found to be lacking one of them—i.e. the important one among them—that it does not attack with its claws; in other words, if it does attack with its claws—it is forever unclean, and there is no need to examine anything further about it.[8] Nor is there any need to add that if it is lacking in all of them—if it has not even one of these marks of cleanness—it is forbidden. Since here even the one singular, important sign prohibits it, as we stated, then all the more certainly [is it forbidden] if it is lacking in all of them. The *nesher* (eagle) is like that: it has not even one of all the signs of cleanness.[9]

If a bird is found lacking in two, i.e. it has only two signs of cleanness, but the other two are missing—if one of the two signs of cleanness found in it is that it is not predatory—any bird that is so is clean [allowed] to be eaten by any person who can recognize the crow and every other species of crow (raven).[10] For among all the unclean kinds there are none like that except the crow and its kind. *It* is like that: it is not predatory, and it has one of the marks of cleanness in its body. This mark of cleanness is not [one] fixed, definite [thing] in every kind of crow and raven. Rather, there are some species of crow that have the extra claw and are not predatory. There are some which have a crop and are not predatory. And some have a gizzard which can be peeled, and are not predatory.[11] The nub of the matter is that in its species these two marks of cleanness are found, and not in any other. So some of the authorities explained it. However, there are those who said[12] that the crow has *two* signs in its body of being clean [kosher] apart from not being predatory.

If a bird was found lacking the three marks of cleanness, and nothing remained for it but the one singular, important sign, i.e. that it is not predatory, it is always clean [kosher]: For among all unclean [non-kosher] fowl, there are none which do not have in their bodies even one

בְּגוּפָם אֶחָד מִכָּל סִימָנֵי הַטָּהֳרָה אֶלָּא שֶׁאֵינוֹ דוֹרֵס, חוּץ מִפֶּרֶס וְעָזְנִיָּה, שֶׁהֵן כֵּן, וְהֵן אֵינָן מְצוּיִין בַּיִּשּׁוּב, וּמִכֵּיוָן שֶׁאֵינָן מְצוּיִין בַּיִּשּׁוּב אֵין לְסַפֵּק בָּהֶן. וְיֵשׁ מִן הַמְּפָרְשִׁים שֶׁאָמְרוּ כִּי לְרַבּוֹתֵינוּ (זִכְרוֹנָם לִבְרָכָה) לֹא הָיוּ מְצוּיִין אֲבָל עַכְשָׁיו מְצוּיִין הֵן; וְקוֹרֵא אֲנִי עֲלֵיהֶם "אַל תְּהִי צַדִּיק הַרְבֵּה", כִּי הֵם אָמְרוּ דְּלָא שְׁכִיחֵי בַּיִּשּׁוּב, כְּלוֹמַר שֶׁמַּרְחִיקִין הֵן לְעוֹלָם מִמְּקוֹמוֹת הַיִּשּׁוּב, וּמִכֵּיוָן שֶׁטִּבְעָם כֵּן, הָאָרֶץ לְעוֹלָם עוֹמֶדֶת, וְהַדִּין שָׁוֶה בְּכָל זְמָן.

נִמְצְאוּ בְגוּפוֹ שְׁלֹשָׁה סִימָנֵי הַטָּהֳרָה, וְהֵם אֶצְבַּע יְתֵרָה וְזֶפֶק וְקֻרְקְבָן נִקְלָף, בְּיָדוּעַ שֶׁהוּא כָשֵׁר, וְגַם הָרְבִיעִי הוּא בוֹ, כְּלוֹמַר שֶׁאֵינוֹ דוֹרֵס — שֶׁאֵין בָּעוֹלָם עוֹף בִּשְׁלֹשָׁה סִימָנִין אֵלּוּ שֶׁיְּהֵא דוֹרֵס, וְאֵין צָרִיךְ לִבְדֹּק אַחֲרָיו כְּלָל אֶלָּא שֶׁיֹּאכְלֶנּוּ מִיָּד; אֲבָל נִמְצְאוּ בוֹ שְׁלֹשָׁה סִימָנֵי טָהֳרָה וְיִהְיֶה אֶחָד מִן הַשְּׁלֹשָׁה שֶׁאֵינוֹ דוֹרֵס, בָּזֶה וַדַּאי יֵשׁ לְסַפֵּק הַרְבֵּה, כִּי רֹב הַטְּמֵאִים הֵם כֵּן, שֶׁיֵּשׁ לָהֶם שְׁלֹשָׁה סִימָנֵי טָהֳרָה כָּאֵלּוּ, וְצָרִיךְ כָּל אָדָם לִשְׁאֹל עַל עוֹף כָּזֶה, אִם אֵינוֹ מַכִּיר כָּל הַטְּמֵאִים הַמְּנוּיִים בַּתּוֹרָה.

נִמְצָא לְפִי דְבָרֵינוּ שֶׁכָּל עוֹף שֶׁיִּסְתַּפֵּק עָלֵינוּ אִם טָמֵא אוֹ טָהוֹר, יִהְיֶה עַל־כָּל־פָּנִים בִּשְׁנֵי צְדָדִין: שֶׁיִּהְיוּ לוֹ שְׁלֹשָׁה סִימָנֵי טָהֳרָה וְהָאֶחָד מֵהֶם אֵינוֹ דוֹרֵס, כְּמוֹ שֶׁאָמַרְנוּ שֶׁיֵּשׁ לְסַפְּקוֹ בְּרֹב מִינֵי הַטְּמֵאִים; אוֹ שֶׁיִּהְיוּ לוֹ שְׁנֵי סִימָנֵי טָהֳרָה וְאֶחָד מֵהֶם אֵינוֹ דוֹרֵס, שֶׁיֵּשׁ לְסַפְּקוֹ בָּעוֹרֵב וּמִינָיו. אֲבָל בְּכָל שְׁאָר הַצְּדָדִין אֵינוֹ בָא לִידֵי הַסָּפֵק אֶלָּא נָדִין אוֹתוֹ אוֹ בְטָהוֹר אוֹ בְטָמֵא מִיָּד.

שִׁית דַּעְתְּךָ בַּדָּבָר כִּי כֵן הוּא לְפִי כְּלָלֵנוּ זֶה. וּכְלָל זֶה כָּתַבְנוּ אוֹתוֹ לְפִי סְבָרַת קְצָת הַמְּפָרְשִׁים, כִּי הַרְבֵּה פֵּרוּשִׁים נִתְפָּרְשׁוּ בְעִנְיָנִים אֵלּוּ שֶׁל עוֹפוֹת. וְכָל הָעוֹפוֹת הַמְּסֻפָּקִים אָמְרוּ זִכְרוֹנָם לִבְרָכָה שֶׁהֵן נֶאֱכָלִין בְּמָסוֹרֶת, כְּלוֹמַר שֶׁאִם קִבְּלוּ בְנֵי הַמָּקוֹם וְנָהֲגוּ בִּפְשִׁיטוּת לְאָכְלוֹ בְּחֶזְקַת טָהוֹר, שֶׁאֵין לְפַקְפֵּק עָלָיו כְּלָל, וְאֵין צָרִיךְ לְבָדְקוֹ. וְיֶתֶר פְּרָטֵי הַמִּצְוָה, בְּפֶרֶק ג׳ מֵחֻלִּין.

13. I.e. if such a fowl is found where people live, there is no need to fear that it may be a *peres* or an *'ozniyah*, and it may be eaten; TB Ḥullin 62a.
14. I.e. in their time and place.
15. So R. Tam, TB Ḥullin 61a, *tosafoth* s.v. *kol.*
16. So R. Moses b. Joseph, cited by Ramban to TB Ḥullin 62a, *et al.*
17. Cf. Rashi to TB Ḥullin 62b, s.v. *v'hani kurk'vanin.*
18. TB Ḥullin 63b.

of all the marks of cleanness but are only not predatory—except the *peres* (ossifrage) and the *'ozniyah* (osprey) (Leviticus 11:13), and they are not found in human settlements; and since they are not found in human habitations, there is no need to have doubts on their account.[13] There are some authorities who said that for our Sages of blessed memory[14] they were not usually found, but now they are quite usual. To them I apply the verse, *Do not be overly righteous* (Ecclesiastes 7:16); for they [the Sages] said that they are not usually found in a human settlement: in other words, they always keep far from the locations of settled communities. Since this is their nature, *the earth abides forever* (*ibid.* 1:4), and the law remains the same at all times.

If the three marks of cleanness were found in its body, i.e. the extra claw, the crop, and the peelable gizzard, it is certainly kosher, and it has the fourth sign also:[15] in other words, it is not predatory. For there is not a bird in the world with these three distinguishing marks which is predatory. Thus there is no need to investigate about it at all, but it may rather be eaten at once.[16] If, however, three marks of cleanness were found in it and one of the three is that it is not predatory, about this there is certainly reason to have great doubt: for most of the unclean [non-kosher] kinds are of this sort—they have three signs of cleanness like that.[17] Then every man must inquire about a bird of this sort, if he does not recognize all the unclean ones listed in the Torah.

What emerges from our words is that every fowl about which we can have doubt if it is unclean or clean [kosher], will be, in every case, in one of two categories: (1) it will have three signs of cleanness, one of which is that it is not predatory—as we said, it can be suspected of being one of the great majority of the unclean kinds; (2) or it has two signs of cleanness, one of which is that it is not predatory: then it is to be suspected of being a crow or one of its [related] species. If it is of any other category, though, it is not a matter of doubt, but we can rather judge it at once to be clean [kosher] or unclean.

Set your mind straight on this, that it is so, according to this rule of ours. We have written this rule according to the view of certain authorities, since many interpretations were given in explanation of these matters concerning fowl. Now, in regard to all fowl in doubt, our Sages of blessed memory taught[18] that they may be eaten by tradition: in other words, if the local inhabitants received a tradition and have simply had the custom to eat it, it is assumed to be clean [kosher], with no need to have any qualms about it, and no need to examine it.

וְנוֹהֶגֶת בְּכָל מָקוֹם וּבְכָל זְמַן, בִּזְכָרִים וּנְקֵבוֹת. וְעוֹבֵר עָלֶיהָ וְאָכַל כַּזַּיִת מֵעוֹף טָמֵא, בְּמֵזִיד לוֹקֶה, בְּשׁוֹגֵג פָּטוּר.

[מִצְוַת בְּדִיקַת סִימָנֵי חֲגָבִים]

קנח לִבְדֹּק בְּסִימָנֵי חֲגָבִים, וְהֵם הַסִּימָנִין שֶׁכְּתוּבִים בַּתּוֹרָה: אֲשֶׁר אֵין לוֹ כְרָעַיִם מִמַּעַל לְרַגְלָיו וְגוֹמֵר, שֶׁנֶּאֱמַר: אֶת זֶה תֹּאכְלוּ מִכֹּל שֶׁרֶץ הָעוֹף. עִנְיַן שָׁרְשָׁהּ כְּמוֹ בִּשְׁאָר הַמִּינִים.

דִּינֶיהָ, פֵּרְשׁוּ זִכְרוֹנָם לִבְרָכָה שֶׁשְּׁמוֹנָה מִינֵי חָגָב טָהוֹר הֵם; וְאֵלּוּ הֵן: אֶחָד שֶׁנִּקְרָא חָגָב, שֵׁנִי שֶׁנִּקְרָא דְּבָנִית, וְהוּא מִין חָגָב, שְׁלִישִׁי שֶׁנִּקְרָא חַרְגֹּל, רְבִיעִי עוּצְרַבְיָא, וְהוּא מִין חַרְגֹּל, חֲמִישִׁי אַרְבֶּה, שִׁשִּׁי צִפֹּרֶת כְּרָמִים, וְהוּא מִין אַרְבֶּה, שְׁבִיעִי סָלְעָם, שְׁמִינִי יוֹחָנָה יְרוּשַׁלְמִית, וְהוּא מִין סָלְעָם. מִי שֶׁהוּא בָקִי בּוֹדֵק בָּהֶן לְפִי בְקִיאוּתוֹ וּבִשְׁמוֹתֵיהֶן וְאוֹכֵל; וְהַצַּיָּד יִשְׂרָאֵל נֶאֱמָן עֲלֵיהֶם וּבָעוֹף; וּמִי שֶׁאֵינוֹ בָקִי בָּהֶן בּוֹדֵק בַּסִּימָנִין שֶׁנָּתְנָה הַתּוֹרָה בָּהֶן.

וּשְׁלֹשָׁה סִימָנִין הֵן, וְאֵלּוּ הֵן: אַרְבַּע כְּנָפַיִם, שֶׁחוֹפוֹת רֹב אֹרֶךְ וְרֹב הֶקֵּף גּוּפוֹ, וְאַרְבַּע רַגְלַיִם, וּשְׁתֵּי כְרָעַיִם לְנַתֵּר בָּהֶן עַל הָאָרֶץ; וְיֵשׁ אוֹמְרִים שֶׁצָּרִיךְ לָדַעַת שֶׁיְּהֵא שְׁמוֹ חָגָב; וְיֶתֶר פְּרָטֶיהָ, מְבֹאָרִים בְּפֶרֶק שְׁלִישִׁי מֵחֻלִּין.

וְנוֹהֶגֶת בְּכָל מָקוֹם וּבְכָל זְמַן, בִּזְכָרִים וּנְקֵבוֹת. וְעוֹבֵר עָלֶיהָ וְאָכַל וְלֹא בָדַק יָפֶה, בִּטֵּל עֲשֵׂה.

[מִצְוַת טֻמְאַת שְׁמֹנָה שְׁרָצִים]

קנט לִהְיוֹת שְׁמֹנָה שְׁרָצִים טְמֵאִים וּמְטַמְּאִים, שֶׁנֶּאֱמַר: וְזֶה לָכֶם הַטָּמֵא בַּשֶּׁרֶץ הַשֹּׁרֵץ עַל הָאָרֶץ הַחֹלֶד וְהָעַכְבָּר וְהַצָּב וְגוֹמֵר.

§158 1. TB Ḥullin 65a; MT *hilchoth ma'achaloth 'asuroth* i 21.

2. The lack of certainty about the names of birds, mentioned in §157, note 4, exists also about the locusts and grasshoppers, etc. in this section. Hence here too the Hebrew or Aramaic names have been retained, and tentative or standard translations are added in parentheses.

3. So the Hebrew in the old manuscripts and the standard editions. In Sifra *perek* 3, 5 it is *'arzibunith* (from the Greek); but in TB Ḥullin 65a and MT (see note 1) it is *razbonith*. TB Ḥullin MS Munich, however, has *duvanith* (*Dikduké Sof'rim*).

4. So the Hebrew in the two oldest manuscripts and the standard editions. One old manuscript and MT ed. Rome 1480 have *'utzranya*; but TB Ḥullin 65a and MT (see note 1) have *'artzuvya* (from the Greek).

5. The oldest manuscript and the first edition have *taḥanah*; *'Aruch haShalém* notes that according to the Arabic it should be *maḥanah*.

6. MT *ibid.* 22, based on TB Ḥullin 63b (*Maggid Mishneh*).

The remaining details of the precept are in chapter 3 of the tractate *Ḥullin*. It is in effect in every time, at every place, for both man and woman. If someone violated it and ate an olive's amount of an unclean [non-kosher] fowl—if it was deliberate, he should receive whiplashes; if inadvertent, he is free of penalty.

[THE PRECEPT OF EXAMINING THE SIGNS OF LOCUSTS, IF THEY ARE KOSHER]

158 to examine the determining marks of grasshoppers, which are the marks written in the Torah: *that have jointed legs above their feet*, etc. (Leviticus 11:21)—as it is stated, *Yet these you may eat of all winged swarming things* (*ibid.*). The theme of its root reason is the same as that of the other species [of edible creatures].

As to its laws, our Sages of blessed memory explained[1] that eight kinds of grasshoppers are clean [kosher]; and they are these: The first is called *ḥagav* (grasshopper).[2] The second is what is called *d'vanith*[3] ("hammer-locust"), a species of *ḥagav*. The third is the one called *ḥargol* (cricket). The fourth is *'utzravya*,[4] a species of *ḥargol*. The fifth is *'arbeh* (locust). The sixth is the "bird of the vineyards," a species of *'arbeh*. The seventh is *sol'am* (the bald locust). The eighth is the Jerusalem *yoḥana*,[5] a species of *sol'am*. Whoever is knowledgeable may examine them according to his expert knowledge and their names, and eat [them]. An Israelite trapper is trusted about them, and about fowl. Whoever has no expert knowledge about them may examine for the determining marks that the Torah has given for them.[6]

There are three distinguishing marks, which are these: four wings which cover most of the length and most of the surface of its body; four legs; and two jointed [upper] legs, *with which to leap on the earth* (Leviticus 11:21).[7] And some say it is necessary to know that its name is *ḥagav*.[8]

The rest of its details are clarified in chapter 3 of the tractate *Ḥullin*. It applies in every place and every time, for both man and woman. If a person violates it and eats without examining [them] well, he disobeys a positive precept.

[THE RITUAL UNCLEANNESS OF EIGHT LOW CRAWLING CREATURES]

159 that eight low crawling creatures are ritually unclean and cause defilement: as it is stated, *And these are what are unclean to you among*

מִשָּׁרְשֵׁי הַמִּצְוָה, הַקְדָּמָה: לֹא יְסֻפַּק כָּל מִי שֶׁיֵּשׁ בּוֹ דֵעָה שֶׁלֹּא הָיָה אָדָם מֵעוֹלָם שֶׁהִשִּׂיג לָדַעַת כָּל הַחָכְמָה עַד סוֹפָהּ, שֶׁלֹּא יִתְעַלֵּם לוֹ מִמֶּנָּה דָבָר, שֶׁהֲרֵי אֲפִלּוּ עַל מֹשֶׁה רַבֵּנוּ עָלָיו הַשָּׁלוֹם אָמְרוּ זִכְרוֹנָם לִבְרָכָה: שִׁשִּׁים שַׁעֲרֵי חָכְמָה הֵן, וְכֻלָּן נִמְסְרוּ לְמֹשֶׁה חוּץ מֵאַחַת; וְכֵן שְׁלֹמֹה הַמֶּלֶךְ הֶחָכָם אָמַר עַל עַצְמוֹ: אָמַרְתִּי אֶחְכָּמָה וְהִיא רְחוֹקָה מִמֶּנִּי; וְכֵן לֹא יְסֻפַּק כָּל שֶׁיֵּשׁ לוֹ מֹחַ בְּקָדְקֳדוֹ כִּי הַשֵּׁם, שֶׁהוּא אַב הַחָכְמָה, וּמֵאִתּוֹ נִמְצֵאת, בּוֹ נִכְלֶלֶת כֻּלָּהּ; וְאֵין שׁוּם סָפֵק גַּם־כֵּן כִּי אַב כָּל הַטּוֹבוֹת לֹא יְצַוֶּה דָבָר אֶת בְּרִיּוֹתָיו רַק לְטוֹבָתָם וּלְתוֹעַלְתָּם, וּלְהַרְחִיק כָּל נֶזֶק מֵעֲלֵיהֶם.

וְעַל־כֵּן כַּאֲשֶׁר נַשִּׂיג בְּחָכְמָתֵנוּ מִן הַמִּצְוֹות לָדַעַת הַתּוֹעָלוֹת הַמַּגִּיעַ לָנוּ בָּהֶן נִשְׂמַח בּוֹ, וְכַאֲשֶׁר אֵין אֲנַחְנוּ מַשִּׂיגִים מֵהֶן בְּחָכְמָתֵנוּ הַתּוֹעֶלֶת שֶׁלָּנוּ בָּהֶן, יֵשׁ לָנוּ לַחְשֹׁב עַל־כָּל־פָּנִים כִּי בְּיִתְרוֹן הַחָכְמָה אֲשֶׁר לַשֵּׁם עַל כָּל בְּרִיָּה, יָדַע הַתּוֹעֶלֶת אֲשֶׁר לָנוּ בְּאוֹתָהּ מִצְוָה, וְעַל כֵּן צִוָּנוּ עָלֶיהָ.

וּכְבָר הוֹדִיעוּנוּ זִכְרוֹנָם לִבְרָכָה לָמָּה לֹא נוֹדַע הַטַּעַם בְּכָל הַמִּצְוֹות, וְאָמְרוּ שֶׁהָיָה הַדָּבָר שֶׁלֹּא יִהְיֶה לָנוּ כִּשָּׁלוֹן בָּזֶה; וְהֵבִיאוּ רְאָיָה, שֶׁהֲרֵי שְׁלֹשָׁה מֵהֶן נִתְגַּלָּה טַעְמָן וְנִכְשַׁל בָּהֶן גְּדוֹל הָעוֹלָם.

וְאַל יַחְשֹׁב תּוֹפֵשׂ לָבוֹא עָלַי עִם הַמָּשָׁל שֶׁאָמְרוּ זִכְרוֹנָם לִבְרָכָה, "כַּפָּא דְחַק נַגָּרָא, בֵּיהּ נִשְׂרוֹף חַרְדְּלָא", בַּמֶּה שֶׁאָמַרְתִּי עַכְשָׁיו שֶׁהַשֵּׁם הֶעֱלִים מִמֶּנּוּ טַעֲמֵי הַמִּצְוֹות, וְאָנֹכִי הֲרִימוֹתִי יָדִי לְדַבֵּר בָּהֶן דָּבָר אֶל נְעָרַי — כִּי כְבָר קְדָמוּנִי רַבּוֹתַי לְדַבֵּר בָּהֶן כַּמָּה דְבָרִים בַּמִּדְרָשִׁים וּבִמְקוֹמוֹת אֲחֵרִים עַל צַד פְּשָׁטָן, וְעֹמֶק חָכְמָתָן וְחֹזֶק בִּינָתָן וְרֹב קְדֻשָּׁתָן גָּנוּז בְּתוֹכָן, אֲפִלּוּ כָּל הָרוּחוֹת לֹא יְזִיזוּ אוֹתָן; וְכָל הַמַּעֲמִיק עֵצָה בִּפְשָׁטֵיהֶן וְיִשְׁתַּדֵּל לְחַדֵּשׁ דָּבָר בַּנִּגְלֶה שֶׁבָּהֶן, כִּי יִכְסֹף לְהָצִיץ

7. MT *ibid.* based on TB Ḥullin 65a and 59a.

8. TB Ḥullin 59a.

§159 1. See § 157, note 4, which applies as well to the names of the creatures in this section.

2. I.e. to master and pass through them; this is evidently from TB Rosh haShanah 21b, but our Talmud editions have "fifty gates of *binah*, understanding."

3. So Rambam, *Guide* III 26.

4. TB Sanhedrin 21b.

5. Deuteronomy 17:16–17; the Talmud reads two instead of three (for the third injunction, Scripture does not give a reason).

6. I.e. King Solomon: according to the Talmud, he decided to ignore the injunctions because he felt invulnerable to the reasons given for them in Scripture; and he subsequently came to grief.

7. TB P'saḥim 28a, as explained by Rashi.

the low crawling things that move upon the earth: the ḥo-led (*weasel*), achbar (*mouse*), *and* tzav (*great lizard*), etc. (Leviticus 11:29).[1]

As to what lies at the root of the precept, [let us start with] a preface: Whoever is possessed of sense can have no doubt that there was never yet a man who attained to know all wisdom, to its very limits, so that nothing remained hidden from him. For you see, even about Moses our Master (peace be upon him) the Sages of blessed memory said: There are sixty gates of wisdom; all were given him,[2] except one. Similarly, the wise King Solomon declared about himself, *I said, "I will get wisdom"; but it was far from me* (Ecclesiastes 7:23). So too, no one with a brain in his skull can doubt that the Eternal Lord is the Father of wisdom, and from Him it has existence, being wholly contained in Him. Nor can there be any doubt whatever that the Father of all goodness would ordain anything for His creatures for anything but their own benefit and good, and in order to remove all harm from them.

Therefore, when we can grasp something from the precepts by our wisdom, to know the benefits we gain from them, let us rejoice in that. And when we cannot grasp by our wisdom what benefit we gain from a particular *mitzvah*, it is for us to realize, in any event, that in His far greater wisdom, beyond that of any being, the Eternal Lord knew the benefit we will have through that precept;[3] and therefore He commanded us about it.

Long before, our Sages of blessed memory informed us[4] why we shall not know the reason for all the precepts: They said it is so in order that we should not come to grief over it; and they brought proof: you see, for three of them the reason was revealed,[5] and a great man of the world suffered disaster through them.[6]

Now, let not some eager questioner think to attack me with the metaphor that the Sages of blessed memory used:[7] "The spoon that the carpenter carved out—with that let him burn his mouth with mustard"—because I have now said that the Eternal Lord concealed from us the reasons for the precepts; yet I have raised my hand to speak a word about them to my young folk. For long ago did our Sages precede me to relate many things about them in the Midrashim and elsewhere, by way of their plain meaning; and their deep wisdom, mighty understanding and great holiness are hidden within them [their words]. Not even all the winds will budge them. Then if anyone delves to find deep counsel in their plain explanations and strives to show something new in their overt meanings, because he yearns to gain a

מִן הַחֲרַכִּים לְהִתְעַנֵּג בְּזֹהַר מַרְאֵיהֶן וְלִלְקֹט מֵעֲלֵיהֶן לַחְגֹּר בָּהֶן, אֵין רָאוּי לָתֵת עָלָיו בָּזֶה אָשָׁם, רַק לְבָרְכוֹ וּלְהַזְכִּירוֹ לְשֶׁבַח בַּאֲשֶׁר הוּא שָׁם.

וְעַתָּה אַחֲרֵי הַקְדָּמָתֵנוּ זֹאת, שֶׁחָכְמַת הָאֵל גָּדְלָה עַל כָּל חָכְמָה, וְכִי לֹא יְצַוֶּה דָּבָר רַק לְטוֹבָה לָנוּ וּלְתוֹעֶלֶת גְּדוֹלָה, אֵין לָנוּ קֻשְׁיָא וְלֹא שְׁאֵלָה בְּכָל אִסּוּר הַמַּאֲכָלוֹת וְהַרְחָקַת הַטֻּמְאָה בְּכָל אֲשֶׁר לֹא יִהְיֶה הַתּוֹעֶלֶת לָנוּ יְדוּעָה וּמֻשָּׂג בַּחֲקִירָה, כִּי יָדַעְנוּ בֶּאֱמֶת שֶׁהַכֹּל לְטוֹב. וְאַל תִּתְמַהּ בְּנִי עַל עִנְיְנֵי הַטֻּמְאָה אִם הוּא נֶעְלָם הַרְבֵּה עַל כָּל בְּרִיָּה, כִּי אֶפְשָׁר שֶׁהַטֻּמְאָה תַזִּיק אֶל הַנֶּפֶשׁ וְתַחְלִיאָהּ קְצָת, וְכֵן שָׁמַעְתִּי הַדָּבָר מִפִּי חֲכָמִים, וּכְעֵין מַה שֶּׁאָמְרוּ זִכְרוֹנָם לִבְרָכָה: "וְנִטְמֵתֶם בָּם", וְנִטַּמְתֶּם כְּתִיב — כְּלוֹמַר שֶׁמַּעְיְנוֹת הַשֵּׂכֶל, שֶׁהוּא הַנֶּפֶשׁ הַקַּיֶּמֶת, מִתְקַלְקְלִים קְצָת בְּעִנְיַן הַטֻּמְאָה.

וְאַל תִּתְמַהּ בְּהִתְקַלְקֵל הַשֵּׂכֶל בָּעִנְיָנִים הַגַּשְׁמִיִּים אַף־עַל־פִּי שֶׁאֵינוֹ מִינוֹ, כִּי מִפְּנֵי שִׁתּוּפָהּ שֶׁל נֶפֶשׁ עִם הַגּוּף יֶאֱרַע לָהּ כֵּן עַל־כָּל־פָּנִים; וְאִם־כֵּן אֲנַחְנוּ בְּנֵי־אִישׁ בַּעֲנִיּוּת דַּעְתֵּנוּ לֹא נֵדַע הַנֶּפֶשׁ וּמַהוּתָהּ, וְאֵיךְ נִלְאֶה לָדַעַת רְפוּאָתָהּ אוֹ מַחֲלָתָהּ מִדֶּרֶךְ הַחֲקִירָה; הֲלֹא לָרוֹפְאִים אֵין תַּחְבּוּלָה בִּרְפוּאָה עַד הַכִּירָם עִקַּר הַמַּחֲלָה.

וְעַל־כֵּן בְּכָל הַרְחָקוֹת הַטֻּמְאָה שֶׁיָּבוֹאוּ בַתּוֹרָה אֵין לָנוּ לְחַטֵּט אַחַר שָׁרְשֵׁיהֶן, עַד בּוֹאֵנוּ אֶל תַּכְלִית הַיְדִיעָה בְּעִנְיְנֵי הַנֶּפֶשׁ, לָדַעַת מַהוּתָהּ וּמוֹצָאָהּ וּמוֹבָאָהּ.

וְהָבֵן זֶה וְדָעֵהוּ, כִּי בוֹ נִמְצָא קְצָת תְּשׁוּבָה עַל כָּל שָׁרְשֵׁי מִצְוֹת הַטֻּמְאָה וְהַטָּהֳרָה, עַד אֲשֶׁר כִּמְעַט יִהְיֶה מַסְוֶה עַל פָּנֵינוּ בְּחִדּוּשׁ פָּרָה אֲדֻמָּה, שֶׁמְּטַמְּאָה הַטָּהוֹר וּמְטַהֶרֶת הַטָּמֵא; וְגַם שָׁם נַאֲרִיךְ בָּעִנְיָן בְּעֶזְרַת הַשֵּׁם, לְקַבֵּל שָׂכָר בִּיגִיעָה לִמְצֹא דִבְרֵי חֵפֶץ.

8. Expression based on Song of Songs 2:9.

9. Cf. Genesis 3:6.

10. TB Yoma 39a.

10a. I.e. to cover our shame (as it were) at being baffled by the antithetical effects of the red heifer, which the author goes on to write.

11. Mishnah, Kélim i 1.

glimpse through the lattice[8] in order to find delight in the radiance of their vision, and [he yearns] to gather of their leaves in order to gird himself with them[9]—it is not proper to put blame on him for this, but rather to bless him and mention him for praise, at his level.

Now, after we have given this preface, that the wisdom of God is greater than any wisdom, and He would command nothing except for our good and for great benefit, we have no difficulty or question about any ban on food or the removal [from permissibility] of anything unclean—any [ban] whose benefit is neither known to us nor to be grasped by probing. For we know that in truth, all is for the good. And do not wonder, my son, about the subject-matter of defilement and ritual uncleanness, if it is greatly hidden from the understanding of any human being. It is possible that this uncleanness will be harmful to the soul and sicken it somewhat; and so I heard the matter from wise scholars. It is akin to what the Sages of blessed memory taught:[10] *v'nitméthem bam* (that you should be defiled by them; Leviticus 11:43)—it is written [without the *'alef*] as *v'nittamtem bam* (that you should be made stupid by them). This is to say that the wellsprings of intelligence, which is the soul that endures, become somewhat impaired by the matter of defilement.

Nor should you wonder that the intelligence can be impaired by physical matters, even if they are not of its kind. Because the soul is united with the body, this can happen to it beyond any doubt. And if we human beings, with our meager understanding, do not know the soul and its nature, how can we seek to the point of exhaustion to know what heals it or sickens it, by way of probing investigation? Even physicians find no plan of healing until they discern the core of the illness.

For this reason, in all instances where uncleanness is removed far [from us], it is not for us to dig after their root reasons, until we attain ultimate knowledge in matters of the soul, to know its nature, its origin and its destination.

Know this and understand it, for thereby we will find some slight answer about all the root reasons for the precepts of defilement and purity, until there will almost be a mask [of equanimity] on our face concerning the novelty [of the precept] of the red heifer (§397),[10a] which defiles the ritually clean and purifies the ritually unclean. But there too we will continue at length about the subject, to receive reward for toiling *to find words of delight* (Ecclesiastes 12:10).

Some laws of the precept are:[11] that the eight swarming creatures

מִדִּינֵי הַמִּצְוָה, שֶׁשְּׁמֹנָה שְׁרָצִים הֵם נִקְרָאִין אַב הַטֻּמְאָה, כְּלוֹמַר שֶׁמְּטַמְּאִין אָדָם וְכֵלִים בְּמַגָּע, וְאִם הַכֵּלִים שֶׁל חֶרֶשׂ מְטַמְּאִין אוֹתוֹ מִכֵּיוָן שֶׁיִּכָּנְסוּ בְתוֹךְ אֲוִירוֹ; וְזֶה הַחִלּוּק שֶׁיֵּשׁ בְּעִנְיַן הַטֻּמְאָה בֵּין מַה שֶּׁנִּקְרָא אָב לְמַה שֶּׁנִּקְרָא וָלָד: שֶׁהַנִּקְרָא אָב מְטַמֵּא אָדָם וְכֵלִים, וְהַנִּקְרָא וָלָד אֵינוֹ מְטַמֵּא אָדָם וְכֵלִים.

וְהַשְּׁרָצִים אֵינָם מְטַמְּאִין עַד שֶׁיָּמוּתוּ, שֶׁנֶּאֱמַר: הַנּוֹגֵעַ בָּהֶם בְּמוֹתָם יִטְמָא. וּשְׁמֹנָה שְׁרָצִים אֵלּוּ דַוְקָא הוּא שֶׁמְּטַמְּאִין, אֲבָל כָּל שְׁאָר שְׁרָצִים, נָחָשׁ וְעַקְרָב וְכַיּוֹצֵא בָהֶן, אֵינָם מְטַמְּאִין כְּלָל. וְדִין הַשְּׁרָצִים הוּא שֶׁאֵינָם מְטַמְּאִין בְּמַשָּׂא בְּלִי מַגָּע; וְהַנּוֹגְעָן, שֶׁאֵינוֹ מְטַמֵּא בְגָדִים שֶׁעָלָיו בִּשְׁעַת מַגָּעוֹ בָהֶן; וְשִׁעוּר טֻמְאַת הַשֶּׁרֶץ בְּכַעֲדָשָׁה, שֶׁהֲרֵי מָצִינוּ שֶׁהַתּוֹרָה טִמְּאָן סְתָם, וְיֵשׁ מֵהֶן שְׁרָצִים שֶׁאֵינָן אֶלָּא כַעֲדָשָׁה; וְכָל הַשְּׁרָצִים מִצְטָרְפִין לְכַעֲדָשָׁה, כְּלוֹמַר אֲפִלּוּ מְעַט מִזֶּה וּמְעַט מִזֶּה מִצְטָרֵף לְכַעֲדָשָׁה לְטַמֵּא, שֶׁלֹּא תֹאמַר אֵין הַחִיּוּב אֶלָּא בְכַעֲדָשָׁה מֵאֶחָד לְבָד.

וְדִין בָּשָׂר חַי הַפּוֹרֵשׁ מִן הַשֶּׁרֶץ, וְאֵבֶר אֶחָד שָׁלֵם, וְהַכּוּלְיָא וְהַכָּבֵד וְהַלָּשׁוֹן; וְדִין דָּמָן וְגִידָן וְצִפָּרְנָן וְעוֹרָן וּבֵיצָתָן; וְדִין כָּל שֶׁנִּטְמָא בָהֶן שֶׁאָסוּר לֶאֱכֹל תְּרוּמָה וְקָדָשִׁים, וְלִכָּנֵס לַמִּקְדָּשׁ, עַד שֶׁיִּטְבֹּל; וְעִנְיַן טְבִילָה הוּא כְּמוֹ שֶׁנִּפְרֵשׁ בְּמִצְוָתוֹ בְּעֶזְרַת הַשֵּׁם; וְאַף לְאַחַר טְבִילָתוֹ אָסוּר לֶאֱכֹל אֲפִלּוּ תְּרוּמָה עַד הֶעֱרֶב הַשֶּׁמֶשׁ, וְאַחַר־כָּךְ טָהוֹר וְאוֹכֵל תְּרוּמָה; וְיֶתֶר פְּרָטֶיהָ, מְבֹאָרִים בְּסֵדֶר טָהֳרוֹת, וּבְרֹב בְּמַסֶּכֶת כֵּלִים וְטָהֳרוֹת.

וְנוֹהֶגֶת בְּכָל מָקוֹם וּבְכָל זְמַן, בִּזְכָרִים וּנְקֵבוֹת, לְעִנְיָן שֶׁכֹּל שֶׁנִּטְמָא בִשְׁרָצִים נִקְרָא טָמֵא, וְלֹא יַעֲלֶה מִטֻּמְאָה עַד שֶׁיִּטְבֹּל בַּמַּיִם כְּדִינוֹ; וּמִכָּל־מָקוֹם עַכְשָׁיו

12. I.e. each vessel; *ibid.* ii 1, etc.
13. But only solid and liquid food; TB Bava Kamma 2b, etc.
14. Sifra on the verse (*sh'mini, perek* 7, 5).
15. Inferred from Mishnah, Kélim i 2.
16. TB Ḥagigah 11a; Sifra *ibid.*
17. TB Me'ilah 15b.
18. TB Ḥullin 128b.
19. Respectively, TB Me'ilah 17a; Sifra, *sh'mini, perek* 10, 2; TB Ḥullin 122a, 126b (on sinews see MY).
20. Leviticus 22:5–6; TB Yevamoth 75b.

are called "a primary cause of uncleanness"; this is to say that they defile a person and objects by contact; but if the objects are earthenware vessels, they defile it[12] once they enter its inner space. Now, this is the difference in regard to ritual uncleanness between what is called a primary cause and what is called a derivative cause: What is called a primary cause defiles a person and objects, while a derivative cause does not defile a person and objects.[13]

These swarming creatures do not cause defilement until they die: for it is stated, *whoever touches them when they are dead, shall be unclean* (Leviticus 11:31).[14] And it is only these eight creatures (*ibid.* 29–30) that cause defilement; but all other swarming creatures, such as a serpent or scorpion, and so on, do not cause defilement at all.[14] The law of these swarming creatures is that they do not cause uncleanness by being carried without being touched;[11] if someone touches them, he does not make the clothing that is on him at the time of his contact defiled by them.[15] The minimal size of a swarming creature that can defile is as a lentil: for here we find that the Torah generally declared them sources of defilement, and there are some creatures among them which are only as [large as] a lentil.[16] All swarming creatures may be conjoined to reach the size of a lentil: in other words, even if there is a bit of this creature and a bit of that, they are considered together, so that if [together] they are the size of a lentil, they cause uncleanness[17]—that you should not think that it is incurred only when there is the size of a lentil in one alone.

Then there is the law of living flesh which becomes separated from a swarming creature, or one whole limb, or a kidney, the liver, or the tongue;[18] the law about their blood, sinews, claws, skin, and eggs;[19] the law that anyone who is defiled by them is forbidden to eat *t'rumah* [the *kohen*'s hallowed portion of all produce] and meat of offerings, or to enter the Sanctuary, until he undergoes ritual immersion.[20] The process of ritual immersion is as we will explain in its precept (§175), with the Eternal Lord's help. Even after his immersion, he is forbidden to eat even *t'rumah* until the sun goes down in the evening; then he is ritually pure and may eat *t'rumah*.[20] The rest of its details are explained in the Talmud, in the order of *Tohoroth*, mainly in the tractates *Kélim* and *Tohoroth*.

It is in effect in every place, at every time, for both man and woman—in the sense that whoever is defiled by the swarming creatures is called unclean. And a person does not emerge from the defilement until

שֶׁאֵין לָנוּ בַּעֲווֹנוֹתֵינוּ לֹא מִקְדָּשׁ וְלֹא טָהֳרוֹת, אֵין לָנוּ לִמְנוֹתָהּ בְּחֶשְׁבּוֹן מִצְווֹת הַנּוֹהֲגוֹת.

וּמִי שֶׁמִּטַּמֵּא אֲפִלּוּ לְדַעַת בְּכָל זְמַן, אֵין עָלָיו חֵטְא בָּזֶה, אֶלָּא שֶׁאֵינוֹ רַשַּׁאי לִגַּע בְּקָדָשִׁים עַד שֶׁיִּטְהַר; וּמִכָּל־מָקוֹם יֵשׁ לְכָל מֵבִין לְהַרְחִיק הַטֻּמְאָה, כִּי הַנֶּפֶשׁ מִתְעַלָּה בְּטָהֳרָה.

וְכָתַב הָרַמְבָּ״ן זִכְרוֹנוֹ לִבְרָכָה שֶׁאֵין לָנוּ לַחְשֹׁב בְּמִנְיַן הַמִּצְווֹת כָּל דִּינֵי הַטֻּמְאוֹת, וּבְסֵפֶר הַמִּצְווֹת שֶׁלּוֹ כָּתַב טַעַם נָכוֹן לִדְבָרָיו, וְהַדַּעַת בָּזֶה נוֹטָה אַחֲרָיו; וּמֵחֶפְצִי בְקִצּוּר בְּחִבּוּר זֶה לֹא רָצִיתִי לִכְתֹּב כָּל טַעֲנוֹתָיו, הִנֵּה בְּמִצְוַת צ״ו בְּסִפְרוֹ תִּמְצָא הָעִנְיָן בַּאֲרֻכָּה. וּבְסוֹף הָעִנְיָן אָמַר שֶׁהַשֵּׁם מְנָעָנוּ מֵעֲשׂוֹת הַדְּבָרִים בְּטֻמְאָה, וְנִשְׁאָר עָלֵינוּ לְהוֹדִיעֵנוּ אֵי זֶה דָבָר הוּא הַטֻּמְאָה; וְאָמַר שֶׁהִיא נְגִיעַת הַמֵּת וְהַשְּׁרָצִים וְזוּלָתָם, כָּל הַנִּזְכָּרִים בַּתּוֹרָה, וְשֶׁאֵין לָנוּ לִמְנוֹתָן בֶּאֱמֶת מִצְווֹת בִּפְנֵי עַצְמָן; וְזֶהוּ כְּאָמְרֵנוּ שֶׁהַקְרָבַת בַּעַל־מוּם נִמְנַעַת, וְנִשְׁאָר עָלֵינוּ לָדַעַת אֵי זֶה דָבָר הֵם הַמּוּמִין, וּבֶאֱמֶת לֹא נִמְנֶה כָּל מוּם וָמוּם מֵהֶם מִצְוָה.

[מִצְוַת עִנְיַן טֻמְאַת אֳכָלִים]

קס שֶׁנִּצְטַוִּינוּ בִּשְׁמִירַת טֻמְאַת אֳכָלִין וּמַשְׁקִין, וּלְהִתְנַהֵג בָּעִנְיָן עַל־פִּי הַתּוֹרָה, שֶׁהוֹדִיעַתְנוּ אֵיךְ נָדִין בְּכָל עִנְיַן טֻמְאַת אֳכָלִין וּמַשְׁקִין וְהַכֵּלִים הַמְּטַמְּאִין עַל יָדָם — שֶׁנֶּאֱמַר: מִכָּל הָאֹכֶל אֲשֶׁר יֵאָכֵל אֲשֶׁר יָבוֹא עָלָיו מַיִם.

מִשָּׁרְשֵׁי הַטֻּמְאָה וְהַטָּהֳרָה בַּמִּצְוָה הַקּוֹדֶמֶת תִּרְאֶה לַהַג הַרְבֵּה, אֵין צֹרֶךְ לְהַחֲזִירוֹ.

מִדִּינֵי הַמִּצְוָה, מַה שֶּׁאָמְרוּ זִכְרוֹנָם לִבְרָכָה שֶׁזֶּה שֶׁנֶּאֱמַר בַּתּוֹרָה ״מִכָּל הָאֹכֶל אֲשֶׁר יֵאָכֵל״, פֵּרוּשׁוֹ שֶׁיֵּאָכֵל לָאָדָם, וּלְפִיכָךְ אָמְרוּ זִכְרוֹנָם לִבְרָכָה שֶׁכָּל אֹכֶל

21. Cf. TB 'Avodah Zarah 20b; ritual purity leads to holiness.

22. In his commentary to ShM positive precept §96.

§160 1. Cf. TB 'Eruvin 21b: *and much study* (lahag) *is a weariness of flesh* (Ecclesiastes 12:12)—whoever meditates studiously (*hogeh*) in them [in words of Torah] will taste the savor of flesh (meat).

2. Sifra on the verse above (*sh'mini, perek* 9, 1).

he undergoes ritual immersion in water, as its law is. But in any case, now that for our sins we have neither Sanctuary nor matters of ritual purity, we cannot count it among the precepts that remain in force.

If a person becomes defiled continually, even if it is deliberate, he commits no sin by this; it is only that he is not permitted to touch sacred objects until he becomes ritually pure. Nevertheless, it is for every understanding person to keep defilement well away: for the soul is exalted by purity.[21]

Now, Ramban of blessed memory wrote that we are not to count all the laws of defilement in the reckoning of the precepts. In his *Book of Precepts* he wrote a sound reason for his words,[22] and the mind in this instance is inclined to follow him. But in my desire for brevity in this work, I did not wish to write all his arguments. There, in precept §96 of his volume,[22] you will find the matter at length. At the end of the discussion he stated that the Eternal Lord restricted us from doing certain things in a state of defilement, and it therefore remained for us to be informed which thing is [a cause of] defilement; and this, he said, is the contact of touch with a corpse or swarming creatures, and apart from these, all that are mentioned in the Torah. But in truth we are not to count them as precepts in their own right. This is akin to our saying that the offering of sacrifices by a blemished *kohen* [with a disfigurement] is forbidden, and it then remains for us to know what things constitute blemishes; but in truth we do not count every single blemish as a precept.

[THE PRECEPT OF THE RITUAL UNCLEANNESS OF FOOD]

160 that we were commanded to observe the ritual uncleanness of solid and liquid food, and to behave in the matter according to the Torah, which informed us how to decide every question of defilement of food and drink, and of the vessels through which they became defiled—as it is stated, *All food in it which may be eaten, on which water comes, shall be unclean* (Leviticus 11:34).

About root reasons for ritual uncleanness and purity, in the precept before this you will see "much study."[1] There is no need to repeat it.

Among the laws of the precept, there is what the Sages of blessed memory taught:[2] that the statement in the Torah, *All food in it which may be eaten*, means which may be eaten by a man. Therefore they

שֶׁאֵינוֹ מְיֻחָד לָאָדָם אֵינוֹ מְקַבֵּל טֻמְאָה כְּלָל. וּפֵרְשׁוּ גַּם־כֵּן שֶׁאֵינוֹ נִקְרָא אֹכֶל לְעִנְיַן קַבָּלַת הַטֻּמְאָה עַד שֶׁיֵּעָקֵר מִן הַקַּרְקַע, אֲבָל כָּל זְמַן שֶׁהוּא מְחֻבָּר אֲפִלּוּ בְּשֹׁרֶשׁ קָטָן שֶׁיָּכוֹל לִחְיוֹת, אֵינוֹ נִקְרָא אֹכֶל לְקַבֵּל טֻמְאָה, וַאֲפִלּוּ נָגְעוּ בוֹ כָּל הַטֻּמְאוֹת טָהוֹר הוּא.

וְכֵן אֵין כָּל אֹכֶל שֶׁבָּעוֹלָם נִקְרָא אֹכֶל לְקַבֵּל טֻמְאָה עַד שֶׁיָּבוֹא עָלָיו מַיִם מֵאַחַר שֶׁנֶּעֱקַר מִן הַקַּרְקַע, וּכְמוֹ שֶׁכָּתוּב: אֲשֶׁר יָבוֹא עָלָיו מַיִם, וְגוֹמֵר. וְאַף־עַל־פִּי שֶׁאָמְרוּ שֶׁזֶּה גְּזֵרַת הַכָּתוּב הוּא, יֵשׁ לְסָמְכוֹ קְצָת אֶל הַטַּעַם לְפִי מַה שֶּׁיַּעֲלֶה בִתְחִלַּת הַמַּחֲשָׁבָה, וְלוֹמַר כִּי הָעִנְיָן לְפִי שֶׁהַתּוֹרָה לֹא תַחֲשֹׁב שׁוּם דָּבָר לִהְיוֹת רָאוּי לְדִינָיו שֶׁבּוֹ עַד שְׁעַת גְּמַר מְלַאכְתָּן, כְּמוֹ שֶׁיָּדוּעַ בְּדִינֵי הַפֵּרוֹת לְעִנְיַן תְּרוּמָה וּמַעַשְׂרוֹת; וְכֵן הַחַלָּה, שֶׁאֵין עוֹנָתָהּ עַד שֶׁתִּתְגַּלְגֵּל הַקֶּמַח, וְזֶהוּ שֶׁהַמַּפְרִישׁ חַלָּתוֹ קֶמַח אֵינָהּ חַלָּה, וְגֶזֶל הִיא בְּיַד כֹּהֵן.

וְעַל־כֵּן גַּם בְּעִנְיַן הַטֻּמְאָה נֹאמַר שֶׁאֵין דִּינֵי טֻמְאַת הַפֵּרוֹת וְטָהֳרָתָן עַד גְּמַר מְלַאכְתָּן, וּלְפִי שֶׁדֶּרֶךְ בְּנֵי־אָדָם בִּקְצָת פֵּרוֹת וִירָקוֹת לַהֲדִיחָן מֵעֲפָרָן טֶרֶם שֶׁיֹּאכְלוּ אוֹתָם, הָיָה הָעִנְיָן לֵאמֹר עַל כֻּלָּן דֶּרֶךְ כְּלָל שֶׁלֹּא יִהְיוּ נִקְרָאִין אֹכֶל עַד שֶׁיֻּכְשְׁרוּ בַּמָּיִם. וּמִן הַטַּעַם הַזֶּה בְּעַצְמוֹ אָמְרוּ שֶׁהֶכְשֵׁרָן הוּא כְּשֶׁהוּדְחוּ בִּרְצוֹן הַבְּעָלִים, כְּלוֹמַר שֶׁהַבְּעָלִים חָשְׁבוּ מַשְׁקֵה הַמַּיִם שֶׁהוּדְחוּ בָהֶן כְּדֶרֶךְ בְּנֵי־אָדָם שֶׁיָּדִיחוּ יַרְקוֹתֵיהֶם בְּמַשְׁקֶה; וְזֶהוּ פֵּרוּשׁ רָצוֹן וְאֹנֶס הַנִּזְכָּר בַּגְּמָרָא בְּעִנְיַן זֶה, לְפִי הַפֵּרוּשִׁים הַטּוֹבִים. וְאִם לֹא יַחְשְׁבוּהוּ לְמַשְׁקֶה, אַף־עַל־פִּי שֶׁהֵן בְּעַצְמָן נְתָנוּהוּ עַל הַפֵּרוֹת אֵין זֶה לְרָצוֹן.

וּלְפִיכָךְ אָמְרוּ זִכְרוֹנָם לִבְרָכָה שֶׁהַטּוֹמֵן פֵּרוֹתָיו בַּמַּיִם מִפְּנֵי הַגַּנָּבִים לֹא הֻכְשְׁרוּ, לְפִי שֶׁאֵין הַמַּיִם חֲשׁוּבִים לַבְּעָלִים לְמַשְׁקֶה, שֶׁלֹּא נְתָנוּם בָּהֶן מֵחֲמַת

3. Mishnah, Tohoroth viii 6.

4. Mishnah, 'Uktzin iii 8.

5. *Ibid.* 1, etc. ("water" is to be understood here in the figurative sense of a liquid: for seven liquids can enable food to become defiled).

6. I.e. with no discernible reason for it.

7. I.e. until they are readied to be used as food.

8. There is no obligation to separate and give them until they have become ready to serve as food; Mishnah, Ma'as'roth i 2.

9. And the *kohen* must give it back; Mishnah, Ḥallah ii 5.

10. Mishnah, Machshirin i 1, etc.

11. I.e. if the wetting was done by the owner's will or consent, or against his will and without his consent.

12. See *Kessef Mishneh* to MT *hilchoth tum'ath 'ochlin* xii 1.

13. Mishnah, Machshirin i 6.

(of blessed memory) ruled[3] that any food which is not particularly intended for man is not subject to defilement at all. They explained too[4] that food is not called so in regard to susceptibility to defilement until it is uprooted from the earth; but as long as it is attached, if only by a small root by which it can live, it is not called food to be able to undergo defilement. Even if all [kinds of] uncleannesses touched it, it is ritually pure.

So too, no food in the world is called food to be able to accept defilement until water falls on it after it has been uprooted from the earth—as it is written, *on which water comes*, etc.[5] Now, even though the Sages said it is a decree of Scripture,[6] it can be somewhat related to a reason, according to what comes to mind at first thought: It can be said that the point is that the Torah would consider nothing ready for the laws that apply to it until the time that its work is completed[7]—as it is known about the laws of produce in regard to *t'rumah* and *ma'asér* (tithes).[8]

So too *ḥallah* [the first of the dough-cake], whose time to be given is not until the flour is kneaded well into a round dough; and this is why, if someone separates his *ḥallah* as flour, it is not *ḥallah*, but [as] the product of robbery in the hands of the *kohen*.[9]

Therefore, regarding defilement likewise, we would say that no laws of the defilement of produce and their purification apply until the completion of their work.[7] And since it is the practice of people with some fruits and vegetables to wash them of their earth before they eat them, it was appropriate to say about all, generally, that they should not be called food until they have been made ready with water. For this very reason it was taught[10] that their preparation [to become subject to defilement] occurs when they are wet by the will or consent of the owner: in other words, if the owner regarded as a [preparatory] liquid the water by which they were rinsed, in keeping with the practice of people, who rinse their vegetables with water. This is the sense of the terms "volition" and "compulsion" mentioned in the Talmud in regard to this,[11] according to the good commentaries.[12] And if he [the owner] does not regard it as a [preparatory] liquid, then even if he himself poured it on the produce, it is not [made defilable] through his will and consent.

Therefore, too, the Sages of blessed memory said[13] that if someone hides produce in water on account of thieves, it does not become readied [to receive defilement]: for the water is not regarded by the owner as liquid [for washing], since he did not put it [the produce] in it

מַשְׁקֶה אֶלָּא לְהַטְמִינָן, כְּמוֹ שֶׁהָיוּ מַטְמִינִים אוֹתָן גַּם־כֵּן בְּתוֹךְ גִּזֵּי צֶמֶר אוֹ בְדָבָר אַחֵר.

וּמֵעִנְיָן זֶה מַה שֶּׁאָמְרוּ זִכְרוֹנָם לִבְרָכָה שֶׁהַכּוֹפֶה קְעָרָה עַל הַכֹּתֶל בְּיוֹם מָטָר, אִם בִּשְׁבִיל שֶׁתּוּדַח הַקְּעָרָה הוּא עוֹשֶׂה, מֵי הַמָּטָר רְאוּיִין לְהַכְשִׁיר, מִפְּנֵי שֶׁעַכְשָׁיו נָדִין מַיִם אֵלּוּ לְמַשְׁקֶה לְדַעַת הַבְּעָלִים, שֶׁדַּרְכּוֹ שֶׁל עוֹלָם לְהָדִיחַ הַדְּבָרִים בְּמַה שֶּׁהוּא מַשְׁקֶה; וְאִם הִנִּיחָהּ שָׁם כְּדֵי שֶׁלֹּא יִלְקֶה הַכֹּתֶל אֵינָם מַכְשִׁירִין.

וְדִינֵי יְדוֹת הָאֳכָלִין רַבִּים; וְיֶתֶר פְּרָטֶיהָ, מְבֹאָרִים בְּמַסֶּכֶת טָהֳרוֹת וְעוּקְצִין וּמַכְשִׁירִין. וְנוֹהֶגֶת בְּכָל מָקוֹם וּבְכָל זְמַן, בִּזְכָרִים וּנְקֵבוֹת, שֶׁנָּדִין בְּעִנְיָן זֶה טֻמְאַת הָאֳכָלִין וְהֶכְשֵׁרָן. וּמִכָּל־מָקוֹם עַכְשָׁיו בְּחוּצָה לָאָרֶץ, שֶׁאֵין לָנוּ בַּעֲווֹנוֹתֵינוּ מִקְדָּשׁ וְקָדָשִׁים, דִּינֵי הַטֻּמְאוֹת בְּטֵלִים אֶצְלֵנוּ. וּמִכָּל־מָקוֹם אִם רָצָה לִנְהֹג בָּהֶם בְּעַצְמוֹ מִנְהַג קְדוֹשִׁים כְּאִלּוּ הָיָה בָאָרֶץ וּלְהִזָּהֵר בָּאֳכָלִין לְאָכְלָן בְּטָהֳרָה, כָּזֶה רָאוּי לָדוּן בָּהֶם.

וּכְבָר כָּתַבְתִּי בַּמִּצְוָה הַקּוֹדֶמֶת דַּעַת הָרַמְבָּ״ן זִכְרוֹנוֹ לִבְרָכָה בְּדִינֵי הַטֻּמְאוֹת, וְהוּא מִתְיַשֵּׁב בְּלֵב שׁוֹמְעוֹ; וְאֵינִי צָרִיךְ לְהַחֲזִירוֹ בְּכָל אַחַת וְאַחַת.

[מִצְוַת עִנְיַן טֻמְאַת נְבֵלָה]

קסא לִהְיוֹת הַנְּבֵלָה טְמֵאָה וּמְטַמְּאָה, שֶׁנֶּאֱמַר: וְכִי יָמוּת מִן הַבְּהֵמָה אֲשֶׁר הִיא לָכֶם לְאָכְלָה וְגוֹמֵר.

כָּתַב הָרַמְבָּ״ם זִכְרוֹנוֹ לִבְרָכָה בַּמִּצְוָה הַזֹּאת, וְזֶה לְשׁוֹנוֹ: וַאֲנִי אַזְכִּיר לְךָ הִנֵּה עַתָּה הַקְדָּמָה, יָאוּת לְךָ שֶׁתִּזְכְּרֶהָ בְּכָל מַה שֶּׁנִּזְכֹּר מִמִּינֵי הַטֻּמְאוֹת, וְהִיא שֶׁזֶּה שֶׁאָנוּ מוֹנִין כָּל מִין וָמִין מֵהַטֻּמְאוֹת מִצְוַת עֲשֵׂה, אֵין עִנְיָנוֹ שֶׁנִּתְחַיֵּב לְהִטַּמֵּא בְטֻמְאָה זוֹ, וְלֹא כְּמוֹ־כֵן אָנוּ נִמְנָעִין מֵהִטָּמֵא בָהּ וְתִהְיֶה מִצְוַת לֹא־תַעֲשֶׂה.

14. *Ibid.* iv 3.
15. I.e. the soft twigs from which fruit hangs on the tree.

§161 1. ShM positive precept §96.

because it was a liquid, but only to hide it—as he might have hidden it in shearings of wool or in something else.

In keeping with this, there is what the Sages of blessed memory said,[14] that if someone turns over a basin [face upward] on a wall in a day of rain, if he does this in order that the basin should be rinsed, then the rainwater is suitable to prepare [produce for possible defilement]—because we now consider this water for washing by the knowledge [and intent] of the owner, as it is the way of the world to rinse things by that which is a liquid. But if he put it there so that the wall should not be damaged, it cannot prepare [food for defilement].

The manifold laws about the "handles" of food,[15] and the rest of its details, are explained in the tractates *Tohoroth*, *'Uktzin* and *Machshirin*. It is in effect in every place and every time, for both man and woman—that we should decide by law about this matter of the ritual uncleanness of foods and their preparation [to be able to receive defilement]. Nevertheless, now, outside the land [of Israel], when for our sins we have no Sanctuary or holinesses, the laws of ritual uncleanness are null and void for us. However, if someone wishes to conduct himself according to them, in a practice of holy people, as though he were in the land [of Israel], and to be careful about food, to eat it in ritual purity, it would be proper to adjudicate in this way about them [the laws].

I have already written, in the preceding precept, the view of Ramban of blessed memory about the laws of ritual uncleanness, which is quite acceptable to the heart of one who hears it. I need not repeat this for each and every one.

[THE PRECEPT OF THE RITUAL UNCLEANNESS OF ANIMAL CARCASSES]

161 that a *n'vélah* [an animal that died without ritual slaying] is ritually unclean and causes defilement: for it is stated, *And if any animal of which you may eat dies*, etc. (Leviticus 11:39).

Rambam of blessed memory wrote about this precept, in these words:[1] Now, here I will relate to you a preface suitable for you, which you should remember in regard to everything we mention about the kinds of defilement. This is that when we list every single kind of defilement as a positive precept, its sense is not that we should be obligated to become defiled by that ritual defilement; and equally, we need not avoid becoming defiled by it, so that it should constitute a negative precept. The truth is that when the Torah states that whoever

וְאוּלָם הֱיוֹת הַתּוֹרָה אוֹמֶרֶת שֶׁמִּי שֶׁקָּרֵב בְּזֶה הַמִּין נִטְמָא אוֹ זֶה הַדָּבָר יִטַּמֵּא עַל עִנְיָן כָּךְ לְמִי שֶׁקָּרֵב אֵלָיו, הוּא מִצְוַת עֲשֵׂה, כְּלוֹמַר זֶה הַדִּין הַמְצֻוֶּה בּוֹ הוּא מִצְוָה, וְהוּא אָמְרֵנוּ שֶׁמִּי שֶׁקָּרֵב בְּכָךְ עַל עִנְיָן כָּךְ, נִטְמָא, וּמִי שֶׁהָיָה עַל עִנְיָן כָּךְ, לֹא יִטָּמֵא. וּבְהִטָּמֵא בְעַצְמוֹ הָרְשׁוּת בְּיַד כָּל אָדָם, כִּי אִם רָצָה יִטָּמֵא וְאִם רָצָה לֹא יִטָּמֵא. וּלְשׁוֹן סִפְרָא: "וּבְנִבְלָתָם לֹא תִגָּעוּ", יָכוֹל אִם נָגַע אָדָם בְּנִבְלָתָם יִלְקֶה אַרְבָּעִים, תַּלְמוּד לוֹמַר "וּלְאֵלֶּה תִּטַּמָּאוּ"; יָכוֹל אִם רָאָה אָדָם נְבֵלָה יֵלֵךְ וְיִטָּמֵא לָהּ, תַּלְמוּד לוֹמַר "וּבְנִבְלָתָם לֹא תִגָּעוּ", הָא כֵּיצַד, הֱוֵי אוֹמֵר, רְשׁוּת. וְהַמִּצְוָה הוּא מַה שֶּׁנֶּאֱמַר לָנוּ בְּאֵלֶּה הַדִּינִין, שֶׁמִּי שֶׁקָּרֵב לָזֶה נִטְמָא וְיִהְיֶה טָמֵא וְיִתְחַיֵּב מַה שֶּׁנִּתְחַיְּבוּ הַטְּמֵאִים, לָצֵאת חוּץ לְמַחֲנֵה שְׁכִינָה וְשֶׁלֹּא יֹאכַל קֹדֶשׁ וְלֹא יִקְרַב אֵלָיו, וְזוּלַת זֶה. וְזֹאת הִיא הַמִּצְוָה, כְּלוֹמַר הֱיוֹתוֹ טָמֵא בְּזֶה הַמִּין כְּשֶׁקָּרֵב אֵלָיו אוֹ כְּשֶׁהָיָה אֶצְלוֹ עַל עִנְיָן כָּךְ. וּזְכֹר זֶה הָעִנְיָן בְּכָל מִין וָמִין מִמִּינֵי הַטֻּמְאָה. עַד כָּאן לְשׁוֹנוֹ.

וְעִם כָּל זֶה לֹא יִתְיַשֵּׁב יָפֶה עִם הַלֵּב שֶׁנַּחֲשֹׁב עִנְיָן זֶה מִצְוָה, וְאָכֵן לֹא נָסוּר מִדֶּרֶךְ רַבֵּנוּ בְּחֶשְׁבּוֹנֵנוּ יָמִין וּשְׂמֹאל, כַּאֲשֶׁר יָעַדְנוּ בַּתְּחִלָּה.

הַשֹּׁרֶשׁ כָּתוּב לְמַעְלָה.

מִדִּינֵי הַמִּצְוָה, מַה שֶּׁאָמְרוּ זִכְרוֹנָם לִבְרָכָה שֶׁהַנְּבֵלָה אָב מֵאֲבוֹת הַטֻּמְאָה, וּכְזַיִת מִבְּשָׂרָהּ מְטַמֵּא אָדָם וְכֵלִים בְּמַגָּע וּכְלִי חֶרֶס בָּאֲוִיר, וּמְטַמֵּא אֶת הָאָדָם בְּמַשָּׂא לְטַמֵּא בְגָדִים. וְאֶחָד בְּהֵמָה וְחַיָּה הַמֻּתָּרוֹת אוֹ הָאֲסוּרוֹת שֶׁמֵּתוּ, כֻּלָּן בְּשָׂרָם מְטַמֵּא בִכְזַיִת, וּשְׁחִיטַת בְּהֵמָה וְחַיָּה טְהוֹרָה מְטַהֶרֶת אוֹתָן וְאֵינָן מְטַמְּאוֹת אַחַר־כֵּן, וַאֲפִלּוּ שְׁחִיטַת חֻלִּין בָּעֲזָרָה וְקָדָשִׁים בַּחוּץ מְטַהֶרֶת אוֹתָן מִידֵי נְבֵלָה.

2. Explained in § 362.
3. See § 159 for our author's reason.
4. Mishnah, Kélim i 2.
5. So Sifra, *sh'mini, parashah* 10, 7.
6. TB Ḥullin 70b.

comes in contact with this particular sort becomes defiled, or that thing defiles in such a manner whatever comes in contact with it, it is a positive precept. In other words, this law which is thereby ordained, is a precept—which, as we said, is that whoever comes in contact with this in such a manner, becomes defiled, and whoever does so in such a manner is not defiled. As for the very matter of becoming defiled, every man has the free right [to choose] if he wishes to become ritually unclean or not. In the language of the Midrash *Sifra:* "and their carcasses you shall not touch" (Leviticus 11:8)—I might think that if a man touched their carcasses, he should receive forty lashes of the whip?—Scripture states, *And by these you shall become unclean* (*ibid.* 24) [and nothing more]. Then I might think that if a man saw a carcass, he should go and be defiled by it?—Scripture states, *and their carcasses you shall not touch.* Then how [is this to be understood]?—you must say it is a free choice. Thus the precept is what we are told about these laws: that whoever comes close to this becomes defiled and is ritually unclean, and he becomes obligated in the duties of the ritually unclean—to go out of the camp of the *shechinah,*[2] that he should not eat sacred food, nor go close to it, and so forth. This, then, is the precept—in other words, that he should be defiled by this sort when he comes in contact with it, or when it is with him in such a manner. Remember this point about every single one of the various kinds of ritual uncleanness. (Thus far his [Rambam's] words.)

Yet with all that, it cannot be accepted well by the heart that we should consider this matter a precept.[3] Nevertheless, we shall not swerve from the way of our master [Rambam] in our reckoning, neither right nor left, as we determined at the beginning.

The root purpose was written above (§159).

Among the laws of the precept, there is what our Sages of blessed memory said:[4] that a *n'vélah* [an animal that died without having been ritually slain] is one of the primary causes of defilement; an olive's amount of its flesh[5] defiles a person and vessels by touch, and an earthenware vessel by being in its space within;[4] it defiles a man upon being carried, to make his clothing ritually unclean.[4] The law is the same for permissible or forbidden domestic or wild animals that died: the flesh of all, in the amount of an olive, causes defilement.[6] However, the ritual slaying of a clean [kosher] domestic or wild animal renders it ritually pure, and they cannot cause defilement afterward. Even the ritual slaying of non-holy animals in the Temple court, or of consecrated

וְכָל שֶׁמֵּתָה מֵאֵלֶיהָ אוֹ שֶׁאֵרַע פְּסוּל בִּשְׁחִיטָתָהּ הֲרֵי הִיא נְבֵלָה, וּכְמוֹ שֶׁאָמְרוּ זִכְרוֹנָם לִבְרָכָה בְּחֻלִּין: זֶה הַכְּלָל, כָּל שֶׁנִּפְסְלָה בִשְׁחִיטָתָהּ, נְבֵלָה, וְכָל שֶׁשְּׁחִיטָתָהּ כָּרָאוּי וְדָבָר אַחֵר גּוֹרֵם לָהּ לְהִפָּסֵל, טְרֵפָה. אֲבָל בְּהֵמָה וְחַיָּה טְמֵאָה אֵין הַשְּׁחִיטָה מְטַהַרְתָּן מִידֵי נְבֵלָה, וּלְפִיכָךְ בְּכָל עִנְיָן שֶׁיָּמוּתוּ נְבֵלוֹת הֵן; וּמִכָּל־מָקוֹם אֵין מְטַמְּאוֹת לֹא הֵן וְלֹא הַטְּהוֹרוֹת עַד שֶׁיָּמוּתוּ לְגַמְרֵי וְלֹא בְעוֹד שֶׁמְּפַרְכְּסוֹת.

וְיֶתֶר רִבֵּי פְּרָטֶיהָ, מְבֹאָרִים בְּסֵדֶר טָהֳרוֹת בְּפִזּוּר, וּבְרֹב בְּמַסֶּכֶת כֵּלִים וּבְמַסֶּכֶת טָהֳרוֹת.

[שֶׁלֹּא לֶאֱכֹל שֶׁרֶץ הָאָרֶץ]

קסב שֶׁלֹּא לֶאֱכֹל שֶׁרֶץ הָאָרֶץ, שֶׁנֶּאֱמַר: וְכָל הַשֶּׁרֶץ הַשֹּׁרֵץ עַל הָאָרֶץ שֶׁקֶץ הוּא לֹא יֵאָכֵל.

מִשָּׁרְשֵׁי מִצְוָה זוֹ, עִם כָּל מַה שֶּׁבָּא בְאִסּוּר הַמַּאֲכָלוֹת, כְּבָר כָּתַבְתִּי לְמַעְלָה מַה שֶּׁיָּדַעְתִּי, אֵין צֹרֶךְ לְהַחֲזִירוֹ בְּכָל אֶחָת.

מִדִּינֵי הַמִּצְוָה, כְּגוֹן הַחִלּוּק שֶׁחָלְקוּ זִכְרוֹנָם לִבְרָכָה בִּשְׁמֹנָה שְׁרָצִים הָאֲמוּרִים בַּתּוֹרָה מִשְּׁאָר שְׁרָצִים, שֶׁהֵם נְחָשִׁים וְעַקְרַבִּים, חִפּוּשִׁית וְנָדָל וְכַיּוֹצֵא בָהֵן: שֶׁאָמְרוּ שֶׁשְּׁמֹנָה שְׁרָצִים הָאֲמוּרִים בַּתּוֹרָה שִׁעוּר חִיּוּב אֲכִילָתָן כְּשִׁעוּר טֻמְאָתָן, שֶׁהִיא כַּעֲדָשָׁה, וְשִׁעוּר הָאֲחֵרִים בִּכְזַיִת; וְכָל הַשִּׁעוּרִין, הֲלָכָה לְמֹשֶׁה מִסִּינַי. וְיֶתֶר פְּרָטֶיהָ, מְבֹאָרִין בְּמַסֶּכֶת חֻלִּין.

וְנוֹהֶגֶת בְּכָל מָקוֹם וּבְכָל זְמַן, בִּזְכָרִים וּנְקֵבוֹת. וְעוֹבֵר עָלֶיהָ וְאָכַל כַּזַּיִת מִתּוֹלָעִים שֶׁבָּאָרֶץ, בְּמֵזִיד לוֹקֶה, וְאִם אָכַל מִשְּׁמֹנָה שְׁרָצִים אֲפִלּוּ כַּעֲדָשָׁה, לוֹקֶה; בְּשׁוֹגֵג פָּטוּר.

7. Which are both forbidden.
8. *Ibid.* 72b.
9. The previous paragraph and this are based on MT *hilchoth 'avoth ha-tum'oth* i 1–2.
10. I.e. a fatal illness or injury, suffered before the completion of the ritual slaying.
11. Mishnah, Oholoth i 6.

§162 1. See §157, note 4.
2. TB Me'ilah 16b.
3. TB 'Eruvin 4a, etc. (The paragraph is based on MT *hilchoth ma'achaloth 'asuroth* ii 6–7).

animals outside it,[7] renders them ritually clean, free from the state of *n'vélah.*[8]

Whatever died of itself, or if something disqualifying happened during its ritual slaying, it is *n'vélah.*[9] As the Sages of blessed memory said in the tractate *Ḥullin* (32a): this is the rule: whatever became disqualified [forbidden to eat] in its ritual slaying, is *n'vélah;* whatever was ritually slain properly, but something else caused it to become disqualified,[10] is *t'réfah;* but as for an unclean [non-kosher kind of] domestic or wild animal, ritual slaying will not purify them from the state of *n'vélah.*[6] Therefore, no matter how they die, they are *n'vélah.* However, neither they nor the clean [kosher] kinds can cause defilement until they die completely, and not while they are yet thrashing about in their death throes.[11]

The rest of its many details are explained in the Mishnah order of *Tohoroth*, scattered about, but mainly in the tractates *Kélim* and *Tohoroth.*

[THE PROHIBITION AGAINST EATING CREATURES THAT SWARM ON THE EARTH]

162 not to eat any swarming creature of the earth: for it is stated, *And every swarming thing that swarms upon the earth is a detestable thing; it shall not be eaten* (Leviticus 11:41).

What lies at the root of this precept, along with all that is involved in the ban on certain foods, I have already written above (§159), as much as I know. There is no need to repeat it in each case.

Among the laws of the precept there is, for instance, the distinction that the Sages of blessed memory made between the eight swarming creatures named in the Torah (§159) and other swarming creatures, i.e. serpents, scorpions, the *ḥipushith* (beetle),[1] the centipede, and so forth; for they said[2] that for the eight swarming creatures mentioned in the Torah, the minimal amount for punishment over eating them is as the minimal amount for them to cause defilement—which is as a lentil; but the minimal amount for the others is as an olive. All the measures are *halachah* (law) given to Moses [orally] at Sinai.[3]

The rest of its details are explained in the tractate *Ḥullin.* It is in force in every time and every place, for both man and woman. If a person violated it and ate an olive's amount of worms of the earth, deliberately, he should be given whiplashes; and if he ate of the eight swarming creatures even the amount of a lentil, he is [likewise] to be given lashes. But if it was inadvertent, he is free of penalty.

[שֶׁלֹּא לֶאֱכֹל מִינֵי שְׁרָצִים דַּקִּים הַנּוֹלָדִים בִּזְרָעִים וּבְפֵרוֹת]

קסג שֶׁלֹּא לֶאֱכֹל מִינֵי שְׁרָצִים דַּקִּים הַנּוֹלָדִין בִּזְרָעִים וּבְפֵרוֹת, מֵעֵת שֶׁיֵּצְאוּ וְיִשְׁרְצוּ בָּאָרֶץ; וְהוּא הַדִּין כָּל זְמַן שֶׁנַּעֲשׂוּ בַּפְּרִי בְּעוֹדוֹ מְחֻבָּר לַקַּרְקַע, אַף־עַל־פִּי שֶׁלֹּא יָצְאוּ וְשָׁרְצוּ עַל הָאָרֶץ, שֶׁשּׁוֹרֵץ עַל הָאָרֶץ נִקְרָא, מִכֵּיוָן שֶׁנַּעֲשָׂה בַּפְּרִי בְּעוֹדוֹ מְחֻבָּר — שֶׁנֶּאֱמַר: לְכָל הַשֶּׁרֶץ הַשֹּׁרֵץ עַל הָאָרֶץ לֹא תֹאכְלוּם.

וְאִם יָצְאוּ עַל הָאָרֶץ, אַף־עַל־פִּי שֶׁחָזְרוּ אַחַר־כָּךְ לְתוֹךְ הַפְּרִי, "שׁוֹרֵץ עַל הָאָרֶץ" נִקְרָא גַּם־כֵּן, מִכֵּיוָן שֶׁיָּצָא. וְכֵן הוּא בְּסִפְרָא: "(ולא תטמאו) [אַל תְּשַׁקְּצוּ] אֶת נַפְשֹׁתֵיכֶם בְּכָל הַשֶּׁרֶץ הַשֹּׁרֵץ", לְהָבִיא אֶת שֶׁפֵּרְשׁוּ עַל הָאָרֶץ וְחָזְרוּ; כְּלוֹמַר אַף־עַל־פִּי שֶׁהֵם עַכְשָׁיו בַּחוֹר שֶׁלָּהֶם, מִכֵּיוָן שֶׁיָּצְאוּ עַל הָאָרֶץ נֶאֶסְרוּ, וְשֶׁרֶץ הָאָרֶץ נִקְרָאִין.

בָּזֶה הַפֵּרוּשׁ שֶׁאֲנִי כּוֹתֵב בְּכָאן כִּי חִיּוּב מִינֵי הַשְּׁרָצִים דַּקִּים הוּא מֵעֵת שֶׁיָּצְאוּ בָּאָרֶץ וְלֹא קֹדֶם לָכֵן, אֲנִי מַעֲלִים עַיִן בַּמֶּה שֶׁכָּתַב בּוֹ הָרַמְבָּ"ם זִכְרוֹנוֹ לִבְרָכָה, אַף־עַל־פִּי שֶׁיָּעַדְתִּי לֶאֱחֹז דַּרְכּוֹ, כִּי הוּא כָּתַב בְּכָאן בְּסֵפֶר הַמִּצְווֹת שֶׁלּוֹ שֶׁהַלָּאו הַזֶּה הוּא מִכֵּיוָן שֶׁיָּצְאוּ לַאֲוִיר הָעוֹלָם אוֹ הָלְכוּ עַל שֶׁטַח הַפְּרִי; וְיֵשׁ לִתְמֹהַּ עָלָיו הַרְבֵּה בְּכָךְ, כִּי בְּפֵרוּשׁ מָצָאנוּ בְּחֻלִּין שֶׁיִּשָּׁאֵר שָׁם עִנְיָן זֶה בְּתֵיקוּ, כְּמוֹ שֶׁבָּא לְשָׁם: בָּעֵי רַב יוֹסֵף: פֵּרְשָׁה לַאֲוִיר הָעוֹלָם מַהוּ, עַל־גַּבֵּי תְמָרָה מַהוּ; וְגַם הָרַב בְּעַצְמוֹ כָּתַב בְּחִבּוּרוֹ הַגָּדוֹל שֶׁעִנְיָן זֶה הוּא סָפֵק וְאֵין לוֹקִין עָלָיו. וְעַל־כֵּן הִנַּחְתִּי פֵּרוּשׁוֹ בְּכָאן, וּכְתַבְתִּיו עַל דֶּרֶךְ הָאֱמֶת. וְגַם־כֵּן מָצָאתִי אַחַר־כֵּן שֶׁהָרַמְבָּ"ן זִכְרוֹנוֹ לִבְרָכָה יִתְמַהּ עָלָיו הַרְבֵּה בִּשְׁגָגָה זוֹ.

מִשָּׁרְשֵׁי הַמִּצְוָה כָּתוּב לְמַעְלָה.

דִּינֶיהָ, כְּגוֹן מַה שֶּׁאָמְרוּ זִכְרוֹנָם לִבְרָכָה: "הַשּׁוֹרֵץ עַל הָאָרֶץ", לְהוֹצִיא זִיזִין שֶׁבַּעֲדָשִׁים וְתוֹלָעִים (שבאוכלוסים) [שֶׁבִּכְלוּסִים], וְהוּא מִין קִטְנִית, וְתוֹלָעִים שֶׁבִּתְמָרִים וּגְרוֹגָרוֹת; וְהוּא הַדִּין לְכָל הַתּוֹלָעִים הַנַּעֲשִׂים בַּפֵּרוֹת אַחַר שֶׁנֶּעֶקְרוּ

§163 1. So TB Ḥullin 67a, and Sifra cited below.

2. *Ibid.* 67b (MT *hilchoth ma'achaloth 'asuroth* ii 15). However, those that are formed within detached (picked) fruit do not become forbidden unless and until they leave and swarm on the earth.

3. In our editions of Sifra, the verse cited is Leviticus 11:43, *You shall not make your souls abhorrent with any swarming thing that swarms* (*sh'mini, perek* 12, 2). The verse in our text is probably a scribal error. (In the old manuscripts, Scriptural verses often have slight inaccuracies, through confusion with other verses.) *N'tziv* suggests, however, that another version of the passage in Sifra may have existed.

4. ShM negative precepts §§178, 179.

5. And were eaten before they touched the ground (literally, "into the air of the world").

[THE PROHIBITION AGAINST EATING MINUTE INSECTS ENGENDERED IN GRAINS AND FRUITS]

163 not to eat any species of tiny swarming creatures that are engendered in plants and fruit, from the time they emerge and swarm on the earth.[1] The same law holds for all the time that they are formed in the fruit while it is yet attached to the ground, even though they have not emerged to swarm on the earth, as they are called "that swarm upon the earth" once they are formed in the fruit while it is attached.[2] For it is stated, *even all the swarming things that swarm upon the earth, you shall not eat* (Leviticus 11:42).

If they emerged onto the earth, then even if they returned afterward into the fruit, they are also called "swarming upon the earth," since they came out. And so is it [taught] in the Midrash *Sifra:* "and you shall not defile your souls with any swarming thing that moves" (Leviticus 11:44)—this is to include those which emerged onto the earth and returned.[3] In other words, even if they are now in their hole, since they came out onto the ground, they became forbidden, and are called swarming things of the earth.

In this explanation that I write here, that guilt for eating tiny species of swarming creatures is incurred from the time they emerge onto the earth and not before that, I am ignoring what Rambam of blessed memory wrote about it, even though I determined to hold to his approach. For he wrote here, in his *Book of Precepts*,[4] that the negative precept applies once they have issued forth into the air[5] or gone onto the fruit's surface. But in this he is greatly to be wondered at, for we find distinctly in the tractate *Ḥullin* (67b) that this matter remains an unresolved question—as it is expressed there: R. Joseph asked: If it came out into the air,[5] what is the law? or if onto the outside of the date, what is the law? Even the master [Rambam] himself wrote in his great work[6] that this is a matter of doubt, and a whipping is not given over it. Therefore I have left aside his explanation here, and written it in the way of the truth. Moreover, I found afterward that Ramban of blessed memory[7] wonders at him greatly in regard to this inadvertent error.

Some part of the root reasons for the precept has been written above (§159).

Its laws are, for example, what the Sages of blessed memory said:[8] "that swarm upon the earth"—this would exclude mites in lentils, worms in *kalusin*, which is a kind of bean, and worms in dates and dried figs. The law is the same for all worms that are formed inside fruit after

וְלֹא פֵּרְשׁוּ מִתּוֹכָן, שֶׁאֵינָן בִּלָאו זֶה דְשׁוֹרֵץ עַל הָאָרֶץ, וְהָיוּ מֻתָּרִין מִן הַדִּין, אֶלָּא שֶׁיֵּשׁ בְּאוֹכֵל אוֹתָן שִׁקּוּץ לַנֶּפֶשׁ קְצָת.

וְאִם יֵשׁ בַּדָּבָר סָפֵק אִם נַעֲשׂוּ הַתּוֹלָעִים בַּפֵּרוֹת קֹדֶם שֶׁנֶּעֶקְרוּ אוֹ אַחַר־כֵּן, יִבְדֹּק אוֹתָם יָפֶה; וְאִם הֵם דַּקִּים מְאֹד עַד שֶׁאֵינוֹ יָכוֹל לִבְדֹּק, יַשְׁהֵא אוֹתָן י״ב חֹדֶשׁ, וְאַחַר־כָּךְ מֻתָּרִין לֶאֱכֹל לְכַתְּחִלָּה בְּלֹא בְדִיקָה, מֵהַכְּלָל שֶׁיָּדוּעַ לְרַבּוֹתֵינוּ זִכְרוֹנָם לִבְרָכָה שֶׁכָּל אוֹתָן תּוֹלְעֵי הַפֵּרוֹת אֵין מִתְקַיְּמִין י״ב חֹדֶשׁ; פֵּרוּשׁ אֵינוֹ מִתְקַיֵּם, כְּלוֹמַר דְּמֵכֵיוָן שֶׁעָבְרוּ עָלָיו י״ב חֹדֶשׁ הֲרֵי הוּא כְּעָפָר גָּמוּר. וּמִפְּנֵי־כֵן אָמְרוּ זִכְרוֹנָם לִבְרָכָה: הַנֵּי תַּמְרֵי דְכַדָּא, בָּתַר תְּרֵי עֲשַׂר יַרְחֵי שַׁתָּא שָׁרְיָין.

וְאִם פֵּרְשׁוּ תוֹלְעֵי הַפֵּרוֹת לָאֲוִיר וְלֹא נָגְעוּ בָאָרֶץ, כְּגוֹן שֶׁיָּצְאוּ מִן הַפְּרִי וְנָפְלוּ לְתוֹךְ פִּיו שֶׁל אוֹכֵל, וְכֵן אִם פֵּרְשׁוּ וְרָחֲשׁוּ עַל גַּב הַפְּרִי, אִם נָדִין גַּב הַפְּרִי כְּמוֹ הָאָרֶץ, וְכֵן אִם פֵּרְשָׁה הַתּוֹלַעַת מִן הַפְּרִי וְנָפְלָה לָאָרֶץ אַחַר שֶׁמֵּתָה, כָּל זֶה אָסוּר מִסָּפֵק אִם נָדִין וְנֹאמַר שֶׁיִּהְיֶה כְּשׁוֹרֵץ עַל הָאָרֶץ אוֹ לֹא.

וְכֵן מַה שֶּׁאָמְרוּ זִכְרוֹנָם לִבְרָכָה שֶׁתּוֹלָעִים הַנִּמְצָאִים בִּמְעֵי הַדָּגִים אֲסוּרִים מִשּׁוּם שֶׁרֶץ, כִּי מִבַּחוּץ הֵם בָּאִים, אֲבָל הַנִּמְצָאִים בָּהֶן בֵּין עוֹר לְבָשָׂר אוֹ בְתוֹךְ הַבָּשָׂר מֻתָּרִין; וְהַנִּמְצָאִין בִּמְעֵי בְהֵמָה אֲסוּרִין, שֶׁמִּבַּחוּץ הֵן בָּאִין; וְאַף הַנִּמְצָאִים בְּמֹחַ הַבְּהֵמָה וּבְתוֹךְ בְּשָׂרָהּ אֲסוּרִין, לְפִי שֶׁאֵין שׁוּם דָּבָר בַּבְּהֵמָה שֶׁיְּהֵא מֻתָּר בְּלֹא שְׁחִיטָה, וְהֵן אֵינָן בְּנֵי שְׁחִיטָה; וְעוֹד שֶׁהַתּוֹרָה רִבְּתָה אוֹתָן לְאִסּוּר, וּכְמוֹ שֶׁאָמְרוּ זִכְרוֹנָם לִבְרָכָה: "וְאֶת נִבְלָתָם תְּשַׁקֵּצוּ", לְרַבּוֹת דִּרְנִין שֶׁבַּבְּהֵמָה.

וְאִם תֹּאמַר: שְׁלִיל אֵיךְ הוּא מֻתָּר בְּלֹא שְׁחִיטָה — מִפְּנֵי שֶׁהַתּוֹרָה הִתִּירָה אוֹתוֹ וְכִדְדָרְשִׁינָן בַּגְּמָרָא מִ"בַּבְּהֵמָה... תֹּאכֵלוּ".

וְכֵן הִתִּירוּ זִכְרוֹנָם לִבְרָכָה בְּמַיִם שֶׁבְּכֵלִים שֶׁהִתְלִיעוּ, אוֹ אֲפִלּוּ בְּבוֹרוֹת שִׁיחִין

6. MT *hilchoth ma'achaloth 'asuroth* ii 16.
7. In his commentary on ShM root principle 9.
8. TB Ḥullin 67b.
9. Inferred from *ibid.*
10. TB Ḥullin 58a.
11. So R. Nissim there.
12. *Ibid.* 58b.
13. See above, the third paragraph.
14. TB Ḥullin 67b.
15. So *tosafoth* s.v. *kukiyani* explains the Talmud's text.
16. I.e. a fully formed unborn animal found alive in the womb just before birth, after the dam (mother animal) was ritually slain.
17. TB Ḥullin 69a.

it has been picked, when they do not leave it: they are not included under this negative precept of "the swarming things that swarm upon the earth." Thus they should be permissible by law, but for one who eats them there is a modicum of abhorrence for the soul.[9]

If there is any doubt in the matter, whether the worms were formed in the fruit before it was picked or afterward, it should be examined well; if they are so minute that it cannot be examined, it should be left for twelve months; after twelve months it may be eaten directly, without examination, by the rule known to our Sages of blessed memory,[10] that all those worms in produce cannot endure twelve months; the sense of "cannot endure" is that it is akin to saying that once twelve months have passed, they are like the soil itself.[11] For this reason our Sages of blessed memory said:[12] These [wormy] dates in the jug—after twelve months of the year they are permitted.

If the worms of fruit emerged into the free air but did not touch the ground—if they left the fruit and fell into the mouth of someone eating; and so likewise if they came out and settled on the outside of the fruit, do we consider the outside of the fruit as the earth?[13] So too, if the worm separated from the fruit and fell to the ground after it was dead[14]—all these are forbidden out of doubt whether we should decide to say that they are as a swarming creature on the ground or not.

Then there is, too, what the Sages of blessed memory said:[14] Worms found in the innards of fish[15] are forbidden under the ban on swarming things, for they come from the outside; but those found in them between the skin and the flesh, or within the flesh, are permitted.[14] Those found in the entrails of an animal are forbidden, since they come from the outside; but even those found in an animal's brain and within its flesh are forbidden: for there is nothing in an animal which can be permitted without ritual slaying, and these are not subject to ritual slaying. Moreover, the Torah particularly added something in order to forbid them: As our Sages of blessed memory said,[14] *v'eth nivlatham t'shakétzu*, "and their carcasses you shall abominate" (Leviticus 11:11)—this is to add *d'ranin*, parasite worms in an animal.

Now, if you should ask, "But how is an embryo[16] permitted without ritual slaying?"—it is because the Torah permitted it, as it is derived in the Talmud[17] from the verse, *among the beasts . . . you may eat* (Leviticus 11:3).

They (of blessed memory) likewise permitted water in vessels that engendered worms, and even pits, ditches and caves [filled with

וּמְעָרוֹת, כְּלוֹמַר כָּל מַיִם מְכֻנָּסִין, וְאָמְרוּ שֶׁאָדָם שׁוֹחֶה וְשׁוֹתֶה מֵהֶן כָּל זְמַן שֶׁלֹּא פֵּרְשׁוּ הַתּוֹלָעִים לְמָקוֹם אַחֵר; וַאֲפִלּוּ פֵּרְשׁוּ לְדָפְנֵי הַכְּלִי אוֹ הַבּוֹר, מִכֵּיוָן שֶׁחָזְרוּ לְתוֹכוֹ שׁוֹתֶה וְאֵינוֹ נִמְנָע, דִּמְקוֹם רְבִיתַיְהוּ הוּא.

וּמִן הַדּוֹמֶה שֶׁאֲפִלּוּ מִשּׁוּם אַל תְּשַׁקְּצוּ אֵין בָּהֶם, וְזֶהוּ אָמְרָם שׁוֹתֶה וְאֵינוֹ נִמְנָע; וְנִרְאֶה שֶׁהַטַּעַם מִפְּנֵי שֶׁמָּצְאוּ לָהֶם הֶתֵּר מְפֹרָשׁ מִן הַכָּתוּב, כְּמוֹ שֶׁדָּרְשׁוּ זִכְרוֹנָם לִבְרָכָה: "בַּיַּמִּים וּבַנְּחָלִים", אֶת שֶׁיֵּשׁ לוֹ אֱכֹל וְשֶׁאֵין לוֹ לֹא תֹאכַל; אֲבָל בְּכֵלִים וְדוֹמֶה לְכֵלִים, בֵּין שֶׁיֵּשׁ לוֹ בֵּין שֶׁאֵין לוֹ מֻתָּר.

וְכֵן מִדִּינֵי הַמִּצְוָה מַה שֶּׁאָמְרוּ זִכְרוֹנָם לִבְרָכָה דְּלָא לִישְׁפֵּי אִינִישׁ שִׁכְרָא בְּצַבְתָּא בְּאוּרְתָּא, מִפְּנֵי חֲשַׁשׁ תּוֹלַעַת, שֶׁיִּשָּׁאֵר בַּצַּבְתָּא וְאַחַר־כָּךְ יִפֹּל לַכּוֹס. וּפֵרוּשׁ צַבְתָּא הוּא תֶּבֶן שֶׁעַל פִּי הַכְּלִי; וּמִכֵּיוָן שֶׁשָּׁרַץ בְּצַבְתָּא דִּינוֹ כְּשׁוֹרֵץ עַל הָאָרֶץ.

וְדִינֵי בְרִיָּה, שֶׁאָמְרוּ זִכְרוֹנָם לִבְרָכָה שֶׁאֵינָהּ בְּטֵלָה לְעוֹלָם, כְּלוֹמַר אֲפִלּוּ נָפְלָה בְּאֶלֶף חֲלָקִים כָּמוֹהָ שֶׁל הֶתֵּר אֵינָהּ בְּטֵלָה בָהֶם וְהַכֹּל אָסוּר: דְּכִי הֵיכִי דַּחֲשִׁיבָא לְעִנְיַן מַלְקוֹת, דְּלוֹקִין עָלֶיהָ בְּכָל שֶׁהִיא, כִּדְאִיתָא בְּמַסֶּכֶת מַכּוֹת, חֲשִׁיבָא נַמֵּי לְעִנְיַן אִסּוּרִין דְּלֹא בְטֵלָה לְעוֹלָם. וְאַף־עַל־גַּב דְּבִירוּשַׁלְמִי דִתְרוּמוֹת פֶּרֶק בָּצָל אָמְרוּ: אוֹרֵי רַבִּי אַבִּין בְּחַד עַכְבְּרָא חַד לְאֶלֶף, גְּמָרָא דִילָן עֲדִיפָא לָן, דְּאָמְרֵי אֲפִלּוּ בְּאֶלֶף לֹא בָטְלָא.

וּפֵרוּשׁ בְּרִיָּה כְּלוֹמַר שׁוּם בַּעַל־חַיִּים, וַאֲפִלּוּ תוֹלַעַת כָּל שֶׁהוּא, כֵּיוָן שֶׁיֵּשׁ בָּהּ חִיּוּת, זֶהוּ עִקַּר פֵּרוּשׁוֹ שֶׁל בְּרִיָּה. וְכֵן נַמֵּי אָמְרוּ זִכְרוֹנָם לִבְרָכָה שֶׁנִּקְרָא בְרִיָּה

18. *Ibid.* 66b.

19. *Ibid.* 67a.

20. More correctly, an alcoholic beverage made of fermented dates; and dates could be wormy (see four paragraphs above, end).

21. TB Ḥullin 99b–100a.

22. This is not stated explicitly, but is inferred from *ibid.* and 96b.

23. So TB Makkoth 17a, and so the explanation is cited explicitly by R. 'Ashér (Rosh) to TB Ḥullin vii, §33.

water]—i.e. any body of collected water; they taught that a man may bend down and drink of them as long as the worms did not go out to some other place.[18] Even if they came out onto the walls of the vessel or the pit, once they return into it he may drink and need not refrain, as this is their place of growth.[19]

It would seem that even the caution, *You shall not make yourself abhorrent* (Leviticus 11:43) does not apply to them, and this is why they [the Sages] said, "and he need not refrain." Apparently the reason is that they found explicit permission out of a Scriptural verse; as the Sages of blessed memory interpreted,[18] "[whatever has fins and scales . . .] in the seas and in the rivers" (Leviticus 11:9)—[there] whatever has [these marks], eat; whatever does not have [them] do not eat; but in vessels and anything similar to vessels, whatever has or does not have [distinguishing marks] is permissible."

So too, among the laws of the precept, there is what the Sages of blessed memory taught:[19] A man should not pour beer[20] slowly over straw at night, for fear of a worm that may remain on the straw and then fall into the cup. The straw is that which is on the mouth of the vessel; and once a swarming thing is in the straw, it is the same in law as though it were moving about on the ground.

There are, furthermore, the laws of a [complete] creature, of which our Sages of blessed memory said[21] that it never becomes nullified [legally]: i.e. even if it fell into 1,000 times its amount of permissible food, it does not become as nothing in the whole [mass], and the whole is forbidden. For just as it is significant in regard to whip-lashes—since a whipping is given for [eating] it, however small it is, as we read in the tractate *Makkoth* (13a)—it is equally significant in regard to forbiddance, in that it never becomes nullified. Even though in the Jerusalem Talmud, chapter 10 of the tractate *T'rumoth*, it was stated, "R. 'Avin ruled about a single mouse that it becomes nullified as one part in a thousand," our Talmud carries more weight for us, wherein it teaches, "and even in a thousand it does not become nullified."[22]

The sense of "a creature" is, in other words, anything alive, even the smallest worm, as long as it is possessed of life: this is the essential meaning of "a creature."[23] And so did our Sages of blessed memory likewise teach that anything which from the beginning of its creation was forbidden, and it is entirely whole as at the time of its creation, is called "a creature" in the sense that it never becomes nullified, even in a

לְעִנְיַן דְּלָא בָטִיל לְעוֹלָם, אֲפִלּוּ בְאֶלֶף, כָּל דָּבָר שֶׁמִּתְּחִלַּת בְּרִיָּתוֹ הוּא אָסוּר וְהוּא שָׁלֵם כֻּלּוֹ כִּבְרִיָּתוֹ; לְאַפּוּקֵי חָסֵר אֲפִלּוּ כָּל שֶׁהוּא, שֶׁאֵין לוֹ דִין בְּרִיָּה וְאֵין לוֹקִין עָלָיו אֶלָּא בִכְזַיִת; וְהוּא מִשֶּׁל בַּעַל־חַיִּים, כְּמוֹ גִּיד הַנָּשֶׁה, שֶׁיֵּשׁ בּוֹ כָּל זֶה, לְאַפּוּקֵי כָּל פְּרִי שֶׁאֵינוֹ בְרִיַּת בַּעַל־חַיִּים, וְכָל כַּיּוֹצֵא בוֹ.

וּבִגְרָרָה דִבְרִיָּה, דְּאַמְרִינָן דַּחֲשִׁיבָא וְלֹא בָטְלָה, נֹאמַר מַה שֶּׁאָמְרוּ זִכְרוֹנָם לִבְרָכָה שֶׁכָּל דָּבָר חָשׁוּב גַּם־כֵּן לֹא בָטִיל, כְּגוֹן אֱגוֹזֵי פֶּרֶךְ וְרִמּוֹנֵי בָאדֶן וְחָבִיּוֹת סְתוּמוֹת וְחִלְפֵי תְרָדִין וְקִלְחֵי כְרוּב וּדְלַעַת יְוָנִית וְכִכְּרוֹת שֶׁל בַּעַל הַבַּיִת. וְהָרַמְבָּ"ם זִכְרוֹנוֹ לִבְרָכָה כָּתַב דְּלָאו דַּוְקָא שִׁבְעָה דְבָרִים אֵלֶּה אֶלָּא כָּל דָּבָר חָשׁוּב, אֲבָל אֵלּוּ הָיוּ הַחֲשׁוּבוֹת בִּזְמַן חַכְמֵי הַמִּשְׁנָה זִכְרוֹנָם לִבְרָכָה.

וְזֶה שֶׁאָמַרְנוּ דִבְרִיָּה לָא בָטְלָא וְכַוָּנָתֵנוּ לוֹמַר בֵּין חַיָּה בֵּין מֵתָה, דַּוְקָא בְרִיָּה שֶׁהָיְתָה אֲסוּרָה מִתְּחִלַּת בְּרִיָּתָהּ, כְּגוֹן בְּהֵמָה טְמֵאָה אוֹ שֶׁרֶץ טָמֵא, וְכֵן גִּיד הַנָּשֶׁה, שֶׁגַּם הוּא אָסוּר מִתְּחִלַּת בְּרִיָּתוֹ; אֲבָל בְּהֵמָה כְשֵׁרָה מִתְּחִלָּתָהּ, דַּוְקָא בְעוֹדָהּ חַיָּה הוּא שֶׁאֵינָהּ בְּטֵלָה, מִשּׁוּם דְּבַעֲלֵי־חַיִּים חֲשִׁיבֵי וְלָא בָטְלֵי, אֲבָל אַחַר שֶׁמֵּתָה וַדַּאי בִּטּוּל יֵשׁ לָהּ, וַאֲפִלּוּ שׁוֹר גָּדוֹל מֵת אַמְרִינָן שֶׁהוּא בָטֵל; וְזֶה יִהְיֶה אַלִּיבָּא דְרַבִּי יוֹחָנָן, דְּהִלְכְתָא כְּוָתֵיהּ, דְּאָמַר בַּגְּמָרָא גַּבֵּי דְבָרִים חֲשׁוּבִים דְּלָא בְטִילֵי: אֶת שֶׁדַּרְכּוֹ לִמָּנוֹת שָׁנִינוּ, כְּלוֹמַר הַדְּבָרִים שֶׁדַּרְכָּן שֶׁל בְּרִיּוֹת לִמְנוֹת דֶּרֶךְ חֲשִׁיבוּת תָּמִיד, שָׁנִינוּ שֶׁאֵין בְּטֵלוֹת, כְּגוֹן אוֹתָן שִׁבְעָה הַמְּנוּיוֹת לְמַעְלָה. אֲבָל שׁוֹר אֶחָד אֵין דַּרְכָּן שֶׁל בְּרִיּוֹת לְהַחֲשִׁיבוֹ בְלִבָּם תָּמִיד, לְפִי שֶׁאֵין רָאוּי לְפִי שָׁעָה וְלֹא קְרוֹבָה הֲנָאָתוֹ לְלֵב בְּנֵי־אָדָם כְּמוֹ אוֹתָן שִׁבְעָה דְבָרִים.

וְאַל תִּתְפַּלֵּא לוֹמַר: חֲתִיכָה אַחַת מִמֶּנּוּ הָרְאוּיָה לְהִתְכַּבֵּד בִּפְנֵי הָאוֹרְחִים תֵּחָשֵׁב וְלֹא תִבָּטֵל, וְכֻלּוֹ בְּיַחַד יִבָּטֵל — כִּי הָאֱמֶת כֵּן הוּא, שֶׁחֲתִיכָה אַחַת מִמֶּנּוּ

24. And hence, if the creature is something forbidden, the whole mass of food is forbidden — as stated above; inferred from TB Ḥullin 99b–100a.

25. Based on TB Nazir 51b.

26. I.e. if it is something forbidden from the start of its creation, e.g. if it was grown with another species (§ 245); TB Makkoth 17a.

27. Mishnah, 'Orlah iii 7.

28. MT *hilchoth ma'achaloth 'asuroth* xvi 9.

29. So TB Z'vaḥim 73a.

30. TB Bétzah 3b, Z'vaḥim 72b.

31. So Rashba (R. Sh'lomoh ibn 'Adreth), *Torath haBa-yith* IV 1.

32. E.g. a fine piece of cooked beef.

thousand [times its amount][24]—which is to exclude something that has even the slightest bit of it missing: That is not "a creature," and lashes are given over it only for the amount of an olive.[25] Yet this holds only if it is from a living being, such as the sinew of the thigh-vein, which has this entire qualification; but we would exclude every fruit,[26] which is not a living creature, and so anything similar.

Now, along with "a creature," which we say is significant and is thus not nullified, let us add something that our Sages of blessed memory said:[27] that anything significant (valued) is similarly not to be nullified—such as cracknuts, the pomegranates of Badan, sealed jugs [of wine], young beet shoots, cabbage stalks, Greek gourds, and home-baked bread. And Rambam of blessed memory wrote[28] that not merely these seven items, but anything of significance and value [is legally the same]; these, however, were the things of eminence at the time of the Sages of the Mishnah, be their memory for a blessing.

Now, what we have stated, that "a creature" is not nullified, by which we mean whether it is living or dead—applies only to a creature that was forbidden from the beginning of its creation: for example, an unclean [non-kosher] animal, or an unclean swarming creature; and so too the sinew of a thigh-vein, which is likewise forbidden from the beginning of its creation. However, when an animal is kosher at the beginning, it is only while it is alive that it cannot be made null and void, because living beings are significant and not to be nullified.[29] After it dies, though, it certainly is capable of being rendered null and void. Even if a great ox dies, we say it can become null and void—this according to R. Yoḥanan, whose view is followed as law. For it was stated in the Talmud[30] about eminent, significant things that are not nullified, "those items which it is the general custom to count, we have stated"; in other words, those things which it is the way of people always to count by virtue of their significance, we have learned that they are not to be nullified—for example, the seven items listed above. As for an ox, however, it is not the way of human beings to set store by it in their hearts at all times, since it is not usable [as food] at a moment's notice, and its pleasurable benefit is not directly in a person's anticipation, as the case is with those seven things.[31]

Now, do not wonder [at this] to ask, "One portion of it [the ox], eminently fit to serve before guests,[32] *is* significant, and will not be made null and void; and the whole of it together *can* be rendered null and void?" For it is truly so: From one portion out of it, there is direct

הֲנָאָתָהּ קְרוֹבָה וְלֵב בְּנֵי־אָדָם קְרוֹבָה אֵלֶיהָ וּמַחֲשִׁיבָהּ, וְעַל־כֵּן אָמְרוּ בָהּ שֶׁלֹּא תִבָּטֵל, וְאַף־עַל־פִּי שֶׁכֻּלּוֹ מֵת יִבָּטֵל. וְדַע זֶה וַהֲבִינֵהוּ.

וְיֵשׁ מִן הַמְּפָרְשִׁים שֶׁאָמְרוּ שֶׁדִּין חֲתִיכָה הָרְאוּיָה לְהִתְכַּבֵּד דְּלָא בָטְלָה לֹא נֶאֱמַר אֶלָּא בִמְבֻשֶּׁלֶת, כִּי אָז רְאוּיָה לְהִתְכַּבֵּד בָּהּ; וְיֵשׁ מֵהֶם שֶׁאָמְרוּ שֶׁאֲפִלּוּ בְחַיָּה נֶאֱמַר. וּמִן הַמְּפָרְשִׁים גַּם־כֵּן שֶׁאָמְרוּ דְּלָא נֶאֱמַר חֲתִיכָה הָרְאוּיָה שֶׁאֵינָהּ בְטֵלָה אֶלָּא כְּשֶׁהִיא אֲסוּרָה מֵחֲמַת עַצְמָהּ, אֲבָל אִם נָפַל אִסּוּר בְּתוֹכָהּ וְנָתַן בָּהּ טַעַם, בְּטֵלָה הַוְיָא, מִפְּנֵי שֶׁאֵין הָאִסּוּר שֶׁבָּהּ רָאוּי לְהִתְכַּבֵּד בִּפְנֵי הָאוֹרְחִין. וְאַף־עַל־גַּב דְּאַשְׁכְּחָן שֶׁאֲפִלּוּ בַחֲתִיכַת בָּשָׂר שֶׁנָּפַל בָּהּ חָלָב אָמְרוּ בַּעֲבוֹדָה זָרָה שֶׁאֵינָהּ בְּטֵלָה, שָׁאנֵי בָשָׂר בְּחָלָב דְּתַעֲרֻבְתָּן עוֹשָׂה אוֹתָהּ כַּחֲתִיכָה הָאֲסוּרָה מֵחֲמַת עַצְמָהּ. וְיֶתֶר רִבֵּי פְרָטֵי עִנְיָנִים אֵלֶּה, בְּחֻלִּין וּבַעֲבוֹדָה זָרָה.

וְנוֹהֶגֶת בְּכָל מָקוֹם וּבְכָל זְמַן, בִּזְכָרִים וּנְקֵבוֹת. וְעוֹבֵר עָלֶיהָ וְאָכַל בְּמֵזִיד בְּרִיָּה שְׁלֵמָה לְגַמְרֵי, טְמֵאָה, בֵּין חַיָּה בֵּין מֵתָה, וַאֲפִלּוּ פְחוּתָה מִן הַחַרְדָּל, וַאֲפִלּוּ הָיְתָה סְרוּחָה, וּבֵין שֶׁהָיְתָה עַל־יְדֵי זָכָר וּנְקֵבָה אוֹ מִכָּל הָעִפּוּשִׁים שֶׁבָּעוֹלָם וְשָׁרְצָה בָּאָרֶץ, מִי שֶׁאֲכָלָהּ כֻּלָּהּ לוֹקֶה עָלֶיהָ; אֲבָל חֲסֵרָה אֲפִלּוּ רֶגֶל אַחַת, אֵינוֹ לוֹקֶה עַד שֶׁיֹּאכַל כַּזַּיִת מִמֶּנָּה.

[שֶׁלֹּא לֶאֱכֹל מִשֶּׁרֶץ הַמַּיִם]

קסד שֶׁלֹּא לֶאֱכֹל מִשֶּׁרֶץ הַמַּיִם, שֶׁנֶּאֱמַר: אַל תְּשַׁקְּצוּ אֶת נַפְשֹׁתֵיכֶם בְּכָל הַשֶּׁרֶץ הַשֹּׁרֵץ וְלֹא תִטַּמְּאוּ בָּהֶם וְנִטְמֵתֶם בָּם. וְשֶׁרֶץ הַמַּיִם יָדוּעַ עִנְיָנוֹ, שֶׁהוּא מִבְּרִיּוֹת דַּקּוֹת הַשָּׁטוֹת בַּמַּיִם וְהֵם נִקְרָאִים שֶׁרֶץ הַמַּיִם. וְזֶה הַלָּאו מְיֻחָד בָּהֶם מִלְּבַד הַלָּאו הַמְיֻחָד לְדָג טָמֵא, שֶׁאֵין אֵלּוּ בִכְלַל דָּגִים כְּלָל, כִּי מִין אֶחָד בִּפְנֵי

33. Literally, commentators—i.e. authors of commentaries on the Talmud, who are, however, regarded as authorities in Jewish law.

34. I.e. which needs to be cooked; cited in *Shulḥan 'Aruch Yoreh Dé'ah* §101, 3.

35. So Rashba (note 31) and R. 'Ashér (*Shulḥan 'Aruch ibid.* 2).

36. So MT *hilchoth ma'achaloth 'asuroth* ii 21; but see *Maggid Mishneh.*

 pleasurable benefit; a person's heart is close to it [in anticipation] and he values it. Hence it was taught about it that it will not become void, as nothing—even though the whole of it, when dead, can be made null and void. Know this and understand it.

Now, there are some authorities[33] who held that the law about a portion fit to be served with honor, which is not to be nullified, was stated only for a cooked item:[32] then it is fit to serve with honor. And there are those who held that it was stated even about a raw portion.[34] Among the authorities[33] there are also those[35] who asserted that we apply the rule about a worthy, significant portion, that it is not nullifiable, only when it is forbidden because of itself; but if something forbidden fell into it, imparting [its] taste to it, it can be nullified, because the forbidden element in it is not a portion worthy of being served guests with honor—this even though we find that even regarding a piece of meat into which milk fell, it was taught in the tractate *'Avodah Zarah* (74a) that it cannot be made null: For meat with milk is different, since their admixture makes them as a piece of food innately forbidden. The remaining many details about these matters are in the Talmud tractates *Ḥullin* and *'Avodah Zarah*.

It is in effect in every place and time, for both man and woman. If someone violated it and willfully ate an entirely whole creature that was unclean (non-kosher), whether it was alive or dead, even if smaller than a mustard seed, even if it was putrid,[36] whether it was [engendered] through a male and a female [creature], or from any decaying matter in the world, and it had swarmed on the ground—if someone ate it entirely, he would be punished with whiplashes. But if it was missing even one leg, he would not be whipped until he ate an olive's amount of it.

[THE PROHIBITION AGAINST EATING CREATURES THAT SWARM IN THE WATER]

164 not to eat any swarming creature of the water: for it is stated, *You shall not make your souls abhorrent with any swarming thing that swarms, nor shall you make yourselves unclean with them, that you should not be defiled by them* (Leviticus 11:43). Now, as to a swarming creature of the water, in substance it is known: it is one of the tiny creatures that swim about in the water, that are called the swarming things of the water. This negative precept is specifically about them alone, apart from the injunction about unclean [non-kosher] fish, since these are not in the

עַצְמוֹ הוּא לְגַמְרֵי. זֶהוּ דַּעַת הָרַמְבָּ״ם זִכְרוֹנוֹ לִבְרָכָה בַּמִּקְרָא הַזֶּה, שֶׁעַל זֶה בָּא לְלַמֵּד.

וְהָרַמְבָּ״ן זִכְרוֹנוֹ לִבְרָכָה חוֹלֵק עָלָיו בָּזֶה, וְכָתַב כִּי הַלָּאו הַזֶּה אֵינֶנּוּ לָאו מְיֻחָד עַל שׁוּם שֶׁרֶץ, אֶלָּא שֶׁהוּא מִן הַלָּאוִין הַכּוֹלְלִים שֶׁאֵין לוֹקִין עֲלֵיהֶם, כְּמוֹ ״לֹא תֹאכַל כָּל תּוֹעֵבָה״ הַכָּתוּב בְּמִשְׁנֵה תוֹרָה בִּתְחִלַּת הַפָּרָשִׁיּוֹת שֶׁל אִסּוּר בַּעֲלֵי־הַחַיִּים; וְכֵן בְּכָאן אָמַר בְּסוֹף כֻּלָּן ״אַל תְּשַׁקְּצוּ אֶת נַפְשֹׁתֵיכֶם״, בְּכָל מְהַלְּכֵי הָאֲדָמָה שֶׁאָסַרְתִּי, וְיִכָּנְסוּ בָזֶה אִסּוּר בְּהֵמָה טְמֵאָה וְאִסּוּר עוֹף טָמֵא וְשֶׁרֶץ הָעוֹף וְשֶׁרֶץ הָאָרֶץ, כִּי כָל הָאָסוּר וְהַמְרֻחָק נִכְלָל בְּשִׁקּוּץ, כְּמוֹ ״כִּי לֹא בָזָה וְלֹא שִׁקַּץ עֱנוּת עָנִי״.

וְהֶאֱרִיכוּ עַל הַלָּאו הַזֶּה שְׁנֵיהֶם זִכְרוֹנָם לִבְרָכָה הַרְבֵּה, וְגִלְגְּלוּ בוֹ מַה שֶּׁאָמְרוּ זִכְרוֹנָם לִבְרָכָה בִּגְמָרָא מַכּוֹת: אָכַל פּוּטִיתָא לוֹקֶה אַרְבַּע, נְמָלָה לוֹקֶה חָמֵשׁ, צִרְעָה לוֹקֶה שֵׁשׁ; וְכָל אֶחָד יְפָרֵשׁ בָּהּ הַנִּרְאֶה אֵלָיו בָּעִנְיָן.

וְאִם בָּאתִי לִכְתֹּב כָּל טַעֲנוֹתָם בַּדָּבָר כְּמוֹת שֶׁהֵן, יֶאֱרַךְ הָעִנְיָן עַד שֶׁלֹּא יְכִילֶנּוּ קְלָף גָּדוֹל, וְאֵצֵא מִגֶּדֶר מְלַאכְתִּי זֹאת. וְאוּלָם לְפִי דַעְתִּי עִקַּר מַחְלְקֻתָּם בָּעִנְיָן תָּלוּי אִם לוֹקִין בְּאִסּוּר אֶחָד שְׁנֵי מַלְקִיּוֹת אִם לֹא: שֶׁהָרַמְבָּ״ם זִכְרוֹנוֹ לִבְרָכָה כָּתַב בְּעִקְּרֵי הַמִּצְוֹת שֶׁעָשָׂה, וְקָבַע בָּהּ מַסְמְרִים, שֶׁלֹּא נִלְקֶה לְעוֹלָם עַל עֲבֵרָה אַחַת שְׁתֵּי מַלְקִיּוֹת, וַאֲפִלּוּ יָבוֹאוּ עָלֶיהָ בַּכָּתוּב כַּמָּה לָאוִין; כְּאִלּוּ תֹאמַר עַל דֶּרֶךְ מָשָׁל שֶׁיָּבוֹא בַתּוֹרָה בַּחֲמֵשׁ מִקְרָאוֹת אוֹ אֲפִלּוּ בְמֵאָה ״לֹא תֹאכַל חֲזִיר״, אִם אֲכָלוֹ לֹא יִלְקֶה לְעוֹלָם בַּאֲכִילָה אַחַת אֶלָּא מַלְקוּת אַחַת. וְאַף־עַל־פִּי שֶׁאוֹתָן הַלָּאוִין לֹא יָבוֹאוּ לִדְרֹשׁ מֵהֶן שׁוּם דָּבָר, רַק לְתוֹסֶפֶת לָאוִין, אַף־עַל־פִּי־כֵן לֹא יִלְקֶה לְעוֹלָם אָדָם עַל אִסּוּר אֶחָד לְבַד רַק מַלְקוּת אֶחָד.

§164　1. ShM negative precept § 179; MT *hilchoth ma'achaloth 'asuroth* iii 12.

2. In his commentary on ShM root principle 9, s.v. *v'ra'ithi.*

3. I.e. of all the forbiddances on certain creatures as food.

4. ShM root principle 9.

5. Literally, and drove nails into it.

 category of fish at all, as they are an entirely separate species. Such is the view of Rambam of blessed memory[1] about the verse, that it comes to teach of this.

However, Ramban of blessed memory differs with him about it.[2] He wrote that this injunction is not a negative precept concerning any swarming creature in particular, but rather is one of the general, omnibus negative precepts, over which no whipping of lashes is given—such as *You shall not eat any abominable thing*, written in Deuteronomy (14:3), at the beginning of the sections on forbidden [non-kosher] living beings. So here too, He has stated at the end of them all,[3] "*You shall not make your souls abhorrent*—with all those that walk the earth which I have forbidden." This would include a ban on an unclean [non-kosher] animal, as well as a ban on unclean fowl, winged swarming beings, and swarming creatures of the earth—since all that is forbidden and removed [from us] is included under the concept of abhorrence and detestation, in the sense of the word in the verse, *For He has not despised nor* abhorred *the lowliness of the poor* (Psalms 22:25).

The both of them (of blessed memory) continued at great length about this negative precept, connecting it with what the Sages of blessed memory said in the Talmud tractate *Makkoth* (16b): If one ate a *putitha* [a small water-creature] he is given whiplashes four times; if an ant, he is whipped five times; if a hornet, he is whipped six times. And each one explains it as the matter appears to him.

Well, if I came to write all their arguments in the matter as they are [in their original form] the subject would grow so long that a large scroll would not contain it, and I would go beyond the proper boundary of this my work. In truth, though, their main difference of opinion in the matter hinges on whether one can be given two whippings (sets of lashes) over one prohibition, or not. For Rambam of blessed memory wrote in the main principles of the precepts that he composed,[4] and made it a hard and fast rule,[5] that we can never be given two whippings for one transgression, even if any number of injunctions are given about it in Scripture. As you might say by way of example, if we found in the Torah in five verses, or even in a hundred, "Do not eat swine," if one ate it he would never be given for one eating any more than one whipping of lashes. Even though those injunctions would then not have been given to derive anything from them, but merely for the addition of injunctions, nevertheless, a man would never receive over one prohibition alone any more than one set of lashes.

וּמִצַּד הַשֹּׁרֶשׁ הַזֶּה הַקָּבוּעַ אֵלָיו, הָיָה לוֹ לִדְחֹק בְּפֵרוּשׁ אוֹתָהּ שְׁמוּעָה דִּגְמָרַת מַכּוֹת הַרְבֵּה, וּלְפָרְשָׁהּ שֶׁלֹּא כְפֵרוּשׁ כָּל הַמְפָרְשִׁים שֶׁקְּדָמוּהוּ, וְהוּא בְעַצְמוֹ כָתַב שֶׁלֹּא רָאָה פֵרוּשׁ אָדָם שֶׁקָּדַם לוֹ שֶׁיְּפָרְשָׁהּ כָּמוֹהוּ.

וּכְלַל פֵּרוּשׁוֹ בַּדָּבָר הוּא שֶׁיַּחֲזֹר לְעוֹלָם, כִּי מַה שֶּׁאָמְרוּ שֶׁאָדָם לוֹקֶה בַּאֲכִילַת בְּרִיָּה אַחַת הַרְבֵּה לָאוִין, שֶׁיִּהְיֶה בְאוֹתָהּ בְּרִיָּה תּוֹסֶפֶת עִנְיָן שֶׁיִּתְיַחֵד הַלָּאו בְּאוֹתוֹ תוֹסֶפֶת, וְלֹא שֶׁיִּלְקֶה לְעוֹלָם מֵאִסּוּר אֶחָד לְבַדּוֹ שְׁתֵּי מַלְקִיּוֹת, וַאֲפִלּוּ נֶאֶמְרוּ עָלָיו בַּתּוֹרָה אֶלֶף לָאוִין, כְּמוֹ שֶׁאָמַרְנוּ; וְלָכֵן יֹאמַר הוּא שֶׁהַבְּרִיָּה שֶׁיְּחַיְּבוּ עָלֶיהָ חֲכָמִים זִכְרוֹנָם לִבְרָכָה הַרְבֵּה מַלְקִיּוֹת הִיא כְּגוֹן שֶׁתִּהְיֶה בְרִיָּה שֶׁיִּתְחַבְּרוּ בְגוּפָהּ הַרְבֵּה מִינִין, כְּגוֹן שֶׁתֹּאמַר שֶׁתִּהְיֶה תְכוּנָתָהּ בְּעִנְיָן שֶׁאֶפְשָׁר לִקְרוֹתָהּ שֶׁרֶץ הָאָרֶץ וְשֶׁרֶץ הָעוֹף, כְּגוֹן שֶׁיִּהְיוּ לָהּ כְּנָפַיִם — וְשֶׁרֶץ הַמַּיִם — שֶׁתָּשׁוּט גַּם־כֵּן בַּמַּיִם עִם הֱיוֹתָהּ מִתְעוֹפֶפֶת בָּאֲוִיר, כְּמוֹ שֶׁנִּרְאֶה כֵן לִפְעָמִים בִּקְצָת מִינֵי הַשְּׁרָצִים. וְעַל הַדֶּרֶךְ הַזֶּה עִם קְצָת דֹּחַק שֶׁיִּדְחֹק בְּפֵרוּשׁוֹ יְפָרֵשׁ שְׁמוּעָה זוֹ דִּגְמָרָא מַכּוֹת: אָכַל פּוּטִיתָא לוֹקֶה אַרְבַּע, נְמָלָה לוֹקֶה חָמֵשׁ, וְכוּלֵי; וְיָגַע לִמְצֹא בְגוּף בְּרִיָּה אַחַת שִׁשָּׁה עִנְיָנִים חֲלוּקִים.

וְהָרַמְבָּ״ן זִכְרוֹנוֹ לִבְרָכָה לֹא נִצְטָרֵךְ לְכָל זֶה, כִּי הוּא יִסְבֹּר שֶׁיֵּשׁ לָנוּ לִלְקוֹת עַל אִסּוּר אֶחָד כַּמָּה מַלְקִיּוֹת אִם יִתְרַבּוּ עָלָיו הַלָּאוִין בַּתּוֹרָה, וְלֹא יִצְטָרְכוּ לָנוּ לִדְרָשׁוֹת אֲחֵרוֹת; וְהַרְבֵּה רְאָיוֹתָיו עַל זֶה רְאָיוֹת חֲזָקוֹת כִּרְאִי מוּצָק לְפִי הַדּוֹמֶה. וּפֵרֵשׁ הַשְּׁמוּעָה דִּגְמָרָא מַכּוֹת כְּפֵרוּשׁ הָרִאשׁוֹנִים יָפֶה.

וְלָאו דְּשֶׁרֶץ הַמַּיִם דָּרִישׁ לֵיהּ הָרַמְבָּ״ן זִכְרוֹנוֹ לִבְרָכָה מִמַּה שֶּׁכָּתוּב בְּפָרָשַׁת אִסּוּר דָּגִים: וְכֹל אֲשֶׁר אֵין לוֹ סְנַפִּיר וְקַשְׂקֶשֶׂת וְכוּלֵי, מִכֹּל שֶׁרֶץ הַמַּיִם וְכוּלֵי, שֶׁקֶץ הֵם לָכֶם; וְזֶה בֶּאֱמֶת יִהְיֶה דָּבָר הַלָּמֵד מֵעִנְיָנוֹ, שֶׁבְּפָרָשָׁה זוֹ יְדַבֵּר בְּאִסּוּר

6. As noted in the first paragraph, Rambam derives it from the verse cited at the beginning; but Ramban regards it as a general, omnibus injunction about all forbidden beings.

7. One of the ways of interpreting Scripture listed by R. Ishmael in the introduction to Sifra.

8. I.e. the teachings of both Rambam and Ramban.

Now, on account of this root principle, which for him is firmly established, he had to take a very forced approach in explaining that teaching [about *putitha*] in the tractate *Makkoth* (16b) and to interpret it in a way that differs from the elucidation of all the commentators who preceded him. Indeed, he himself wrote that he did not see the explanation of any man before him that should clarify it as he did.

The crux of his explanation of the matter is what he forever reiterates, that when the Sages said that for one act of eating, a man should receive whiplashes on account of many negative precepts, there is some additional feature about that being [which he ate] to which feature [each additional] negative precept applies, but not that he should ever be whipped over one prohibition with two sets of lashes, even if a thousand injunctions were stated about it in the Torah—as we said. Therefore he would assert that a creature over which the Sages of blessed memory imposed many whippings is, for example, an organism in whose body many species are found combined: for instance, as you might say, if its structure and nature is such that it can be called a swarming creature of the earth and a flying swarming being—for instance, if it has wings—and a swarming creature of the water, which also swims in water in addition to flying in the air—as we see at times with some kinds of swarming beings. By this approach, with some straining as he forces his interpretation, he explains this teaching in the Talmud tractate *Makkoth* (16b): If someone ate a *putitha*, he is whipped four times; if an ant, he is whipped five times; etc. And he labored to find six different natures in the body of one creature.

Ramban of blessed memory has no need of all this. For he holds that we are to give any number of whippings over one prohibition, if there are many injunctions about it in the Torah, and they are not necessary for us to derive other teachings [from them]. He adduced many proofs of his for this—proofs, it would seem, *hard as a cast-metal mirror* (Job 37:18). And he elucidated well the teaching in the tractate *Makkoth* (16b) in keeping with the explanation of the earlier authorities.

As for an injunction about swarming creatures of the water,[6] Ramban of blessed memory derives it from a verse in the section about the ban on [forbidden] fish: *And anything that has not fins and scales . . . of all the swarming creatures of the water . . . is an abhorrence to you* (Leviticus 11:10). This is truly "something learned from its subject":[7] for in this section [Scripture] speaks of a ban on fish that grow in the water; then it speaks there also of the swarming creatures of the water. Listen to them,[8]

דָּגִים שֶׁגְּדֵלִים בַּמַּיִם, וְשָׁם יְדַבֵּר גַּם־כֵּן מִשֶּׁרֶץ הַמַּיִם. שְׁמָעֶנָּה בְּנִי, וְאִם תִּזְכֶּה בְּחַר לְךָ לְדַעְתְּךָ; אֵלּוּ וָאֵלּוּ דִבְרֵי אֱלֹהִים חַיִּים הֵם.

מִשָּׁרְשֵׁי אִסּוּר הַמַּאֲכָלִים כָּתַבְנוּ לְמַעְלָה. דִּינֶיהָ קְצָרִים, וּכְלַל הָעִנְיָן כִּי כָל אוֹתָן הַבְּרִיּוֹת קְטַנּוֹת כְּמוֹ הַתּוֹלָעִים וְהָעֲלוּקָה וְכַיּוֹצֵא בָם שֶׁגְּדֵלִים בַּמַּיִם נִקְרָאִים שֶׁרֶץ הַמָּיִם.

וְנוֹהֶגֶת בְּכָל מָקוֹם וּבְכָל זְמַן, בִּזְכָרִים וּנְקֵבוֹת. וְעוֹבֵר עָלֶיהָ וְאָכַל בְּרִיָּה אַחַת שְׁלֵמָה מֵהֶן, וַאֲפִלּוּ קְטַנָּה בְּיוֹתֵר, לוֹקֶה; וְאִם אֵינָהּ שְׁלֵמָה, אֵינוֹ לוֹקֶה עַד שֶׁיֹּאכַל מֵהֶן כַּזַּיִת; וּמִכָּל־מָקוֹם אָסוּר לֶאֱכֹל מֵהֶן דְּבַר תּוֹרָה אֲפִלּוּ פָּחוֹת מִכְּזַיִת, שֶׁחֲצִי שִׁעוּר, דְּאוֹרַיְתָא הוּא אָסוּר, אֲבָל אֵין חִיּוּב הַמַּלְקוֹת אֶלָּא עַל אֲכִילַת הַשִּׁעוּר הַמְקֻבָּל.

[שֶׁלֹּא לֶאֱכֹל מִן הַשְּׁרָצִים הַמִּתְהַוִּים מִן הָעִפּוּשׁ]

קסה שֶׁלֹּא לֶאֱכֹל מִן הַשְּׁרָצִים הַמִּתְהַוִּים מִן הָעִפּוּשִׁים, אַף־עַל־פִּי שֶׁאֵינוֹ מִין יָדוּעַ וְלֹא יִתְהַוֶּה מִזָּכָר וּנְקֵבָה, שֶׁנֶּאֱמַר: וְלֹא תְטַמְּאוּ אֶת נַפְשֹׁתֵיכֶם בְּכָל הַשֶּׁרֶץ הָרֹמֵשׂ עַל הָאָרֶץ. וּלְשׁוֹן סִפְרָא: "הַשֶּׁרֶץ הָרֹמֵשׂ עַל הָאָרֶץ", אַף־עַל־פִּי שֶׁאֵינוֹ פָּרֶה וְרָבֶה.

וְכָתַב הָרַמְבָּ"ם זִכְרוֹנוֹ לִבְרָכָה כִּי בְּשֶׁרֶץ הַנּוֹלָד מִזְּכָרִים וּנְקֵבוֹת נֶאֱמַר שׁוֹרֵץ, וַאֲשֶׁר הוּא נַעֲשָׂה מִן הָעִפּוּשׁ נֶאֱמַר עָלָיו רוֹמֵשׂ. וְהָרַמְבָּ"ן זִכְרוֹנוֹ לִבְרָכָה הִקְשָׁה עָלָיו מִן הַמִּקְרָאוֹת דִּכְתִיב, וְכָתַב כִּי בְּכֻלָּן יֵאָמֵר רוֹמֵשׂ וְשׁוֹרֵץ.

הַשֹּׁרֶשׁ יָדוּעַ.

דִּינֶיהָ קְצָרִים, שֶׁכָּל פְּרָטֶיהָ יִכָּנְסוּ בִּכְלָל אֶחָד, שֶׁנֶּאֶסְרוּ לָנוּ כָּל שִׁרְצֵי הָעִפּוּשִׁים שֶׁבָּעוֹלָם הָרוֹמְשִׂים בָּאָרֶץ, חוּץ מִשִּׁרְצֵי עִפּוּשֵׁי הַפֵּרוֹת שֶׁנַּעֲשׂוּ שָׁם אַחַר שֶׁנֶּעֶקְרוּ, וְשִׁרְצֵי עִפּוּשֵׁי הַמַּיִם שֶׁבַּכֵּלִים, הַכֹּל כְּמוֹ שֶׁאָמַרְנוּ לְמַעְלָה.

וְנוֹהֶגֶת בְּכָל מָקוֹם וּבְכָל זְמַן, בִּזְכָרִים וּנְקֵבוֹת. וְעוֹבֵר עָלֶיהָ וְאָכַל בְּרִיָּה מִכָּל הָעִפּוּשִׁים שֶׁבָּאַשְׁפּוֹת וּבְכָל הַמְּקוֹמוֹת, אֲפִלּוּ קְטַנָּה שֶׁבַּקְּטַנּוֹת, מִכֵּיוָן שֶׁאֲכָלָהּ וְהִיא שְׁלֵמָה, לוֹקֶה עָלֶיהָ; וְאִם אֵינָהּ שְׁלֵמָה, שִׁעוּרָהּ בִּכְזַיִת, כְּמוֹ שֶׁאָמַרְנוּ.

9. I.e. which to follow. At the end of his preface our author wrote that he conceived this work with his young son (and the son's friends) in mind.

10. A Talmudic expression about the conflicting rulings of the School of Hillel and the School of Shammai; TB 'Eruvin 13b.

11. So TB Yoma 74a, etc.

§165 1. ShM negative precept §177; MT *hilchoth ma'achaloth 'asuroth* ii 13.

2. E.g. Genesis 7:14; commentary on ShM root principle 9, s.v. *v'ha-périush*.

my son; and if you shall merit [to understand them], choose for yourself, by your mind.[9] Both these and those are words of the living God.[10]

The purpose that lies at the root of the ban on certain foods, we have written above (§§73, 154). Its laws are brief, the nub of the matter being that all those small creatures such as worms, leeches, and so on, which grow in the water, are called swarming beings of the water.

It is in force in every place and every time, for both man and woman. If someone violated it and ate one whole creature of them, even of the smallest size, he should receive whiplashes; if it was not whole, he would receive no lashes until he ate an olive's amount of them. However, by the law of the Torah it is forbidden to eat of them even less than the amount of an olive: for half a minimal amount is prohibited by the Torah;[11] but the punishment of whiplashes is for eating not less than the minimal amount received [taught in the Oral Tradition].

[THE PROHIBITION AGAINST EATING SWARMING CREATURES ENGENDERED IN DECAY]

165 not to eat of swarming beings engendered from decay, even though they are not a known species and are not engendered from male and female. For it is stated, *and you shall not defile your souls with any swarming thing that crawls upon the earth* (Leviticus 11:44); and in the language of the Midrash *Sifra:* "any swarming thing that crawls upon the earth"—even if it does not reproduce.

Rambam of blessed memory wrote[1] that of a swarming creature born of male and female, the term *sho-rétz*, "swarms," is used, while for one formed in decay, the term *ro-més*, "crawls," is used. But Ramban of blessed memory disputed him by [citing] verses of Scripture,[2] and he wrote that about all of them both *sho-rétz* and *ro-més* are used.

The root reason is known. Its laws are brief: for all its details can be summed up under the rule that all swarming creatures from decay in the world which crawl on the earth were forbidden us, except for swarming creatures in decayed fruit that formed there after it was picked, and swarming beings in rancid water contained in vessels—all as we have stated above (§163).

It applies in every place, at every time, for both male and female. If a person violated it and ate any creature engendered in the decay of garbage or anywhere else, even the very tiniest, as long as he ate it and it was whole, he should receive whiplashes for it; and if it was not whole, the minimal amount [for lashes] is as an olive, as we stated.

אִשָּׁה כִּי תַזְרִיעַ

יֵשׁ בָּהּ שֶׁבַע מִצְוֹת: חָמֵשׁ מִצְווֹת עֲשֵׂה וּשְׁתֵּי מִצְווֹת לֹא־תַעֲשֶׂה

[מִצְוַת עִנְיַן טֻמְאַת יוֹלֶדֶת]

קסו לְטַמֵּא הַיּוֹלֶדֶת, כְּלוֹמַר הָאִשָּׁה כְּשֶׁתֵּלֵד שֶׁתִּהְיֶה טְמֵאָה לְבַעְלָהּ, וְכָל־שֶׁכֵּן לְטָהֳרוֹת — שִׁבְעָה יָמִים כְּשֶׁתֵּלֵד זָכָר, וּשְׁבוּעַיִם כְּשֶׁתֵּלֵד נְקֵבָה — שֶׁנֶּאֱמַר: אִשָּׁה כִּי תַזְרִיעַ וְיָלְדָה זָכָר וְטָמְאָה שִׁבְעַת יָמִים וְגוֹמֵר, וְאִם נְקֵבָה תֵלֵד וְטָמְאָה שְׁבֻעַיִם וְגוֹמֵר.

מִשָּׁרְשֵׁי הַמִּצְוָה, הַקְדָּמָה: אֵין סָפֵק כִּי חֳלָיֵי בְנֵי־אָדָם יָבוֹאוּ אוֹ מִפְּנֵי מוֹתָר שֶׁבַּגּוּף אוֹ מִפְּנֵי חִסָּרוֹן, אוֹ מִצַּד הֶפְסֵד שֶׁיְּקַבֵּל מֵאֵי זוֹ סִבָּה שֶׁתִּהְיֶה; כִּי בֶאֱמֶת כָּל זְמַן שֶׁהַטֶּבַע יָשָׁר בְּתַכְלִית הַיֹּשֶׁר וְלֹא קִבֵּל הֶפְסֵד דָּבָר, לֹא יֶחֱלֶה הַגּוּף, וְחֵטְא בְנֵי־אָדָם יְבִיאֵם לְהַעְדִּיף אוֹ לְהַחְסִיר בְּמַה שֶּׁצָּרִיךְ לְטִבְעָם, וְיֶחֱלוּ.

וּכְבָר אָמַרְנוּ בְּאַזְהָרַת טְרֵפָה וְאִסּוּרֵי מַאֲכָלוֹת כִּי הָאֵל בָּרוּךְ הוּא רִחֵק עַמּוֹ אֲשֶׁר בָּחַר מִכָּל הַדְּבָרִים הַמַּזִּיקִים אֶת הַגּוּף, בַּעֲבוּר הֱיוֹתוֹ כְּלִי לַנֶּפֶשׁ הַיּוֹדַעַת יוֹצְרָהּ; וּכְמוֹ־כֵן מִן הַשֹּׁרֶשׁ הַזֶּה הִרְחִיקָנוּ מִן הַיּוֹלֶדֶת וּמִן הַנִּדָּה וְהַזָּבָה יָמִים מִסְפָּר, עַד שֶׁיִּתְנַקּוּ מֵאוֹתוֹ הַמּוֹתָר שֶׁבָּהֶן, שֶׁהוּא דָבָר רַע וּמַחֲלִיא, וּכְמוֹ שֶׁאָמַרְנוּ כִּי כָּל מוֹתָר מִשֹּׁרֶשׁ מַחֲלָה הוּא. וְעַל־כֵּן אָמְרוּ זִכְרוֹנָם לִבְרָכָה שֶׁאֵין אִשָּׁה רוֹאָה דָם שֶׁלֹּא יְהוּ רֹאשָׁהּ וְאֵבָרֶיהָ כְּבֵדִים עָלֶיהָ; וְאֵין סָפֵק כִּי בְאוֹתוֹ הַמּוֹתָר מַחֲלָה לָהֶן וּלְכָל הַקָּרֵב בָּהֶן שׁוּם קִרְבָה, וְכָל־שֶׁכֵּן בְּתַשְׁמִישׁ, שֶׁהוּא תַכְלִית הַקִּרְבָה הַחָמְרִית; וְגַם הַוָּלָד הַנּוֹצָר בְּעוֹד שֶׁאוֹתוֹ הַמּוֹתָר מִתְגַּבֵּר עֲלֵיהֶם מְעֻתָּד לָחֳלָאִים רָעִים.

וּמִן הַשֹּׁרֶשׁ הַזֶּה שֶׁאָמַרְנוּ, מִצַּד הַמּוֹתָר, צִוְּתָה הַתּוֹרָה לִהְיוֹת טְמֵאָה מִן הַזָּכָר

§166 1. So Rashi, Leviticus 12:2, based on TB Niddah 9a and 63b; cf. also MT *hilchoth 'issuré bi'ah* viii 2, and *Maggid Mishneh* on *ibid.* 1.

sidrah thazri'a

(Leviticus 12–13)

It contains seven precepts: five positive and two negative precepts.

[THE PRECEPT ABOUT THE RITUAL UNCLEANNESS OF A WOMAN AFTER CHILDBEARING]

166 to declare ritually unclean a woman who gives birth; in other words, that a woman should be unclean [impermissible] to her husband, and all the more certainly in regard to matters of ritual purity, for seven days when she bears a male child, and for two weeks when she gives birth to a female—as it is stated, *If a woman conceives and bears a male child, then she shall be unclean seven days . . . But if she bears a female child, then she shall be unclean two weeks* (Leviticus 12:2, 5).

Now, as to the root purpose of the precept, first a preface: There is no doubt that human illnesses come either on account of an excess in the body or a deficiency, or on account of some damage or deterioration which it suffers from whatever cause there may be For in truth, as long as its nature is straight (balanced) to the utmost degree and it has not suffered any sort of damage, the body will not sicken; but the sin of people will lead them to have an excess or a lack in what is needed for their nature, and they will fall ill.

We stated earlier, at the injunction about the *t'réfah* (§73) and about forbidden foods (§§147–48) that God, blessed is He, removed His people, whom He chose, from all the things that harm the body, because it is an instrument for the soul that knows its Maker. Similarly, for the same root reason, he removed us from a woman who gave birth, as well as from one unclean on account of the menses, and one who has a discharge for a few days, until they are cleansed of that excess which is in them, which is a bad thing, and causes illness. As we said, every excess is a root cause of illness. For this reason our Sages of blessed memory said that no woman sees blood [of the menses] without her head and limbs being heavy on her.[1] Then without any doubt, in that excess lies illness for them and for anyone who comes at all close to them, and all the more certainly [for anyone close] in conjugal intimacy, which is the utmost kind of physical proximity. The child too, formed while this excess dominates them, is prone to many ills.

For this root reason that we have stated, because of the excess, the Torah ordained that she should be unclean on account of a male

שִׁבְעָה, וּמִן הַנְּקֵבָה שְׁבוּעַיִם, שֶׁאֵין סָפֵק כִּי מוֹתְרֵי הַיּוֹלֶדֶת נְקֵבָה גְּדוֹלִים מִן הַיּוֹלֶדֶת זָכָר, לְפִי שֶׁהֶרְיוֹן הַזָּכָר יוֹרֶה חֹם בַּנְּקֵבָה, וּכְמוֹ שֶׁאָמְרוּ זִכְרוֹנָם לִבְרָכָה: "כִּי תַזְרִיעַ וְיָלְדָה זָכָר", אִשָּׁה מַזְרַעַת תְּחִלָּה יוֹלֶדֶת זָכָר; וְיָדוּעַ כִּי הַחֹלִי חֹם, מוֹתָרָיו מְעַטִּים וִימַהֵר פְּעֻלָּתוֹ לְעוֹלָם, דָּבָר מֻשְׂכָּל הוּא; וְעַל־כֵּן יַסְפִּיק לָנוּ בְּהֶרְיוֹן הַזָּכָר נְקָיוֹן שֶׁל שִׁבְעָה יָמִים.

וְהֶרְיוֹן הַנְּקֵבָה תוֹרֶה עַל קְרִירוּת טֶבַע הַנְּקֵבָה, וּבִקְרִירוּת יִרְבּוּ הַמּוֹתָרוֹת, וְלָכֵן תִּצְטָרֵךְ שְׁבוּעַיִם לִנְקִיּוּן גּוּפָהּ. וְכֵן מָצָאתִי הָעִנְיָן אַחֲרֵי כָּתְבִי זֶה לְהָרַמְבָּ"ן זִכְרוֹנוֹ לִבְרָכָה, וְזֶה לְשׁוֹנוֹ: בַּעֲבוּר כִּי טֶבַע הַנְּקֵבָה קַר וְלַח וְהַלְּבָנָה בְּרֶחֶם הָאֵם רַבָּה מְאֹד וְקָרָה, וְעַל־כֵּן יָלְדָה נְקֵבָה, וּלְפִיכָךְ הִיא צְרִיכָה נְקָיוֹן גָּדוֹל, מִפְּנֵי רִבּוּי הַלֵּחוֹת וְהַדָּם הַמְעֻפָּשׁ שֶׁבָּהֶן וּמִפְּנֵי קְרִירוּתָן, בְּיָדוּעַ כִּי הֶחֳלָאִים הַקָּרִים צְרִיכִים בְּנִקְיוֹנָן אֲרִיכוּת זְמַן יוֹתֵר מִן הַחַמִּים. עַד כָּאן.

וּבְדוֹמֶה לָזֶה יִהְיֶה הָעִנְיָן גַּם־כֵּן בְּנִדָּה וְזָבָה, כִּי הַנִּדָּה תִטְהַר לְשִׁבְעַת יָמִים, וַאֲפִלּוּ שׁוֹפַעַת כָּל שִׁבְעָה, וּבִלְבַד שֶׁתִּפְסֹק בַּשְּׁבִיעִי מִבְּעוֹד יוֹם, מִדִּין תּוֹרָה; וְהַזָּבָה צְרִיכָה שִׁבְעָה נְקִיִּים, לְפִי שֶׁהַזָּבָה תוֹרֶה עַל רֹב מוֹתְרֵי הָאִשָּׁה, וְזֶהוּ הֶמְשֵׁךְ הֲרָקַת דָּמֶיהָ יָמִים רַבִּים אַחַר הַשִּׁבְעָה יָמִים הַנְּהוּגִים בְּרֹב הַנָּשִׁים.

וְאֶפְשָׁר לָנוּ לוֹמַר שֶׁחֹלִי הֲרָקַת הַדָּמִים בְּנָשִׁים מֵחֹדֶשׁ לְחֹדֶשׁ הָיָה כְּדֵי שֶׁלֹּא תָזוּחַ דַּעְתָּן הַקַּלָּה עֲלֵיהֶן, אוֹ כְּדֵי לְהַרְחִיק קִרְבָתָן קְצָת מִן הָאָדָם שֶׁלֹּא יְהֵא רָץ אַחֲרֵיהֶן כָּל הַיָּמִים, כִּי יִתְגַּנּוּ בְּעֵינָיו קְצָת בִּדְבַר הַלִּכְלוּךְ הַהוּא שֶׁיֵּדַע בָּהֶם וְלֹא יִשְׁגֶּה תָמִיד בְּאַהֲבָתָן.

וְרַבּוֹתֵינוּ זִכְרוֹנָם לִבְרָכָה אָמְרוּ בְּנִדָּה עַל צַד הַפְּשָׁט, רְצוֹנִי לוֹמַר שֶׁכִּוְּנוּ לְגַלּוֹת אֶחָד מִן הַתּוֹעָלוֹת הַגְּדוֹלוֹת שֶׁיֵּשׁ בַּמִּצְוָה מִלְּבַד רֹב עִקָּרֶיהָ הַגְּדוֹלִים

2. TB B'rachoth 60a.
3. Commentary, Leviticus 12:4.
4. Literally, from month to month.
5. A quality attributed to them in TB Shabbath 33b.

[child] seven days, and on account of a female, two weeks. For past any doubt, the excess substances in a woman who bears a female are greater than in one who bears a male: because the conception of a male indicates a warmth in the woman. As our Sages of blessed memory said,[2] "If a woman conceives and bears a male child"—if the woman completes her share in the conception first, she gives birth to a boy. Now, it is known that when an illness is with temperature, its excess substances are few, and it always hastens its activity; this is something logical, understandable. Hence, for the conception of a male, a cleansing period of seven days is enough for us.

However, the conception of a female indicates coldness in the woman's physical nature, and in coldness the excess substances increase. Therefore she needs two weeks for the cleansing of her body. And so, after writing this, I found the matter [comprehended] by Ramban of blessed memory. These are his words:[3] Because the physical nature of the woman was cold and moist, and the white humor in the mother's womb was of large amount and cold, she therefore bore a female. Hence she needs great cleansing, on account of the accretion of humors and the foul blood in them, and on account of their coldness. It is known that cold illnesses require for their cleansing a greater length of time than those with heat. Thus far his words.

Quite like this, as well, is the theme of the menstruant and a woman with a discharge [*zavah*]: for the menstruant becomes ritually pure in seven days, even if she experiences a flow all seven, provided it stops on the seventh while it is yet day—this by the law of the Torah. A woman with a discharge, however, requires seven clean days: for the discharge indicates a large excess of substances in the woman, and this is why there is a continuation of the issue of her blood many days after the seven which are usual with most women.

Now, we could say that the malady of the emission of blood in women every month[4] is in order that they should not become conceited in their light-headedness,[5] or in order to remove their proximity somewhat from the man, so that he should not be pursuing them all the time: for they will become slightly depreciated in his sight, on account of that sullying which he knows in regard to them, and he will not be constantly occupied with a love for them.

Our Sages of blessed memory wrote about the menstruant by way of the plain meaning—by which I mean that they intended to reveal one of the great benefits that lie in the precept, apart from its great

וְהַחֲזָקִים, וְכָתְבוּ שֶׁיֵּשׁ תּוֹעֶלֶת בְּהַרְחָקַת הָאִשָּׁה קְצָת זְמַן כְּדֵי שֶׁתִּתְחַבֵּב עַל בַּעְלָהּ יוֹתֵר בַּזְּמַן הַמֻּכְשָׁר, וְלֹא יָקוּצוּ זֶה מִזֶּה לְרֹב הַתְמָדַת קִרְבָתָן וְיִתְּנוּ עֵינֵיהֶם בְּגוּפִים אֲחֵרִים, וּכְמוֹ שֶׁיַּעֲשׂוּ רֹב הָאֻמּוֹת שֶׁאֵינָם גְּדוּרִים בִּגְדָרֵינוּ הַחֲמוּרִים. וּכְמוֹ־כֵן יַסְפִּיק טַעְמָם זֶה עַל צַד הַפְּשָׁט בַּיּוֹלֶדֶת, שֶׁלֹּא יִתְנַוֵּל בָּהּ מִיָּד, וְשֶׁמָּא תִתְגַּנֶּה בְעֵינָיו וְיָקוּץ בָּהּ, כְּמוֹ שֶׁאָמְרוּ בְּנִדָּה.

מִדִּינֵי הַמִּצְוָה, (כְּגוֹן) מַה שֶּׁאָמְרוּ זִכְרוֹנָם לִבְרָכָה שֶׁכָּל הַיּוֹלְדוֹת טְמֵאוֹת וְאַף־עַל־פִּי שֶׁלֹּא רָאוּ דָם, שֶׁאִי אֶפְשָׁר לִפְתִיחַת הַקֶּבֶר בְּלֹא דָם; וְאֶחָד הַיּוֹלֶדֶת חַי אוֹ מֵת וַאֲפִלּוּ נֵפֶל, וְהוּא שֶׁתִּגָּמֵר צוּרָתוֹ, טְמֵאָה טֻמְאַת לֵדָה; וַאֲפִלּוּ הִפִּילָה שִׁלְיָא אוֹ שָׁפִיר מָלֵא מַיִם אוֹ דָם, הֲרֵי זוֹ חוֹשֶׁשֶׁת לְלֵדָה, דְּקַיְמָא לָן אֵין שִׁלְיָא בְּלֹא וָלָד; וְאַף־עַל־פִּי שֶׁאֵין מוֹצְאִין עַכְשָׁיו הַוָּלָד בַּשִּׁלְיָא, חוֹשְׁשִׁין שֶׁמָּא נִמּוֹק בְּתוֹכוֹ; וְתֵשֵׁב מִסָּפֵק יְמֵי טֻמְאָה שֶׁל נְקֵבָה, שֶׁהֵם שְׁבוּעַיִם, וִימֵי טֹהַר שֶׁל זָכָר, שֶׁהֵם ל״ג יוֹם, וְלֹא יוֹתֵר, דְּמִסָּפֵק אַזְלִינָן הָכָא וְהָכָא לְהַחְמִיר.

וְזֶה שֶׁאָנוּ אוֹמְרִים שֶׁצְּרִיכָה לָחוּשׁ לַוָּלָד, דַּוְקָא שֶׁעָבְרוּ עָלֶיהָ אַרְבָּעִים יוֹם מִשֶּׁנִּתְעַבְּרָה, אֲבָל לֹא עָבְרוּ עָלֶיהָ אַרְבָּעִים יוֹם אֵינָהּ חוֹשֶׁשֶׁת לְלֵדָה, וַאֲפִלּוּ בְּיוֹם אַרְבָּעִים מַמָּשׁ, שֶׁיּוֹם אַרְבָּעִים כְּלִפְנֵי אַרְבָּעִים הוּא חָשׁוּב. וּמִכָּל־מָקוֹם אַף־עַל־פִּי שֶׁאֵינָהּ חוֹשֶׁשֶׁת לְלֵדָה, כְּלוֹמַר וְלֹא יִהְיוּ לָהּ יְמֵי טֹהַר כְּמוֹ בְיוֹלֶדֶת, חוֹשֶׁשֶׁת הִיא מִכָּל־מָקוֹם לְטֻמְאַת נִדָּה. וְאַף־עַל־פִּי שֶׁיָּלְדָה לֵדָה יְבֵשָׁה, כְּלוֹמַר שֶׁלֹּא רָאֲתָה דָם כְּלָל, אָנוּ אוֹמְרִים: מִכֵּיוָן שֶׁיָּלְדָה, אִי אֶפְשָׁר לִפְתִיחַת הָרֶחֶם בְּלֹא דָם, וְשֶׁמָּא הָיָה מוּעָט וְנֶאֱבַד.

וְכָל אִשָּׁה שֶׁיֵּשׁ לָהּ יְמֵי לֵדָה לְטֻמְאָה יֵשׁ לָהּ יְמֵי טֹהַר מִדִּין תּוֹרָה, וִימֵי הַטֹּהַר הֵם ל״ג לְזָכָר וס״ו לִנְקֵבָה. וְהָעִנְיָן הוּא כֵן: דִּין תּוֹרָה, שֶׁהָאִשָּׁה אַחַר שֶׁיָּלְדָה,

6. E.g. observing a precept of the Torah in obedience to the Divine will, and thus growing in merit and virtue.

7. TB Niddah 31b.

7a. The two oldest manuscripts have *ha-ḥamudim* (the cherished, precious) instead of *ha-ḥamurim*, the stringent.

8. I.e. if a childbirth was apparently without bleeding.

9. So Rava, TB Niddah 66a.

10. Sifra on Leviticus 12:2.

11. I.e. if it had assumed the basic form of an embryo, which it would forty days after conception; MT *hilchoth 'issuré bi'ah* x 1.

12. Derived from R. Dimi's statement, TB Niddah 45a.

13. This is explained two paragraphs below.

14. I.e. in the first question we rule as if a female child had been born, and in the second as if it had been a male—in order to be strict always, because it is a matter of doubt.

15. See note 11.

and mighty main values;[6] they wrote[7] that there is an advantage in keeping a woman distant for a short time: [it is] so that she should be the more beloved to her husband in the proper, felicitous time, and they should not grow disgusted with one another on account of the too great constancy of their closeness, and thus cast their eyes on other bodies—as do most of the nations that are not bound by our stringent[7a] "fences" (protective restrictions). This reason of theirs will likewise be enough, by way of the plain meaning, for a woman giving birth [to explain it]: that he should not be distastefully intimate with her at once, for fear that she may become degraded in his eyes and he will be disgusted with her, as we stated about a menstruant.

Among the laws of the precept, there is, for example, what the Sages of blessed memory said: that all women who give birth are ritually unclean, even if they saw no blood[8]—because it is impossible for the womb to open without bleeding.[9] It is all one whether a woman bears a live or dead child, or even an aborted fetus,[10] provided its form was completed:[11] she is then unclean by the defilement of delivery. Even if she dropped a placenta or an amniotic sac filled with water or blood, she is to suspect that there was a birth; for we have an established rule: there is no placenta without a fetus.[12] Hence, even if a fetus is not found in the placenta now, we suspect that perhaps it was mashed to a pulp within it; and in the doubt she should observe the days of uncleanness for a female child, which means two weeks, and the days of purity[13] for a male child, which are thirty-three days and no more—for in doubt, we go both this way and that way to be stringent.[14]

Now, when we say that she must suspect that there may have been an embryo, this is only if [at least] forty days passed by since she became pregnant; but if forty days did not pass by, she need not suspect a birth[15]—and this even on the fortieth day itself: for the fortieth day is reckoned as though before the forty. However, even if she does not suspect a birth—which means that she will not have days of ritual purity[16] as a woman who gives birth has—she must yet suspect defilement as a menstruant. Even if she had a dry delivery, i.e. if she saw no blood at all, we say: since she gave birth, it is impossible for the womb to open without bleeding; and so perhaps there was a little bit and it was lost.[17]

Every woman who has "days of birth" [to observe] in defilement has days of ritual purity by the law of the Torah. These days of purity are thirty-three for a male child, and sixty-six for a female. In substance,

מוֹנָה שִׁבְעָה יָמִים מִיּוֹם שֶׁיָּלְדָה; וּבֵין שֶׁיָּלְדָה בִתְחִלַּת הַלַּיְלָה אוֹ בַחֲצִי הַיּוֹם, אוֹ אֲפִלּוּ סָמוּךְ לִשְׁקִיעַת הַחַמָּה, מוֹנָה אוֹתוֹ הַיּוֹם שֶׁל לֵדָה יוֹם אֶחָד, וּמַשְׁלִים עָלָיו שֵׁשֶׁת יָמִים; וּבֵין רוֹאָה קְצָת יָמִים מִן הַשִּׁבְעָה אוֹ כָּל הַשִּׁבְעָה, לָעֶרֶב שֶׁל שְׁבִיעִי שֶׁהוּא לֵיל שְׁמִינִי טוֹבֶלֶת וּטְהוֹרָה לְבַעֲלָהּ; וַאֲפִלּוּ שׁוֹפַעַת דָּם בְּאוֹתוֹ לֵיל שְׁמִינִי, טוֹבֶלֶת וּטְהוֹרָה (לְבַעֲלָהּ), שֶׁהַתּוֹרָה הִתִּירָה כָּל הַדָּמִים שֶׁתִּרְאֶה הַיּוֹלֶדֶת אַחַר שִׁבְעָה יָמִים לְזָכָר בְּתוֹךְ ל״ג יוֹם, וְאַחַר י״ד לִנְקֵבָה בְּתוֹךְ ס״ו יוֹם.

וְעַל זֶה אָמְרוּ זִכְרוֹנָם לִבְרָכָה כִּי מַעְיָן אֶחָד הוּא וְהַתּוֹרָה טִמְּאַתּוּ וְהַתּוֹרָה טִהֲרַתּוּ; כְּלוֹמַר שֶׁדְּמֵי הַלֵּדָה שֶׁטִּמְּאָה הַתּוֹרָה וּדְמֵי הַטֹּהַר שֶׁטִּהֲרָה הַתּוֹרָה, מִמָּקוֹם אֶחָד, וְהוּא מִן הַמָּקוֹר, שֶׁהוּא מְקוֹם טֻמְאָה, יוֹצְאוֹת שְׁנֵיהֶן, אֶלָּא שֶׁהַתּוֹרָה תִתְלֶה הָעִנְיָן בַּזְּמַן, וּתְטַמֵּא הַדָּם הַיּוֹצֵא מִמֶּנָּה בִּזְמַן אֶחָד, וּתְטַהֵר הַשֵּׁנִי. וּבָרוּךְ הַיּוֹדֵעַ כָּל הַחָכְמָה כִּי הַכֹּל עָשָׂה בְטַעַם נָכוֹן וּמְחֻיָּב, וְהוּא בָרוּךְ הוּא יָדַע שֶׁעַד אוֹתוֹ הַזְּמַן הַדָּמִים מַזִּיקִין וּמִשָּׁם וָאֵילָךְ לֹא יַזִּיקוּ.

וְעַכְשָׁיו נָהֲגוּ כָּל יִשְׂרָאֵל וְגָדְרוּ עַצְמָן לִנְהֹג טֻמְאָה בִדְמֵי טֹהַר כְּמוֹ בִדְמֵי טֻמְאָה. וּכְלַל הָעִנְיָן שֶׁאֵין הָאִשָּׁה עַכְשָׁיו עוֹלָה מִטֻּמְאָתָהּ לְעוֹלָם עַד שֶׁתַּעֲמֹד שִׁבְעָה יָמִים שְׁלֵמִים נְקִיִּים מִכָּל דָּם, וְתַתְחִיל לִמְנוֹתָן מִבָּעֶרֶב; זֶהוּ כְּלָל גָּדוֹל וְטוֹב בְּכָל מְקוֹמוֹת יִשְׂרָאֵל הַכְּשֵׁרִים, וּבָזֶה נִצַּלְנוּ מִכַּמָּה סְפֵקוֹת.

וְדִינֵי הַסְּפֵקוֹת הַמִּתְחַדְּשׁוֹת לִפְעָמִים עַל הַיּוֹלֶדֶת, כְּגוֹן אִם תִּתְחַיֵּב לֵישֵׁב עַל טֻמְאַת זָכָר אוֹ עַל טֻמְאַת נְקֵבָה, שֶׁפְּעָמִים תִּצְטָרֵךְ מִתּוֹךְ הַסָּפֵק לֵישֵׁב לְזָכָר וְלִנְקֵבָה וְגַם לְנִדָּה; וְדִין הַמַּפֶּלֶת כְּמִין בְּהֵמָה חַיָּה וָעוֹף מַה דִּינָהּ, וְאִם פְּנֵיהֶם

16. Explained in the next paragraph.

17. I.e. it passed out unseen; so Rabad, *Ba'alé haNefesh, sha'ar ha-p'rishah.*

18. Because in Jewish reckoning, a day begins at nightfall on the previous evening.

19. So Rashi, Leviticus 12:4.

20. TB Niddah 35b.

21. I.e. if there is any discharge of blood during the thirty-three days for a male child or the sixty-six for a female.

22. From the time of the *ge'onim*; MT *hilchoth 'issuré bi'ah* xi 6.

23. I.e. if she aborted something which may or may not have been a true fetus; TB Niddah 24a.

24. *Ibid.* 21a.

it means this: It is the law of the Torah that after she has borne [a son] a woman counts seven days from the day she gave birth; whether she delivered at the beginning of the night or at midday, or even close to sunset, she counts that day of birth as one day, and completes [the period] with it [by observing another] six days. Then, whether she saw [blood] some days of the seven, or even all seven, on the evening of the seventh, which is the night of the eighth,[18] she undergoes immersion and is ritually clean [permitted] to her husband. Even if she has a discharge of blood that very night of the eighth day, she undergoes immersion and is ritually pure (to her husband): For the Torah ruled permissible [non-defiling] all blood that a woman giving birth will see after seven days, within [the next] thirty-three days, for a male child; and after fourteen days for a female, within [the next] sixty-six days.[19]

About this the Sages of blessed memory said that it is one fountain, but the Torah declared it defiled, and the Torah declared it ritually clean.[20] In other words, the blood of birth, which the Torah declared ritually unclean, and the blood of purity, which the Torah ruled ritually clean, are from one place: i.e. from the uterine origin, meaning the place of defilement, both of them issue; it is only that the Torah would make the matter depend on the time, declaring the blood that issues from it at one time ritually unclean, and the second ritually clean. Then blessed is He who knows all wisdom, that He did all with a right and essential reason. He (blessed is He) knew that until such time the blood is harmful, and from then on it is not harmful.

Now, however, all Jewry has adopted the practice and fenced itself about [with the protective resolution] to observe the laws of defilement over the blood of ritual purity[21] just as over blood of impurity. The crux of the matter is that now a woman does not ever rise out of her ritual uncleanness until she experiences seven whole days free of any blood, beginning to count them from the evening. This is a great and good rule followed in all locations of worthy, observant Jewry;[22] and by it we are saved from many doubts.

In addition, we have laws on doubts which arise at times about a woman who gave birth: for example, whether she is duty-bound to observe a period of defilement for a male child or for a female, in which case at times she may need, because of the doubt, to observe the period for a male and a female, and also for menstruation.[23] And there is the law for one who aborts something like [the embryo of] a domestic or wild animal, or a fowl—what is the ruling for her;[24] and if their

כִּפְנֵי אָדָם אוֹ אֵין פְּנֵיהֶם כִּפְנֵי אָדָם מַה דִּינָהּ; וְהַמַּפֶּלֶת כְּמִין יַבְחוּשִׁין, כְּמִין שְׂעָרוֹת, וְהַמַּפֶּלֶת דְּמוּת אָדָם שֶׁיֵּשׁ לוֹ כְנָפַיִם שֶׁל בָּשָׂר, וְכֵן הַמַּפֶּלֶת דְּמוּת אָדָם בְּעַיִן אַחַת וְיָרֵךְ אַחַת, וְהַמַּפֶּלֶת זָכָר וְסַנְדָּל עִמּוֹ, וְהִיא הַבְּרִיָּה שֶׁאֵינָהּ נִכֶּרֶת אִם זָכָר אוֹ נְקֵבָה; וְדִין הָאִשָּׁה שֶׁיָּצְאָה מְלֵאָה וּבָאת רֵיקָנִית וְהִיא טוֹעָה בְחֶשְׁבּוֹנָהּ; וְיֶתֶר רִבֵּי הַפְּרָטִים בְּעִנְיְנֵי טֻמְאָתָהּ, הַכֹּל בְּמַסֶּכֶת נִדָּה. וְעִנְיַן דִּינֵי קָרְבָּנָהּ מְפֻזָּרִים בְּהַרְבֵּה מַסֶּכְתּוֹת, וּמֵהֶן הַרְבֵּה בִּזְבָחִים וַעֲרָכִים וּכְרֵתוֹת וְקִנִּין וּנְגָעִים.

וְנוֹהֶגֶת מִצְוָה זוֹ בְּכָל מָקוֹם וּבְכָל זְמַן לְעִנְיָן שֶׁהַיּוֹלְדוֹת טְמֵאוֹת. וְהָעוֹבֵר וּבָא עָלֶיהָ בְּמֵזִיד בְּתוֹךְ הַזְּמַן הַמְּגֻבָּל לְאִסּוּר אוֹ אֲפִלּוּ אַחַר הַזְּמַן הַמְּגֻבָּל כָּל זְמַן שֶׁלֹּא טָבְלָה, בִּטֵּל עֲשֵׂה זֶה, וְגַם עָבַר עַל לָאו כְּמוֹ בְנִדָּה, וּכְעִנְיָן שֶׁכָּתוּב: כִּימֵי נִדַּת דְּוֹתָהּ תִּטְמָא, וְחַיָּב כָּרֵת; בְּשׁוֹגֵג חַיָּב לְהָבִיא חַטָּאת קְבוּעָה בִּזְמַן הַבַּיִת.

[שֶׁלֹּא יֹאכַל טָמֵא מִן הַקֳּדָשִׁים]

קסז שֶׁלֹּא יֹאכַל טָמֵא מִן הַקֳּדָשִׁים עַד שֶׁיִּטְבֹּל וְיַעֲרִיב שִׁמְשׁוֹ, וְאִם הוּא טָמֵא שֶׁצָּרִיךְ כַּפָּרָה, עַד שֶׁיָּבִיא כַּפָּרָתוֹ — שֶׁנֶּאֱמַר: בְּכָל קֹדֶשׁ לֹא תִגָּע. וּלְשׁוֹן סִפְרָא: "בְּכָל קֹדֶשׁ לֹא תִגָּע וְאֶל הַמִּקְדָּשׁ לֹא תָבֹא", מַה מִּקְדָּשׁ הַנִּכְנָס לוֹ בְטֻמְאָה עָנוּשׁ כָּרֵת, אַף הָאוֹכֵל קָדָשִׁים בְּטֻמְאָה עָנוּשׁ כָּרֵת.

וְאַמְרִינָן בְּמַכּוֹת: "בְּכָל קֹדֶשׁ לֹא תִגָּע", אַזְהָרָה לָאוֹכֵל; אַתָּה אוֹמֵר לָאוֹכֵל, אוֹ אֵינוֹ אֶלָּא לַנּוֹגֵעַ, וְכוּלֵּי, כִּדְאִיתָא הָתָם.

25. *Ibid.* 23b.
26. *Ibid.* 24b.
27. *Ibid.* 24b, 25b.
28. I.e. exactly how long ago the birth was; TB Niddah 29b.
29. Leviticus 12:6.
30. But not in regard to the offering she should bring (note 29), since she can do that only when the Temple stands.
31. Explained in §121.

§167
1. I.e. in the evening after the immersion; Leviticus 22:7.
2. So ShM negative precept §129; the version in our editions differs.

faces are like human visages or are not like human visages, what is the law for her.[25] [Further, there are laws for] one who aborts something like gnats or something like hair;[24] one who aborts a human form that has wings of flesh;[26] likewise, one who aborts a human form with one eye and one thigh;[25] and one who aborts a male fetus and a flat fish shape with it—which is the creature that cannot be identified as male or female.[27] Then we have the law of a woman who went out full (pregnant) and came back empty [long after her delivery] and she is uncertain in her reckoning.[28] [These] and the rest of the many details in regard to her defilement are all in the Talmud tractate *Niddah*. As to the laws of her offering,[29] they are scattered in many tractates, a good number of them being in *Z'vaḥim*, *'Arachin*, *K'rithoth*, *Kinim* and *N'ga'im*.

This precept is in force in every place and every time, to the effect that women who give birth are ritually impure.[30] If someone violates this and is conjugally intimate with her deliberately within the time defined as forbidden, or even after the time so restricted, as long as she did not undergo immersion, he thus disobeys a positive precept, and also transgresses a negative precept as with a menstruant, in keeping with the verse, *as in the days of her menstrual illness* (Leviticus 12:2)—and he is punishable by *karéth* [Divine severance of existence]. If it was inadvertent, he is obligated to bring a standard unvarying *ḥattath* (sin-offering)[31] when the Temple is extant.

[A RITUALLY UNCLEAN PERSON IS NOT TO EAT MEAT OF HOLY SACRIFICES]

167 that a ritually impure person should not eat of holy offerings until he undergoes immersion and his sun sets;[1] and if he is a defiled person who needs atonement, until he brings his atonement. For it is written, *she shall not touch any hallowed thing* (Leviticus 12:4); and in the words of the Midrash *Sifra*: "she shall not touch any hallowed thing, nor come into the sanctuary"—just as with the Sanctuary, whoever enters it while ritually unclean is punished by *karéth* [Divine severance of existence], so is one who eats holy offerings while unclean punished by *karéth*.[2]

It was taught, too, in the Talmud tractate *Makkoth* (14b): "she shall not touch any hallowed thing"—this is an admonition to one who eats [of offerings while defiled]. You say it is for one who eats; perhaps it is not so but rather for one who touches [a hallowed thing

מִשָּׁרְשֵׁי הַמִּצְוָה, מַה שֶּׁכָּתַבְנוּ לְמַעְלָה, לִקְבֹּעַ בְּנַפְשׁוֹתֵינוּ יִרְאַת הַמִּקְדָּשׁ וְקָדָשָׁיו, וְלָכֵן אֵין רָאוּי שֶׁיֹּאכְלוּם רַק הַטְּהוֹרִים, כִּי הַטָּהֳרָה מַעֲלָה וְכָבוֹד בָּאָדָם, כַּיָּדוּעַ לְכָל מֵבִין.

מִדִּינֵי הַמִּצְוָה, מַה שֶּׁאָמְרוּ זִכְרוֹנָם לִבְרָכָה שֶׁהַטֻּמְאָה שֶׁחַיָּבִין עָלֶיהָ הִיא שֶׁנִּטְמָא בְטֻמְאָה דְאוֹרַיְתָא שֶׁחַיָּבִין עָלֶיהָ כָּרֵת עַל בִּיאַת מִקְדָּשׁ וְקָדָשָׁיו, כְּמוֹ שֶׁכָּתַבְנוּ לְמַעְלָה; וּמַה שֶּׁאָמְרוּ זִכְרוֹנָם לִבְרָכָה שֶׁאֵין חַיָּבִין עַל אֲכִילַת קֹדֶשׁ שֶׁיֵּשׁ לוֹ מַתִּירִין עַד שֶׁיִּקָּרְבוּ מַתִּירָיו, כְּלוֹמַר הָאֵמוּרִין; וּכְמוֹ־כֵן הוֹרוּנוּ זִכְרוֹנָם לִבְרָכָה שֶׁכָּל שֶׁיֵּשׁ לוֹ מַתִּירִין אֵין חַיָּבִין עָלָיו מִשּׁוּם פִּגּוּל אוֹ נוֹתָר אוֹ מִשּׁוּם טָמֵא עַד שֶׁיִּקָּרְבוּ מַתִּירָיו כְּהִלְכָתָן; וְכָל שֶׁאֵין לוֹ מַתִּירִין, כֵּיוָן שֶׁקָּדַשׁ בִּכְלִי חַיָּבִין עָלָיו; וְיֶתֶר פְּרָטֶיהָ, מְבֹאָרִים בְּפֶרֶק י״ג מִזְּבָחִים.

וְנוֹהֶגֶת בִּזְמַן הַבַּיִת, בִּזְכָרִים וּנְקֵבוֹת. וְעוֹבֵר עָלֶיהָ וְאָכַל כַּזַּיִת בְּשַׂר קֹדֶשׁ טָהוֹר אוֹ בְּשַׂר קֹדֶשׁ טָמֵא בְעוֹדֶנּוּ טָמֵא טֻמְאָה דְאוֹרַיְתָא, בְּמֵזִיד קֹדֶם שֶׁיִּטְבֹּל, חַיָּב כָּרֵת; בְּשׁוֹגֵג מֵבִיא קָרְבָּן עוֹלֶה וְיוֹרֵד — כְּמוֹ שֶׁכָּתַבְנוּ לְמַעְלָה. וְאִם אָכַל אַחַר שֶׁטָּבַל קֹדֶם שֶׁיַּעֲרִיב שִׁמְשׁוֹ אוֹ קֹדֶם שֶׁיָּבִיא כַפָּרָתוֹ, כְּמוֹ הַיּוֹלֶדֶת שֶׁצְּרִיכָה לְהָבִיא כַפָּרָה, וְכֵן כָּל הַצָּרִיךְ לְכַפָּרָה, לוֹקֶה וְאֵינוֹ חַיָּב כָּרֵת, שֶׁנֶּאֱמַר בְּעִנְיַן כָּרֵת זֶה "וְטֻמְאָתוֹ עָלָיו", וּפֵרְשׁוּ זִכְרוֹנָם לִבְרָכָה: עַד שֶׁתִּהְיֶה כָּל טֻמְאָתוֹ עָלָיו. וְאִם

3. Since a defiled person who enters is punishable by *karéth* (Rashi). This last sentence is omitted in the Hebrew, as our author breaks off with *v'chulé* ("etc.").

4. MS Vatican and the first edition have *she-nitme'ah*, "where *she* became defiled" —i.e. a woman who gave birth.

5. It is clear from the sources that this is a scribal error for the blood of the offering: when this is sprinkled on the altar, it makes the *'émurim* permitted to be burnt on the altar, and the flesh to be eaten; TB Z'vaḥim 34a; MT *hilchoth p'sulé ha-mukdashin* xviii 16.

6. I.e. the blood of animal offerings, and the handful of flour and the frankincense of *minḥah* (meal) offerings; TB Me'ilah 10a.

7. E.g. the handful of flour from a *minḥah:* it has nothing to make it permitted for any purpose.

8. So TB Z'vaḥim 106a.

9. See note 1.

while defiled]?—Scripture states, *and to the sanctuary she shall not come*: it equates hallowed things with the Sanctuary: just as the Sanctuary is something that can lead to the loss of life,[3] so does "any hallowed thing" mean what can lead to the loss of life; and if it applies to touching, is there then loss of life for anything but eating?

At the root of the precept lies the purpose that we wrote above (§95): to establish in our spirits a reverent fear for the Sanctuary and its holy offerings. It is therefore not fitting that any but the ritually pure should eat them, since purity is a quality of excellence and honor for a man, as any understanding person knows.

Among the laws of the precept, there is what the Sages of blessed memory said: that the ritual impurity with which punishment is incurred is in a case where one became defiled[4] by a source of uncleanness by the law of the Torah, for which there is a penalty of *karéth* for entering the Sanctuary and on account of its holy offerings, as we wrote above (§123). Then there is what the Sages of blessed memory taught: that for eating a holy offering which has something that makes it permitted, no punishment is incurred until that which makes it permitted has been offered up—i.e. the *'émurim* [parts for burning on the altar].[5] Similarly, our Sages of blessed memory taught us that whatever has parts which make it permitted,[6] no penalty is incurred over it on account of *piggul* (§144) or *nothar* (§142), or because of ritual uncleanness, until those parts have been offered up in their proper way. But whatever has no parts that make it permitted,[7] once it has been consecrated in a vessel, there is punishment over it. The rest of its details are clarified in chapter 13 of the tractate *Z'vaḥim*.

It is in effect when the Temple exists, for both man and woman. If a person violated it and ate an olive's amount of ritually pure sacred meat, or defiled sacred meat, while he was yet impure through a defilement by Torah law—if deliberately, before he underwent immersion, he would be punishable by *karéth* [Divine severance of existence]; if it was unwitting, he would bring an offering of greater or lesser value, as we wrote above (§123).[8] If he ate it after he had ritual immersion but before his sun set,[9] or before he brought his atoning offering—for example, a woman who gave birth, who would have to bring an atoning offering; and so anyone who was in need of atonement—he would receive whiplashes and would not be punishable by *karéth:* for it is stated about this punishment of *karéth*, *while his uncleanness is upon him* (Leviticus 7:20)—which our Sages of blessed memory explained

הָיָה טָמֵא בְטֻמְאָה שֶׁל דִּבְרֵיהֶם אֵינוֹ לוֹקֶה, וְאֵין צָרִיךְ לוֹמַר שֶׁאֵין חַיָּב כָּרֵת, אֶלָּא מַכִּין אוֹתוֹ מַכַּת מַרְדּוּת.

[מִצְוַת קָרְבַּן יוֹלֶדֶת]

קסח שֶׁתַּקְרִיב הַיּוֹלֶדֶת קָרְבָּן כְּשֶׁיִּשְׁלְמוּ יְמֵי הַטֹּהַר לְבֵן אוֹ לְבַת, וְהוּא כֶּבֶשׂ בֶּן שְׁנָתוֹ לְעוֹלָה וּבֶן יוֹנָה אוֹ תוֹר לְחַטָּאת; וְאִם הִיא עֲנִיָּה תַּקְרִיב שְׁתֵּי תוֹרִים אוֹ שְׁנֵי בְנֵי יוֹנָה, אֶחָד לְעוֹלָה וְאֶחָד לְחַטָּאת — שֶׁנֶּאֱמַר: וּבִמְלֹאת יְמֵי טָהֳרָהּ לְבֵן אוֹ לְבַת תָּבִיא וְגוֹמֵר, וְהִיא מְחֻסֶּרֶת כַּפָּרָה עַד שֶׁתַּקְרִיב קָרְבָּנָהּ.

מִשָּׁרְשֵׁי הַמִּצְוָה, כְּדֵי שֶׁתִּתְעוֹרֵר מִתּוֹךְ הַפְּעֻלָּה לָתֵת הוֹדָאָה לַיי בָּרוּךְ הוּא שֶׁהִצִּילָהּ מֵחֶבְלֵי יוֹלֵדָה, שֶׁהוּא דָּבָר נִסִּי. וְעוֹד אָמְרוּ זִכְרוֹנָם לִבְרָכָה שֶׁהָאִשָּׁה קוֹפֶצֶת וְנִשְׁבַּעַת בְּעֵת צִירֶיהָ שֶׁלֹּא תִזָּקֵק עוֹד לְאִישׁ, וּלְפִיכָךְ צְרִיכָה כַּפָּרָה; וְעַל־כֵּן יִקָּרֵא קָרְבָּנָהּ חַטָּאת, וְנֶאֱמַר בּוֹ: וְכִפֶּר עָלֶיהָ הַכֹּהֵן.

מִדִּינֶיהָ, (כְּגוֹן) מַה שֶּׁאָמְרוּ זִכְרוֹנָם לִבְרָכָה שֶׁאֵין הַיּוֹלֶדֶת מְבִיאָה קָרְבָּנָהּ בְּיוֹם אַרְבָּעִים לְזָכָר וּבְיוֹם שְׁמֹנִים לִנְקֵבָה אֶלָּא לְמָחָר, שֶׁהוּא יוֹם אַרְבָּעִים וְאֶחָד, וְכֵן בְּיוֹם שְׁמֹנִים וְאֶחָד — שֶׁנֶּאֱמַר: וּבִמְלֹאת יְמֵי טָהֳרָהּ, כְּלוֹמַר שֶׁיִּהְיוּ שְׁלֵמִים לְגַמְרֵי; וְאִם הֱבִיאַתּוּ בְּתוֹךְ יְמֵי מְלֹאת, לֹא יָצְאָה יְדֵי חוֹבָתָהּ; עָבַר זְמַן זֶה וְלֹא הֵבִיאָה כַּפָּרָתָהּ, מְבִיאָה לְאַחַר זְמַן: וְכָל זְמַן שֶׁלֹּא הֵבִיאָה, אֲסוּרָה לֶאֱכֹל בַּקֳּדָשִׁים, וּכְמוֹ שֶׁאָמְרוּ זִכְרוֹנָם לִבְרָכָה, הֵבִיא כַּפָּרָתוֹ אוֹכֵל בַּקֳּדָשִׁים; וְכָל מְחֻסְּרֵי כַפָּרָה דִּינָם שָׁוֶה בָּזֶה; וְכָל מְחֻיְּבֵי קָרְבָּן אֵין מַקְרִיבִין קָרְבָּנָן אֶלָּא מִדַּעְתָּן, חוּץ מִמְּחֻסְּרֵי כַפָּרָה, שֶׁאֵין צְרִיכִין דַּעַת בְּעָלִים; וְיֶתֶר פְּרָטֶיהָ, בְּמַסֶּכֶת נִדָּה.

10. Literally, until.

11. But if he underwent immersion and was waiting for the sun to set, or for the time to bring his offering, "all his defilement" was no longer upon him; MT *hilchoth p'sulé ha-mukdashin* xviii 14.

12. I.e. he contracted the defilement from something which only the decree of the Sages makes a source of ritual impurity.

13. See § 12, note 4.

§168

1. See § 166, tenth and eleventh paragraphs.
2. The paragraph is based on ShM positive precept §76.
3. I.e. that she survived them.
4. TB Niddah 31b.
5. TB Z'vaḥim 112b.
6. Mishnah, N'ga'im xiv 3.
7. See §176.
8. TB N'darim 35b.

[to mean], not unless[10] all his defilement was upon him.[11] If he was ritually unclean through defilement by decree of the Sages,[12] he would receive no whiplashes; and there is no need to say that he would not be liable to *karéth;* but he should be given "lashes of disobedience."[13]

168 [THE PRECEPT OF A WOMAN'S OFFERING AFTER GIVING BIRTH]

that a woman who gave birth should bring an offering when the "days of purity"[1] over a son or a daughter are completed, this being *a lamb in its first year for an* 'olah *(burnt-offering), and a young pigeon or a turtledove for a sin-offering* (Leviticus 12:6); and if she is poor, *she shall bring two turtledoves or two young pigeons, one for an* 'olah *and one for a sin-offering* (*ibid.* 8); as it is written, *And when the days of her purification are completed, for a son or for a daughter, she shall bring*, etc. (*ibid.* 6); and she remains lacking in atonement until she brings her offering.[2]

At the root of the precept lies the purpose that she should be stirred as a result of the activity, to give thanks to the Lord, blessed is He, that He rescued her from the birth pangs,[3] which is a miraculous thing. Moreover, our Sages of blessed memory said[4] that a woman rashly vows during her labor throes that she will no longer be drawn conjugally to a man; therefore she needs atonement, and for this reason her offering is called *ḥattath* (a sin-offering); so it is stated about it, *the* kohen *shall make atonement for her* (Leviticus 12:8).

Among its laws, there is, for instance, what the Sages of blessed memory said: that a woman who gave birth does not bring her offering on the fortieth day for a male child and on the eightieth day for a female, but on the morrow, which is the forty-first day, and similarly the eighty-first day: For it is stated, *And when the days of her purification are completed* (Leviticus 12:6)—which is to say, they should be entirely complete and whole; and if she brought it within the days of completion, she would not acquit herself of her obligation.[5] If this time passed and she did not bring her atoning offering, she was to bring it after the time; but as long as she did not bring it, she would be forbidden to eat of sacred offerings; as our Sages of blessed memory said:[6] if he brought his atoning offering, he might eat of holy food; and in this, the law is the same for all who lacked atonement.[7] All those who bore the obligation of an offering could bring the offering only by their own will and consent, except those who lacked atonement: [their offerings] did not need the will and consent of the owners.[8] The rest of its details are in the Talmud tractate *Niddah.*

וְנוֹהֶגֶת בִּזְמַן הַבַּיִת, בִּנְקֵבוֹת. וְהָעוֹבֶרֶת עַל זֶה וְלֹא קֵרְבָה קָרְבָּנָהּ, בִּטְּלָה עֲשֵׂה, וְהִיא מְחֻסֶּרֶת כַּפָּרָה וַאֲסוּרָה לֶאֱכֹל בְּקָדָשִׁים; וְאוֹי לָהּ אִם תָּמוּת קֹדֶם שֶׁתַּקְרִיבֶנּוּ, וְתִשָּׂא עֲוֹנָהּ עַל נַפְשָׁהּ.

[מִצְוַת עִנְיַן טֻמְאַת מְצֹרָע]

קסט לְטַמֵּא אָדָם מְצֹרָע, כְּלוֹמַר שֶׁמִּצְוָה הִיא עָלֵינוּ שֶׁכָּל מִי שֶׁיִּהְיֶה מְצֹרָע שֶׁיָּבוֹא אֶל הַכֹּהֵן לִשְׁאֹל עַל צָרַעְתּוֹ וְהַכֹּהֵן יְטַמְּאֶנּוּ אוֹ יְטַהֲרֶנּוּ, וְהוּא יִתְנַהֵג עַל־פִּי הַתּוֹרָה הַכְּתוּבָה כַּאֲשֶׁר יְצַוֶּנּוּ הַכֹּהֵן; וְלֹא יִקַּח הַדָּבָר כְּחֹלִי הַבָּא בְמִקְרֶה, אֶלָּא יִתֵּן לֵב עָלָיו וְיֵדַע כִּי גֹדֶל עֲווֹנוֹ גָּרַם אוֹתוֹ — שֶׁנֶּאֱמַר: אָדָם כִּי יִהְיֶה בְעוֹר בְּשָׂרוֹ וְגוֹמֵר, וְהוּבָא אֶל אַהֲרֹן הַכֹּהֵן אוֹ אֶל אַחַד מִבָּנָיו הַכֹּהֲנִים.

וּמִצְוָה זוֹ כּוֹלֶלֶת כָּל מִשְׁפְּטֵי צָרַעַת אָדָם, מַה שֶׁמִּמֶּנָּה טָמֵא וּמַה שֶּׁמִּמֶּנָּה טָהוֹר, וּמַה שֶּׁמִּמֶּנָּה צָרִיךְ הֶסְגֵּר וּמַה שֶּׁאֵינוֹ צָרִיךְ הֶסְגֵּר, וּמַה שֶּׁצָּרִיךְ עִם הַהֶסְגֵּר גִּלּוּחַ אוֹ אֵינוֹ צָרִיךְ גִּלּוּחַ, כְּלוֹמַר תִּגְלַחַת הַנֶּתֶק, וּמִלְּבַד זֶה דִּינִין הַרְבֵּה.

וְעִנְיַן הַצָּרַעַת, שֶׁיַּלְבִּין מָקוֹם אֶחָד אוֹ הַרְבֵּה מְקוֹמוֹת בְּעוֹר בְּשַׂר הָאָדָם וְיִהְיוּ אוֹתָן הַמְּקוֹמוֹת לְבָנִים הַרְבֵּה עַד שֶׁיִּדְמֶה הַלֹּבֶן שֶׁלָּהֶם לְלֹבֶן קְרוּם בֵּיצָה וּלְמַעְלָה מִמֶּנּוּ בְּלַבְנִינוּת; אֲבָל כָּל זְמַן שֶׁיִּהְיֶה כֵּהֶה לְמַטָּה מִמַּרְאֵה קְרוּם בֵּיצָה, אֵין צָרַעַת אֶלָּא בֹּהַק הוּא, כְּלוֹמַר חֹלִי אַחֵר שֶׁאֵינוֹ מִמִּין צָרַעַת כְּלָל, אֶלָּא כְּמִינֵי הַגָּרָב וּשְׁאָר מִינֵי נְגָעִים הַנַּעֲשִׂים בָּאָדָם.

וְאַרְבַּע מַרְאוֹת לֹבֶן שֶׁל צָרַעַת הֵן בְּעוֹר בְּשַׂר הָאָדָם: הַשְּׁתַּיִם הֵן אָבוֹת, וְהֵן שְׂאֵת וּבַהֶרֶת, וְהַשְּׁתַּיִם תּוֹלָדוֹת לָהֶן, כְּלוֹמַר שֶׁהֵן לְמַטָּה בְלֹבֶן מֵאֵלּוּ הַשְּׁתַּיִם שֶׁנִּקְרָאִים אָבוֹת; וְזֶהוּ אָמְרָם זִכְרוֹנָם לִבְרָכָה: מַרְאוֹת נְגָעִים שְׁתַּיִם שֶׁהֵן אַרְבַּע, בַּהֶרֶת וְסַפַּחְתָּהּ, שְׂאֵת וְסַפַּחְתָּהּ; וּפֵרוּשׁ סַפַּחְתָּהּ כְּלוֹמַר תּוֹלַדְתָּהּ, שֶׁאֵין לְשׁוֹן סַפַּחַת אֶלָּא לְשׁוֹן טְפֵלָה.

9. I.e. of remaining without atonement.

§169 1. Or mange (both conjectural); Leviticus 13:33. The first two paragraphs are based on ShM positive precept §101. It should be noted that throughout, the Hebrew terms *tzara'ath* and *m'tzora* have been so left, in transliteration. The standard translations of "leprosy" and "leper" derive from the fact that the Greek *lepra* originally meant certain skin diseases and was later used for leprosy (see e.g. E.V. Hulse, "The nature of biblical 'leprosy'," *Palestine Exploration Quarterly*, July-December 1975, pp. 88–90). The Torah's term *tzara'ath* may possibly mean some types of psoriasis (which, tantalizingly, has a slight phonetic similarity) and favus, but no certain conclusions can be reached from present-day knowledge. (Cf. also Julius Preuss, *Biblisch-talmudische Medizin*, Berlin 1911, chapter 12.)

It is in effect when the Temple exists, for women. If one violated it and did not bring her offering, she would thus disobey a positive precept, and she would be forbidden to eat of holy offerings. And woe to her if she should die before bringing it, thus bearing the sin[9] on her soul.

[THE PRECEPT REGARDING THE RITUAL UNCLEANNESS OF A M'TZORA]

169 to declare a *m'tzora* unclean: in other words, it is a religious duty for us that whoever has an affliction of *tzara'ath* should come to the *kohen* to ask about his skin ailment, and the *kohen* will declare him ritually impure or pure. He should behave in accord with the Written Torah, as the *kohen* will command him, and not take the matter as an illness that occurs by chance; rather he should give thought to it and know that the enormity of his wrongdoing caused it. For it is stated, *When a man shall have on the skin of his flesh . . . then he shall be brought to Aaron the* kohen *or to one of his sons the* kohanim (Leviticus 13:2).

This precept includes all the rules of human *tzara'ath* afflictions: which kinds are ritually unclean, and which clean; which kinds require quarantine, and which do not require quarantine; which require, with the quarantine, shaving the hair, and which do not require it—i.e. the shaving for a *nethek* (alopecia);[1] and many laws apart from this.

In substance, it is a *tzara'ath* ailment when one or many places on the skin of a man's flesh turn white, those places being so very light that their whiteness resembles the whiteness of the membrane about an egg, or even goes beyond it in lightness. But as long as it is duller than the appearance of an egg's membrane, this is not a *tzara'ath* ailment but rather *bohak* (a dull-bright shiny patch of skin):[2] in other words, another illness which is not any kind of *tzara'ath* disease at all, but like the varieties of rashes and other sorts of afflictions that form in the human being.[3]

There are four appearances [shades] of white for *tzara'ath* in the skin of a man's flesh: Two are major, primary types, i.e. *se'éth* (heightening) and *bahereth* (shiny white); and two are derivatives of them: i.e. in degree of whiteness they are lower than these two, which are called primary types. This is why our Sages of blessed memory said:[2] The appearances of *tzara'ath* afflictions are two which are four: the *bahereth* and its *sapaḥath*, the *se'éth* and its *sapaḥath*. The meaning of "its *sapaḥath*" is in the sense of "its derivative": for the term is nothing more than an expression for an adjunct (something auxiliary).

וְאַרְבַּע הַמַּרְאוֹת אֵלּוּ דִּמּוּ אוֹתָן חֲכָמִים אַחַת לְצֶמֶר לָבָן נָקִי, וְזֶהוּ שְׂאֵת, וְאַחַת לְשֶׁלֶג, וְזֶהוּ בַּהֶרֶת, וְאַחַת לְסִיד הַהֵיכָל, וְהִיא תוֹלֶדֶת בַּהֶרֶת, וְאַחַת לִקְרוּם בֵּיצָה, וְהִיא תוֹלֶדֶת שְׂאֵת. אַרְבַּע מַרְאוֹת אֵלֶּה הֵם הַטְּמֵאִים, וּמִצְטָרְפִין זֶה עִם זֶה לְטַמֵּא. וְכָל שֶׁאֵין מַכִּיר אוֹתָן בְּחִלּוּקֵיהֶן וּשְׁמוֹתֵיהֶן אֵינוֹ דָן אֶת הַנֶּגַע אֶלָּא עַל־פִּי מַכִּיר, וּכְמוֹ שֶׁנֹּאמַר לְמַטָּה בְּדִינֵי הַמִּצְוָה.

מִשָּׁרְשֵׁי הַמִּצְוָה, לִקְבֹּעַ בְּנַפְשׁוֹתֵינוּ כִּי הַשְׁגָּחַת הַשֵּׁם בָּרוּךְ הוּא פְּרָטִית עַל כָּל אֶחָד וְאֶחָד מִבְּנֵי־אָדָם, וְכִי עֵינָיו פְּקוּחוֹת עַל כָּל דַּרְכֵיהֶם, כְּמוֹ שֶׁכָּתוּב: כִּי עֵינָיו עַל דַּרְכֵי אִישׁ וְכָל צְעָדָיו יִרְאֶה; וְלָכֵן הֻזְהַרְנוּ לָתֵת לֵב אֶל הַחֳלִי הָרַע וְלַחְשֹׁב כִּי הַחֵטְא גָּרַם אוֹתוֹ; וּכְבָר אָמְרוּ זִכְרוֹנָם לִבְרָכָה כִּי בְחֵטְא לָשׁוֹן הָרָע יָבוֹא בָּרֹב, וְלֹא נִקָּחֶנּוּ דֶּרֶךְ מִקְרֶה; וְיֵשׁ לָנוּ לָבוֹא אֶל הַכֹּהֵן, שֶׁהוּא הָעוֹמֵד לְכַפָּרַת הַחוֹטְאִים, וְעִם חֶבְרַת הַמְכַפֵּר אוּלַי יְהַרְהֵר בִּתְשׁוּבָה וְיִסָּגֵר קְצָת יָמִים כְּדֵי שֶׁיָּשִׁיב אֶל לִבּוֹ עִנְיָנָיו בְּמָתוּן, וִיפַשְׁפֵּשׁ בְּמַעֲשָׂיו.

וְלִפְעָמִים יִסָּגֵר שְׁנֵי הֶסְגֵּרִין, שֶׁמָּא הִרְהֵר תְּשׁוּבָה וְלֹא תְשׁוּבָה שְׁלֵמָה לְגַמְרֵי, כְּאִלּוּ תֹּאמַר עַל דֶּרֶךְ מָשָׁל שֶׁחָשַׁב לְהַחֲזִיר מַחֲצִית גְּזֵלָתוֹ, וְאָז יְחַדֵּשׁ בּוֹ הַשֵּׁם קְצָת סִימָנִין שֶׁיִּסָּגֵר שֵׁנִית, אוּלַי יַשְׁלִים תְּשׁוּבָתוֹ וְיִטָּהֵר לְגַמְרֵי.

וְכָל עִנְיַן הֶסְגֵּרִין אֵלּוּ יוֹרֶה הַשְׁגָּחָתוֹ בָּרוּךְ הוּא עַל כָּל דַּרְכֵי הָאָדָם, אַחַת לְאַחַת. וּלְפִי שֶׁהַדֵּעוֹת רַבּוֹת בְּהַשְׁגָּחַת הָאֵל עַל כָּל בְּרוּאָיו, יָבוֹאוּ בָהּ הַרְבֵּה פְּסוּקִים בַּמִּקְרָא, וְהַרְבֵּה מִצְווֹת לְהוֹרוֹת עַל הָעִנְיָן, מִהְיוֹתוֹ פִּנָּה גְדוֹלָה בְּתוֹרָתֵנוּ.

שֶׁיֵּשׁ כִּתּוֹת בְּנֵי־אָדָם יַחְשְׁבוּ כִּי הַשְׁגָּחַת הַשֵּׁם בָּרוּךְ הוּא עַל כָּל הַמִּינִין בִּפְרָט, בֵּין אֲנָשִׁים אוֹ כָּל שְׁאָר בַּעֲלֵי־חַיִּים; וְיֵשׁ מֵהֶן כִּתּוֹת יַחְשְׁבוּ כִּי הַשְׁגָּחַת

2. Mishnah, N'ga'im i 1. In general, the parenthetical translations in this section are based on this source and on S.R. Hirsch on Pentateuch. On *se'éth* see MT *hilchoth tum'ath tzara'ath* i 6.

3. The paragraph is based on MT *ibid.* 1.

3a. I.e. the entrance-hall and two holy chambers of the Sanctuary, whose walls were whitewashed anew every Passover (Mishnah, Middoth iii 4).

4. I.e. if half the minimal area has one kind and half has another kind, the two are considered together as one *tzara'ath* condition; Mishnah *ibid.* 3.

5. I.e. among the *kohanim*, whose task it was to judge *tzara'ath*.

6. TB Sh'vu'oth 6a.

7. Literally, the evil tongue; TB 'Arachin 15b.

8. Leviticus 13:4.

9. *Ibid.* 5.

As regards these four appearances [shades], our Sages likened one to pure white wool—i.e. the *se'éth* (heightening); one to snow, i.e. the *bahereth* (shiny white); one to the plaster in the *héchal*,[3a] i.e. the derivative of the *bahereth;* and one to the membrane of an egg, i.e. the derivative of *se'éth*. These four appearances are of the ritually unclean kinds, and they can be considered together, as one,[4] to declare [the person] defiled. But whoever[5] cannot recognize them by their differences and their names is not to judge a *tzara'ath* ailment [himself] but only through someone who does recognize them,[6] as we will state below, among the laws of the precept.

At the root of the precept lies the purpose to establish firmly in our spirits that the watchful care of the Eternal Lord is individual, over each and every one among human beings, and His eyes are open to observe all their ways: as it is written, *For His eyes are upon the ways of a man, and He sees all his steps* (Job 34:21). Hence He adjured us to give thought to this evil disease and to consider that sin caused it. Long ago our Sages of blessed memory said that it comes mostly for the sin of evil gossip,[7] and we should not assume it [to happen] by way of chance. We are then to come to the *kohen*, who stands [as minister] for the atonement of sinners. In the company of the agent of atonement, perhaps he [the sinner] will meditate on repentance. Then he will be shut away (quarantined) for a few days,[8] so that he can think over his affairs unhurriedly, and examine his deeds.

At times he will be shut away for two periods of quarantine:[9] Perhaps [the first time] he meditated on repentance but there was no complete return in penitence—as you might say, by way of example, that he decided to return half of what he had seized in robbery; whereupon the Eternal Lord would create in him anew a few signs [of affliction] so that he should be quarantined a second time: perhaps he will complete his repentance, and thus become completely purified.

Now, the whole subject of these quarantines indicates His providential watch (blessed is He) over all the ways of a man, one by one. But because there are many opinions about God's providential care for all His creatures, there are many verses that apply to it in Scripture, and many precepts to teach about the subject, since it is a great cornerstone principle in our Torah.

For there are certain groups of people who think that the watchful care of the Eternal Lord (blessed is He) is over all species individually, both over humans and over other living creatures. Then there are

הַשֵּׁם בָּרוּךְ הוּא עַל כָּל עִנְיְנֵי הָעוֹלָם, בֵּין בַּעֲלֵי־חַיִּים אוֹ כָּל שְׁאָר דְּבָרִים, כְּלוֹמַר שֶׁלֹּא יִתְנוֹעֵעַ דָּבָר אֶחָד קָטָן בָּעוֹלָם הַזֶּה רַק בְּחֶפְצוֹ בָּרוּךְ הוּא וּבִגְזֵרָתוֹ, עַד שֶׁיַּחְשְׁבוּ כִּי בִנְפֹל עָלֶה אֶחָד מִן הָאִילָן, הוּא גָזַר עָלָיו שֶׁיִּפֹּל, וְאִי אֶפְשָׁר שֶׁיִּתְאַחֵר אוֹ יִקְדַּם זְמַן נְפִילָתָהּ אֲפִלּוּ רֶגַע; וְזֶה דַעַת רָחוֹק הַרְבֵּה מִן הַשֵּׂכֶל.

וְיֵשׁ כִּתּוֹת רָעוֹת יַחְשְׁבוּ שֶׁלֹּא יָשִׂים הַשְׁגָּחָתוֹ בָּרוּךְ הוּא כְּלָל בְּכָל עִנְיְנֵי הָעוֹלָם הַשָּׁפֵל, בֵּין בָּאֲנָשִׁים אוֹ בִשְׁאָר בַּעֲלֵי־חַיִּים; וְהוּא דַעַת הַכּוֹפְרִים, רַע וָמָר.

וַאֲנַחְנוּ בַּעֲלֵי הַדָּת הָאֲמִתִּית, לְפִי מַה שֶּׁשָּׁמַעְתִּי, נָשִׂים הַשְׁגָּחָתוֹ בָּרוּךְ הוּא עַל כָּל מִינֵי בַּעֲלֵי־הַחַיִּים בִּכְלָל, כְּלוֹמַר שֶׁכָּל מִין מִן הַמִּינִין הַנִּבְרָאִין בָּעוֹלָם יִתְקַיֵּם לְעוֹלָם, לֹא יִכְלֶה וְיֹאבַד כֻּלּוֹ, כִּי בְהַשְׁגָּחָתוֹ יִמָּצֵא קִיּוּם לְכָל דָּבָר; וּבְמִין הָאָדָם נַאֲמִין כִּי הַשְׁגָּחָתוֹ בָּרוּךְ הוּא עַל כָּל אֶחָד וְאֶחָד בִּפְרָט, וְהוּא הַמֵּבִין אֶל כָּל מַעֲשֵׂיהֶם. וְכֵן קִבַּלְנוּ מִגְּדוֹלֵינוּ, וְגַם נִמְצָא עַל זֶה הַרְבֵּה כְתוּבִים יוֹרוּ כִּי הָעִנְיָן כֵּן.

וְלָכֵן הִזְהִירַתְנוּ הַתּוֹרָה כִּי בְהַגִּיעַ אֶל הָאָדָם הַחֹלִי הָרַע, וְהוּא הַצָּרַעַת, שֶׁלֹּא יִקָּחֶנּוּ דֶּרֶךְ מִקְרֶה, רַק יַחְשֹׁב מִיָּד כִּי עֲווֹנוֹתָיו גָּרְמוּ, וְיַרְחִיק מֵחֶבְרַת בְּנֵי־אָדָם כְּאָדָם הַמֻּרְחָק מֵרֹעַ מַעֲשָׂיו, וְיִתְחַבֵּר אֶל הַמְכַפֵּר הַמְרַפֵּא שֶׁבֶר הַחֵטְא וְיַרְאֶה אֵלָיו נִגְעוֹ, וּבַעֲצָתוֹ וּבִדְבָרָיו וּבְפִשְׁפּוּשׁ מַעֲשָׂיו יוּסַר מֵעָלָיו הַנֶּגַע; כִּי הָאֵל בָּרוּךְ הוּא שֶׁמַּשְׁגִּיחַ עָלָיו תָּמִיד יִרְאֶה מַעֲשֵׂה תְשׁוּבָתוֹ וְיִרְפָּאֵהוּ; וְזֶהוּ עִנְיַן הַהֶסְגֵּרִין כְּמוֹ שֶׁאָמַרְנוּ.

מִדִּינֵי הַמִּצְוָה, כְּגוֹן מַה שֶּׁאָמְרוּ זִכְרוֹנָם לִבְרָכָה שֶׁאֵין מַרְאוֹת נְגָעִים אֵלּוּ שֶׁאָמַרְנוּ מְטַמְּאִין עַד שֶׁיֵּרָאוּ עֲמֻקִּין מִן הָעוֹר, וְלֹא שֶׁיִּהְיוּ עֲמֻקִּין מַמָּשׁ בְּמִשּׁוּשׁ אֶלָּא שֶׁיֵּרָאוּ כֵן בִּרְאִיַּת הָעַיִן, כְּעֵין מַרְאֵה הַחַמָּה, שֶׁנִּדְמֵית לָרוֹאִים עֲמֻקָּה מִן

10. I.e. from the great scholars and teachers; this and the past two paragraphs are based on Rambam, *Guide* III 17.

11. TB Sh'vu'oth 6b; MT *hilchoth tum'ath tzara'ath* i 6.

12. Mishnah, N'ga'im vi 1; MT *ibid.* 7.

groups among them who believe that the watchful care of the Eternal Lord (blessed is He) is over all things of the world, whether living creatures or any other things: In other words, not one small entity will move in this world except by His desire (blessed is He) and by His decree—to such an extent that they believe that when one leaf falls from a tree, He decreed over it that it should fall; and it is impossible for the time of its fall to be delayed or advanced by even a moment. But this view is very removed from human reason.

Then there are evil groups that think He (blessed is He) does not set His watchful care at all about any matters of this lowly world, whether about humans or other living creatures. This is the view of the heretics—evil and bitter.

However, according to what I have heard,[10] we, masters of the true religion, assume His watchful care (blessed is He) to be over all species of living creatures generally: In other words, every one of the species created in the world will permanently endure; it will never end and perish entirely, as by His providential care a way of existence will be found for everything. As for the human species, [it is our belief] that His providential care (blessed is He) is for each and every one individually, and it is He *who understands all their doings* (Psalms 33:15). So we received [the teaching] from our great luminaries; and we will also find many verses about it which show that the matter is so.

Therefore the Torah cautioned us that when this evil disease befalls a man, namely, a *tzara'ath* affliction, he should not take it as a chance happening, but rather think at once that his sins caused it. So let him draw apart from people's company, like a man who becomes outcast for the evil of his deeds. And let him associate with the one who makes atonement, who heals the injury of the sin, and let him show him his affliction. By his counsel and his words, and by his own examination of his deeds, the affliction will be removed from him: for God (blessed is He) who keeps watch over him constantly, will see the act of his repentance and will heal him. This is the reason for the quarantines, as we have stated.

Among the laws of the precept, there is what the Sages of blessed memory taught:[11] that these appearances of afflictions which we described do not render a person defiled until they seem deeper than the skin—not that they should actually be deeper to the touch, but they should seem so in the eye's sight, just as the light of the sun appears to the observer deeper than the shade. Then there is what they said,[12]

הַצֵּל; וּמַה שֶּׁאָמְרוּ שֶׁשִּׁעוּר הַצָּרַעַת הוּא כִּגְרִיס הַקִּלְקִי, כְּלוֹמַר שֶׁאִם יֵרָאוּ בְעוֹר בְּשַׂר הָאָדָם מֵאוֹתָן מַרְאוֹת כְּשִׁעוּר זֶה, נִקְרָא צָרַעַת, אֲבָל פָּחוֹת מִזֶּה הַשִּׁעוּר אֵין זֶה צָרַעַת; וְהַשִּׁעוּר הַזֶּה הוּא מָקוֹם מְרֻבָּע בָּעוֹר מַחֲזִיק שֵׁשׁ שְׂעָרוֹת רֹחַב וְשֵׁשׁ אֹרֶךְ, שֶׁהוּא בְתִשְׁבֹּרֶת מְקוֹם שְׁלֹשִׁים וָשֵׁשׁ שְׂעָרוֹת. הָיָה בְרָחְבּוֹ חָמֵשׁ שְׂעָרוֹת, אֲפִלּוּ אָרְכּוֹ אַמָּה אֵין זֶה צָרַעַת, דְּרֹחַב שֵׁשׁ שְׂעָרוֹת בָּעִינָן.

כָּל מָקוֹם שֶׁנֶּאֱמַר בַּתּוֹרָה בַּהֶרֶת, הוּא הַדִּין לְאַרְבַּע הַמַּרְאוֹת. וּשְׁלֹשָׁה סִימָנֵי טֻמְאָה הֵן: שֵׂעָר לָבָן, מִחְיַת בָּשָׂר חַי, פִּשְׂיוֹן. כֵּיצַד, מִי שֶׁנּוֹלַד בּוֹ שְׂאֵת אוֹ סַפַּחַת אוֹ בַהֶרֶת וּבָהּ שֵׂעָר לָבָן אוֹ מִחְיַת בָּשָׂר חַי, כְּשֶׁיִּרְאֶנּוּ הַכֹּהֵן יֹאמַר לוֹ מִיָּד שֶׁטָּמֵא מֻחְלָט הוּא. לֹא הָיָה בוֹ שֵׂעָר לָבָן וְלֹא מִחְיָה, יַסְגִּירֶנּוּ שִׁבְעַת יָמִים; וְאִם פָּשָׂה הַנֶּגַע, יַחְלִיטֶנּוּ מִיָּד גַּם־כֵּן, שֶׁגַּם הַפִּשְׂיוֹן הוּא סִימַן טֻמְאָה, כְּמוֹ שֶׁאָמַרְנוּ. לֹא נוֹלַד בּוֹ אֶחָד מִשְּׁלֹשָׁה סִימָנֵי טֻמְאָה בְּשָׁבוּעַ שֶׁל הֶסְגֵּר רִאשׁוֹן, יַסְגִּירֶנּוּ שָׁבוּעַ שֵׁנִי, וְאִם נוֹלַד בּוֹ אֶחָד מִשְּׁלֹשָׁה סִימָנֵי טֻמְאָה אֵלּוּ יַחְלִיטֶנּוּ לְטֻמְאָה, וְאִם לָאו יְטַהֲרֶנּוּ; שֶׁאֵין הֶסְגֵּר לְצָרַעַת עוֹר בָּשָׂר יוֹתֵר מִשְּׁנֵי שָׁבוּעוֹת. וְאִם אַחַר כָּךְ שֶׁטִּהֵר אוֹתוֹ יִוָּלֵד בּוֹ אֶחָד מִשְּׁלֹשָׁה סִימָנֵי הַטֻּמְאָה, יְטַמְּאֶנּוּ מִיָּד גַּם־כֵּן, שֶׁאוֹתָם שְׁלֹשָׁה סִימָנֵי הַטֻּמְאָה לְעוֹלָם מְטַמְּאִין, בֵּין בִּתְחִלָּה בֵּין אַחַר הַהֶסְגֵּרִין.

נֶגַע הַצָּרַעַת שֶׁהָיְתָה לְבָנָה הַרְבֵּה, כְּמוֹ הַצֶּמֶר הַלָּבָן וְהַשֶּׁלֶג, וְאַחַר־כָּךְ כֵּהָה וְחָזְרָה כְּמַרְאֵה קְרוּם הַבֵּיצָה וְסִיד הַהֵיכָל, אֵין זֶה סִימַן טָהֳרָה כְּלָל אֶלָּא הֲרֵי הִיא בְטֻמְאָתָהּ מַמָּשׁ כְּמוֹ בַתְּחִלָּה, עַד שֶׁיִּכְהֶה לְמַטָּה מִלֹּבֶן קְרוּם בֵּיצָה; וְאָז הוּא נִקְרָא בֹּהַק, וְטָהוֹר.

וְאִם תִּשְׁאַל: אִם כֵּן, מַהוּ שֶׁנֶּאֱמַר בַּתּוֹרָה: וְהִנֵּה כֵּהָה הַנֶּגַע וְלֹא פָשָׂה הַנֶּגַע בָּעוֹר וְטִהֲרוֹ הַכֹּהֵן — תְּשׁוּבָתְךָ, שֶׁזֶּה נֶאֱמַר בְּשֶׁכֵּהָה הַנֶּגַע לְמַטָּה מִקְּרוּם בֵּיצָה,

13. MT *ibid.* 9.
14. I.e. a derivative adjunct; see above, fourth paragraph.
15. MT *ibid.* 10, based on Mishnah, N'ga'im iii 3, vii 3, etc.
16. Mishnah, N'ga'im iv 7; MT *ibid.* 11.

that the minimal size of an affliction is as a Cilician bean: in other words, if any of these phenomena appear on the skin of a man's flesh on an area of this size, it is called *tzara'ath*, but if on less than this amount, it is not. In surface measure it is a square area on the skin that can contain six hairs in the breadth and six hairs in the length, which means an area of thirty-six square hairsbreadths. But if there were only five hairsbreadths in the width, then even if the length is a cubit, it is not a *tzara'ath* affliction—for a width of six hairsbreadths is a required condition.

Wherever the term *bahereth* (shiny white) is stated in the Torah, the law is the same for all four appearances [shades of white].[13] There are three signs of ritual impurity: white hair, raw flesh, and spreading. How [is this rule implemented]? When there arises on a person's body a *se'éth* (heightening), *sapaḥath*,[14] or *bahereth*, if there is white hair or quick raw flesh in it, when the *kohen* sees it, he is to tell him at once that this is absolutely unclean. If there was no white hair or quick flesh in it, he is to shut him away in quarantine for seven days. If the affliction then spreads, he likewise rules it at once [to be ritually unclean]: for spreading is also a sign of defilement, as we stated. If not one of the three signs of impurity arose in it in this [first] week of quarantine, he is to shut him away for a second week. If one of the three signs of uncleanness developed in it then, he rules it ritually unclean; if not, he declares him ritually pure: for there can be no quarantine over a *tzara'ath* ailment of the skin of the flesh for more than two weeks. If after the time he declared him ritually clean, one of the three signs of impurity develops, he is to declare him, likewise, defiled at once:[15] for those three signs of ritual impurity always bring defilement, whether originally or after quarantines.

If a *tzara'ath* ailment was intensely white, like white wool or snow, after which it became dulled and appeared in turn like the appearance of an egg's membrane or plaster of the *héchal*—this is not a sign of ritual purification at all. It is rather in its actual impurity, as at the beginning, until it becomes duller than the brightness of an egg's membrane. Then it is called *bohak* (tetter), and it is ritually clean.[16]

Now, you might ask: If so, in what sense is it stated in the Torah, *and behold, if the affliction has become dim and the affliction has not spread in the skin, then the* kohen *shall pronounce him clean* (Lev. 13:6)? The answer for you is that this was stated about a case where the affliction became duller than the membrane of an egg; but if it is as an egg's membrane or

אֲבָל בִּקְרוּם בֵּיצָה וּלְמַעְלָה מִמֶּנּוּ אֵין זֶה כֵהוּי, שֶׁעֲדַיִן מִכְּלַל מַרְאוֹת הַטְּמֵאִים הוּא.

וּמַה שֶּׁנֶּאֱמַר "וְלֹא פָשָׂה הַנֶּגַע בָּעוֹר וְטִהֲרוֹ", יוֹרֶה שֶׁכָּל זְמַן שֶׁלֹּא פָשָׂה כְּלָל וְלֹא נוֹלַד בּוֹ אֶחָד מִשְּׁלֹשָׁה סִימָנֵי הַטֻּמְאָה שֶׁאָמַרְנוּ, אַף־עַל־פִּי שֶׁלֹּא כֵהָה אֶלָּא עָמַד בְּעֵינָיו, מִכֵּיוָן שֶׁלֹּא פָשָׂה טָהוֹר הוּא.

וְדִינֵי הַמְּקוֹמוֹת שֶׁבָּאָדָם שֶׁאֵין מִתְטַמְּאִין מִשּׁוּם צָרַעַת, וְדִינֵי שִׂעוּרֵי מִחְיָה וּפִשְׂיוֹן וְשֵׂעָר לָבָן גַּם־כֵּן, בְּכַמָּה מְטַמֵּא; וְדִינֵי נִגְעֵי הָרֹאשׁ וְהַזָּקָן, וְעִנְיָנוֹ שֶׁהוּא נְפִילַת הַשֵּׂעָר שֶׁבָּהֶם מֵעִקָּרוֹ וְיִשָּׁאֵר מָקוֹם פָּנוּי, וְזֶהוּ נֶתֶק, וְאֵין נֶתֶק פָּחוּת מִכִּגְרִיס; וְדִינֵי כֵּיצַד מְגַלְּחִין אוֹתָהּ, וְסִימָנֵי טֻמְאָתוֹ וְטָהֳרָתוֹ; וְדִין מַה שֶּׁאָמְרוּ שֶׁהַכֹּל מִתְטַמְּאִין בִּנְגָעִים, וַאֲפִלּוּ קָטָן בֶּן יוֹמוֹ וְהָעֲבָדִים, אֲבָל לֹא גוֹיִים וְלֹא גֵר תּוֹשָׁב; וְדִין מַה שֶּׁאָמְרוּ שֶׁהַכֹּל כְּשֵׁרִים לִרְאוֹת הַנְּגָעִים, אֲבָל הַטֻּמְאָה וְהַטָּהֳרָה תְּלוּיָה בְּיַד כֹּהֵן; כֵּיצַד, כֹּהֵן שֶׁאֵינוֹ יוֹדֵעַ לִרְאוֹת, חָכָם יִשְׂרָאֵל רוֹאֵהוּ וְאוֹמֵר לוֹ לַכֹּהֵן "אֱמֹר טָמֵא" וְהוּא אוֹמֵר טָמֵא, אוֹ "אֱמֹר טָהוֹר" וְהוּא אוֹמֵר טָהוֹר; וְיֶתֶר רִבֵּי פְרָטֶיהָ, מְבֹאָרִים בְּמַסֶּכֶת נְגָעִים.

וְנוֹהֶגֶת דִּינֵי צָרַעַת בִּזְכָרִים וּנְקֵבוֹת, בְּכָל זְמַן שֶׁיִּהְיוּ לָנוּ הַכֹּהֲנִים בְּקִיאִין רוֹאִין אוֹתָם; כֵּן נִרְאֶה מִדִּבְרֵי הָרַמְבָּ"ם זִכְרוֹנוֹ לִבְרָכָה. וְאַף־עַל־פִּי שֶׁאִי אֶפְשָׁר לְהָבִיא קָרְבָּן עַכְשָׁיו, לִכְשֶׁיִּבָּנֶה בֵּית הַמִּקְדָּשׁ וְיִהְיֶה אֶפְשָׁר לְהָבִיא קָרְבָּן בְּטָהֳרָתוֹ מִצָּרַעְתּוֹ יָבִיא קָרְבָּן. וְכָל מִי שֶׁנִּצְטָרַע וְלֹא הִתְנַהֵג עַל־פִּי הַתּוֹרָה הַכְּתוּבָה בִּמְצֹרָע, אֶלָּא שֶׁלָּקַח הַדָּבָר בְּדֶרֶךְ מִקְרֶה וְלֹא חָשׁ לָבוֹא אֶל הַכֹּהֵן וּלְהַרְאוֹתָהּ לוֹ, בִּטֵּל עֲשֵׂה זֶה; וּמִן הַדּוֹמֶה שֶׁיִּהְיֶה עָנְשׁוֹ שֶׁתִּדְבַּק בּוֹ הַצָּרַעַת לְעוֹלָם; וְלַטּוֹבִים יֵיטִיב הַשֵּׁם וִירַפֵּא.

וּכְבָר כָּתַבְתִּי לְמַעְלָה, סֵדֶר "בַּיּוֹם הַשְּׁמִינִי" בְּטֻמְאַת שְׁמֹנָה שְׁרָצִים מִצְוָה ד׳

17. MT *ibid.*
18. Mishnah, N'ga'im vi 8.
19. *Ibid.* i 5, iv 1 and 6, etc.
20. *Ibid.* i 5, iv 4.
21. MT *hilchoth tum'ath tzara'ath* viii 1, based on Sifra to Leviticus 13:31.
22. Sifra *ibid.* (*thazri'a, perek* 8).
23. Mishnah, N'ga'im x 5.
24. *Ibid.* 1, 3, 9.
25. *Ibid.* iii 1, TB 'Arachin 3a; MT *ibid.* ix 1.
26. Mishnah, N'ga'im iii 1.
27. MT *hilchoth tum'ath tzara'ath* xi 6.
28. As a *m'tzora* is required to do when he becomes ritually clean: Leviticus 14:10.

whiter, this is not dulling: for it is still in the category of the impure appearances [shades].[17]

As to the statement, *and the affliction has not spread in the skin, then the* kohen *shall pronounce him clean*, this teaches that as long as it did not spread at all, and none of the three signs of impurity which we mentioned developed, then even if it did not grow duller but stayed in its state of appearance, since it did not spread it is ritually clean.[17]

Then there are the laws of those [body] areas of a man which do not bring defilement on account of *tzara'ath* infection;[18] the laws of the minimal areas for quick raw flesh and spreading,[19] and for white hair as well[20]—in what coverage it defiles. And [we have] the laws of afflictions of the head [pate] and the beard: in substance, they are the falling out of their hair by the roots, leaving a bald (hairless) area, which is a *nethek* (alopecia).[21] There can be no *nethek* [deserving the name, on an area] smaller than a *garis* (bean).[22] And we have laws on how it is to be shaved,[23] and the signs of its ritual uncleanness and purity;[24] the law that the Sages said:[25] that all can become defiled by the afflictions, even a one-day-old child and servants, but not heathens or a *gér toshav* (a heathen who renounced idolatry); and the law that they taught, that all are fit (authorized) to discern afflictions, but declaring them ritually unclean or clean lies only in the power of the *kohen*. How [would they work]? If a *kohen* does not know how to discern it, a learned Israelite scrutinizes it, and he tells the *kohen* "Say: unclean"; and he says, "Unclean." Or, "Say: clean," and he says, "Clean."[26]

[These] and its many other details are explained in the Mishnah tractate *N'ga'im*. The laws of *tzara'ath* are in force at any time that we have *kohanim* of clear lineage to examine them; so it appears from the words of Rambam of blessed memory.[27] And though it is not possible to bring an offering now,[28] when the Sanctuary is rebuilt and it will be possible to bring an offering on becoming ritually cleansed of his ailment, he will bring an offering. If anyone became a *m'tzora* and did not conduct himself according to what is written in the Torah about a man with this affliction, but took the matter as a chance happening and did not hasten to come to the *kohen* and show it to him, he would disobey this positive precept. And as it seems, his punishment should be that the *tzara'ath* should cling to him forever. But to the good, the Eternal Lord will do good, and He will give healing.

Now, I have already written above, in *sidrah sh'mini*, in connection with the defilement of eight swarming creatures—the fourth positive

[סי׳ קנ״ט], שֶׁהָרַמְבָּ״ן זִכְרוֹנוֹ לִבְרָכָה לֹא יִמְנֶה בְּחֶשְׁבּוֹן הַמִּצְווֹת דִּינֵי הַטֻּמְאוֹת כֻּלָּן, כְּגוֹן טֻמְאַת נְבֵלוֹת וּשְׁרָצִים וְאוֹכְלִין וּמַשְׁקִין, נִדָּה וְיוֹלֶדֶת וְזָבָה וְזָב וְשִׁכְבַת זֶרַע וְצָרַעַת אָדָם וּבַיִת וּבֶגֶד, וְטֻמְאַת מֵת וְטֻמְאַת מֵי נִדָּה וְטָהֳרָתָן; וְהוּא כָתַב בְּסֵפֶר הַמִּצְווֹת שֶׁלּוֹ רְאָיוֹת בְּרוּרוֹת בְּזֶה הָעִנְיָן, מוֹשְׁכוֹת כָּל לֵב שׁוֹמְעָן. וְעִם כָּל זֶה מִדֶּרֶךְ הָרַמְבָּ״ם זִכְרוֹנוֹ לִבְרָכָה לֹא נָטָה בַּמִּנְיָן, כַּאֲשֶׁר יָעַדְתִּי בִּתְחִלַּת הַבִּנְיָן.

[שֶׁלֹּא לְגַלֵּחַ שְׂעַר הַנֶּתֶק]

קע שֶׁלֹּא לְגַלֵּחַ שְׂעַר הַנֶּתֶק, שֶׁנֶּאֱמַר: וְאֶת הַנֶּתֶק לֹא יְגַלֵּחַ, כְּלוֹמַר אוֹתוֹ שֵׂעָר שֶׁעַל מְקוֹם הַנֶּתֶק לֹא יְגַלֵּחַ. וּלְשׁוֹן סִפְרָא: מִנַּיִן לְתוֹלֵשׁ סִימָנֵי טֻמְאָה מִתּוֹךְ נְתָקוֹ שֶׁעוֹבֵר בְּלֹא תַעֲשֶׂה, שֶׁנֶּאֱמַר: וְאֶת הַנֶּתֶק לֹא יְגַלֵּחַ. וְהָעִנְיָן כְּדֵי שֶׁיַּכִּיר הַכֹּהֵן סִימָנֵי הַטֻּמְאָה בַּשְּׂעָרוֹת.

מִשָּׁרְשֵׁי הַמִּצְוָה, לִרְמֹז שֶׁיְּסַבֵּל כָּל אָדָם אֵי זֶה צַעַר וְאֵי זֶה עֹנֶשׁ שֶׁיַּעֲנִישֵׁהוּ הַשֵּׁם בָּרוּךְ הוּא וְלֹא יִבְעַט בָּהֶם, וְאַל יַחְשֹׁב שֶׁיִּהְיֶה יְכֹלֶת בְּיָדוֹ לְבַטֵּל אוֹתָם וּלְהַעֲלִימָם מִן הַבְּרִיּוֹת, רַק יֵשׁ לוֹ לְבַקֵּשׁ תְּחִנָּה מֵאֵת הָאֵל (בָּרוּךְ הוּא) שֶׁיִּרַפֵּא מַחַץ מַכּוֹתָיו. וְזֶה הַשֹּׁרֶשׁ יַסְפִּיק גַּם־כֵּן לְלָאו דְּלֹא יָקֹץ בַּהֶרְתּוֹ שֶׁבְּסֵדֶר כִּי תֵצֵא [סי׳ תקפ״ד].

מִדִּינֵי הַמִּצְוָה, מַה שֶּׁאָמְרוּ זִכְרוֹנָם לִבְרָכָה: כֵּיצַד מְגַלְּחִין הַנֶּתֶק, מְגַלֵּחַ חוּצָה לוֹ וּמַנִּיחַ שְׁתֵּי שְׂעָרוֹת סָמוּךְ לוֹ, כְּדֵי שֶׁיִּהְיֶה מַכִּיר הַפִּשְׂיוֹן; וּמַה שֶּׁאָמְרוּ גַּם־כֵּן שֶׁהַתִּגְלַחַת כְּשֵׁרָה בְּכָל אָדָם, שֶׁנֶּאֱמַר "וְהִתְגַּלָּח", וּמִן הַסְּתָם מַשְׁמַע בְּכָל אָדָם; וּמַה שֶּׁאָמְרוּ שֶׁאֵין חַיָּב עַד שֶׁיְּגַלֵּחַ כָּל הַנֶּתֶק בְּתַעַר; וְיֶתֶר פְּרָטֶיהָ, מְבֹאָרִים בְּמַסֶּכֶת נְגָעִים.

29. Commentary to ShM positive precept §96.

§170 1. About the parenthetical translations of biblical terms in this section, see §169, note 2.

2. The paragraph is based on ShM negative precept §307.

3. Literally, kick out.

4. Literally, from the arrow.

5. I.e. surrounding it; Mishnah, N'ga'im x 5.

6. Sifra on the verse that follows.

7. While the verse is sometimes translated, "then he shall shave himself," the verb is in the reflexive (*hithpa'él*), and rather has this sense.

8. Of removing the signs of possible uncleanness (see first paragraph); MT *hilchoth tum'ath tzara'ath* x 1, based on Sifra to Leviticus 13:33 (*Kessef Mishneh*).

precept (§159)—that Ramban of blessed memory does not count in the reckoning of the precepts all the laws of ritual uncleannesses, such as the defilement of carcasses and swarming creatures, and solid and liquid food, the menstruant and the woman giving birth, a man and a woman with a discharge; semen; the *tzara'ath* ailment of a man, a house or a garment; the defilement of a corpse, and defilement and purification with the lustral water for impurity. He wrote, in his *Book of Precepts,*[29] clear proofs in this matter which draw the heart of all who hear them. Yet with all that, from the path of Rambam of blessed memory we shall not swerve in the list [of the precepts], as I determined at the start of the structure [of this work].

[THE PROHIBITION AGAINST SHAVING THE AREA OF A NETHEK]

170 not to shave the hair of a *nethek* (alopecia)[1]—as it is stated, *but the* nethek *he shall not shave* (Leviticus 13:33); in other words, that hair which is in the area of the *nethek*, he shall not shave. In the language of the Midrash *Sifra:* How do we know that if someone plucks out the signs of ritual uncleanness from the midst of his *nethek*, he transgresses a negative precept?—because it is stated, *but the* nethek *he shall not shave.* The reason is so that the *kohen* will [be able to] discern the signs of defilement in the hair.[2]

At the root of the precept lies the purpose to imply that every man should bear whatever pain and whatever punishment the Eternal Lord imposes on him, and not lash out[3] in protest against them. Nor should he think that he will have the ability to nullify them and conceal them from people. He can only entreat God, blessed is He, for gracious mercy, that he should be healed from the stinging wound[4] of his afflictions. And this reason will suffice, as well, for the injunction not to cut away one's *bahereth* (snowy-white spot;[1] §584) in *sidrah ki thétzé.*

Among the laws of the precept, there is what the Sages of blessed memory said: How is a *nethek* shaved? One shaves about it, leaving two hairbreadths near it,[5] so that spreading can be perceived. Then there is what they said, likewise,[6] that the shaving may properly be done by any man; for it is stated, *then he shall be shaven*[7] (Leviticus 13:33), and the general, unspecific expression implies [that it may be done] by any man. There is, too, what the Sages said, that one is not guilty[8] until he shaves the entire *nethek* with a razor. The rest of its details are clarified in the Mishnah tractate *N'ga'im.*

וְנוֹהֶגֶת בִּזְכָרִים וּנְקֵבוֹת, בְּכָל מָקוֹם וּבְכָל זְמַן שֶׁיֵּשׁ כֹּהֵן חָכָם לִרְאוֹת הַנְּגָעִים. וְעוֹבֵר עָלֶיהָ וְגִלַּח אֶת הַנֶּתֶק, לוֹקֶה.

[מִצְוַת הַנְהָגַת הַמְּצֹרָע וְכָל מְטַמְּאֵי אָדָם בִּקְרִיעָה וּפְרִימָה]

קעא שֶׁיִּתְנַהֵג הַמְּצֹרָע כְּמִשְׁפַּט הַכָּתוּב בַּפָּרָשָׁה, שֶׁנֶּאֱמַר: בְּגָדָיו יִהְיוּ פְרֻמִים וְרֹאשׁוֹ יִהְיֶה פָרוּעַ; וְכֵן כָּל שְׁאָר הַטְּמֵאִים גַּם־כֵּן צְרִיכִין לְהוֹדִיעַ אֶת עַצְמָן. וּלְשׁוֹן סִפְרָא: טְמֵא מֵת וּבוֹעֵל נִדָּה וְכָל הַמְּטַמְּאִין אֶת הָאָדָם מִנַּיִן, תַּלְמוּד לוֹמַר: וְטָמֵא טָמֵא יִקְרָא. וְהַקְּרִיאָה הִיא שֶׁיַּעֲשֶׂה בְגוּפוֹ עִנְיָן שֶׁיֻּכַּר לִבְנֵי־אָדָם בּוֹ שֶׁהוּא טָמֵא, וְיָסוּרוּ מִמֶּנּוּ.

מִשָּׁרְשֵׁי הַמִּצְוָה, שֶׁיִּקַּח דִּמְיוֹן בְּנַפְשׁוֹ בְּהַרְחָקָתוֹ מִבְּנֵי־אָדָם כִּי בְסִבַּת הַחֵטְא יִרְחַק הָאָדָם מִכָּל טוּב, לְמַעַן יָשׁוּב מִדַּרְכּוֹ הָרָעָה. וְזֶהוּ אָמְרָם זִכְרוֹנָם לִבְרָכָה: הוּא הִבְדִּיל בִּלְשׁוֹן הָרָע בֵּין אִישׁ לְאִשְׁתּוֹ, בֵּין אָדָם לַחֲבֵרוֹ, וּלְפִיכָךְ מִחוּץ לַמַּחֲנֶה אָהֳלוֹ. וְלָכֵן רָאוּי שֶׁיִּקְרָא לְכָל אָדָם שֶׁיָּסוּרוּ מִמֶּנּוּ.

וּכְלָל גָּדוֹל בְּכָל הַדְּבָרִים: בְּמִדָּה שֶׁאָדָם מוֹדֵד בָּהּ מוֹדְדִים לוֹ. וּפֵרוּשׁ דָּבָר זֶה לֹא יְדָעוּהוּ רַבִּים, כִּי יַחְשְׁבוּ לְפָרֵשׁ דָּבָר זֶה אֵצֶל הַשֵּׁם בָּרוּךְ הוּא בְּדֻגְמַת גְּמוּל בְּנֵי־אָדָם, שֶׁכָּל אֶחָד יְשַׁלֵּם אֶת חֲבֵרוֹ גְמוּל כְּפִי הַטּוֹבָה שֶׁעָשָׂה עִמּוֹ אוֹ כְפִי הָרָעָה; וְלֹא כֵן הָעִנְיָן אֵצֶל הַשֵּׁם בָּרוּךְ הוּא חָלִילָה, כִּי אֵין עִם הַשֵּׁם בָּרוּךְ הוּא כִּי אִם טוֹבָה וָחֶסֶד וְרַחֲמִים לְעוֹלָם, וּבְכָל עֵת וּבְכָל שָׁעָה טוּבוֹ מוּכָן אֶל כָּל הָרָאוּי לְקַבְּלוֹ, וְלֹא יָנוּם וְלֹא יִישָׁן שׁוֹמֵר יִשְׂרָאֵל. וּמַה שֶּׁאָמְרוּ זִכְרוֹנָם לִבְרָכָה אֶצְלוֹ בָּרוּךְ הוּא "בְּמִדָּה שֶׁאָדָם מוֹדֵד בָּהּ מוֹדְדִין לוֹ", הַכַּוָּנָה לוֹמַר כִּי כְפִי מַעֲשֵׂה

9. See § 169, paragraph before last (note 27).

§171 1. If it referred only to a *m'tzora*, Scripture could have written "Unclean" only once; now it can be understood to mean: every unclean person shall cry, "Unclean" (Malbim).

2. The paragraph is based on ShM positive precept §112.

3. TB 'Arachin 16b.

4. I.e. let him be divided—separated and ostracized—from the community.

5. TB Sotah 8b.

It applies to both man and woman, in every place and at every time that there is a *kohen* of clear lineage to appraise afflictions.[9] If someone violated it and shaved the *nethek*, he should receive whiplashes.

[THAT ONE WITH A TZARA'ATH CONDITION, ET AL. SHOULD REND HIS CLOTHES]

171 that a person with a *tzara'ath* ailment should conduct himself by the rules written in the Scriptural section—as it is stated, *his clothes shall be torn and his head shall be unshorn* (Leviticus 13:45); and so must all other defiled persons make themselves known. In the language of the Midrash *Sifra:* How do we know [it applies equally to] someone defiled by a corpse, one who was conjugally intimate with a woman unclean from the menses, or anyone [with a ritual uncleanness by which he] can defile [another] person—for Scripture states, *and "Unclean, unclean" he shall cry* (*ibid.*).[1] This "crying" (proclamation) means that he should do something with his body so that it will be evident to people that he is defiled, and they will get away from him.[2]

At the root of the precept lies the purpose that a person should realize the analogy in his soul, as he withdraws from people, that on account of a sin a person withdraws from all good—so that he should turn back from his evil way. In this vein our Sages of blessed memory said:[3] With his evil gossip he brought division between a man and his wife, between a man and his fellow; therefore let his tent be outside the camp.[4] And it is therefore fitting that he should call out to every man to turn away from him.

One great rule prevails in all these matters: By the yardstick with which a man measures, by that is he measured.[5] Now, many do not know the meaning of this apothegm, for they believe it is to be explained in regard to the Eternal Lord, blessed is He, by the example of human recompense: because everyone pays his fellow back according to the good that he does for him, or according to the evil. But this is *not* the case with the Eternal Lord (blessed is He)—perish the thought! For with the Eternal Lord, blessed is He, there is nothing but goodness, kindness and mercy always. At every time, at every hour, His goodness is prepared for everyone who is worthy to receive it; *the guardian of Israel neither slumbers nor sleeps* (Psalms 121:4). Hence, when the Sages of blessed memory said about Him (blessed is He),[5] "By the yardstick with which a man measures, by that he is measured," it was meant to convey that according to a man's action, whether for goodness or for

הָאָדָם, אִם לְטוֹבָה אִם לְהֶפֶךְ, יִתָּכֵן לְקַבָּלַת הַגְּמוּל, כִּי לְעוֹלָם בְּאוֹתוֹ הָעִנְיָן שֶׁיָּשִׂים כָּל מַחְשְׁבוֹתָיו וְיַעֲשֶׂה מַעֲשָׂיו, בְּדֻגְמָתוֹ מַמָּשׁ תִּמָּשֵׁךְ עָלָיו הַבְּרָכָה אוֹ הַהֵפֶךְ.

וְכֵן אָמַר הַכָּתוּב: כִּי לֹא עִנָּה מִלִּבּוֹ וַיַּגֶּה בְּנֵי אִישׁ, וּכְתִיב גַּם־כֵּן: כִּי לֹא אֵל חָפֵץ רֶשַׁע אָתָּה, כְּלוֹמַר שֶׁהַשֵּׁם יִתְבָּרֵךְ לֹא יְחַיֵּב בְּרִיָּה מֵחֶפְצוֹ בְּחִיּוּב, כִּי הָאֵל הַטּוֹב חָפֵץ בְּטוּב לָעוֹלָם; אֲבָל הָאָדָם הוּא שֶׁמְּחַיֵּב אֶת עַצְמוֹ בִּנְטוֹתוֹ מִן הַיֹּשֶׁר וְיָסִיר מִגּוּפוֹ הַהֲכָנוֹת הַמַּכְשִׁירוֹת אוֹתוֹ לְקַבֵּל הַטּוֹבָה. וְהַמָּשָׁל עַל זֶה הַהוֹלֵךְ בְּדֶרֶךְ יָשָׁר וּפָנוּי מֵאֲבָנִים וּמִכָּל דָּבָר הַמַּכְשִׁיל וְיֵשׁ לַדֶּרֶךְ גֶּדֶר קוֹצִים מִכָּאן וּמִכָּאן, וְעָבַר אֶחָד וְנִתְחַכֵּךְ בַּגָּדֵר וְנִכְוָה. בֶּאֱמֶת אֵין לוֹמַר עַל הָאִישׁ הַזֶּה שֶׁהַשֵּׁם חָפֵץ בִּכְוִיָּתוֹ, אֲבָל הוּא הַגּוֹרֵם, כִּי לֹא נִזְהַר לָלֶכֶת בְּיֹשֶׁר.

וּכְמוֹ־כֵן בַּעַל הַחֵטְא מִדַּת הַדִּין תְּחַיְּבֶנּוּ עַל חֶטְאוֹ עַל־כָּל־פָּנִים, וְאֵין לוֹמַר עָלָיו שֶׁהָאֵל הַטּוֹב יַחְפֹּץ בְּחִיּוּבוֹ, אֲבָל בְּהִמָּנַע מִמֶּנּוּ הַטּוֹב מִצַּד חֶטְאוֹ יִמָּצֵא אֵלָיו הָרָע. וּכְעֵין דָּבָר זֶה אָמְרוּ זִכְרוֹנָם לִבְרָכָה: אֵין דָּבָר רַע יוֹרֵד מִלְמַעְלָה.

וּכְלַל דְּבָרֵינוּ, כִּי כָל הַמִּקְרֶה הָרַע הַמִּתְחַדֵּשׁ בָּאָדָם הוּא פְּעֻלָּה הַמִּתְחַדֶּשֶׁת בָּאָדָם בְּהַסְתָּרַת פְּנֵי הַשֵּׁם מִן הָאִישׁ, כְּלוֹמַר שֶׁהַשֵּׁם מֵסִיר שְׁמִירָתוֹ מֵעָלָיו מִצַּד חֶטְאוֹ עַד שֶׁיְּקַבֵּל הָעֹנֶשׁ הָרָאוּי לוֹ לְפִי הַחֵטְא, וְאָז יְצַוֶּה מַלְאָכָיו לְשָׁמְרוֹ כַּאֲשֶׁר בַּתְּחִלָּה, וּכְמוֹ שֶׁכָּתוּב: וְהִסְתַּרְתִּי פָנַי מֵהֶם וְהָיָה לֶאֱכֹל, וּמְצָאֻהוּ רָעוֹת רַבּוֹת וְצָרוֹת, וְאָמַר בַּיּוֹם הַהוּא הֲלֹא עַל כִּי אֵין אֱלֹהַי בְּקִרְבִּי מְצָאוּנִי הָרָעוֹת הָאֵלֶּה. וְכָתַב חָכָם אֶחָד: יָדַעְנוּ כִּי הַשֵּׁם אֶחָד, וְהַשִּׁנּוּי יָבוֹא מֵהַמְקַבְּלִים, וְהַשֵּׁם לֹא יְשַׁנֶּה מַעֲשָׂיו, כִּי כֻלָּם הֵם בְּחָכְמָה.

מִדִּינֵי הַמִּצְוָה, מַה שֶּׁאָמְרוּ זִכְרוֹנָם לִבְרָכָה: אֵין בֵּין מְצֹרָע מֻסְגָּר לִמְצֹרָע מֻחְלָט אֶלָּא פְּרִיעָה וּפְרִימָה וְתִגְלַחַת וְצִפֳּרִים, כְּלוֹמַר שֶׁהַמֻּסְגָּר אֵינוֹ פּוֹרֵעַ

6. B'réshith Rabbah 51, 3.

7. R. Judah haLévi, *Kuzari* IV 3.

8. I.e. the human beings who receive the impact of His presence and respond to their encounter with Him. They can be receptive to His word and His grace, or they can reject Him.

9. TB M'gillah 8b.

10. I.e. one declared absolutely unclean.

the opposite, he is gauged to receive reward. For always, within that subject on which a person sets all his thoughts and does his activity, by his very example will blessing be drawn to him, or the reverse.

Thus Scripture states, *For He does not afflict out of His heart or grieve the sons of men* (Lamentations 3:33); and it is written, likewise, *For Thou are not a God who delights in wickedness* (Psalms 5:5). In other words, the Eternal Lord (be He blessed) will not declare any human being guilty out of a desire of His for condemnation, since the good God delights in goodness for the world. It is but man who sentences himself when he swerves from the upright path and removes from himself the preparations that made him ready to receive goodness. An illustration for this would be a man walking on a straightforward path free of stones or anything that might cause stumbling, but the path had a fence of thorns on either side; along he came and scratched himself on the fence, and he was bruised. It truly cannot be said about this man that the Eternal Lord had any wish for his bruise. Rather, he was the cause, because he was not careful to walk straight.

So too a man who sinned: the quality of justice will sentence him for his sin, in any event; but it cannot be said of him that the good God delights in his sentence. Rather, as goodness is withheld from him on account of his sin, evil will befall him. Our Sages of blessed memory said something akin to this:[6] Nothing evil descends from above.

The sum of our words is that every new evil event that befalls a man is an occurrence that arises for the person as the visage of the Eternal Lord is hidden from him: in other words, the Eternal Lord removes His protection from him on account of his sin, until he receives the punishment he deserves according to the sin. Then He will command His angels to guard him as at the beginning. As it is written: *and I will hide My face from them, and they will be devoured; and many evils and troubles will come upon them, so that they will say in that day, "Have these evils not come upon us because our God is not among us?"* (Deuteronomy 31:17). And one learned scholar wrote:[7] We know that the Eternal Lord is one, and change comes from the receivers;[8] but the Eternal Lord will not change His deeds; for they are all [wrought] with wisdom.

Among the laws of the precept, there is what the Sages of blessed memory taught:[9] that there is no difference between a quarantined *m'tzora* and a definite, absolute *m'tzora*[10] other than neglecting the hair and tearing the clothes, shaving [the body] (§174), and the birds (§173). In other words, a person quarantined does not let his hair grow

וּפוֹרֵם — וּפֵרוּשׁ פּוֹרֵעַ, גִּדּוּל שֵׂעָר; וּפוֹרֵם, שֶׁיִּקְרַע בְּגָדָיו — וְהַטָּהוֹר מִתּוֹךְ הֶסְגֵּר פָּטוּר מִתִּגְלַחַת וּצִפֳּרִים, וְהַטָּהוֹר מִתּוֹךְ הֶחְלֵט חַיָּב בְּתִגְלַחַת וְצִפֳּרִים; אֲבָל טֻמְאַת שְׁנֵיהֶם שָׁוָה לְכָל דָּבָר. וְעִנְיְנֵי טֻמְאָתָן כַּמָּה וְכֵיצַד, וְאִם אֲסוּרִין בִּשְׁאִילַת שָׁלוֹם, וְאִם הֵן מֻתָּרִין לִשְׁנוֹת בְּעוֹדָן בְּטֻמְאָתָן, וְאִם אֲסוּרִין לְסַפֵּר וּלְכַבֵּס, וְאִם מֻתָּרִין בִּרְחִיצָה וּבְסִיכָה וּבִנְעִילַת הַסַּנְדָּל וּבְתַשְׁמִישׁ הַמִּטָּה, וְדִין הַמְּצֹרַעַת כֵּיצַד דִּינָהּ וְהַנְהָגָתָהּ; וְיֶתֶר פְּרָטֶיהָ, מְבֹאָרִים בִּנְגָעִים.

וְנוֹהֶגֶת בְּכָל זְמַן שֶׁיִּהְיוּ לָנוּ כֹּהֲנִים וַחֲכָמִים שֶׁיּוֹדְעִין הַנְּגָעִים, שֶׁרְאוּיִין לְטַהֵר וּלְטַמֵּא. וְעוֹבֵר עַל זֶה וְלֹא עָשָׂה בְּעַצְמוֹ כַּמִּשְׁפָּט הַזֶּה, בִּטֵּל עֲשֵׂה זֶה.

[מִצְוַת עִנְיַן נֶגַע בְּגָדִים]

קעב לַעֲשׂוֹת בְּנִגְעֵי בְגָדִים כַּמִּשְׁפָּט הַכָּתוּב בַּפָּרָשָׁה, שֶׁנֶּאֱמַר: וְהַבֶּגֶד כִּי יִהְיֶה בוֹ נֶגַע וְגוֹמֵר. וּמִצְוָה זוֹ כּוֹלֶלֶת כָּל דִּינֵי צָרַעַת בְּגָדִים, אֵיךְ יְטַמְּאוּ וְאֵיךְ לֹא יְטַמְּאוּ, וּמַה מֵּהֶם צָרִיךְ הֶסְגֵּר אוֹ קְרִיעָה אוֹ שְׂרֵפָה וּרְחִיצָה וְטָהֳרָה.

מִשָּׁרְשֵׁי הַמִּצְוָה, שֶׁרָצָה הָאֵל (בָּרוּךְ הוּא) בְּטוּבוֹ הַגָּדוֹל לְיַסְּרֵנוּ כַּאֲשֶׁר יְיַסֵּר אִישׁ אֶת בְּנוֹ: כִּי זֶה הָעִנְיָן אֵינֶנּוּ בַּטֶּבַע, אֲבָל מוֹפֵת הוּא בָּאֻמָּה הַקְּדוֹשָׁה, לְמַעַן יִלְמְדוּ וְיִקְחוּ מוּסָר בְּהִשְׁתַּנּוֹת הַכֵּלִים הַמְיֻחָדִים לְתַשְׁמִישָׁם, וְהֵם הַבְּגָדִים שֶׁל צֶמֶר וּפִשְׁתִּים, כִּי בָהֶם רֹב תַּשְׁמִישׁ בְּנֵי־אָדָם, וְיָשׁוּבוּ מִתּוֹךְ כָּךְ מִדַּרְכָּם הָרָעָה טֶרֶם יִזְרַח הַצָּרַעַת גַּם בְּגוּפָם.

מִדִּינֵי הַמִּצְוָה, מַה שֶּׁאָמְרוּ זִכְרוֹנָם לִבְרָכָה שֶׁאֵין מִטַּמֵּא בִנְגָעִים אֶלָּא בִגְדֵי צֶמֶר וּפִשְׁתִּים בִּלְבַד, וְשִׁעוּר טֻמְאָתָן כִּגְרִיס, כַּשִּׁעוּר בָּאָדָם. וּשְׁלֹשָׁה סִימָנֵי

11. The Hebrew text now adds the explanation of *p'rimah* as "tearing the clothes."

12. Mishnah, Kélim i 1, Zavim v 6; Sifra to Leviticus 14:8.

13. TB Mo'éd Katan 15a (see MY).

14. A practice in Middle East and oriental countries, to help withstand the hot climate.

15. Literally, the sandal.

16. MT *hilchoth tum'ath tzara'ath* x 6, based on TB Mo'éd Katan 15b, 7b (*Kessef Mishneh*).

17. TB Sotah 23a; MT *ibid.* 8.

18. See § 169, third and second paragraphs before the end.

§172 1. I.e. the affected part of the garment: Leviticus 13:56. The sentence is based on ShM positive precept § 102.

2. I.e. *tzara'ath* infection in clothing. What our author goes on to state is to be found in MT *hilchoth tum'ath tzara'ath* xvi 10.

3. Sifra to Leviticus 13:47 (*thazri'a, perek* 13, 1); TB Shabbath 26b.

unshorn or rend his clothes—the meaning of *poré'a* being to let the hair grow long.[11] A man pronounced ritually clean out of quarantine is free of the duty of shaving and the birds, while a person pronounced absolutely unclean has the duty of shaving and the birds. But the defilement of both is the same in every respect. Then there are the topics of their defilement—to what degree and in what way [they are ritually unclean];[12] if they are forbidden to give a greeting;[13] if they are permitted to study [Torah] while they are yet in their defilement;[13] if they are forbidden to cut their hair and wash their clothes;[13] if they are allowed bathing, applying oil to the skin,[14] wearing shoes,[15] and having conjugal relations.[16] Then there is the law of a woman with a *tzara'ath* disease: what her procedure and conduct should be.[17] [These] and its further details are explained in the Mishnah tractate *N'ga'im*.

It is in force at every time when we have *kohanim* and learned scholars who know the afflictions, thus being fit to pronounce a person ritually clean or unclean.[18] If someone violated it and did not conduct himself by this rule, he would disobey this positive precept.

172 [THE PRECEPT ON TZARA'ATH IN CLOTH]

to deal with afflictions in clothes according to the procedure written in the Scriptural section—as it is written, *And when there is an affliction of* tzara'ath *in a garment*, etc. (Leviticus 13:47). This precept includes all the laws of *tzara'ath* infection of clothes: how they become defiled and how they do not become defiled; which of them requires quarantine, tearing out,[1] or burning; or washing and purification [by *t'vilah*, ritual immersion].

At the root of the precept lies the reason that in His great goodness, God, blessed is He, desired to chastise us *as a man chastises his son* (Deuteronomy 8:5). For this phenomenon[2] is not something natural but a wonder amid this holy people, that they may learn and accept the chastening lesson when objects for their particular use become changed [supernaturally]—i.e. garments of wool or linen, since people make use of them mostly. In consequence of this, they will turn back from their evil way before *tzara'ath* flares up in their bodies too.

Among the laws of the precept, there is what the Sages of blessed memory taught:[3] that nothing can become defiled by *tzara'ath* afflictions but garments of wool or linen alone. The minimal area for their defilement is as a *garis* (bean), like the minimal area for *tzara'ath* ailment

טֻמְאָה יֵשׁ בָּהֶם: יְרַקְרַק, אֲדַמְדָּם, פִּשְׁיוֹן. פֵּרוּשׁ יְרַקְרַק, יָרֹק שֶׁבַּיְּרֻקִּין כִּכְנַף הַטַּוָּס; וַאֲדַמְדָּם, אָדֹם שֶׁבָּאֲדֻמִּים כְּמוֹ הַזְּהוֹרִית; וְדִינֵי הַפִּשְׁיוֹן, וְדִין יָרֹק שֶׁפָּשָׂה אָדֹם, אוֹ אָדֹם שֶׁפָּשָׂה יָרֹק; וְדִין כָּל כְּלִי הָרָאוּי לְהִתְטַמֵּא, שֶׁאָמְרוּ זִכְרוֹנָם לִבְרָכָה שֶׁהוּא מְטַמֵּא בִנְגָעִים אַף־עַל־פִּי שֶׁאֵינוֹ מְטַמֵּא בְּמִדְרַס הַזָּב, כְּגוֹן קְלָעִים שֶׁל סְפִינָה וְהַפָּרֹכֶת (ושבכיס) [וְשָׁבִיס] שֶׁל שְׂבָכָה וּמִטְפְּחוֹת סוֹפְרִים וְהָאַבְנֵט, וּרְצוּעוֹת מִנְעָל וְסַנְדָּל שֶׁיֵּשׁ בָּהֶן רֹחַב כִּגְרִיס, וְכָל כַּיּוֹצֵא בָהֶן, וְאֵין צָרִיךְ לוֹמַר שְׁאָר הַכֵּלִים כְּגוֹן כָּרִים וּכְסָתוֹת; וְיֶתֶר פְּרָטֶיהָ, מְבֹאָרִים בְּטָהֳרוֹת, וְהָרֹב מֵהֶן בְּמַסֶּכֶת נְגָעִים.

וְנוֹהֶגֶת בְּבִגְדֵי זְכָרִים וּנְקֵבוֹת. וְעוֹבֵר עָלֶיהָ וְלֹא הִתְנַהֵג בְּעִנְיָן זֶה כְּדִין הַכָּתוּב בַּפָּרָשָׁה, בִּטֵּל עֲשֵׂה.

זֹאת תִּהְיֶה תּוֹרַת הַמְּצֹרָע

יֵשׁ בָּהּ אַחַת־עֶשְׂרֵה מִצְווֹת עֲשֵׂה

[מִצְוַת הַטָּהֳרָה מִן הַצָּרַעַת שֶׁתִּהְיֶה בְּמִינִים יְדוּעִים]

קעג לִהְיוֹת הַטָּהֳרָה מִן הַצָּרַעַת, בֵּין צָרַעַת אָדָם אוֹ בֶגֶד אוֹ בַיִת, בְּעֵץ אֶרֶז וְאֵזוֹב וּשְׁנִי תוֹלַעַת וּשְׁתֵּי צִפֳּרִים וּמַיִם חַיִּים, וְשֶׁיַּעֲשֶׂה בָהֶם כָּל מַה שֶּׁכָּתוּב בָּעִנְיָן, שֶׁנֶּאֱמַר: זֹאת תִּהְיֶה תּוֹרַת הַמְּצֹרָע וְגוֹמֵר, כָּל הַפָּרָשָׁה.

וּשְׁלֹשֶׁת מִינִין שֶׁל טָהֳרָה הֻזְכְּרוּ בַּתּוֹרָה, וְאֵלּוּ הֵן: מַיִם, וְזֶה הַמִּין שֶׁל מַיִם יִכְלֹל טָהֳרַת כָּל טָמֵא, כְּלוֹמַר שֶׁאִי אֶפְשָׁר לְכָל טָמֵא לַעֲלוֹת מִטֻּמְאָה כִּי־אִם בְּמַיִם; וְהַמִּין הַשֵּׁנִי מֵי נִדָּה, וְהוּא הַמִּין שֶׁל טָהֳרָה הַמְיֻחָד בְּטֻמְאַת מֵת; וְהַמִּין

4. Sifra *ibid.* (*perek* 14, 1).

5. Mishnah, N'ga'im iii 7.

6. Tosefta cited by R. Samson of Sens in his commentary, *ibid.* xi 4.

7. Mishnah, N'ga'im xi 7.

8. *Ibid.* 4.

9. Literally, the "treading" of a person with a discharge: i.e. any seat, couch, bed, etc. which he has used (Leviticus 15:4); *ibid.* 11.

10. Used as a hanging in a doorway.

11. For wrapping scrolls.

§173 1. There is a slight imprecision in this general statement: birds are prescribed for the cleansing of a man or a house, but not a garment (MH). (This and the next paragraph are based on ShM positive precept §110.)

in a man.[4] There are three signs of ritual uncleanness in them: greened, reddened, or spreading.[5] The meaning of "greened" is the greenest of green, like the wing of a peacock; "reddened" means the reddest of red, like crimson silk.[6] Then there are the laws of spreading;[7] the law of green that spread in red, or red that spread in green;[8] the law on any cloth object that is capable of being defiled, about which the Sages of blessed memory said that it becomes ritually impure through *tzara'ath* infections, even if it does not become defiled by the resting-place of a person with a discharge[9]—such as the sails of a ship, a curtain,[10] the band of a hair-net, bands of scribes,[11] a sash, laces for shoes and sandals which have the width of a *garis* (bean), and so anything similar; and there is no need to add the other [more usual] cloth objects like mattresses and pillows. The rest of its details are explained in the Mishnah order *Tohoroth*, most of them in the tractate *N'ga'im*.

It applies to the garments of both man and woman. If a person violated it and did not conduct himself in this matter according to the law of the Writ in this section, he would thus disobey a positive precept.

sidrah m'tzora

(Leviticus 14–15)

There are eleven positive precepts in it.

[THE PRECEPT THAT RITUAL CLEANSING FROM TZARA'ATH AFFLICTION SHOULD BE THROUGH CERTAIN INGREDIENTS]

173 that there should be purification from *tzara'ath*—whether it is such a distemper of a man, a garment, or a house—with cedar-wood, hyssop, scarlet stuff, two birds, and running spring water;[1] and that one should do with them all that is written about the subject—as it is stated, *This shall be the law of the man with a* tzara'ath *disease* (Leviticus 14:2), and so on, to the end of the section.

Three kinds of purification were mentioned in the Torah. These are: [first] water; this kind, by water, is involved in the purification of every defiled person; in other words, it is impossible for any ritually unclean person to ascend from uncleanness except with water. The second kind is sprinkling water for impurity (§376); this is the kind for the particular purification of defilement by a corpse. The third

הַשְּׁלִישִׁי עֵץ אֶרֶז וְאֵזוֹב וּשְׁנִי תוֹלַעַת וּשְׁתֵּי צִפֳּרִים וּמַיִם חַיִּים, וְזֶה הַמִּין מְיֻחָד לַצָּרַעַת.

קְצָת רֶמֶז בְּעִנְיְנֵי טָהֳרָתוֹ שֶׁל מְצֹרָע בִּדְבָרִים אֵלֶּה הוֹדִיעוּנוּ חֲכָמִים עַל צַד הַפְּשָׁט, שֶׁאָמְרוּ זִכְרוֹנָם לִבְרָכָה שֶׁהָעִנְיָן הוּא לִקְבֹּעַ בְּנַפְשׁוֹ שֶׁל מְצֹרָע, שֶׁאִם הָיָה טֶרֶם בָּא עָלָיו הַחֹלִי גְּבַהּ לֵב כְּמוֹ הָאֶרֶז, עַל דֶּרֶךְ מָשָׁל, שֶׁהוּא אִילָן גָּבוֹהַּ, יַשְׁפִּיל עַצְמוֹ כְּאֵזוֹב; וְאָמְרוּ בְטַעַם צִפֳּרִים: הוּא עָשָׂה מַעֲשֵׂה פָּטִיט, כְּלוֹמַר שֶׁהִרְבָּה דְבָרִים בְּלָשׁוֹן הָרָע, לְפִיכָךְ יַקְרִיב צִפֳּרִים, שֶׁהֵם מְצַפְצְפִים תָּמִיד.

וּבִשְׁנִי הַתּוֹלַעַת אֵינִי יוֹדֵעַ וְנִזְכָּר שֶׁאָמְרוּ זִכְרוֹנָם לִבְרָכָה עָלָיו דָּבָר; וְאֶפְשָׁר גַּם־כֵּן שֶׁהוּא רֶמֶז שֶׁיַּשְׁפִּיל עַצְמוֹ, וְיִהְיֶה הָרֶמֶז מִצַּד הַשֵּׁם שֶׁל תּוֹלַעַת.

וּבְטַעַם הַמַּיִם שֶׁיְּטַהֲרוּ כָּל טָמֵא, אֶחְשֹׁב עַל צַד הַפְּשָׁט, כִּי הָעִנְיָן הוּא כְּדֵי שֶׁיִּרְאֶה הָאָדָם אֶת עַצְמוֹ אַחַר הַטְּבִילָה כְּאִלּוּ נִבְרָא בְּאוֹתָהּ שָׁעָה, כְּמוֹ שֶׁהָיָה הָעוֹלָם כֻּלּוֹ מַיִם טֶרֶם הֱיוֹת בּוֹ אָדָם, וּכְמוֹ שֶׁכָּתוּב: וְרוּחַ אֱלֹהִים מְרַחֶפֶת עַל פְּנֵי הַמָּיִם; וְיִתֵּן אֶל לִבּוֹ בְּדִמְיוֹן כִּי כְמוֹ שֶׁנִּתְחַדֵּשׁ בְּגוּפוֹ יְחַדֵּשׁ גַּם־כֵּן פְּעֻלּוֹתָיו לְטוֹב, וְיַכְשִׁיר מַעֲשָׂיו, וְיִדַקְדֵּק בְּדַרְכֵי הַשֵּׁם בָּרוּךְ הוּא.

וְעַל־כֵּן אָמְרוּ חֲכָמִים שֶׁלֹּא תִכְשַׁר הַטָּהֳרָה בְּמַיִם שֶׁבִּכְלִי, רַק בְּמַיִם חַיִּים אוֹ מְכֻנָּסִין שֶׁהֵן עַל קַרְקַע וְלֹא בִכְלִי מִכָּל־מָקוֹם, כְּדֵי לָתֵת אֶל לִבּוֹ בְּמַחֲשָׁבָה כְּאִלּוּ הָעוֹלָם כֻּלּוֹ מַיִם, וְהוּא נִתְחַדֵּשׁ בַּעֲלוֹתוֹ מֵהֶן, כְּמוֹ שֶׁאָמַרְנוּ. וְאִם יִהְיוּ הַמַּיִם בִּכְלִי, אוֹ אֲפִלּוּ עָבְרוּ עַל כְּלִי, לֹא יִתָּכֵן הָעִנְיָן הַזֶּה שֶׁאָמַרְנוּ אֶל מַחֲשֶׁבֶת הַטּוֹבֵל, כִּי יֵשׁ גְּבוּל אֶל כָּל אֲשֶׁר הוּא בִכְלִי, שֶׁהוּא מַעֲשֵׂה יְדֵי אָדָם, וְעַל כֵּן לֹא יַחְשֹׁב בְּטָבְלוֹ בִּכְלִי, כָּל הָעוֹלָם לְמַיִם כַּאֲשֶׁר בַּתְּחִלָּה, וְשֶׁהוּא נִתְחַדֵּשׁ לְשַׁעְתּוֹ. וְהַשּׁוֹמֵעַ יִשְׁמַע וְהֶחָדֵל יֶחְדָּל.

2. P'sikta d'R. Kahana 4 (ed. Buber, 35a).

3. TB 'Arachin 16b.

4. The Hebrew term for scarlet stuff is "thread of the worm," i.e. the silkworm. It evidently escaped our author's attention that Rashi makes this point (on Leviticus 14:4).

kind is [with] cedarwood, hyssop, scarlet stuff, two birds, and running spring water—which is the particular kind for a man with a *tzara'ath* affliction.

Now, the Sages gave us, by way of the plain meaning, some hint of the significance of a man's purification from *tzara'ath* ailment by these things. For they (of blessed memory) said[2] that the purport is to impress on the afflicted man's spirit that if before the illness befell him he was "tall" and haughty of heart, like the cedar—by way of simile, since it is a tall tree—let him abase himself [to be as low] as hyssop. Then they said about a reason for the birds:[3] He did an act of chattering—i.e. he multiplied words in evil gossip; let him therefore bring an offering of birds, which always chatter.

As to the scarlet stuff, I do not know or remember that our Sages of blessed memory said anything about it. Perhaps it is likewise a hint that he should humble himself, the implication being by way of the name *tola'ath,*[4] which means a worm.

As to a reason for water, why it should purify every defiled person, I would think, by way of the plain meaning, that it is in order that a man should perceive himself after the immersion as though he had been created at that moment—just as the world was entirely water before there was any man in it: as it is written, *and the spirit of God was hovering over the face of the waters* (Genesis 1:2). Thus he will ponder in his reflection that just as he becomes renewed in his body, so let him make all his actions equally new, for the good. Let him make his deeds worthy, carefully observing the ways of the Eternal Lord, blessed is He.

Hence the Sages said that the purification cannot be proper and acceptable with water in a vessel but only with running spring water or collected water that is on the ground, but not, under any circumstances, in a vessel—so that he should conceive in his thought as though the world were entirely water, and he becomes a new person when he ascends from it—as we stated. But if the water is in a vessel, or if it even passed through one, the thought of the person undergoing immersion could not hold this concept: for there is a boundary, a limit to whatever is in a vessel, which is a man's handiwork. Hence, while immersing himself in a vessel, he cannot imagine all the world to be water, as at the beginning, and that he has become a new person at that moment. He who would hearken [to this], let him hearken; and he who would reject it, let him reject it (Ezekiel 3:27).

⟨235⟩ Among the laws of the precept, there is what the Sages of blessed

מִדִּינֵי הַמִּצְוָה, מַה שֶּׁאָמְרוּ זִכְרוֹנָם לִבְרָכָה: כֵּיצַד מְטַהֲרִין אֶת הַמְּצֹרָע, מֵבִיא מִזְרָק שֶׁל חֶרֶשׂ שֶׁהוּא חָדָשׁ וְנוֹתֵן לְתוֹכוֹ רְבִיעִית מַיִם חַיִּים הָרְאוּיִין לְקַדֵּשׁ אוֹתָן לְמֵי חַטָּאת; וְשִׁעוּר זֶה מִדִּבְרֵי סוֹפְרִים; וּמֵבִיא שְׁתֵּי צִפֳּרִים דְּרוֹר טְהוֹרוֹת לְשֵׁם טָהֳרַת הַמְּצֹרָע, שֶׁנֶּאֱמַר: וְלָקַח לַמִּטַּהֵר, וְשׁוֹחֵט אֶת הַבְּרוּרָה שֶׁבִּשְׁתֵּיהֶן עַל הַמַּיִם שֶׁבַּכְּלִי־חֶרֶשׂ וּמְמַצֶּה עַד שֶׁיִּהְיֶה הַדָּם נִכָּר בַּמַּיִם, וְחוֹפֵר וְקוֹבֵר הַצִּפּוֹר הַשְּׁחוּטָה בְּפָנָיו — וְדָבָר זֶה קַבָּלָה מִפִּי הַשְּׁמוּעָה.

וְנוֹטֵל עֵץ אֶרֶז, וּמִצְוָתוֹ שֶׁיִּהְיֶה אָרְכּוֹ אַמָּה וְעָבְיוֹ כִּרְבִיעַ כֶּרַע מִכַּרְעֵי הַמִּטָּה; וְאֵזוֹב שֶׁאֵין לוֹ שֵׁם לְוַי, וְלֹא יְהֵא פָּחוֹת מִטֶּפַח; וּשְׁנִי תוֹלַעַת, מִשְׁקָלוֹ שֶׁקֶל — וְאִם טְעָמוֹ פְּסָלוֹ, כִּצְבִיעוּת הַתְּכֵלֶת, שֶׁנִּפְסָל בִּטְעִימָה; וְכָל הַשִּׁעוּרִין הֲלָכָה.

וְלוֹקֵחַ עִם שְׁלָשְׁתָּן הַצִּפּוֹר הַחַיָּה; וְאַרְבַּעַת מִינִין אֵלּוּ מְעַכְּבִין זֶה אֶת זֶה; וְעֵץ אֶרֶז וְאֵזוֹב שֶׁנִּתְקַלְּפוּ פְּסוּלִין; וְכוֹרֵךְ הָאֵזוֹב עִם הָאֶרֶז בִּלְשׁוֹן שֶׁל זְהוֹרִית, וּמַקִּיף לָהֶם רָאשֵׁי אֲגַפַּיִם וְרֹאשׁ הַזָּנָב שֶׁל צִפּוֹר הַחַיָּה, וְטוֹבֵל אַרְבַּעְתָּן בַּמַּיִם שֶׁבַּכְּלִי וּבַדָּם שֶׁעֲלֵיהֶם, וּמַזֶּה שֶׁבַע פְּעָמִים עַל גַּב יָדוֹ שֶׁל מְצֹרָע, וּמְשַׁלֵּחַ אֶת הַצִּפּוֹר. וְכֵיצַד מְשַׁלְּחָהּ, עוֹמֵד בָּעִיר וְזוֹרְקָהּ חוּץ לַחוֹמָה, וְאֵינוֹ הוֹפֵךְ פָּנָיו לָאֳהָלִים וְלֹא לָעִיר אֶלָּא לַמִּדְבָּר, שֶׁנֶּאֱמַר: אֶל מִחוּץ לָעִיר אֶל פְּנֵי הַשָּׂדֶה. שִׁלְּחָהּ וְחָזְרָה, חוֹזֵר וּמְשַׁלְּחָהּ, אֲפִלּוּ מֵאָה פְעָמִים.

וְאַחַר־כָּךְ מְגַלֵּחַ הַכֹּהֵן אֶת הַמְּצֹרָע; וְכֵיצַד מְגַלְּחוֹ, מַעֲבִיר תַּעַר עַל בְּשָׂרוֹ הַנִּרְאֶה, וַאֲפִלּוּ בֵּית הַשֶּׁחִי וּבֵית הָעֶרְוָה וּשְׁאָר כָּל הַגּוּף, עַד שֶׁיֵּעָשֶׂה כִּדְלַעַת, שֶׁנֶּאֱמַר: אֶת כָּל שְׂעָרוֹ. אִם־כֵּן, לָמָּה נֶאֱמַר "רֹאשׁוֹ וּזְקָנוֹ וְגַבֹּת עֵינָיו" — לְרַבּוֹת כָּל כַּיּוֹצֵא בָהֶן וּלְמַעֵט שֵׂעָר שֶׁבְּתוֹךְ הַחֹטֶם, לְפִי שֶׁאֵינוֹ נִרְאֶה.

5. Mishnah, N'ga'im xiv 1; MT *hilchoth tum'ath tzara'ath* xi 1.

6. TB Sotah 16b.

7. Mishnah, N'ga'im xiv 1; Sifra, *m'tzora, parashah* 1, 10.

8. Sifra, *m'tzora, perek* 1, 2.

9. Mishnah, N'ga'im xiv 1.

10. More correctly, an eighth: one fourth of its half, after it is divided in two; Mishnah, N'ga'im xiv 6.

11. E.g. Greek or Roman hyssop; *ibid.*

12. TB Niddah 26a.

13. I.e. 9.6 grams; TB Yoma 42a.

14. Sifra, *m'tzora, parashah* 1, 15.

15. One thread of which was used in the *tzitzith*, the tassels at the corners of a four-cornered garment (Numbers 15:38).

16. TB 'Eruvin 4a.

17. I.e. if any one is missing or unacceptable, all are unacceptable, and it is as if none were brought; TB M'naḥoth 27a.

18. TB Sotah 15b.

memory said:[5] How is the man with a *tzara'ath* ailment made ritually clean? One brings an earthenware bowl which is new, and puts in it a *r'vi'ith* of running spring water which is fit to be hallowed as water for purifying—this measure is by the ruling of the Scribes.[6] Then he brings two free, uncaged birds that are undefiled, for the purpose of purifying the leprously afflicted man[7]—as it is stated, *and it shall be taken for him that is to be cleansed* (Leviticus 14:4); and he ritually slays the choicer (healthier) one of the two[8] over the water in the earthenware vessel (Leviticus 14:5), draining it until the blood is discernible in the water.[6] He then digs [in the earth] and buries the slain bird in his [the cured *m'tzora's*] presence;[9] this matter is a teaching received in the Oral Tradition.

He then takes cedarwood, which the precept requires to be a cubit in length, while its width should be about one fourth that of the leg of a bed;[10] and [he should take] hyssop which has no accompanying name,[11] and which should not be less than a handbreadth;[12] and scarlet stuff weighing a *shekel.*[13] If it had its color mixed, it was thus disqualified,[14] as in the dyeing of *t'chéleth*, purple-blue wool,[15] which becomes disqualified by the mixing of the color. All these measures are *halachah* (normative oral law).[16]

With the three he takes the live bird; and these four items can withhold one another [from being acceptable].[17] If the cedarwood or hyssop was peeled, it would be disqualified.[18] Then he wraps the hyssop with the cedarwood in the scarlet stuff, and places next to them the tips of the wings and the tip of the tail of the living bird; and thus he immerses all four in the water in the vessel and in the blood that is on it. He sprinkles this seven times onto the back of the afflicted man's hand, and lets the bird go.[19] How does he let it go? He stands in the city and throws it beyond the wall, turning his face neither to the tents nor to the city, but toward the wilderness—for it is stated, *out of the city into the open field* (Leviticus 14:53).[19] If he let it go and it returned, he is to send it away again, [and so] even a hundred times.[20]

Afterward the *kohen* shaves the man who had *tzara'ath*. How does he shave him?—he passes a razor over his visible flesh, even [over] the armpits and the pubic area, and so the rest of the body, until he becomes [as hairless] as a gourd: For it is stated, *all his hair* (Leviticus 14:9); in that case, why does it say, *his head and his beard and his eyebrows* (*ibid.*)?—to add everything similar to them, and to exclude hair within the nostrils, because it is not visible.[21]

וְאַחַר־כָּךְ מְכַבֵּס בְּגָדָיו וְטוֹבֵל, וְיִטְהַר בְּכָךְ מִלְּטַמֵּא בְּבִיאָה וּמִלְּטַמֵּא בְּמִשְׁכָּב וּבְמוֹשָׁב, וְיִכָּנֵס לִפְנִים מִן הַחוֹמָה; וּמוֹנֶה שִׁבְעַת יָמִים, וְהוּא אָסוּר בְּשִׁבְעַת הַיָּמִים אֵלּוּ בְּתַשְׁמִישׁ הַמִּטָּה, שֶׁנֶּאֱמַר: מִחוּץ לְאָהֳלוֹ — מְלַמֵּד שֶׁאָסוּר בְּתַשְׁמִישׁ הַמִּטָּה; אֲבָל מְצֹרַעַת מֻתֶּרֶת בְּתַשְׁמִישׁ הַמִּטָּה.

כָּל שִׁבְעַת הַיָּמִים אֵלּוּ עֲדַיִן הוּא אַב הַטֻּמְאָה, וּמְטַמֵּא אָדָם וְכֵלִים בְּמַגָּע וְאֵינוֹ מְטַמֵּא בְּמַשָּׂא, שֶׁהֲרֵי הוּא אוֹמֵר: וְהָיָה בַּיּוֹם הַשְּׁבִיעִי וְגוֹמֵר, וְכִבֶּס אֶת בְּגָדָיו, מְלַמֵּד שֶׁהָיָה מְטַמֵּא בְגָדִים, וּכְשֵׁם שֶׁהָיָה מְטַמֵּא בְגָדִים בְּמַגָּע כָּךְ מְטַמֵּא אָדָם בְּמַגָּע, שֶׁכָּל הַמְטַמֵּא אָדָם מְטַמֵּא בְגָדִים וְשֶׁאֵינוֹ מְטַמֵּא אָדָם אֵינוֹ מְטַמֵּא בְגָדִים.

וּבַיּוֹם הַשְּׁבִיעִי מְגַלְּחוֹ הַכֹּהֵן תִּגְלַחַת שְׁנִיָּה כְּתִגְלַחַת רִאשׁוֹנָה, וּמְכַבֵּס בְּגָדָיו וְטוֹבֵל, וְיִטְהַר מִלְּטַמֵּא אֲחֵרִים; וַהֲרֵי הוּא כְּכָל טְבוּלֵי יוֹם, וְאוֹכֵל בְּמַעֲשֵׂר; הֶעֱרִיב שִׁמְשׁוֹ, אוֹכֵל בִּתְרוּמָה; הֵבִיא כַּפָּרָתוֹ, אוֹכֵל בַּקֳּדָשִׁים.

שְׁחִיטַת הַצִּפּוֹר וְהַתִּגְלַחַת וְהַהַזָּאָה בַּיּוֹם, וּשְׁאָר כָּל מַעֲשָׂיו בֵּין בַּיּוֹם בֵּין בַּלַּיְלָה; וְאֵלּוּ בַּאֲנָשִׁים, וְכָל הַשְּׁאָר אֲפִלּוּ נָשִׁים; וְאֵלּוּ בַּכֹּהֲנִים, וְכָל הַשְּׁאָר אֲפִלּוּ עַל־יְדֵי יִשְׂרָאֵל; וְאוֹתוֹ כֹהֵן שֶׁטִּמְּאוֹ מִצְוָה לְטַהֲרוֹ, שֶׁנֶּאֱמַר: לְטַהֲרוֹ אוֹ לְטַמְּאוֹ; וְיֶתֶר פְּרָטֶיהָ, בְּמַסֶּכֶת נְגָעִים.

וְנוֹהֶגֶת טָהֳרָה זוֹ בְּכָל מָקוֹם וּבְכָל זְמַן שֶׁיֵּשׁ כֹּהֵן חָכָם בִּנְגָעִים, כֵּן פֵּרֵשׁ הָרַמְבַּ״ם זִכְרוֹנוֹ לִבְרָכָה (וְכֵן רָאִיתִי בְּסִפְרָא). וְעוֹבֵר עָלֶיהָ וְלֹא עֲשָׂאָהּ כַּמִּשְׁפָּט, בִּטֵּל עֲשֵׂה.

[מִצְוַת תִּגְלַחַת מְצֹרָע בַּיּוֹם הַשְּׁבִיעִי]

קעד שֶׁיְּגַלַּח הַמְצֹרָע אֶת כָּל שְׂעָרוֹ, וְהִיא הַטָּהֳרָה הַשְּׁנִיָּה, כְּמוֹ שֶׁאָמְרוּ

19. Although the verse occurs about the purification of an infected house, it is taken to apply equally to the ritual cleansing of a man with a *tzara'ath* infection; TB Kiddushin 57b; Mishnah, N'ga'im xiv 2.

20. Tosefta, N'ga'im viii.

21. TB Sotah 16a–b.

21a. I.e. subjects them to ritual immersion (in a *mikveh*); see MT *hilchoth mikva'oth* i 2.

22. Mishnah, N'ga'im xiv 2; Sifra, *m'tzora, parashah* 2, 6.

23. TB K'rithoth 8b.

24. Mishnah, Kélim i 1.

25. I.e. *ma'asér shéni* (the Second Tithe), which its owner was to eat (either itself or its equivalent value in food) in Jerusalem.

26. Mishnah, N'ga'im xiv 3.

27. Sifra, *m'tzora, parashah* 1, 3; MT *hilchoth tum'ath tzara'ath* xi 5.

After that he washes his clothes[21a] and undergoes immersion, and with that he becomes cleansed, so that he no longer causes defilement by entering [a house], and no longer causes defilement through his couch or seat. He enters within the wall [of the city] and counts seven days, being forbidden conjugal intimacy, since it is stated, *outside his tent* (ibid. 8), which teaches that conjugal intimacy is forbidden him.[22] A woman with *tzara'ath*, however, is permitted conjugal intimacy.[23]

All these seven days, he is yet a primary cause of ritual impurity, who defiles people and objects by touch, but does not defile them by carrying:[24] for here it says, *And it shall be on the seventh day . . . he shall wash his clothes* (ibid. 9), which teaches that [until then] he could defile clothing—and just as he could render clothing ritually unclean by [his] touch, so could he make people unclean by touch. For whoever can defile a person can defile clothing, and whoever does not defile people does not defile clothing.

On the seventh day, the *kohen* shaves him again, as at the first shaving. He washes his clothes, undergoes immersion, and is thus purified from [his state of] defiling others. Now he is like all who bathe by day and wait for nightfall, and he may eat *ma'asér* (the tithe);[25] when his sun has set [and night comes] he may eat *t'rumah;* when he has brought his atoning offering, he may eat of holy offerings.[26]

The ritual slaying of the bird, the shaving, and the sprinkling [must be] by day; the rest of his acts [for purification may be] either by day or at night. These [three actions] are for men; all the rest are for women as well. These [three must be done] by *kohanim;* all the rest [may be done] even by Israelites (non-*kohanim*).[27] And it is a religious duty for that *kohen* who declared him ritually unclean to cleanse him: for it is stated, *to pronounce it clean or to pronounce it unclean* (Leviticus 13:59).[28] The rest of its details are in the Mishnah tractate *N'ga'im.*

This purification is in effect in every place and every time that there is a *kohen* learned in leprous afflictions. So Rambam of blessed memory explained,[29] (and so I saw in the Midrash *Sifra*).[30] If a person transgressed it and did not observe it properly, he would disobey a positive precept.

[THE SHAVING OF A HEALED M'TZORA ON THE SEVENTH DAY]

174 that the man with *tzara'ath* should shave all his hair, which is the second purification, as our Sages of blessed memory said in the

זִכְרוֹנָם לִבְרָכָה בִּנְגָעִים, שֶׁנֶּאֱמַר: וְהָיָה בַיּוֹם הַשְּׁבִיעִי יְגַלַּח אֶת כָּל שְׂעָרוֹ וְגוֹמֵר; וְאָמְרוּ זִכְרוֹנָם לִבְרָכָה: שְׁלֹשָׁה מְגַלְּחִין וְתִגְלַחְתָּן מִצְוָה, הַנָּזִיר וְהַמְּצֹרָע וְהַלְוִיִּם. וּלְוִיִּם צְרִיכִין תִּגְלַחַת כַּמְּצֹרָע, וְזֶה הָיָה בַּמִּדְבָּר.

מִשָּׁרְשֵׁי הַמִּצְוָה, קְצָת מִן הַטַּעַם שֶׁאָמַרְנוּ לְמַעְלָה בַּמַּיִם, כְּדֵי שֶׁיִּרְאֶה הָאָדָם כְּאִלּוּ הַיּוֹם נִבְרָא וְהַיּוֹם מַתְחִיל שְׂעָרוֹ לִצְמֹחַ, וִיחַדֵּשׁ מַעֲשָׂיו לְטוֹב. כִּי בִּהְיוֹת הָאָדָם מְנֻקֶּה מִכָּל שֵׂעָר, אָז יִנָּקֶה יָפֶה מִכָּל לִכְלוּךְ, וְלָכֵן רָאוּי לוֹ לַעֲלוֹתוֹ מִטֻּמְאַת צָרַעְתּוֹ לַעֲשׂוֹת בְּעַצְמוֹ מַעֲשֵׂה הַנְּקִיּוּת בְּכָל כֹּחוֹ, כְּדֵי שֶׁיְּנַקֶּה מַעֲשָׂיו גַּם־כֵּן בְּכָל כֹּחוֹ וְיַהַפְכֵם מֵרָעָה לְטוֹבָה וּלְהַכְשִׁיר.

מִדִּינֵי הַמִּצְוָה, מַה שֶּׁאָמְרוּ זִכְרוֹנָם לִבְרָכָה: כֵּיצַד הוּא הַגִּלּוּחַ, מַעֲבִיר תַּעַר עַל כָּל בְּשָׂרוֹ הַנִּרְאֶה, וַאֲפִלּוּ בֵּית הַשֶּׁחִי וּבֵית הָעֶרְוָה, וְכָל שְׁאָר הַגּוּף, עַד שֶׁיֵּעָשֶׂה כִּדְלַעַת, שֶׁנֶּאֱמַר: אֶת כָּל שְׂעָרוֹ; וּכְשֶׁהוּא מְגַלֵּחַ בִּשְׁתֵּי הַתִּגְלָחוֹת, אֵינוֹ מְגַלֵּחַ אֶלָּא בְתַעַר; וְאִם גִּלַּח שֶׁלֹּא בְתַעַר אוֹ שֶׁהִנִּיחַ שְׁתֵּי שְׂעָרוֹת, לֹא עָשָׂה כְלוּם; וְיֶתֶר פְּרָטֶיהָ, בְּמַסֶּכֶת נְגָעִים.

וְאָמַר הָרַמְבָּ"ם זִכְרוֹנוֹ לִבְרָכָה בְּזוֹ הַמִּצְוָה, וְזֶהוּ לְשׁוֹן הַמַּעְתִּיק: וַאֲבָאֵר עַתָּה מַה הַסִּבָּה אֶצְלֵנוּ בְּתִגְלַחַת מְצֹרָע מִצְוָה בִּפְנֵי עַצְמָהּ וַהֲבָאַת קָרְבְּנוֹתָיו מִצְוָה בִּפְנֵי עַצְמָהּ, וְלֹא עָשִׂינוּ כֵן בְּנָזִיר אֲבָל שַׂמְנוּ תִגְלַחְתּוֹ וַהֲבָאַת קָרְבְּנוֹתָיו מִצְוָה אַחַת. וְזֶהוּ שֶׁהַמְּצֹרָע אֵין קֶשֶׁר לְתִגְלַחְתּוֹ עִם הֲבָאַת קָרְבְּנוֹתָיו, וְהַתַּכְלִית הַמַּגַּעַת מִתִּגְלַחְתּוֹ בִּלְתִּי הַתַּכְלִית הַמַּגַּעַת מֵהֲבָאַת קָרְבְּנוֹתָיו, וְזֶהוּ שֶׁהַמְּצֹרָע טָהֳרָתוֹ תְּלוּיָה בְתִגְלַחְתּוֹ; וּבְפֶרֶק שִׁשִּׁי מִנְּזִירוּת אָמְרוּ: מַה בֵּין נָזִיר לִמְצֹרָע, אֶלָּא שֶׁזֶּה טָהֳרָתוֹ תְּלוּיָה בְיָמָיו, כְּלוֹמַר הַנָּזִיר, וּמְצֹרָע טָהֳרָתוֹ תְּלוּיָה בְתִגְלַחְתּוֹ. וּכְשֶׁיְּגַלַּח הַמְּצֹרָע וְתִשְׁלַם תִּגְלַחְתּוֹ הַשְּׁנִיָּה, טָהַר מִלְּטַמֵּא כְּשֶׁרֶץ, כְּמוֹ שֶׁהִתְבָּאֵר בְּסוֹף

28. Thus Scripture indicates that there should be this link between the two acts; Sifra, *thazri'a, perek* 15, 13; MT *ibid.*

29. MT *ibid.* 6.

30. Sifra, *thazri'a*, beginning. This phrase is not in the old manuscripts, and is apparently a later marginal note that was incorporated.

§174 1. Mishnah, N'ga'im xiv 4.

2. I.e. once only—when they were consecrated to serve at the *mishkan* (Tabernacle) in place of the firstborn: Numbers 8:7. (The paragraph is based on ShM positive precept §111).

3. TB Sotah 16a (MT *hilchoth tum'ath tzara'ath* xi 1).

4. Once when he is healed of his disease, and once after counting seven days (Leviticus 14:8–9).

5. ShM positive precept §111.

tractate *N'ga'im* (xiv 3)—for it is stated, *And it shall be on the seventh day, that he shall shave all his hair*, etc. (Leviticus 14:9). Our Sages of blessed memory taught:[1] Three shave, and their shaving is a religious obligation: the *nazir* (Numbers 6:18), the [healed] *m'tzora*, and the Levites. The Levites required shaving like a man with *tzara'ath* ailment; it was in the wilderness.[2]

At the root of the precept lies a bit of the reason that we stated above about water (§173): it is in order that the man should consider it as though he were created this day, and today his hair begins to grow; and so let him change his deeds anew, for the good. For when a man is shaved clean of all hair, then he can be cleaned well of every besmirching. It is therefore appropriate for him, as he ascends from the ritual uncleanness of his *tzara'ath* ailment, to effect for himself the act of cleansing with all his power, so that he shall cleanse his deeds as well, and change them from bad to good and make them worthy.

Among the laws of the precept, there is what the Sages of blessed memory taught:[3] How is the shaving [done]? He passes a razor across all his visible flesh, even the armpits and pubic area, and all the rest of his body, until he is made [hairless] like a gourd; for it says, *all his hair*. When he is shaved the two times,[4] he is shaved only with a razor. If he shaved without a razor, or if he left two hairs, he [as much as] did nothing.[1] The rest of its details are in *N'ga'im*.

Now, Rambam of blessed memory stated about this precept,[5] in these words of the transcriber:[6] I will now elucidate what the reason is that we list the shaving of the person with *tzara'ath* as a precept by itself and the bringing of his offering as a precept by itself, although we did not do so with the *nazir*, but rather set down his shaving and the bringing of his offerings as one precept (§377): It is because with the [cured] *m'tzora* there is no connection between his shaving and the presentation of his offerings; the end attained by shaving him is not the end attained by bringing his offerings. The reason is that with the *m'tzora*, his purification depends on his shaving; thus, in chapter 6 of the Talmud tractate *Nazir* (44b) it was taught: What is the difference [in law] between a *nazir* and a [healed] *m'tzora*? It is only that with this one, his purification depends on his days—i.e. the *nazir;* while for the *m'tzora*, his purification depends on his shaving. And when the *m'tzora* is shaven and his second shaving is completed, he is cleansed from [his state of] causing defilement like a swarming creature, as it is elucidated toward the end of the Mishnah tractate

נְגָעִים, וְיִשָּׁאֵר מְחֻסַּר כִּפּוּרִים עַד שֶׁיָּבִיא קָרְבְּנוֹתָיו, כִּשְׁאָר מְחֻסְּרֵי כִפּוּרִים, כְּמוֹ שֶׁנִּתְבָּאֵר שָׁם.

וְהוּא תַכְלִית תִּגְלַחְתּוֹ טָהֳרָתוֹ מִלְּטַמֵּא כְּשֶׁרֶץ, הֵבִיא קָרְבְּנוֹתָיו אוֹ לֹא הֵבִיא, וְתַכְלִית הֲבָאַת קָרְבְּנוֹתָיו תַּשְׁלוּם כַּפָּרָתוֹ כִּשְׁאָר מְחֻסְּרֵי כַפָּרָה, כְּלוֹמַר זָב וְזָבָה וְיוֹלֶדֶת; וּכְבָר קָדַם לָנוּ לְשׁוֹן מַאֲמָרָם, "אַרְבָּעָה מְחֻסְּרֵי כַפָּרָה"; וְשָׁם נִתְבָּאֵר שֶׁהַנָּזִיר אֵינוֹ מְחֻסַּר כַּפָּרָה, אֲבָל הַמְּלָאכָה הַהִיא בִכְלָלָהּ, כְּמוֹ הַתִּגְלַחַת וַהֲבָאַת הַקָּרְבָּן, יַתִּירוּ לוֹ שְׁתִיַּת הַיַּיִן, וְלֹא יַסְפִּיק הָאֶחָד מֵהֶם בִּלְתִּי הָאַחֵר; וְתִגְלַחַת קְשׁוּרָה בַּקָּרְבָּן וְהַקָּרְבָּן תָּלוּי בַּתִּגְלַחַת, וּבְקִבּוּצָם תַּגִּיעַ הַתַּכְלִית כְּאַחַת, וְהוּא שֶׁיַּתִּירוּ לוֹ הַדְּבָרִים שֶׁהָיוּ נִמְנָעִים מִמֶּנּוּ בִּימֵי נִזְרוֹ. וּבְפֶרֶק שְׁשִׁי מִנְּזִירוּת אָמְרוּ: גִּלַּח עַל הַזֶּבַח וְנִמְצָא פָּסוּל, תִּגְלַחְתּוֹ פְסוּלָה וּזְבָחָיו לֹא עָלוּ לוֹ. וְהִנֵּה הִתְבָּאֵר שֶׁתִּגְלַחַת הִיא מִתְּנָאֵי הַזֶּבַח, וְהַזֶּבַח מִתְּנָאֶיהָ.

וּבַתּוֹסֶפְתָּא נִתְבָּאֵר כְּמוֹ־כֵן שֶׁנָּזִיר שֶׁכָּלוּ יָמָיו אָסוּר לְגַלֵּחַ וְלִשְׁתּוֹת יַיִן וְלִטַּמֵּא לְמֵתִים עַד שֶׁיַּעֲשֶׂה הַמְּלָאכָה הַהִיא כֻלָּהּ; וְהִיא תִגְלַחַת טָהֳרָה, כְּמוֹ שֶׁהִתְבָּאֵר בְּפֶרֶק שְׁשִׁי מִנְּזִירוּת, וְהוּא שֶׁיְּגַלַּח פֶּתַח אֹהֶל מוֹעֵד, וְיַשְׁלִיךְ שְׂעָרוֹ תַּחַת הַדּוּד; וְיַקְרִיב הַקָּרְבָּנוֹת כְּפִי מַה שֶּׁבָּא בַכָּתוּב; וְאַתָּה תִּמְצָאֵם (בְּסוֹף הַמִּצְווֹת) [בְּרֹב מְקוֹמוֹת] יִקְרְאוּ הֲבָאַת הַקָּרְבָּנוֹת תִּגְלַחַת, וּבְבֵאוּר אָמְרוּ בְּמִצְוַת הַמִּשְׁנָה: "הֲרֵינִי נָזִיר וְעָלַי לְגַלֵּחַ נָזִיר", יִרְצֶה לוֹמַר בָּזֶה שֶׁיָּבִיא קָרְבְּנוֹת נָזִיר וְיַקְרִיבֵם בַּעֲדוֹ. הִנֵּה הִתְבָּאֵר לְךָ שֶׁהַתִּגְלַחַת נוֹפֶלֶת עַל הֲבָאַת הַקָּרְבָּנוֹת, וְהַטַּעַם בָּזֶה הֱיוֹתָהּ חֵלֶק מֵהֶם כְּמוֹ שֶׁבֵּאַרְנוּ; וּבְקִבּוּצָם יוּסַר דִּין הַנְּזִירוּת וְיִשְׁתֶּה הַנָּזִיר יַיִן; אָמְנָם תִּגְלַחַת טֻמְאָה הִיא מִדִּקְדּוּק, פֵּרוּשׁ מֵעִנְיַן הַמִּצְוָה, וְלֹא מִצְוָה בִפְנֵי עַצְמָהּ, כְּמוֹ שֶׁבֵּאַרְנוּ בְּמַה שֶּׁקָּדַם. עַד כָּאן.

6. See §151, note 3. In this citation, the *nazir* is one who has become *ta-mé* (ritually defiled) during the period that he was obligated to be a *nazir*. He counts seven days, and then, like the healed *m'tzora*, he is completely shaven, and the next day he brings his required offerings (Numbers 6:9–10). Yet there is a difference between the two cases, as explained herewith.

7. TB K'rithoth 8b.

8. Numbers 6:18 (but see Rashi). On the *nazir*'s "shaving in his purity" (two lines above) see §377.

9. In which his *sh'lamim* (peace-offering) was cooked; TB Nazir 45b.

10. Mishnah, Nazir ii 5.

N'ga'im (xiv 3); he [merely] remains lacking atonement until he brings his offerings, like all who lack atonement—as it is explained there.

Thus the end purpose of his shaving is his purification, so that he should not cause defilement like a swarming creature—whether he brought his offerings or not. And the end purpose of presenting his offerings is the completion of his atonement, as for all who lack atonement—i.e. a man or a woman with a discharge, or a woman who gave birth. The expression of their [the Sages'] teaching already preceded us:[7] There are four lacking in atonement. And it is explained there that the *nazir* is not lacking in atonement, but rather that task in its entirety, i.e. the shaving and the presentation of the offering, permits him to drink wine; one of them without the other does not suffice: The shaving is bound up with the offering, and the offering is bound up with the shaving. With the both together, the end purpose is reached at once, i.e. that those things which were barred to him during his days as *nazir* become permitted him. Thus in chapter 6 of the tractate *Nazir* (46b) it was taught: If he shaved in conjunction with the offering and it was found to be disqualified, his shaving is unacceptable and his sacrifices are not accredited for him. Here, then, it has been clarified that shaving is among the conditions for [making] the sacrifice [acceptable], while the sacrifice is one of *its* conditions [to make *it* acceptable].

In the Tosefta (ii end) it is similarly clarified that if the [consecrated] days of a *nazir* have ended, he is forbidden to shave, drink wine, or become defiled by the dead, until that task will be done in entirety. This means the shaving in [his] purity, as explained in chapter 6 of the Talmud tractate *Nazir* (45a–b): i.e. that he should shave at the entrance to the Tent of Meeting[8] and throw his hair under the pot,[9] and then present the offerings in accord with what is stated in Scripture. So you will find that in most instances they call the presentation of the offerings "shaving." In clarification, it was taught about a religious obligation in the Mishnah:[10] [If someone says] "I shall be a *nazir*, and I take it upon myself to shave a *nazir*"—he means to say by this that he will bring the offerings of [another] *nazir* and offer them up for him. Thus it has been shown you that shaving is an expression for the presentation of the offerings—the reason for this being that it is a part of them, as we explained. And when they occur jointly, the restrictive state of the *nazir* is removed from him, and he may drink wine. In truth, shaving on account of uncleanness is a detail, i.e. part of the precept, and not a

וְנוֹהֶגֶת בִּזְכָרִים וּנְקֵבוֹת, בְּכָל מָקוֹם וּבְכָל זְמַן שֶׁיֵּשׁ כֹּהֲנִים חֲכָמִים גְּדוֹלִים רְאוּיִים לְהוֹרוֹת בְּצָרַעַת. וְעוֹבֵר עָלֶיהָ וְלֹא גִלַּח, בִּטֵּל עֲשֵׂה, וְהוּא טָמֵא.

[מִצְוַת טְבִילָה לַטְּמֵאִים]

קעה שֶׁנִּטְבֹּל בְּמֵי מִקְוֶה וְאָז נִטַּהֵר בְּאֵי זֶה מִין מִמִּינֵי הַטֻּמְאוֹת שֶׁנִּטְמֵאנוּ בוֹ, שֶׁנֶּאֱמַר: וְרָחַץ אֶת בְּשָׂרוֹ, וּבָאָה הַקַּבָּלָה: מַיִם שֶׁכָּל בְּשָׂרוֹ עוֹלֶה בָהֶן; וְשִׁעֲרוּ חֲכָמִים שֶׁהֵן אַרְבָּעִים סְאָה, וְזֶהוּ שִׁעוּר מִקְוֶה.

וּמִן הַתּוֹרָה, בֵּין שֶׁיִּהְיוּ הַמַּיִם שְׁאוּבִין אוֹ שֶׁהִמְשִׁיכוּ אוֹתָן מִן הַמַּעְיָנוֹת אוֹ מִן הַגְּשָׁמִים, הַכֹּל כָּשֵׁר, שֶׁהַתּוֹרָה אָמְרָה "מִקְוֵה מַיִם", מִכָּל מָקוֹם; אֲבָל חֲכָמִים פָּסְלוּ כָּל מִקְוֶה שֶׁמֵּימָיו שְׁאוּבִין, וְלֹא עוֹד אֶלָּא אֲפִלּוּ עָבְרוּ בִכְלִי שָׁלֵם בְּעֵת שֶׁמַּמְשִׁיכִין אוֹתָן לְתוֹךְ הַחֲפִירָה, פְּסָלוּהוּ.

וְזֶה הַשִּׁעוּר שֶׁל אַרְבָּעִים סְאָה בָּעֵינָן בְּמֵי מִקְוֶה אֲפִלּוּ לְהַטְבִּיל בּוֹ מַחַט, לְדַעַת קְצָת מִן הַמְפָרְשִׁים; אֲבָל בְּמַיִם נוֹבְעִים, כְּלוֹמַר מַיִם הַיּוֹצְאִין מִמַּעְיָנוֹת, אֵין לָהֶם שִׁעוּר כְּלָל, אֶלָּא כָּל זְמַן שֶׁיִּתְכַּסֶּה הָאָדָם כָּל גּוּפוֹ בָהֶן בְּיַחַד, אוֹ שֶׁיִּתְכַּסּוּ בוֹ הַכֵּלִים הַטְּמֵאִים בְּיַחַד, רָאוּי לִטְבֹּל בּוֹ.

וְכָתַב הָרַמְבָּ"ם זִכְרוֹנוֹ לִבְרָכָה: וְאֵין כַּוָּנָתֵנוּ בְּאָמְרֵנוּ שֶׁהַטְּבִילָה מִצְוַת עֲשֵׂה, שֶׁיִּהְיֶה מְצֻוֶּה עַל כָּל טָמֵא שֶׁיִּטְהַר עַל־כָּל־פָּנִים, כְּמוֹ שֶׁחַיָּב כָּל מִי שֶׁיִּתְכַּסֶּה בִכְסוּת שֶׁיַּעֲשֶׂה צִיצִית — פֵּרוּשׁ לְפֵרוּשׁוֹ, בִּכְסוּת אַרְבַּע כְּנָפַיִם — וְכֵן כָּל מִי שֶׁיֵּשׁ לוֹ גַג שֶׁחַיָּב לַעֲשׂוֹת לוֹ מַעֲקֶה; אֲבָל הָעִנְיָן הוּא שֶׁהוֹדִיעַתְנוּ הַתּוֹרָה: מִי שֶׁיִּרְצֶה לְהִטַּהֵר מִטֻּמְאָה לֹא יִתָּכֵן לוֹ זֶה אֶלָּא בִטְבִילָה בְמַיִם, וְצִוַּתְנוּ לְקַבֵּל הָעִנְיָן וְלַעֲשׂוֹתוֹ כֵן כְּשֶׁנִּרְצֶה לְהִטַּהֵר; אֲבָל אִם יִרְצֶה לְהִשָּׁאֵר בְּטֻמְאָתוֹ וְלֹא יִכָּנֵס לְמַחֲנֵה שְׁכִינָה זְמַן רָב, הָרְשׁוּת בְּיָדוֹ.

11. See §169, paragraph before last (note 27), and §173, end (notes 29–30).

§175
1. TB 'Eruvin 4b, P'saḥim 109b.
2. So TB Bava Bathra 66a and Tosefta, Mikva'oth ii beginning (cited in *tosafoth* there, s.v. *mik'lal*).
3. Mishnah, Mikva'oth iv 2.
4. So *tosafoth*, TB Nazir 38a, s.v. *bar*.
5. So Rambam and Rabad, as cited by Rashba, *Torath haBa-yith* VII (188a).
6. ShM positive precept §109.
7. This means a garment with four corners; Numbers 15:38; §386.
8. Deuteronomy 22:8, §546.

precept in its own right [for the defiled *nazir*]—as we have explained earlier. Thus far [the words of Rambam].

It applies to both man and woman, in every place, at every time that there are great learned *kohanim*, properly fit to rule about *tzara'ath* affliction.[11] If a person violated it and did not shave, he would disobey a positive precept, and would [continue to] be ritually unclean.

[THE PRECEPT OF RITUAL IMMERSION FOR CLEANSING THE DEFILED]

175 that we should immerse ourselves in a *mikveh* [collected body of] water, and then we will be cleansed of any kind of ritual impurity with which we were defiled—as it is stated, *and he shall bathe his flesh* (Leviticus 14:9). It was taught in the Oral Tradition[1] what the amount of water is into which all "his flesh" can go: our Sages estimated that it is forty *se'ah*—so that this is the measure of a *mikveh*.

Now, by the law of the Torah, whether the water was collected manually or made to flow from springs or the rains, it is all fit and acceptable:[2] for the Torah stated, *a gathering of water* (Leviticus 11:36)—under any conditions. However, the Sages disqualified any *mikveh* whose water was manually collected; moreover, if it even passed over by way of a complete vessel at the time it was drawn into the dug-out place in the ground, that would disqualify it.[3]

This measure of forty *se'ah* is required for the water of a *mikveh*, even [if only] to immerse a needle in it, in the view of some authorities.[4] For flowing water, however—in other words, water that comes out of springs—there is no minimum measure at all; rather, as long as a man can have his entire body covered by it at once, or defiled objects can be covered by it altogether, it is fit to use for immersion.[5]

Now, Rambam of blessed memory wrote:[6] When we say that ritual immersion is a positive precept, it is not our meaning that it is to be a religious obligation for every defiled person to become ritually cleansed under any circumstances, in the way that anyone who covers himself with a garment is to put *tzitzith* [tassels, at the corners],[7] and similarly, whoever has a roof is obligated to make a balustrade for it.[8] Its substance is rather that the Torah informed us that when someone wishes to be cleansed of ritual defilement, this cannot be effected for him by any other means than immersion in water. It commanded us to accept this matter and so carry it out when we will want to be cleansed.

But should someone wish to remain in his defilement, and thus not

תּוֹסֶפֶת: וּמִכָּל־מָקוֹם אֵין זֶה מִמִּדַּת הַחֲסִידִים וְאַנְשֵׁי מַעֲשֶׂה לִהְיוֹתָם מְטַמְּעִים בְּטֻמְאָתָם, כִּי הַטֻּמְאָה מְאוּסָה, וְהַטָּהֳרָה אֲהוּבָה, וְנַפְשׁוֹ שֶׁל אָדָם מִתְעַלָּה וּמִזְדַּכֶּכֶת בְּטָהֳרָה. עַד כָּאן.

וּלְשׁוֹן סִפְרָא: "וְרָחַץ אֶת בְּשָׂרוֹ", יָכוֹל גְּזֵרַת מֶלֶךְ, תַּלְמוּד לוֹמַר "וְאַחַר יָבֹא אֶל הַמַּחֲנֶה". כְּלוֹמַר שֶׁאֵין הָאָדָם מְצֻוֶּה לְהִטַּהֵר, אֲבָל כְּשֶׁיִּרְצֶה לְהִטַּהֵר, מִצְוָה עָלָיו לַעֲשׂוֹת זֶה הַמַּעֲשֶׂה לְטָהֳרָתוֹ.

מִשָּׁרְשֵׁי הַמִּצְוָה זוֹ שֶׁל טָהֳרַת הַמַּיִם, מַה שֶּׁכָּתַבְנוּ לְמַעְלָה בְּרֹאשׁ הַסֵּדֶר [סי׳ קע״ג], לְהָשִׁיב אֶת הַיְלָדִים כִּפְשָׁטָן שֶׁל דְּבָרִים כְּדֶרֶךְ הַפַּשְׁטָנִים, עַד שֶׁיִּגְדְּלוּ וְיָבִינוּ אֶת אֲשֶׁר יָבִינוּ. וְעוֹד נֹאמַר בָּעִנְיָן, שֶׁיֵּשׁ בַּטְּבִילָה רֶמֶז אֶל הַטּוֹבֵל שֶׁיְּנַקֶּה נַפְשׁוֹ מִכָּל חֵטְא, כְּמוֹ שֶׁטֶּבַע הַמַּיִם לְנַקּוֹת כָּל דָּבָר הַמִּתְכַּבֵּס בָּהֶן.

מִדִּינֵי הַמִּצְוָה, מַה שֶּׁאָמְרוּ זִכְרוֹנָם לִבְרָכָה שֶׁמֵּי מִקְוֶה רְאוּיִים לְהִטַּהֵר בָּהֶם מִכָּל טֻמְאָה, כְּגוֹן נִדָּה וְזָבָה וּשְׁאָר כָּל הַטֻּמְאוֹת שֶׁל אָדָם וְכֵלִים, חוּץ מִטֻּמְאַת זָב לְבַד, לְפִי שֶׁהַכָּתוּב פֵּרֵשׁ בּוֹ לְבַד "מַיִם חַיִּים" לְטָהֳרָתוֹ, פֵּרוּשׁ מַיִם נוֹבְעִין. וְכֵן מַה שֶּׁאָמְרוּ זִכְרוֹנָם לִבְרָכָה שֶׁאַף־עַל־פִּי שֶׁטְּבִילַת קְצָתָם בַּיּוֹם, לֹא תִשְׁלַם טָהֳרָתָם עַד הֶעֱרֵב הַשֶּׁמֶשׁ, כְּמוֹ שֶׁכָּתוּב: בַּמַּיִם יוּבָא וְטָמֵא עַד הָעֶרֶב וְטָהֵר.

וְשֶׁצָּרִיךְ לִטְבֹּל גּוּפוֹ מְגֻלֶּה, כְּלוֹמַר שֶׁנּוֹגֵעַ לְשֶׁטַח הַמַּיִם כֻּלּוֹ, כְּלוֹמַר שֶׁלֹּא יְהֵא שׁוּם דָּבָר חוֹצֵץ בֵּין כָּל הַגּוּף וְהַמַּיִם; וְאִם טָבְלוּ בְּבִגְדֵיהֶם, דִּיעֲבַד עָלְתָה לָהֶם

9. I.e. originally that part of the camp of the Israelites in the wilderness which contained the *mishkan* (Tabernacle); the corresponding part in the land of Israel was the Sanctuary.

10. The Hebrew reads literally, "Addition:"

11. Sifra, *aḥaré moth, parashah* 5, 3. This paragraph continues the quotation from ShM positive precept §109.

12. So MT *hilchoth mikva'oth* xi 12.

13. Mishnah, Mikva'oth i 8.

14. Leviticus 15:13.

15. Sifra, *sh'mini, perek* 8, 9; TB Yevamoth 75a.

enter "the camp of the *shechinah*"[9] a long time, the right [to do so] is in his hands.

But let us [the author] add a word:[10] In any case, though, it is not a trait of the pious and the scrupulously observant to remain wallowing in their ritual uncleanness: For uncleanness is repulsive, while ritual purity is beloved, and a man's spirit is exalted and purified by ritual cleanness. Thus far [our addition].

In the language of the Midrash *Sifra*:[11] "and he shall bathe his body" (Leviticus 14:8)—I might think it is a Royal [Divine] decree?—Scripture states, *and after that he may come into the camp* (ibid.). In other words, the man is not commanded to purify himself; but when he will want to become ritually clean, it is a religious law for him to carry out this action for his purification.

At the root of this precept of ritual cleansing by water lies the point we have written above, at the beginning of the *sidrah* (§173), to give the children a satisfying explanation, according to the direct meaning of the subject, in the way of those who explain simply—until they grow up and understand what they will understand. Let us say, furthermore, about the matter, that in ritual immersion lies a hint to the one undergoing it that he should cleanse his spirit from every sin, even as it is the nature of water to cleanse everything that is washed in it.[12]

Among the laws of the precept, there is what the Sages of blessed memory taught:[13] that the water of the *mikveh* is suitable for purification from every kind of defilement—for instance, a woman unclean from the menses or from an irregular discharge, and all other instances of uncleanness in a person or objects—except solely for the uncleanness of a man with a discharge: because for him alone Scripture designated "living water" for his purification,[14] which means welling, flowing (spring) water. There is, likewise, what the Sages of blessed memory said:[15] that although the immersion of some is properly by day, their purification is not completed until the setting of the sun; as it is written, *it must be put into water; and it shall be unclean until the evening; then it shall be clean* (Leviticus 11:32).

Then [we have the law] that one must immerse his body uncovered, i.e. all of it touching the expanse of the water—which means that there should be nothing intervening between the entire body and the water. If, however, they immersed themselves in their clothes, then after the fact, having been done, the bathing is valid and effective for them, since the water penetrates them [the clothes]. Even a woman unclean from the

טְבִילָה, מִפְּנֵי שֶׁהַמַּיִם בָּאִין בָּהֶם; וְגַם הַנִּדָּה בְּדִין זֶה דִיעֲבַד, וּמֻתֶּרֶת לְבַעְלָהּ; וְהוּא שֶׁלֹּא יִהְיוּ הַבְּגָדִים מְהֻדָּקִים יוֹתֵר מִדַּי.

וְכָל חַיָּבֵי טְבִילוֹת טְבִילָתָן בַּיּוֹם, חוּץ מִנִּדָּה וְיוֹלֶדֶת, שֶׁטְּבִילָתָן בַּלַּיְלָה; וּבַעַל קֶרִי טוֹבֵל וְהוֹלֵךְ כָּל הַיּוֹם כֻּלּוֹ, וַאֲפִלּוּ מִתְּחִלַּת הַלַּיְלָה עַד הֶעֱרֵב הַשֶּׁמֶשׁ. וְדִינֵי חֲצִיצָה, שֶׁאָמְרוּ זִכְרוֹנָם לִבְרָכָה כִּי דְּבַר תּוֹרָה, אִם הָיָה דָבָר חוֹצֵץ חוֹפֶה אֶת רֹב הָאָדָם אוֹ רֹב הַכְּלִי, לֹא עָלְתָה לָהֶם טְבִילָה; וְהוּא שֶׁיַּקְפִּיד הָאָדָם בַּדָּבָר, אֲבָל אִם אֵינוֹ מַקְפִּיד עָלְתָה לוֹ טְבִילָה; וְאִם הַדָּבָר הַחוֹצֵץ אֵינוֹ אֶלָּא עַל מִעוּטוֹ, אֲפִלּוּ מַקְפִּיד עָלְתָה לוֹ טְבִילָה דִּין תּוֹרָה.

אֲבָל מִדִּבְרֵי סוֹפְרִים, שֶׁכָּל דָּבָר הַחוֹצֵץ, וַאֲפִלּוּ כָּל שֶׁהוּא, אִם מַקְפִּיד עָלָיו לֹא עָלְתָה לוֹ טְבִילָה, גְּזֵרָה מִעוּטוֹ מִשּׁוּם רֻבּוֹ, שֶׁהוּא אָסוּר מִן הַתּוֹרָה כְּשֶׁמַּקְפִּיד; וְאִם הָיָה דָבָר הַחוֹצֵץ חוֹפֶה רֻבּוֹ, אַף־עַל־פִּי שֶׁאֵינוֹ מַקְפִּיד לֹא עָלְתָה לוֹ טְבִילָה, גְּזֵרָה רֹב שֶׁאֵינוֹ מַקְפִּיד מִשּׁוּם רֹב הַמַּקְפִּיד, שֶׁאָסוּר דְּבַר תּוֹרָה.

נִמְצָא לְפִי זֶה שֶׁאִם הָיָה דָבָר חוֹצֵץ עַל מִעוּטוֹ וְאֵינוֹ מַקְפִּיד, עָלְתָה לוֹ טְבִילָה אֲפִלּוּ מִדְּרַבָּנָן, דְּהַשְׁתָּא יֵשׁ בַּדָּבָר תַּרְתֵּי לְטִיבוּתָא.

וְדִינֵי מִקְוָאוֹת רַבִּים, וְדִין מַיִם שְׁאוּבִין בְּכַמָּה פּוֹסְלִין הַמִּקְוֶה, וְכֵיצַד, וּבְאֵי זֶה כְּלִי יִקָּרְאוּ הַמַּיִם שְׁאוּבִין, שֶׁאִלּוּ שְׁאָבוּהָ בִּכְלִי נָקוּב בְּמוֹצִיא רִמּוֹן אֵין אֵלּוּ נִקְרָאִים מַיִם שְׁאוּבִין, שֶׁאֵין עָלָיו תּוֹרַת כְּלִי מֵעַתָּה; וַאֲפִלּוּ סָתְמוּ הַנֶּקֶב סְתִימָה שֶׁאֵינָהּ יָפָה, כְּגוֹן שֶׁנָּתְנוּ בוֹ אֶבֶן אוֹ פְרִי לְפִי שָׁעָה שֶׁאֵינוֹ סוֹתְמוֹ סְתִימָה יָפָה,

16. TB Bétzah 18a.

17. TB Yoma 6a.

18. TB Shabbath 121a.

19. I.e. if there was anything attached or clinging to the body to get in the way and not permit the water to reach that part of the body.

20. And he wished to remove the interference.

21. Since he had no wish to remove it, it is considered as though part of him (Rashi, TB Sukkah 6b, s.v. *'én*).

22. I.e. not covering the greater part of his body.

23. TB 'Eruvin 4b, etc. (MT *hilchoth mikva'oth* i 6.)

24. I.e. if people were accustomed to bathing ritually with something covering a lesser part of the body, they could well become lax about interferences covering the greater part of the body—especially if they were uncertain if a majority of the body area was actually covered.

25. I.e. if people were accustomed to bathing ritually with the greater part of their body covered by something they did not mind, they could become lax when they found such a covering annoying but did not wish to trouble themselves to remove it.

26. Mishnah, Mikva'oth ii 4, etc.

27. *Ibid.* iii 4; MT *hilchoth mikva'oth* v 1.

menses is included in this law of [validity] after the fact, and she is permitted to her husband—but this, if the clothes were not fastened unduly tight.[16]

All those obligated to have ritual immersion are to have the bathing done by day, except a woman unclean from the menses and one who has given birth, whose ritual bathing is to be at night,[17] while a man who had a pollution may undergo the immersion at any time of the day at all, even from the beginning of the night to the setting of the sun.[18] We have, too, the laws of interference,[19] about which the Sages of blessed memory taught that by the law of the Torah, if some intervening substance was covering most of the man or most of the object, the immersion would be of no value for them, provided the man minded about the matter.[20] But if he did not mind, the immersion was effective for him.[21] On the other hand, if the interfering object was only on a small part of him,[22] then even if he objected to it, the ritual immersion was effective for him, by the law of the Torah.[23]

By the ruling of the Scribes, however, if there is anything at all that intervenes, even the smallest thing, if he but objects to it, the immersion has no validity for him. It is an edict of restriction about a small part of the person on account of the greater part of him[24]—when it is forbidden by Torah law when he minds. If the interfering thing covered most of him, then even if he did not mind, the ritual bathing is of no value to him—[by] an edict [of the Sages when there is something interfering covering] the greater part, which he does not mind, on account of [an interference over] the greater part that he does mind,[25] which is forbidden by the law of the Torah.[23]

Consequently, according to this, if there was something intervening over the lesser part of a person and he did not mind, the ritual bathing would be valid for him even by the law of the Sages: For now there are two things in its favor.[23]

And many [further] laws about *mikveh*: We have the law of manually collected water: in what quantity it disqualifies a *mikveh* [if used as part of its water],[26] and in what way;[27] in what kind of a vessel the water is called collected—for if it was gathered in a vessel with a hole big enough to let a pomegranate through, it would not be called collected water, since as of now it is not considered as a vessel.[28] Even if the hole was stopped up with an unsatisfactory filling temporarily—for instance, if a stone or a fruit was placed in it, which does not block it up well and properly, since holes and cracks are left. If [a vessel] was

שֶׁעֲדַיִן יִשָּׁאֲרוּ בוֹ נְקָבִים וּסְדָקִים. [וְאִם נִקַּב] בְּכוֹנֵס מַשְׁקֶה, גַּם בָּזֶה שָׁמַעְתִּי מִמּוֹרַי: יֵשׁ אוֹמְרִים שֶׁלֹּא תִקָּרֵא שְׁאוּבָה, וּרְאוּיָה לִטְבֹּל בָּהּ.

וְדִין חָקַק הַכְּלִי עַד שֶׁלֹּא קְבָעוֹ אוֹ קְבָעוֹ וְאַחַר־כָּךְ חֲקָקוֹ; וְכַמָּה חֶקֶק רָאוּי לִפְסֹל; וְהַחִלּוּק שֶׁבֵּין כְּלִי חֶרֶס לִשְׁאָר כֵּלִים, שֶׁכְּלִי חֶרֶס אֵינוֹ פוֹסֵל עַד שֶׁיִּהְיֶה הַחֶקֶק כְּדֵי לְקַבֵּל רְבִיעִית, וּכְלִי עֵץ פָּסוּל בְּכָל שֶׁהוּא.

וּמַה שֶּׁאָמְרוּ שֶׁאֵין הַמִּקְוֶה נִפְסָל לֹא בְשִׁנּוּי הָרֵיחַ וְלֹא בְשִׁנּוּי הַטַּעַם, אֶלָּא בְשִׁנּוּי מַרְאֶה בִּלְבָד; וְכָל דָּבָר שֶׁאֵין עוֹשִׂין בּוֹ מִקְוֶה לְכַתְּחִלָּה פּוֹסֵל אֶת הַמִּקְוֶה בְּשִׁנּוּי מַרְאֶה, כְּגוֹן הַיַּיִן וְהֶחָלָב וְהַדָּם, וּמֵי כָּל פֵּרוֹת גַּם־כֵּן; אֲבָל נָפְלוּ מֵהֶם לַמִּקְוֶה וְלֹא שִׁנּוּ מַרְאָיו אֵינָם פּוֹסְלִין, דְּדַוְקָא בְּמַיִם שְׁאוּבִין גָּזְרוּ וְאָמְרוּ שֶׁשְּׁלֹשֶׁת לֻגִּין מֵהֶן פּוֹסְלִין, אֲבָל לֹא מֵי פֵּרוֹת, עַד שֶׁיִּשְׁתַּנֶּה מַרְאֵה הַמַּיִם בַּעֲבוּרָן.

וְדִינֵי חֲצִיצוֹת רַבִּים, וְסוֹף הַדְּבָרִים הַכְּלָל הַצָּרִיךְ אֵלֵינוּ זֶהוּ: מִדִּין תּוֹרָה הָיְתָה צְרִיכָה כָּל אִשָּׁה לְעַיֵּן כָּל גּוּפָהּ סָמוּךְ לִטְבִילָתָהּ שֶׁלֹּא יְהֵא דָבָר חוֹצֵץ בְּגוּפָהּ, וְדַיָּהּ; וְעֶזְרָא וּבֵית דִּינוֹ תִּקְּנוּ שֶׁתְּהֵא חוֹפֶפֶת בְּכָל מְקוֹם שֵׂעָר שֶׁבָּהּ בְּמַיִם חַמִּים, וּמְסָרֶקֶת אוֹ מְפַסְפֶּסֶת שַׂעֲרוֹתֶיהָ בְּיָדֶיהָ — אוֹ בְמַסְרֵק אִם יֵשׁ לָהּ — יָפֶה יָפֶה, כְּדֵי שֶׁאִם הָיוּ שַׂעֲרוֹתֶיהָ נִקְשָׁרִים תַּתִּיר אוֹתָם; וּבְנוֹת יִשְׂרָאֵל הֶחְמִירוּ עַל עַצְמָן לִשְׁטֹף כָּל גּוּפָן בְּחַמִּין, וְכָל הַמְשַׁנֶּה מִמִּנְהָגָן יִמָּתַח עַל הָעַמּוּד.

וַחֲפִיפָה זוֹ צְרִיכָה סָמוּךְ לַטְּבִילָה, כְּלוֹמַר שֶׁלֹּא תִתְעַסֵּק בְּדָבָר אַחֵר בֵּינְתַיִם; וּמִכָּל־מָקוֹם אִם נִזְדַּמְּנָה לְאִשָּׁה טְבִילָה בְּלֵילֵי שַׁבָּת וְיוֹם־טוֹב, הִתִּירוּ אֲפִלּוּ לְכַתְּחִלָּה שֶׁתְּהֵא חוֹפֶפֶת בַּיּוֹם וְטוֹבֶלֶת בַּלַּיְלָה; וְכֵן מִפְּנֵי חֲשָׁשׁ שֶׁיִּכָּנְסוּ הַמַּיִם בְּכָל מָקוֹם שֶׁבְּגוּפָהּ, אָמְרוּ זִכְרוֹנָם לִבְרָכָה שֶׁצְּרִיכָה הָאִשָּׁה לַעֲמֹד בִּשְׁעַת טְבִילָה

28. MY cites Séfer Roké-aḥ §377, that with a hole of this size, no vessel can be considered a proper receptacle at all; hence it cannot be considered a source of "collected" water to disqualify a *mikveh*. From Mishnah, Mikva'oth iv 5, it appears that a hole as big as the opening of a leather water-bottle is enough to invalidate a vessel, but according to Séfer Roké-aḥ that is only when the vessel is in the water (MY).

28a. The Hebrew text of this sentence has been emended per MH, who refers to a view cited in *Beth Yosef* to *Tur Yoreh Dé'ah* §201.

29. In the latter case it is considered as part of the earth from the start, and water coming from it into a *mikveh* is not regarded as "collected water"; Mishnah, Mikva'oth iv 5; TB Bava Kamma 67a.

30. By making it a vessel properly fit for collecting water; explained in what follows.

31. Mishnah, Mikva'oth iv 3.

32. TB Shabbath 24a, Ḥullin 106a; Mishnah, Mikva'oth vii 3 (MT *hilchoth mikva'oth* vii 1).

broached enough to let liquid enter, about this too I heard from my master teacher that some say [water gathered in it] would not be called manually collected, and it would be suitable for ritual bathing.[28a]

We have, moreover, the law if a vessel was hollowed out before it was set in the ground, or if it was set into the ground and then hollowed out;[29] how much hollowing out is a fit amount to disqualify it;[30] the difference [in law] between an earthenware vessel and other vessels—that an earthenware vessel is not disqualified until the hollow is enough to hold a *r'vi'ith;* whereas a wooden vessel is disqualified with any [hollow] at all.[31]

In addition, there is what the Sages said, that a *mikveh* does not become disqualified by a change in smell or a change in taste [of the water], but only by a change in the appearance.[32] Anything from which a *mikveh* may not be formed originally can disqualify the *mikveh* [water] by changing the appearance:[33] for example, wine, milk, blood, and the juice of all fruits as well. However, if any of these fell into a *mikveh* and did not change its appearance, they do not disqualify it.[34] For only on manually collected water did the Sages decree and say that three *log* of it cause disqualification; but not so fruit juices; [they have no effect] until the appearance of the water changes on their account.[35]

There are, too, many laws about intervening objects.[19] But when all is said and done, the rule we need is this: By the law of the Torah, every woman would have to examine her entire body shortly before her immersion, that there should be no interfering object on her body; and that would be enough. However, Ezra and his *beth din* [court of scholars] established the rule that she should wash her every area with hair with warm water, and then comb or part her hair with her hands—or with a comb, if she has one—very thoroughly, so that if her hairs were tangled, she would loosen them.[36] The daughters of Israel (Jewry), though, adopted for themselves the more stringent practice to wash their entire body with warm water.[37] Whoever will diverge from their practice should be stretched on the stand [to receive punishment].

This washing of the hair needs [to be done] directly before the immersion; in other words, she should not busy herself with anything else in between. However, if a ritual immersion fell due for a woman on on the evening of a Sabbath or a festival day,[38] the Sages permitted even at the start[39] that she should wash her hair by day and bathe ritually at night.[40] Likewise, on account of doubt whether the water will reach her body at every point, our Sages of blessed memory said that a

בְּעִנְיָן שֶׁתְּהֵא נִרְאֵית כְּאוֹרֶגֶת וּכְמֵינֶקֶת אֶת בְּנָהּ שֶׁעוֹמֵד תַּחַת הַדָּד.

וּצְרִיכָה לְהִזָּהֵר גַּם־כֵּן בְּטַבָּעוֹת שֶׁבְּיָדָהּ, וְהַצְּמִידִים, אִם הֵם מְהֻדָּקִין כְּלָל לִטְּלָן מִיָּדֶיהָ בִּשְׁעַת טְבִילָה, וְכֵן הָרְצוּעוֹת שֶׁבְּרֹאשָׁהּ לְהַתִּירָן, וְתָדִיחַ אֶת פִּיהָ וְשִׁנֶּיהָ, שֶׁאַף־עַל־פִּי שֶׁכָּל הַמְּקוֹמוֹת שֶׁבְּבֵית הַסְּתָרִים אֵין צְרִיכִין שֶׁיָּבוֹאוּ בָהֶן מַיִם, צְרִיכִין הֵם לִהְיוֹתָם רְאוּיִים לְבִיאַת מַיִם; וּמַעֲשֶׂה הָיָה בְּאִשָּׁה שֶׁטָּבְלָה וְנִמְצָא לָהּ עֶצֶם בֵּין שִׁנֶּיהָ, וְהִצְרִיכוּהָ חֲכָמִים טְבִילָה אַחֶרֶת.

טָבְלָה וְנִמְצָא עָלֶיהָ שׁוּם דָּבָר חוֹצֵץ כְּגוֹן בָּצֵק אוֹ זֶפֶת אוֹ דָם יָבֵשׁ וְכַיּוֹצֵא בָהֶן, מִכָּל הַדְּבָרִים שֶׁמָּנוּ חֲכָמִים שֶׁחוֹצְצִין, אֲפִלּוּ כְּטִפַּת חַרְדָּל, כָּל זְמַן שֶׁמַּקְפֶּדֶת עָלֶיהָ וְדַרְכָּהּ לְהַעֲבִירָהּ לֹא עָלְתָה לָהּ טְבִילָה; וַאֲפִלּוּ הָיָה הַדָּבָר הַחוֹצֵץ תַּחַת הַצִּפֹּרֶן וַאֲפִלּוּ כְּנֶגֶד הַבָּשָׂר, מִכֵּיוָן שֶׁמַּקְפֶּדֶת חוֹצֵץ; וּלְפִיכָךְ נָהֲגוּ בְּנוֹת יִשְׂרָאֵל לִטֹּל צִפָּרְנָן בִּשְׁעַת טְבִילָה; וְיֶתֶר רִבֵּי פְּרָטִים שֶׁל דִּינֵי חֲצִיצָה וְדִינֵי מִקְוָאוֹת וּטְבוּל יוֹם, מְבֹאָרִים בְּמַסֶּכֶת מִקְוָאוֹת וּבְמַסֶּכֶת טְבוּל יוֹם.

וְנוֹהֶגֶת מִצְוָה זוֹ שֶׁל טְבִילָה בְּכָל מָקוֹם וּבְכָל זְמַן, בִּזְכָרִים וּנְקֵבוֹת, שֶׁמִּצְוָה עֲלֵיהֶם כְּשֶׁיִּרְצוּ לְהִטַּהֵר מִטֻּמְאָתָן שֶׁיִּטְבְּלוּ בַמַּיִם, כְּעִנְיָן שֶׁאָמַרְנוּ בְּמַיִם רְאוּיִין, וְשֶׁלֹּא יְהֵא בָהֶן דָּבָר חוֹצֵץ, וְיֶתֶר הָעִנְיָנִים שֶׁכָּתַבְנוּ; אֲבָל מִכָּל־מָקוֹם אֵין הַמִּצְוָה שֶׁיִּטַּהֲרוּ עַצְמָן עַל־כָּל־פָּנִים אִם רָצוּ לְהִשָּׁאֵר בְּטֻמְאָתָן, אֶלָּא־אִם־כֵּן בָּא לִכָּנֵס לַמִּקְדָּשׁ אוֹ לֶאֱכֹל קֹדֶשׁ, וְזֶהוּ בִזְמַן הַבַּיִת, כִּי אָז בַּזְּמַן הַהוּא אִם עָשָׂה כֵן בִּטֵּל עֲשֵׂה זֶה, מִלְּבַד הַחִיּוּב שֶׁעָלָיו בְּאָכְלוֹ קֹדֶשׁ בְּטֻמְאָה וְהִכָּנְסוֹ לַמִּקְדָּשׁ, כְּמוֹ שֶׁכָּתַבְנוּ לְמַעְלָה.

33. TB Shabbath 144b.

34. Mishnah, Mikva'oth vii 5, etc. (see MY).

35. MT *ibid.*

36. TB Bava Kamma 82a, Niddah 66b; *She'iltoth d'R. Aḥa'i Ga'on,* §96; Rabad, *Ba'alé Nefesh, sha'ar ha-t'villah, diné ḥafifah,* beginning; Ramban, *hilchoth niddah* ix 2.

37. Rabad *ibid.*; Ramban *ibid.* 3.

38. I.e. the evening before the Sabbath or festival day, which begins the day—since a day in Jewish reckoning begins at nightfall and ends at sunset.

39. I.e. not merely after the fact, if the deed was already done.

40. TB Niddah 68a; *She'iltoth d'R. Aḥa'i Ga'on,* §96.

41. TB Niddah 67a.

42. Tosefta, Mikva'oth x.

43. Mishnah, Mikva'oth ix 1.

44. TB Niddah 66b.

45. Which invalidates the immersion; Mishnah, Mikva'oth ix 2, 5: TB Shabbath 120b; TB 'Eruvin 4b.

46. Ramban, *hilchoth niddah* ix 12.

woman must stand during the immersion, in such a manner that she should seem like one weaving or nursing her son as he stays [held] under the breast.[41]

She also needs to be careful about rings on her hand, and bracelets: if they are at all fastened [on her] she is to remove them from her hands for the time of the immersion.[42] So too, bands on her head should be untied;[43] and she should rinse her mouth and teeth. For even though none of the places in the hidden parts of the body require that the water should reach them, they have to be fit for the water to be able to reach them.[44] It happened once that a woman had ritual immersion, and a bone was found between her teeth—and the Sages required her to have another immersion.[44]

If a woman had her immersion and something intervening was then found upon her, such as dough, tar, dried blood, or anything similar, of all the things the Sages listed as forming a separation even in the size of a drop of mustard—so long as she finds it objectionable and would generally remove it, the ritual immersion is of no avail to her. Even if the intervening thing was under a fingernail or even against the flesh, since she minds it, it is an interference.[45] For this reason, the daughters of Israel (Jewry) adopted the practice of cutting their fingernails at the time of the immersion.[46] The remaining host of details of the laws of interfering things, the laws of the *mikveh*, and one who needs ritual immersion by day [becoming purified in the evening], are explained in the Mishnah tractates *Mikva'oth* and *T'vul Yom*.

This *mitzvah* of ritual bathing remains in force in every place, at every time, for both man and woman: it is an ordained procedure for them, when they wish to be cleansed of their defilement, that they should undergo immersion in the way we have described, in properly constituted water; and there should be nothing intervening about them [on their bodies]; and so the other matters that we have written. But in any event, the commandment is not that they should cleanse themselves under all circumstances, if they wished to remain in their defilement—unless one came to enter the Sanctuary or eat hallowed food, which means at the time the Temple is in existence. For then, at that time, if someone acted so, he would disobey this positive precept—this apart from the guilt he would incur by eating sacred food in defilement or thus entering the Sanctuary, as we wrote above (§167).

[מִצְוַת קָרְבַּן מְצֹרָע כְּשֶׁיִּתְרַפֵּא מִצָּרַעְתּוֹ]

קעו שֶׁיַּקְרִיב כָּל מְצֹרָע קָרְבָּן כְּשֶׁיֵּרָפֵא מֵחָלְיוֹ, וְהוּא שָׁלֹשׁ בְּהֵמוֹת, אַחַת לְעוֹלָה וְאַחַת לְחַטָּאת וְאַחַת לְאָשָׁם, וְעוֹד לֹג שֶׁמֶן; וְאִם הוּא עָנִי, כֶּבֶשׂ אֶחָד לְאָשָׁם וְעִשָּׂרוֹן סֹלֶת וְלֹג שֶׁמֶן וּשְׁתֵּי תוֹרִים אוֹ שְׁנֵי בְּנֵי יוֹנָה, הָאֶחָד חַטָּאת וְהָאֶחָד עוֹלָה — שֶׁנֶּאֱמַר: וּבַיּוֹם הַשְּׁמִינִי יִקַּח שְׁנֵי כְבָשִׂים תְּמִימִם וְכַבְשָׂה אַחַת, וְכָתַב בַּפָּרָשָׁה שֶׁאַחַר זוֹ: וְאִם דַּל הוּא וְגוֹמֵר; וְזֶה הַמְּצֹרָע נִקְרָא מְחֻסַּר כַּפָּרָה עַד שֶׁיַּקְרִיב זֶה הַקָּרְבָּן.

וְאַרְבָּעָה מְחֻסְּרֵי כַפָּרָה הֵן: זֶה שֶׁאָמַרְנוּ וְזָב וְזָבָה וְיוֹלֶדֶת. וְהָעִנְיָן שֶׁנִּקְרְאוּ מְחֻסְּרֵי כַפָּרָה הוּא לוֹמַר שֶׁכָּל אֶחָד מֵהֶם, אַף־עַל־פִּי שֶׁטָּהַר מִטֻּמְאָתוֹ וְטָבַל וְהֶעֱרִיב שִׁמְשׁוֹ בַּיּוֹם הַשְּׁבִיעִי, עֲדַיִן הוּא חָסֵר כַּפָּרָה זוֹ, וְאֵינוֹ יָכוֹל לֶאֱכֹל בְּקָדָשִׁים עַד שֶׁיַּקְרִיבֶנָּה בַּיּוֹם הַשְּׁמִינִי.

וְאַל יִקְשֶׁה עָלֶיךָ לָמָּה אָנוּ מוֹנִין קָרְבַּן כָּל אֶחָד מֵאַרְבָּעָה אֵלֶּה מִצְוָה אַחַת וְלֹא נִכְלְלוּ כֻּלָּן בְּמִצְוָה אַחַת, שֶׁנֹּאמַר שֶׁיַּקְרִיבוּ אַרְבָּעָה מְחֻסְּרֵי כַפָּרָה וְאַחַר־כָּךְ יִהְיוּ מְכֻפָּרִין — כְּמוֹ שֶׁאָנוּ אוֹמְרִים בְּטָהֳרַת מֵי מִקְוֶה שֶׁיִּטְבֹּל כָּל טָמֵא וְאַחַר־כָּךְ יִטְהַר, וְאֵין אָנוּ מְחַלְּקִין בְּעִנְיְנֵי הַטֻּמְאוֹת לַחֲשֹׁב טָהֳרַת כָּל אַחַת מִצְוָה. כִּי הָעִנְיָן הוּא מִפְּנֵי שֶׁקָּרְבְּנוֹת אַרְבָּעָה אֵלֶּה אֵינָם שָׁוִים, וְנִמְצָא שֶׁהַדָּבָר שֶׁיַּשְׁלִים כַּפָּרָתוֹ שֶׁל אֶחָד מֵהֶם לֹא יַשְׁלִים כַּפָּרַת הָאַחֵר, וְלָכֵן יִמְנוּ כָל אֶחָד מִצְוָה, מַה שֶּׁאֵין כֵּן בְּמֵי מִקְוֶה, שֶׁהַטָּהֳרָה שָׁוָה בַכֹּל; כֵּן תֵּרֵץ הַדָּבָר הָרַמְבָּ"ם זִכְרוֹנוֹ לִבְרָכָה.

מִשָּׁרְשֵׁי עִנְיַן הַקָּרְבָּן, כָּתַבְנוּ לְמַעְלָה עַל צַד הַפְּשָׁט, כִּי בוֹ דִּמְיוֹן לְהַשְׁפִּיל יֵצֶר הַגּוּף הַחוֹטֵא וּלְהַגְדִּיל מַעֲלַת הַנֶּפֶשׁ; וְלָכֵן הַמְּצֹרָע חַיָּב בּוֹ, כִּי הַצָּרַעַת לֹא יִהְיֶה

§176

1. The paragraph is based on ShM positive precept §77.
2. So TB K'rithoth 8b.
3. So MT *hilchoth m'ḥus'ré kapparah* i 1.
4. ShM positive precept §77.

[THE PRECEPT OF THE OFFERING OF A M'TZORA, WHEN HE IS HEALED]

176 that every person with a *tzara'ath* ailment should bring an offering when he is healed of his disease, this being three animals: one for an *'olah* (burnt-offering), one for a *ḥattath* (sin-offering), and one for an *'asham* (guilt-offering); and in addition, a *log* of oil. If he is poor, [he brings] one sheep for an *'asham*, an *'issaron* of fine flour, a *log* of oil, and two turtledoves or two young pigeons—one for a *ḥattath* and one for an *'olah*. For it is stated, *And on the eighth day he shall take two male lambs without blemish, and one ewe-lamb* (Leviticus 14:10); then it is written in the section after this, *And if he is poor*, etc. (*ibid.* 21). This man with the *tzara'ath* disease is called "lacking in atonement" until he brings this offering.[1]

There are four "lacking in atonement": this one whom we noted, a man and a woman with a discharge, and a woman who gives birth.[2] In essence they are called lacking in atonement to convey that even though each was purified of his defilement and had ritual immersion, and his sun set on the seventh day, every one of them yet lacks this atonement, and he may not eat of holy offerings until he brings his offering on the eighth day.[3]

Now, let it not be a difficulty for you why we count the offering of each of these four as a separate precept, and all were not included in one precept: After all, we ought to say that the four lacking in atonement should bring an offering, and then they will have found atonement, as we say about purification in the water of a *mikveh*, that every defiled person should undergo ritual immersion, and after that he will be ritually pure; and we do not differentiate in regard to defilements to consider the ritual cleansing of each one a [separate] precept. But the reason is that the offerings of these four are not identical, and consequently, what completes the atonement of one will not complete the atonement of another. Hence each is counted as a precept, which is not the case with the water of the *mikveh*, where the purification is the same for everyone.

So Rambam of blessed memory answered it.[4]

At the root of the subject of the offering lies the point we wrote above, by way of the plain meaning: that in it there is an implicit metaphor to humble the inclination of the sinner's body and magnify the noble side of the spirit. Therefore is it required of a person with a *tzara'ath* ailment: for this disease will not befall a man except for the

בָּאָדָם רַק מִצַּד הֶמְשֵׁכוֹ אַחַר תַּאֲוֹת הַגּוּף אוֹ בְדִבּוּר אוֹ בְמַעֲשֶׂה, וְרָאוּי לְהִתְיַסֵּר.

מִדִּינֵי הַמִּצְוָה, מַה שֶּׁאָמְרוּ זִכְרוֹנָם לִבְרָכָה שֶׁכָּל מְחֻיְּבֵי קָרְבָּן אֵין מַקְרִיבִין אֲחֵרִים קָרְבָּנָן אֶלָּא מִדַּעְתָּן, חוּץ מִמְּחֻסְּרֵי כַפָּרָה, שֶׁאֵין צְרִיכִין דַּעַת בְּעָלִים; וּמִפְּנֵי־כֵן אָמְרוּ שֶׁאָדָם מֵבִיא קָרְבָּן עַל בָּנָיו וּבְנוֹתָיו הַקְּטַנִּים אִם הָיוּ מְחֻסְּרֵי כַפָּרָה, וּמַאֲכִילָן בִּזְבָחִים; וְיֶתֶר פְּרָטֶיהָ, מְבֹאָרִים בְּהַרְבֵּה מְקוֹמוֹת בַּתַּלְמוּד, וְעִקָּר בִּזְבָחִים בְּפֶרֶק שֵׁנִי וַעֲרָכִין פֶּרֶק שֵׁנִי וּכְרֵתוֹת פֶּרֶק א׳ וּבְנָזִיר פֶּרֶק ח׳ וּבְסוֹף נְגָעִים וְקִנִּין.

וְנוֹהֶגֶת בִּזְמַן הַבַּיִת, בִּזְכָרִים וּנְקֵבוֹת. וְעוֹבֵר עָלֶיהָ וְלֹא הִקְרִיב קָרְבָּנוֹ בִּזְמַנּוֹ, בִּטֵּל עֲשֵׂה.

[מִצְוַת עִנְיַן טֻמְאַת בַּיִת שֶׁיִּהְיֶה בּוֹ נֶגַע]

קעז לְטַמֵּא בַּיִת מְנֻגָּע, כְּלוֹמַר שֶׁנַּעֲשֶׂה בְּבַיִת שֶׁיִּהְיֶה בּוֹ צָרַעַת כַּמִּשְׁפָּט הַכָּתוּב בַּפָּרָשָׁה, כְּמוֹ שֶׁנֶּאֱמַר: וּבָא אֲשֶׁר לוֹ הַבַּיִת וְגוֹמֵר, כְּמוֹ שֶׁכָּתוּב שָׁם; וְשֶׁנַּחֲזִיק מִי שֶׁנִּכְנַס לַבַּיִת בְּטָמֵא, כְּמוֹ שֶׁכָּתוּב בַּפָּרָשָׁה: וְהַבָּא אֶל הַבַּיִת... יִטְמָא וְגוֹמֵר.

וּמִצְוָה זוֹ כּוֹלֶלֶת כָּל עִנְיְנֵי טֻמְאַת הַבַּיִת, אֵי זֶה צָרִיךְ הֶסְגֵּר אוֹ הֲרִיסָה בִּקְצָת הַקִּירוֹת, אוֹ בְכֻלָּן. וְזֶה הָעִנְיָן שֶׁל צָרַעַת הַהוֹוֶה בָאֲבָנִים, שָׁמַעְתִּי שֶׁאֵינֶנּוּ דָבָר טִבְעִי, אֲבָל הוּא עִנְיָן מוֹפְתִי, יָבוֹא לִפְעָמִים לְבָתֵּי יִשְׂרָאֵל לְהוֹכִיחָם, כִּי מֵאַהֲבַת הַשֵּׁם אוֹתָם יוֹדִיעֵם מוּסָרוֹ בְּמַה שֶּׁהוּא חוּץ לְגוּפָם, כְּדֵי שֶׁיַּחְזְרוּ בִתְשׁוּבָה טֶרֶם יִתְחַיְּבוּ לַעֲנֹשׁ אוֹתָם בְּגוּפָם. וְכֵן הָיָה הָעִנְיָן, שֶׁאִם לֹא עָשָׂה תְשׁוּבָה, יִתְפַּשֵּׁט הַנֶּגַע גַּם בִּבְגָדָיו; לֹא הִרְגִּישׁ עֲדַיִן, יִתְפַּשֵּׁט גַּם בְּגוּפוֹ.

וְעוֹד אָמְרוּ זִכְרוֹנָם לִבְרָכָה כִּי בַתְּחִלָּה כְּשֶׁכָּבְשׁוּ הָאָרֶץ הֵבִיא הַשֵּׁם בִּקְצָת

5. TB N'darim 35b.

6. Literally, the knowledge of the owner—i.e. the one for whom the offering is sacrificed; MT *ibid.* 5.

§177 1. So MT *hilchoth tum'ath tzara'ath* xvi 10, and Ramban, Leviticus 13:47. Cf. Ruth Rabbah 2, 10: The Master of mercy never exacts punishment from souls (lives) first . . . and so it is with *tzara'ath* distempers: at first they attack one's house . . . if he turns back [from his evil], good; if not, they attack his clothes . . . after that they attack his body.

2. Va-yikra Rabbah 17, 6. (The word *nissim*, "miracles," near the end of the paragraph, is the reading of the three oldest manuscripts and the first edition. In the fourth manuscript it is missing, but written in the margin by another hand. In the second edition, Venice 1600, it is simply missing. In later editions the gap has been filled by the word *tovah*, "good.")

reason that he was drawn after the body's cravings, either in speech or in action; and he thus deserved to be chastised.

Among the laws of the precept, there is what the Sages of blessed memory said:[5] that whoever has the obligation of an offering, others may not bring the offering for him unless it was with his knowledge—except for those lacking in atonement: [their offerings] do not require their consent.[6] For this reason the Sages ruled[5] that a man may bring an offering for his young sons and daughters if they were lacking in atonement, and may then feed them [meat] of sacrifices. The rest of its details are explained in many places in the Talmud, primarily in *Z'vaḥim*, chapter 2; *Arachin*, chapter 2; *K'rithoth*, chapter 1; *Nazir*, chapter 8; and toward the end of the Mishnah tractates *N'ga'im* and *Kinnim*.

It is in effect when the Temple is extant, for both man and woman. If someone violated it and did not bring his offering at its time, he would thus disobey a positive precept.

[THE RITUAL UNCLEANNESS OF A HOUSE CONTAMINATED WITH TZARA'ATH INFECTION]

177 to declare ritually unclean a house with a *tzara'ath* infection: in other words, that we should treat a house in which there is contamination of *tzara'ath* in the proper way written in the *sidrah*—as it is stated, *then he whose house it is shall come*, etc. (Leviticus 14:35), as it is written there; and that we should hold anyone who enters the house to be defiled, as it is written in the section, *And he that goes into the house . . . shall be unclean*, etc. (*ibid.* 46).

This precept includes all matters regarding the ritual uncleanness of a house: which requires shutting up, or demolition, either of some of the walls or of all. Now, this matter of *tzara'ath* infection that occurs in stones—I heard that it is not something natural, but rather something wondrous [supernatural] that would happen at times to the houses of Israelites to reprove them. For out of the Eternal Lord's love for them, He would impart His chastisement to them through objects apart from their bodies, so that they would return in repentance before they incurred guilt to be punished in their bodies. And this is the reason why, if a person did not attain repentance, the affliction would spread to his clothes as well. If he yet did not sense [the chastisement] it would spread to his body as well.[1]

Moreover, the Sages of blessed memory said[2] that originally, when they conquered the land, the Lord brought a plague of *tzara'ath*

בָּתִּים נֶגַע צָרַעַת לְטוֹבָתָם, כְּדֵי שֶׁיַּהַרְסוּ הַבַּיִת וְיִתְגַּלֶּה לָהֶם מַטְמוֹן שֶׁטָּמְנוּ שָׁם הָאֱמוֹרִיִּים; וְאַף־עַל־פִּי שֶׁהָיָה אֶפְשָׁר לְהוֹדִיעָם זֶה עַל יְדֵי נָבִיא מִבְּלִי נֶגַע, יָדוּעַ שֶׁהָאֵל יַעֲשֶׂה נִסִּים לִבְנֵי־אָדָם דֶּרֶךְ סֵתֶר, כְּמוֹ שֶׁכָּתַבְנוּ לְמַעְלָה.

מִדִּינֵי הַמִּצְוָה, מַה שֶּׁאָמְרוּ זִכְרוֹנָם לִבְרָכָה שֶׁשִּׁעוּר נִגְעֵי בָתִּים כִּשְׁנֵי גְרִיסִין זֶה בְּצַד זֶה; וּשְׁלֹשָׁה סִימָנֵי טֻמְאָה בְּבַיִת: יְרַקְרַק אֲדַמְדָּם וּפִשְׁיוֹן, וְכֻלָּן מְפֹרָשִׁין בַּכָּתוּב; וּשְׁתֵּי הַמַּרְאוֹת מִצְטָרְפִין זֶה עִם זֶה לְשִׁעוּר שְׁנֵי גְרִיסִין; וְכָל הַשִּׁעוּרִין הֲלָכָה לְמֹשֶׁה מִסִּינַי.

וּכְשֶׁיֵּרָאֶה נֶגַע בְּבַיִת, אֲפִלּוּ חָכָם שֶׁיּוֹדֵעַ שֶׁהוּא נֶגַע לֹא יִגְזֹר וְיֹאמַר "נֶגַע נִרְאָה לִי" אֶלָּא "כְּנֶגַע", כִּי לַכֹּהֵן נִתָּן לְטַמֵּא וּלְטַהֵר נְגָעִים, וְלֹא לְאָדָם אַחֵר. וְאֵין בַּיִת אָפֵל מִטַּמֵּא בְנֶגַע, לְפִי שֶׁאֵין פּוֹתְחִין בּוֹ חַלּוֹנוֹת לִרְאוֹת בּוֹ נֶגַע— שֶׁנֶּאֱמַר: נִרְאָה לִי, וּפֵרְשׁוּ זִכְרוֹנָם לִבְרָכָה: לִי וְלֹא לְאוֹרִי. שֶׁמָּא תֹאמַר יִרְאֶה אֶת הַנֶּגַע בְּנֵר, הָרְאִיָּה בְּנֵר אֵינָהּ שְׁלֵמָה, וּלְפִיכָךְ בַּיִת אָפֵל אֵין מִטַּמֵּא לְעוֹלָם בְּנֶגַע.

וְכֵן אֵין הַבַּיִת מִטַּמֵּא בְנֶגַע עַד שֶׁיְּהֵא בוֹ אַרְבַּע אַמּוֹת עַל אַרְבַּע אַמּוֹת אוֹ יוֹתֵר, שֶׁאֵין קָרוּי בַּיִת בְּפָחוּת מִכֵּן, וְהַתּוֹרָה אָמְרָה "בַּיִת"; וְכֵן בָּעִינָן שֶׁיְּהֵא לוֹ אַרְבָּעָה כְתָלִים וּבָנוּי עַל הָאָרֶץ בַּאֲבָנִים וְעֵצִים וְעָפָר, שֶׁנֶּאֱמַר: אֶת אֲבָנָיו וְאֶת עֵצָיו וְאֵת כָּל עֲפַר הַבָּיִת; וְהַלְּבֵנִים וְהַשַּׁיִשׁ אֵינָן חֲשׁוּבִים כַּאֲבָנִים. וִירוּשָׁלַיִם וְחוּצָה לָאָרֶץ גַּם־כֵּן אֵין בָּהֶם דִּין טֻמְאַת בָּתִּים, שֶׁנֶּאֱמַר: בְּבֵית אֶרֶץ אֲחֻזַּתְכֶם, וְחוּצָה לָאָרֶץ אֵינָהּ אֲחֻזָּה, וִירוּשָׁלַיִם גַּם־כֵּן לֹא נִתְחַלְּקָה לִשְׁבָטִים, וּלְפִיכָךְ אֵינָהּ בִּכְלַל אֲחֻזַּתְכֶם; וְיֶתֶר פְּרָטֶיהָ, בִּנְגָעִים.

וְנוֹהֶגֶת בְּבַיִת שֶׁל זָכָר אוֹ נְקֵבָה בָּאָרֶץ, וּבְכָל זְמַן שֶׁיֵּשׁ כֹּהֲנִים רְאוּיִין לַדָּבָר. וְעוֹבֵר עָלֶיהָ, בִּטֵּל עֲשֵׂה.

3. Mishnah, N'ga'im xiv 3.

4. *Ibid.* iii 8 (see § 172, third paragraph).

5. E.g. if an area the size of a bean is very red, and next to it an equal area is very green, the house is defiled; MT *hilchoth tum'ath tzara'ath* xiv 2, derived from Sifra, *thazri'a, perek* 14, 2 (*Kessef Mishneh*).

6. Mishnah, N'ga'im xii 5.

7. *Ibid.* ii 3.

8. Sifra on the verse (*m'tzora, parashah* 5, 11).

9. TB Sukkah 3a.

10. I.e. if it is to come under the law of defilement.

11. TB Bava Bathra 164b; Mishnah, N'ga'im xii 2; MT *hilchoth tum'ath tzara'ath* xiv 6.

12. Mishnah *ibid.* MT *ibid.* 8.

13. Mishnah *ibid.* 4.

14. TB Yoma 12a, etc.

15. MT *ibid.* 11.

to some houses for their good, so that a house would be demolished, and treasure which the Amorites had hidden there would be revealed. Although it was possible to inform them of this through a prophet, without a plague, it is a known matter that God works miracles for people in hidden ways, as we wrote above.

Among the laws of the precept, there is what the Sages of blessed memory taught,[3] that the minimal area for plagues of houses is the size of two *garis* beans next to one another. There are three signs of ritual impurity in a house: greened, reddened, and spreading;[4] and all are explained in the Writ. Two different appearances may be added together to make up the minimal size of two *garis* beans.[5] Minimal sizes are *halachah* (law) [given orally] to Moses at Sinai.

When someone sees an infection in a house, even if he is a learned scholar who knows it is a plague, let him not decide and say, "A plague has appeared before me," but rather "Something like a plague"; for it was given to the *kohen* to declare cases of *tzara'ath* unclean or clean, and not to any other man.[6] A dark house does not become defiled by the infection, for windows are not opened in it so as to see the distemper in it,[7] since it is stated, *appears to me to be* (Leviticus 14:35), and our Sages of blessed memory interpreted:[8] "to me," and not "by my light." But perhaps you might say, "Let him observe the plague by lamplight"?—examination by lamplight is not complete (thorough). Therefore a dark house can never become defiled by a distemper.

Likewise, a house does not become defiled by the plague unless it measures four cubits by four cubits, or more: for it is not called a house if it is smaller than that, and the Torah said "a house."[9] Similarly, it is required[10] to have four walls and be built on the ground out of stone, wood and earth (loam): for it is stated, *its stones and its timber and all the mortar of the house* (Leviticus 14:45).[11] Bricks and marble are not considered as stones.[12] In Jerusalem and outside the land [of Israel] there is likewise no law of ritual uncleanness of houses:[13] for it is stated, *in a house of the land of your possession* (*ibid.* 34), and outside the land there is no possession; and similarly, Jerusalem was not parceled out to the tribes [of Israel][14]—and it is therefore not in the category of "your possession."[15]

The rest of its details are in the Mishnah tractate *N'ga'im*. It applies to the house of either a man or a woman in the land [of Israel], at any time that there are *kohanim* fit (qualified) for the subject. Whoever transgresses it disobeys a positive precept.

[מִצְוַת עִנְיַן טֻמְאַת זָב לִהְיוֹת טָמֵא וּמְטַמֵּא]

קעח שֶׁיְּהֵא הַזָּב טָמֵא וּמְטַמֵּא אֶת אֲחֵרִים, שֶׁנֶּאֱמַר: אִישׁ אִישׁ כִּי יִהְיֶה זָב מִבְּשָׂרוֹ וְכוּלֵי וְזֹאת תִּהְיֶה טֻמְאָתוֹ וְגוֹמֵר; וּבָא הַפֵּרוּשׁ: "מִבְּשָׂרוֹ", כְּלוֹמַר זָב מִפִּי הָאַמָּה, וּכְמוֹ שֶׁדָּרְשׁוּ זִכְרוֹנָם לִבְרָכָה: "כִּי יִהְיֶה זָב", יָכוֹל זָב מִכָּל מָקוֹם יְהֵא טָמֵא, תַּלְמוּד לוֹמַר "מִבְּשָׂרוֹ" וְלֹא כָל בְּשָׂרוֹ; אַחַר שֶׁחִלֵּק הַכָּתוּב בֵּין בָּשָׂר לְבָשָׂר זָכִיתִי לָדוּן: טִמֵּא בְזָב טִמֵּא בְזָבָה, מַה זָּבָה מִן הַמָּקוֹם שֶׁהִיא מְטַמְּאָה וְכוּלֵי.

וְעִנְיַן זִיבָה הוּא שֶׁיּוֹצֵא מִן הָאָדָם מִפִּי הָאַמָּה כְּעֵין לֵחָה, וְאֵין לוֹ בִיצִיאָתוֹ תַּאֲוָה וְלֹא הֲנָאָה; וְאָמְרוּ זִכְרוֹנָם לִבְרָכָה שֶׁהוּא דוֹמֶה לְמֵי בָצֵק שֶׁל שְׂעוֹרִים, וּכְמוֹ־כֵן דוֹמֶה לְלֹבֶן בֵּיצָה הַמּוּזֶרֶת; וְשִׁכְבַת זֶרַע אֵינוֹ כֵן, כִּי הוּא יִדְמֶה לְלֹבֶן בֵּיצָה שֶׁאֵינָהּ מוּזֶרֶת, וְזֶהוּ הַחִלּוּק בָּהֶן לְהַכִּיר בֵּין זֶה לָזֶה.

וְצִוָּה הַכָּתוּב שֶׁכָּל מִי שֶׁיִּקְרֶה בוֹ עִנְיָן זֶה, שֶׁיֵּצֵא מִמֶּנּוּ זִיבָה, שֶׁיְּהֵא טָמֵא וּמְטַמֵּא עַד שֶׁיִּטְהַר; וּבָא הַפֵּרוּשׁ שֶׁאֵינוֹ טָמֵא מִשּׁוּם רְאִיַּת פַּעַם אַחַת לְבַד אֶלָּא בִשְׁתֵּי רְאִיּוֹת, כְּלוֹמַר שֶׁיָּזוּב מִמֶּנּוּ אוֹתוֹ עִנְיָן שְׁתֵּי פְעָמִים, בֵּין סְמוּכִין אוֹ חֲלוּקִין, וּבִלְבַד שֶׁיִּהְיוּ בְיוֹם אֶחָד וְשֶׁלֹּא יָזוּב בְּפַעַם אַחַת מַמָּשׁ; וְאֵין לוֹ שִׁעוּר, אֶלָּא אֲפִלּוּ כָּל־שֶׁהוּא. וְזֶהוּ אָמְרָם זִכְרוֹנָם לִבְרָכָה: מָנָה הַכָּתוּב שְׁתַּיִם וְקָרָא טָמֵא, שָׁלֹשׁ וְקָרָא טָמֵא; הָא כֵיצַד, שְׁתַּיִם לְטֻמְאָה וְשָׁלֹשׁ לְקָרְבָּן; כְּלוֹמַר שֶׁאַף־

§178 1. Sifra on the verse (*m'tzora, zavim, parashah* 1, 3–4).

2. TB Niddah 43b.

3. "Light" because she does not need to observe seven "clean" days (in which she sees no flow at all of blood) and then bring an offering.

4. Which requires seven "clean" days and an offering to remove the defilement.

5. MT *hilchoth m'ḥus'ré kapparah* ii 1. Rambam describes it as a flow of "unmatured" semen due to a weakness *qua* illness of the seminal organs or vesicles (MT *ibid.* and Commentary to Mishnah, Zavim ii 2). However, Preuss (an Orthodox physician who devoted years of study to medical matters in the Bible and Talmud) flatly calls it gonorrhea, and notes that in early medicine, gonorrheal discharges were considered seminal without question (*op. cit.* in §169 note 1, p. 411). Actually, the nub of the matter lies in the word gonorrhea (which, incidentally, is the Septuagint's translation for **זוב**). It was Galen's Greek name for the illness, *because* he considered the discharge to be seminal: *gonos*=semen; *rrhoe*=flow. Only in 1879 was it finally established that the discharge is caused by a micro-organism and has no connection with semen. It might be noted in retrospect that Leviticus 15:32 indicates that this flow and seminal emission are two distinct matters; and so too Tosefta, Zavim ii 4. (See *Entziklopedya Ivrith* XVI s.v. *zivah*.)

6. TB Niddah 35b.

7. Mishnah, Zavim i 1.

[ON THE RITUAL UNCLEANNESS OF A MAN WITH A GONORRHEAL DISCHARGE]

178 that a man with a discharge is ritually unclean and capable of defiling others: for it is stated, *When any man has a discharge from his flesh, his discharge is unclean; and this shall be his uncleanness*, etc. (Leviticus 15:2–3); and the explanation was given [in the Oral Tradition]:[1] "from his flesh"—i.e. a flow from the opening of the generative organ. As our Sages of blessed memory taught:[2] "When any man has a discharge"—I might think it means that with a discharge from anywhere [in his body] he should be ritually unclean?—Scripture states, *from his flesh*, and not all his flesh. Since Scripture has differentiated between flesh and flesh, I have merited to learn it by a deduction: It has declared a man unclean by a discharge, and so a woman. Just as in the case of a woman, from the place whereby she incurs a light impurity,[3] by the menses, she incurs a major impurity[4] by the [irregular] discharge, so with the male: from the place whereby he incurs a light impurity, by seminal emission, he incurs a major one, by a [gonorrheal] discharge.

In substance, this discharge is something that issues from a man out of the opening of the generative organ, as a kind of liquid, and at its emission he feels neither lust nor pleasure.[5] Our Sages of blessed memory taught[6] that it resembles the liquid of dough from barley flour; and it likewise resembles the white of a rotten unfertilized egg. Semen, however, is not so, being like the white of a sound fertilized egg. This, then, is the difference between them, so that one can be distinguished from the other.

Well, Scripture ordained that any man who suffers this fate, that [gonorrheal] discharge issues from him, is to be ritually unclean and cause defilement, until he is purified. The explanation was given [in the Oral Tradition][7] that one does not become impure by seeing only one discharge, but only on seeing two—i.e. that this substance flows from him two times, whether one directly after the other or at different times, provided a whole day did not intervene,[8] and that they should not have flowed actually at one time.[9] There is no minimal amount for it [the discharge]; it can be any quantity at all.[10] And thus our Sages of blessed memory said:[11] Scripture listed two occasions, and called him unclean;[12] then three occasions, and it called him unclean.[13] Then how [is this to be understood]? Twice is [the minimum] for defilement, and three times, for an offering. In other words, although a person becomes ritually unclean with two [discharges], he does not

עַל־פִּי שֶׁהוּא טָמֵא בִשְׁתַּיִם לֹא יִתְחַיֵּב לְהָבִיא קָרְבָּן בְּטָהֳרָתוֹ עַד שָׁלֹשׁ. וּמִכָּל־מָקוֹם, אִם רָאָה רְאִיָּה אַחַת אֲרֻכָּה כְּשָׁלֹשׁ רְאִיּוֹת, שֶׁנִּמְצָא מִתְּחִלָּתָהּ וְעַד סוֹפָהּ כִּשְׁתֵּי טְבִילוֹת וּשְׁנֵי סְפוּגִין, הֲרֵי זוֹ נֶחְשֶׁבֶת כְּשָׁלֹשׁ רְאִיּוֹת, וּמֵבִיא קָרְבָּן.

מִשָּׁרְשֵׁי הַמִּצְוָה, לְפִי שֶׁהַשֵּׁם בָּרוּךְ הוּא הִרְחִיקָנוּ מְאֹד מִן הַמּוֹתָרוֹת, וְצִוָּנוּ לִהְיוֹת קְדוֹשִׁים וִישָׁרִים בְּעִנְיַן הַמַּאֲכָל וְהַמִּשְׁתֶּה וּבְכָל שְׁאָר עִנְיְנֵי הָאָדָם, וְאֵין סָפֵק כִּי עִנְיַן הַזִּיבָה יִקְרֶה בָּאָדָם בְּצֵאתוֹ מִדֶּרֶךְ הַיֹּשֶׁר בְּהַתְמָדָה בְּמַאֲכָלָיו וְשִׁקּוּיָיו, וְיִגְדַּל בְּגוּפוֹ מִתּוֹךְ כָּךְ אוֹתוֹ הַמּוֹתָר הַסָּרוּחַ הַמָּאוּס וְהַטָּמֵא, וּכְמוֹ שֶׁאָמְרוּ זִכְרוֹנָם לִבְרָכָה: דַּרְכָּא דְמֵיכְלָא יְתֵירָא לְאַיְתוּיֵי לִידֵי זִיבָה; וְהוֹדִיעַתְנוּ הַתּוֹרָה שֶׁהָאָדָם שֶׁיִּהְיֶה בוֹ כֵן נִקְרָא טָמֵא, וְהַטֻּמְאָה שֵׁם כּוֹלֵל כָּל דָּבָר נִמְאָס וְנֶאֱלָח; וּבְהַרְחִיקֵנוּ מִזֶּה נִקְנֶה בְנַפְשֵׁנוּ מִדַּת הַיֹּשֶׁר וְהַשְׁוָיָה בְּכָל דַּעְתֵּנוּ וּבְכָל כֹּחֵנוּ.

וּמִזֶּה הָעִנְיָן הוּא שֶׁאֵינוֹ טָמֵא בִרְאִיָּה אַחַת, לְפִי שֶׁלֹּא נִתְחַזְּקָה בְגוּפוֹ אוֹתָהּ הַלֵּחָה כָּל־כָּךְ, וְהַמִּעוּט הַזֶּה אֵינֶנּוּ הוֹרָאָה לִהְיוֹתוֹ מֻרְגָּל הַרְבֵּה לָצֵאת מִדֶּרֶךְ הַיֹּשֶׁר; וְכֵיוָן שֶׁכֵּן, אֵין רָאוּי לְטַמְּאוֹ בְמוּעָט, כִּי הָאָדָם בָּנוּי בְעִנְיָן שֶׁאִי אֶפְשָׁר לוֹ בְשׁוּם צַד לְהִנָּצֵל שֶׁלֹּא לָצֵאת מִקַּו הַיֹּשֶׁר כְּלוּם, אֲבָל בְּצֵאתוֹ הַרְבֵּה אָז יִקָּרֵא אָשֵׁם וְרָאוּי לִהְיוֹתוֹ טָמֵא. וְאַף־עַל־פִּי שֶׁאָמְרוּ זִכְרוֹנָם לִבְרָכָה: בְּשִׁבְעָה דְרָכִים בּוֹדְקִין אֶת הַזָּב, בְּמַאֲכָל וּבְמִשְׁתֶּה בִּקְפִיצָה בְּמַשָּׂא בְּחֹלִי בְּמַרְאֶה בְּהִרְהוּר, כְּלוֹמַר וְאִם אֵרַע לוֹ מִפְּנֵי זֶה אֵינוֹ טָמֵא, לֹא תִסָּתֵר טַעֲנָתֵנוּ זֹאת בָּזֶה, כִּי הָעִנְיָן הוּא שֶׁיֵּשׁ לָנוּ לִבְדֹּק אִם נִהְיְתָה הַזִּיבָה בוֹ בְּדֶרֶךְ מִקְרֶה שֶׁל פַּעַם אַחַת, וְאֵין לְטַמְּאוֹ בָהּ, אוֹ נִהְיְתָה חֲזָקָה בְגוּפוֹ מִתּוֹךְ הֶרְגֵּל רַע שֶׁהֻרְגַּל פְּעָמִים רַבּוֹת, וְרָאוּי לְטַמְּאוֹ.

וְכֵן כָּתַב הָרַמְבָּ״ן זִכְרוֹנוֹ לִבְרָכָה, וְזֶה לְשׁוֹנוֹ: וְטַעַם טֻמְאַת הַזּוֹב מִפְּנֵי הֱיוֹתוֹ

8. The Hebrew reads, "provided they were both in one day"—but it is clear from the Talmud and MT that this must be a scribal error: TB Bava Kamma 24a, Mishnah, Zavim i 1; MT *ibid.* 7–8.

9. I.e. with no real pause between the two.

10. TB Niddah 40a.

11. TB M'gillah 8a.

12. In Leviticus 15:2: *When any man has a discharge from his flesh, his discharge is unclean*—"discharge" is mentioned twice, denoting two flows.

13. In *ibid.* 3: *And this shall be his uncleanness for his* discharge: *whether his flesh runs with his* discharge, *or his flesh is stopped from his* discharge, *it is his uncleanness.*

14. Mishnah, Zavim i 5.

15. TB Kiddushin 2b.

16. Mishnah, Zavim ii 2.

become obligated to bring an offering upon becoming purified until [there have been at least] three. Nevertheless, if he saw one discharge that took as long as three manifestations [of discharge], such that from its beginning to its end there was time for ritual immersion twice and rubbing the body dry twice, it is then reckoned as three appearances [of discharge] and he is to bring an offering.[14]

At the root of the precept lies the reason that the Eternal Lord, blessed is He, removed us from excesses, and commanded us to be holy and decent in regard to food and drink, and in all other human activities. There can be no doubt that this matter of discharge will happen to a person when he persistently leaves the straight and decent path in his eating and drinking, amassing in his body, as a result, that putrid, abhorrent, unclean excess. As the Sages of blessed memory said:[15] It is the way of excessive food to lead to [such] discharge. So the Torah informed us that a man who has this condition is called unclean, uncleanness being a term that covers everything repulsive and corrupt. By keeping ourselves distant from this, we will acquire in our spirit the quality of straightness, decency and balance in all our thought and all our strength.

From this concept it follows that a person is not unclean on seeing one discharge—since that liquid has not become so strongly contained in his body. The small amount is not an indication that he is very accustomed to go off the straight and decent path; and in that case, it is not right to declare him unclean for that small quantity [of discharge]. For man is so constituted that it is impossible for him in any way to be saved from going out of the straight and proper line at all. But when he goes far out, he is then called guilty, and he deserves to be [declared] ritually unclean. Although our Sages of blessed memory said,[16] "In seven ways is a man with a discharge examined: by food, drink, jumping, a burden, illness, a sight, or improper fantasy," i.e. if he suffered it on account of this, he is not defiled[17]—our argument is not refuted by this: For the meaning is that it is for us to investigate if the discharge happened to him as an event of a single time, and he is then not to be declared defiled by it, or if this became entrenched in his body by force of a bad habit, to which he became accustomed by many repetitions, and it is proper to declare him unclean.

So, indeed, Ramban of blessed memory wrote, expressing it thus:[18] The reason for the ritual uncleanness of the discharge is on account of its being a severe sickness, of the contagious diseases. Thus

חֹלִי כָּבֵד מִן הֶחֳלָאִים הַנִּדְבָּקִים, עַד כָּאן. וְאִלּוּ יִהְיֶה מִצַּד מִקְרֶה, כְּלוֹמַר מֵאַחַת מִן הַדְּרָכִים הַיְּדוּעִים, לֹא יִהְיֶה חֹלִי נִדְבָּק, וְאֵין רָאוּי לְטַמְּאוֹ. וְזֹאת הַבְּדִיקָה אֵין עוֹשִׂין אוֹתָהּ כִּי אִם בִּרְאִיָּה שְׁנִיָּה, לְפִי שֶׁאֵין טֻמְאַת זִיבָה אֶלָּא בִשְׁתֵּי רְאִיּוֹת, כְּמוֹ שֶׁאָמַרְנוּ, שֶׁכֵּן בָּא לָנוּ הַפֵּרוּשׁ הָאֲמִתִּי.

מִדִּינֵי הַמִּצְוָה, מַה שֶּׁאָמְרוּ זִכְרוֹנָם לִבְרָכָה שֶׁהַזָּב מְטַמֵּא הַמִּשְׁכָּב וְהַמּוֹשָׁב וְהַמֶּרְכָּב בַּחֲמִשָּׁה דְרָכִים, וְאֵלּוּ הֵן: עוֹמֵד יוֹשֵׁב שׁוֹכֵב נִתְלֶה נִשְׁעָן; וּפֵרוּשׁ מֶרְכָּב הוּא אוֹתוֹ הַלּוּחַ שֶׁהוּא בִכְלִי הֶעָשׂוּי לִרְכִיבָה הַנִּקְרָא אַרְצוֹן; שֶׁאֵין לוֹמַר שֶׁיְּהֵא אוֹתוֹ שֶׁיּוֹשְׁבִין עָלָיו, דְּאִם כֵּן הַיְנוּ מוֹשָׁב, וְזֶה דָבָר בָּרוּר; וְיֶתֶר פְּרָטֶיהָ רַבִּים, מְבֹאָרִים בַּמַּסֶּכְתָּא הַבְּנוּיָה עַל זֶה וְהִיא מַסֶּכֶת זָבִים.

וְנוֹהֵג עִנְיָן זֶה, שֶׁבַּעַל זִיבָה נִקְרָא טָמֵא, בְּכָל מָקוֹם וּבְכָל זְמַן; אֲבָל עַכְשָׁיו בַּעֲווֹנוֹתֵינוּ שֶׁאֵין לָנוּ מִקְדָּשׁ וְלֹא טָהֳרוֹת, אֵין לָנוּ לַחֲשֹׁב טֻמְאַת הַזָּב בְּמִצְוָה נוֹהֶגֶת, לְפִי שֶׁאֵין לָנוּ לַעֲשׂוֹת בְּעִנְיַן הַזִּיבָה שׁוּם דָּבָר; וּבִזְמַן הַבַּיִת נוֹהֵג, לְהָבִיא עָלֶיהָ קָרְבָּן. וְעוֹבֵר עָלֶיהָ וְנִכְנָס לַמִּקְדָּשׁ אוֹ אָכַל קֹדֶשׁ קֹדֶם שֶׁיִּטְהַר, בִּטֵּל עֲשֵׂה, מִלְּבַד שֶׁיֵּשׁ עָלָיו עֹנֶשׁ, כְּמוֹ שֶׁכָּתוּב לְמַעְלָה.

[מִצְוַת קָרְבַּן זָב כְּשֶׁיִּתְרַפֵּא מִזּוֹבוֹ]

קעט לְהַקְרִיב הַזָּב קָרְבָּן אַחַר שֶׁיִּתְרַפֵּא מִזּוֹבוֹ, שֶׁנֶּאֱמַר: וְכִי יִטְהַר הַזָּב מִזּוֹבוֹ וְגוֹמֵר וּבַיּוֹם הַשְּׁמִינִי יִקַּח לוֹ שְׁתֵּי תֹרִים וְגוֹמֵר. וְהַקָּרְבָּן הַהוּא הוּא שְׁתֵּי תוֹרִים אוֹ שְׁנֵי בְנֵי יוֹנָה, אֶחָד לְחַטָּאת וְאֶחָד לְעוֹלָה, וְהוּא נִקְרָא מְחֻסַּר כַּפָּרָה עַד שֶׁיַּקְרִיבֵהוּ.

מִשָּׁרְשֵׁי הַמִּצְוָה, מַה שֶּׁכָּתַבְנוּ לְמַעְלָה כִּי עִנְיַן הַקָּרְבָּן לְרֶמֶז לְהַשְׁפָּלַת יֵצֶר הַגּוּף הַמִּתְאַוֶּה וְלַעֲלוֹת נֶפֶשׁ הַשֵּׂכֶל; וְלָכֵן כְּשֶׁנִּתְרַפֵּא הַזָּב רָאוּי לוֹ לְהַכִּיר רֹעַ תַּאֲוָתוֹ, וּלְהַיְשִׁיר גּוּפוֹ בְּכָל כֹּחוֹ, וּבְעִנְיַן הַקָּרְבָּן יַתְחִיל לָקַחַת מוּסָר.

17. I.e. if the discharge occurred because a man ate or drank excessively, jumped, carried a too heavy burden, was ill, saw an attractive woman, or indulged in improper fantasies, there was a specific cause for the discharge, and it is not the symptom of an illness for which he should be pronounced unclean.

18. Ramban, commentary, Leviticus 15:11.

19. With one discharge, though, there is light defilement, as with any pollution; TB Niddah 35a.

20. Mishnah, Zavim ii 4.

21. I.e. a board to which the rider holds fast (as to a bar or a strap); so Rashi, Leviticus 15:9, and TB 'Eruvin 27a, s.v. *tafus*.

§179 1. So TB K'rithoth 8b.

far his words. Well, if it should happen by way of chance, i.e. through one of the [seven] known ways, it is not a contagious disease, and it would not be right to pronounce him defiled. Then this examination is made only upon the second appearance, since there can be uncleanness through a discharge for nothing less than two manifestations, as we stated.[19] For so the true explanation was transmitted to us.

Among the laws of the precept are what the Sages of blessed memory said:[20] that a man with a discharge renders unclean a couch, a seat and a hold in five ways, these being: standing, sitting, lying, hanging, leaning. The meaning of "a hold" is that board which is in the equipage made for riding, which is called *arçon*;[21] for it cannot be said to be the part on which one sits, since in that case it is identical with a seat; this is something clear. The rest of its many details are explained in the Mishnah tractate composed about this theme, i.e. the tractate *Zavim*.

This rule, that a person with a discharge is called unclean, applies in every place and every time. However, now that for our sins we have no Sanctuary or practices of ritual cleanness, we cannot reckon the defilement of a man with a discharge as a precept in force—since there is nothing at all for us to do in regard to the discharge. When the Temple exists, the rule is in effect to bring an offering over it. And if someone violated it [the precept] and entered the Sanctuary or ate hallowed food before becoming ritually pure, he would thus disobey a positive precept, apart from incurring punishment, as written above (§167).

[ON THE OFFERING BY A MAN WITH A GONORRHEAL DISCHARGE, WHEN HE IS HEALED]

179 that a man with a discharge is to bring an offering after he becomes cured of his discharge: for it is stated, *And when he that has a discharge is cleansed of his discharge . . . And on the eighth day he shall take for himself two turtledoves*, etc. (Leviticus 15:13–14). This offering is two turtledoves or two young pigeons, one for a *ḥattath* (sin-offering) and one for an *'olah* (burnt-offering). And he is called "lacking in atonement" until he offers it up.[1]

At the root of the precept lies what we have written above, that the significance of an offering is to hint at the degradation of the body's desiring inclination, and the exaltation of the spirit of intelligence. Thus, when a man with a discharge is cured, it is fitting for him to realize the evil of his craving[2] and to set his body straight with all his

דִּינֵי הַמִּצְוָה, כְּגוֹן מַה שֶּׁאָמְרוּ זִכְרוֹנָם לִבְרָכָה שֶׁקָּרְבַּן מְחֻסַּר כַּפָּרָה אֵינוֹ צָרִיךְ דַּעַת בְּעָלִים, כְּמוֹ שֶׁכָּתַבְנוּ לְמַעְלָה; וְיֶתֶר פְּרָטֶיהָ, מְבֹאָרִים בַּמְּקוֹמוֹת שֶׁכָּתַבְנוּ לְמַעְלָה בְּקָרְבַּן מְצֹרָע.

וְנוֹהֶגֶת בִּזְמַן הַבַּיִת. וְעוֹבֵר עָלֶיהָ וְלֹא הִקְרִיב קָרְבָּן בִּטֵּל עֲשֵׂה, וְהוּא מְחֻסַּר כַּפָּרָה; וַחֲבַל עַל רֵישֵׁיהּ אִי מָאִית וְיִשָּׂא עֲוֹנוֹ בְנַפְשׁוֹ.

[מִצְוַת עִנְיַן טֻמְאַת שִׁכְבַת זֶרַע שֶׁהוּא טָמֵא וּמְטַמֵּא]

קפ לִהְיוֹת שִׁכְבַת זֶרַע טָמֵא וּמְטַמֵּא, שֶׁנֶּאֱמַר: וְאִישׁ כִּי תֵצֵא מִמֶּנּוּ שִׁכְבַת זָרַע [וְכוּלֵּי].

מִשָּׁרְשֵׁי הַמִּצְוָה, לְפִי שֶׁעִנְיָן זֶה לֹא יִקְרֶה רַק מִצַּד מַחֲשֶׁבֶת הַתַּאֲווֹת הַגּוּפָנִיּוֹת, הוֹדִיעַתְנוּ הַתּוֹרָה הַשְּׁלֵמָה כִּי הַגּוּף נִקְרָא טָמֵא בָהֶן; כִּי עִקַּר הֱיוֹתוֹ בָּעוֹלָם אֵינוֹ רַק לְהָבִין בַּמֻּשְׂכָּלוֹת וְלַעֲבֹד בּוֹרְאוֹ; לְפִיכָךְ כְּשֶׁיִּקְרֶה בוֹ אוֹתוֹ דָבָר שֶׁמַּרְאֶה בוֹ הַטָּיָתוֹ אֶל הַתַּאֲוָה הַחָמְרִית, רָאוּי לַעֲמֹד יוֹם אֶחָד בְּטֻמְאָתוֹ כְּדֵי שֶׁתִּתְנַקֶּה מַחֲשַׁבְתּוֹ יָפֶה, וְאַחַר־כָּךְ יִטְהָר.

מִדִּינֵי הַמִּצְוָה, מַה שֶּׁאָמְרוּ זִכְרוֹנָם לִבְרָכָה שֶׁשִּׁעוּרוֹ לַנּוֹגֵעַ בְּכַעֲדָשָׁה, וּלְרוֹאֶה הַקֶּרִי בְּכָל־שֶׁהוּא; וְאֶחָד רוֹאֶה קֶרִי בְּאֹנֶס אוֹ בְרָצוֹן, טָמֵא; וְזֶרַע שֶׁל קָטָן אֵינוֹ מְטַמֵּא; וְזֶרַע אָדֹם אֵינוֹ טָמֵא, אֶלָּא לָבָן; וְכָל זֶרַע שֶׁאֵין הָאָדָם מַרְגִּישׁ בּוֹ לֹא בַתְּחִלָּה וְלֹא בַסּוֹף אֵינוֹ טָמֵא; וְהַמְּהַרְהֵר בַּלַּיְלָה וְרָאָה שֶׁשִּׁמֵּשׁ בַּחֲלוֹם וְעָמַד וּמָצָא בְשָׂרוֹ חַם, אַף־עַל־פִּי שֶׁלֹּא רָאָה שִׁכְבַת זֶרַע, טָמֵא; וְיֶתֶר פְּרָטֶיהָ, מְבֹאָרִים בְּמַסֶּכֶת זָבִים.

וְנוֹהֶגֶת טֻמְאַת שִׁכְבַת זֶרַע בְּכָל מָקוֹם וּבְכָל זְמַן; אֲבָל עַכְשָׁיו בַּעֲווֹנוֹתֵינוּ

2. See § 178, fourth paragraph, that its cause is held to be excessive eating and drinking.

3. Literally, the owner—i.e. the person for whom it is brought; TB N'darim 35b.

§ 180

1. TB Niddah 43b.

2. *Ibid.* 35a.

3. *Ibid.* 32b.

4. *Ibid.* 43a. (The paragraph is based on MT *hilchoth 'avoth ha-tum'oth* v 1–4.)

power. By the significance of the offering he will begin to learn his moral lesson.

The laws of the precept are, for example, what the Sages of blessed memory taught: that the offering of one lacking in atonement does not need the knowledge and consent of its person,[3] as we have written above (§§168, 176). The rest of its details are explained in the places we mentioned above, in the precept of the *m'tzora*'s offering (§176).

It is in effect when the Temple is extant. If someone violated it and did not bring an offering, he would thus disobey a positive precept, and would be lacking in atonement. And woe upon his head if he were to die and bear his sin in his soul.

180 [ON THE RITUAL UNCLEANNESS OF SEMINAL FLUID]

that semen is ritually unclean and causes defilement: for it is stated, *And if a flow of seed goes out from a man*, etc. (Leviticus 15:16).

At the root of the precept lies the reason that this matter will occur only on account of the thought of physical desires. Hence the complete, perfect Torah informed us that the body is considered defiled by it. For a person's being in the world is primarily for no other purpose but to understand the concepts of reason and to serve his Creator. Therefore, when this matter happens to him, which indicates in him his turning to physical desire, he should properly stay one day in his impurity, so that his thought will be well cleansed, and then he will become ritually clean.

Among the laws of the precept there is what the Sages of blessed memory taught:[1] that its minimal amount to [defile] one who touches it is as a lentil, but to [defile] one who sees [has] the emission, it can be any amount at all. It is all one whether a person sees [has] a pollution by accident or by desire: he becomes impure.[2] The semen of a child does not defile.[3] A red emission is not ritually unclean; only white is.[3] Any emission with which a man experiences no sensation, neither at the beginning nor at the end, is not ritually unclean.[4] If someone fantasied at night and saw himself in conjugal intimacy in a dream, and he arose and found his flesh warm, then even though he did not see any seminal emission, he is ritually unclean.[4] The rest of its details are explained in the Mishnah tractate *Zavim*.

The uncleanness of semen is in effect in every place and every time. However, now that for our sins we have neither Sanctuary nor holy

שֶׁאֵין לָנוּ לֹא מִקְדָּשׁ וְלֹא קָדָשִׁים אֵין אָנוּ צְרִיכִין לְהִזָּהֵר בְּעִנְיַן הַטֻּמְאָה. וְאַף־עַל־פִּי־כֵן עֶזְרָא תִקֵּן טְבִילָה לְבַעֲלֵי קְרָיִין, כְּדֵי שֶׁיִּהְיוּ נְקִיִּים וּטְהוֹרִים יוֹתֵר בְּמַחֲשַׁבְתָּן, וְלֹא יִהְיוּ בְנֵי־אָדָם מְצוּיִין עִם נְשׁוֹתֵיהֶן כְּתַרְנְגוֹלִין. וּבִזְמַנּוֹ לֹא הָיָה אָדָם מִתְפַּלֵּל וְשׁוֹנֶה בַּתּוֹרָה עַד אַחַר טְבִילָה; וּבַזְּמַן הַזֶּה פָּסְקִנוּ בַּגְּמָרָא דְּבַטְּלוּהָ חֲכָמִים לִטְבִילוּתָא, וְאֵין אָדָם נִמְנָע מִלְּהִתְפַּלֵּל וְלִשְׁנוֹת, גַּם לְהָנִיחַ תְּפִלִּין, בִּשְׁבִיל קֶרִי; וַאֲפִלּוּ לִנְטִילוּתָא, דְּהַיְנוּ הֲדָחַת הַגּוּף בְּתִשְׁעָה קַבִּין מַיִם, גַּם־כֵּן בִּטְּלוּ, וְעַכְשָׁיו לֹא יִטְבְּלוּ וְלֹא יָדִיחוּ כְּלָל. וְאָמְנָם בַּעַל נֶפֶשׁ הַמִּטַּהֵר לְקִרְיוֹ גַּם הַיּוֹם מִדָּה טוֹבָה וּמְשֻׁבַּחַת הִיא לוֹ וְתָבוֹא עָלָיו בְּרָכָה; וְיוֹדֵעַ דֶּרֶךְ הַטָּהֳרָה וְרֹב טוּבָהּ יַחֲזִיק בָּהּ.

[מִצְוַת עִנְיַן טֻמְאַת נִדָּה שֶׁטְּמֵאָה וּמְטַמְּאָה]

קפא לִהְיוֹת הַנִּדָּה טְמֵאָה וּמְטַמְּאָה אֲחֵרִים, שֶׁנֶּאֱמַר: וְכָל הַנֹּגֵעַ בָּהּ יִטְמָא עַד הָעָרֶב.

שֹׁרֶשׁ הַמִּצְוָה וּקְצָת פְּרָטֶיהָ נִכְתֹּב כְּמִנְהָגֵנוּ בַּלָּאו דְּנִדָּה בְּסֵדֶר אַחֲרֵי מוֹת [סי׳ ר״ז] בְּעֶזְרַת הַשֵּׁם.

וְנוֹהֶגֶת בְּכָל מָקוֹם וּבְכָל זְמַן. וְעוֹבֵר עָלֶיהָ וְלֹא הִתְנַהֵג עִמָּהּ בְּטֻמְאָה, וְכֵן הִיא שֶׁנָּהֲגָה בְעַצְמָהּ מִנְהַג טָהֳרָה, בִּטֵּל עֲשֵׂה זֶה, מִלְּבַד הָעֹנֶשׁ שֶׁיֵּשׁ בָּהּ, כְּמוֹ שֶׁנִּכְתֹּב לְמַטָּה בְּעֶזְרַת הַשֵּׁם.

[מִצְוַת עִנְיַן טֻמְאַת זָבָה שֶׁטְּמֵאָה וּמְטַמְּאָה]

קפב לִהְיוֹת הַזָּבָה טְמֵאָה וּמְטַמְּאָה, שֶׁנֶּאֱמַר: וְאִשָּׁה כִּי יָזוּב זוֹב דָּמָהּ יָמִים רַבִּים וְגוֹמֵר.

רֶמֶז שֹׁרֶשׁ הַמִּצְוָה כְּתַבְתִּיו בְּיוֹלֶדֶת, כִּי עִנְיַן הָרִחוּק מֵהֶן וְטֻמְאָתָן מִפְּנֵי

5. TB Bava Kamma 82a; see also B'rachoth 22a.

6. Since conjugal intimacy is as defiling as a pollution; TB B'rachoth 22a.

7. *Ibid.*

8. A *kav* (singular of *kavim*) measures 1,382 cubic centimeters according to one view, 2,389 cubic centimeters according to another.

9. So Rabad, cited in *Tur 'Oraḥ Ḥayyim* §88, toward the end—supported by TJ Yoma viii 1.

10. So TB B'rachoth 22a.

offerings, we do not need to be careful in regard to the ritual uncleanness. Nevertheless, Ezra instituted the rule of ritual immersion for those who have pollutions,[5] so that they should be more cleansed and pure in their thought, and people should not be so frequently with their wives, like roosters.[6] In his time, a man would not pray or study Torah until after ritual immersion. But for our time we have the ruling in the Talmud that the Sages nullified [the need for] immersion.[7] Hence a man need not refrain now from praying and studying, or even from putting on *t'fillin* (phylacteries), on account of a pollution. Even the practice of washing, i.e. washing the body with nine *kavim*[8] of water, the Sages equally nullified.[9] Thus now one does not undergo immersion or wash [for it] at all. However, if a spiritual person purifies himself of his pollutions even today, it is a good and praiseworthy way of behavior for him, and blessing will be bestowed upon him.[10] Then whoever knows the way of purity and its manifold goodness, let him hold fast to it.

[THE PRECEPT OF THE RITUAL UNCLEANNESS OF A MENSTRUANT]

181 that a woman with the menses is ritually unclean and defiles others: as it is stated, *and whoever touches her shall be unclean until the evening* (Leviticus 15:19).

The root purpose of the precept and some of its laws, we will write, as is our custom, in the negative precept of the menstruant (§207) in *sidrah aḥaré moth*, with the Eternal Lord's help.

It is in force in every place and every time. If someone violates it and does not deal with her as in a state of defilement, and so too if she conducts herself in a way of ritual purity, he [or she] has disobeyed this positive precept, and this apart from the punishment it entails, which we will write below, with the Eternal Lord's help.

[ON THE RITUAL UNCLEANNESS OF A WOMAN WITH AN IRREGULAR DISCHARGE]

182 that a woman with a discharge (*zavah*) is to be ritually unclean and a source of defilement: as it is stated, *And if a woman has a discharge of her blood many days*, etc. (Leviticus 15:25).

I have written a hint of the root purpose of the precept in connection with a woman who gave birth (§166)—that the matter of keeping distant from them and their uncleanness is on account of the

הַמַּחֲלָה שֶׁבָּהֶן, שֶׁמַּזֶּקֶת הַרְבֵּה בְּנֵי־אָדָם, וְכָל שֶׁכֵּן הַשּׁוֹכֵב אוֹתָן, כִּי לְפִי רֹב קִרְבָתוֹ עִמָּהֶן הַהֶזֵּק יוֹתֵר.

מִדִּינֵי הַמִּצְוָה, מַה שֶּׁאָמְרוּ זִכְרוֹנָם לִבְרָכָה שֶׁאַחַד־עָשָׂר יוֹם הֵם שֶׁהֵם בֵּין נִדָּה לְנִדָּה, כְּלוֹמַר שֶׁהָאִשָּׁה נַעֲשֵׂית בָּהֶם זָבָה; כָּךְ הִיא הֲלָכָה לְמֹשֶׁה מִסִּינָי. וּפֵרוּשׁ הַדָּבָר כָּךְ הוּא: שֶׁכָּל אִשָּׁה בְּעֵת שֶׁתִּרְאֶה דָם, בִּתְחִלַּת רְאִיָּתָהּ תִּקָּרֵא נִדָּה. וְעִנְיַן הַנִּדּוּת כָּךְ דִּינוֹ: שֶׁאִם תִּרְאֶה יוֹם אֶחָד דָּם, אוֹ אֲפִלּוּ שִׁבְעָה יָמִים רְצוּפִים, כָּל זְמַן שֶׁתִּפְסֹק הַדָּם בַּיּוֹם הַשְּׁבִיעִי מִבְּעוֹד יוֹם טוֹבֶלֶת לָעֶרֶב, דְּהַיְנוּ הַלַּיְלָה שֶׁמָּחֳרָתוֹ יוֹם שְׁמִינִי לִתְחִלַּת רְאִיָּתָהּ; וְאַחַר טְבִילָתָהּ טְהוֹרָה לְבַעְלָהּ.

וְאַחַר שִׁבְעַת יְמֵי הַנִּדּוּת, אִם תִּרְאֶה דָם בְּתוֹךְ אַחַד־עָשָׂר יוֹם אַחַר הַשִּׁבְעָה, יִקָּרֵא אוֹתוֹ הַדָּם דַּם זִיבָה; וְדִינוֹ כֵּן: שֶׁאִם תִּרְאֶה מִמֶּנּוּ יוֹם אֶחָד, בֵּין שֶׁתִּרְאֶה בִתְחִלַּת הַלַּיְלָה אוֹ בְסוֹף הַיּוֹם, מְשַׁמֶּרֶת יוֹם אֶחָד כְּנֶגְדּוֹ וְטוֹבֶלֶת, וּטְהוֹרָה לְבַעְלָהּ לָעֶרֶב; וּטְבִילָתָהּ אֲפִלּוּ בַּיּוֹם מִשֶּׁתָּנֵץ הַחַמָּה; וְזֹאת הִיא זָבָה קְטַנָּה. וְכֵן אִם תִּרְאֶה דָם שְׁנֵי יָמִים וְתִפְסֹק בַּשְּׁלִישִׁי דִּינָהּ כְּמוֹ־כֵן לִשְׁמֹר יוֹם אֶחָד, וּבְכֵן יַסְפִּיק לָהּ אֲפִלּוּ לִשְׁנֵי יָמִים וְתִטְהַר, וְזֹאת גַּם־כֵּן תִּקָּרֵא זָבָה קְטַנָּה.

וְאִם תִּרְאֶה דָם בְּתוֹךְ אַחַד־עָשָׂר יוֹם אֵלּוּ שְׁלֹשָׁה יָמִים רְצוּפִים, תִּקָּרֵא זָבָה גְדוֹלָה, וּצְרִיכָה לֵישֵׁב שִׁבְעָה יָמִים נְקִיִּים, וְאַחַר־כָּךְ טוֹבֶלֶת וּטְהוֹרָה לְבַעְלָהּ.

וְאַחַר אַחַד־עָשָׂר יוֹם אֵלּוּ, אִם תִּרְאֶה, חוֹזֶרֶת לִתְחִלַּת נִדּוּת וְיֵשׁ לָהּ שִׁבְעָה יָמִים כְּדִין נִדָּה, כְּמוֹ שֶׁאָמַרְנוּ לְמַעְלָה. וְכֵן יִהְיֶה הַדָּבָר לְעוֹלָם, שֶׁאַחַר הַנִּדּוּת יֵשׁ לָהּ אַחַד־עָשָׂר יוֹם שֶׁבָּהֶן נַעֲשֵׂית זָבָה, וְאַחַר שֶׁעָבְרוּ אוֹתָן הי״א יוֹם אֵינָהּ נַעֲשֵׂית זָבָה לְעוֹלָם עַד שֶׁעָבְרוּ עָלֶיהָ שִׁבְעָה יְמֵי נִדּוּת.

וּמִפְּנֵי שֶׁכְּבָר טָעוּ בָזֶה אֲחֵרִים וְחָשְׁבוּ שֶׁהַחֶשְׁבּוֹן הוּא שֶׁתִּמְנֶה שִׁבְעָה יָמִים

§182 1. TB Niddah 72b.

2. Literally, at the beginning of her seeing.

3. So Sifra, *m'tzora, zavim, parashah* 4, 5.

4. I.e. if there was no discharge during the night, she may undergo immersion at sunrise, and if there is no discharge during the day, she is permitted to her husband after nightfall (MT *hilchoth 'issuré bi'ah* vi 9).

5. I.e. a night and a day after the two days; if there was no discharge during this time, she is permissible to her husband the following evening (MT *ibid.* 10).

6. Literally, to sit seven clean ones — i.e. to wait and see when seven days in a row have passed without the occurrence of discharge.

7. What she sees (experiences) is considered the beginning of the menses.

8. So Ramban, commentary to TB Niddah 54a.

9. I.e. MT *hilchoth 'issuré bi'ah* vi 4, and those who follow Rambam.

illness in them, which is greatly injurious to people, and especially so to anyone who lies carnally with them. For the closer one is to them, the greater the injurious effect.

Among the laws of the precept, there is what the Sages of blessed memory taught:[1] that there are eleven days between one menstruation and another—i.e., in which a woman can have a discharge [that is considered irregular]; so is the law [as given orally] to Moses at Sinai. Now, this is the explanation of the matter: When any woman sees blood, at the beginning of its appearance[2] she is called *niddah*, a menstruant; and such is the rule for menstruants: If she sees blood one day or even seven days, as long as the blood ceases on the seventh while it is still day, she undergoes ritual immersion in the evening,[3] i.e. the evening whose following morning will be the eighth day since she began seeing blood. And after her ritual bathing she is pure (permitted) to her husband.

Now, after the seven days of the menstruant, if she should see blood during eleven days after the seven, that is called blood of discharge; and this is its law: If she sees it for one day, whether she sees it at the beginning of the night or the end of the day, she observes one day [of cleanness] in apposition to it, and undergoes ritual immersion, whereupon she is pure (permitted) to her husband in the evening. Her immersion may be even by day, from the time the sun rises.[4] This is a woman with a minor discharge. So too, if she sees blood two days and it stops on the third, the law for her is, likewise, to observe one day.[5] So this is enough for her even for two days [of discharge], and she becomes ritually clean. And she too is called a woman with a minor discharge.

Now, if, during these eleven days, she should see blood for three days in a row, she is called a woman with a major discharge, and she needs to observe seven clean days;[6] after that she undergoes ritual immersion and is pure (permitted) to her husband.

After these eleven days, if she should see [blood] she returns to the beginning of menstruation,[7] and she has seven days [to wait], as the law is for a menstruant, as we stated above. So the matter remains always: after the period of menstrual uncleanness, she has eleven days in which she can become a woman with a discharge. After those eleven days, she can never become a woman with a discharge until she has passed [again] through seven days of menstrual uncleanness.[8]

Others have previously erred about this,[9] and thought the reckoning should be so: that she should count seven days of menstrual

שֶׁל נִדּוּת וְאַחַד־עָשָׂר יוֹם שֶׁל זִיבוּת, וְשֶׁבַע שֶׁל נִדּוּת וי״א שֶׁל זִיבוּת, וְכֵן לְעוֹלָם, הֶאֱרַכְתִּי בָעִנְיָן לוֹמַר שֶׁאֵינוֹ כֵן, אֶלָּא לְעוֹלָם אֵין יְמֵי זִיבָה אֶלָּא אַחַד־עָשָׂר יוֹם אַחַר שִׁבְעָה שֶׁל נִדּוּת, וְלֹא אַחַר כָּךְ לְעוֹלָם עַד שֶׁתַּחֲזוֹר לִתְחִלַּת הַנִּדּוּת; רְצוֹנִי לוֹמַר שֶׁאִם תַּעֲמֹד וְלֹא תִרְאֶה אַחַר הי״א יוֹם אֲפִלּוּ שָׁנָה, אֵין לָהּ דִּין זָבָה עַד שֶׁיַּעַבְרוּ עָלֶיהָ שִׁבְעַת יְמֵי נִדּוּת.

וְיֶתֶר פְּרָטֶיהָ בְּמַסֶּכֶת זָבִים, וּבְמַסֶּכֶת נִדָּה גַּם־כֵּן קְצָת מִדִּינֵי זִיבָה. וּבְלָאו דְּנִדָּה בְּסֵדֶר אַחֲרֵי מוֹת [סי׳ ר״ז] נִכְתֹּב בְּעֶזְרַת הַשֵּׁם מַה שֶּׁנָּהוּג הַיּוֹם בְּעִנְיָנִים אֵלֶּה. וְעוֹבֵר עַל מִצְוָה זוֹ וְהוּא מֵקֵל בְּעִנְיַן טֻמְאָתָהּ, בִּטֵּל עֲשֵׂה זֶה, מִלְּבַד הָעֹנֶשׁ שֶׁהַשּׁוֹכֵב עִמָּהּ הוּא בְכָרֵת, כְּמוֹ שֶׁנִּכְתֹּב בְּלָאו דְּנִדָּה בְּעֶזְרַת הַשֵּׁם.

[מִצְוַת קָרְבַּן זָבָה כְּשֶׁתִּתְרַפֵּא מִזּוֹבָהּ]

קפג שֶׁתַּקְרִיב הַזָּבָה קָרְבָּן כְּשֶׁתִּתְרַפֵּא מִזּוֹבָהּ, וְהוּא שְׁתֵּי תוֹרִים אוֹ שְׁנֵי בְנֵי יוֹנָה, שֶׁנֶּאֱמַר: וְאִם טָהֲרָה מִזּוֹבָהּ וְגוֹמֵר, וּבַיּוֹם הַשְּׁמִינִי תִּקַּח לָהּ שְׁתֵּי תֹרִים וְגוֹמֵר.

שֹׁרֶשׁ הַמִּצְוָה זוֹ וּקְצָת פְּרָטֶיהָ כְּעֵין מַה שֶּׁכָּתַבְנוּ לְמַעְלָה בְּקָרְבַּן הַזָּב. וְכָתַב הָרַמְבָּ״ם זִכְרוֹנוֹ לִבְרָכָה כִּי מִפְּנֵי־כֵן נֶחֱשַׁב לִשְׁתֵּי מִצְווֹת שְׁתֵּי קָרְבָּנוֹת אֵלּוּ שֶׁל זָב וְשֶׁל זָבָה, וְאַף־עַל־פִּי שֶׁהֵן קָרְבָּן אֶחָד מַמָּשׁ, מַה שֶּׁלֹּא עָשִׂינוּ כֵן בִּשְׁאָר קָרְבָּנוֹת הַרְבֵּה, שֶׁאֵין אָנוּ חוֹשְׁשִׁין לִמְנוֹת מִצְוָה בִּפְנֵי עַצְמָהּ כָּל קָרְבָּן וְקָרְבָּן בִּשְׁבִיל חִלּוּק הַמְּבִיאִים אוֹתָן, כָּל זְמַן שֶׁהַקָּרְבָּן אֶחָד — לְפִי שֶׁטֻּמְאָתָן שֶׁל אֵלּוּ אֵינָהּ שָׁוָה כְּלָל, שֶׁהָאִישׁ מִטַּמֵּא בְלֹבֶן וְהָאִשָּׁה בְּאֹדֶם, וּבְהֶפֶךְ לֹא יִטְמָא לֹא זֶה

§183 1. ShM positive precept §75.

uncleanness and eleven days of [possible irregular] discharge, then seven days for [possible] menstrual uncleanness and eleven days of [possible] discharge, and so on forever. I have therefore written at length about the matter, to state that it is not so. Rather, in truth, the days of [possible irregular] discharge are never other than eleven after the seven of menstrual uncleanness, and then no more after that, ever, until she returns to the beginning of menstrual uncleanness. By this I mean that if she should remain the same and not see [any blood] after the eleven days for even a year, no law of a woman with a discharge applies to her, until seven days of menstrual uncleanness pass by for her.

The rest of its details are in the Mishnah tractate *Zavim;* and in the Talmud tractate *Niddah* there are also some laws of [irregular] discharge. In the negative precept of the menstruant in *sidrah aḥaré moth* (§207) we will write, with the Eternal Lord's help, what is in force today of these matters. If someone transgresses this precept and treats the matter of her ritual uncleanness unduly lightly, he has disobeyed this positive precept—this apart from the punishment for one who lies carnally with her, which is *karéth* [Divine severance of existence], as we will write in the negative precept of the menstruant (§207), with the Eternal Lord's help.

[ON THE OFFERING BY A WOMAN WITH AN IRREGULAR DISCHARGE, WHEN SHE RECOVERS]

183 that a woman with a discharge should bring an offering when she is healed of her discharge, this being two turtledoves or two young pigeons: as it is stated, *But if she is cleansed of her discharge . . . And on the eighth day she shall take two turtledoves*, etc. (Leviticus 15:28–29).

The root reason for this precept, and some of its laws, are akin to what we wrote above about the offering of a man with a discharge (§179). Now, Rambam of blessed memory wrote[1] that for this reason we reckon as two precepts these two offerings of the man and the woman with discharges, although they are actually one and the same offering—which we have not done with many other offerings, since we do not scruple to count every single offering as a separate precept because of differences among those who bring them, as long as it is one kind of offering—because the ritual uncleannesses of these two are not at all alike: The man becomes impure with a white discharge, and the woman with red [blood]; should it be the reverse, neither one nor the other

וְלֹא זֶה; וְכֵיוָן שֶׁהֵם חֲלוּקִים כָּל־כָּךְ רָאוּי לִמְנוֹתָם לִשְׁתֵּי מִצְווֹת.

וְאֵין דּוֹמֶה עִנְיָן זֶה כְּלָל לְעִנְיַן מְצֹרָע וּמְצֹרַעַת, שֶׁהוּא נֶחְשָׁב לְמִצְוָה אַחַת, שֶׁהַצָּרַעַת דָּבָר שָׁוֶה בְּכֻלָּן. וְהֵבִיא רְאָיָה קְצָת לִדְבָרָיו מִמַּה שֶּׁאָמְרוּ בִּכְרֵתוֹת: אַרְבָּעָה מְחֻסְּרֵי כַפָּרָה, וְאֵלּוּ הֵן, הַזָּב וְהַזָּבָה וְהַיּוֹלֶדֶת וְהַמְּצֹרָע — הֲרֵי שֶׁחָשְׁבוּ זָב וְזָבָה בִּשְׁנַיִם, לְפִי שֶׁחֲלוּקִין בְּחָלְיָן, וּמְצֹרַעַת וּמְצֹרָע כְּאֶחָד לְפִי שֶׁהַחֹלִי שָׁוֶה בִּשְׁנֵיהֶם.

וְנוֹהֶגֶת בִּזְמַן הַבַּיִת. וְהָעוֹבֶרֶת וְלֹא תַקְרִיב קָרְבָּנָהּ כְּשֶׁתִּתְרַפֵּא מִזּוֹבָהּ, בִּטְּלָה עֲשֵׂה זֶה, מִלְּבַד שֶׁהִיא מְחֻסֶּרֶת כַּפָּרָה.

אַחֲרֵי מוֹת

יֵשׁ בָּהּ כ״ח מִצְווֹת: ב׳ מִצְווֹת עֲשֵׂה וכ״ו מִצְווֹת לֹא־תַעֲשֶׂה

[שֶׁלֹּא יִכָּנְסוּ הַכֹּהֲנִים בְּכָל עֵת בַּמִּקְדָּשׁ וְכָל־שֶׁכֵּן זָרִים]

קפד שֶׁלֹּא יִכָּנְסוּ הַכֹּהֲנִים בְּכָל עֵת אֶל הַמִּקְדָּשׁ, אֶלָּא בְּעֵת הָעֲבוֹדָה, שֶׁנֶּאֱמַר: וְאַל יָבֹא בְכָל עֵת. וְיַזְהִיר בְּכָאן כֹּהֵן גָּדוֹל מֵהִכָּנֵס בְּבֵית קֹדֶשׁ הַקֳּדָשִׁים, וַאֲפִלּוּ בְּיוֹם הַכִּפּוּרִים, אֶלָּא בִּזְמַן הָעֲבוֹדָה; וְכֵן יִכָּנֵס בָּאַזְהָרָה כֹּהֵן הֶדְיוֹט מֵהִכָּנֵס בַּהֵיכָל כָּל הַשָּׁנָה אֶלָּא בִּזְמַן הָעֲבוֹדָה. וִיהְיֶה בֵּאוּר עִנְיַן הַמְּנִיעָה לוֹמַר שֶׁכָּל כֹּהֵן לֹא יִכָּנֵס בְּמָקוֹם שֶׁהוּא רָאוּי אֶלָּא בַּזְּמַן שֶׁהוּא רָאוּי לְהִכָּנֵס בּוֹ, דְּהַיְנוּ בִּשְׁעַת עֲבוֹדָה.

וּלְשׁוֹן סִפְרָא: ״וְאַל יָבֹא בְכָל עֵת״, זֶה יוֹם הַכִּפּוּרִים; ״אֶל הַקֹּדֶשׁ״ לְרַבּוֹת

§184 1. The "Temple palace," which includes the *'ulam* (entrance hall), the holy chamber, and the holy of holies (§95).

2. Sifra, *aḥaré moth, parashah* 1, 8 and 10.

becomes impure. Then since they are so very differentiated, it is proper to reckon these as two precepts.

Nor is this matter at all similar to the case of a man and a woman with a *tzara'ath* disease, who are both included under one precept—for *tzara'ath* is the same thing with all. He brought some proof for his words from what the Sages said in the Talmud tractate *K'rithoth* (8b): There are four who are lacking in atonement; these are a man and a woman with a discharge, a woman who gave birth, and a person with a *tzara'ath* ailment. Well, you see that they reckoned the man and the woman with a discharge as two [separate categories], because they are different in their illness, but a man and a woman afflicted with *tzara'ath* as one, because the illness is the same in both.

It is in force when the Temple exists. If a woman violates it and does not bring her offering when she is cured of her discharge, she disobeys this positive precept, apart from remaining lacking in atonement.

sidrah 'aḥaré moth

(Leviticus 16–18)

It contains twenty-eight precepts: two positive, and twenty-six negative precepts.

[THAT THE KOHANIM SHOULD ENTER THE INNER SANCTUARY ONLY FOR THE TEMPLE SERVICE]

184 that the *kohanim* should not enter the inner Sanctuary all the time, but only at an instance of Temple service: for it is stated, *that he should not come at all times* (Leviticus 16:2). Here the *kohen gadol* is warned against entering the chamber of the holy of holies, even on the Day of Atonement, except at the time of the service. But so does the warning include an ordinary *kohen*, that he should not enter the *héchal*[1] the entire year except at a time of service. It would define the theme of the restriction to say that no *kohen* is to enter the place where he belongs at any but the time when it is proper for him to enter there: i.e., at the time of Temple service.

In the language of the Midrash *Sifra:*[2] "that he should not come at all times"—this refers to the Day of Atonement; "into the holy place" (*ibid.*)—this is to extend it to the other days of the year; "within

שְׁאָר יְמוֹת הַשָּׁנָה; "מִבֵּית לַפָּרֹכֶת" לְהַזְהִיר עַל כָּל הַבַּיִת. יָכוֹל כָּל הַבַּיִת בְּמִיתָה, תַּלְמוּד לוֹמַר: אֶל פְּנֵי הַכַּפֹּרֶת אֲשֶׁר עַל הָאָרֹן וְלֹא יָמוּת. הָא כֵיצַד, אֶל פְּנֵי הַכַּפֹּרֶת בְּמִיתָה, וְעַל שְׁאָר כָּל הַבַּיִת בְּאַזְהָרָה. וּבִגְמָרָא מְנָחוֹת אָמְרוּ זִכְרוֹנָם לִבְרָכָה: עַל הַהֵיכָל בְּאַרְבָּעִים.

מִשָּׁרְשֵׁי הַמִּצְוָה, שֶׁיִּקְבְּעוּ הַמְשָׁרְתִים בְּנַפְשׁוֹתָם גְּדֻלַּת הַמָּקוֹם וּמַעֲלָתוֹ, וְתִהְיֶה יִרְאָתוֹ תָמִיד עַל פְּנֵיהֶם.

מִדִּינֵי הַמִּצְוָה, מַה שֶּׁאָמְרוּ זִכְרוֹנָם לִבְרָכָה שֶׁכֹּהֵן גָּדוֹל אֵינוֹ נִכְנָס לְקֹדֶשׁ הַקֳּדָשִׁים אֶלָּא בְּיוֹם הַכִּפּוּרִים, שֶׁנִּכְנָס אַרְבַּע פְּעָמִים וְלֹא יוֹתֵר, שֶׁאִם נִכְנַס חֲמִישִׁית חַיָּב מִיתָה בִּידֵי שָׁמַיִם; וְכֹהֵן הֶדְיוֹט נִכְנָס בַּהֵיכָל לַעֲבוֹדָה בְּכָל יוֹם; וְכָל הַנִּכְנָס לַהֵיכָל שֶׁלֹּא לְצֹרֶךְ עֲבוֹדָה, בֵּין כֹּהֵן גָּדוֹל אוֹ כֹהֵן הֶדְיוֹט, כְּגוֹן שֶׁיִּכָּנֵס אֲפִלּוּ לְהִשְׁתַּחֲווֹת, לוֹקֶה וְאֵינוֹ חַיָּב מִיתָה, שֶׁנֶּאֱמַר: אֶל פְּנֵי הַכַּפֹּרֶת... וְלֹא יָמוּת; עַל קֹדֶשׁ הַקֳּדָשִׁים בְּמִיתָה וְעַל שְׁאָר הַבַּיִת בְּלָאו. זֶהוּ דַּעַת הָרַמְבָּ"ם זִכְרוֹנוֹ לִבְרָכָה בַּלָּאו הַזֶּה.

וּכְבָר כָּתַבְתִּי לְמַעְלָה דַעַת הָרַמְבָּ"ן זִכְרוֹנוֹ לִבְרָכָה, שֶׁאָמַר שֶׁהַכְּנִיסָה בַבַּיִת שֶׁלֹּא לַעֲבוֹדָה בִּפְרוּעַ רֹאשׁ וּקְרוּעַ בְּגָדִים מַעֲלָה הִיא מִדִּבְרֵיהֶם. וְאִם־כֵּן, לְדַעְתּוֹ כָּל שֶׁנִּכְנָס לְהִשְׁתַּחֲווֹת אֶפְשָׁר שֶׁאֵינוֹ בְמַלְקוֹת כְּלָל, וְאִסּוּר זֶה דְ"אַל יָבֹא" יִהְיֶה בְבִיאָה רֵיקָנִית לְגַמְרֵי, לְפִי שֶׁזֶּה זִלְזוּל בִּכְבוֹד הַבַּיִת לְהִכָּנֵס בּוֹ חִנָּם. וְיֶתֶר פְּרָטֶיהָ, מְבֹאָרִים בִּמְנָחוֹת וּבְסִפְרָא.

וְנוֹהֶגֶת בִּזְמַן הַבַּיִת בַּכֹּהֲנִים; וַאֲפִלּוּ עַכְשָׁיו, שֶׁלֹּא בִזְמַן הַבַּיִת, אָמְרוּ זִכְרוֹנָם לִבְרָכָה שֶׁמֻּזְהָרִים אָנוּ שֶׁלֹּא לְהִכָּנֵס לַמִּקְדָּשׁ, וְדָרְשׁוּ הַדָּבָר מִדִּכְתִיב "וַהֲשִׁמּוֹתִי

3. Hence improper entry in the rest of the Temple is punishable by a whipping of lashes ("before the ark-cover" means in the holy of holies).

4. Here *héchal* denotes only the *'ulam* and the holy chamber. (The first two paragraphs are based on ShM negative precept §68.)

5. Mishnah, Kélim i 9.

6. Tosefta, Kélim i.

7. MT *hilchoth bi'ath ha-mikdash* ii 4.

8. I.e. not to walk on its site; MT *hilchoth béth ha-b'ḥirah* vi 16, based on TB M'gillah 28a.

the veil" (*ibid.*)—to apply the warning to the entire Temple. I might think that [improper entry] anywhere in the Temple is [punishable] by death?—Scripture writes, *before the ark-cover which is upon the ark, that he should not die* (ibid.). Then how [is it to be understood]?—"before the ark-cover" is punishable by death; over all the rest of the Temple, there is an injunction.[3] And in the Talmud tractate *M'naḥoth* (27b) the Sages of blessed memory said: For [improperly entering] the *héchal*, [there is punishment] by forty [lashes of the whip].[4]

At the root of the precept lies the purpose that the [Temple] ministers should realize firmly in their souls the grandeur of the place and its exalted level, and reverent fear for Him should be constantly before their eyes.

Among the laws of the precept, there is what the Sages of blessed memory taught: that the *kohen gadol* was to enter the holy of holies at no other time but the Day of Atonement;[5] that he was to enter four times and no more; and if he entered a fifth time he would be punishable by death at Heaven's hands.[6] An ordinary *kohen* might enter the *héchal*[4] for Temple service every day. But whoever entered the *héchal* without any need for Temple service, whether he was the *kohen gadol* or an ordinary *kohen*—for example, if he entered even to bow down in worship—he would receive whiplashes, but would not be punished by death: for it is stated, *before the ark-cover . . . that he should not die* (Leviticus 16:2)—for the holy of holies, the punishment is by death; for the rest of the Temple, it is a negative precept. This is the view of Rambam of blessed memory about this injunction.[7]

I have already written above (§§149, 150) the view of Ramban of blessed memory, who said that [the ban on] entering the Temple without the purpose of service, with overgrown head, or with torn clothes, is [merely] a higher standard [of respectful behavior] set by a ruling of the Sages. Hence, by his view, whoever enters to bow down in worship may perhaps not be punishable by whiplashes at all; and this prohibition, *that he should not come* (Leviticus 16:2), would apply to entry completely devoid of purpose, since this constitutes a disregard for the honor of the Temple, to enter it for nothing.

The rest of its details are explained in the Talmud tractate *M'naḥoth* and the Midrash *Sifra*. It is in effect when the Temple exists, for the *kohanim*. Yet even now, when the Temple is not in existence, our Sages of blessed memory said that we are adjured not to enter the Sanctuary.[8]

They derived the matter from the fact that it is written, *and I will*

אֶת מִקְדְּשֵׁיכֶם" וְלֹא אָמַר "מִקְדְּשֵׁיכֶם אָשִׂים שְׁמָמָה", דְּמַשְׁמַע קְדֻשָּׁתָן עֲלֵיהֶן אֲפִלּוּ כְּשֶׁהֵן שׁוֹמְמִין. וְכֵיוָן שֶׁכֵּן, יֵשׁ לִי לִמְנוֹת אִסּוּר זֶה בִּכְלַל אִסּוּרִין הַנּוֹהֲגִין הַיּוֹם.

[מִצְוַת עֲבוֹדַת יוֹם הַכִּפּוּרִים]

קפה שֶׁיַּעֲשֶׂה כֹּהֵן גָּדוֹל כָּל מַעֲשֵׂה יוֹם הַכִּפּוּרִים עַל סֵדֶר, הַקָּרְבָּנוֹת וְהַוִּדּוּיִין וְשִׁלּוּחַ הַשָּׂעִיר וּשְׁאָר הָעֲבוֹדָה, כְּמוֹ שֶׁכָּתוּב בַּפָּרָשָׁה, שֶׁנֶּאֱמַר: בְּזֹאת יָבֹא אַהֲרֹן אֶל הַקֹּדֶשׁ, וְגוֹמֵר, כָּל הַפָּרָשָׁה.

מִשָּׁרְשֵׁי הַמִּצְוָה, שֶׁהָיָה מֵחַסְדֵי הָאֵל עַל בְּרִיּוֹתָיו לִקְבֹּעַ לָהֶן יוֹם אֶחָד בַּשָּׁנָה לְכַפָּרָה עַל הַחֲטָאִים עִם הַתְּשׁוּבָה שֶׁיָּשׁוּבוּ, שֶׁאִלּוּ יִתְקַבְּצוּ עֲוֹנוֹת הַבְּרִיּוֹת שָׁנָה שָׁנָה תִּתְמַלֵּא סְאָתָם לְסוֹף שְׁנָתַיִם אוֹ שָׁלֹשׁ אוֹ יוֹתֵר וְיִתְחַיֵּב הָעוֹלָם כְּלָיָה; עַל כֵּן רָאָה בְחָכְמָתוֹ בָּרוּךְ הוּא, לְקִיּוּם הָעוֹלָם, לִקְבֹּעַ יוֹם אֶחָד בַּשָּׁנָה לְכַפָּרַת חֲטָאִים לַשָּׁבִים. וּמִתְּחִלַּת בְּרִיאַת הָעוֹלָם יְעָדוֹ וְקִדְּשׁוֹ לְכָךְ, וְאַחַר שֶׁיְּעָדוֹ הָאֵל בָּרוּךְ הוּא אוֹתוֹ הַיּוֹם לְכַפָּרָה, נִתְקַדֵּשׁ הַיּוֹם וְקִבֵּל כֹּחַ הַזַּכּוּת מֵאִתּוֹ יִתְעַלֶּה עַד שֶׁהוּא מְסַיֵּעַ בְּכַפָּרָה. וְזֶהוּ אָמְרָם זִכְרוֹנָם לִבְרָכָה בְּהַרְבֵּה מְקוֹמוֹת: וְיוֹם הַכִּפּוּרִים מְכַפֵּר, כְּלוֹמַר שֶׁיֵּשׁ כֹּחַ לַיּוֹם בְּעַצְמוֹ בְּכַפָּרָה בַּעֲבֵרוֹת קַלּוֹת.

מִדִּינֵי הַמִּצְוָה, מַה שֶּׁאָמְרוּ זִכְרוֹנָם לִבְרָכָה שֶׁבְּיוֹם זֶה הָיוּ מַקְרִיבִין תָּמִיד בַּשַּׁחַר וְתָמִיד בֵּין הָעַרְבַּיִם כְּסֵדֶר כָּל יוֹם וָיוֹם; וּמַקְרִיבִין מוּסַף הַיּוֹם, פָּר וָאַיִל וְשִׁבְעָה כְבָשִׂים, הַכֹּל עוֹלוֹת; וְשָׂעִיר לְחַטָּאת וְנַעֲשָׂה בַחוּץ, וְהוּא נֶאֱכָל לָעֶרֶב. וְעוֹד מַקְרִיבִין יֶתֶר עַל זֶה פַּר בֶּן בָּקָר לְחַטָּאת, וְהוּא נִשְׂרָף, וְאַיִל לְעוֹלָה, וּשְׁנֵיהֶם מִשֶּׁל כֹּהֵן גָּדוֹל; וְאַיִל הַבָּא מִשֶּׁל צִבּוּר הָאָמוּר בְּפָרָשָׁה זוֹ הוּא הָאַיִל הָאָמוּר

§185 1. The view of the Sages, TB Sh'vu'oth 13a, and R. Ishmael, Yoma 86a.

2. Cf. TB 'Avodah Zarah 4a: I will give you a parable: to what is the matter like?—to a man who is collecting debts from two people, one his friend and one his enemy. From his friend he takes payment bit by bit; from his enemy he exacts payment all at once.

3. Cf. B'réshith Rabbah 2, 3: "one day" (Genesis 1:5)—which the Holy One, blessed is He, gave him [Jacob]; which was it?—the Day of Atonement. In B'réshith Rabbah 3, 8 it is again so interpreted, as the day He gave the wicked and the righteous.

4. E.g. TB Yoma 85b.

5. See §365.

6. Numbers 29:11; TB Yoma 70a.

7. *Ibid.* 8; TB *ibid.*

8. I.e. its blood was sprinkled on the altar outside the *héchal*.

9. TB M'naḥoth 99b.

10. I.e. his property, or bought from his funds; Leviticus 16:3, 27; TB Yoma 3b. The *ḥattath* was burned outside the Sanctuary; the *'olah*, on the altar.

make desolate your sanctuaries (Leviticus 26:31), and it does not say, "your sanctuaries will I make a desolation," so that it implies that their holiness remains upon them even when they are forsaken ruins. That being so, it is for me to list this prohibition among the bans that are in effect today.

[THE PRECEPT OF THE TEMPLE SERVICE ON THE DAY OF ATONEMENT]

185 that the *kohen gadol* should carry out the entire service of the Day of Atonement in proper order: the offerings and confessions, the sending away of the goat, and the rest of the service—as it is written in the *sidrah:* for it is stated, *Herewith shall Aaron come into the holy place*, and so on through the entire section.

At the root of the precept lies the reason that it is of God's loving-kindness toward His human beings to establish one day in the year for them for atonement of sins in accord with the repentance that they will undergo.[1] For if the transgressions of human beings were to accumulate year by year, their measure would become full at the end of two or three years or more, and the world would become sentenced to destruction.[2] Therefore, in His wisdom (blessed is He), He saw fit, for the endurance of the world, to set one day in the year for the atonement of the sins of the repentant. From the beginning of the creation of the world, He designated it and consecrated it for this.[3] And since God, blessed is He, designated that day for atonement, the day became hallowed, and it received the force of purification from Himself (be He exalted), so much so that *it assists* in the atonement. This is why the Sages of blessed memory said in many instances,[4] "and the Day of Atonement atones"; in other words, the day has power of itself to atone for light (minor) transgressions.[5]

Among the laws of the precept, there is what our Sages of blessed memory said: that on this day the daily *'olah* (burnt-offering) would be offered up in the morning, and the daily *'olah* in the evening, as in the routine of every day;[6] the *musaf* (additional) offerings of the day would be offered up—a bullock, a ram, and seven sheep—all *'olah* (burnt) offerings,[7] and a goat for a *ḥattath* (sin-offering),[6] which is sacrificed outside[8] and eaten in the evening.[9] Moreover, in addition, a young bullock would be offered up as a *ḥattath*, which was burned, and a ram for an *'olah*. Both of these were from the *kohen gadol*,[10] whereas the ram that was brought from the community,[11] which is

בְּחֹמֶשׁ הַפְּקוּדִים בִּכְלַל הַמּוּסָף, וְהוּא הַנִּקְרָא אֵיל הָעָם. וְעוֹד מְבִיאִין מִשֶּׁל צִבּוּר שְׁנֵי שְׂעִירֵי עִזִּים: אֶחָד הָיוּ מַקְרִיבִין חַטָּאת וְהוּא הַנִּשְׂרָף, וְהַשֵּׁנִי שָׂעִיר הַמִּשְׁתַּלֵּחַ.

נִמְצְאוּ כָּל הַבְּהֵמוֹת הַקְּרֵבִין בְּיוֹם הַצּוֹם, מִלְּבַד שָׂעִיר הַמִּשְׁתַּלֵּחַ, שֶׁהוּא אֵינוֹ קָרֵב, חֲמֵשׁ־עֶשְׂרֵה: שְׁנֵי תְמִידִין וּפַר וּשְׁנֵי אֵילִים וְשִׁבְעָה כְבָשִׂים, כֻּלָּן עוֹלוֹת, וּשְׁנֵי שְׂעִירֵי חַטָּאת, אֶחָד נַעֲשֶׂה בַּחוּץ וְנֶאֱכָל לָעֶרֶב וְהַשֵּׁנִי נַעֲשֶׂה בִּפְנִים וְנִשְׂרָף, וְעוֹד פַּר בֶּן בָּקָר לְחַטָּאת.

עֲבוֹדַת כָּל חֲמֵשׁ־עֶשְׂרֵה בְהֵמוֹת אֵלּוּ הַקְּרֵבִין בְּיוֹם זֶה אֵינָהּ אֶלָּא בְּכֹהֵן גָּדוֹל בִּלְבָד, אֶחָד כֹּהֵן הַמָּשׁוּחַ בְּשֶׁמֶן הַמִּשְׁחָה אוֹ הַמְּרֻבֶּה בִּבְגָדִים. וְאִם הָיָה שַׁבָּת, אַף מוּסָף אֵין מַקְרִיב אוֹתוֹ אֶלָּא כֹּהֵן גָּדוֹל; וְכֵן שְׁאָר הָעֲבוֹדוֹת שֶׁל יוֹם, כְּגוֹן הַקְּטֹרֶת שֶׁל כָּל יוֹם וַהֲטָבַת הַנֵּרוֹת, הַכֹּל בְּכֹהֵן גָּדוֹל נָשׂוּי, שֶׁנֶּאֱמַר: וְכִפֶּר בַּעֲדוֹ וּבְעַד בֵּיתוֹ, זוֹ אִשְׁתּוֹ.

וְיֶתֶר כָּל הָעֲבוֹדוֹת, וַחֲלִיפַת הַבְּגָדִים מִבִּגְדֵי לָבָן לְבִגְדֵי זָהָב וּמִבִּגְדֵי זָהָב לְבִגְדֵי לָבָן, וְחָמֵשׁ טְבִילוֹת שֶׁהָיָה טוֹבֵל בְּיוֹם זֶה, וְעֶשֶׂר פְּעָמִים שֶׁמְּקַדֵּשׁ יָדָיו וְרַגְלָיו, וְעִנְיַן הַהַפְרָשָׁה שֶׁמַּפְרִישִׁין אוֹתוֹ קֹדֶם לְיוֹם הַצּוֹם שִׁבְעָה יָמִים, וְהַכָּבוֹד שֶׁהָיוּ נוֹהֲגִין בּוֹ, וְהַוִּדּוּיִין שֶׁהָיָה אוֹמֵר, וְכָל שְׁאָר דִּינֵי יוֹם זֶה, הַכֹּל בַּמַּסֶּכְתָּא הַבְּנוּיָה עַל זֶה, וְהִיא מַסֶּכֶת יוֹמָא.

וְנוֹהֶגֶת כָּל מִצְוָה זוֹ בִּזְמַן הַבַּיִת. וְעַכְשָׁיו בַּעֲווֹנוֹתֵינוּ שֶׁאֵין לָנוּ לֹא מִקְדָּשׁ וְלֹא כֹהֵן גָּדוֹל וְלֹא בִגְדֵי שְׂרָד וְלֹא קָרְבָּנוֹת, נָהֲגוּ כָּל יִשְׂרָאֵל לַעֲבֹד בְּיוֹם זֶה בִּתְפִלּוֹת וּבְתַחֲנוּנִים, וּכְמוֹ שֶׁכָּתוּב: וּנְשַׁלְּמָה פָרִים שְׂפָתֵינוּ.

11. I.e. bought from communal funds.

12. TB Yoma 3a.

13. Leviticus 18:7, etc.

14. I.e. its blood was sprinkled.

15. Outside the Sanctuary.

16. But not anointed with the oil (which was not extant at the time of the second Temple); TB Horayoth 12b.

17. I.e. if the Day of Atonement fell on a Sabbath.

18. TB Horayoth 12b.

19. Hence, to fulfill this verse, he must be married; TB Yoma 2a. The last three paragraphs are based on MT *hilchoth 'avodath yom ha-kippurim* i 1–2.

20. I.e. embroidered with gold thread; see §99.

21. As stated in §99, for any task on the Day of Atonement that took the *kohen gadol* into the holy of holies, he had to wear only his four white (linen) garments. For his other tasks he wore eight, including the four with gold thread.

22. Mishnah, Yoma iii 3.

23. *Ibid.* i 1.

mentioned in this *sidrah* (Leviticus 16:3), is the ram mentioned in the *Book of Numbers* (29:8) among the *musaf* (additional) offerings, which was called "the ram of the people."[12] Furthermore, from the community,[11] two male goats were brought: one was offered up as a *ḥattath*, and was burned, while the second was the goat sent away.[13]

Thus, all the animals offered up on this day of fasting, except the goat sent away, which was not offered up, are found to be fifteen: the two daily offerings, a bullock, two rams, and seven sheep—all *'olah* (burnt) offerings; two goats for sin-offerings—one sacrificed[14] [on the altar] outside and eaten in the evening, and one sacrificed[14] [on the altar] within, and burned;[15] and an additional young bullock, for a *ḥattath* (sin-offering).

The service of all these fifteen animals that were offered up on this day was to be done by none but the *kohen gadol* alone, whether he was [raised to this rank by becoming] the *kohen* anointed with the anointing oil, or [by becoming] the one with the additional garments.[16] And if it was the Sabbath,[17] then none but the *kohen gadol* was to offer up its *musaf* (additional) offerings.[18] So too the other Divine tasks of the day, such as the daily incense and the kindling (*hattavah*) of the lights [in the *menorah*]—all [was to be done] by a married *kohen gadol:* for it is stated, *and he shall make atonement for himself and for his house* (Leviticus 16:11), which denotes his wife.[19]

Then there are all the other tasks of the service, the changing of the clothes, from white garments to gold,[20] and from gold garments to white;[21] the five instances of ritual immersion which he would undergo on this day;[22] the ten times that he would sanctify (rinse) his hands and feet.[22] And there was the matter of separation: that seven days before the day of fasting he was separated [to be kept apart];[23] the honor with which he was treated;[24] the confessions he would make; and all the other laws of this day—all [to be found] in the Talmud tractate composed about this subject: the tractate *Yoma.*

This entire precept is in effect when the Temple is extant. Now, when for our sins we have neither Sanctuary nor *kohen gadol*, neither wrapping-cloths[25] nor offerings, all Jewry has the custom to worship on this day with prayers and supplications, in keeping with the verse, *so will we render for bullocks the offering of our lips* (Hosea 14:3).

[שֶׁלֹּא לִשְׁחֹט קָדָשִׁים חוּץ לָעֲזָרָה]

קפו שֶׁלֹּא לִזְבֹּחַ קָדָשִׁים חוּץ לָעֲזָרָה, וְזֶה יִקָּרֵא שׁוֹחֵט בַּחוּץ, שֶׁנֶּאֱמַר: אֲשֶׁר יִשְׁחַט שׁוֹר אוֹ כֶשֶׂב אוֹ עֵז וְגוֹמֵר, וְאֶל פֶּתַח אֹהֶל מוֹעֵד לֹא הֱבִיאוֹ וְגוֹמֵר, דָּם שָׁפָךְ וְנִכְרַת. וְאֵין הָאַזְהָרָה לָנוּ מִזֶּה הַכָּתוּב, כִּי הַכָּתוּב הַזֶּה לֹא יְפָרֵשׁ כִּי־אִם הָעֹנֶשׁ, וְקַיְמָא לָן: לֹא עָנַשׁ אֶלָּא אִם־כֵּן הִזְהִיר.

וְאָמְרוּ זִכְרוֹנָם לִבְרָכָה שֶׁאַזְהָרָה בָּזֶה נִלְמְדָה בְהֶקֵּשׁ, כִּדְאִיתָא בִגְמָרָא זְבָחִים, שֶׁאָמְרוּ זִכְרוֹנָם לִבְרָכָה שָׁם: הַשּׁוֹחֵט וְהַמַּעֲלֶה בַחוּץ חַיָּב עַל הַשְּׁחִיטָה וְחַיָּב עַל הָעֲלִיָּה; פֵּרוּשׁ עֲלִיָּה, שְׂרֵפָה בָאֵשׁ. וְהִקְשׁוּ שָׁם: בִּשְׁלָמָא הַעֲלָאָה כְּתִיב עֹנֶשׁ וּכְתִיב אַזְהָרָה; עֹנֶשׁ: וְאֶל פֶּתַח אֹהֶל מוֹעֵד לֹא הֱבִיאוֹ ... וְנִכְרַת; אַזְהָרָה: הִשָּׁמֶר לְךָ פֶּן תַּעֲלֶה עֹלֹתֶיךָ; וְכִדְרַבִּי אַבִּין, דְּאָמַר רַבִּי אַבִּין אָמַר רַבִּי אֶלְעָה: כָּל מָקוֹם שֶׁנֶּאֱמַר "הִשָּׁמֶר", "פֶּן" וְ"אַל", אֵינוֹ אֶלָּא מִצְוַת לֹא־תַעֲשֶׂה; אֶלָּא שְׁחִיטָה, בִּשְׁלָמָא עֹנֶשׁ כְּתִיב: וְאֶל פֶּתַח וְגוֹמֵר, אֶלָּא אַזְהָרָה מְנָא לָן.

וְאַחַר יְגִיעָה רַבָּה אָמְרוּ שָׁם כִּי הַכָּתוּב אָמַר "שָׁם תַּעֲלֶה ... וְשָׁם תַּעֲשֶׂה", מַקִּישׁ עֲלִיָּה לַעֲשִׂיָּה: מָה עֲלִיָּה עָנַשׁ וְהִזְהִיר, אַף עֲשִׂיָּה עָנַשׁ וְהִזְהִיר. פֵּרוּשׁ, עֲשִׂיָּה תִּכְלֹל הַכֹּל, בֵּין זְבִיחָה בֵּין שְׂרֵפָה.

מִשָּׁרְשֵׁי הַמִּצְוָה, לְפִי שֶׁהַשֵּׁם בָּרוּךְ הוּא קָבַע מָקוֹם לְיִשְׂרָאֵל לְהָבִיא שָׁם קָרְבְּנוֹתָם וּלְהָכִין שָׁם לְבָבָם אֵלָיו, וּמִתּוֹךְ קְבִיעוּת הַמָּקוֹם וְהַגְדָּלָתוֹ וְיִרְאָתוֹ אֶל לֵב בְּנֵי־אָדָם, נַפְשָׁם מִתְפַּעֶלֶת שָׁם לְטוֹב, וְהַלְּבָבוֹת מִתְרַכְּכִים וְנִכְנָעִים לְקַבֵּל שָׁם מַלְכוּת שָׁמַיִם שְׁלֵמָה; עַל־כֵּן מְנָעָנוּ הַשֵּׁם מֵעֲשׂוֹת מַעֲשֵׂה הַקָּרְבָּנוֹת רַק בַּמָּקוֹם הַהוּא, כְּדֵי שֶׁתְּהֵא כַפָּרָה שְׁלֵמָה לָנוּ.

24. *Ibid.* vii 4.
25. See Rashi, Exodus 35:19.

§186

1. TB Sanhedrin 56b; TJ Yoma i 5.
2. So the old manuscripts and the first edition; but our editions of the Talmud have "in the name of R. 'Ila'a."
3. Hence an admonition.
4. From the beginning to here is based on ShM negative precept §90.

[NOT TO RITUALLY SLAY HOLY OFFERINGS OUTSIDE THE SANCTUARY FORECOURT]

186 not to sacrifice holy offerings outside the Temple court—which is called "ritual slaying outside"—for it is stated: *Whatever man . . . that slays an ox or lamb or goat . . . and to the door of the tent of meeting he has not brought it . . . he has shed blood; and that man shall be cut off from among his people* (Leviticus 17:3–4). Now, we do not learn the admonition from this verse, since this verse conveys only the penalty; yet we have an established rule[1] that He does not punish unless He cautions.

Well, our Sages of blessed memory taught that an admonition about this is to be learned by equation, as it is given in the tractate *Z'vaḥim* (106a). For our Sages of blessed memory said there: If someone ritually slays and sends up in flames [an offering] outside [the Temple court], he is punishable for the ritual slaying, and punishable for the burning. The difficulty was then raised there: About burning all is well and good—the punishment is written, and the admonition is written; the punishment: *and to the door of the tent of meeting he has not brought it . . . and that man shall be cut off;* the admonition: *Take heed to yourself lest you send up your burnt-offerings in flames at every place that you see* (Deuteronomy 12:13)—and this as R. 'Avin taught: For R. 'Avin said in R. Elia's name:[2] Wherever it is stated [in Scripture] *Take heed, lest,* or *Do not,* it denotes nothing other than a negative precept.[3] For ritual slaying, though, granted that the punishment is written—*and to the door,* etc.—but from where do we derive an admonition?

After great toil, our Sages concluded there that Scripture states, *there you shall send up your burnt-offerings, and there you shall do* (Deuteronomy 12:14): it equates sending up in flames to "doing"; just as for burning [an offering outside the Temple court] He gave the punishment and an admonition, so for "doing" did He give the punishment and an admonition. The meaning of "doing" includes everything, whether ritual slaying or burning.[4]

At the root of the precept lies the reason that the Eternal Lord, blessed is He, set a fixed place for the Israelites to bring their offerings, and to direct their heart to Him there. Because of the permanence of the place and its glorification, and its awe in people's hearts, their spirit would be influenced there for the good. The heart would be softened and humbled to receive there Heaven's kingship completely. Therefore the Eternal Lord restricted us from sacrificing the offerings anywhere but at that place, so that there should be complete atonement for us.

וּכְלַל הַדְּבָרִים כִּי כָל אֲשֶׁר צִוָּנוּ לְטוֹב לָנוּ, כְּמוֹ שֶׁכָּתַבְנוּ, כִּי הָאֵל חָפֵץ בְּטוֹבַת בְּרִיּוֹתָיו בְּטוּבוֹ הַגָּדוֹל; וְאָמַר כִּי מִי שֶׁיַּקְרִיב חוּץ לְאוֹתוֹ הַמָּקוֹם הַנִּבְחָר, דָּם יֵחָשֵׁב לוֹ. וְהָעִנְיָן הוּא כִּי הַשֵּׁם לֹא הִתִּיר לִבְנֵי־אָדָם בְּשַׂר בַּעֲלֵי־חַיִּים רַק לְכַפָּרָה אוֹ לְצָרְכֵי בְנֵי־אָדָם, כְּגוֹן מָזוֹן אוֹ רְפוּאָה, אוֹ כָּל דָּבָר שֶׁיֵּשׁ בּוֹ שׁוּם צֹרֶךְ בְּנֵי־אָדָם; אֲבָל לַהֲמִיתָם מִבְּלִי שׁוּם תּוֹעֶלֶת כְּלָל, יֵשׁ בַּדָּבָר הַשְׁחָתָה וְנִקְרָא שׁוֹפֵךְ דָּם. וְאַף־עַל־פִּי שֶׁאֵינוֹ כִשְׁפִיכוּת דַּם הָאָדָם, לְמַעֲלַת הָאָדָם וּפְחִיתוּת הַבְּהֵמָה, מִכָּל־מָקוֹם שְׁפִיכוּת דָּם יִקָּרֵא, מֵאַחַר שֶׁלֹּא הִתִּירוֹ הַכָּתוּב לְשָׁפְכוֹ לְלֹא תוֹעֶלֶת; וְעַל־כֵּן אָמַר סְתָם שֶׁהוּא כִשְׁפִיכוּת דָּם, אַחַר שֶׁהוּא שׁוֹפֵךְ דָּמָהּ בְּמָקוֹם שֶׁלֹּא נִצְטַוָּה לְשָׁחֲטָהּ, וְאֵין בְּאוֹתָהּ שְׁחִיטָה תּוֹעֶלֶת כְּלָל, אֲבָל יֵשׁ בַּדָּבָר נֶזֶק שֶׁעָבַר עַל מִצְוַת בּוֹרְאוֹ; וְלָכֵן עֲנָשׁוֹ הַכָּתוּב בְּכָרֵת.

מִדִּינֵי הַמִּצְוָה, (כְּגוֹן) מַה שֶּׁאָמְרוּ זִכְרוֹנָם לִבְרָכָה שֶׁאִם שָׁחַט בַּחוּץ, אַף־עַל־פִּי שֶׁהֶעֱלָה בִפְנִים, חַיָּב, לְפִי שֶׁהַשְּׁחִיטָה וְהָעֲלִיָּה בְּכָל אֶחָד לָאו בִּפְנֵי עַצְמוֹ; וְלָאו דַּעֲלִיָּה בְסֵדֶר רְאֵה אָנֹכִי ב׳ [סי׳ תל״ט]; וְאֵין אָדָם חַיָּב אֶלָּא עַל שְׁחִיטַת קָדָשִׁים הָרְאוּיִין לִקָּרֵב עַל הַמִּזְבֵּחַ, אֲבָל הַשּׁוֹחֵט בַּחוּץ אֶחָד מֵאִסּוּרֵי מִזְבֵּחַ הֲרֵי זֶה פָּטוּר, שֶׁנֶּאֱמַר: לִפְנֵי מִשְׁכַּן יי, כָּל שֶׁאֵינוֹ רָאוּי לָבוֹא אֶל מִשְׁכַּן יי אֵין חַיָּבִין עָלָיו; וְיֶתֶר פְּרָטֶיהָ, מְבֹאָרִין בְּפֶרֶק י״ג מִזְּבָחִים.

וְנוֹהֵג אִסּוּר זְבִיחָה בַחוּץ בְּכָל מָקוֹם וּבְכָל זְמַן, שֶׁאֲפִלּוּ הַשּׁוֹחֵט בְּהֵמָה הַיּוֹם לְשֵׁם קָדָשִׁים חַיָּב; וְהָכִי אַמְרִינָן בַּגְּמָרָא בְמַסֶּכֶת זְבָחִים בְּמַעֲלֶה בַחוּץ בַּזְּמַן הַזֶּה, רַבִּי יוֹחָנָן אוֹמֵר חַיָּב; וְכֵן הֲלָכָה. וְעוֹבֵר עָלֶיהָ וְשָׁחַט קָדָשִׁים בַּחוּץ בְּמֵזִיד, חַיָּב

5. TB Z'vaḥim 106a (MT *hilchoth ma'aséh ha-korbanoth* xviii 5).

6. *Ibid.* 112a.

7. In the two oldest manuscripts and the first three editions, "Z'vaḥim" is missing; but in MS Parma 928 (the oldest) there is a mark indicating that a correction is required; and in MS Casanatense 134 the word is present.

The crux of the matter is that all He commanded us is for our good, as we have written, because God has delight in the good fortune of His human creatures, in His great goodness. And so He said that whoever will sacrifice an offering anywhere outside that chosen place, it will be reckoned for him as a blood crime. The reason is that the Eternal Lord permitted the flesh of living creatures to people for no other purpose than atonement or human needs, such as food or healing preparations, or anything of which human beings have need. But to kill them without any useful purpose at all—there is destruction in this, and it is called spilling blood. Even though it is not like spilling human blood, in view of man's superior level and the animal's inferiority, it is called shedding blood nevertheless, since the Writ did not permit spilling it to no useful purpose. Therefore it stated generally that this is as the shedding of blood, since one spills its blood at a location where he was not commanded to slay it ritually, and there is no benefit whatever in that ritual slaying. Rather, there is damage in the matter, since he has transgressed the commandment of his Creator. Hence Scripture gave his punishment as *karéth* ["cutting off": Divine severance of existence].

Among the laws of the precept there are, for example, what the Sages of blessed memory said: [5] that if a person ritually slew [an offering] outside, then even if he burned it within [the Temple court] he deserves punishment—because ritual slaying and burning have each a separate negative precept about it, the one on burning being the second in *sidrah r'éh*, §439. A man incurs punishment only for the ritual slaying of consecrated animals that are fit to be offered up on the altar; but if someone ritually slays outside [the Temple court] one of those kinds forbidden on the altar, he is free of punishment: [6] For it is stated, *before the tabernacle of the Lord* (Leviticus 17:4): whatever is not fit to come [be brought] to the *mishkan* (Tabernacle) of the Lord, there is no punishment over it. The rest of its details are explained in chapter 13 of the Talmud tractate *Z'vaḥim.*

The ban on sacrificing an animal outside [the Temple court] applies in every place and every time. For even if someone ritually slays an animal today, purposing it to be a holy offering, he incurs punishment; and thus it was taught in the Talmud tractate *Z'vaḥim* (107b) [7] about a person who sends up an animal in flames [as an offering] in our time: R. Yoḥanan says, he is punishable—and so the law remains. If a person transgressed it and ritually slew a consecrated animal outside [the Temple court] deliberately, he would deserve *karéth* [Divine

כָּרֵת; וְאַף־עַל־פִּי שֶׁלֹּא הֶעֱלָה אוֹתָן, מֵעֵת שֶׁשְּׁחָטָן חַיָּב; וְכֵן אָמְרוּ זִכְרוֹנָם לִבְרָכָה: חַיָּב עַל הַשְּׁחִיטָה וְחַיָּב עַל הָעֲלִיָּה. וְאִם עָבַר וְשָׁחַט בְּשׁוֹגֵג, חַיָּב לְהָבִיא חַטָּאת קְבוּעָה בִּזְמַן הַבַּיִת.

[מִצְוַת כִּסּוּי הַדָּם]

קפז לְכַסּוֹת הַדָּם אַחַר זְבִיחַת חַיָּה אוֹ עוֹף, שֶׁנֶּאֱמַר: אֲשֶׁר יָצוּד צֵיד חַיָּה אוֹ עוֹף אֲשֶׁר יֵאָכֵל וְשָׁפַךְ אֶת דָּמוֹ וְכִסָּהוּ בֶּעָפָר.

מִשָּׁרְשֵׁי הַמִּצְוָה, לְפִי שֶׁהַנֶּפֶשׁ תְּלוּיָה בַדָּם, כְּמוֹ שֶׁאָמַרְנוּ בְּאִסּוּר דָּם, וְלָכֵן רָאוּי לָנוּ לְכַסּוֹת הַנֶּפֶשׁ וּלְהַסְתִּירוֹ מֵעֵין רוֹאָיו טֶרֶם נֹאכַל הַבָּשָׂר; כִּי גַם בָּזֶה נִקְנֶה קְצָת אַכְזָרִיּוּת בְּנַפְשֵׁנוּ, לֶאֱכֹל הַבָּשָׂר וְהַנֶּפֶשׁ נִשְׁפָּךְ לְפָנֵינוּ.

וּבַבְּהֵמוֹת לֹא נִצְטַוֵּינוּ כָּךְ, לְפִי שֶׁדַּם הַבְּהֵמָה נִתָּן לְקָרְבָּן לְכַפָּרָה עַל נַפְשׁוֹתֵינוּ וְאִי אֶפְשָׁר לְכַסּוֹתוֹ, וְאַחַר שֶׁכֵּן לֹא רָצְתָה הַתּוֹרָה לְחַלֵּק לָנוּ בֵּין מֻקְדָּשִׁין לְחֻלִּין. וְאִם גַּם בְּמִין הָעוֹפוֹת יֵשׁ מֵהֶן קָרֵב לְגַבֵּי מִזְבֵּחַ, מוּעָט הוּא, וּלְדָבָר מוּעָט לֹא תָחוּשׁ הַתּוֹרָה לְעוֹלָם; וּמִפְּנֵי־כֵן חִיְּבַתְנוּ בְּכִסּוּי דַם הָעוֹפוֹת בְּכֻלָּן.

מִדִּינֵי הַמִּצְוָה, מַה שֶּׁאָמְרוּ זִכְרוֹנָם לִבְרָכָה שֶׁכִּסּוּי הַדָּם נוֹהֵג בְּכָל עוֹף וּבְכָל חַיָּה, בִּמְזֻמָּן וּבְשֶׁאֵינוֹ מְזֻמָּן, וְלֹא נֶאֱמַר "אֲשֶׁר יָצוּד" אֶלָּא בַּהוֹוֶה; וְנוֹהֵג בְּחֻלִּין אֲבָל לֹא בְמֻקְדָּשִׁין; וְנוֹהֵג בְּכוֹי מִפְּנֵי שֶׁהוּא סָפֵק אִם מִין חַיָּה אוֹ בְהֵמָה, וְאֵין מְבָרְכִין בְּכִסּוּיוֹ מִסָּפֵק; וְדַם הַנִּתָּז וְשֶׁעַל הַסַּכִּין חַיָּב לְכַסּוֹת בְּשֶׁאֵין דָּם אֶלָּא הוּא, אֲבָל יֵשׁ דָּם כְּלָל שֶׁלֹּא הוּא אֵינוֹ צָרִיךְ, דִּכְתִיב: וְשָׁפַךְ אֶת דָּמוֹ וְכִסָּהוּ בֶּעָפָר,

8. The paragraph is largely based on ShM negative precept §90.

§187
1. So Rambam, *Guide* III 34.
2. So Ramban, commentary, Leviticus 17:11.
3. TB Ḥullin 83b.
4. I.e. tame, raised on one's home grounds; *ibid.* 84a.
5. Evidently a species of bearded deer or antelope; according to *'Aruch*, following one view in the Talmud, it is the male issue of a gazelle sired by a goat; by a later view it is the species *antilope picta* (see *'Aruch haShalém* s.v. *koy*).
6. MT *hilchoth sheḥittah* xiv 4.
7. TB Ḥullin 87b.

severance of existence]. Even if he did not send it up in flames, from the time he ritually slew it he is punishable. And so our Sages of blessed memory taught:[5] One is punishable for ritual slaying and punishable for burning it. If someone transgressed it and ritually slew [a consecrated animal] inadvertently, he would be obligated to bring a standard unvarying *ḥattath* (sin-offering) when the Temple is in existence.[8]

[THE PRECEPT OF COVERING THE BLOOD IN THE RITUAL SLAYING OF AN ANIMAL]

187 to cover the blood after the ritual slaying of a wild animal or fowl: for it is stated, *And whatever man . . . that takes in hunting any beast or bird that may be eaten, he shall pour out its blood and cover it with dust* (Leviticus 17:13).

At the root of the precept lies the reason that the life-spirit is integrally bound up with the blood, as we stated in regard to the prohibition on blood (§148). It is therefore fitting for us to cover the life-spirit and conceal it from the eyes of those who [might] see it before we eat the meat. For by this too we would acquire a slight cruelty in our spirit, eating the meat while the life-spirit lies poured out before us.

With domestic animals we were not thus commanded, because the blood of a domestic animal is used for an offering to obtain atonement for our souls, and it is not possible to cover that. And that being the case, the Torah did not wish to set a difference for us between consecrated animals and ordinary, non-holy ones. Now, if among the species of fowl there are some which can be offered up on the altar, they are very few; and about a small, limited matter the Torah is never concerned.[1] For this reason it gave us the obligation of covering the blood of fowl for all of them.[2]

Among the laws of the precept, there is, for instance, what the Sages of blessed memory said,[3] that covering the blood is an obligation that applies to every fowl and every wild animal, whether it is at hand [in one's possession][4] or not; "that takes in hunting" was stated only because that is the usual way. It applies to ordinary, non-holy animals, but not to consecrated ones.[3] It applies to a *koy*,[5] because it is uncertain if it is a species of wild or domestic animal;[3] but no blessing is recited over covering it, because of the doubt.[6] Blood which sprays [onto a wall] and which is on the knife is required to be covered when there is no blood but that; but if there is general blood apart from that, it need not [be covered]:[7] for it is stated, *he shall pour out its blood and cover*

פֵּרוּשׁ וַאֲפִלּוּ מִקְצָת דָּמוֹ; וְצָרִיךְ הַמְּכַסֶּה לִתֵּן עָפָר לְמַטָּה וּלְמַעְלָה; וְכָל עָפָר בָּעוֹלָם שֶׁהוּא דַק בִּכְדֵי שֶׁאֵין הַיּוֹצֵר צָרִיךְ לְכָתְשׁוֹ, רָאוּי לְכִסּוּי; וְכֵן כָּל מַה שֶּׁנִּקְרָא עָפָר, אַף־עַל־פִּי שֶׁאֵינוֹ עָפָר מַמָּשׁ, מְכַסִּין בּוֹ — כְּגוֹן זָהָב שָׁחוּק, שֶׁנִּקְרָא עָפָר, שֶׁנֶּאֱמַר: וְעַפְרֹת זָהָב לוֹ; וּמִי שֶׁרָאָה חֲבֵרוֹ שֶׁשָּׁחַט וְלֹא כִסָּה, חַיָּב הוּא לְכַסּוֹת, שֶׁנֶּאֱמַר בְּמִצְוָה זוֹ: וְאֹמַר לִבְנֵי יִשְׂרָאֵל, וְדָרְשׁוּ זִכְרוֹנָם לִבְרָכָה: מִצְוָה זוֹ עַל כָּל בְּנֵי־יִשְׂרָאֵל; וְיֶתֶר פְּרָטֶיהָ, בְּחֻלִּין בְּפֶרֶק כִּסּוּי הַדָּם.

וְנוֹהֶגֶת בְּכָל מָקוֹם וּבְכָל זְמַן, בִּזְכָרִים וּנְקֵבוֹת. וְעוֹבֵר עָלֶיהָ וְלֹא כִסָּה דַּם חַיָּה וָעוֹף, בִּטֵּל עֲשֵׂה.

[שֶׁלֹּא לְהִתְעַדֵּן בְּאַחַת מִכָּל הָעֲרָיוֹת]

קפח שֶׁלֹּא לְהִתְעַדֵּן בְּאַחַת מִכָּל הָעֲרָיוֹת, וְהֵן קְרוֹבוֹת וְאֵשֶׁת אִישׁ וְנִדָּה, וַאֲפִלּוּ בְלֹא בִיאָה, כְּגוֹן חִבּוּק וְנִשּׁוּק וְכָל הַדּוֹמֶה לְאֵלּוּ הָרָעוֹת שֶׁמַּעֲמִיקִין בָּהֶן בַּעֲלֵי הַזִּמָּה הַהוֹלְכִים אַחֲרֵי הַהֶבֶל וַיֶּהְבָּלוּ — שֶׁנֶּאֱמַר: אִישׁ אִישׁ אֶל כָּל שְׁאֵר בְּשָׂרוֹ לֹא תִקְרְבוּ לְגַלּוֹת עֶרְוָה, וּפֵרוּשׁוֹ כְּאִלּוּ אָמַר לֹא תַעֲשׂוּ שׁוּם קְרִיבָה שֶׁהִיא הַגּוֹרֶמֶת וְהַמְּבִיאָה הָאָדָם לְגַלּוֹת עֶרְוָה. וְכֵן דָּרְשׁוּ זִכְרוֹנָם לִבְרָכָה: "לֹא תִקְרְבוּ לְגַלּוֹת", אֵין לִי אֶלָּא שֶׁלֹּא יְגַלֶּה; מִנַּיִן שֶׁלֹּא יִקְרַב, תַּלְמוּד לוֹמַר: וְאֶל אִשָּׁה בְּנִדַּת טֻמְאָתָהּ לֹא תִקְרַב. אֵין לִי אֶלָּא נִדָּה בְלֹא תִקְרַב וּבַל תְּגַלֶּה; מִנַּיִן לְכָל הָעֲרָיוֹת, תַּלְמוּד לוֹמַר: לֹא תִקְרְבוּ לְגַלּוֹת; וְשָׁם נֶאֱמַר: וְנִכְרְתוּ הַנְּפָשׁוֹת הָעֹשֹׂת; שֶׁמָּא תֹאמַר יִהְיוּ חַיָּבִין כָּרֵת עַל הַקְּרִיבָה לְבָד, תַּלְמוּד לוֹמַר "הָעֹשֹׂת", וְלֹא הַקְּרֵבוֹת.

וְנִכְפַּל הַלָּאו בְּאִסּוּר זֶה בְּאָמְרוֹ: וְלֹא תַעֲשׂוּ מִכֹּל הַתּוֹעֵבֹת, שֶׁיִּכְלֹל כָּל עִנְיָנִים

8. I.e. that is sufficient; *ibid.* 87a.
9. *Ibid.* 28a.
10. *Ibid.* 88b.
11. *Ibid.* 87a.

§188
1. Expression based on Jeremiah 2:5.
2. Sifra, *aḥaré moth, perek* 13, 15 and 21 ("uncovering nakedness" is the standard expression in Scripture to refer to absolutely forbidden conjugal intimacy).
3. I.e. both acts are forbidden; and this is in the general injunction, which applies to all.

it with dust, which means even some of its blood.[8] The one who covers it has to put dust (earth) below and above it.[3] Any dust in the world which is fine enough so that a potter would not need to pound it, is suitable for the covering.[9] So too anything that is called dust, even if it is not real, actual dust, may be used for covering—such as ground gold, which is called dust, as it is stated, *and it has dust of gold* (Job 28:6).[10] If someone saw his fellow do ritual slaying and not cover [the blood], he is duty-bound to cover it: for it is stated in regard to this precept, *therefore I said to the Israelites* (Leviticus 17:14), and our Sages of blessed memory interpreted:[11] This precept is [an obligation that lies] on all Israelites (Jews). The rest of its details are in the tractate *Ḥullin*, chapter 6.

It is in effect in every place, at every time, for both man and woman. If someone violates it and does not cover the blood of an undomesticated animal or of fowl, he disobeys a positive precept.

[THE PROHIBITION OF PLEASURE WITH ANY WOMAN RANKED AS 'ERVAH]

188 not to have pleasure with any one of the maritally forbidden women, who are consanguineous relations, a married woman, and one defiled by the menses—and this even without conjugal intimacy: for example, embracing, kissing, and anything similar to these evil actions, in which lechers engross themselves, who go after vapidity and become worthless.[1] For it is stated, *No man among you shall approach anyone near of kin to him to uncover nakedness* (Leviticus 18:6); and its import is as though it said, "Do not do any act of intimacy which is what causes and brings a man to uncover nakedness." And so our Sages of blessed memory interpreted:[2] "you shall not approach to uncover"—thus I know only that one should not uncover; how do I know that he should not approach or draw near?—Scripture states, *And you shall not draw close to a woman while she is in her menstrual uncleanness* (*ibid.* 19). Thus I know only that a woman defiled by the menses is forbidden by the injunctions, "you shall not draw close" and "to uncover"; how do I know this about all forbidden women?—Scripture states, "you shall not approach to uncover."[3] Now, it is stated there, *the souls that do them shall be cut off* (*ibid.* 29). Perhaps you would think they should be punished by *karéth* [Divine severance of existence] for drawing close alone?—Scripture states, "that do them," and not "that draw close."

The injunction about this prohibition was doubled by Scripture's statement, *and you shall do none of these abominations* (Leviticus 18:26):

אֵלֶּה שֶׁהֵם תּוֹעֲבַת יי, כְּלוֹמַר שֶׁהָעוֹשֶׂה אוֹתָן יִתְרַחֵק מִן הַטּוֹבָה וּמֵסִיר מֵעָלָיו הַשְׁגָּחַת הַשֵּׁם בָּרוּךְ הוּא. וְזֶהוּ פֵּרוּשׁ תִּעוּב הַשֵּׁם בְּכָל מָקוֹם, לְפִי מַה שֶּׁשָּׁמַעְתִּי. וְגַם־כֵּן מַה שֶּׁכָּתוּב בְּסוֹף הָעִנְיָן: כִּי אֶת כָּל הַתּוֹעֵבֹת הָאֵל עָשׂוּ אַנְשֵׁי הָאָרֶץ אֲשֶׁר לִפְנֵיכֶם וָאָקוּץ בָּם, הָעִנְיָן לוֹמַר שֶׁהַמִּדָּה מְגֻנָּה מְאֹד, וְכָל דָּבָר רַע וּמָאוּס בְּיוֹתֵר יְכַנֶּה הַכָּתוּב כְּאִלּוּ הַשֵּׁם שׂוֹנֵא אוֹתוֹ, וְהַכֹּל עַל הָעִנְיָן שֶׁאָמַרְנוּ; וּכְעֵין מַה שֶּׁאָמְרוּ זִכְרוֹנָם לִבְרָכָה בְּכָל מָקוֹם: כְּדֵי לְשַׁבֵּר אֶת הָאֹזֶן מַה שֶּׁהִיא יְכוֹלָה לִשְׁמֹעַ.

וּלְשׁוֹן סִפְרָא: ״כְּמַעֲשֵׂה אֶרֶץ מִצְרַיִם... וּכְמַעֲשֵׂה אֶרֶץ כְּנַעַן״ וְגוֹמֵר, יָכוֹל לֹא יִבְנוּ בִנְיָנוֹת כְּמוֹתָם, תַּלְמוּד לוֹמַר ״וּבְחֻקֹּתֵיהֶם לֹא תֵלֵכוּ״, לֹא אָמַרְתִּי אֶלָּא בְּחֻקִּים הַחֲקוּקִים לָהֶם וְלֹא בְנְיָנוֹתֵיהֶם. וְשָׁם נֶאֱמַר: מֶה הָיוּ עוֹשִׂין, הָאִישׁ נוֹשֵׂא אִישׁ וְאִשָּׁה נוֹשֵׂאת אִשָּׁה, וְאִשָּׁה נִשֵּׂאת לִשְׁנֵי אֲנָשִׁים.

מִשָּׁרְשֵׁי הַרְחָקַת הַזִּמָּה כָּתַבְתִּי בְּפָרָשַׁת וַיִּשְׁמַע יִתְרוֹ בְּלָאו דְּלֹא תִנְאָף ח׳ [סי׳ ל״ה] מַה שֶּׁיָּדַעְתִּי. וְזֹאת הַמִּצְוָה גַּם־כֵּן מֵאוֹתוֹ הַשֹּׁרֶשׁ הוּא, שֶׁנִּמְנַעְנוּ מֵהִתְקָרֵב עִם הָעֶרְוָה שׁוּם קֻרְבָה, לְפִי שֶׁיָּדוּעַ כִּי הַקֻּרְבָה סִבָּה אֶל גִּלּוּי עֶרְוָה, וּבְגִלּוּי הָעֶרְוָה יִמָּצְאוּ כַּמָּה תַקָּלוֹת וְכַמָּה הֶפְסֵדִים, כְּמוֹ שֶׁכָּתַבְתִּי שָׁם. וְאָמְנָם אוֹתוֹ הַטַּעַם יַסְפִּיק בְּאֵשֶׁת אִישׁ, אֲבָל בִּקְרוֹבוֹת עֲדַיִן צְרִיכִין אָנוּ לְטַעַם אַחֵר, וּבְאַזְהָרַת עֶרְוַת אֵם [סי׳ ק״צ] נִכְתֹּב בּוֹ מַה שֶּׁנֵּדַע בְּעֶזְרַת הַשֵּׁם.

מִדִּינֵי הַמִּצְוָה, מַה שֶּׁאָסְרוּ חֲכָמִים זִכְרוֹנָם לִבְרָכָה בָּזֶה לְגָדֵר, וְהוּא שֶׁלֹּא יִקְרֹץ אָדָם בְּיָדָיו וְיִרְמֹז בְּעֵינָיו לְאַחַת מִן הָעֲרָיוֹת, וְשֶׁלֹּא לִשְׂחֹק עִמָּהֶם כְּלָל, וַאֲפִלּוּ לְהָרִיחַ בִּשָׂמִים שֶׁעֲלֵיהֶם אָסְרוּ, וְשֶׁלֹּא לְהַבִּיט בְּנָשִׁים כְּלָל וַאֲפִלּוּ בִפְנֵי כַלָּה בְּכַוָּנַת הֲנָאָה; וַאֲפִלּוּ בְאֶצְבַּע קְטַנָּה שֶׁלָּהֶן אָסְרוּ לְהִסְתַּכֵּל, חוּץ מֵאִשְׁתּוֹ שֶׁל

4. Where the term occurs in Scripture.
5. I.e. that this conveys a truth about the quality or trait in a human being, but not in the Almighty, who is beyond human emotion and human comprehension.
6. E.g. Mechilta, Exodus 19:18.
7. From the beginning to here is based on ShM negative precept §353.
8. MT *hilchoth 'issuré bi'ah* xxi 2, based on *'Avoth d'R. Nathan (Kessef Mishneh)*
9. Mishnah, 'Avoth iii 13.
10. MT *ibid.* based on TB Shabbath 62b.
11. TB K'thuboth 17a.
12. TB Shabbath 64b.

this includes all these matters, which are an abomination to the Lord; in other words, anyone who does them becomes removed far from goodness and removes from himself the watchful care of the Eternal Lord, blessed is He. This is the meaning of abomination to the Eternal Lord in every instance,[4] according to what I heard. So likewise, what is written at the end of the matter: *for all these abominations the men of the land did who were before you (ibid. 27) and I abhorred them* (Leviticus 20:23). Its sense is to convey that the quality is most ugly; every unusually bad and repulsive thing, Scripture describes as though the Eternal Lord detests it, all along the lines that we have stated,[5] and in the vein of what the Sages of blessed memory said in every instance:[6] in order to convey intelligibly to the ear what it is able to hear.

In the language of the Midrash *Sifra:* "As the activity of the land of Egypt . . . and as the activity of the land of Canaan" (Leviticus 18:3)—I might think they should not build structures like them?—Scripture states, *and in their statutes you shall not walk* (*ibid.*): I did not state this about anything but the statutes they enacted, and not about their buildings. And it is said there [further]: What would they do? A man would marry a man, and a woman would marry a woman; and one woman would be married to two men.[7]

On root reasons for putting licentiousness at a far distance [from us], I have written in *sidrah yithro*, in the negative precept, *you shall not commit adultery* (Exodus 20:13; §35) what I know [concerning it]. This precept is likewise for that root reason: we have been restricted from drawing close to a forbidden woman in any affectionate intimacy, because it is known that such intimacy is a cause that leads to uncovering nakedness; and from uncovering nakedness many misfortunes and many harms result, as I wrote there. Actually, though, this reason will be enough [to explain] about a married woman; but for consanguineous relations we still need another reason. In the injunction against uncovering the nakedness of a mother (§190) we will write about it what we know, with the Eternal Lord's help.

Among the laws of the precept, there is what the Sages of blessed memory forbade as a "fence" (protective restriction): i.e. that a man should not signal with his hands or hint with his eyes to any one of the forbidden women,[8] and should not laugh (flirt) with them at all;[9] even to smell the perfume on them, the Sages forbade.[10] And one is not to gaze at women at all, even at the face of a bride, with the intent of pleasure.[11] Even to gaze at a small finger of theirs, the Sages forbade[12]

אָדָם, שֶׁמֻּתָּר לוֹ לְהַבִּיט בְּיָפְיָהּ, וַאֲפִלּוּ בְעוֹדָהּ נִדָּה, מִפְּנֵי שֶׁהִיא מֻתֶּרֶת לוֹ לְאַחַר זְמַן, וַחֲזָקָה בְּיִשְׂרָאֵל שֶׁיִּצְרוֹ מָסוּר בְּיָדוֹ בִכְגוֹן דָּבָר זֶה שֶׁתָּלוּי בִּזְמָן. וְדַוְקָא בְּמָקוֹם מְגֻלֶּה שֶׁבָּהּ הִתִּירוּ לְהִסְתַּכֵּל בְּעוֹדָהּ נִדָּה, אֲבָל לֹא בִמְכֻסֶּה, כְּדֵי שֶׁלֹּא יִלְבְּשֶׁנּוּ יֵצֶר הָרָע.

וְאָמְרוּ זִכְרוֹנָם לִבְרָכָה גַּם־כֵּן שֶׁאָסוּר לְהִסְתַּכֵּל אֲפִלּוּ בִשְׂעָרָהּ שֶׁל אִשָּׁה הָאֲסוּרָה לוֹ, וַאֲפִלּוּ לִשְׁמֹעַ קוֹלָהּ לְכַוָּנָה שֶׁיֵּהָנֶה בָהּ אָסוּר; וַאֲפִלּוּ לְהִסְתַּכֵּל בְּבִגְדֵי צֶבַע שֶׁל אִשָּׁה, כְּלוֹמַר בְּגָדִים נָאִים שֶׁדַּרְכָּן לַעֲשׂוֹתָן מִבְּגָדִים צְבוּעִים, אָסוּר לְהִסְתַּכֵּל בָּהֶן כָּל זְמַן שֶׁמַּכִּיר הָאִשָּׁה הַלּוֹבֶשֶׁת אוֹתָן, לְפִי שֶׁמִּתּוֹךְ רְאִיַּת הַמַּלְבּוּשׁ יָבוֹא לְהַרְהֵר בָּהּ.

וְהִרְחִיקוּ גַּם־כֵּן שֶׁלֹּא לִשְׁאֹל בִּשְׁלוֹם אֵשֶׁת אִישׁ כְּלָל, וַאֲפִלּוּ עַל־יְדֵי בַעְלָהּ; וְרִבּוּי פְּרָטֵי הָרִחוּקִין שֶׁהִזְהִירוּ עֲלֵיהֶן בְּעִנְיָן זֶה; אֲבָל כְּלַל הַדָּבָר הוּא שֶׁלֹּא יַעֲשֶׂה הָאָדָם שׁוּם דָּבָר בָּעוֹלָם הַמְּבִיאוֹ לִידֵי הִרְהוּר בְּנָשִׁים, לֹא בְמַעֲשֶׂה וְלֹא בְדִבּוּר וְלֹא שׁוּם רֶמֶז לְקָרֵב דַּעַת הָאִשָּׁה הַקַּל עִם דַּעְתּוֹ, אֶלָּא בְאִשְׁתּוֹ לְבָד. וּבְעִנְיָן זֶה הָיָה מוֹכִיחַ הַנָּבִיא אַנְשֵׁי דוֹרוֹ בְּאָמְרוֹ לָהֶם: אִישׁ אֶל אֵשֶׁת רֵעֵהוּ יִצְהָלוּ, כְּלוֹמַר לְפִי דַרְכָּם שֶׁנִּרְאֶה כְאִלּוּ אֵינָם מִתְכַּוְּנִים לְכָךְ יִרְמְזוּ לִנְשֵׁי רֵעֵיהֶם רְמִיזוֹת שֶׁל נִאוּף וּמַגְבִּיהִין קוֹלָן בְּעִנְיָן שֶׁיִּשְׁמְעוּ אוֹתָן הַנָּשִׁים וְיִתְעוֹרֵר יִצְרָן אֶל אַהֲבַת הַנּוֹאֵף. וְאֵין בְּאֶפְשָׁר לְהַגִּיד פְּרָטֵי הָעִנְיָנִים שֶׁיֵּדַע הָאָדָם לַעֲשׂוֹת לְקָרֵב אֵלָיו דַּעַת הָאִשָּׁה, שֶׁהוּא קַל; וְלָכֵן הִזְכִּירוּ זִכְרוֹנָם לִבְרָכָה מֵהֶם קְצָת, וּבִשְׁאָר יִזָּהֵר כָּל אֶחָד וְאֶחָד לִשְׁמֹר עַצְמוֹ לְפִי מַה שֶּׁיִּמְצָא אֶת גּוּפוֹ, כִּי הַשֵּׁם יִרְאֶה לַלֵּבָב.

וּמִכָּל־מָקוֹם, לְפִי הַדּוֹמֶה מִכָּל מַה שֶּׁהִזְהִירוּ זִכְרוֹנָם לִבְרָכָה, אֵין אָדָם רַשַּׁאי לָזוּז מִמּוּסָרָם הַטּוֹב; וְאַף־עַל־פִּי שֶׁהוּא מוֹצֵא עַצְמוֹ חֲשׂוּךְ הַתַּאֲוָה קְצָת, לֹא

13. MT *ibid.* 4, based on TB N'darim 20a (*Kessef Mishneh*), and TB Sanhedrin 37a.
14. TB N'darim 20a.
15. TB B'rachoth 24a.
16. TB ‘Avodah Zarah 20a.
17. Literally, they removed far.
18. TB Kiddushin 70b; see *tosafoth* there s.v. *d'ha*.
19. Literally, of removals, or distancings.
20. I.e. whether they seem relevant to him or not.

—except for a man's wife: he is permitted to gaze at her beauty, even while she is ritually unclean from the menses, because she is permitted to him after a while, and it is an established tenet about a Jew that his passion is under his control in such an instance, where it is a matter of time.[13] However, only at a generally exposed part of her did the Sages permit him to gaze while she is yet menstrually unclean, but not at what is generally hidden, so that the evil impulse should not possess him.[14]

Our Sages of blessed memory taught further that it is forbidden to gaze even at the hair of a woman who is banned to him; and so is it forbidden even to listen to her voice with the intention of deriving enjoyment from it.[15] Even to gaze at the colored clothing of a woman, i.e. the beautiful garments that it is their custom to make from colored cloth—it is forbidden to stare at them as long as he recognizes the woman who [generally] wears them, because as a result of seeing the garment, he can be led to immoral fantasy about her.[16]

So too, the Sages set a barrier[17] not to ask after the welfare of a married woman at all, even through her husband.[18] There are many details of protective barriers[19] about which the Sages enjoined us in this regard. The heart of the matter, though, is that a man should do absolutely nothing in the world that can lead him into the grip of immoral fantasy about women, neither by action nor by speech, nor by any hint to bring the light (unserious) mind of a woman into intimacy with his mind—except with his wife alone.

About this the prophet would chastise the people of his generation, telling them, *they neigh every one to his neighbor's wife* (Jeremiah 5:8); in other words, in their normal way, where it seems as if they do not intend this, they send hints to their neighbors' wives—little signals of immorality, and raise their voices in such a way that the women will hear them and their passion will be aroused toward the philanderer. It is not possible to relate the details of these matters, that a man can know to do in order to attract the mind of a woman, which is fickle. Therefore the Sages of blessed memory mentioned some of them, and about the rest, let everyone take care to watch himself according to what he finds [happening within] himself—for *the Eternal Lord sees the heart* (I Samuel 16:7).

In any event, apparently, from all that the Sages of blessed memory adjured us, a man is not permitted to budge—from their good ethical teaching.[20] Even if he finds himself somewhat devoid of desire, he

יֹאמַר "כֵּיוָן שֶׁאֲנִי מוֹצֵא עַצְמִי כֵּן, מַה אִכְפַּת לִי אִם אֶסְתַּכֵּל בְּנָשִׁים, כִּי יוֹדֵעַ אֲנִי בְעַצְמִי שֶׁלֹּא יִתְעוֹרֵר יִצְרִי בְכָךְ", שֶׁהַרְבֵּה אָמְרוּ כֵן וְנִכְשְׁלוּ. וְעַל זֶה רָמְזוּ זִכְרוֹנָם לִבְרָכָה בְּאָמְרָם כִּי הַיֵּצֶר בַּתְּחִלָּה חַלָּשׁ מְאֹד וְהוֹלֵךְ וּמִתְחַזֵּק עַל הָאָדָם הַרְבֵּה.

וְאַתָּה בְּנִי הִזָּהֵר עַל זֶה מְאֹד וְאַל יַבְטִיחֲךָ יִצְרְךָ, וְאִם אֶלֶף עֲרֵבִים יִתֵּן לְךָ. וְזֶה שֶׁאַתָּה מוֹצֵא קְצָת מַעֲשִׂים בַּגְּמָרָא מַרְאִים סוֹתְרִים דִּבְרֵי אֵלֶּה, כְּלוֹמַר שֶׁאֲפִלּוּ בַּמֶּה שֶׁאָסְרוּ זִכְרוֹנָם לִבְרָכָה בְּנָשִׁים לֹא הָיוּ קְצָת מֵהֶן חוֹשְׁשִׁין, אֵין זֶה סְתִירָה כְּלָל לִדְבָרַי, דִּבְמָקוֹם מִצְוָה הוּא דַוְקָא שֶׁהָיוּ מְקִלִּין קְצָת, כְּמוֹ שֶׁמָּצִינוּ בְרַבִּי יוֹחָנָן דַּהֲוָה יָתִיב אַשַּׁעֲרֵי טְבִילָה כְּדֵי שֶׁיִּסְתַּכְּלוּ בוֹ הַנָּשִׁים וְיוֹלִידוּ בָנִים נָאִים כְּמוֹתוֹ, וְהוּא לֹא הָיָה מִסְתַּכֵּל בָּהֶן חָלִילָה; וְרַבִּי דַהֲוָה נָקִיט כַּלָּתָא אַכְּתְפֵיהּ, לְמִצְוָה הוּא שֶׁהָיָה עוֹשֶׂה כֵן, כְּדֵי לְשַׂמְּחָהּ; וּקְצָת עִנְיָנִים כַּיּוֹצֵא בָאֵלּוּ.

וְעוֹד שֶׁהֵם זִכְרוֹנָם לִבְרָכָה הָיוּ כְמַלְאָכִים, שֶׁלֹּא הָיָה עִסְקָם אֲפִלּוּ שָׁעָה קַלָּה כִּי־אִם בַּתּוֹרָה וּבַמִּצְווֹת, וְהָיְתָה מְפֻרְסֶמֶת כַּוָּנָתָם לְכָל הָעוֹלָם כַּשֶּׁמֶשׁ, וְלֹא הָיוּ מַרְגִּישִׁים הֶרְגֵּשׁ רַע בְּשׁוּם דָּבָר, מֵרֹב דְּבֵקוּתָם בַּתּוֹרָה וּבַמִּצְווֹת. אֲבָל אֲנַחְנוּ עַכְשָׁיו אֵין לָנוּ לִפְרֹץ אֲפִלּוּ גָּדֵר קָטָן בְּעִנְיָנִים אֵלּוּ כְּלָל, אֶלָּא לִשְׁמֹר כָּל הַהַרְחָקִים שֶׁהוֹדִיעוּנוּ זִכְרוֹנָם לִבְרָכָה בִּפְרָט; וּבַמֶּה שֶׁלֹּא הִזְכִּירוּ הֵם יֵשׁ עַל כָּל אֶחָד וְאֶחָד לַעֲשׂוֹת כְּפִי מַה שֶּׁיִּמְצָא אֶת גּוּפוֹ מוּכָן , כְּמוֹ שֶׁאָמַרְנוּ, שֶׁאִם הוּא מוֹצֵא עַצְמוֹ שֶׁצָּרִיךְ גָּדֵר אַף עַל הַמֻּתָּר יִגְדֹּר עַצְמוֹ, כְּמוֹ שֶׁמָּצִינוּ אֶחָד מִן הַחֲכָמִים שֶׁאָמַר, "הִזָּהֲרוּ בִי מִפְּנֵי בִתִּי"; וְאַף־עַל־פִּי שֶׁמֻּתָּר לְאָדָם לְהִתְיַחֵד עִם בִּתּוֹ, כְּמוֹ שֶׁנִּכְתֹּב בְּעֶזְרַת הַשֵּׁם, לְפִי שֶׁעִנְיָן זֶה קָשֶׁה מְאֹד וְיֵצֶר הָרַע חָזָק בּוֹ, עַל כֵּן צָרִיךְ כָּל אָדָם לְהַרְבּוֹת בִּשְׁמִירָה.

וְאִם יַחְשֹׁב הָאִישׁ בְּפָגְעוֹ בְאִשָּׁה נָאָה כִּי גֵיהִנֹּם פָּתוּחַ בֵּין רִיסֵי עֵינֶיהָ, וּבְאֵשׁ

21. TB Sukkah 52a: At first the evil inclination is like a gossamer thread of a spider's web; at the end it is like wagon ropes.

22. TB B'rachoth 20a.

23. So to dance at the wedding celebration; TB K'thuboth 17a (our editions of the Talmud have R. Aḥa).

24. Literally, removals, or distancings.

25. I.e. do not let me be alone with her; TB Kiddushin 81b.

should not say, "Since I find myself to be so, what does it matter to me if I gaze at women? I know of myself that my passion will not be aroused by it"—for many thought so, and they came to grief. Our Sages of blessed memory hinted at this when they said that the evil inclination is very weak at first, and it goes on gradually to become very powerful over a man.[21]

Then you, my son, take great care about this, and let not your inclination give you any assurance, even if it should give you a thousand guarantees. The fact that you find some incidents in the Talmud which seem to contradict these words of mine—in other words, that even about what the Sages of blessed memory forbade in regard to women, some of them seemed to take no notice—this is not a contradiction to my words at all: For it was specifically in an instance of a religious purpose that they would be slightly lenient. Thus we find that R. Yoḥanan would sit at the gates of the place of ritual immersion, so that the women should gaze at him and bear sons as handsome as he was;[22] but he would not gaze at them, perish the thought. Rabbi [Judah haNassi] would take a bride on his shoulder:[23] it was for a religious purpose that he would do so, in order to make her happy; and so a few other acts like these.

Moreover, they (of blessed memory) were as angels, as their occupation, even for a brief moment, was never with anything but the Torah and the precepts; their intention was as clear as the sun to all, and they would feel no evil sensation in anything, in their great bond of devotion to Torah and *mitzvoth*. But as for us at present, it is not for us to break through even one small fence (protective restriction) whatever in these matters, but only to observe all the protective barriers[24] that our Sages of blessed memory taught us in detail; and regarding [restrictions] that they did not mention, it is for each and every one to act as he finds his nature responding—as we stated. For if a person discovers himself to need a "fence" even about something permissible, let him so "fence" himself about—as we find that one of the Sages said, "Take care about me on account of my daughter."[25] Even though it would be permissible for a man to be alone with his own daughter, as we will write [below] with the Eternal Lord's help, because it is a very difficult matter, the evil impulse being strong within a person, a man therefore needs to multiply the protective guard.

If a man would but think upon encountering a beautiful woman that Gehinnom (purgatory) opens between her eyelids, and whoever

תָּמִיד תּוּקַד כָּל הַקָּרֵב אֵלֶיהָ, וְיַחֲזִיר כָּל מַחְשְׁבוֹתָיו אֶל הַדְּבָרִים הָאֵלֶּה, לֹא תִהְיֶה לוֹ לְפוּקָה. וְאָמְרוּ זִכְרוֹנָם לִבְרָכָה שֶׁאִם אֵין כֹּחַ בְּיָדוֹ לְהָמִית הַיֵּצֶר וּלְהַרְחִיק מַחֲשַׁבְתּוֹ מִמֶּנּוּ, שֶׁיִּקְרָא קְרִיַּת שְׁמַע אוֹ יַעֲסֹק בַּתּוֹרָה, וְהוֹדִיעוּנוּ שֶׁעַל־כָּל־פָּנִים יָמוּת בְּכָךְ, כְּמוֹ שֶׁאָמְרוּ זִכְרוֹנָם לִבְרָכָה, שֶׁאִם אֶבֶן הוּא נִמּוֹחַ, וְאִם בַּרְזֶל מִתְפּוֹצֵץ, שֶׁנֶּאֱמַר: הֲלֹא כֹה דְבָרִי כָּאֵשׁ וְגוֹמֵר.

וְעוֹד אָמְרוּ רַבּוֹתֵינוּ זִכְרוֹנָם לִבְרָכָה בְּמִצְוָה זוֹ שֶׁאָסוּר לְהִתְיַחֵד עִם כָּל הָעֲרָיוֹת, רְצוֹנִי לוֹמַר עִם כָּל הָעֲרָיוֹת דְּבַר תּוֹרָה, בֵּין זְקֵנָה בֵּין יַלְדָּה, שֶׁהַיִּחוּד, לְגַלּוֹת עֶרְוָה הוּא גוֹרֵם; חוּץ מִן הָאֵם עִם בְּנָהּ וְהָאָב עִם בִּתּוֹ וְהַבַּעַל עִם אִשְׁתּוֹ נִדָּה, שֶׁמֻּתָּרִין; חוּץ מֵחָתָן שֶׁפֵּרְשָׁה אִשְׁתּוֹ נִדָּה קֹדֶם שֶׁיִּבְעֹל; וּמֻתָּר לְהִתְיַחֵד עִם הַזָּכוּר וְעִם הַבְּהֵמָה, שֶׁלֹּא נֶחְשְׁדוּ יִשְׂרָאֵל עַל כָּךְ.

כְּשֶׁאֵרַע מַעֲשֵׂה אַמְנוֹן וְתָמָר, גָּזַר דָּוִד וּבֵית דִּינוֹ עַל יִחוּד דִּפְנוּיָה. שַׁמַּאי וְהִלֵּל גָּזְרוּ עַל יִחוּד גּוֹיִים. וְהִתִּירוּ זִכְרוֹנָם לִבְרָכָה לְהִסְתַּכֵּל בִּפְנֵי פְנוּיָה לְמִי שֶׁמִּסְתַּכֵּל בָּהּ לָדַעַת שֶׁיִּשָּׂא אוֹתָהּ לְאִשָּׁה אִם תִּהְיֶה נָאָה בְעֵינָיו. וְגַם אָמְרוּ שֶׁרָאוּי לַעֲשׂוֹת כֵּן, שֶׁלֹּא יִשָּׂא אָדָם אִשָּׁה עַד שֶׁיִּרְאֶנָּה, כְּדֵי שֶׁלֹּא יָבוֹא לְגָרְשָׁהּ אַחַר־כֵּן אִם תִּתְגַּנֶּה בְעֵינָיו; וְיֶתֶר פְּרָטֵי הַמִּצְוָה, מְבֹאָרִים בְּהַרְבֵּה מְקוֹמוֹת בַּתַּלְמוּד בְּפִזּוּר.

וְנוֹהֶגֶת בְּכָל מָקוֹם וּבְכָל זְמַן בִּזְכָרִים וּנְקֵבוֹת, שֶׁגַּם לָהֶן אָסוּר לְהַרְהֵר אַחַר הָאֲנָשִׁים זוּלָתִי בְּבַעְלֵיהֶן, שֶׁעֲלֵיהֶם רָאוּי לָהֶן לְהַמְשִׁיךְ כָּל חֶשְׁקָן וְחֶפְצָן, וְכֵן יַעֲשׂוּ בְנוֹת יִשְׂרָאֵל הַכְּשֵׁרוֹת. וְעוֹבֵר עָלֶיהָ וְקָרֵב אֶל הָעֶרְוָה קֵרוּב בָּשָׂר כְּדֵי שֶׁיֵּהָנֶה מִמֶּנָּה, בְּמֵזִיד וּבְהַתְרָאָה לוֹקֶה; וְאִם עָבַר עַל שְׁאָר הַדְּבָרִים שֶׁאָסְרוּ

26. TB B’rachoth 5a.

27. Deuteronomy 4:6–11.

28. TB Kiddushin 30b–31a.

29. *Ibid.* 80b, Sanhedrin 21b, ‘Avodah Zarah 36b.

30. The phrase רצוני לומר עם כל העריות (“by which I mean all those severely banned”) is found only in the second oldest manuscript (MS Vatican 163/1) and in the first edition. As I indicated in my preface to the first volume (p. xii), these two show some kinship (very possibly they derive from one “forefather” manuscript), and in quite a few instances this MS Vatican has proven the most accurate. Here, in any case, it is most unlikely that the words in question are a later interpolation from some scholar’s note in the margin of his copy of the work. Far more likely, the phrase is the author’s, and was afterward omitted by a scribe or scribes, by a jump of the eye between two identical phrases close together.

Now, with the phrase omitted in the standard editions, MH understands from the text that our author holds this ban on seclusion with women ranked as ‘*arayoth* (severely forbidden, on pain of *karéth*) to be a law of the Torah, which is the view of *tosafoth* (TB Shabbath 13a, s.v. *d’ha*; Sanhedrin 37a, s.v. *ha-torah*; Sotah 7a, s.v. *niddah*). With this comes intimately close at all to her will be burned on a steady fire—if he will turn all his thoughts to these concepts, she will not be a stumbling-block to him. Our Sages of blessed memory said, too,[26] that if a person has not the power to kill the evil impulse and remove his thought from it, he should recite the *Sh'ma*[27] or engage in Torah study; and they informed us that under any circumstances, it will thus succumb; as our Sages of blessed memory said,[28] if it [the evil impulse] is of stone, it will be pulverized; if it is of iron, it will be smashed: for it is stated, *Is not My word as fire? says the Lord; and like a hammer that smashes the rock?* (Jeremiah 23:29).

Moreover, our Sages of blessed memory taught about this precept[29] that it is prohibited to be alone with any of the severely forbidden women, by which I mean all those severely banned by the Torah's law,[30] whether she is very old or very young, as seclusion leads to the uncovering of nakedness—except for a mother with her son, a father with his daughter, and a husband with his menstrually impure wife, who are permitted, with the exception of a bridegroom whose wife's menstruation began before they consummated the marriage.[31] A man is equally permitted to be alone with a male and with an animal, as Israelites are not suspected about this.[32]

When the incident of Amnon and Tamar occurred, David and his *beth din* decreed against seclusion with an unmarried woman.[33] Shammai and Hillel decreed against seclusion with heathens.[33] And the Sages of blessed memory permitted looking at the face of an unmarried woman for one who would regard her to know if he would take her for a wife, if she is beautiful in his eyes. Our Sages said, furthermore, that it is proper to do so: for a man should not marry a woman until he sees her, so that he should not come to divorce her afterward if she will prove repulsive in his eyes.[34] The remaining details of the precept are elucidated in many places in the Talmud, scattered about.

It is in force in every place and every time, for both man and woman—since it is equally forbidden for them to think with yearning about any men other than their husbands, on whom it is fitting for them to set all their desire and delight; and so proper, worthy Jewish daughters do. If someone transgresses it and draws close to a forbidden woman in bodily intimacy in order to derive enjoyment from her—if it was deliberate and with a [prior] warning, he is given lashes of the whip. If he transgressed any of the other prohibitions which the Sages of blessed memory imposed to [maintain a safe] distance—for example, laughter

זִכְרוֹנָם לִבְרָכָה לְהַרְחָקָה, כְּגוֹן הַשְּׂחוֹק עִמָּהֶן וְקַלּוּת רֹאשׁ, וְהִתְרוּ בוֹ וְלֹא נִמְנַע, מַכִּין אוֹתוֹ מַכַּת מַרְדּוּת.

וְהָרַמְבָּ״ן זִכְרוֹנוֹ לִבְרָכָה כָּתַב שֶׁלֹּא נִמְנֶה לָאו זֶה דִּקְרִיבָה בְּמִנְיַן הַלָּאוִין, שֶׁכָּל הֶרְחֵק הַקְּרִיבָה דְּרַבָּנָן הִיא. וְהָרְאָיָה מַה שֶּׁאָמְרוּ זִכְרוֹנָם לִבְרָכָה: אָמַר רַבִּי יוֹסִי בְּרַבִּי בּוּן: הִיא בַּל תִּקְרַב הִיא בַּל תְּגַלֶּה, כְּלוֹמַר שֶׁאֵין בִּקְרִיבָה לָאו, אֶלָּא לָאו דְּגִלּוּי. וְיֶתֶר רְאָיוֹתָיו רַבּוֹת בְּסִפְרוֹ בְּמִצְוַת שמ״ז.

[שֶׁלֹּא לְגַלּוֹת עֶרְוַת אָב]

קפט שֶׁלֹּא יְגַלֶּה אָדָם עֶרְוַת אָבִיו, כְּלוֹמַר שֶׁלֹּא יִשְׁכַּב אוֹתוֹ מִשְׁכְּבֵי אִשָּׁה, שֶׁנֶּאֱמַר: עֶרְוַת אָבִיךָ ... לֹא תְגַלֵּה. וְזֹאת הָאַזְהָרָה נוֹסֶפֶת בְּשׁוֹכֵב אֶת אָבִיו עַל הָאַזְהָרָה הַכּוֹלֶלֶת מִשְׁכַּב זָכוּר בְּכָל אָדָם, שֶׁנֶּאֶמְרָה בְּמָקוֹם אַחֵר, כְּמוֹ שֶׁנֶּאֱמַר: וְאֶת זָכָר לֹא תִשְׁכַּב מִשְׁכְּבֵי אִשָּׁה.

וְכֵן אָמְרוּ זִכְרוֹנָם לִבְרָכָה בְּסַנְהֶדְרִין: עֶרְוַת אָבִיךָ ... לֹא תְגַלֵּה, אָבִיךָ מַמָּשׁ. וְשָׁאֲלוּ שָׁם: הַאי מִ״וְאֶת זָכָר לֹא תִשְׁכַּב״ נָפְקָא מִינֵהּ. וְהֵשִׁיב הַמֵּשִׁיב: כְּדֵי לְחַיֵּב שְׁתַּיִם, וְכִדְרַבִּי יְהוּדָה, דְּאָמַר: גּוֹי הַבָּא עַל אָבִיו חַיָּב שְׁתַּיִם; וְשָׁם בֵּאֲרוּ וְאָמְרוּ: מִסְתַּבְּרָא מִילְתֵיהּ דְּרַב יְהוּדָה בְּיִשְׂרָאֵל וּבְשׁוֹגֵג וּלְקָרְבָּן. וְהַאי דְּקָאָמַר גּוֹי, לִישְׁנָא מַעַלְיָא נָקַט, כְּלוֹמַר שֶׁלֹּא רָצָה לְהַזְכִּיר הָעִנְיָן הַמְגֻנֶּה בְּיִשְׂרָאֵל, כֵּיוָן שֶׁאֶפְשָׁר לְהַעֲמִידוֹ בְגוֹי, שֶׁאַף הֵן מְצֻוִּין בַּעֲרָיוֹת; אֲבָל הוּא הַדִּין בְּיִשְׂרָאֵל שֶׁחַיָּב שְׁתַּיִם בְּאָבִיו, כְּלוֹמַר שֶׁאִם שָׁכַב אוֹתוֹ בְשׁוֹגֵג חַיָּב לְהָבִיא שְׁתֵּי חַטָּאוֹת.

עִנְיַן הָאַזְהָרָה זוֹ נִגְלֶה הוּא, אֵין לְהַאֲרִיךְ בְּשָׁרְשָׁהּ, כִּי הַכִּעוּר הַגָּדוֹל כָּזֶה רָאוּי

phrase, however, our author's meaning is evidently that the original ban on seclusion (before the additional bans noted in the next paragraph) applies to those women ranked as *‘arayoth* by the Torah. This is in keeping with the Talmudic source (see note 29), which concludes, "a son may be in private with his mother, but one is not to be closeted with any of the [other] *‘arayoth* in the Torah."

31. TB K'thuboth 4b.
32. TB Kiddushin 82a.
33. TB ‘Avodah Zarah 36b.
34. TB Kiddushin 41a.
35. See § 24, note 14.
36. In his commentary to ShM negative precept §353.
37. TJ Sanhedrin vii 7.
38. Since the first is prelude to the second.

§189 1. E.g. if he did not know it is forbidden by the Torah.

2. I.e. since two injunctions (negative precepts) were violated, two offerings are needed; but for willful transgressions the punishment is death; hence the second injunction would make no difference, since a man can be killed only once.

with them, or frivolity—if he was warned and he did not refrain, he is given punishment for disobedience.[35]

Now, Ramban of blessed memory wrote[36] that we should not count this prohibition on general intimacy in the list of negative precepts, because the entire matter of keeping away from such intimacy is by the ruling of the Sages. The proof is what they (of blessed memory) taught:[37] R. Yosé b. R. Bon said: The injunction not to approach is the same as the injunction not to uncover. In other words, there is no other negative precept about approaching but the one about uncovering.[38] The rest of his many proofs are in his work,[36] in [negative] precept §353.

[THE PROHIBITION ON UNCOVERING THE NAKEDNESS OF ONE'S FATHER]

189 that a man should not uncover the nakedness of his father: in other words, he should not lie carnally with him as with a woman—as it is stated, *The nakedness of your father . . . you shall not uncover* (Leviticus 18:7). This injunction is added, if one lies with his father, to the general injunction against homosexual connection which applies to any man, that is stated elsewhere, as we read, *And with a male you shall not lie as with a woman* (*ibid.* 22).

And so our Sages of blessed memory taught in the tractate *Sanhedrin* (54a): "The nakedness of your father . . . you shall not uncover"—literally your father. It was then asked there: But this can be derived from the verse, *And with a male you shall not lie*, etc.? The answer was given: It is in order to impose punishment for [violating] two precepts; and it is in keeping with the view of R. Judah, who said: If a heathen had carnal connection with his father, he is punishable for [violating] two injunctions. It was then explained there thus: It stands to reason that the teaching of R. Judah is about an Israelite who acted inadvertently,[1] and in regard to an [atoning] offering;[2] and as for his saying a heathen, he used a euphemism. In other words, he did not wish to speak of this disgraceful matter in regard to an Israelite since it is possible to illustrate it with a heathen, as they too are enjoined about forbidden conjugal relations; but the law is the same for an Israelite, that he is punishable for two [precepts] over his father. This is to say that if he had carnal connection with him unwittingly,[1] he is duty-bound to bring two *ḥattath* (sin) offerings.

The significance of this injunction is obvious. There is no need to

לְהַרְחִיקוֹ מִבְּנֵי־אָדָם וְלַעֲנֹשׁ עָלָיו הָעוֹבֵר עֹנֶשׁ גָּדוֹל, וְלָכֵן יְחַיְּבֶנּוּ בִסְקִילָה.

מִדִּינֵי הַמִּצְוָה, מַה שֶּׁאָמְרוּ זִכְרוֹנָם לִבְרָכָה שֶׁהַחִיּוּב הוּא בְהַכְנָסַת הָעֲטָרָה מִיָּד וְלֹא קֹדֶם לָכֵן; וְהוּא הַדִּין בְּכָל הָעֲרָיוֹת, שֶׁהַחִיּוּב בָּהֶן בְּהַכְנָסַת הָעֲטָרָה מִיָּד, חוּץ מִן הַבָּא עַל הַשִּׁפְחָה, שֶׁהַחִיּוּב בָּהּ בְּגוֹמֵר בִּיאָתוֹ; וְיֶתֶר פְּרָטֶיהָ, בְּסוֹף הַסֵּדֶר נוֹדִיעַ מְקוֹמָן, עִם פְּרָטֵי שְׁאָר כָּל הָעֲרָיוֹת, בְּעֶזְרַת הַשֵּׁם.

וְנוֹהֵג אִסּוּר זֶה בְּכָל מָקוֹם וּבְכָל זְמָן. וְעוֹבֵר עַל זֶה וְשָׁכַב אֶת אָבִיו, מִכֵּיוָן שֶׁהִכְנִיס רֹאשׁ הָעֲטָרָה בְמֵזִיד וְיֵשׁ עֵדִים וְהַתְרָאָה, נִסְקָל; בְּשׁוֹגֵג מֵבִיא שְׁנֵי חַטָּאוֹת בִּזְמַן הַבַּיִת, אֶחָד מִשּׁוּם לָאו דְּאָבִיו וְאֶחָד מִשּׁוּם לָאו דְּזָכָר.

[שֶׁלֹּא לְגַלּוֹת עֶרְוַת אֵם]

קצ שֶׁלֹּא יְגַלֶּה הַבֵּן עֶרְוַת הָאֵם, שֶׁנֶּאֱמַר: אִמְּךָ הִיא לֹא תְגַלֶּה עֶרְוָתָהּ. בְּטַעַם אִסּוּר הַקְּרוֹבוֹת כָּתַב הָרַמְבָּ״ם זִכְרוֹנוֹ לִבְרָכָה שֶׁהָעִנְיָן הוּא לְפִי שֶׁהַתּוֹרָה תַרְחִיק הַמִּשְׁגָּל מִבְּנֵי־אָדָם לְבַד מַה שֶּׁצָּרִיךְ לִפְרִיָּה וּרְבִיָּה אוֹ לְמִצְוָה, וְלָכֵן אָסְרָה לָנוּ הַתּוֹרָה הַקְּרוֹבוֹת, לְפִי שֶׁהַכִּשָּׁלוֹן יִמָּצֵא בָהֶן יוֹתֵר מִפְּנֵי שֶׁהֵן מְצוּיוֹת אֶצְלוֹ תָּמִיד.

וְהָרַמְבָּ״ן זִכְרוֹנוֹ לִבְרָכָה אָמַר כִּי הַטַּעַם הַזֶּה חָלוּשׁ מְאֹד שֶׁיְּחַיֵּב הַכָּתוּב כָּרֵת עַל אֵלֶּה מִפְּנֵי הִמָּצְאָם אֶצְלוֹ תָמִיד, וְיַתִּיר מִצַּד אַחֵר שֶׁיִּשָּׂא אָדָם אֶחָד מֵאָה נָשִׁים אִם יִרְצֶה, אוֹ אֶלֶף. וְאָמַר הוּא זִכְרוֹנוֹ לִבְרָכָה, וְזֶה לְשׁוֹנוֹ: אֲבָל כְּפִי הַסְּבָרָא כִּי יֵשׁ בָּעִנְיָן סוֹד מִסּוֹדוֹת הַיְצִירָה דָּבוּק בַּנֶּפֶשׁ, וְהוּא מִכְּלַל סוֹד הָעִבּוּר שֶׁכְּבָר רָמַזְנוּ לוֹ. עַד כָּאן.

3. TB Yevamoth 53b, 55b.

4. TB K'rithoth 10b; Sifra, *k'doshim, perek* 5, 2.

§190 1. Rambam, *Guide* III 49.

2. I.e. if it was permitted to marry them and the only barrier to conjugal intimacy with them was the lack of marriage (*ibid.*).

3. Ramban, commentary, Leviticus 18:6.

4. I.e. if the Torah forbids such intimacy because it wishes to restrict conjugal relations to a necessary minimum, why is one free to take any number of wives?

5. Ramban evidently alludes here to his *Sha'ar haG'mul*, where he uses the term "mystery of impregnation" (*sod ha'ibbur*) in reference to the fact that children of closely related parents are frequently feeble-minded or otherwise defective.

write at length about its root reason: for it is fitting to remove this great ugliness from human beings and to punish a transgressor for it with a great penalty. He is therefore sentenced to death by stoning.

Among the laws of the precept there is what the Sages of blessed memory said:[3] that guilt is incurred at once upon the intromission of the corona, but not before that; and this is the law with all forbidden conjugal relations, that guilt for them comes at once with the intromission of the corona, except for one who is conjugally intimate with a [betrothed] maidservant (§129), who incurs guilt at the end of the intimacy.[4] As to the remaining details of the law, we shall give their location at the end of the *sidrah* (§211), with the details of other forbidden conjugal relations, with the Eternal Lord's help.

This prohibition is in force in every place, at every time. If someone violated it and had carnal connection with his father, once he intromitted the corona willfully, and there were witnesses and a [prior] warning, he would be stoned to death. If it was inadvertent,[1] he would bring two *ḥattath* (sin) offerings when the Temple exists: one because of the injunction about his father, and one for the injunction about a male.

[THE PROHIBITION ON UNCOVERING ONE'S MOTHER'S NAKEDNESS]

190 that a son should not uncover the nakedness of a mother, as it is stated, *she is your mother; you shall not uncover her nakedness* (Leviticus 18:7). As to the reason for the ban on consanguineous relations, Rambam of blessed memory wrote[1] that in substance it is because the Torah would remove conjugal intimacy from human beings, except what is necessary for reproduction or for a religious duty. Therefore the Torah prohibited near relations to us, because one is the more likely to succumb to misfortune with them,[2] since they are about us constantly.

Ramban of blessed memory wrote, however,[3] that this reason is very weak—that the Writ should impose over these the penalty of *karéth* [Divine severance of existence—merely] on account of their being about one constantly, and on the other hand it permits one man to marry a hundred women if he wishes, or [even] a thousand.[4] And he (of blessed memory) stated [the purpose] in these words: According to reason, though, there is in the matter one of the mysteries of creation that is attached to the soul. It is part of the general mystery of impregnation to which we have alluded previously.[5] Thus far his words.

וַאֲנִי רָאִיתִי לָרַמְבָּ"ם זִכְרוֹנוֹ לִבְרָכָה שֶׁכָּתַב עוֹד טַעַם אַחֵר בָּעִנְיָן, עַל צַד הַפְּשָׁט לְדַעְתִּי: אָמַר כִּי תַרְחִיק הַתּוֹרָה שֶׁלֹּא יָעִיז פָּנָיו הָאָדָם לָבוֹא עַל הָאִשָּׁה שֶׁרָאוּי לִנְהֹג בָּהּ כָּבוֹד; וְיִדְחֹק לְפָרֵשׁ רְבָּן עַל הַצַּד הַזֶּה, כְּלוֹמַר מִטַּעַם מִדַּת הַבֹּשֶׁת, הַכֹּל כְּמוֹ שֶׁבָּא בְסִפְרוֹ; יַאֲרִיךְ הָעִנְיָן אִם בָּאנוּ לִכְתֹּב הַכֹּל.

מִדִּינֵי הַמִּצְוָה, מַה שֶּׁאָמְרוּ זִכְרוֹנָם לִבְרָכָה שֶׁאִסּוּר הָאֵם אֲפִלּוּ הָיְתָה אֲנוּסַת אָבִיו, שֶׁהֲרֵי מִכָּל־מָקוֹם אִמּוֹ הִיא; וְכֵן מַה שֶּׁאָמְרוּ שֶׁהַבָּא עַל אִמּוֹ שֶׁהִיא אֵשֶׁת אָבִיו כְּלוֹמַר שֶׁלֹּא הָיְתָה אֲנוּסָתוֹ, חַיָּב שְׁתַּיִם, מִשּׁוּם אִמּוֹ וּמִשּׁוּם אֵשֶׁת אָבִיו; וְאֵין חִלּוּק בָּזֶה בֵּין שֶׁבָּא עָלֶיהָ בְּחַיֵּי אָבִיו אוֹ לְאַחַר מוֹתוֹ, דִּלְעוֹלָם אֵשֶׁת אָבִיו נִקְרֵאת, וְחַיָּב בָּהּ שְׁתַּיִם כְּמוֹ שֶׁאָמַרְנוּ.

וְכֵן מַה שֶּׁאָסְרוּ רַבּוֹתֵינוּ זִכְרוֹנָם לִבְרָכָה לְגֶדֶר אִסּוּר זֶה שֶׁל אֵם, אֵם אִמּוֹ, כְּלוֹמַר זְקֵנָתוֹ; וְכֵן אֵם זְקֵנָתוֹ, וְכֵן אֵם אֵם זְקֵנָתוֹ, עַד מַעְלָה מַעְלָה, אֲפִלּוּ אֶלֶף דּוֹר אִם יִהְיֶה בְּאֶפְשָׁר לִרְאוֹתָן — כֻּלָּן אֲסוּרוֹת מִדִּבְרֵי סוֹפְרִים. וְכֵן אָסְרוּ לְגֶדֶר הָאֵם, אֵם אָבִיו, שֶׁהִיא זְקֵנָתוֹ מִצַּד אָב, וְכֵן אֵם זְקֵנָתוֹ עַד מַעְלָה מַעְלָה לְעוֹלָם; וְכֵן אָסְרוּ לְגֶדֶר זֶה שֶׁל אֵם, אֵם אֲבִי אָבִיו בִּלְבַד, וְאֵם אֲבִי אִמּוֹ בִּלְבָד. וְיֵשׁ שֶׁפֵּרְשׁוּ שֶׁגַּם אֵלּוּ אֲסוּרוֹת לְמַעְלָה לְעוֹלָם.

וְאִם תִּשְׁאַל, לָמָּה יִתְפַּשֵּׁט הָאִסּוּר עַד לְמַעְלָה בָּרִאשׁוֹנוֹת, כְּדַעַת הָרִאשׁוֹן, יוֹתֵר מִבִּשְׁתֵּי אֵלּוּ הָאַחֲרוֹנוֹת, הַטַּעַם לְפִי שֶׁהָרִאשׁוֹנוֹת תִּקְרַבְנָה אֶל אִסּוּר הָאֵם, שֶׁהוּא עִקַּר הָאִסּוּר, שֶׁהֲרֵי יֵשׁ בָּהֶן זְקֵנָה אֲסוּרָה, דְּהַיְנוּ אֵם הָאֵם וְאֵם הָאָב; וְעַל־כֵּן רָאוּי לִגְזֹר בָּהֶן אֲפִלּוּ עַד לְמַעְלָה; אֲבָל בִּשְׁתֵּי אֵלּוּ הָאַחֲרוֹנוֹת אֵין בָּהֶן זְקֵנָה

6. TB Sanhedrin 54a, etc.

7. *Ibid.* 53a.

8. TB Yevamoth 21a.

9. But not the mother of his grandfather's father; TJ Yevamoth ii, 4; MT *hilchoth 'ishuth* i 6.

10. Rashi, TB Yevamoth 21a, s.v. *'arba nashim.*

Now, I have seen that Rambam of blessed memory wrote another reason, as well, about the matter[1]—by way of the plain meaning, to my mind. He stated that the Torah imposes a barrier in order that a man should not be so arrogant as to be conjugally intimate with a woman whom, properly, he ought to treat with respect. And he strains to explain most of them in this vein, i.e. on account of the quality of shame—all as it is set forth in his work. But it would draw the subject out unduly if we undertook to write the whole thing.

Among the laws of the precept, there is what the Sages of blessed memory taught:[6] that the ban on the mother holds even if she was one's father's victim of compulsion (rape), since in any event she is his mother. So is there the law they stated:[7] that if someone was conjugally intimate with his mother who is his father's wife—i.e. she was not his victim of compulsion—he is guilty of two infractions: because she is his mother, and because she is his father's wife (Leviticus 18:8; §191). It makes no difference in this regard whether he was conjugally intimate with her in his father's lifetime or after his death, since she is always called his father's wife; and he is thus punishable for two sins on her account, as we stated.

So too, there is the ban which our Sages of blessed memory imposed as a "fence" (protective restriction) about the prohibition of the mother: the mother of one's mother, i.e. his grandmother; and so too his grandmother's mother, and likewise his grandmother's maternal grandmother, and so on further back, even through a thousand generations: if it is possible to see them, all are forbidden by the ruling of the Scribes.[8] So too as a "fence" about the mother, they forbade the mother of one's father, who is his paternal grandmother; and similarly the mother of this grandmother of his, and so on back endlessly. Likewise, as a "fence" about this precept of the mother, they banned the mother of his father's father alone,[9] and the mother of his mother's father alone.[9] There are those who explained, however,[10] that these are also forbidden further back without limit.

Now, you might ask: Why should the ban extend further back for the first ones, according to the view of the first authority, more so than for these two last ones? The reason is that the first ones are closer to the prohibition on the mother, which is the main forbiddance—for they have [at their center] a forbidden grandmother, i.e. the mother's mother and the father's mother. It is therefore fitting to decree them forbidden all the way further back. In these last two instances, however,

אֲסוּרָה, וְכֵיוָן שֶׁאֵין הָעִנְיָן מִתְקָרֵב לָאֻמּוֹת, שֶׁהוּא עִקַּר הָאִסּוּר, רָאוּ זִכְרוֹנָם לִבְרָכָה כִּי דַּי לָנוּ שֶׁנִּגְזֹר בִּשְׁתֵּי אֵלּוּ לְבָד. וְדִבְרֵי פִּי חֲכָמִים חֵן.

וְאֵלּוּ שֶׁאֲסוּרוֹת מִדְּרַבָּנָן נִקְרָאוֹת שְׁנִיּוֹת, כְּלוֹמַר שֶׁהֵן שְׁנִיּוֹת לְאוֹתָן עֲרָיוֹת שֶׁאָסְרָה הַתּוֹרָה.

וְנוֹהֵג אִסּוּר זֶה בְּכָל מָקוֹם וּבְכָל זְמָן. וְעוֹבֵר עַל זֶה וְשָׁכַב עִם אִמּוֹ בְּמֵזִיד, חַיָּב כָּרֵת, וּבְעֵדִים נִסְקָל. בְּשׁוֹגֵג, חַיָּב לְהָבִיא חַטָּאת קְבוּעָה בִּזְמַן הַבַּיִת. וְאִם שָׁכַב עִם אַחַת מִן הַשְּׁנִיּוֹת, לוֹקֶה מַכַּת מַרְדּוּת.

וְזֹאת מִן הָעֲרָיוֹת שֶׁנִּצְטַוּוּ עָלֶיהָ כָּל בְּנֵי הָעוֹלָם בִּכְלָל; אֲבָל חִלּוּק יֵשׁ בֵּין יִשְׂרָאֵל לִשְׁאָר הָאֻמּוֹת בְּעִנְיַן הַשְּׁנִיּוֹת, כִּי יִשְׂרָאֵל גָּדְרוּ גָּדֵר בְּעִנְיַן הַשְּׁנִיּוֹת, אֲבָל שְׁאָר הָאֻמּוֹת אֵין אִסּוּר עֲלֵיהֶם אֶלָּא הָאֵם לְבָד.

[שֶׁלֹּא לְגַלּוֹת עֶרְוַת אֵשֶׁת אָב וְאַף־עַל־פִּי שֶׁאֵינָהּ אִמּוֹ]

קצא שֶׁלֹּא לְגַלּוֹת עֶרְוַת אֵשֶׁת אָב וְאַף־עַל־פִּי שֶׁאֵינָהּ אִמּוֹ, שֶׁנֶּאֱמַר: עֶרְוַת אֵשֶׁת אָבִיךָ לֹא תְגַלֵּה.

מִשָּׁרְשֵׁי הַמִּצְוָה, מַה שֶּׁכָּתַבְנוּ בְּעִנְיַן הַקְּרוֹבוֹת. וְעוֹד יֵשׁ לָנוּ לוֹמַר כִּי הַטַּעַם בָּזֶה לְפִי שֶׁיִּהְיֶה בַּדָּבָר קָלוֹן אֵצֶל אָבִיו, וּכְבָר כָּתַבְנוּ בְּמִצְוַת כִּבּוּד אָב הַתּוֹעֶלֶת הַנִּמְצָא לָנוּ בְּכִבּוּד הָאָבוֹת.

מִדִּינֵי הַמִּצְוָה, מַה שֶּׁאָמְרוּ זִכְרוֹנָם לִבְרָכָה שֶׁאֵשֶׁת אָבִיו אֲסוּרָה מִן הַתּוֹרָה בֵּין מִן הָאֵרוּסִין, פֵּרוּשׁ מִן הַקִּדּוּשִׁין, בֵּין מִן הַנִּשּׂוּאִין, בֵּין בְּחַיֵּי אָבִיו וַאֲפִלּוּ גֵּרְשָׁהּ, בֵּין אַחַר מוֹתוֹ. וְכֵן מַה שֶּׁאָסְרוּ לְגֶדֶר אִסּוּר זֶה אֵשֶׁת אֲבִי אָבִיו, כְּלוֹמַר

11. Expression based on Ecclesiastes 10:12.
12. And they gave him a prior warning, which he defiantly ignored.
13. See §24, note 14.
14. TB Sanhedrin 58a.

§191 1. TB Sanhedrin 53a.
2. See §35, note 8.

there is no forbidden grandmother; and since the subject contains nothing close to mothers, who are the main focus of the prohibition, our Sages of blessed memory considered it enough for us to decree these two alone forbidden. The words of the mouth of Sages are gracious.[11]

Those forbidden by the Sages are called "secondary ones"; i.e. they are secondary to those consanguineous relations that the Torah forbade.

This prohibition is in force in every place, at every time. If someone violated it and was conjugally intimate with his mother willfully, he is punishable by *karéth* [Divine severance of existence]; if there were witnesses,[12] he should be stoned to death; and if it was inadvertent, he would be obligated to bring a standard unvarying *ḥattath* (sin-offering) at the time the Temple exists. If someone was thus intimate with any of the "secondary ones," he should receive a whipping for disobedience.[13]

This is among the forbidden consanguineous relations about which all mankind generally was commanded.[14] However, there is a difference between the Israelites and the other nations, in regard to the secondary ones: For the Israelites have erected a "fence" (protective restriction) concerning the secondary ones, while among the other nations there is no ban on them, but on a mother alone.

[THE PROHIBITION ON CONJUGAL INTIMACY WITH ONE'S FATHER'S WIFE EVEN IF SHE IS NOT HIS MOTHER]

191 not to uncover the nakedness of one's father's wife even if she is not his mother: for it is stated, *The nakedness of your father's wife you shall not uncover* (Leviticus 18:8).

At the root of the precept lies the reason we have written regarding [all] near relations (§ 190). We could say, moreover, that the reason for this is that there would be a disgrace for one's father in the matter. And we have written previously, in the precept of respect for one's father (§ 33) the useful benefit we obtain from esteem for parents.

Among the laws of the precept, there is what the Sages of blessed memory said:[1] that the wife of one's father is forbidden by the law of the Torah both after betrothal, i.e. consecration, and after marriage;[2] both in his father's lifetime, even if he divorced her, and after his death. There is, further, the prohibition they decreed, as a protective "fence" about this forbiddance, on the wife of one's father's father, i.e. his grandfather's

אֵשֶׁת זְקֵנוֹ אַף־עַל־פִּי שֶׁאֵינָהּ זְקֶנְתּוֹ, וְכֵן אָסְרוּ גַם־כֵּן אֵשֶׁת אֲבִי זְקֵנוֹ, וְכֵן אֵשֶׁת אֲבִי אֲבִי זְקֵנוֹ, וְכֵן עַד מַעְלָה מַעְלָה אֲפִלּוּ עַד יַעֲקֹב.

וְאָסְרוּ גַם־כֵּן לְגֶדֶר אִסּוּר זֶה אֵשֶׁת אֲבִי אִמּוֹ בִּלְבָד; וְהַטַּעַם לְפִי שֶׁעִקַּר אִסּוּר זֶה הוּא מִצַּד אָבוֹת, דְּהַיְנוּ אֵשֶׁת אָב, עַל־כֵּן הֶחְמִירוּ זִכְרוֹנָם לִבְרָכָה יוֹתֵר בְּצַד הָאָבוֹת, וְאָמְרוּ שֶׁיְּהֵא אָסוּר לְמַעְלָה עַד לְעוֹלָם; וּבְצַד הָאֵם לֹא גָזְרוּ אֶלָּא בְאֵשֶׁת אֲבִי אִמּוֹ לְבַד; וְהוּא כְעֵין הַחִלּוּק שֶׁכָּתַבְנוּ לְמַעְלָה בְּאִסּוּר הָאֵם; וְיֶתֶר פְּרָטֶיהָ, הֵם בַּמְּקוֹמוֹת שֶׁנִּכְתֹּב לְמַטָּה בְּסוֹף הַסֵּדֶר.

וְזֹאת מִן הָעֲרָיוֹת שֶׁנִּצְטַוּוּ עָלֶיהָ כָּל בְּנֵי הָעוֹלָם בִּכְלָל, אֲבָל יֵשׁ חִלּוּק בֵּין יִשְׂרָאֵל לִשְׁאָר הָאֻמּוֹת, שֶׁבִּשְׁאָר הָאֻמּוֹת אֵין נִקְרֵאת אֵשֶׁת אָבִיו אֶלָּא עַל־יְדֵי בְעִילָה. וּבְיִשְׂרָאֵל אֲפִלּוּ בְקִדּוּשִׁין; וְכֵן בְּעִנְיַן הַשְּׁנִיּוֹת, שֶׁאֵין אִסּוּר שְׁנִיּוֹת בָּאֻמּוֹת, כְּמוֹ שֶׁאָמַרְנוּ.

וְנוֹהֵג אִסּוּר זֶה בְּכָל מָקוֹם וּבְכָל זְמָן. וְעוֹבֵר עָלֶיהָ וְשָׁכַב אֶת אֵשֶׁת אָבִיו בְּמֵזִיד, חַיָּב כָּרֵת; וּבְעֵדִים וּבְהַתְרָאָה נִסְקָל. בְּשׁוֹגֵג חַיָּב לְהָבִיא חַטָּאת קְבוּעָה בִּזְמַן הַבַּיִת. וְאִם שָׁכַב עִם אַחַת מִן הַשְּׁנִיּוֹת, לוֹקֶה מַכַּת מַרְדּוּת.

[שֶׁלֹּא לְגַלּוֹת עֶרְוַת אָחוֹת בְּכָל צַד שֶׁהִיא אָחוֹת]

קצב שֶׁלֹּא לְגַלּוֹת עֶרְוַת אָחוֹת, בֵּין שֶׁהִיא אָחוֹת מֵאָב לְבַד בֵּין שֶׁהִיא אָחוֹת מֵאֵם לְבַד, וּבֵין שֶׁהִיא אָחוֹת מֵאֲנוּסַת אָבִיו וּבֵין שֶׁהִיא אָחוֹת מֵאֵם מִן הַזְּנוּת, בְּכָל צְדָדִין אֵלּוּ נִקְרֵאת אָחוֹת, וְחַיָּבִין עָלֶיהָ, שֶׁנֶּאֱמַר: עֶרְוַת אֲחוֹתְךָ בַת אָבִיךָ אוֹ

3. TB Yevamoth 21a.

4. In the first edition this phrase, *'ésheth 'avi 'avi z'kéno*, appears as *'ésheth 'avi 'immo z'kéno*, "the wife of his mother's father, his grandfather." Not only is this out of place here, but it is mentioned in the very next sentence. In subsequent editions the phrase was omitted (it is likewise absent in MS Parma 741).

5. I.e. but not the wife of a mother's grandfather; so Ze'iri in TB Sanhedrin 53a, and MT *hilchoth 'ishuth* i 6.

6. TB Sanhedrin 58a.

7. *Ibid.* 57b.

8. I.e. those banned only by the Sages; see two and three paragraphs above.

9. See §24, note 14.

wife, even if she is not his grandmother.[3] So too, they banned the wife of one's paternal great-grandfather; and likewise the wife of one's paternal grandfather's paternal grandfather;[4] and so on further back, even to Jacob the Patriarch.[3]

Similarly, as a protective "fence" about this prohibition, they banned the wife of one's mother's father alone,[5] the reason [for not extending it further back] being that the core of this prohibition concerns the fathers, specifically the father's wife. Therefore they (of blessed memory) were more stringent on the side of the fathers, and they ruled that there the ban should extend back endlessly. On the mother's side, however, they decreed a ban on none but the wife of the mother's father alone. This is similar to the distinction of which we wrote above, about the ban on the mother (§190). The rest of its details are in those places that we will list below, at the end of the *sidrah* (§211).

This is one of the forbidden consanguineous relations about which all mankind generally was commanded.[6] Yet there is a difference [in this] between the Israelites and the other nations: For among the other nations, [a woman] is not called one's father's wife except by virtue of [their] conjugal intimacy;[7] while among Israelites it is even by virtue of *kiddushin* ("consecration," betrothal).[2] So too [are they different] in regard to the secondary ones:[8] for there is no ban on secondary ones among the nations, as we said (§190, end).

This prohibition is in effect in every place and every time. If someone violated it and was conjugally intimate with his father's wife—if deliberately, he would incur *karéth* [Divine severance of existence]; if there were witnesses and a [prior] warning, he should be stoned to death; if it was inadvertent, he would be obligated to bring a standard unvarying *ḥattath* when the Temple is in existence. If someone was conjugally intimate with one of the secondary ones,[8] he should receive a whipping for disobedience.[9]

[NOT TO UNCOVER A SISTER'S NAKEDNESS, IF SHE IS ONE'S SISTER IN ANY WAY]

192 not to uncover the nakedness of a sister, whether she is a sister from a common father only, a sister from a common mother only, a sister from the victim of one's father's rape, or a sister from a common mother through immorality. In all these instances she is called a sister, and there is guilt on her account: for it is stated, *The nakedness of your*

בַּת אִמֶּךָ מוֹלֶדֶת בַּיִת אוֹ מוֹלֶדֶת חוּץ [לֹא תְגַלֶּה].

וְאִם תֹּאמַר, אִם־כֵּן מַה זֶּה שֶׁנֶּאֱמַר בַּתּוֹרָה "עֶרְוַת בַּת אֵשֶׁת אָבִיךָ... לֹא תְגַלֶּה", וְלָמָּה הָיָה צָרִיךְ זֶה הַמִּקְרָא, וַהֲלֹא מִשּׁוּם אֲחוֹתוֹ חַיָּב עָלֶיהָ? בֶּאֱמֶת זֶה הַמִּקְרָא לֹא נֶאֱמַר אֶלָּא כְּדֵי שֶׁיָּשִׂים בַּת אֵשֶׁת הָאָב כְּשֶׁתִּהְיֶה אֲחוֹתוֹ עֶרְוָה בִּפְנֵי עַצְמָהּ, וּכְמוֹ שֶׁנִּכְתֹּב לְמַטָּה בִּמְקוֹמוֹ. וְנִמְצָא שֶׁהַבָּא עַל אֲחוֹתוֹ שֶׁהִיא בַּת נְשׂוּאַת אָבִיו שֶׁחַיָּב שְׁתַּיִם, מִשּׁוּם עֶרְוַת אֲחוֹתוֹ וּמִשּׁוּם עֶרְוַת בַּת אֵשֶׁת אָבִיו. וְאִם בָּא עָלֶיהָ בְּשׁוֹגֵג, חַיָּב לְהָבִיא שְׁנֵי חַטָּאוֹת.

מִשָּׁרְשֵׁי אִסּוּר הַקְּרוֹבוֹת, כָּתַבְנוּ בְּעֶרְוַת אֵם מַה שֶּׁיָּדַעְנוּ בָּהֶן.

מִדִּינֵי הַמִּצְוָה, מַה שֶּׁאָמְרוּ זִכְרוֹנָם לִבְרָכָה דַּוְקָא בַּת אֵשֶׁת אָבִיו שֶׁהִיא אֲחוֹתוֹ, כְּלוֹמַר שֶׁהוֹלִידָהּ אָבִיו, הִיא אֲסוּרָה עָלָיו; אֲבָל בַּת אֵשֶׁת אָבִיו שֶׁאֵינָהּ אֲחוֹתוֹ, כְּגוֹן שֶׁאֵשֶׁת אָבִיו (היה) [הָיְתָה] לָהּ בַּת מֵאִישׁ אַחֵר, זוֹ אֵינָהּ אֲסוּרָה כְּלָל, אֶלָּא מֻתָּר לוֹ לָאָדָם לִשָּׂא אוֹתָהּ לְכַתְּחִלָּה, וְלָא גָזְרִינָן אַטּוּ אֲחוֹתוֹ, שֶׁאֵין כָּאן מָקוֹם לִגְזֵרָה כְּלָל.

וְנוֹהֶגֶת בְּכָל מָקוֹם וּבְכָל זְמָן. וְעוֹבֵר עָלֶיהָ וְשָׁכַב אֶת אֲחוֹתוֹ בְּמֵזִיד, חַיָּב כָּרֵת לְבַד, כְּלוֹמַר שֶׁאֲפִלּוּ בְעֵדִים וְהַתְרָאָה אֵין בַּדָּבָר אֶלָּא חִיּוּב כָּרֵת; וּבְשׁוֹגֵג מֵבִיא חַטָּאת קְבוּעָה.

וְזֹאת מִן הָעֲרָיוֹת שֶׁנִּצְטַוּוּ עָלֶיהָ כָּל בְּנֵי הָעוֹלָם בִּכְלָל, אֲבָל חִלּוּק יֵשׁ בָּהּ בֵּין יִשְׂרָאֵל לִשְׁאָר הָאֻמּוֹת, שֶׁבִּשְׁאָר הָאֻמּוֹת אֵין אָסוּר עֲלֵיהֶם אֶלָּא אֲחוֹתָם מֵאֵם לְבַד, וּבְיִשְׂרָאֵל בֵּין מֵאָב בֵּין מֵאֵם. וּכְלָל זֶה יִהְיֶה בְיָדְךָ בְּכָל מַה שֶּׁנִּצְטַוּוּ הָאֻמּוֹת, שֶׁכָּל זְמַן שֶׁהֵם תַּחַת יָדֵינוּ עָלֵינוּ לַעֲשׂוֹת דִּין בָּהֶם בְּעָבְרָם עַל מִצְוָתָם. וּכְבָר

§192 1. I.e. because she is his father's wife's daughter as well as his sister, which she would not be if she was born out of wedlock.

2. So TB Yevamoth 22b.

3. TB Sotah 43b.

4. I.e. we do not fear that if a person is allowed to marry his father's wife's daughter by another man, people will think any sister is permitted.

5. Explained in §121.

6. TB Sanhedrin 58b; MT *hilchoth m'lachim* ix 5.

sister, the daughter of your father or the daughter of your mother, whether born at home or born abroad [*you shall not uncover*] (Leviticus 18:9).

Now, you might ask: In that case, what is this that the Torah states: *The nakedness of your father's wife's daughter . . . you shall not uncover* (*ibid.* 11)? Why was this verse needed? Is one not punishable for her because she is his sister? Well, in truth, this verse was stated only to make the daughter of one's father's wife, when she is his sister, a forbidden consanguineous relation in that respect,[1] as we will write below, in its proper place (§ 196). Consequently, if anyone is conjugally intimate with his sister who is his father's daughter in wedlock, he is punishable for two violations:[2] because of the nakedness of his sister, and because of the nakedness of his father's wife's daughter. And if he was conjugally intimate with her inadvertently, he would be obligated to bring two *ḥattath* (sin) offerings.

About the root reasons for the ban on consanguineous relations, we wrote in connection with the forbiddenness of the mother (§ 190), what we know of them.

Among the laws of the precept, there is what the Sages of blessed memory taught:[3] that only the daughter of one's father's wife who is his sister, i.e. whom his father sired, is forbidden to him; but a daughter of one's father's wife who is not his sister—for instance, if his father's wife had a daughter by another man—she is not forbidden at all, but is rather permitted for a man to marry from the start. We do not decree any ban [as a "fence" of protective restriction] on account of one's sister;[4] for there is no place here for a protective decree at all.[3]

It applies in every place and every time. If a person violated it and was conjugally intimate with his sister—if deliberately, he is punishable by *karéth* [Divine severance of existence] alone: this means that even if there were witnesses and a [prior] warning, the matter entails nothing other than the punishment of *karéth*. If it was unwitting, he should bring a standard unvarying *ḥattath* (sin-offering).[5]

This is among the forbidden relations about which all mankind was generally commanded; but there is a difference [in the law] between the Israelites and the other nations: For among the other nations, none but a sister from a common mother is forbidden,[6] while for the Israelites the law holds for a sister from either the same father or the same mother. This rule should be ever in your hand about all that the heathen nations were commanded: As long as they are under our dominion, it is for us to enforce the law over them if they

כָּתַבְתִּי לְמַעְלָה בְּסֵדֶר וַיִּשְׁמַע יִתְרוֹ [סי' י"ט] שֶׁהַדִּין שֶׁלָּהֶם לְעוֹלָם הִיא מִיתָה בֵּין מְזִידִין בֵּין שׁוֹגְגִין, וְשֶׁאֵין צְרִיכִין הַתְרָאָה, אֲבָל שְׁנֵי עֵדִים צְרִיכִין אוֹ הוֹדָאַת פִּיהֶם. וּמִן הַדּוֹמֶה שֶׁאַף־עַל־פִּי שֶׁהֵם אֵינָם כְּשֵׁרִים לְהָעִיד עַל יִשְׂרָאֵל, רְאוּיִים הֵם לְהָעִיד זֶה עַל זֶה; וְכֵן הוֹרָה זָקֵן.

[שֶׁלֹּא לְגַלּוֹת עֶרְוַת בַּת הַבֵּן]

קצג שֶׁלֹּא לְגַלּוֹת עֶרְוַת בַּת הַבֵּן, שֶׁנֶּאֱמַר: עֶרְוַת בַּת בִּנְךָ וְכוּלֵי לֹא תְגַלֶּה. וּלְפִי הַדּוֹמֶה כִּי הָאִסּוּר הוּא בֵּין שֶׁהַבֵּן כָּשֵׁר אוֹ אֲפִלּוּ מַמְזֵר, בְּנוֹ הוּא מִכָּל מָקוֹם, וּבֵין שֶׁבַּת הַבֵּן גַּם־כֵּן כְּשֵׁרָה אוֹ אֲפִלּוּ מַמְזֶרֶת.

שֹׁרֶשׁ אִסּוּר הַקְּרוֹבוֹת כְּתַבְתִּיהוּ בְּאִסּוּר עֶרְוַת אֵם [סי' ק"צ].

מִדִּינֵי הַמִּצְוָה, מַה שֶּׁאָסְרוּ זִכְרוֹנָם לִבְרָכָה לְגֶדֶר אִסּוּר זֶה, וְהִיא בַּת בַּת בְּנוֹ בִּלְבַד, וְכֵן בַּת בֶּן בְּנוֹ בִּלְבָד; וְיֵשׁ אוֹמְרִים שֶׁאֵין הֶפְסֵק לְאִסּוּר אֵלּוּ לְעוֹלָם, כִּי כָל יוֹצְאֵי יְרֵכוֹ שֶׁל אָדָם אָסְרוּ עָלָיו עַד סוֹף כָּל הַדּוֹרוֹת; וְיֶתֶר פְּרָטֶיהָ, בְּסוֹף הַסֵּדֶר תִּרְאֶה הֵיכָן הֵם.

וְנוֹהֵג אִסּוּר זֶה בְּכָל מָקוֹם וּבְכָל זְמָן. וְעוֹבֵר עָלֶיהָ וְשָׁכַב אֶת בַּת בְּנוֹ בְּמֵזִיד וְיֵשׁ עֵדִים, חַיָּב שְׂרֵפָה, כְּמוֹ שֶׁאָמְרוּ זִכְרוֹנָם לִבְרָכָה בְּסַנְהֶדְרִין; וְאִם אֵין עֵדִים, חַיָּב כָּרֵת; בְּשׁוֹגֵג, מֵבִיא חַטָּאת קְבוּעָה בִּזְמַן הַבַּיִת; וְאִם שָׁכַב אֶת בַּת בַּת בְּנוֹ, וְכֵן כָּל שְׁאָר הַשְּׁנִיּוֹת, לוֹקֶה מַכַּת מַרְדּוּת.

7. TB *ibid.* 57b.
8. This is probably a scribal error: two witnesses are generally required in Jewish law, but it is clear from *ibid.* that here one is sufficient.
9. Evident from *ibid.*
10. I.e. MT *hilchoth m'lachim* ix 14.

§193 1. Apparent from TB Yevamoth 22a. In Jewish law the term "bastard" (*mamzér*) generally means one born from a forbidden consanguineous relation or through adultery.
2. I.e. but not on a son's great-granddaughter; MT *hilchoth 'ishuth* i 6, based on TB Yevamoth 22a.
3. So Ramban, as cited in *Maggid Mishneh* to MT *ibid.*
4. See §190, note 12.
5. Explained in §121.
6. I.e. those banned only by the Sages.
7. See §24, note 14.

transgress their commandments. I have previously written, above, in *sidrah yithro* (§19), that the proper sentence for them is always death, whether they act deliberately or inadvertently, and they do not require a warning [to be punishable];[7] but there have to be two witnesses[8] or their own confession. And as it seems, although they are not qualified to testify about an Israelite, they are fit to testify about one another;[9] and so the elder scholar [Rambam] ruled.[10]

[THE PROHIBITION OF CONJUGAL INTIMACY WITH THE DAUGHTER OF A SON]

193 not to uncover the nakedness of a son's daughter: as it is stated, *The nakedness of your son's daughter . . . you shall not uncover* (Leviticus 18:10). And it would seem that this ban applies whether the son is legitimate or even a bastard—he is one's son in any case; and so whether the son's daughter is equally legitimate or even a bastard.[1]

As to the root reason for the ban on near relations, I wrote it in connection with the forbiddenness of the mother (§190).

Among the laws of the precept, there is the ban which the Sages decreed, as a "fence" about this prohibition, which is on the daughter of a son's daughter only, and so too on the daughter of a son's son alone.[2] Some say, however, that there is no terminal point ever to the ban on these: because all the descendants of a person were forbidden to him, till the end of all the generations.[3] As to the rest of its details, at the end of the *sidrah* (§211) you will see where they are [located].

This prohibition is in force in every place and every time. If someone transgressed it and was conjugally intimate with his son's daughter willfully, and there were witnesses,[4] he deserves death by burning, as the Sages of blessed memory said in the Talmud tractate *Sanhedrin* (75a). If there were no witnesses, he is punishable by *karéth* [Divine severance of existence]; if it was inadvertent, he should bring a standard unvarying *ḥattath* (sin-offering)[5] when the Temple is in existence. If one had carnal connection with the daughter of his son's daughter, or equally with any other of the secondary ones,[6] he should be whipped with lashes for disobedience.[7]

[שֶׁלֹּא לְגַלּוֹת עֶרְוַת בַּת הַבַּת]

קצד שֶׁלֹּא לְגַלּוֹת עֶרְוַת בַּת הַבַּת, שֶׁנֶּאֱמַר: אוֹ בַת בִּתְּךָ לֹא תְגַלֶּה עֶרְוָתָן כִּי עֶרְוָתְךָ הֵנָּה.

כָּל דִּינֶיהָ כְּדִין בַּת הַבֵּן, וּשְׁנִיּוֹת לָהּ גַּם־כֵּן בַּת בַּת בִּתּוֹ, וְכֵן בַּת בֶּן בִּתּוֹ; וְיֵשׁ שֶׁאוֹמְרִים שֶׁאֵין לָהֶם הֶפְסֵק לְעוֹלָם.

[שֶׁלֹּא לְגַלּוֹת עֶרְוַת הַבַּת]

קצה שֶׁלֹּא לְגַלּוֹת עֶרְוַת הַבַּת; וְזֹאת לֹא נִתְבָּאֲרָה בִּלְשׁוֹן הַתּוֹרָה, שֶׁיֹּאמַר הַכָּתוּב "עֶרְוַת בִּתְּךָ לֹא תְגַלֶּה"; וּמִפְּנֵי־כֵן לֹא בָא עָלֶיהָ כָּתוּב מְפֹרָשׁ, לְפִי שֶׁאֵין צֹרֶךְ בּוֹ; דְּכֵיוָן שֶׁאָסְרָה הַתּוֹרָה בַּת הַבֵּן וּבַת הַבַּת, שֶׁהֵן רְחוֹקוֹת מִמֶּנָּה, אֵין צָרִיךְ לוֹמַר שֶׁהִיא אֲסוּרָה, דְּקַל וָחֹמֶר הוּא. וְעוֹד לְמָדוּהָ זִכְרוֹנָם לִבְרָכָה מִגְּזֵרָה שָׁוָה, דְּאִי מִקַּל וָחֹמֶר גְּרֵידָא הֲוָה יַלְפִינָן לָהּ לֹא הָיָה אָדָם נִדּוֹן עָלֶיהָ, דְּקַיְמָא לָן אֵין עוֹנְשִׁים מִן הַדִּין.

מִשָּׁרְשֵׁי הַמִּצְוָה כָּתַבְנוּ לְמַעְלָה מַה שֶּׁיָּכֹלְנוּ דֶּרֶךְ כְּלָל בְּכָל הָעֲרָיוֹת.

דִּינֵי מִצְוָה זוֹ, כְּלוֹמַר אֵיךְ לְמָדוּהָ זִכְרוֹנָם לִבְרָכָה, וּמֵאֵי זֶה כָּתוּב, בִּגְמָרָא יְבָמוֹת הוּא, שֶׁאָמְרוּ שָׁם בִּתּוֹ עִקַּר אִסּוּרָא מִדְּרָשָׁא אַתְיָה, דְּאָמַר רָבָא: אָמַר לִי רַב יִצְחָק בַּר אַבְדִּימִי: אַתְיָא הֵנָּה הֵנָּה, אַתְיָא זִמָּה זִמָּה, כְּלוֹמַר שֶׁהַכָּתוּב אָמַר בְּבַת הַבֵּן וּבְבַת הַבַּת "עֶרְוָתְךָ הֵנָּה", וְאָמַר בְּאִסּוּר אִשָּׁה וּבִתָּהּ וּבַת בְּנָהּ וּבַת בִּתָּהּ לְשׁוֹן "הֵנָּה", כְּמוֹ שֶׁכָּתוּב בְּסוֹף הַפָּרָשָׁה "שַׁאֲרָה הֵנָּה"; מַה לְּהַלָּן מְפֹרָשׁ שֶׁנֶּאֶסְרָה בִּתָּהּ, שֶׁהֲרֵי בְּפֵרוּשׁ נִכְתְּבָה שָׁם, אַף כָּאן שֶׁאָסַר הַכָּתוּב בַּת בְּנוֹ הוּא

§194 1. I.e. those banned by the Sages, so that no one should think that because they are permissible, the ones prohibited by the Torah are equally permissible.

2. Source in §193, note 2.

3. I.e. the ban of the Sages applies to any female descendant; source in §193, n. 3.

§195 1. From the beginning to here is based on ShM negative precept §336.

2. TB Sanhedrin 76a.

3. The first edition reads *bitto mé'anusatho*, "one's daughter from the victim of his rape" (but this is not in the oldest manuscripts, and would thus seem to be an incorporated later gloss). It is clear from TB Ḥagigah 12b, Sanhedrin 87b and K'rithoth 5a that this is the daughter meant here (so also Rashi in Yevamoth 3a s.v. *'ikar 'isuraihu*); for as our author explains below, a daughter from a lawfully wedded wife is forbidden under the ban of Leviticus 18:17.

[THE PROHIBITION OF CONJUGAL INTIMACY WITH A DAUGHTER'S DAUGHTER]

194 not to uncover the nakedness of a daughter's daughter: for it is written, *or of your daughter's daughter, even their nakedness you shall not uncover, for theirs is your own nakedness* (Leviticus 18:10).

All its laws are as the laws of a son's daughter. Its "secondary ones"[1] are likewise the daughter of one's daughter's daughter, and so too the daughter of one's daughter's son;[2] and some say there is no terminal point for them ever.[3]

[THE PROHIBITION OF CONJUGAL INTIMACY WITH A DAUGHTER]

195 not to uncover a daughter's nakedness. This was not made clear in the text of the Torah, by the Writ's saying, "the nakedness of your daughter you shall not uncover." But no verse was given for it explicitly for the [simple] reason that there is no need for it: Since the Torah forbade a son's daughter and a daughter's daughter, who are more distant relations than she is, there is no need to declare that she is forbidden, as it is a *kal va-ḥomer*, an inference by reasoning *a fortiori*, from the less to the more.[1] In addition, our Sages of blessed memory learned it by a *g'zérah shavah*, a deduction from identical terms in two verses. For if we derived it from a *kal va-ḥomer* alone, no man would be sentenced for it, since we have an established rule:[2] no punishment is given over something inferred by reasoning *a fortiori*.

What lies at the root of the precept, we wrote above (§190), what we were able to in a general way, about all the forbidden women.

The laws of this precept, i.e. how the Sages of blessed memory derived it, and from which verse—this is [all] in the Talmud tractate *Yevamoth* (3a). It was stated there: As to one's daughter,[3] the essential prohibition is derived from an inference. For Rava said: R. Yitzḥak b. 'Avdimi told me: It is derived from the common term *hénah* ("they are"), and from the common term *zimmah* ("lewdness"). That is to say: the Writ states about both a son's daughter and a daughter's daughter, *ervath'cha hénah* (theirs is your own nakedness; Leviticus 18:10); and it states about the prohibition of marrying a woman and her daughter or her son's daughter or daughter's daughter, the term *hénah*—as it is written at the end of the section, *sha'arah hénah* (they are near kinswomen; *ibid.* 17). Just as it is explicit there (verse 17) that her daughter is forbidden, since it is written distinctly there, so

הַדִּין לְבִתּוֹ, אַף־עַל־פִּי שֶׁלֹּא פֵּרְשָׁהּ הַכָּתוּב, דְּגָמְרִינָן לָהּ בִּגְזֵרָה שָׁוָה זוֹ.

וְעוֹד לָמְדוּ זִכְרוֹנָם לִבְרָכָה מִכֹּחַ גְּזֵרָה שָׁוָה זוֹ, בְּאֵי זוֹ מִיתָה נִדּוֹן הַבָּא עַל בִּתּוֹ אוֹ עַל בַּת בְּנוֹ וּבַת בִּתּוֹ; וְאַף־עַל־פִּי שֶׁאֵין מִשְׁפַּט הַמִּיתָה כָּתוּב בַּמִּקְרָא שֶׁל עֶרְוַת אִשָּׁה וּבִתָּהּ וּבַת בְּנָהּ וּבַת בִּתָּהּ, לְמָדוּהָ זִכְרוֹנָם לִבְרָכָה מִמֶּנּוּ אַחַר שֶׁנִּלְמַד בּוֹ מִמָּקוֹם אַחֵר; וּמֵאֵי זֶה מָקוֹם אַחֵר נִלְמַד בּוֹ, מִמַּה שֶּׁכָּתוּב: וְאִישׁ אֲשֶׁר יִקַּח אֶת אִשָּׁה וְאֶת אִמָּהּ זִמָּה הִיא בָּאֵשׁ יִשְׂרְפוּ אֹתוֹ וְאֶתְהֶן, וְאָמְרוּ זִכְרוֹנָם לִבְרָכָה: מַה הָתָם, בְּאִשָּׁה וְאִמָּהּ, דִּכְתִיב בְּהוּ זִמָּה, בִּשְׂרֵפָה, אַף הָכָא בְּאִשָּׁה וּבִתָּהּ וּבַת בְּנָהּ וּבַת בִּתָּהּ, דִּכְתִיב בְּהוּ "שַׁאֲרָה הֵנָּה זִמָּה הִיא" נִדּוֹן בִּשְׂרֵפָה.

וּמֵעַתָּה, אַחַר שֶׁמָּצָאנוּ כִּי מִשְׁפַּט אִשָּׁה וּבִתָּהּ וּבַת בְּנָהּ וּבַת בִּתָּהּ בִּשְׂרֵפָה, מִכֹּחַ גְּזֵרָה שָׁוָה זוֹ דְזִמָּה זִמָּה, יֵשׁ לָנוּ לִלְמֹד גַּם־כֵּן כִּי מִשְׁפַּט הַבָּא עַל בִּתּוֹ וּבַת בְּנוֹ וּבַת בִּתּוֹ בִּשְׂרֵפָה, לְפִי שֶׁכְּבָר לָמַדְנוּ מִמֶּנּוּ אִסּוּר עַל בִּתּוֹ בִּגְזֵרָה שָׁוָה דְהֵנָּה הֵנָּה, וְכֵיוָן שֶׁלָּמַדְנוּ מִמֶּנָּה דָּבָר אֶחָד, נִלְמַד מִמֶּנּוּ עוֹד כָּל שְׁאָר הַדִּינִין שֶׁבּוֹ, וְנֹאמַר שֶׁמִּשְׁפַּט הַבָּא עַל בִּתּוֹ גַּם־כֵּן בִּשְׂרֵפָה.

וְעַל כַּיּוֹצֵא בָזֶה יֹאמְרוּ בַּגְּמָרָא: דּוֹן מִנָּהּ וּמִנָּהּ, כְּלוֹמַר כְּשֶׁנִּלְמַד כָּתוּב אֶחָד מֵחֲבֵרוֹ לֹא לְדָבָר אֶחָד שֶׁבּוֹ לְבַד נִלְמְדֵהוּ אֶלָּא לְכָל מִשְׁפָּטָיו נִלְמְדֵהוּ מִמֶּנּוּ; וְאַף־עַל־פִּי שֶׁאוֹתָן מִשְׁפָּטִים שֶׁבּוֹ אֵינָם כְּמַשְׁמָעוּתוֹ שֶׁלַּכָּתוּב בְּעַצְמוֹ אֶלָּא שֶׁנִּלְמְדֵם מִכְּתוּבִים אֲחֵרִים, אַף־עַל־פִּי־כֵן כָּל מַה שֶּׁיֵּשׁ בּוֹ, בֵּין מִגּוּפֵיהּ דִּקְרָא בֵּין שֶׁנִּלְמַד מִמָּקוֹם אַחֵר, נִלְמַד מִמֶּנּוּ.

וְאָמְרוּ זִכְרוֹנָם לִבְרָכָה בִּגְמָרָא כְּרֵתוֹת: אַל תְּהִי גְזֵרָה שָׁוָה קַלָּה בְעֵינֶיךָ, שֶׁהֲרֵי

4. I.e. from the case of conjugal intimacy with a mother and her daughter, etc. (to which the incest of father and daughter is equated by the *g'zérah shavah*). The next "this" refers to the death-penalty for mating with both a mother and her daughter; as the author notes, it is not given explicitly in the Scriptural verse about the transgression.

5. TB Sanhedrin 75b.

6. E.g. TB Yevamoth 78b, Bava Kamma 25a.

here too (verse 10), where the Writ forbade one's son's daughter, the same law holds for one's daughter, even if Scripture did not state it openly—since we learn it from this *g'zérah shavah* (equivalence of terms).

Our Sages learned further, on the strength of this *g'zérah shavah*, to which death one is sentenced for conjugal intimacy with his daughter, his son's daughter, or his daughter's daughter. Even though the form of death is not written in the verse about forbidden intimacy with a woman and her daughter, her son's daughter, or her daughter's daughter, they (of blessed memory) derived it from this[4] after we learned this from another place. From which other place do we learn this?—from the verse, *And if a man takes a wife and her mother also, it is* zimmah, *lewdness; they shall be burned with fire, both he and they* (Leviticus 20:14). And so our Sages of blessed memory said:[5] Just as there, in the case of a woman and her mother, where the term *zimmah* is written, the death is by burning, so here too, in the case of a woman and her daughter, her son's daughter, or her daughter's daughter, where it is written, *they are near kinswomen; it is* zimmah, *lewdness* (Leviticus 18:17), the sentence is by burning.

Hence, now that we have found that the verdict for a woman and her daughter, her son's daughter, or her daughter's daughter, is death by burning, on the strength of this *g'zérah shavah*, the identity of the term *zimmah* [in the two verses], we can learn likewise that the sentence of one who is conjugally intimate with his daughter, his son's daughter, or his daughter's daughter, is death by burning—since we have already learned from it [Leviticus 18:17] the prohibition on his daughter by the *g'zérah shavah* (identity) of the term *hénah*; and once we have learned one thing from it, we can learn from it all the other laws that it contains, and so conclude that the verdict for one who is conjugally intimate with his daughter is death by burning.

About something like this it would be said in the Talmud,[6] "Learn from it, and [again] from it." In other words, when we learn about one verse from another, it is not for one point alone in it that we learn from it, but we are to derive all its rules from it. And even if these rules about it are not in the direct meaning of the verse itself but are derived from other verses, nevertheless, all that is valid about it, whether [known] from the verse itself or learned from somewhere else, we may derive from it.

⟨315⟩ In the Talmud tractate *K'rithoth* (5a) our Sages of blessed memory

בִּתּוֹ אֶחָד מִגּוּפֵי תּוֹרָה הִיא וְלֹא לְמָדָהּ הַכָּתוּב אֶלָּא בִּגְזֵרָה שָׁוָה, אָתְיָא הֵנָּה הֵנָּה אָתְיָא זִמָּה זִמָּה — כְּלוֹמַר שֶׁבִּשְׁתֵּי גְזֵרוֹת שָׁווֹת אֵלּוּ לָמַדְנוּ אִסּוּרָהּ וּמִשְׁפָּטָהּ, וּכְמוֹ שֶׁפֵּרַשְׁנוּ.

(אֲבָל בִּתּוֹ מִנְּשׂוּאָתוֹ מְפֹרָשׁ הִיא בַּמִּקְרָא, מִדִּכְתִיב: עֶרְוַת אִשָּׁה וּבִתָּהּ; וְאֵין חִלּוּק בֵּין שֶׁהִיא בִּתּוֹ וּבִתָּהּ אוֹ מֵאִישׁ אַחֵר; וְזֶה מְדַבֵּר בִּנְשׂוּאָה מִדִּכְתִיב "אִשָּׁה" דְּמַשְׁמַע לְשׁוֹן אִישׁוּת, וּכְתִיב נָמֵי "לֹא תִקָּח", וְקִיחָה מַשְׁמַע גַּם־כֵּן דֶּרֶךְ אִישׁוּת; אֲבָל גַּבֵּי בִּתּוֹ מֵאֲנוּסָתוֹ וּבַת בְּנוֹ וּבַת בִּתּוֹ לָא כְתִיב אֶלָּא "לֹא תְגַלֶּה".)

וְכָתַב הָרַמְבַּ"ם זִכְרוֹנוֹ לִבְרָכָה: הַבֵּט אָמְרָם זִכְרוֹנָם לִבְרָכָה "לֹא לְמָדָהּ הַכָּתוּב", וְלֹא אָמְרוּ "וְלֹא לְמַדְנוּהָ", לְפִי שֶׁאֵלֶּה הָעִנְיָנִים כֻּלָּם הֵם קַבָּלָה מֵהַשָּׁלִיחַ עָלָיו הַשָּׁלוֹם, שֶׁמָּסַר הַפֵּרוּשׁ אֶל הַזְּקֵנִים; וְזֶהוּ אָמְרָם עַל זֶה גּוּף תּוֹרָה.

וְהֵבִיאוּ לָרַב זִכְרוֹנוֹ לִבְרָכָה לִכְתֹּב דָּבָר זֶה, הָעִקָּר הַקָּבוּעַ לוֹ שֶׁאֵין בְּחֶשְׁבּוֹן תרי"ג הַמִּצְווֹת אֶלָּא מַה שֶּׁמְּפֹרָשׁ בַּכָּתוּב, אוֹ מַה שֶּׁיֹּאמְרוּ זִכְרוֹנָם לִבְרָכָה עָלָיו בְּפֵרוּשׁ שֶׁהוּא מִן הַתּוֹרָה, אֲבָל לֹא כָל מַה שֶּׁנִּלְמַד בִּשְׁלֹש־עֶשְׂרֵה מִדּוֹת. וּכְבָר סָתַר הָרַמְבַּ"ן זִכְרוֹנוֹ לִבְרָכָה עִנְיָן זֶה בִּרְאָיוֹת בְּרוּרוֹת.

דִּינֵי הַמִּצְוָה בְּסוֹף הַסֵּדֶר נִכְתֹּב מְקוֹמָן, עִם כָּל הָעֲרָיוֹת בִּכְלָל.

וְנוֹהֵג אִסּוּר זֶה בְּכָל מָקוֹם וּבְכָל זְמָן. וְעוֹבֵר עַל זֶה וְשָׁכַב אֶת בִּתּוֹ מֵאֲנוּסָתוֹ בְּמֵזִיד וְיֵשׁ עֵדִים, נִדּוֹן בִּשְׂרֵפָה; בְּלֹא עֵדִים חַיָּב כָּרֵת, בְּשׁוֹגֵג חַיָּב חַטָּאת קְבוּעָה.

7. Here again the first edition has *bitto mé'anusatho*, in keeping with our editions of the Talmud; but neither is this in the oldest manuscripts. See note 3.

7a. This paragraph is not in the oldest manuscripts, and would thus seem a later addition.

8. ShM negative precept §336.

9. So ShM root principle 2. Hence he must insist that Moses gave the law explicitly, but only orally; and the *g'zérah shavah* would thus merely provide support for it.

10. In his commentary (*hassagoth*) to *ibid.*

said: Let not *g'zérah shavah* be a trivial matter in your eyes, for here [the ban on] one's daughter[7] is one of the main laws of the Torah, and Scripture did not teach it by any other means but *g'zérah shavah*: there are the identical terms *hénah*, and the identical terms *zimmah*. This is to say that with these two instances of *g'zérah shavah* we learn its prohibition and its death sentence, as we have explained.

Now, one's daughter by his lawfully married wife is, on the other hand, dealt with explicitly in Scripture, since it is written, *The nakedness of a woman and her daughter* (Leviticus 18:17), and it makes no difference if she is both his and her daughter or [her daughter] by another man; and this speaks of a married woman, since it is written, *'ishah* (a woman), which connotes one married. It is written, further, *do not take* (*ibid.*), which similarly connotes by marriage. However, about one's daughter from a victim of his rape, his son's daughter, or his daughter's daughter, we find written nothing but *you shall not uncover* (Leviticus 18:10).[7a]

Well, Rambam of blessed memory wrote:[8] Notice that the Sages of blessed memory said, "and Scripture did not teach it," but they did not say, "and we did not learn it"—because all these matters are elements of Oral Tradition from the messenger [of the Eternal Lord, Moses] peace be with him, who transmitted the explanation to the elders. In this sense they spoke of it as "a main law of the Torah."

What moved the master (of blessed memory) to write this thought is a main principle that is firmly established for him, that the reckoning of the 613 precepts may include no more than what is given explicitly in the Writ, or something about which the Sages of blessed memory said distinctly that is a law of the Torah, but not anything that we derive by the thirteen rules of Scriptural interpretation.[9] Long ago, however, Ramban of blessed memory disproved this thesis with clear proofs.[10]

As to the laws of the precept, at the end of the *sidrah* (§211) we will write their location [in the Talmud], together with all those forbidden, in general. This prohibition is in force in every time and every place. If a person transgresses it and is conjugally intimate with his daughter from a victim of his rape, if it was deliberate and there were witnesses, he is sentenced to death by burning. If it was without witnesses, he is punishable by *karéth* [Divine severance of existence]; and if it was inadvertent, he is obligated to bring a standard unvarying *ḥattath* (sin-offering).

If a person was conjugally intimate with his daughter from his

וְאִם שָׁכַב אֶת בִּתּוֹ מִנְּשׂוּאָתוֹ חַיָּב שְׁתֵּי חַטָּאוֹת, אַחַת מִשּׁוּם בִּתּוֹ וְאַחַת מִשּׁוּם עֶרְוַת אִשָּׁה וּבִתָּהּ, שֶׁאֵין חִיּוּב עֶרְוַת אִשָּׁה וּבִתָּהּ אֶלָּא בִנְשׂוּאֵי הָרִאשׁוֹנָה, שֶׁהֲרֵי בְּפֵרוּשׁ כְּתִיב בָּהֶן "לֹא תִקַּח", בֵּין בִּמְקוֹם הָאַזְהָרָה עֲלֵיהֶן בֵּין בִּמְקוֹם הָעֹנֶשׁ, וּלְשׁוֹן קִיחָה מַשְׁמָע לָן לְשׁוֹן נִשּׂוּאִין.

וּמִפְּנֵי־כֵן אָמְרוּ זִכְרוֹנָם לִבְרָכָה כִּי מִדִּין הַתּוֹרָה הוּא שֶׁאִם אָנַס אָדָם אִשָּׁה מֻתָּר הָיָה לִשָּׂא בִתָּהּ, אֶלָּא שֶׁחֲכָמִים זִכְרוֹנָם לִבְרָכָה גָּדְרוּ גָדֵר וְאָסְרוּ הַדָּבָר, וְאָמְרוּ שֶׁמִּי שֶׁנָּאַף אִשָּׁה אָסוּר לִשָּׂא אַחַת מִן הַשֶּׁבַע נָשִׁים קְרוֹבוֹתֶיהָ הַיְּדוּעוֹת כָּל זְמַן שֶׁהַזּוֹנָה קַיֶּמֶת, מִפְּנֵי שֶׁהַזּוֹנָה בָּאָה לְבַקֵּר אוֹתָן, וְהוּא מִתְיַחֵד עִמָּהּ וְלִבּוֹ גַס בָּהּ, וְיָבוֹא לִידֵי עֲבֵרָה שֶׁיִּבְעַל הָעֶרְוָה; וְלֹא עוֹד אֶלָּא אֲפִלּוּ נִטְעַן עַל אִשָּׁה הֲרֵי זֶה לֹא יִשָּׂא אַחַת מִקְּרוֹבוֹתֶיהָ עַד שֶׁתָּמוּת זוֹ שֶׁנִּטְעַן עָלֶיהָ. וּמִכָּל־מָקוֹם אִם כְּנָסָהּ לָזוֹ שֶׁקְּרוֹבָה לְאוֹתָהּ שֶׁזָּנְתָה עִמּוֹ, אֵין מַצְרִיכִין אוֹתוֹ לְהוֹצִיאָהּ.

וְעוֹד אָמְרוּ זִכְרוֹנָם לִבְרָכָה בְּעִנְיָן זֶה שֶׁכָּל מִי שֶׁנִּטְעַן עַל עֶרְוָה אוֹ שֶׁיָּצָא לוֹ שֵׁם רַע עִמָּהּ, שֶׁלֹּא יָדוּר עִמָּהּ בְּמָבוֹי אֶחָד וְלֹא יֵרָאֶה בְאוֹתָהּ הַשְּׁכוּנָה. אָנַס אָבִיו אוֹ בְנוֹ אוֹ אָחִיו אִשָּׁה, אוֹ פִתּוּ אוֹתָהּ, הֲרֵי זוֹ מֻתֶּרֶת לִשָּׂא אוֹתָהּ, שֶׁלֹּא נֶאֶסְרוּ אֶלָּא דֶרֶךְ אִישׁוּת, וְאֵין כָּאן אִישׁוּת; וְלֹא הֶחְמִירוּ זִכְרוֹנָם לִבְרָכָה גַּם־כֵּן לַעֲשׂוֹת גָּדֵר לְאֶחָד מִשּׁוּם זְנוּת שֶׁל קְרוֹבוֹ.

[שֶׁלֹּא לְגַלּוֹת עֶרְוַת אָחוֹת מִן הָאָב וְהִיא בַת אֵשֶׁת אָבִיו]

קצו שֶׁלֹּא לְגַלּוֹת עֶרְוַת בַּת אֵשֶׁת אָבִיו כְּשֶׁתִּהְיֶה אֲחוֹתוֹ, כְּלוֹמַר שֶׁהִיא בַת

11. So MT *hilchoth 'issuré bi'ah* ii 6.

12. So TB Yevamoth 97a.

13. Leviticus 18:17.

14. Leviticus 20:14 (i.e. the verb "taking" is equally used there).

15. TB Yevamoth 97a.

16. *Ibid.*

17. I.e. her mother, two grandmothers, daughter, son's daughter, daughter's daughter, and her sister; TB Yevamoth 40b.

18. TB Yevamoth 97a.

19. Tosefta, Yevamoth iv; MT *hilchoth 'issuré bi'ah* ii 11.

20. MT *ibid.* 12, derived from TB Kiddushin 12b (*Maggid Mishneh*).

21. TB Yevamoth 97a, 26a; MT *ibid.* 13.

lawfully wedded wife, he would be obligated to bring two *hattath* (sin) offerings: one because she was his daughter, and one on account of "the nakedness of a woman and her daughter" (Leviticus 18:17);[11] for there is no guilt for "the nakedness of a woman and her daughter" unless there was marriage with the first [of them],[12] since it is expressly written about them, *you shall not take* (*ibid.*), both at the place of the admonition about them[13] and where the punishment is specified;[14] and the expression of "taking" denotes for us the sense of marriage.

For this reason the Sages of blessed memory taught that by the law of the Torah, if a man raped a woman, he should be permitted to marry her daughter [by another man];[15] but the Sages of blessed memory erected a "fence" and banned the matter,[16] ruling that if someone had immoral conjugal relations with a woman, he is forbidden to marry any one of her seven known female relatives[17] as long as the immoral woman is alive:[18] because the immoral woman will come to visit them, and he will be alone with her, and since his heart is overly familiar with her, he will be led into the grip of sin, and be conjugally intimate with an absolutely forbidden woman. Nay, even more: if a man is but suspected of immorality with a woman, he is not to marry any of her near relatives until the one about whom he is suspected dies. Nevertheless, if he did wed a woman who is closely related to the one with whom he was immorally intimate, he is not required [or compelled] to divorce her.[19]

Further, our Sages of blessed memory taught on this subject[18] that if anyone is suspected about a forbidden woman, or if a bad reputation has spread about him in regard to her, he should not live with her in one lane, nor appear in that neigborhood.[20] If a person's father, son, or brother raped a woman, or if any of them seduced her, she is permitted to him to marry her: for they [such women] were not forbidden except through marriage, and there was no marriage here; and the Sages of blessed memory likewise were not stringent to add a "fence" (protective restriction) [to forbid a woman] to a person on account of immorality with his near relative.[21]

[THE PROHIBITION OF CONJUGAL RELATIONS WITH A SISTER ON THE FATHER'S SIDE WHO IS THE FATHER'S WIFE'S DAUGHTER]

196 not to uncover the nakedness of the daughter of one's father's

wife in the event that she is his sister: in other words, if she is his father's

אָבִיו, שֶׁאִלּוּ בַּת אֵשֶׁת אָבִיו שֶׁאֵינָהּ אֲחוֹתוֹ, כְּבָר אָמַרְנוּ לְמַעְלָה שֶׁמֻּתָּר לִשָּׂא אוֹתָהּ לְאִשָּׁה לְכַתְּחִלָּה, אֶלָּא פֵּרוּשׁוֹ בַּת אֵשֶׁת אָבִיו וְהִיא אֲחוֹתוֹ — שֶׁנֶּאֱמַר: עֶרְוַת בַּת אֵשֶׁת אָבִיךָ ... לֹא תְגַלֶּה.

וּכְבָר כָּתַבְתִּי לְמַעְלָה בְּעֶרְוַת אָחוֹת, שֶׁהַלָּאו הַזֶּה בָּא כְּדֵי שֶׁיָּשִׂים אֲחוֹתוֹ מִנְּשׂוּאַת אָבִיו עֶרְוָה בִּפְנֵי עַצְמָהּ, וּכְעֵין מַה שֶּׁאָמַרְנוּ בְּאִמּוֹ שֶׁאִם הִיא אֵשֶׁת אָב חַיָּב בָּהּ שְׁתַּיִם, מִשּׁוּם אֵם וּמִשּׁוּם אֵשֶׁת אָב. וְהָרְאָיָה מַה שֶּׁאָמְרוּ זִכְרוֹנָם לִבְרָכָה בִּיבָמוֹת: תָּנוּ רַבָּנָן: הַבָּא עַל אֲחוֹתוֹ וְהִיא בַּת אֵשֶׁת אָבִיו, חַיָּב מִשּׁוּם אָחוֹת וּמִשּׁוּם בַּת אֵשֶׁת אָבִיו. רַבִּי יוֹסֵי בְּרַבִּי יְהוּדָה אוֹמֵר: אֵינוֹ חַיָּב אֶלָּא מִשּׁוּם אֲחוֹתוֹ בִּלְבָד. מַאי טַעְמַיְהוּ דְּרַבָּנָן, אָמְרֵי: מִכְּדִי כְּתִיב "עֶרְוַת אֲחוֹתְךָ בַת אָבִיךָ" וְגוֹמֵר, "עֶרְוַת בַּת אֵשֶׁת אָבִיךָ מוֹלֶדֶת אָבִיךָ" לָמָּה לִי? שְׁמַע מִנָּהּ לְחַיְּבוֹ מִשּׁוּם אֲחוֹתוֹ וּמִשּׁוּם בַּת אֵשֶׁת אָבִיו.

נִמְצָא שֶׁהַשּׁוֹכֵב עִם אָחוֹת שֶׁהִיא מֵאֲנוּסַת אָבִיו, אֵין בָּהּ אֶלָּא לָאו אֶחָד, וְהַשּׁוֹכֵב עִם אָחוֹת שֶׁהִיא מִנְּשׂוּאַת אָבִיו יִתְחַיֵּב שְׁנֵי לָאוִין, וּבְשׁוֹגֵג חַיָּב לְהָבִיא שְׁתֵּי חַטָּאוֹת. וּמִשְׁפְּטֵי הַשֵּׁם צָדְקוּ, כִּי אַחַר שֶׁתַּרְחִיק הַתּוֹרָה קִרְבַת הָאָחוֹת, רָאוּי לְהַחְמִיר בְּאוֹתָהּ שֶׁהִיא אָחוֹת גְּמוּרָה, רְצוֹנִי לוֹמַר מִן הַנְּשׂוּאִין, כִּי הִיא נִקְרֵאת אָחוֹת אֱמֶת. וּכְעִנְיָן זֶה כָּתַב הָרַמְבָּ"ן זִכְרוֹנוֹ לִבְרָכָה.

דִּינֵי הַמִּצְוָה, בְּסוֹף הַסֵּדֶר תִּרְאֶה הֵיכָן הֵם. וְנוֹהֵג אִסּוּר זֶה בְּכָל מָקוֹם וּבְכָל זְמַן. וְעוֹבֵר עַל זֶה וְשָׁכַב אֶת אֲחוֹתוֹ מִנְּשׂוּאַת אָבִיו בְּמֵזִיד, חַיָּב כָּרֵת; בְּשׁוֹגֵג מֵבִיא שְׁתֵּי חַטָּאוֹת, כְּמוֹ שֶׁאָמַרְנוּ.

§196 1. The oldest manuscripts and first edition read "his father's wife's daughter," but this is clearly a scribal error.

2. From the beginning to here is based on ShM negative precept §333.

3. Expression based on Psalms 19:10.

4. Ramban, commentary, Leviticus 18:9.

daughter;[1] for if she is a daughter of his father's wife who is not his sister, we have already stated above (§192) that he is permitted from the start to take her for a wife. Thus it only means a daughter of his father's wife who is his sister—as it is stated, *The nakedness of your father's wife's daughter, begotten of your father . . . you shall not uncover* (Leviticus 18:11).

I have already written, above, about the forbiddance of a sister (§192), that this injunction was given to make a daughter from one's father's marriage forbidden by a separate [extra] ban. It is akin to what we said about one's mother, that if she is the father's wife, he is guilty of two sins on her account: because of "mother" and because of "father's wife." Proof of this lies in what the Sages of blessed memory said in the tractate *Yevamoth* (22b): Our Sages taught: If someone was conjugally intimate with his sister who was the daughter of his father's wife, he is punishable on account of "sister" and on account of "the daughter of his father's wife." R. Yosé b. R. Judah said: He is guilty solely because she is his sister. What is the Sages' reason?—they would say: Since it is written, *The nakedness of your sister, the daughter of your father*, etc. (Leviticus 18:9), why do I need the verse, *The nakedness of your father's wife's daughter, begotten of your father*? Then infer from it to impose punishment on him because she is his sister and because she is his father's wife's daughter.

Consequently, if someone is conjugally intimate with a sister who was born to a victim of his father's rape, there is no more than one negative precept about her. But if one is thus intimate with a sister from his father's wife, he is punishable over two negative precepts; and if he acted unwittingly, he would be obligated to bring two *ḥattath* (sin) offerings.[2] And the ordinances of the Eternal Lord are righteous:[3] for after the Torah rules out intimacy with a sister, it is right to be more stringent about one who is a real sister, by which I mean by [the father's] marriage; for she is called a true sister. And in this vein Ramban of blessed memory wrote.[4]

As to the laws of the precept, at the end of the *sidrah* (§211) you will see where they are [to be found]. This prohibition is in effect in every place and time. If someone violated it and was conjugally intimate with his sister from his father's marriage—if deliberately, he deserves *karéth* [Divine severance of existence]; if unwittingly, he should bring two *ḥattath* (sin) offerings, as we stated.

[שֶׁלֹּא לְגַלּוֹת עֶרְוַת אֲחוֹת אָב]

קצז שֶׁלֹּא לָבוֹא עַל אֲחוֹת הָאָב, שֶׁנֶּאֱמַר: עֶרְוַת אֲחוֹת אָבִיךָ לֹא תְגַלֵּה וְגוֹמֵר.

מִשָּׁרְשֵׁי הָעֲרָיוֹת, כָּתַבְנוּ מַה שֶּׁיָּדַעְנוּ.

מִדִּינֵי הַמִּצְוָה, מַה שֶּׁאָמְרוּ זִכְרוֹנָם לִבְרָכָה שֶׁאִסּוּר אֲחוֹת אָב, בֵּין שֶׁהִיא אָחוֹת לְאָבִיו מִן הָאָב לְבַד אוֹ מִן הָאֵם לְבַד, וּבֵין שֶׁהִיא אֲחוֹתוֹ מִן הַנִּשּׂוּאִין בֵּין מִן הַזְּנוּת, שֶׁכָּל אַחַת מֵאֵלּוּ מִכָּל־מָקוֹם אֲחוֹת אָבִיו נִקְרֵאת. וְאֵין כָּאן מָקוֹם לִשְׁנִיּוֹת.

דִּינֵי הַמִּצְוָה, בְּסוֹף הַסֵּדֶר תִּרְאֶה מְקוֹמָן.

וְנוֹהֵג אִסּוּר זֶה בְּכָל מָקוֹם וּבְכָל זְמָן. וְעוֹבֵר עָלֶיהָ וְשָׁכַב אֶת אֲחוֹת אָבִיו, בְּמֵזִיד חַיָּב כָּרֵת, בְּשׁוֹגֵג מֵבִיא חַטָּאת קְבוּעָה.

[שֶׁלֹּא לְגַלּוֹת עֶרְוַת אֲחוֹת אֵם]

קצח שֶׁלֹּא לָבוֹא עַל אֲחוֹת אֵם, שֶׁנֶּאֱמַר: עֶרְוַת אֲחוֹת אִמְּךָ לֹא תְגַלֵּה וְגוֹמֵר. כָּל עִנְיָנָהּ כְּמוֹ אֲחוֹת אָב.

[שֶׁלֹּא לָבוֹא עַל אֲחִי הָאָב]

קצט שֶׁלֹּא לָבוֹא עַל אֲחִי הָאָב, וּמִן הַדּוֹמֶה שֶׁאֵין הֶפְרֵשׁ בֵּין שֶׁיִּהְיֶה אֲחִי אָבִיו מִן הָאָב אוֹ מִן הָאֵם, בֵּין מִן הַנִּשּׂוּאִים בֵּין מִן הַזְּנוּת, שֶׁנֶּאֱמַר: עֶרְוַת אֲחִי אָבִיךָ לֹא תְגַלֵּה, וַאֲחִי אָבִיו נִקְרָא מִכָּל־מָקוֹם. וְאַף־עַל־פִּי שֶׁהַבָּא עַל כָּל זָכָר חַיָּב מִשּׁוּם "וְאֶת זָכָר לֹא תִשְׁכַּב" וְגוֹמֵר, זֶה הַלָּאו הוּא נוֹסָף בְּמִי שֶׁבָּא עַל אֲחִי אָבִיו, וְאִם יִהְיֶה שׁוֹגֵג יִתְחַיֵּב עָלָיו שְׁתֵּי חַטָּאוֹת, מִשּׁוּם לָאו דְּבָא עַל הַזָּכָר וְלָאו

§197 1. TB Yevamoth 54b.
2. Evident from *ibid.* 22a, 23a.
3. See §191, note 8.
4. Explained in §121.

§199 1. Apparent from TB Yevamoth 54b (see MY; but see also notes of R. Judah Rosanes, author of *Mishneh l'Melech* on MT, *ad loc.*).

[THE PROHIBITION OF CONJUGAL INTIMACY WITH A FATHER'S SISTER]

197 not to be conjugally intimate with a father's sister: for it is stated, *You shall not uncover the nakedness of your father's sister*, etc. (Leviticus 18:12).

About root reasons for the bans on forbidden conjugal relations, we have written what we know (§190).

Among the laws of the precept, there is, what the Sages of blessed memory taught:[1] that the ban on a father's sister applies whether she is a sister of one's father from the same father alone or from the same mother alone; and so too whether she is his sister from [their father's] marriage or from [his] immorality;[2] for every one of these is called, in any case, his father's sister. Here there is no place for "secondary ones."[3]

As to the laws of the precept, you will find their location at the end of the *sidrah* (§211). This prohibition remains in effect in every place and time. If someone violated it and was conjugally intimate with a sister of his father, if it was deliberate, he deserves *karéth* [Divine severance of existence]; if it was unwitting, he should bring a standard unvarying *ḥattath* (sin-offering).[4]

[THE PROHIBITION OF CONJUGAL INTIMACY WITH A MOTHER'S SISTER]

198 not to be conjugally intimate with a mother's sister: for it is stated, *You shall not uncover the nakedness of your mother's sister*, etc. (Leviticus 18:13). In its entire substance it is like [the precept] about a father's sister (§197).

[THE PROHIBITION OF CARNAL RELATIONS WITH A FATHER'S BROTHER]

199 not to have unnatural connection with a father's brother; and it would seem that it makes no difference whether he is one's father's brother from one father or from one mother, or whether from [the parent's] marriage or from [his] immorality; for it is stated, *You shall not uncover the nakedness of your father's brother* (Leviticus 18:14), and he is called his father's brother in any case.[1] Now, even though anyone who has such relations with any male is guilty by virtue of the verse, *And with a male you shall not lie carnally*, etc. (ibid. 22), this injunction is additional, for one who had carnal connection with his father's brother; and if he should sin thus unwittingly, he would owe two *ḥattath* (sin) offerings over it: on account of the injunction

דְּבָא עַל אֲחִי אָבִיו, וּכְמוֹ שֶׁאָמַרְנוּ גַּם־כֵּן בְּאָבִיו. וּבִגְמָרָא סַנְהֶדְרִין אָמְרוּ זִכְרוֹנָם לִבְרָכָה: הַבָּא עַל אֲחִי אָבִיו חַיָּב שְׁתַּיִם לְדִבְרֵי הַכֹּל.

וְנוֹהֵג אִסּוּר זֶה בְּכָל מָקוֹם וּבְכָל זְמָן. וְעוֹבֵר עָלֶיהָ וְשָׁכַב עִם אֲחִי אָבִיו, שְׁנֵיהֶם נִסְקָלִין, הַשּׁוֹכֵב וְהַנִּשְׁכָּב, אִם שְׁנֵיהֶם מְזִידִין וּבְעֵדִים וְהַתְרָאָה; וְאִם אֵין עֵדִים, שְׁנֵיהֶם בְּכָרֵת; וּבְשׁוֹגֵג חַיָּב הָאֶחָד שְׁתֵּי חַטָּאוֹת כְּמוֹ שֶׁאָמַרְנוּ, שֶׁהַבָּא עַל אֲחִי אָבִיו שֶׁחַיָּב שְׁתֵּי חַטָּאוֹת, וְהָאֶחָד חַטָּאת אֶחָת.

[שֶׁלֹּא לָבוֹא עַל אֵשֶׁת אֲחִי הָאָב]

ר שֶׁלֹּא לָבוֹא עַל אֵשֶׁת אֲחִי הָאָב, וְזֹאת נִקְרֵאת בַּכָּתוּב דּוֹדָתוֹ, לְפִי שֶׁהִיא אֵשֶׁת דּוֹדוֹ, שֶׁנֶּאֱמַר: אֶל אִשְׁתּוֹ לֹא תִקְרָב דֹּדָתְךָ הִיא. וְאַזְהָרָה זוֹ מִכֵּיוָן שֶׁנִּתְאָרְסָה לְדוֹדוֹ, כְּלוֹמַר שֶׁנִּתְקַדְּשָׁה לוֹ, וְאֵין צָרִיךְ לוֹמַר אַחַר שֶׁנִּשֵּׂאת לוֹ, וּבֵין בְּחַיֵּי דוֹדוֹ וַאֲפִלּוּ גֵרְשָׁהּ, וּבֵין אַחַר מִיתָתוֹ.

מִשָּׁרְשֵׁי הַמִּצְוָה כָּתַבְנוּ לְמַעְלָה.

מִדִּינֵי הַמִּצְוָה, מַה שֶּׁאָמְרוּ זִכְרוֹנָם לִבְרָכָה שֶׁאֲחִי אָבִיו נִקְרָא לְעִנְיַן אִסּוּר זֶה שֶׁל אִשְׁתּוֹ, כְּשֶׁהוּא אֲחִי אָבִיו מִצַּד אָב; אֲבָל אֲחִי אָבִיו מִצַּד אֵם אֵינוֹ בְאִסּוּר זֶה שֶׁל "אֶל אִשְׁתּוֹ לֹא תִקְרָב" מִדִּין תּוֹרָה, אֶלָּא שֶׁחֲכָמִים גָּדְרוּ גָדֵר וְאָסְרוּ אֲפִלּוּ אֵשֶׁת אֲחִי אָבִיו מִצַּד אֵם, כְּדֵי לְהַרְחִיקֵנוּ הַרְבֵּה שֶׁלֹּא לִגַּע לְאִסּוּר תּוֹרָה. וְכֵן אָסְרוּ גַּם־כֵּן אֵשֶׁת אֲחִי אִמּוֹ בֵּין שֶׁהוּא אָחִיהָ מִצַּד אָב לְבַד אוֹ מִצַּד אֵם לְבַד;

2. I.e. the father's brother, who participates passively—because he transgresses only the general ban on homosexual relations; in all other cases of severely forbidden carnal intimacy, though, both partners are equally subject to the penalty. See Rashi, TB K'rithoth 3a, s.v. *d'amar*.

§200 1. TB Sanhedrin 53a (see Rashi, s.v. *bén*; see also §35, note 8).
2. TB Yevamoth 97a end.
3. *Ibid.* 54b.
4. *Ibid.* 21a–b.

against having immoral relations with a male, and the injunction against having immoral relations with a father's brother—as we said, likewise, about one's father (§189). Thus in the Talmud tractate *Sanhedrin* (54a) the Sages of blessed memory taught: If someone had carnal relations with his father's brother, he incurs two guilts by the view of everyone.

This prohibition is in force in every place, at every time. If a person transgressed it and lay carnally with his father's brother, both would be put to death by stoning—the one who acted and the one who was receptive—if the deed of both was deliberate, and there were witnesses and a [prior] warning. If there were no witnesses, both incur *karéth* [Divine severance of existence]. If it was done unwittingly, one is required to bring two *ḥattath* (sin) offerings—as we stated, that a person who acts immorally with his father's brother owes two sin-offerings—and one,[2] only one *ḥattath*.

[THE PROHIBITION OF CONJUGAL RELATIONS WITH THE WIFE OF A FATHER'S BROTHER]

200 not to be conjugally intimate with the wife of a father's brother, who is the one called his aunt in Scripture, because she is his uncle's wife: for it is stated, *you shall not approach his wife; she is your aunt* (Leviticus 18:14). This injunction takes effect once she becomes betrothed to his uncle, i.e. when she is consecrated to him; and there is no need to add, after she is married to him;[1] and [it remains in effect] both in his uncle's lifetime, even if he divorces her, and after his death.[2]

About its root reasons, we have written above (§190).

Among the laws of the precept, there is, for example, what the Sages of blessed memory said:[3] that a person is called one's father's brother in respect of this prohibition on his wife, when he is his father's brother on the father's side [his father and his uncle have a common father]; but one's father's brother on the mother's side [when his father and his uncle have a common mother] is not included under this prohibition, *you shall not approach his wife*, by the law of the Torah. However, the Sages erected a "fence" (protective restriction) and banned even the wife of one's father's brother on the mother's side, so as to move us to a very safe distance, that we should not impinge on a prohibition of the Torah.[4] So too, they likewise banned the wife of one's mother's brother, whether he is her brother on the father's

וְאַף־עַל־פִּי שֶׁאֵשֶׁת אֲחִי אִמּוֹ אֵינָהּ אֲסוּרָה כְּלָל דְּבַר תּוֹרָה, מִפְּנֵי שֶׁאָסְרָה הַתּוֹרָה אֵשֶׁת אֲחִי אָבִיו מִצַּד אָב שֶׁנִּקְרָא דוֹדוֹ, הוֹסִיפוּ הֵם בָּאִסּוּר לְגֶדֶר כָּל אֶחָד מֵאֵלּוּ הַדּוֹמִים לוֹ.

וְנוֹהֵג אִסּוּר זֶה בְּכָל מָקוֹם וּבְכָל זְמָן. וְעוֹבֵר עָלֶיהָ וְשָׁכַב אֶת אֵשֶׁת אֲחִי אָבִיו מִצַּד אָב בְּחַיֵּי דוֹדוֹ בְּמֵזִיד, וְיֵשׁ עֵדִים, מִיתַת שְׁנֵיהֶם בְּחֶנֶק, שֶׁכֵּן הוּא דִין הַבָּא עַל אֵשֶׁת אִישׁ, בְּחֶנֶק. וְאִם שָׁכַב אוֹתָהּ אַחַר מוֹת דוֹדוֹ, בְּמֵזִיד חַיָּב כָּרֵת, וְאִם יֵשׁ עֵדִים לוֹקֶה; בְּשׁוֹגֵג מֵבִיא חַטָּאת קְבוּעָה, כְּמוֹ שֶׁיָּדוּעַ לָנוּ דְּכָל שֶׁבִּזְדוֹנוֹ כָּרֵת בְּשִׁגְגָתוֹ חַטָּאת. וְאִם שָׁכַב אֵשֶׁת אֲחִי אָבִיו מִצַּד אֵם, אוֹ אֵשֶׁת אֲחִי אִמּוֹ בֵּין מִצַּד אָב אוֹ מִצַּד אֵם, בְּמֵזִיד מַכִּין אוֹתוֹ מַכַּת מַרְדּוּת, בְּשׁוֹגֵג פָּטוּר.

[שֶׁלֹּא לָבוֹא עַל אֵשֶׁת הַבֵּן]

רא שֶׁלֹּא לָבוֹא עַל אֵשֶׁת הַבֵּן שֶׁתִּהְיֶה אִשְׁתּוֹ מִן הָאֵרוּסִין, וְכָל־שֶׁכֵּן מִן הַנִּשּׂוּאִין, בֵּין בְּחַיָּיו וַאֲפִלּוּ גֵרְשָׁהּ, בֵּין אַחַר מוֹתוֹ; בְּכָל עִנְיָן זֶה נִקְרֵאת אֵשֶׁת בְּנוֹ, וַאֲסוּרָה עָלָיו, שֶׁנֶּאֱמַר: עֶרְוַת כַּלָּתְךָ לֹא תְגַלֵּה. וּמִן הַדּוֹמֶה שֶׁהַחִיּוּב אֲפִלּוּ בְּבֵן מַמְזֵר, בְּנוֹ הוּא מִכָּל־מָקוֹם, אֲבָל בֶּן שִׁפְחָה וְנָכְרִית אֵין זֶה נִקְרָא בְנוֹ לְשׁוּם דָּבָר.

שֹׁרֶשׁ אִסּוּר הָעֲרָיוֹת כְּתַבְנוּהוּ.

מִדִּינֵי הַמִּצְוָה, מַה שֶּׁאָסְרוּ זִכְרוֹנָם לִבְרָכָה לְגֶדֶר זֶה כַּלַּת בְּנוֹ, וְכֵן כַּלַּת בֶּן בְּנוֹ,

5. I.e. to forbid the wife of anyone called one's uncle, so as to prevent confusion and mistaken assumptions.
6. Explained in § 121.
7. See §24, note 14.

§201 1. So TB Sanhedrin 53a. See §35, note 8.
2. I.e. the wife of a son born to him from an *'ervah* (a forbidden consanguineous relation or a married woman) with whom conjugal intimacy is punishable by *karéth*.
3. Since such a son is not reckoned a Jew.

side alone or on the mother's side alone.[4] Even though the wife of one's mother's brother is not at all forbidden by Torah law, because the Torah banned the wife of one's father's brother on the father's side, since he is called his uncle, the Sages added to the prohibition, fencing each of these about [with their restriction], who are similar to him.[5]

This prohibition is in force in every place and every time. If a person transgressed it and was conjugally intimate with the wife of his father's brother on the father's side, while his uncle was living, deliberately, and there were witnesses, the death sentence for both is by strangulation: for this is the penalty for one who is conjugally intimate with a married woman—death by strangulation. If he was thus intimate with her after his uncle's death, if it was done willfully, he incurs *karéth* [Divine severance of existence]; and if there were witnesses, he should be given whiplashes; should it have occurred unwittingly, he is to bring a standard unvarying *ḥattath* (sin-offering)[6]—as we know that for anything punishable by *karéth* if done deliberately, a *ḥattath* is due if it is done unwittingly. If someone was conjugally intimate with the wife of his father's brother on his mother's side, or with the wife of his mother's brother, whether on her father's or mother's side—if it was deliberate, he is given a whipping for disobedience;[7] and if it was unwitting, he is free of penalty.

[THE PROHIBITION OF CONJUGAL RELATIONS WITH THE WIFE OF A SON]

201 not to be conjugally intimate with a son's wife, if she is his wife by betrothal, and all the more certainly if by marriage, [and this] both in his lifetime, even if he divorced her, and after her death.[1] Under all these conditions she is called his son's wife, and is forbidden to him: for it is stated, *You shall not uncover the nakedness of your daughter-in-law* (Leviticus 18:15). And it would seem that guilt is incurred even with a bastard son,[2] since he is his son in any case; but the son of a maidservant or a non-Jewish woman would not be called his son in any respect.[3]

As to the root reason for the ban on the forbidden women, I have written it (§190).

Among the laws of the precept there is the ban which the Sages of blessed memory imposed as a "fence" about this—on one's son's

עַד סוֹף הָעוֹלָם; וְאָסְרוּ גַּם־כֵּן כַּלַּת בִּתּוֹ בִּלְבָד. וְהַטַּעַם כְּעֵין מַה שֶּׁאָמַרְנוּ לְמַעְלָה: לְפִי שֶׁהָאִסּוּר בָּא בַכָּתוּב בְּכַלָּתוֹ, גָּזְרוּ הֵם בְּכָל הַכַּלּוֹת הַבָּאוֹת מֵחֲמַת הַבֵּן, וְגָזְרוּ בְכַלַּת בִּתּוֹ בִּלְבַד, וְדַי לָנוּ בְכָךְ, וְאֵלּוּ נִקְרָאוֹת שְׁנִיּוֹת.

וְנוֹהֵג אִסּוּר זֶה בְּכָל מָקוֹם וּבְכָל זְמָן. וְעוֹבֵר עָלֶיהָ וְשָׁכַב אֶת כַּלָּתוֹ בְּמֵזִיד וְיֵשׁ עֵדִים וְהַתְרָאָה, בִּסְקִילָה; וְאִם אֵין עֵדִים, בְּכָרֵת; בְּשׁוֹגֵג מֵבִיא חַטָּאת קְבוּעָה. וְאִם שָׁכַב אֶת כַּלַּת בְּנוֹ אוֹ בֶן בְּנוֹ עַד סוֹף הָעוֹלָם, אוֹ כַּלַּת בִּתּוֹ, מַכִּין אוֹתוֹ מַכַּת מַרְדּוּת.

[שֶׁלֹּא לָבוֹא עַל אֵשֶׁת אָח]

רב שֶׁלֹּא לָבוֹא עַל אֵשֶׁת אָחִיו, שֶׁנֶּאֱמַר: עֶרְוַת אֵשֶׁת אָחִיךָ לֹא תְגַלֵּה; וְאֶחָד אָחִיו מֵאָבִיו לְבַד אוֹ מֵאִמּוֹ לְבַד, וּבֵין מִן הַנִּשּׂוּאִין בֵּין מִן הַזְּנוּת, אִשְׁתּוֹ עֶרְוָה עָלָיו, שֶׁאָחִיו נִקְרָא מִכָּל־מָקוֹם; וּמִכֵּיוָן שֶׁאֵרְסָהּ נִקְרֵאת אֵשֶׁת אָח וַאֲסוּרָה, וְכָל־שֶׁכֵּן אַחַר שֶׁנְּשָׂאָהּ; וּבֵין בְּחַיֵּי אָחִיו בֵּין אַחַר מוֹתוֹ הִיא אֲסוּרָה עָלָיו מִשּׁוּם אֵשֶׁת אָח — חוּץ מֵאֵשֶׁת אָח שֶׁלֹּא הִנִּיחַ בֵּן, שֶׁהַתּוֹרָה צִוְּתָה עַל זוֹ בְּפֵרוּשׁ שֶׁיִּשָּׂאֶנָּה הָאָח, וְזֹאת הִיא מִצְוַת יִבּוּם, כְּמוֹ שֶׁנְּפָרֵשׁ בְּעֶזְרַת הַשֵּׁם.

וְנוֹהֵג אִסּוּר זֶה בְּכָל מָקוֹם וּבְכָל זְמָן. וְעוֹבֵר עָלֶיהָ וְשָׁכַב אֶת אֵשֶׁת אָחִיו, חַיָּב כָּרֵת אִם הָיָה מֵזִיד, וְאִם שׁוֹגֵג חַיָּב לְהָבִיא חַטָּאת קְבוּעָה; וְזֶה יִהְיֶה אַחַר מוֹת

4. Literally, till the end of the world; TB Yevamoth 21b.
5. But not the daughter-in-law of any child or grandchild of the daughter; *ibid.*
6. Because they are forbidden only by the Sages.
7. Explained in §121.
8. See §24, note 14.

§202 1. So TB Yevamoth 55a.
2. As explained in §35 note 8, for want of better terms *'érusin* and *nissu'in* have been rendered as "betrothal" and "marriage"; these terms have a technical meaning of their own where Jewish law is concerned: By "betrothal" (*'érusin*) a couple become legally bound as man and wife, but may not live together until their "marriage" (*nissu'in*). In olden times a year generally separated the two ceremonies, to give the bride time to prepare what she would need in her marital home. Later it became the practice for both to take place together under the wedding canopy.

daughter-in-law, and so on his son's son's daughter-in-law, and so down to the end of time.[4] And they equally banned one's daughter's daughter-in-law alone.[5] The reason [why this ban is not extended to further generations] is akin to what I stated above (§190): Because the prohibition found in the Writ is on one's daughter-in-law, the Sages decreed a ban on all daughters-in-law that enter the family through the line of the son; then they decreed a ban on one's daughter's daughter-in-law, and that is enough for us. And these are called the secondary ones.[6]

This prohibition is in effect in every place, at every time. If a person transgressed it and was conjugally intimate with his daughter-in-law: if it was willful and there were witnesses and a [prior] warning, he should be stoned to death. If there were no witnesses, he is subject to *karéth* [Divine severance of existence]. If it was done unwittingly, he should bring a standard unvarying *ḥattath* (sin-offering).[7] If he was conjugally intimate with the daughter-in-law of his son or his son's son, and so on down without limit, he should be punished with lashes of the whip for disobedience.[8]

[THE PROHIBITION OF CONJUGAL RELATIONS WITH A BROTHER'S WIFE]

202 not to be conjugally intimate with one's brother's wife: for it is stated, *You shall not uncover the nakedness of your brother's wife* (Leviticus 18:16). It is all one whether he is a brother only from the same father or only from the same mother,[1] and whether from [their father's] marriage or from his immorality—his [brother's] wife is a forbidden woman to him, since he is called his brother in any event. Once he [the brother] betroths her, she is called a brother's wife and is forbidden, and all the more certainly so after he has married her;[2] then both during his brother's lifetime and after his death, she is forbidden to him under the ban on a brother's wife[1]—except in the case of the wife of a brother who left no child [at his death], since the Torah explicitly commanded about her that the [surviving] brother should marry her. This is the precept of levirate marriage (§598), as we will explain, with the Eternal Lord's help.

This prohibition is in effect in every time and every place. If a person violated it and was conjugally intimate with his brother's wife, he is punishable by *karéth* [Divine severance of existence] if he acted willfully. If it was inadvertent, he is obligated to bring a standard

אָחִיו וְנִשְׁאֲרוּ לוֹ בָנִים, אוֹ אַחַר שֶׁגֵּרְשָׁהּ, שֶׁאִלּוּ בְּחַיָּיו, בְּעוֹדָהּ תַּחְתָּיו, יָדוּעַ הוּא שֶׁדִּין הַשּׁוֹכֵב אֶת אֵשֶׁת אִישׁ מִיתָתָן בְּחֶנֶק. וְאֵין בְּאִסּוּר אֵשֶׁת אָח מָקוֹם לְאִסּוּר שְׁנִיּוֹת.

[שֶׁלֹּא לָבוֹא עַל אִשָּׁה וּבִתָּהּ]

רג שֶׁלֹּא לְגַלּוֹת עֶרְוַת אִשָּׁה וּבִתָּהּ, שֶׁנֶּאֱמַר: עֶרְוַת אִשָּׁה וּבִתָּהּ לֹא תְגַלֵּה; וּבָא הַפֵּרוּשׁ שֶׁאֵין הַחִיּוּב אֶלָּא כְּגוֹן שֶׁנָּשָׂא הָאַחַת תְּחִלָּה, וְאַחַר־כֵּן כְּשֶׁבָּא עַל הַשְּׁנִיָּה הוּא מִתְחַיֵּב, אֲבָל אִם לֹא נָשָׂא אַחַת מֵהֶן לֹא יִתְחַיֵּב עֲלֵיהֶן, לְפִי שֶׁכָּתוּב בָּהֶן לְשׁוֹן קִיחָה דְּמַשְׁמָע עַל־יְדֵי נִשּׂוּאִין, דְּהָכִי מַשְׁמָע לָן לְשׁוֹן קִיחָה בְּכָל מָקוֹם, לְשׁוֹן נִשּׂוּאִין. (אֲבָל חֲכָמִים גָּדְרוּ גָדֵר וְאָמְרוּ שֶׁאִם נָאַף אָדָם עִם אִשָּׁה אָסוּר לִשָּׂא בִתָּהּ — כָּל הַשֶּׁבַע נָשִׁים קְרוֹבוֹתֶיהָ — כָּל זְמַן שֶׁהַזּוֹנָה קַיֶּמֶת, מִפְּנֵי שֶׁהַזּוֹנָה בָּאָה לְבַקֵּר אוֹתָן, וְלִבּוֹ גַס בָּהּ, וְשֶׁמָּא יָבוֹא לִידֵי עֲבֵרָה).

וְנוֹהֵג אִסּוּר זֶה בְּכָל מָקוֹם וּבְכָל זְמַן. וְעוֹבֵר עָלֶיהָ וְשָׁכַב אֶת אִשָּׁה וּבִתָּהּ, שְׁנֵיהֶם נִשְׂרָפִין, הוּא וְאוֹתָהּ שֶׁשָּׁכַב אַחֲרוֹנָה, שֶׁאֵין לָרִאשׁוֹנָה חֵטְא, שֶׁהֲרֵי בְּהֶתֵּר נְשָׂאָהּ. וְאִם בָּא עַל הַשְּׁנִיָּה לְאַחַר מִיתַת אִשְׁתּוֹ הָרִאשׁוֹנָה הֲרֵי אֵלּוּ בְּכָרֵת, וְאֵין בָּהֶן מִיתַת בֵּית־דִּין, שֶׁנֶּאֱמַר בְּמָקוֹם אַחֵר בְּסֵדֶר קְדוֹשִׁים תִּהְיוּ: בָּאֵשׁ יִשְׂרְפוּ אֹתוֹ וְאֶתְהֶן, וּפֵרֵשׁ רַבִּי אֱלִיעֶזֶר בְּסַנְהֶדְרִין: בָּאֵשׁ יִשְׂרְפוּ אוֹתוֹ וְאַחַת מֵהֶן, דְּהַיְנוּ הָאַחֲרוֹנָה, כְּמוֹ שֶׁאָמַרְנוּ. וְדַוְקָא כְּשֶׁשְּׁתֵּיהֶן קַיָּמוֹת, שֶׁכֵּן בָּא הַפֵּרוּשׁ, אֲבָל כְּשֶׁאֵין שְׁתֵּיהֶן קַיָּמוֹת אֵין שָׁם שְׂרֵפָה, אֶלָּא שֶׁהֵן בְּחִיּוּב כָּרֵת בְּמֵזִיד, וּבְשׁוֹגֵג בְּחִיּוּב

3. Explained in § 121.
4. I.e. other women prohibited by the Sages, as a protective measure to make sure the Torah's prohibition will be in no danger of violation.

§203 1. TB Yevamoth 97a.
2. *Ibid.* (MT *hilchoth 'issuré bi'ah* ii 11). This part in parentheses is not in the oldest manuscripts, and would thus seem a later addition.

unvarying *ḥattath* (sin-offering).[3] This is [the law] after one's brother's death if he left children or after he divorced her; for if it was in his lifetime while she was yet with him, it is known that the sentence for one who is conjugally intimate with a married woman is death by strangulation. With the prohibition on a brother's wife there is no place for a ban on "secondary ones."[4]

[THE PROHIBITION OF CONJUGAL RELATIONS WITH BOTH A WOMAN AND HER DAUGHTER]

203 not to uncover the nakedness of a woman and her daughter: for it is stated, *You shall not uncover the nakedness of a woman and her daughter* (Leviticus 18:17); and the interpretation was given [in the Oral Tradition][1] that guilt is not incurred unless it was a case where a person married one first; afterward, when he is conjugally intimate with the other, he becomes punishable. But if he did not marry one of them, he incurs no guilt on their account—because an expression of "taking" is written about them, which means by the procedure of marriage; for this is what the expression of "taking" denotes everywhere: the sense of marriage. (However, the Sages erected a "fence" and ruled that if a man had immoral relations with a woman, he becomes forbidden to marry her daughter—[indeed] any of her seven close female relatives—as long as the immoral woman is alive: because the immoral woman will come to visit them, and his heart is overly familiar with her, and thus he may perhaps be led into the grip of sin.)[2]

This prohibition is in effect in every place, at every time. If a person violated it and was conjugally intimate with a woman and her daughter, the two of them should be put to death by burning: he, and the one with whom he was intimate later. For with the first one there was no sin, since he married her permissibly. If he was conjugally intimate with the second after his wife, the first one, died, they are punishable by *karéth* [Divine severance of existence]; but they are not liable to a death sentence by the court. For it is written elsewhere, in *sidrah k'doshim, they shall be burned with fire, both he and they* (Leviticus 20:14), and R. 'Eli'ezer explained in the tractate *Sanhedrin* (76b), "they shall be burned with fire, he and one of them"—i.e. the later one, as we have stated. However, this applies only when both women are alive, since the interpretation was thus given [in the Oral Tradition]; but when both of them are not alive, there is no death by burning; rather, they are subject to the punishment of *karéth* [Divine severance

חַטָּאת קְבוּעָה. וְרַבִּי עֲקִיבָא מְפָרֵשׁ שָׁם: אוֹתוֹ וּשְׁתֵּיהֶן, וּכְגוֹן שֶׁנָּשָׂא הַשְּׁתַּיִם בְּאִסּוּר, וְיִמָּצֵא זֶה כְּשֶׁנָּשָׂא הַבַּת וְאִמָּהּ וְאֵם אִמָּהּ. וְשָׁם מִתְבָּאֵר בְּמַאי פְּלִיגִי.

[שֶׁלֹּא לְגַלּוֹת עֶרְוַת אִשָּׁה וּבַת בְּנָהּ]

רד שֶׁלֹּא לְגַלּוֹת עֶרְוַת אִשָּׁה וּבַת בְּנָהּ; וּכְבָר אָמַרְנוּ שֶׁאִסּוּר זֶה הוּא לְעוֹלָם בְּנִשּׂוּאֵי הָרִאשׁוֹנָה; שֶׁנֶּאֱמַר: אֶת בַּת בְּנָהּ... לֹא תִקַּח וְגוֹמֵר.

מִדִּינֵי הַמִּצְוָה, מַה שֶּׁאָסְרוּ זִכְרוֹנָם לִבְרָכָה לְגֶדֶר זֶה, בַּת בֶּן בְּנָהּ, וְהִיא מִכְּלַל הַשְּׁנִיּוֹת, כְּמוֹ שֶׁאָמַרְנוּ שֶׁכָּל שֶׁאִסּוּרָהּ מִדִּבְרֵי סוֹפְרִים תִּקָּרֵא שְׁנִיָּה. וְכֵן אָסְרוּ אֵם אֵם אֲבִי אִשְׁתּוֹ בִּלְבַד, וְכֵן אֵם אַב אֲבִי אִשְׁתּוֹ בִּלְבַד.

וְנוֹהֵג אִסּוּר זֶה בְּכָל מָקוֹם וּבְכָל זְמַן. וְעוֹבֵר עָלֶיהָ וְשָׁכַב אִשָּׁה וּבַת בְּנָהּ בְּנִשּׂוּאֵי הָרִאשׁוֹנָה, שְׁנֵיהֶם נִשְׂרָפִין בְּחַיֵּי הָרִאשׁוֹנָה; וְאִם מֵתָה הָרִאשׁוֹנָה שְׁנֵיהֶם בְּכָרֵת בְּמֵזִיד, בְּשׁוֹגֵג מְבִיאִין חַטָּאת קְבוּעָה. וְאִם שָׁכַב אֶת הַשְּׁנִיָּה, לוֹקֶה מַכַּת מַרְדּוּת מִדְּרַבָּנָן.

[שֶׁלֹּא לְגַלּוֹת עֶרְוַת אִשָּׁה וּבַת בִּתָּהּ]

רה שֶׁלֹּא לְגַלּוֹת עֶרְוַת אִשָּׁה וּבַת בִּתָּהּ, וּכְבָר אָמַרְנוּ שֶׁאִסּוּר זֶה בְּנִשּׂוּאֵי הָרִאשׁוֹנָה, שֶׁנֶּאֱמַר: וְאֶת בַּת בִּתָּהּ לֹא תִקַּח וְגוֹמֵר, וּלְשׁוֹן קִיחָה מַשְׁמַע לָן לְשׁוֹן נִשּׂוּאִין.

מִדִּינֵי הַמִּצְוָה, מַה שֶּׁאָסְרוּ זִכְרוֹנָם לִבְרָכָה לְגֶדֶר זֶה בַּת בַּת בִּתָּהּ בִּלְבַד, וְאֵם

§204 1. TB Yevamoth 22a.

2. I.e. but not the grandmother or great-grandmother, etc. According to MT *hilchoth 'ishuth* 1 6, this word "alone" should equally apply two sentences above, about "the daughter of a son of her son": there too, the ban of the Sages does not extend to a granddaughter or great-granddaughter (see TB Yevamoth 21a).

3. I.e. but not the grandmother, great-grandmother, etc. (TB *ibid.*)

4. Explained in §121.

5. I.e. one of those banned by the Sages, listed in the previous paragraph.

6. See §24, note 14.

of existence] if it was willful; and if it was inadvertent, to the obligation of a standard unvarying *ḥattath* (sin-offering). R. 'Akiva, though, explains [the verse] there to mean both him and the two women—in a case where he married the two under conditions of prohibition. This can occur when one married a daughter, her mother, and the mother's mother. It is clarified there in what their difference of opinion consists.

[THE PROHIBITION OF CONJUGAL INTIMACY WITH BOTH A WOMAN AND HER SON'S DAUGHTER]

204 not to uncover the nakedness of a woman and her son's daughter; and we have stated previously (§203) that this ban always applies upon marriage with the first one—for it is stated, *her son's daughter . . . you shall not take* (Leviticus 18:17) [i.e. in marriage].

Among the laws of the precept there is the restriction that the Sages of blessed memory decreed[1] as a "fence" about this, on the daughter of a son of her son—who is thus included among the "secondary" ones. As we stated, any woman banned by a ruling of the Sages is called a secondary one. So too, they prohibited the mother of the mother of one's father-in-law alone,[2] and likewise the mother of the father of one's father-in-law alone.[3]

This prohibition is in force everywhere, and at every time. If someone violated it and was conjugally intimate with a woman and her son's daughter, having married the first [of them], the both are to be burned to death [if they thus sinned] during the first one's life. If the first one had been dead, the two are punishable by *karéth* [Divine severance of existence] if they acted willfully; if it was done unwittingly, they should bring a standard unvarying *ḥattath* (sin-offering).[4] If a person was conjugally intimate with a secondary one,[5] he should be whipped with lashes for disobedience, by the Sages' edict.[6]

[THE PROHIBITION OF CONJUGAL INTIMACY WITH BOTH A WOMAN AND HER DAUGHTER'S DAUGHTER]

205 not to uncover the nakedness of a woman and her daughter's daughter; we have already said that this prohibition applies upon marriage with the first woman; for it is stated, *and her daughter's daughter you shall not take*, etc. (Leviticus 18:17), and the expression of "taking" denotes for us the sense of marriage.

Among the laws of the precept, there is the ban that the Sages of blessed memory decreed as a "fence" about this: on the daughter of her

אֵם אִשְׁתּוֹ בִּלְבַד, וְאֵם אַב אֵם אִשְׁתּוֹ בִּלְבָד. כְּלַל הָעִנְיָן שֶׁל אִסּוּר אִשָּׁה וּבִתָּהּ וּבַת בְּנָהּ וּבַת בִּתָּהּ, כִּי הַתּוֹרָה תֶּאֱסֹר לָאָדָם מִלִּשָּׂא שֵׁשׁ קְרוֹבוֹת שֶׁל אִשְׁתּוֹ מִלְּבַד הָאָחוֹת: שָׁלֹשׁ לְמַעְלָה, דְּהַיְנוּ אִמָּהּ וּשְׁתֵּי זְקֵנוֹתֶיהָ, וְשָׁלֹשׁ לְמַטָּה, דְּהַיְנוּ בִּתָּהּ וּבַת בִּתָּהּ וּבַת בְּנָהּ; וַחֲכָמִים הוֹסִיפוּ עֲלֵיהֶן גַּם־כֵּן לְגָדֵר, שֵׁשׁ אֲחֵרוֹת: אַרְבַּע לְמַעְלָה וּשְׁתַּיִם לְמַטָּה, כִּי כֵן יָאוּת הָעִנְיָן לִהְיוֹת בְּהֶכְרֵחַ, כִּי שְׁתֵּי הַזְּקֵנוֹת גּוֹרְרוֹת אַרְבַּע אֲחֵרוֹת לְגָדֵר לָהֶן, אֲבָל בַּת בְּנָהּ וּבַת בִּתָּהּ אִי אֶפְשָׁר לָהֶן לִגְדֹּר אֶלָּא שְׁתַּיִם כְּמוֹתָן, וְהָאֵם וְהַבַּת אֵין לְהוֹסִיף עֲלֵיהֶן לְגָדֵר, שֶׁהֲרֵי יֵשׁ נָשִׁים אֲסוּרוֹת מִן הַתּוֹרָה לְמַטָּן וּלְמַעְלָן. עַיֵּן בַּדָּבָר כִּי כֵן הוּא בְּהֶכְרֵחַ.

וְנוֹהֶגֶת בְּכָל מָקוֹם וּבְכָל זְמַן. וְעוֹבֵר עָלֶיהָ וְשָׁכַב אִשָּׁה וּבַת בִּתָּהּ, שְׁנֵיהֶם נִשְׂרָפִין בְּחַיֵּי רִאשׁוֹנָה; וְאִם מֵתָה רִאשׁוֹנָה, שְׁנֵיהֶם בְּכָרֵת בְּמֵזִיד, וּבְשׁוֹגֵג מְבִיאִין חַטָּאת קְבוּעָה. וְאִם שָׁכַב אֶת הַשְּׁנִיּוֹת, מַלְקִין אוֹתוֹ מַכַּת מַרְדּוּת.

[שֶׁלֹּא לָבוֹא עַל שְׁתֵּי אֲחָיוֹת מֵחַיִּים]

רו שֶׁלֹּא לָבוֹא עַל שְׁתֵּי אֲחָיוֹת, כְּלוֹמַר שֶׁלֹּא יִשָּׂא אָדָם שְׁתֵּי אֲחָיוֹת בְּיַחַד, וְלֹא אֲפִלּוּ זוֹ אַחַר זוֹ בְּחַיֵּי הָרִאשׁוֹנָה, וַאֲפִלּוּ גֵּרְשָׁהּ לָרִאשׁוֹנָה, שֶׁנֶּאֱמַר: וְאִשָּׁה אֶל אֲחֹתָהּ לֹא תִקָּח לִצְרֹר לְגַלּוֹת עֶרְוָתָהּ עָלֶיהָ בְּחַיֶּיהָ. פֵּרוּשׁ: וְאִשָּׁה עִם אֲחוֹתָהּ, בְּיַחַד; לֹא תִקָּח לִצְרֹר, לְשׁוֹן צָרָה, כְּלוֹמַר כְּדֵי שֶׁלֹּא תֵּעָשֶׂה הָאַחַת צָרָה לַחֲבֶרְתָּהּ; בְּחַיֶּיהָ, בָּא וְלִמֵּד שֶׁאֲפִלּוּ גֵּרְשָׁהּ לָרִאשׁוֹנָה לֹא יִשָּׂא אֲחוֹתָהּ, וְזֶהוּ לְשׁוֹן בְּחַיֶּיהָ, כְּלוֹמַר כָּל זְמַן שֶׁהִיא בַּחַיִּים; אֲבָל אַחַר מוֹת הָאַחַת אֵין סָפֵק שֶׁמֻּתָּר

§205 1. I.e. but not the granddaughter, great-granddaughter, etc. TB Yevamoth 21a. So MT *hilchoth 'ishuth* i 6. Hence the daughter of her son's daughter or of her daughter's son is not forbidden him by Rabbinic law. MY queries this, however: In the Sages' ban on a wife's great-grandmother, she is forbidden to a man in all four possibilities: whether she is the paternal or maternal grandmother of his wife's father or mother. Why is a differentiation by line of descent made here? Two lines below, our author writes, "but as for her son's daughter and her daughter's son, it is impossible to 'fence' them about with any more than two like them." Yet indeed why not? MY replies that while people would use the term "grandmother" equally for both a father's and a mother's mother (as borne out by TB Yevamoth 21b—so that the Sages had to forbid both to prevent any confusion and error about a man's own or his wife's grandmother), in referring to a grandchild, people would specify whether it was from a person's son or daughter. Therefore a ban on the daughter of her son's daughter and of her daughter's son would not serve as a protective "fence" for the Torah's prohibition of a wife's son's daughter or daughter's daughter, since they are dissimilar in name. *Kessef Mishneh* to MT *ibid.*, however, poses another difficulty: Why is a man's own great-granddaughter forbidden to him in all four possibilities (see §§193, 194), if his wife's great-granddaughter is not? And he leaves the query unanswered. Perhaps it might be suggested that in the case of a direct descendant the Sages saw fit to be more stringent.

daughter's daughter alone,[1] the maternal grandmother of one's mother-in-law alone,[2] and the paternal grandmother of one's mother-in-law alone.[2] The rule concerning the ban on [marrying] a woman and her daugher, or her son's daughter or daughter's daughter, is that the Torah forbids a man to marry six near relatives of his wife, apart from a sister: three above—i.e. her mother and two grandmothers; and three below—i.e. her daughter, daughter's daughter, and son's daughter. Then the Sages added to these, as well, six others as a "fence" (protective restriction): four above,[3] and two below.[4] For so is it right for the matter to be, necessarily: the two grandmothers require four others to serve as a "fence" for them; but as for her son's daughter and her daughter's daughter, it is impossible to "fence" them about with any more than two like them. As to the mother and daughter [of one's wife] none can be added to them as a "fence," since there are women forbidden by the Torah above and below them.[5] Ponder the matter, for it is necessarily so.

It applies everywhere, and at every time. If someone transgressed it and was conjugally intimate with a woman and her daughter's daughter, the two of them[6] are to be burned to death [if they thus sinned] during the first [of the two women's] lifetime; and if the first one [the wife] had been dead, the two are subject to *karéth* [Divine severance of existence] if they acted willfully. If it was inadvertent, they should bring a standard unvarying *ḥattath* (sin-offering).[7] If someone was conjugally intimate with [any of] the secondary ones,[8] he is to be given lashes of disobedience.[9]

[THE PROHIBITION OF CONJUGAL RELATIONS WITH TWO SISTERS WHILE BOTH ARE ALIVE]

206 not to be conjugally intimate with two sisters; in other words, that a man should not marry two sisters together, nor one after the other in the lifetime of the first one, even if he divorced the first one—as it is stated, *And you shall not take a woman after her sister to be a rival, to uncover her nakedness beside the other in her lifetime* (Leviticus 18:18)—which means a woman and her sister together: "you shall not take *litz'ror*" denotes that you should not make one a *tzarah*, a rival, to the other; "in her lifetime"—come and learn that even if he divorced the first one, he is not to marry her sister,[1] since this is the significance of "in her lifetime," i.e. as long as she is alive. But after the death of one, there is no doubt that he is permitted to marry the other: this is why

לִשָּׂא הָאַחֶרֶת, דְּהַיְנוּ שֶׁאָמַר הַכָּתוּב "בְּחַיֶּיהָ"; וְכֵן הַשּׁוֹכֵב דֶּרֶךְ זְנוּת עִם הָאָחוֹת אַחַר שֶׁנָּשָׂא הָרִאשׁוֹנָה אוֹ קִדְּשָׁהּ, גַּם־כֵּן בִּכְלַל הָאִסּוּר, כִּי בְנִשּׂוּאֵי הָרִאשׁוֹנָה הִקְפִּידָה תוֹרָה.

מִשָּׁרְשֵׁי עִנְיַן הָעֲרָיוֹת כָּתַבְנוּ לְמַעְלָה מַה שֶּׁיָּדַעְנוּ. וְעוֹד אוֹמֵר לִי לִבִּי בְּעִנְיָן זֶה שֶׁאָסַר הַכָּתוּב מִלִּשָּׂא שְׁתֵּי אֲחָיוֹת, כִּי אֲדוֹן הַשָּׁלוֹם יַחְפֹּץ בִּשְׁלוֹם כָּל בְּרִיּוֹתָיו, וְכָל־שֶׁכֵּן בִּשְׁלוֹם אוֹתָן בְּרִיּוֹת שֶׁהַטֶּבַע וְהַשֵּׂכֶל מְחַיְּבִין לִהְיוֹת שָׁלוֹם בֵּינֵיהֶם וְלֹא קְטָטָה וְתַחֲרוּת תָּמִיד כָּל הַיּוֹם.

מִדִּינֵי הַמִּצְוָה, מַה שֶּׁפֵּרְשׁוּ זִכְרוֹנָם לִבְרָכָה שֶׁאֲחוֹת אִשְׁתּוֹ נִקְרֵאת בֵּין אֲחוֹתָהּ מֵאִמָּהּ בֵּין אֲחוֹתָהּ מֵאָבִיהָ, בֵּין מִן הַנִּשּׂוּאִין בֵּין מִן הַזְּנוּת. וּפֵרְשׁוּ גַּם־כֵּן שֶׁהָאִסּוּר יָחוּל מִכֵּיוָן שֶׁיְּקַדְּשֶׁנָּה, וְכִדְמַשְׁמַע לָן לְשׁוֹן קִיחָה בְּאִשָּׁה לְעוֹלָם, כְּמוֹ שֶׁאָמַרְנוּ.

וְכֵן מַה שֶּׁאָסְרוּ זִכְרוֹנָם לִבְרָכָה לְגֶדֶר אִסּוּר זֶה אֲחוֹת זְקוּקָתוֹ. פֵּרוּשׁ זְקוּקָתוֹ, כְּגוֹן מִי שֶׁהָיָה לוֹ אָח וָמֵת וְלֹא הִנִּיחַ בָּנִים, שֶׁהוּא חַיָּב לִשָּׂא אִשְׁתּוֹ מִן הַתּוֹרָה אוֹ לַחֲלֹץ לָהּ, כְּמוֹ שֶׁבָּא הַמִּצְוָה בַּכָּתוּב בְּפֵרוּשׁ. וְזֹאת הָאִשָּׁה שֶׁהִיא זְקוּקָה לָאָח, כְּלוֹמַר שֶׁהִיא בִרְשׁוּת הָאָח לִשָּׂא אוֹתָהּ אִם יִרְצֶה, כִּי מִן הַשָּׁמַיִם הִקְנוּהָ לוֹ, תִּקָּרֵא זְקוּקָתוֹ, וְאָסְרוּ זִכְרוֹנָם לִבְרָכָה מִלִּשָּׂא אֲחוֹתָהּ מִכֵּיוָן שֶׁהִיא זְקוּקָה אֵלָיו, אַף־עַל־פִּי שֶׁלֹּא קִדְּשָׁהּ וְלֹא עָשָׂה בָהּ שׁוּם עִנְיָן.

וְכֵן אָסְרוּ עָלָיו גַּם־כֵּן לְגֶדֶר זֶה אֲחוֹת חֲלוּצָתוֹ, כְּלוֹמַר אֲפִלּוּ אַחַר שֶׁחָלַץ לָהּ אָסְרוּ עָלָיו מִלִּשָּׂא אֲחוֹתָהּ. כְּמוֹ שֶׁאָסַר הַכָּתוּב אֲחוֹת גְּרוּשָׁתוֹ, כְּמוֹ שֶׁפֵּרַשְׁנוּ, כֵּן אָסְרוּ הֵם גַּם־כֵּן אֲחוֹת חֲלוּצָתוֹ, שֶׁהַחֲלִיצָה כְּעֵין גֵּט הִיא. וּמִכָּל־מָקוֹם אִסּוּר

2. I.e. but not the great-grandmother, etc. *Ibid.*

3. The mother-in-law's maternal grandmother, the mother-in-law's paternal grandmother, the father-in-law's maternal grandmother, and the father-in-law's paternal grandmother.

4. The daughter of her son's son, and the daughter of her daughter's daughter.

5. I.e. the grandmother and the granddaughter, since the Torah forbids taking a woman and her granddaughter (Leviticus 18:17).

6. The man and his wife's granddaughter.

7. Explained in §121.

8. I.e. those forbidden by the decree of the Sages.

9. See §24, note 14.

§206 1. The interpretation of the verse till here is derived from Rashi *ad loc.* which is based on TB Kiddushin 50b and Yevamoth 8b.

2. So TB Yevamoth 97a. (On "betrothed," two lines above, see §202, note 2).

3. I.e. it would be inhuman cruelty to take two sisters and make them lifelong rivals for the affection of one man. Cf. Ramban, commentary, Leviticus 18:18.

Scripture stated "in her lifetime." So too, if a person was conjugally intimate with one sister immorally after he married or betrothed the first one, this is likewise included under the prohibition. For the Torah is strict in respect of marriage to the first one.[2]

As to the root reason behind the subject of [these] forbidden women, we have written above (§190) what we know. Furthermore, my heart tells me about this prohibition that the Torah imposed on marrying two sisters, that the Lord of peace has delight in peace for all His human creatures, and all the more certainly in the serenity of those human beings for whom nature and reason would require that there should be peace between them, and not quarrel and contention constantly, all the day.[3]

Among the laws of the precept, there is what the Sages of blessed memory explained:[4] that one's wife's sister is thus called whether she is her sister from one mother or from one father, whether from [the parent's] marriage, or from [his] immorality. They explained, furthermore,[2] that the prohibition takes effect once he consecrates (betroths) her,[5] as the expression "taking" in regard to a woman always signifies this for us, as we stated.

So too, there is the ban that the Sages of blessed memory decreed as a "fence" about this prohibition—on the sister of one bound to him for levirate marriage: which means, for instance, if he had a brother who died leaving no children, so that he has a duty to marry his [brother's] wife by the law of the Torah, or to release her by *ḥalitzah* (§§597–599), as the commandment is explained clearly in Scripture. This woman is bound to the brother for levirate marriage: in other words, she is in the power of the brother, for him to marry if he wishes;[6] for since by Heaven she is confined to him, she is called "his *z'kukah*"—bound to him for levirate marriage. Well, the Sages of blessed memory prohibited [a man in this situation] from marrying her sister, since she is bound to him for marriage—even though he did not consecrate (betroth) her or do anything at all in regard to her.[7]

Similarly, the Sages banned to a man, as a "fence" about this, the sister of his *ḥalutzah*, a woman whom he released from her bond for levirate marriage. In other words, even after he released her by the ritual of *ḥalitzah* (§599), the Sages forbade him to marry her sister.[8] Just as the Writ forbids marrying the sister of one's divorced wife, as we explained, so they similarly banned the sister of one whom he released from the bond for levirate marriage, since *ḥalitzah* is akin

אֲחוֹת חֲלוּצָתוֹ וַאֲפִלּוּ אֲחוֹת זְקוּקָתוֹ קַיְמָא לָן אַלִּיבָּא דְהִלְכְתָא דְמִדְּרַבָּנָן הוּא, כִּי הַתּוֹרָה לֹא אָסְרָה כִּי אִם אֲחוֹת נְשׂוּאָתוֹ אוֹ אֲרוּסָתוֹ; אֲבָל הַזְּקוּקָה לוֹ, אַף־עַל־פִּי שֶׁמִּן הַשָּׁמַיִם הִקְנוּהָ לוֹ אֵין אֲחוֹתָהּ בִּכְלַל אִסּוּר תּוֹרָה, אֶלָּא שֶׁהֵם זִכְרוֹנָם לִבְרָכָה אֲסָרוּהָ, שֶׁלֹּא לִגַּע לְאִסּוּרָא דְאוֹרַיְתָא.

וּמִפְּנֵי שֶׁאִסּוּר זֶה הוּא מִדִּבְרֵיהֶם, כְּמוֹ שֶׁאָמַרְנוּ, הֵקֵלּוּ בָּעִנְיָן קְצָת לִפְעָמִים, עַד שֶׁאָמְרוּ זִכְרוֹנָם לִבְרָכָה כִּי אֶחָד מִן הַיְּבָמִין שֶׁקִּדֵּשׁ אֲחוֹת יְבִמְתּוֹ שֶׁאוֹמְרִים לוֹ: הַמְתֵּן, אַל תְּגָרְשֶׁנָּה וְאַל תִּשָּׂאֶנָּה עַד שֶׁיְּיַבֵּם אָחִיךָ אוֹ יַחֲלֹץ לִיבָמָה זוֹ הַזְּקוּקָה לְכֻלְּכֶם. חָלַץ לָהּ אָחִיו אוֹ יִבְּמָהּ אוֹ שֶׁמֵּתָה הַיְבָמָה, הֲרֵי הוּא יִכְנֹס אֲרוּסָתוֹ, אֲבָל אִם מֵתוּ הָאַחִים כֻּלָּם מוֹצִיא אֶת אֲרוּסָתוֹ בְּגֵט וִיבִמְתּוֹ בַּחֲלִיצָה; וְאִם מֵתָה אֲרוּסָתוֹ, בֵּין שֶׁמֵּתָה קֹדֶם מִיתַת הָאַחִין בֵּין שֶׁמֵּתָה לְאַחַר מִיתָתָם חָזְרָה הַיְבָמָה לְהֶתֵּרָהּ, רָצָה חוֹלֵץ רָצָה מְיַבֵּם. וּבְמִצְוַת יִבּוּם נִכְתֹּב עוֹד מְעַט בְּעִנְיָנִים אֵלֶּה כְּמִנְהָגֵנוּ בְּעֶזְרַת הַשֵּׁם, שֶׁאֵין כָּאן מְקוֹמָן.

וְנוֹהֶגֶת אַזְהָרָה זוֹ בְּכָל מָקוֹם וּבְכָל זְמַן. וְעוֹבֵר עָלֶיהָ וְשָׁכַב עִם הָאָחוֹת, בֵּין עַל יְדֵי נִשּׂוּאִין בֵּין דֶּרֶךְ זְנוּת, בְּחַיֵּי הָרִאשׁוֹנָה, בְּמֵזִיד חַיָּב כָּרֵת, וְאִם יֵשׁ עֵדִים וְהַתְרָאָה לוֹקֶה; בְּשׁוֹגֵג מֵבִיא חַטָּאת קְבוּעָה. וְאִם שָׁכַב עִם אֲחוֹת זְקוּקָתוֹ אוֹ אֲחוֹת חֲלוּצָתוֹ, לוֹקֶה מַכַּת מַרְדּוּת דְּרַבָּנָן.

וּמִכָּל־מָקוֹם אֵין אִשְׁתּוֹ דְּהַיְנוּ הָאָחוֹת שֶׁנָּשָׂא הָרִאשׁוֹנָה אֲסוּרָה עָלָיו מִפְּנֵי נִשּׂוּאֵי שְׁנִיָּה אוֹ זִמָּתָהּ, אֶלָּא אִשְׁתּוֹ מֻתֶּרֶת לוֹ וְזֹאת הַשֵּׁנִית תֵּלֵךְ לָהּ; וַאֲפִלּוּ

4. TB Yevamoth 54b.
5. See § 202, note 2.
6. Until he either marries her or releases her, she may marry no one else.
7. TB Yevamoth 41a, etc.
8. *Ibid.* 40a.
9. *Ibid.* 28b, 41a, etc.
10. Since the Sages equated to a marital tie the bond between a man and his dead brother's childless wife (until he either takes her to wife or releases her by *ḥalitzah*; TB Yevamoth 17b), and they likewise equated her release by *ḥalitzah* to divorce (*ibid.* 40b), whether he divorces his betrothed and takes his sister-in-law or he releases his sister-in-law and marries his betrothed, he is in effect marrying a wife's sister; TB Yevamoth 41a; MT *hilchoth yibbum* vii 8.
11. TB *ibid.* MT *ibid.*
12. Explained in § 121.
13. See § 24, note 14.

to a divorce. However, [despite this similarity] the ban on the sister of one released from the bond, and even on the sister of one bound to a man for levirate marriage, as the rule of the accepted law is established for us, is only by the decree of the Sages.[9] For the Torah forbade no more than the sister of one's married or betrothed wife; but as for one bound to him for levirate marriage, even though Heaven placed her in his power,[6] her sister is not included under the prohibition of the Torah. It is only that the Sages of blessed memory forbade her, so that a prohibition of the Torah should not be impinged upon.

Now, because this ban is by the Sages' ruling, as we stated, they were somewhat lenient in the matter at times, to the extent that they (of blessed memory) said that if one of several brothers duty-bound to take a woman in levirate marriage consecrated (betrothed) her sister,[5] he is told, "Wait: do not divorce her and do not marry her, until a brother of yours will either marry or release by *ḥalitzah* this woman who is bound to you all for levirate marriage." Then, if a brother of his released her with *ḥalitzah* or took her in levirate marriage, or if this dead brother's wife died, he may marry his betrothed. If, however, all the brothers died, he is to release his betrothed with a divorce and the original dead brother's wife with *ḥalitzah*.[10] If his betrothed died, whether she passed away before the brothers died or after their death, the woman bound for levirate marriage returns to her state of permissibility: If he wishes, he may release her by *ḥalitzah*, and if he wishes, he may take her in levirate marriage.[11] In the precept of levirate marriage (§598) we will write a bit more on these topics, as our custom is, with the Eternal Lord's help; for this is not its proper place.

This injunction is in force in every place and every time. If someone transgresses it and is conjugally intimate with a [wife's] sister, whether in marriage or in immorality, in the lifetime of the first [sister]—if it was willful, he incurs *karéth* [Divine severance of existence]; if there were witnesses and a [prior] warning, he should be given whiplashes; if it was inadvertent, he should bring a standard unvarying *ḥattath* (sin-offering).[12] If someone was conjugally intimate with the sister of a woman bound to him for levirate marriage, or the sister of one whom he released from the bond by *ḥalitzah*, he should be given whiplashes as punishment for disobedience, by the ruling of the Sages.[13]

In any event, though, the man's wife, meaning the sister whom he married first, does not become forbidden to him on account of marriage or immoral relations with the second one. Rather, his

נְשָׂאָהּ עַל־יְדֵי חֻפָּה וְקִדּוּשִׁין אֵינָהּ צְרִיכָה מִמֶּנּוּ גֵט, שֶׁאֵין קִדּוּשִׁין תּוֹפְסִין בָּעֲרָיוֹת לְהַצְרִיכָן גֵט; אֲבָל מִכָּל־מָקוֹם מִתְחַיֵּב הָעוֹשֶׂה בָהֶן מַעֲשֵׂה הַקִּדּוּשִׁין, שֶׁהַתּוֹרָה אָמְרָה "לֹא תִקָּח", וּמַשְׁמָע לְשׁוֹן קִדּוּשִׁין; וְאַף־עַל־גַּב דְּאִם עָבַר וְלָקַח, כְּלוֹמַר שֶׁקִּדֵּשׁ, לָא מְהַנֵּי לֵיהּ, כְּלוֹמַר שֶׁאֵינָהּ לְקוּחָתוֹ לְשׁוּם דָּבָר וְאֵינָהּ צְרִיכָה מִמֶּנּוּ גֵּט, מִכָּל־מָקוֹם נִתְחַיֵּב בְּכָךְ, כְּמוֹ שֶׁאָמַרְנוּ.

וְזֶה הַדִּין אֵינוֹ בַּאֲחָיוֹת לְבַד, אֶלָּא אַף בְּכָל שְׁאָר הָעֲרָיוֹת הוּא, שֶׁאִם נְשָׂאָן בְּחֶזְקַת הֶתֵּר וְנִמְצְאוּ עֲרָיוֹת, שֶׁאֵינָן צְרִיכוֹת גֵּט מִן הַטַּעַם שֶׁאָמַרְנוּ, שֶׁאֵין קִדּוּשִׁין תּוֹפְסִין בָּעֲרָיוֹת.

וְכֵן אִם נָשָׂא אוֹ עָבַר וְנָאַף עִם אַחַת מִן הַשֵּׁשׁ נָשִׁים שֶׁכָּתַבְנוּ לְמַעְלָה שֶׁהֵן עֲרָיוֹת עָלָיו מִן הַתּוֹרָה מֵחֲמַת אִשְׁתּוֹ, אֵינָן אוֹסְרוֹת אִשְׁתּוֹ עָלָיו אֶלָּא יֵלְכוּ לָהֶן בְּלֹא גֵט וְתִשָּׁאֵר אִשְׁתּוֹ מֻתֶּרֶת לוֹ, כְּמוֹ שֶׁאָמַרְנוּ; זוּלָתִי בַּאֲחוֹת אֲרוּסָתוֹ, שֶׁהֶחְמִירוּ חֲכָמִים וְאָסְרוּ אַף הָרִאשׁוֹנָה מִפְּנֵי נִשּׂוּאֵי הַשְּׁנִיָּה, שֶׁאָמְרוּ זִכְרוֹנָם לִבְרָכָה שֶׁאִם אֵרַס אָדָם אִשָּׁה, כְּלוֹמַר שֶׁקִּדְּשָׁהּ, וְאַחַר־כָּךְ נָשָׂא אֲחוֹתָהּ, שֶׁשְּׁתֵּיהֶן אֲסוּרוֹת עָלָיו וּצְרִיכוֹת מִמֶּנּוּ גֵט.

וּמִפְּנֵי־מַה אָמְרוּ כֵן וְלֹא אָמְרוּ שֶׁיִּשָּׂא הָרִאשׁוֹנָה וְהַשֵּׁנִית תֵּלֵךְ לָהּ בְּלֹא גֵט, כְּמוֹ שֶׁאָמַרְנוּ לְמַעְלָה? לְפִי שֶׁחָשְׁשׁוּ חֲכָמִים שֶׁמָּא יֹאמְרוּ הַבְּרִיּוֹת — אַחַר שֶׁלֹּא הָיָה לוֹ בָּרִאשׁוֹנָה אֶלָּא קִדּוּשִׁין לְבַד — כִּי בְאוֹתָן קִדּוּשִׁין הָיָה שׁוּם תְּנַאי, וְעַל־כֵּן נָשָׂא הַשֵּׁנִית וּבְדִין נְשָׂאָהּ; וּלְפִיכָךְ הִצְרִיכוּ בָהּ גֵּט, וְאַחַר שֶׁהִצְרִיכוּ בָּאַחֲרוֹנָה גֵט מִפְּנֵי זֶה הַחֲשָׁשׁ שֶׁאָמַרְנוּ, הָיָה לָהֶם לֶאֱסֹר גַּם־כֵּן אֲרוּסָתוֹ הָרִאשׁוֹנָה כְּדֵי שֶׁלֹּא יֹאמְרוּ הַבְּרִיּוֹת נָשָׂא אֲחוֹת גְּרוּשָׁתוֹ.

14. TB Yevamoth 94a.

15. *Ibid.* 94b.

16. Evidently derived from TB Kiddushin 67b, although Rambam apparently differs (MY). (Again, "betrothal" here has solely the meaning explained in §202, note 2.)

17. So R. 'Akiva, TB Yevamoth 94b, and so MT *hilchoth gĕrushin* x 9–10.

18. I.e. he probably became betrothed to her only conditionally, and the stipulated condition was not fulfilled.

19. So that people should not think that some women may go free and remarry without a divorce. MH notes that if he merely had immoral carnal relations with the second but formed no marital tie, she would not require a divorce, since this reason would not apply. Alternately, the reason would apparently apply as well with other close relatives of his wife, as long as his tie to her was only *'ērusin* (betrothal) — in which case people could assume that a condition had been stipulated and not fulfilled.

wife is permitted to him, and this second one is to go her way.[14] Even if he married her by consecration under the bridal canopy, she needs no divorce from him, for consecration (betrothal) is of no effect for absolutely forbidden women, to make them require a divorce.[15] Yet, nevertheless, any man who carries through an act of consecration (betrothal) with them incurs guilt: for the Torah said "you shall not take," which denotes the sense of betrothal. Even though, if someone transgressed and did take, i.e. betroth [one of these forbidden women], the act is of no avail to him—in other words, she does not become his in any respect, and she needs no divorce from him—he incurs guilt for it nevertheless, as we stated.[16]

This law applies not to sisters alone, but to all other absolutely forbidden women as well: If one married any of them on the assumption that they were permissible, and they were found to be thus forbidden, they require no divorce, for the reason that we stated—that consecration (betrothal) does not take effect with severely forbidden women.

Likewise, if a man married or was immorally intimate with any of the six women whom we mentioned above (§205), who are absolutely forbidden to him by the Torah's law on account of his wife, they do not make his wife forbidden to him, but they should rather go without a divorce, and his wife should remain permitted to him, as we stated—except in the case of a sister of someone betrothed to him: There the Sages were stringent and forbade the first one too, on account of marriage with the second. For the Sages of blessed memory taught that if a man betrothed a woman, i.e. he consecrated her, and afterward he married her sister, both are forbidden to him, and both require a divorce from him.[17]

Now, why did they rule so, and did not say that he should marry the first one, and the second [sister] should go her way without a divorce, as we stated above? It is because the Sages feared that people might say, "Since there was nothing more than consecration (betrothal) between him and the first one, there must have been some condition stipulated in that consecration,[18] and he therefore married the second one, taking her to wife according to law." Therefore the Sages required a divorce for her.[19] And once they made a divorce necessary for the later one, on account of this fear that we stated, they had to forbid his first, betrothed wife [to him], so that people should not say, "He married the sister of his divorced wife."

[שֶׁלֹּא לָבוֹא עַל אִשָּׁה נִדָּה]

רז שֶׁלֹּא לָבוֹא עַל אִשָּׁה בְּעֵת שֶׁהִיא נִדָּה, שֶׁנֶּאֱמַר: וְאֶל אִשָּׁה בְּנִדַּת טֻמְאָתָהּ לֹא תִקְרַב. וּזְמַן נִדּוּתָהּ נִמְשָׁךְ שִׁבְעָה יָמִים, כִּדְכְתִיב: שִׁבְעַת יָמִים תִּהְיֶה בְנִדָּתָהּ. וּבֵין שֶׁתִּרְאֶה פַּעַם אַחַת בָּהֶן אוֹ שׁוֹפַעַת כָּל הַשִּׁבְעָה, נִדָּה הִיא; וְכָל זְמַן שֶׁלֹּא תִטְבֹּל אַף אַחַר הַשִּׁבְעָה הִיא נִדָּה לְעוֹלָם, כִּי בְיָמִים וּטְבִילָה תָּלָה הַכָּתוּב, שֶׁנֶּאֱמַר בַּטְּמֵאִים: וְרָחֲצוּ בַמַּיִם, וְאָמְרוּ זִכְרוֹנָם לִבְרָכָה: בִּנְיַן אָב לְכָל טָמֵא שֶׁהוּא בְטֻמְאָה עַד שֶׁיִּטְבֹּל; וְכֵן גַּם־כֵּן דָּרְשׁוּ זִכְרוֹנָם לִבְרָכָה: "תִּהְיֶה בְנִדָּתָהּ", תְּהֵא בְנִדָּתָהּ עַד שֶׁתָּבוֹא בַמָּיִם.

וְעִנְיַן הַנִּדּוּת הוּא כִּי יֵשׁ בַּנָּשִׁים עִנְיָן שֶׁיָּזוּב דָּם מֵהֶן דֶּרֶךְ עֶרְוָתָן בְּכָל חֹדֶשׁ וְחֹדֶשׁ שְׁנֵי יָמִים אוֹ שְׁלֹשָׁה אוֹ יוֹתֵר, עַד שִׁבְעָה; וְצִוָּה הַכָּתוּב דְּבֵין שֶׁיָּזוּב הַדָּם מִמֶּנָּה יוֹם אֶחָד לְבַד אוֹ אֲפִלּוּ כָּל הַשִּׁבְעָה יִהְיֶה הַדִּין שָׁוֶה בָהֶן, שֶׁאִם זָב כָּל שִׁבְעָה וּפָסַק מִבְּעוֹד יוֹם בַּשְּׁבִיעִי, טוֹבֶלֶת לָעֶרֶב, שֶׁהוּא לֵיל שֶׁמָּחֳרָתָהּ יוֹם שְׁמִינִי, וּטְהוֹרָה; וְכֵן אִם לֹא זָב אֶלָּא יוֹם אֶחָד מִכָּל הַשִּׁבְעָה וַאֲפִלּוּ דָם טִפָּה כְּחַרְדָּל, מְצַפָּה שִׁבְעַת יָמִים, וְלָעֶרֶב שֶׁהוּא לֵיל שְׁמִינִי טוֹבֶלֶת, וּטְהוֹרָה לְבַעְלָהּ.

מִשָּׁרְשֵׁי הַנִּדָּה, כָּתַבְתִּי בְּפָרָשַׁת זֹאת תִּהְיֶה עַל עִנְיַן זָבָה [סי׳ קס״ו, קפ״ב] מַה שֶּׁיָּדַעְתִּי. וּכְלַל הָעִנְיָן כִּי הַשֵּׁם יַרְחִיק מֵעַמּוֹ אֲשֶׁר בָּחַר, כָּל טֻמְאָה וְכָל לִכְלוּךְ וְכָל נֶזֶק; גַּם אָמַרְתִּי שָׁם מַה יִּהְיֶה הָעִנְיָן לְפִי הַדּוֹמֶה שֶׁהֶחֱלִיאָן הַשֵּׁם לַנָּשִׁים בָּחֳלִי זֶה.

§207

1. So TB Niddah 73a, and Sifra, *m'tzora, zavim, parashah* 4, 5.
2. Literally, "[it is] a father-structure," i.e. it establishes a standard rule.
3. So MT *hilchoth 'issuré bi'ah* iv 3.
4. TB Shabbath 64b.

[THE PROHIBITION OF CONJUGAL INTIMACY WITH A MENSTRUOUS WOMAN]

207 not to be conjugally intimate with a woman when she is ritually unclean from the menses: as it is is stated, *And you shall not approach a woman to uncover her nakedness while she is impure by her uncleanness* (Leviticus 18:19). The time of her menstrual impurity lasts seven days, for it is written, *she shall be in her impurity seven days* (Leviticus 15:19). Whether she sees [menstrual stains] once in these days or there is a flow all the seven, she is [equally] menstrually unclean;[1] and as long as she does not undergo ritual immersion, even after the seven she remains forever menstrually impure; for Scripture made the matter depend on days and ritual bathing: It is stated about the ritually unclean, *they shall bathe themselves in water* (*ibid.* 18), and the Sages of blessed memory taught: This establishes a rule[2] for everyone ritually impure that he remains thus unclean until he undergoes ritual immersion.[3] So too the Sages of blessed memory interpreted the verse, *she shall be in her impurity* (*ibid.* 19):[4] she is to remain in her state of menstrual defilement until she enters water [for ritual immersion].

The matter of menstrual uncleanness is that it is a characteristic of women that blood should flow from them through the uterine canal every single month for two or three days, or more, up to seven. Well, Scripture ordained that whether blood flows from her one day alone or even all seven, the law should be the same in all instances: For if it flowed all seven [days] and stopped on the seventh while it was yet day, she may undergo ritual immersion in the evening, which is the night whose morning will be the eighth day, and she is then ritually clean. So too if it flowed for no more than one day alone out of the seven, and even if [there was then but] a drop of blood the size of a mustard seed: she is to wait seven days, and in the evening, which is the night of the eighth, she is to undergo ritual immersion, and she is then permitted to her husband.

As to the root reason for menstrual uncleanness, I wrote in *sidrah m'tzora*, on the subject of a woman with an irregular discharge (§§166, 182) what I know. The crux of the matter is that the Eternal Lord would remove from His people, whom He chose, every uncleanness, every besmirching, and every harm. I likewise stated there (§166) what the purpose of the matter would seem to be, that the Eternal Lord made women ill with this malady.

Among the laws of the precept, there is what the Sages of blessed

מִדִּינֵי הַמִּצְוָה, מַה שֶּׁאָמְרוּ זִכְרוֹנָם לִבְרָכָה שֶׁהָאִשָּׁה מְטַמְּאָה בְנִדָּה וַאֲפִלּוּ בְּיוֹם לִדְתָּהּ, מַה שֶּׁאֵין הַדִּין כֵּן בְּזָבָה, שֶׁאֵין הָאִשָּׁה מְטַמְּאָה בְזִיבָה עַד עֲשָׂרָה יָמִים; וְדָבָר זֶה מִפִּי הַשְּׁמוּעָה.

וְכָל הַנָּשִׁים בִּכְלַל אִסּוּר זֶה; וַאֲפִלּוּ שְׁפָחוֹת, כְּלוֹמַר שְׁפָחוֹת כְּנַעֲנִיּוֹת, מִכֵּיוָן שֶׁהֵן בִּכְלַל הַמִּצְווֹת הֲרֵי הֵן כְּיִשְׂרְאֵלִיּוֹת לְעִנְיָן זֶה. אֲבָל הַנָּשִׁים שֶׁל אֻמּוֹת הָעוֹלָם אֵינָן בִּכְלַל אִסּוּר נִדּוּת וְזִיבוּת אֶלָּא מִדְּרַבָּנָן, שֶׁגָּזְרוּ עֲלֵיהֶן בֵּין בִּזְכָרִים בֵּין בִּנְקֵבוֹת שֶׁיִּהְיוּ כְזָבִין לְכָל דִּבְרֵיהֶם. וְזֶה שֶׁאָמְרוּ בַגְּמָרָא שֶׁהַבָּא עַל הַגּוֹיָה חַיָּב עָלֶיהָ מִשּׁוּם נשג״ז, פֵּרוּשׁ: נִדָּה, שִׁפְחָה, גּוֹיָה, זוֹנָה; זֶה הַחִיּוּב אֵינוֹ אֶלָּא מִדְּרַבָּנָן בְּאִישׁ יִשְׂרָאֵל, אֲבָל בְּאִישׁ כֹּהֵן חַיָּב עָלֶיהָ מִדְּאוֹרַיְתָא מִשּׁוּם זוֹנָה וְלוֹקֶה עָלֶיהָ.

וּמַה שֶּׁאָמְרוּ זִכְרוֹנָם לִבְרָכָה גַּם־כֵּן שֶׁחֲמִשָּׁה מַרְאוֹת דָּמִים הֵן שֶׁטִּמְּאָה הַתּוֹרָה, וּשְׁאָר מַרְאוֹת הַדָּמִים טְהוֹרִים; וְהָעִנְיָן הוּא לְפִי שֶׁחֲכָמִים יָדְעוּ בְחָכְמָתָן שֶׁכָּל דָּם שֶׁאֵינוֹ מֵאוֹתָן חֲמִשָּׁה מַרְאוֹת אֵינוֹ בָא מִמָּקוֹם טָמֵא, כִּי מָקוֹם יָדוּעַ בָּאִשָּׁה שֶׁהַדָּם הַבָּא מִמֶּנּוּ בִּלְבַד טָמֵא, הוּא הַנִּקְרָא מָקוֹר, וּבִלְשׁוֹן חֲכָמִים קָרוּי חֶדֶר.

וּבִימֵיהֶם, שֶׁהָיוּ בְקִיאִין בְּכָל חָכְמָה, הָיוּ הַנָּשִׁים מַרְאוֹת דָּמָן לַחֲכָמִים וּמְטַהֲרִין אוֹתָן אוֹ מְטַמְּאִין לְפִי מַה שֶּׁהֵן; וּבְאוֹתָן הַיָּמִים הָיוּ כָל הַנָּשִׁים נוֹהֲגוֹת בְּדִין תּוֹרָה לְנִדּוּת וּלְזִיבוּת, שֶׁהַזָּבָה הָיְתָה יוֹשֶׁבֶת שִׁבְעָה יָמִים נְקִיִּים וְהַנִּדָּה טוֹבֶלֶת בְּלֵיל שְׁמִינִי, וַאֲפִלּוּ שׁוֹפַעַת כָּל שִׁבְעָה, מִכֵּיוָן שֶׁפָּסַק הַדָּם בַּשְּׁבִיעִי מִבְּעוֹד יוֹם.

וּמִשֶּׁרַבּוּ הַצָּרוֹת נִתְמַעֲטוּ לִבָּן שֶׁל חֲכָמִים וְיוֹדְעֵי הַתּוֹרָה וְלֹא רָצוּ לִסְמֹךְ

5. TB Niddah 32a (MT *ibid.* 1).

6. Since they are owned by Jews, they become obligated by ritual immersion to observe the precepts like Jewish women, except those precepts from which Scripture excludes them specifically. And whenever a heathen maidservant is freed, she becomes a Jewess automatically upon ritual immersion. Sifra, *m'tzora, zavim, parashah* 5, 1.

7. I.e. with the same degree of ritual uncleanness; TB Niddah 34a.

8. I.e. as though he had been thus intimate with all four; TB 'Avodah Zarah 36b.

9. So Rava in TB T'murah 29b.

10. TB Niddah 19a.

11. Literally, sit seven clean days (this is the standard idiom, or "sit seven clean ones"): i.e. watch and wait to make sure seven days in a row go by with no appearance of blood.

memory taught:[5] that a female can become ritually unclean from the menses even on the day of her birth—which is not the law for a woman with an irregular discharge: for a female does not become ritually impure by an irregular discharge until the age of ten days. This matter is known through the Oral Tradition.

All women are included under this prohibition, even maidservants, meaning female Canaanite slaves: since they are included under the obligation of the precepts, they are like Israelite women in this regard.[6] Women of the nations of the world, however, are not subject to the prohibition of those unclean from the menses or irregular discharge—except by the ruling of the Sages, who decreed about them, both man and woman, that they should be as people with irregular discharges in all respects.[7] This is why it was stated in the Talmud that if someone is conjugally intimate with a non-Jewish woman, he incurs guilt of four kinds on her account: as for one menstrually unclean, for a heathen maidservant, a non-Jewish woman, and a harlot.[8] Now, this guilt lies only by the ruling of the Sages on an ordinary Israelite; but a *kohen* becomes guilty on her account by the law of the Torah, as for a harlot (§266), and he receives whiplashes because of her.[9]

There is, likewise, what the Sages of blessed memory taught:[10] that there are five appearances (hues) of blood which the Torah has ruled to be ritually defiling, while all other appearances (hues) of blood are ritually clean. The reason is that the Sages knew by their wisdom that any blood which is not of those five hues does not come from an unclean source. For there is a certain place in the woman, from which origin alone the blood that issues is ritually unclean, that is called "the source"; and in the terminology of the Sages it is called "the chamber."

In their days, when they [the Sages] were expert in every wisdom, the women would show their [emissions of] blood to the Sages, and they would declare them ritually clean or unclean, according to what they were. And in those days, all women would behave according to the law of the Torah for women with the menses and irregular discharges: One with a discharge would observe seven clean days,[11] while a menstruant would undergo ritual immersion on the night of the eighth, even if the flow persisted through all seven, as long as the blood stopped on the seventh while it was yet day.

However, when the tribulations multiplied, the heart of the Sages and Torah scholars diminished, and they did not wish to rely on their

בְּדַעְתָּן לָדוּן מַרְאוֹת הַדָּמִים בִּכְלָל. וּלְפִיכָךְ עַכְשָׁיו בַּזְּמַן הַזֶּה כָּל שֶׁיֵּשׁ בּוֹ מַרְאֶה אֲדַמְדַּמִית כְּלָל אוֹ מַרְאֵה שַׁחֲרוּת, בֵּין שֶׁהוּא עָמֹק הַרְבֵּה אוֹ דֵיהֶא, כְּלוֹמַר שֶׁאֵינוֹ עָמֹק, טָמֵא; אֲבָל הַיָּרֹק וְהַלָּבָן, אַף־עַל־פִּי שֶׁהוּא עָבֶה כְּמוֹ דָם, הֲרֵי זֶה טָהוֹר. וְנֶאֱמֶנֶת אִשָּׁה לוֹמַר: כְּמַרְאֶה זֶה רָאִיתִי וְאִבַּדְתִּיו. וְאִם אָמְרָה: יָרֹק אוֹ לָבָן הָיָה, מְטַהֲרִין לָהּ.

וּכְשֶׁבָּא רַבִּי וְרָאָה שֶׁנִּתְמַעֲטָה הַחָכְמָה בָּעוֹלָם וְאֵין הַחֲכָמִים בְּקִיאִין בְּמַרְאוֹת הַדָּמִים, וְכִי הַנָּשִׁים הָיוּ נוֹהֲגוֹת בְּדִין תּוֹרָה שֶׁהָיוּ מוֹנוֹת יְמֵי נִדָּה לְנִדָּה וִימֵי זִיבָה לְזִיבָה, חָשַׁשׁ לַדָּבָר שֶׁמָּא לִפְעָמִים תִּרְאֶה הָאִשָּׁה דָם שֶׁהוּא מִדִּין תּוֹרָה טָהוֹר, וּמִפְּנֵי שֶׁלֹּא תִמְצָא חָכָם שֶׁיַּכִּיר בּוֹ תָחוּשׁ לוֹ מִן הַסָּפֵק וְתֵשֵׁב עָלָיו; וְאִם אַתָּה מַנְהִיגָהּ כְּדִין תּוֹרָה הֲרֵי שֶׁתִּהְיֶה מוֹנָה מֵאוֹתוֹ יוֹם שֶׁתַּתְחִיל לִרְאוֹת שִׁבְעָה יָמִים, וּבְלֵיל שְׁמִינִי אַף־עַל־פִּי שֶׁשָּׁפְעָה כָּל שִׁבְעָה אִם פָּסְקָה בְּיוֹם שְׁבִיעִי טוֹבֶלֶת לָעֶרֶב, כְּמוֹ שֶׁאָמַרְנוּ לְמַעְלָה.

וְנִמְצָא לִפְעָמִים שֶׁבָּאִין עָלֶיהָ לִידֵי אִסּוּר כָּרֵת, כִּי יֵשׁ לָחוּשׁ שֶׁמָּא כָּל הַדָּם שֶׁרָאֲתָה כָּל שִׁשָּׁה יָמִים הוּא דָם טָהוֹר וְשֶׁל יוֹם הַשְּׁבִיעִי הָיָה דָם טָמֵא, וְהִיא הִתְחִילָה לִמְנוֹת שִׁבְעַת יְמֵי נִדּוּת מִיּוֹם רִאשׁוֹן שֶׁרָאֲתָה וְהָיָה לָהּ לְהַתְחִיל וְלִמְנוֹתָם מִיּוֹם שְׁבִיעִי, כִּי הוּא הַתְחָלַת נִדּוּתָהּ, שֶׁהָיָה דָם טָמֵא.

וְעַל יְדֵי טָעוּת זוֹ בָּאָה לִטְעוּת הַרְבֵּה פְּעָמִים מִנִּדָּה לְזָבָה וּמִזָּבָה לְנִדָּה, שֶׁתְּהֵא סְבוּרָה לִהְיוֹת בִּימֵי נִדּוּת וּתְהֵא בִימֵי זִיבוּת.

לְפִיכָךְ עָמַד רַבִּי וְתִקֵּן שֶׁכָּל אִשָּׁה שֶׁרוֹאָה יוֹם אֶחָד תֵּשֵׁב שִׁשָּׁה יָמִים נְקִיִּים,

12. *Ibid.* 20b.

13. As our author explained in §182, this is the original law: When a woman saw blood, it was taken as the beginning of the menses. She waited seven days, and if the flow stopped definitely during those days, she underwent ritual immersion and was then purified. For the next eleven days, if any blood appeared, it was regarded as an irregular discharge. If such blood appeared for one or two days, it was a minor discharge: she had to observe one day of cleanness (free of any flow) and undergo ritual immersion. If blood thus appeared for three days, it was a major discharge: she would have to observe seven clean days and then undergo ritual immersion. After the eleven days, any bleeding would mark the recurrence of the menses.

14. Literally, and she would sit over it (see note 11); i.e. she would regard it as the onset of the menses, and she would then conduct herself accordingly (see note 13).

knowledge to judge the appearances (hues) of blood at all.[12] Therefore, now, at the present time, whatever has any appearance of redness at all, or any shade of black, whether it is very dark or light, i.e. not deep, it is ritually impure. However, anything greenish or white, even if it is as thick as blood, is ritually pure. And a woman is believed to say, "Such a hue did I see, and I lost it"; and if she said [it had been] greenish or white, she would be pronounced ritually clean.[12]

Now, Rabbi [Judah haNassi] came along and saw that wisdom had grown diminished in the world, and the sage scholars were not expert in the appearances of blood, while the women were conducting themselves according to the law of the Torah, counting the days of menstrual uncleanness for the menses, and the days of discharge-uncleanness for one with an irregular discharge.[13] He was then afraid about the matter: Perhaps at times a woman would see blood which was ritually pure by the law of the Torah, and because she could find no scholar who could recognize it, in her doubt she would suspect it [of being impure] and would observe the days over it accordingly.[14] Well, if you would have her follow the Torah's law, from the day she began seeing [blood] she should count seven days, and then, even if it flowed all the seven, if it but stopped on the seventh day, on the night of the eighth day she would undergo ritual immersion in the evening, as we stated above.

Then the result is that at times one could become punishable by *karéth* [Divine severance of existence] on her account: For it should be suspected that perhaps all the blood she saw all six days was ritually pure blood, and that of the seventh day was impure. Yet she began to count the seven days of menstrual uncleanness from the first day she saw [the blood], while she should have begun counting from the seventh day, as that marked the beginning of her menstrual uncleanness, when there was ritually impure blood.

Well, from this error she could go on to further error many times—from menstrual uncleanness to irregular-discharge-uncleanness, and from the ritual uncleanness of irregular discharge to that of the menses: for she could believe herself to be in the days of menstrual uncleanness when she was actually in the days of uncleanness from irregular discharge.

Therefore Rabbi [Judah haNassi] arose and established the rule that any woman who sees [blood] one day should observe six clean days; and so too if she saw [a flow] for two days, she should likewise

וְכֵן אִם רָאֲתָה שְׁנֵי יָמִים תֵּשֵׁב גַּם־כֵּן שִׁשָּׁה נְקִיִּים; שֶׁכָּל זְמַן שֶׁאֵינָהּ רוֹאָה יוֹתֵר מִשְּׁנֵי יָמִים, כְּשֶׁהִיא יוֹשֶׁבֶת עֲלֵיהֶן שִׁשָּׁה יָמִים נְקִיִּים אֵין בָּהֶן מְקוֹם סָפֵק מֵעַתָּה: שֶׁאִם אוֹתָן הַיָּמִים שְׁנֵיהֶם בִּימֵי נִדָּה הֵן, לְסוֹף שִׁבְעָה טְהוֹרָה הִיא, וְאִם שְׁנֵיהֶן בִּימֵי זִיבָה הֵן לֹא הָיְתָה צְרִיכָה אֶלָּא יוֹם אֶחָד. וַאֲפִלּוּ הָרִאשׁוֹן בִּימֵי זִיבָה וְהַשֵּׁנִי בִּימֵי נִדָּה אֵין בְּכָךְ כְּלוּם, שֶׁהֲרֵי הִיא יוֹשֶׁבֶת אַחַר־מִכֵּן שִׁשָּׁה נְקִיִּים, וְהָאֶחָד מֵאוֹתָן שִׁשָּׁה נְקִיִּים עוֹלֶה לְאוֹתוֹ יוֹם שֶׁל זִיבָה, וְאַף־עַל־פִּי שֶׁכֻּלָּן בִּימֵי נִדָּה הֵן, שֶׁהֲלָכָה הִיא: יְמֵי נִדָּה שֶׁאֵינָהּ רוֹאָה בָהֶן עוֹלִין לִימֵי זִיבָה.

וְאִם רָאֲתָה שְׁלֹשָׁה יָמִים, תִּקֵּן הוּא שֶׁתְּהֵא יוֹשֶׁבֶת שִׁבְעָה נְקִיִּים, מִפְּנֵי שֶׁיֵּשׁ לָחוּשׁ שֶׁכָּל הַשְּׁלֹשָׁה בִימֵי זִיבָה הָיוּ, וַהֲרֵי הִיא זָבָה גְדוֹלָה, שֶׁצְּרִיכָה לֵישֵׁב שִׁבְעָה נְקִיִּים מִדִּין תּוֹרָה.

זֹאת הָיְתָה תַקָּנָתוֹ שֶׁל רַבִּי, וְעִם תַּקָּנָה זוֹ לֹא נִשְׁאָר שׁוּם סָפֵק בָּעִנְיָן. וְאַחַר תַּקָּנָה זוֹ הוֹסִיפוּ עוֹד בְּנוֹת יִשְׂרָאֵל וְהֶחְמִירוּ עַל עַצְמָן שֶׁאֲפִלּוּ רוֹאוֹת דָּם טִפָּה כְּחַרְדָּל, כְּלוֹמַר אֲפִלּוּ בִרְאִיָּה אַחַת, הָיוּ יוֹשְׁבוֹת שִׁבְעָה נְקִיִּים, שֶׁלֹּא רָצוּ לַחֲלֹק בֵּין רוֹאָה דָם יוֹם אֶחָד אוֹ שְׁנַיִם לְרוֹאָה שְׁלֹשָׁה יָמִים. וְאֵין עִנְיַן הַחֻמְרָא שֶׁהֶחְמִירוּ הֵן מִשּׁוּם דָּם מוּעָט כְּחַרְדָּל, כִּי מִדִּין תּוֹרָה אֵין חִלּוּק לְעִנְיַן יְמֵי נִדּוּת בֵּין דָּם מוּעָט לְדָם מְרֻבֶּה, כִּי לְעוֹלָם צְרִיכָה לֵישֵׁב שִׁבְעַת יָמִים רְצוּפִים, כְּמוֹ שֶׁאָמַרְנוּ; אֲבָל הַחֻמְרָא הִיא שֶׁעָשׂוּ עַצְמָן כְּזָבוֹת אֲפִלּוּ בִרְאִיָּה אַחַת. וְחֻמְרָא זוֹ שֶׁקִּבְּלוּ עַל עַצְמָן הִיא מֻזְכֶּרֶת בְּהַרְבֵּה מְקוֹמוֹת בַּתַּלְמוּד, וְנִרְאֶה מִתּוֹךְ כָּךְ שֶׁחֲכָמִים רָאוּ חֻמְרָתָן טוֹבָה וּצְרִיכָה, וְהוֹדוּ לְדִבְרֵיהֶן.

נִמְצָא שֶׁכָּל הַנָּשִׁים הַיּוֹם, אֲפִלּוּ בִרְאִיָּה אַחַת דִּינָן כְּזָבוֹת גְּדוֹלוֹת וּצְרִיכוֹת לִסְפֹּר שִׁבְעָה יָמִים נְקִיִּים. וְכֵן כָּל אִשָּׁה שֶׁמּוֹצְאָה כֶּתֶם בְּמָקוֹם שֶׁרָאוּי לָחוּשׁ לוֹ,

15. I.e. upon ritual immersion (see first paragraph).

16. As cited in TB Niddah 66a and explained by Ramban (quoted by *Maggid Mishneh* to MT *hilchoth 'issuré bi'ah* xi 3). R. Judah haNassi was about the last of the *tanna'im* (Sages of the Mishnah); he codified the Mishnah into organic, authoritative form, in the second century CE. As his title *nassi* (patriarch) indicates, he was the religious head of Jewry in the land of Israel. On account of his great learning and piety, he is called in the Talmud simply *Rabbi*.

17. TB Niddah 66a.

observe six clean days. For as long as she sees [blood] no more than two days, when she observes six clean days for them, there is henceforth no room for doubt about them: If both of those days were in her period of menstrual uncleanness, at the end of seven she is ritually pure;[15] and if both were during days of irregular discharge, she needed no more than one day [without any flow]. Even if the first was in the days of irregular discharge, and the second in the menses, it is of no matter: for here she observes six clean days afterward, and one of those six clean ones counts against that day of irregular discharge, even though all [the six] are in the days of menstrual uncleanness—for it is a principle of law: days of menstrual uncleanness in which she sees no blood can count against that day of irregular discharge.

Now, if [a woman] saw [a flow] for three days, Rabbi [Judah haNassi] established the rule that she should observe seven clean days: for it can be suspected that all three were in the days of irregular discharge, and then she is "a woman with a major discharge," who is required to observe seven clean days by the law of the Torah.

This was the rule that Rabbi established;[16] and with this rule no doubt whatever can remain in the matter. Yet after this rule was established, the daughters of Israel (Jewish women) went further and made a stricter rule for themselves: that even if they should see a drop of blood the size of a mustard seed—in other words, even upon one manifestation of blood—they would observe seven clean days.[17] For they did not want to differentiate between one who sees blood one or two days, and one who sees it for three days.

Now, their extra strictness that they imposed on themselves is not in regard to the little bit of blood the size of a mustard seed: For by the law of the Torah there is no difference in respect of the days of menstrual uncleanness between a little blood and a great amount: [the woman] must always observe seven days in a row, as we have stated. The extra stringency is rather that they undertook to regard themselves as women with an irregular major discharge even at a single manifestation [of blood]. This extra strictness that they imposed on themselves is mentioned in many places in the Talmud, from which it would appear that the Sages saw their added stringency as something good and necessary, and gratefully consented to their amendment.

As a result, all women today, even upon one appearance [of blood], are regarded under the law as women with a major discharge, and they have to count seven clean days. So too any woman who

אַף־עַל־פִּי שֶׁהַכְּתָמִים מִדְּרַבָּנָן, כִּי מִן הַתּוֹרָה אֵין אִשָּׁה מִתְטַמְּאָה עַד שֶׁתַּרְגִּישׁ בְּעַצְמָהּ דַּם טֻמְאָתָהּ, שֶׁנֶּאֱמַר: דָּם יִהְיֶה זֹבָהּ בִּבְשָׂרָהּ, כְּלוֹמַר שֶׁתַּרְגִּישׁ אוֹתוֹ, אַף־עַל־פִּי־כֵן כְּבָר הֶחְמִירוּ חֲכָמִים עַל הַכְּתָמִים וְהִצְרִיכוּ סְפִירַת שִׁבְעָה עֲלֵיהֶם וְהֶפְסֵק טָהֳרָה. וּלְפִיכָךְ אִם מָצְאָה כֶּתֶם כְּשִׁעוּר הָאוֹסֵר בְּמָקוֹם שֶׁרָאוּי לָחוּשׁ בּוֹ, צְרִיכָה לֵישֵׁב עָלָיו גַּם־כֵּן שִׁבְעָה נְקִיִּים.

וּמֵאֵימָתַי הָאִשָּׁה מוֹנָה שִׁבְעָה יָמִים נְקִיִּים, מִמָּחֳרַת יוֹם שֶׁפָּסַק הַדָּם לְגַמְרֵי. כֵּיצַד, רָאֲתָה שְׁנֵי יָמִים אוֹ שְׁלֹשָׁה, בּוֹדֶקֶת עַצְמָהּ תָּדִיר: אִם פָּסַק הַדָּם בְּיוֹם שֵׁנִי אוֹ בְיוֹם שְׁלִישִׁי אֲפִלּוּ בְּשַׁחֲרִית, אֵינָהּ מוֹנָה שִׁבְעָה מֵאוֹתוֹ יוֹם שֶׁפָּסַק הַדָּם בּוֹ, אֶלָּא לְמָחָר בּוֹדֶקֶת עַצְמָהּ פַּעַם אַחֶרֶת וּמַתְחֶלֶת לִסְפֹּר שִׁבְעָה מֵאוֹתוֹ הַיּוֹם.

וּבַמֶּה דְּבָרִים אֲמוּרִים, שֶׁרָאֲתָה שְׁנֵי יָמִים אוֹ שְׁלֹשָׁה אוֹ עוֹד, אֲבָל לֹא רָאֲתָה אֶלָּא יוֹם אֶחָד, אַף־עַל־פִּי שֶׁבְּאוֹתוֹ הַיּוֹם בָּדְקָה עַצְמָהּ וְהִפְסִיקָה בְטָהֳרָה אֵינָהּ מוֹנָה מִיּוֹם הַמָּחֳרָת, שֶׁחֶזְקַת הַיּוֹם הָרִאשׁוֹן כֻּלּוֹ טָמֵא, וְהֻחְזַק מַעְיָן פָּתוּחַ כָּל אוֹתוֹ הַיּוֹם, וְחוֹשְׁשִׁין שֶׁמָּא דָמֶיהָ חָזְרוּ לָהּ לְאַחַר בְּדִיקָתָהּ וְשָׁפְעָה כָּל הַלַּיְלָה, וְאֵין יוֹם שֵׁנִי זֶה לִרְאִיָּתָהּ מִן הַמִּנְיָן. וַאֲפִלּוּ בָּדְקָה עַצְמָהּ מִבָּעֶרֶב, חוֹשְׁשִׁין שֶׁמָּא עִם סִלּוּק יָדֶיהָ רָאֲתָה, אֶלָּא־אִם־כֵּן הָיוּ יָדֶיהָ בֵּין עֵינֶיהָ כָּל בֵּין הַשְּׁמָשׁוֹת, כְּלוֹמַר שֶׁבָּדְקָה עַצְמָהּ וְהִנִּיחָה הָעֵד בִּפְנִים מִבְּעוֹד יוֹם וְעָמַד שָׁם בֵּין הַשְּׁמָשׁוֹת עַד הַלַּיְלָה וְלֹא מָצְאָה עָלָיו דָּם כְּלָל, בְּעִנְיָן זֶה אֶפְשָׁר שֶׁנֹּאמַר שֶׁתַּתְחִיל לִמְנוֹת מִיּוֹם הַמָּחֳרָת.

וְהַמּוֹצְאָה כֶּתֶם אֵין מַחְמִירִין בָּהּ כָּל־כָּךְ שֶׁנַּצְרִיךְ אוֹתָהּ יוֹם הֶפְסֵק טָהֳרָה מִלְּבַד הַיּוֹם שֶׁמָּצְאָה בוֹ הַכֶּתֶם, כְּמוֹ שֶׁאָמַרְנוּ בְּרוֹאָה יוֹם אֶחָד לְבָד, אֶלָּא וַדַּאי מִכֵּיוָן שֶׁבָּדְקָה עַצְמָהּ אַחַר שֶׁמָּצְאָה הַכֶּתֶם וּמָצְאָה טָהוֹר, מוֹנָה שִׁבְעָה נְקִיִּים

18. *Ibid.* 58b.

19. Literal translation, denoting that her irregular discharge consists of blood.

20. *Ibid.* 57b: she must sense it "in her flesh."

21. I.e. the woman must know for certain that all blood and stains ceased during the "clean" days.

22. I.e. of a minimal size—as a *garis* (bean)—that would render her menstrually unclean if it was definitely menstrual blood.

23. So Rabad, Ramban and Rashba, cited by *Maggid Mishneh* to MT *hilchoth 'issuré bi'ah* xi 11. This means that the stringent rule adopted by Jewish women applies to stains as well, although the original restrictions which stains impose are only by the Sages' decree.

24. Based on TB Niddah 69a and 33a.

25. So MT *ibid.* vi 20.

26. Because there is no firm evidence to end the assumption of the "open fountain" (of blood) that was definitely established the first day.

finds a stain in a place where suspicion [that it is menstrual] is warranted. Even though stains [bring ritual uncleanness only] by decree of the Sages,[18] for by the law of the Torah, a woman does not become ritually impure until she senses in herself the blood of her uncleanness—as it is stated, *blood shall be her discharge in her flesh*[19] (Leviticus 15:19): in other words, she should sense it[20]—nevertheless the Sages imposed a stringent rule long ago about stains, and required the counting of seven days for them, and cessation for ritual purity.[21] Therefore, if a woman found a stain of a size that imposes the prohibition,[22] in a place where suspicion [that it is menstrual blood] is warranted, she needs to observe seven clean days for it as well.[23]

Now, from when does a woman count the seven clean days?—from the day after the one on which the blood ceased completely. How so?—If she saw [blood] for two or three days, she is to examine herself constantly. If the blood stopped on the second or third day, even in the morning, she is not to count the seven from that day on which the blood ceased, but rather the next day she examines herself yet another time, and begins to count seven from that day.[24]

When does this rule apply, though?—If she saw [blood] two or three days or more. But if she saw it for no more than one day, even if she examined herself [regularly] and it stopped [that day, leaving her] in purity, she is not to count from the next day: For the established status of the first day is that it was entirely unclean, and there was thus a firm assumption of an "open fountain" that entire day.[25] Hence we suspect that perhaps her [menstrual] blood returned to her after her examination, and it flowed all night;[26] then this second day, after she saw [the blood], cannot be in the reckoning [of the seven clean days]. Even if she examined herself in the evening, we suspect that perhaps on removing her hands there was an appearance [of blood]—unless "her hands were between her eyes" the entire twilight: in other words, if she examined herself and left the tampon within while it was yet day, and it remained there through twilight till night, and she found no blood on it at all.[27] In such a case we can perhaps say that she should begin counting from the next day.

If a woman finds a stain, however, we are not so very stringent with her, that we should require her to have a day of interruption for ritual cleanness,[28] apart from the day on which she found the stain, as we said regarding a woman who sees [blood] for one day only. Rather, without any doubt, since she examined herself after she found

חוּץ מֵאוֹתוֹ יוֹם שֶׁמָּצְאָה הַכֶּתֶם, כְּלוֹמַר שֶׁמַּתְחֶלֶת מִנְיָנָהּ לְמָחֳרָתוֹ שֶׁל יוֹם שֶׁמָּצְאָה בוֹ הַכֶּתֶם, כְּדִין אִשָּׁה שֶׁרָאֲתָה דָם שְׁנֵי יָמִים אוֹ שְׁלֹשָׁה, כְּמוֹ שֶׁאָמַרְנוּ לְמַעְלָה.

כָּל שִׁבְעָה יָמִים צְרִיכָה הָאִשָּׁה בְּדִיקָה לְכַתְּחִלָּה בְּכָל יוֹם וָיוֹם; וּבְדִיעֲבַד אִם בָּדְקָה יוֹם רִאשׁוֹן בִּלְבַד, שֶׁהוּא מָחֳרַת הַיּוֹם שֶׁהִפְסִיקָה, וְשׁוּב לֹא בָדְקָה, אֲפִלּוּ עָבְרוּ עָלֶיהָ כַּמָּה יָמִים אַחַר הַשִּׁבְעָה, בּוֹדֶקֶת עַצְמָהּ בִּשְׁעַת טְבִילָה וְדַיָּהּ, שֶׁכְּבָר הִפְסִיקָה בְּטָהֳרָה קֹדֶם לָכֵן. לֹא בָדְקָה עַצְמָהּ בְּיוֹם רִאשׁוֹן אֶלָּא בְּיוֹם הֶפְסֵקָהּ בִּלְבַד, לְיוֹם שְׁבִיעִי בּוֹדֶקֶת עַצְמָהּ וְדַיָּהּ וְטוֹבֶלֶת בְּלֵיל שְׁמִינִי. לֹא בָדְקָה עַצְמָהּ לֹא בְיוֹם רִאשׁוֹן וְלֹא בְיוֹם שְׁבִיעִי, אֲפִלּוּ בָּדְקָה בְּלֵיל שְׁמִינִי, אַף־עַל־פִּי שֶׁהִפְסִיקָה בְטָהֳרָה מִקֹּדֶם לָכֵן, אֵין עוֹלִין לָהּ כְּלָל אוֹתָן שִׁבְעָה יָמִים שֶׁעָבְרוּ, מִכֵּיוָן שֶׁלֹּא בָדְקָה בָהֶן לֹא בַתְּחִלָּה וְלֹא בַסּוֹף, וּצְרִיכָה לִמְנוֹת מֵעֵת שֶׁבָּדְקָה שִׁבְעָה יָמִים נְקִיִּים.

וְאֶפְשָׁר שֶׁעִקַּר דָּבָר זֶה מִכֵּיוָן שֶׁהַתּוֹרָה צִוְּתָה "וְסָפְרָה לָּהּ... וְאַחַר תִּטְהָר", וּמִכֵּיוָן שֶׁלֹּא בָדְקָה לֹא בַתְּחִלָּה וְלֹא בַסּוֹף אֵין כָּאן סְפִירָה.

וּבְדִיקָה זוֹ צְרִיכָה הָאִשָּׁה לַעֲשׂוֹתָהּ בְּצֶמֶר גֶּפֶן נָקִי הַנִּקְרָא בְּלַעַז קוֹטוֹן אוֹ בְּצֶמֶר לָבָן נָקִי וָרַךְ אוֹ בְּבֶגֶד פִּשְׁתָּן יָשָׁן שֶׁמֵּחֲמַת יָשְׁנוֹ הוּא רַךְ, וְכֻלָּן יִהְיוּ לְבָנִים, כְּדֵי שֶׁיְּהֵא נִכָּר יָפֶה בָהֶן כָּל מַרְאֶה אַדְמִימוּת. וְאֵלֶּה הַבְּגָדִים שֶׁבּוֹדֶקֶת בָּהֶן נִקְרָאִין בַּתַּלְמוּד עִדִּים. וּכְשֶׁבּוֹדֶקֶת צְרִיכָה לְהַכְנִיס הָעֵד בְּכָל חוֹרִין וּסְדָקִין שֶׁבְּאוֹתוֹ מָקוֹם, וְאִם מָצְאָה עָלָיו אַחַר־כֵּן שׁוּם מַרְאֶה אָדֹם, טְמֵאָה. כָּל בְּדִיקָה שֶׁאֵינָהּ עֲשׂוּיָה כָּךְ אֵינָהּ בְּדִיקָה; אֲפִלּוּ הִכְנִיסָה הָעֵד בְּאוֹתוֹ מָקוֹם וְלֹא בָדְקָה בַּחוֹרִין וּסְדָקִין, אֵינָהּ בְּדִיקָה יָפָה, שֶׁאֵין זֶה קָרוּי אֶלָּא קִנּוּחַ; וְכָל־שֶׁכֵּן שֶׁאֵין שִׁנּוּי חֲלוּקָהּ עוֹלֶה לָהּ לִבְדִיקָה.

27. Then the second day, beginning with nightfall, starts with a firm assumption of cleanness, and the prior assumption of the "open fountain" is no longer valid; Ramban, cited in *Maggid Mishneh* to MT *ibid.*

28. I.e. not to allow her to start counting days of cleanness from the very next day.

29. So *tosafoth* to TB Niddah 7b, s.v. *R. 'Eli'ezer.*

30. TB Niddah 68b. It should be noted that in such an instance the examination on the first day must have been thorough, to establish a state of cleanness past all doubt.

31. I.e. the examination on the first day following the day the flow ceased, ended her status as one with bleeding, and established an assumption of cleanness.

32. So Ramban and Rashba, cited in *Maggid Mishneh* to MT *hilchoth 'issuré bi'ah* vi 21.

33. There must be an examination on the first or the last of the seven days to establish that she has counted days of cleanness.

34. Source in note 32, based on TB Niddah 17a.

the stain, and found herself clean, she may count seven clean days apart from that day when she found the stain. That is: she begins her counting the day after the one when the stain was found,[23] as the law is for a woman who saw blood for two or three days, as we said above.

During the entire seven days, the woman is required to make an examination, initially, every single day.[29] After the fact, though, if she made the examination the first day alone, i.e. the day after the one on which she stopped, and then she did not examine herself again, even if several days passed by thereafter, after the seven she is to examine herself at the time of the ritual immersion, and this is enough for her:[30] for she already severed connection [with the bleeding] by cleanness before this.[31] If she did not examine herself the first day [of the seven] but only on the day of the cessation [of the flow], on the seventh day she is to examine herself, and it is enough; and she may undergo ritual immersion on the night of the eighth. If she examined herself neither the first day [of the seven] nor the seventh, then even if she examined herself on the night of the eighth, and although she severed connection [with the menses] by cleanness before that, those seven days that passed were of no effect for her at all, since she did not make her examination either at the beginning or at the end;[32] and she has to count seven clean days from the time she examined herself.

It could be that the main reason for this is that the Torah commanded, *then she shall count for herself . . . and after that she shall be clean* (Leviticus 15:28), and since she made no examination either at the beginning or at the end, there was no "counting" here.[33]

As to this examination, the woman has to make it with clean cotton [cloth], called *cotón* in the foreign tongue [Spanish], or with clean, soft white wool [cloth], or with old linen cloth which, because of its age, is soft. All should be white, so that any appearance of redness will be well discerned on it.[34] These cloths with which she examines herself, are called in the Talmud "witnesses."[35] When she examines, she is required to introduce the "witness" into all the hollows and crevices of that place, and if she found on it any appearance of redness afterward, she is ritually unclean. Any examination that was not done so is no examination; even if she introduced the "witness" into that place, but did not investigate the hollows and crevices, it is not a proper examination, for this is called nothing more than cleansing.[36] And all the more certainly is changing her garment of no avail to her

〈353〉 for the examination.

שִׁבְעָה יָמִים נְקִיִּים אֵלּוּ צְרִיכִין שֶׁיִּהְיוּ רְצוּפִין, שֶׁלֹּא תַפְסִק טֻמְאָה בֵּינֵיהֶם. אֲפִלּוּ יָשְׁבָה לָהּ כָּל הַיָּמִים וְלֹא רָאֲתָה, וּבַיּוֹם הַשְּׁבִיעִי אֲפִלּוּ מִבָּעֶרֶב רָאֲתָה, הֲרֵי זוֹ סוֹתֶרֶת כָּל מִנְיָנָהּ וּצְרִיכָה לִסְפֹּר אַחַר־כָּךְ שִׁבְעָה יָמִים נְקִיִּים רְצוּפִים.

וְדִינֵי שִׁעוּרֵי הַכֶּתֶם, וּבְאֵיזֶה עִנְיָן תּוֹלָה בַכֶּתֶם אוֹ אֵינָהּ תּוֹלָה; וּמִי שֶׁיֵּשׁ לָהּ מַכָּה בְּאוֹתוֹ מָקוֹם, אִם תּוֹלָה בָהּ דָּמֶיהָ עַד שֶׁתִּחְיֶה הַמַּכָּה; וְעִנְיַן קְטַנָּה שֶׁנִּבְעֲלָה וְהַדָּם שׁוֹתֵת מִמֶּנָּה, מַה דִּינָהּ; וְדַם בְּתוּלִים, שֶׁדָּנוּ אוֹתָן חֲכָמִים כְּדַם נִדָּה.

וְדִינֵי הַוְּסָתוֹת רַבִּים; וְדִין פְּרִישָׁה מִן הָאִשָּׁה סָמוּךְ לְוִסְתָּהּ עוֹנָה, כְּלוֹמַר אוֹתוֹ הַיּוֹם אוֹ אוֹתוֹ הַלַּיְלָה שֶׁהִיא רְגִילָה לִרְאוֹת בָּהֶן, אֲסוּרָה בְתַשְׁמִישׁ, מִדִּכְתִיב: וְהִזַּרְתֶּם אֶת בְּנֵי יִשְׂרָאֵל מִטֻּמְאָתָם, וּבָא הַפֵּרוּשׁ שֶׁיִּפְרְשׁוּ מִנְּשׁוֹתֵיהֶן סָמוּךְ לְוִסְתָּן; אֲבָל אַחַר שֶׁעָבְרָה עוֹנַת הַוֶּסֶת מֻתָּרִין לְשַׁמֵּשׁ.

וְעִנְיַן הַהַרְחָקָה מִן הָאִשָּׁה שֶׁצִּוּוּ זִכְרוֹנָם לִבְרָכָה בְּעִנְיַן הַנִּדּוּת, כְּדֵי שֶׁלֹּא יִכָּשֵׁל אָדָם בַּעֲבֵרָה, וְהוּא שֶׁלֹּא יֹאכַל אָדָם עִם אִשְׁתּוֹ נִדָּה בִּקְעָרָה אַחַת וְלֹא יוֹשִׁיט דָּבָר מִיָּדוֹ לְיָדָהּ וְלֹא יְדַבֵּר עִמָּהּ דְּבָרִים שֶׁל הֶרְגֵּל עֲבֵרָה, וְכַיּוֹצֵא בִדְבָרִים אֵלּוּ.

וְעִנְיַן טְבִילָתָן שֶׁהִצְרִיכוּ אוֹתָן חֲכָמִים לִטְבֹּל בַּלַּיְלָה; וְאַף־עַל־פִּי שֶׁטְּבִילַת הַזָּבָה אֲפִלּוּ בַיּוֹם מִדִּין תּוֹרָה, וְהֵן כֻּלָּן הַיּוֹם כְּזָבוֹת, אַף־עַל־פִּי־כֵן אָמְרוּ חֲכָמִים שֶׁטְּבִילַת כֻּלָּן בַּלַּיְלָה, מִשּׁוּם סְרָךְ בִּתָּהּ, וּכְמוֹ שֶׁמְּפֹרָשׁ הָעִנְיָן בַּגְּמָרָא. וּבִמְקוֹם דֹּחַק כְּגוֹן שֶׁדַּלְתוֹת מְדִינָה נִנְעָלוֹת בַּלַּיְלָה וְכַיּוֹצֵא בָזֶה, הִתִּירוּ לִטְבֹּל אֲפִלּוּ בַיּוֹם; וּמִכָּל־מָקוֹם אֲסוּרָה לְשַׁמֵּשׁ עַד הַלַּיְלָה, שֶׁמָּא תִּרְאֶה וְתִסְתֹּר כָּל מִנְיָנָהּ, וְנִמְצָא

35. Because they provide the evidence for cleanness or uncleanness.

36. So Rashba, *Torath haBa-yith*, VII 5.

37. TB Niddah 37a.

38. Which can bring a state of uncleanness; *ibid.* 58b.

39. *Ibid.*

40. TB Niddah 64b.

41. *Ibid.* 65b.

42. *Ibid.* 63b.

43. MT *hilchoth 'issuré bi'ah* xi 18, based on TB Shabbath 13a.

44. *Tosafoth* to TB Shabbath 13b, s.v. *bimé*.

45. See Mishnah, 'Avoth i 5, and commentaries of R. 'Obadiah Bertinoro and Rambam.

46. I.e because a daughter is close to her mother and takes her as a model for her own later behavior. The source in the Talmud (Niddah 67b) reads: R. Yoḥanan said: Whether in its proper time or not, she is not to undergo ritual immersion other than at night, because of "the attachment of her daughter." Now, as our author explained above, at some time in our past history it became the accepted practice of Jewish women to conduct themselves as if with an irregular discharge even upon the appearance of a small

These seven clean days have to be consecutive (in a row), with no ritual uncleanness interrupting them. Even if a woman sat through all the days and saw no blood, and on the seventh day, only toward evening, she did see, this upsets all her counting, and she has to count seven consecutive clean days after that.[37]

Then there are the laws of minimal sizes of a stain,[38] and in which cases we attribute [what appears] to a stain, or do not attribute it to a stain.[39] Then too, if a woman has a wound at that place, if she should attribute her bleeding to it until the wound heals.[39] And we have the subject of a child who participated in conjugal intimacy and the blood pours from her, what her law is;[40] and the blood of terminated virginity, which the Sages regarded in law as blood of the menses.[41]

Then there are the many laws of periods of the menses; and the law of separating from one's wife close to the time for her regular period: in other words, that day or that night when she is wont to see [menstrual blood], conjugal intimacy is forbidden, since it is written, *Thus you shall separate the Israelites from their uncleanness* (Leviticus 15:31), for which the explanation was given [in the Oral Tradition][42] that they should separate from their wives close to their periods. But after the period [of likely bleeding] before the time for the menses has passed [and there is no bleeding] they are permitted conjugal intimacy.

There is, further, the matter of maintaining distance from one's wife, which the Sages of blessed memory commanded in regard to menstruants, so that a man should not come to grief with sin: This means that he should not eat with his menstrually unclean wife out of one plate;[43] he should not give over anything [directly] from his hand to hers;[44] he should not speak with her any words that could lead to the habit of sinning;[45] and so anything similar to these.

We have, too, the matter of their ritual immersion, which the Sages have required them to undergo at night. Even though the ritual immersion of a woman with an irregular discharge may be even by day by the law of the Torah, and today they are all like women with irregular discharges [under the law], nevertheless the Sages ruled that the ritual immersion of all is to be at night, because of "the attachment of her daughter"—as the subject is explained in the Talmud.[46] Where there are pressing circumstances, though—for example, if the gates of the city are locked at night, or anything similar—they are permitted ritual immersion even by day. Nevertheless, she is forbidden conjugal intimacy until the night: perhaps she will see [blood] and thus

שֶׁבָּא עַל הַטְּמֵאָה, לְפִי שֶׁטָּהֳרָתָהּ תָּלָה הַכָּתוּב בְּיָמִים וּטְבִילָה.

וְנוֹהֵג אִסּוּר זֶה בְּכָל מָקוֹם וּבְכָל זְמַן. וְעוֹבֵר עָלֶיהָ וְשָׁכַב אֶת הַנִּדָּה בְּמֵזִיד, מִכֵּיוָן שֶׁהֶעֱרָה בָהּ חַיָּב כָּרֵת; בְּשׁוֹגֵג, מֵבִיא חַטָּאת קְבוּעָה. וּבֶן הַנִּדָּה אֵינוֹ נִקְרָא מַמְזֵר אֶלָּא וָלָד פָּגוּם, וּבְלָאו דְּ״לֹא יָבוֹא מַמְזֵר״ נְבָאֵר זֶה בְּעֶזְרַת הַשֵּׁם, בְּסֵדֶר כִּי תֵצֵא [סי׳ תק״ס].

[שֶׁלֹּא נִתֵּן מִזַּרְעֵנוּ לַמֹּלֶךְ]

רח שֶׁלֹּא נִתֵּן קְצָת מִבָּנֵינוּ לְהַעֲבִירָם לִפְנֵי עֲבוֹדָה זָרָה שֶׁהָיוּ עוֹשִׂין בְּנֵי־אָדָם בִּזְמַן מַתַּן תּוֹרָה שֶׁהָיָה שְׁמוֹ מֹלֶךְ, שֶׁנֶּאֱמַר: וּמִזַּרְעֲךָ לֹא תִתֵּן לְהַעֲבִיר לַמֹּלֶךְ, כְּלוֹמַר מִקְּצָת זַרְעֲךָ. וְנִכְפְּלָה הָאַזְהָרָה, דִּכְתִיב בְּמָקוֹם אַחֵר: לֹא יִמָּצֵא בְךָ מַעֲבִיר בְּנוֹ וּבִתּוֹ בָּאֵשׁ.

וְכָךְ הָיוּ עוֹשִׂין: הָאָב מוֹסְרוֹ לַכּוֹמָרִים לְשֵׁם שִׁקּוּצָם, כְּעֵין מַה שֶּׁכָּתוּב בְּקָרְבָּנוֹת כְּשֵׁרִים ״וּנְתָנָם אֶל הַכֹּהֵן״; וְאֶפְשָׁר שֶׁהַכּוֹמָרִים עוֹשִׂין בּוֹ תְנוּפָה אוֹ הַגָּשָׁה לִפְנֵי הַמֹּלֶךְ; וְאַחַר־כָּךְ מַחֲזִירִין אוֹתוֹ לָאָב וּמַבְעִירִין אֵשׁ גְּדוֹלָה לִפְנֵי הָעֲבוֹדָה זָרָה, וְהָאָב לוֹקֵחַ בְּנוֹ וּמַעֲבִירוֹ בְּלַהַב הָאֵשׁ. וְכָךְ אָמְרוּ בִירוּשַׁלְמִי: אֵינוֹ חַיָּב עַד שֶׁיִּמְסֹר לַכּוֹמָרִים וְיִטְּלֵנוּ וְיַעֲבִירֶנּוּ.

וְדַעַת הָרַב רַשִׁ״י זִכְרוֹנוֹ לִבְרָכָה וְהָרַמְבָּ״ם זִכְרוֹנוֹ לִבְרָכָה שֶׁלֹּא הָיָה שׂוֹרְפוֹ אֶלָּא הָעֲבוֹדָה הָיְתָה לְהַעֲבִירוֹ לְבַד, וּמִכֵּיוָן שֶׁהֶעֱבִירוֹ כְּמוֹ שֶׁהָיָה דַרְכָּם לְהַעֲבִירוֹ, חַיָּב. וְדַעַת הָרַמְבָּ״ן זִכְרוֹנוֹ לִבְרָכָה שֶׁהָיָה מַעֲבִירוֹ בַּלַּהַב עַד שֶׁנִּשְׁמָתוֹ יוֹצֵאת, וּרְאָיוֹתָיו בְּפֵרוּשׁ הַחֻמָּשׁ שֶׁעָשָׂה.

bloodstain: i.e. they then observe seven clean days and undergo ritual immersion. As such authorities as Me'iri (TB *ad loc.*) and Rashba (believed to be our author's main instructor in Talmud and *halachah*; TB *ad loc.* and *Torath haBa-yith* VII 7, ed. Josefov 30b) apply the Talmudic rule to this later, continuing period in Jewish life, it means that even on her eighth clean day a woman is not to have her immersion by day, because her daughter may believe it was the seventh day, and at a later time she may go for her own ritual immersion on her seventh day of cleanness; and afterward she may cohabit with her husband, only to find a reappearance of blood before the day's end. By the rule given four paragraphs above, her seven clean days would then become null and void, and she would have to observe a new period of cleanness. Consequently, her act of cohabitation would remain a severe transgression which incurs *karéth* if done deliberately. Hence any woman is forbidden to undergo her ritual immersion by day, even after her period of clean days has passed.

This is how Me'iri and Rashba apply R. Yoḥanan's ruling in the Talmud as regards "not in its proper time"; "in its proper time" would then mean as the seven clean days approach their end: i.e. on the seventh day. It will be clear from the foregoing, however, that while "the attachment of her daughter" would still be a consideration (as above), upset all her counting, and the result will be that [her husband] was conjugally intimate with a ritually unclean woman, since Scripture made her ritual purification depend on days and ritual immersion.[47]

This prohibition is in force everywhere and at every time. If someone violates it and is conjugally intimate with a menstrually unclean woman deliberately, once he has intromitted the membrum, he is punishable by *karéth* [Divine severance of existence]. If it was inadvertent, he is to bring a standard unvarying *ḥattath* (sin-offering).[48] The son of a menstrually unclean woman is not called (reckoned) a bastard but merely a child of inferior rank. In the negative precept that a bastard is not to enter the community (§560) we will clarify this, with the Eternal Lord's help, in *sidrah ki thétzé*.

[NOT TO GIVE ANY OF OUR CHILDREN TO THE IDOL MOLECH]

208 that we should not give some of our sons to pass them before an idol that people used to make at the time the Torah was given, whose name was Molech—as it is written, *And you shall not give of your offspring to transport them to Molech* (Leviticus 18:21), which means "some of your offspring."[1] The injunction was repeated, as it is written elsewhere, *There shall not be found among you any one that makes his son or his daughter pass through the fire* (Deuteronomy 18:10).

This is what they would do: The father would hand him over to the priests for the sake of their abomination,[2] paralleling what is written of worthy, acceptable offerings: *and he shall give them to the* kohen (Leviticus 15:14). It is possible that the priests would lift him up or bring him near before Molech, and then would return him to his father.[3] Then they would kindle a great fire before the idol; and the father would take his son and pass him through the flame of the fire. And so it was taught in the Jerusalem Talmud:[4] One is not guilty until he hands [his son] over to the priests, takes him and passes him across.

Now, the view of Rashi and Rambam of blessed memory is that he would not burn him; rather, the way of worship was merely to pass him through.[5] So once he passed him through [the flames] as it was their way to take him through, he would be punishable. But the view of Ramban of blessed memory[6] is that he would take him through the flames until his soul would expire; his proofs are in the commentary to the Pentateuch that he composed.[6]

רֶמֶז מִשָּׁרְשֵׁי רִחוּק עֲבוֹדָה זָרָה דֶּרֶךְ כְּלָל כָּתַבְתִּי לְמַעְלָה בוֹ מַה שֶׁיָּדַעְתִּי, בְּסֵדֶר וַיִּשְׁמַע יִתְרוֹ. וְהָעִנְיָן הַזֶּה שֶׁל עֲבוֹדָה זָרָה זוֹ שֶׁל מֹלֶךְ, לְפִי שֶׁהָיְתָה עֲבוֹדָה רָעָה בְּיוֹתֵר וְהָיוּ אֲדוּקִין בָּהּ הַרְבֵּה בְּאוֹתוֹ זְמַן, נִתְיַחֲדָה בָהּ אַזְהָרָה מִלְּבַד כָּל אַזְהָרוֹת עֲבוֹדָה זָרָה הַרְבֵּה שֶׁבַּתּוֹרָה; וְזֶה נֹאמַר לְדַעַת הָרַמְבָּ״ם זִכְרוֹנוֹ לִבְרָכָה.

אֲבָל לְפִי הַנִּרְאֶה, לְדַעַת הָרַמְבָּ״ן זִכְרוֹנוֹ לִבְרָכָה לֹא נִצְטָרֵךְ לָזֶה, כִּי הוּא סוֹבֵר שֶׁעִנְיָן מְחֻדָּשׁ יֵשׁ בָּעֲבוֹדָה זוֹ שֶׁל מֹלֶךְ מִכָּל שְׁאָר עֲבוֹדוֹת זָרוֹת: שֶׁבְּכָל עֲבוֹדָה זָרָה לֹא יִתְחַיֵּב הָעוֹבְדָהּ בְּשֶׁלֹּא כְדַרְכָּהּ אֶלָּא בְּאַרְבַּע עֲבוֹדוֹת הַיְּדוּעוֹת, אֲבָל בְּעִנְיָן זֶה שֶׁל מֹלֶךְ יִתְחַיֵּב הָעוֹשֶׂה מַעֲשֶׂה זֶה שֶׁל מֹלֶךְ בְּכָל עֲבוֹדָה זָרָה; וּלְפִיכָךְ נִתְיַחֲדָה הָאַזְהָרָה בוֹ. וּלְפִי שֶׁהָעִנְיָן מְכֹעָר בְּיוֹתֵר הֶחְמִירָה הַתּוֹרָה בוֹ כָּל־כָּךְ לְחַיֵּב הָעוֹשֶׂה כֵן בְּכָל עֲבוֹדָה זָרָה אַף־עַל־פִּי שֶׁאֵינוֹ דַרְכָּהּ בְּכָךְ. זֶהוּ הַנִּרְאֶה לִי מִכְּלַל דְּבָרָיו.

וְזֶה הָעִנְיָן שֶׁאֵין הַחִיּוּב בָּא אֶלָּא בְּמִקְצָת הַזֶּרַע וְלֹא בְכֻלּוֹ, אֶפְשָׁר שֶׁהָיָה מִפְּנֵי שֶׁהַכּוֹמָרִים הַשַּׁקְרָנִים הָיוּ מַבְטִיחִין אֲבִי הַבֵּן כִּי עַל־יְדֵי תִקְרֹבֶת בֵּן זֶה יַצְלִיחַ שְׁאָר זַרְעוֹ בְּכֹל אֲשֶׁר יִפְנֶה, וְתִהְיֶה הַבְּרָכָה וְהַטּוֹבָה מְצוּיָה בְּבֵיתוֹ; וּלְרֹב תַּרְמִיתָם לֹא רָצוּ מִתְּחִלָּה לִקְבֹּעַ הַחֹק רַק בְּמִי שֶׁיִּשָּׁאֵר לוֹ זֶרַע מִלְּבַד אוֹתוֹ שֶׁהוּא נוֹתֵן לָהֶם, פֶּן יְמָאֲנוּ מִלִּשְׁמֹעַ אֲלֵיהֶם, הֵן לְשָׂרְפוֹ לְגַמְרֵי הֵן לְהַעֲבִירוֹ בְּתוֹךְ הַלַּהַב וּלְסַכְּנוֹ כְּדַעַת קְצָת הַמְפָרְשִׁים, וּלְמַעַן יַבְטִיחוּ גַם־כֵּן עַל הַבְּרָכָה וְהַטּוֹבָה בַּנִּשְׁאָרִים וְיִתְפַּתּוּ אֲלֵיהֶם מִתּוֹךְ כָּךְ הַפְּתָאִים; וְלָכֵן לֹא חִיְּבָה הַתּוֹרָה בָּעִנְיָן רַק כְּשֶׁהוּא כְעֵין עֲבוֹדָתָן וְלֹא בְצַד אַחֵר.

מִדִּינֵי הַמִּצְוָה, מַה שֶּׁאָמְרוּ זִכְרוֹנָם לִבְרָכָה: מָסַר וְלֹא הֶעֱבִיר, הֶעֱבִיר וְלֹא מָסַר, פָּטוּר; וְשֶׁאֵינוֹ חַיָּב עַד שֶׁיַּעֲבִיר מִקְצָת זַרְעוֹ וְיַנִּיחַ מִקְצָתוֹ, כְּמוֹ שֶׁאָמַרְנוּ;

there is a prior reason for forbidding a woman her ritual immersion on her seventh day of cleanness: she herself may cohabit with her husband afterward, and then find a reappearance of blood before the day's end.

Yet just as R. Yoḥanan gave his one reason for both "in its proper time" and afterward, so has our author left his wording general, without specifying details. (Very possibly he deliberately left it vague for his son and the young student's friends—for whom, as he states, he wrote this work—to fathom the details in their own further study.) The ruling that follows, however, refers specifically to the seventh day, and not afterwards (see note 47). Hence MY understands this ruling too to apply only to the seventh day; and he explains it as follows: Sometimes a woman may be certain that her flow is not an irregular discharge (i.e. at the first flow after forty days following the birth of a boy, or after eighty days following the birth of a girl). Then she may go by the pure rule of the Torah, and observe only seven days (clean or not) beginning from the onset of the flow. Having seen her mother go for her ritual immersion within the last of her "days of counting," she may go to the *mikveh* on *her* last "day of counting," and in her case,

A hint of the root reason for removing idolatry in general, I wrote above, what I know of it, in *sidrah yithro* (§26). As to the reason concerning this idol-worship of Molech, because the worship was extremely evil, and people were very devout in it, a particular injunction was given about it apart from all the many admonitions about idolatry in the Torah. This we would say according to the view of Rambam of blessed memory.

According to the view of Ramban of blessed memory, however,[7] we evidently will not have need of this [reason], for he holds that there is a new element in this worship of Molech, unlike every other idol-worship: With any other idol, a person who worships it in a way that is not usual for it will incur punishment only with the four known ways of worship.[8] But as regards this matter of Molech, anyone who does this act of Molech in the worship of any idol, incurs guilt.[9] Therefore this particular injunction was given about it. And because the matter is so intensely revolting, the Torah was so very stringent about it, to impose the punishment on any person who does this toward any idol, even if this is not its way of worship. This is how it seems to me from the general sum of his words.

As to the reason why guilt is incurred only for [sacrificing] some of one's offspring, but not for (sacrificing) all[10]—it is possibly because the lying priests used to assure the father of the son that by the sacrifice of this son, his other children would succeed wherever they turned, and blessing and goodness would be found [constantly] in his house. Thus, in their great deceitfulness, they did not wish to establish this practice for any but a person who would leave over offspring apart from the one he would give them—for fear that people would refuse to listen to them, whether it was to burn him completely, or to pass him through the flame, and thus put his life into danger, according to the view of some authorities;[11] and also in order that they should rely on the [promised] blessing and goodness for the remaining ones; and so, as a result, the foolish people would be persuaded by them. Hence the Torah imposed guilt in this matter only when it was in a way resembling their worship, but not in any other way.

Among the laws of the precept, there is what the Sages of blessed memory taught:[12] If [a father] handed over [a son to the priests] but did not pass [him through the fire], or if he passed [him through the fire] but did not hand [him] over, he is free of guilt. He is not punishable until he passes some of his offspring through [the flames]

וְשֶׁחַיָּב בֵּין עַל זַרְעוֹ כָּשֵׁר בֵּין עַל זַרְעוֹ פָּסוּל; וְשֶׁחַיָּב עַל כָּל יוֹצְאֵי יְרֵכוֹ, בָּנִים אוֹ בָנוֹת, בֵּין בָּנִים אוֹ בְנֵי בָנִים, עַד לְעוֹלָם, אֲבָל אִם הֶעֱבִיר אֶחָיו אוֹ אַחְיוֹתָיו אוֹ אֲבוֹתָיו אוֹ שֶׁהֶעֱבִיר עַצְמוֹ פָּטוּר; וְיֶתֶר פְּרָטֶיהָ, בְּפֶרֶק שְׁבִיעִי מִסַּנְהֶדְרִין.

וְנוֹהֶגֶת בְּכָל מָקוֹם וּבְכָל זְמַן בִּזְכָרִים וּנְקֵבוֹת. וְעוֹבֵר עַל לָאו זֶה בְּמֵזִיד וְיֵשׁ עֵדִים וְהַתְרָאָה, נִסְקָל בִּזְמַן שֶׁדָּנִין דִּינֵי נְפָשׁוֹת; וְאִם אֵין עֵדִים וְהַתְרָאָה, חַיָּב כָּרֵת; וּבְשׁוֹגֵג, חַיָּב לְהָבִיא חַטָּאת קְבוּעָה. וּכְבָר כָּתַבְתִּי לְמַעְלָה בְּסֵדֶר וַיִּשְׁמַע יִתְרוֹ [סי׳ כ״ו] שֶׁאִסּוּר עֲבוֹדָה זָרָה הוּא עַל כָּל בְּנֵי הָעוֹלָם בִּכְלָל.

[שֶׁלֹּא לָבוֹא עַל הַזְּכָרִים]

רט שֶׁלֹּא לָבוֹא עַל הַזְּכָרִים, שֶׁנֶּאֱמַר: וְאֶת זָכָר לֹא תִשְׁכַּב מִשְׁכְּבֵי אִשָּׁה, תּוֹעֵבָה הִיא.

וְכָתַב הָרַמְבָּ״ם זִכְרוֹנוֹ לִבְרָכָה: וְנִכְפַּל זֶה הַלָּאו בָּזֶה הָעִנְיָן בְּעַצְמוֹ בְּמָקוֹם אַחֵר, דִּכְתִיב: וְלֹא יִהְיֶה קָדֵשׁ מִבְּנֵי יִשְׂרָאֵל. נִרְאֶה כִּי לֹא הִסְכִּים הָרַב זִכְרוֹנוֹ לִבְרָכָה בְּכָאן עִם מַה שֶּׁתִּרְגֵּם אוּנְקְלוֹס, שֶׁתִּרְגֵּם ״וְלָא יִסַּב גַּבְרָא מִבְּנֵי יִשְׂרָאֵל אִתְּתָא אָמָה״, פֵּרוּשׁ שִׁפְחָה כְנַעֲנִית, אֶלָּא דַעְתּוֹ דְ״לֹא יִהְיֶה קָדֵשׁ״, לֹא יָבוֹא רַק לְתוֹסֶפֶת לָאוִין לְמִשְׁכַּב זָכוּר, כְּמוֹ שֶׁיֵּשׁ כַּמָּה אַזְהָרוֹת בַּתּוֹרָה כְּפוּלוֹת בְּמִלּוֹת שׁוֹנוֹת.

וְרָאִיתִי לָרַמְבָּ״ן זִכְרוֹנוֹ לִבְרָכָה שֶׁלֹּא יַסְכִּים גַּם הוּא בַּלָּאו הַזֶּה עִם הַתִּרְגּוּם, אֲבָל יֹאמַר כִּי לָאו דְ״לֹא יִהְיֶה קָדֵשׁ״ יָבוֹא לְהַזְהִיר שֶׁלֹּא נַנִּיחַ לִהְיוֹת בֵּינֵינוּ, עַם הַקֹּדֶשׁ, קָדֵשׁ, וְהוּא הָאִישׁ הַמְזֻמָּן לִהְיוֹת נִשְׁכָּב מִן הַזְּכָרִים, כַּיָּדוּעַ מֵהֶם בְּאַרְצוֹת הַיִּשְׁמְעֵאלִים עַד הַיּוֹם. וּמִפְּנֵי־כֵן אָמַר ״מִבְּנֵי יִשְׂרָאֵל״ לוֹמַר שֶׁאֵין אֲנַחְנוּ

her defilement will remain by the law of the Torah! As for a woman going to the *mikveh* on the eighth day of her cleanness (or on a later day), MY writes that in our author's view it would not be forbidden on account of "the attachment of her daughter" as explained in the preceding paragraph — because the possibility of transgression described there is too remote a contingency.

47. Although our author has left also this ruling unspecific, it obviously refers only to the seventh of the clean days. After the seven, even if she cohabits and blood appears later in the day, it does not leave her, retroactively, ritually unclean, but merely begins a new period of ritual defilement, since there have been seven full days of cleanness and ritual immersion. Our author follows here the view of R. Aaron haLévi in his *Bedek haBa-yith* (commentary on Rashba, *Torath haBa-yith*, VII 7; ed Josefov 30b; s.v. *garsinan b'niddah*). Other early authorities, including *Tur Yoreh Dé'ah* §197, understand the Talmudic source differently and rule more stringently: that in pressing circumstances the ritual immersion may be in the daytime only after the seven clean days have passed; and immersion during the seventh day is valid only after the fact, having been done, but is not permissible initially even under pressing circumstances.

and leaves some over, as we stated.[10] He is punishable both over legitimate offspring and illegitimate offspring.[12] He is guilty over anyone who issued from his loins [who is descended from him]: sons or daughters, children or grandchildren, and so down without limit.[12] But if one passed his brothers, sisters or parents, or even himself [through the fire], he is free of guilt.[12] The rest of its details are in chapter 7 of the Talmud tractate *Sanhedrin*.

It is in effect in every place and every time, for both man and woman. If someone transgressed this negative precept deliberately, and there were witnesses and a [prior] warning, he would be stoned to death at a time when capital cases are tried; and if there were no witnesses with a warning, he would be punishable by *karéth* [Divine severance of existence]. If it was done unwittingly, he would be obligated to bring a standard unvarying *ḥattath* (sin-offering).[13] I wrote previously, above in *sidrah yithro* (§26), that the ban on idolatry applies to all mankind generally.

[THE PROHIBITION OF CARNAL RELATIONS WITH ANY MALE]

209 not to have carnal connection with males: for it is stated, *And with a male you shall not lie carnally as with a woman; it is an abomination* (Leviticus 18:22).

Now, Rambam of blessed memory wrote,[1] "This injunction was repeated, about this very subject, in another place: for it is written, *neither shall there be a* kadésh *of the sons of Israel* (Deuteronomy 23:18)." Evidently the master of blessed memory does not agree here with the rendering of Onkelos [for the latter verse]: "neither shall a man of the Israelites marry a maidservant"—i.e. a Canaanite (heathen) maidservant;[2] but his view is rather that the verse "neither shall there be a *kadésh*" comes only to add an injunction about male carnal connection, just as there are many injunctions in the Torah which are repeated in different words.

Well, I saw that neither does Ramban of blessed memory agree with the interpretation of Onkelos,[3] but rather states that the injunction "neither shall there be a *kadésh*" is given to adjure us that we should not permit a male prostitute to exist among us, the holy people[4]—i.e. a man prepared to be used by males for carnal relations, such as are known to exist in the lands of the Ishmaelites to this day. Then for this reason does Scripture state, *of the sons of Israel* (*ibid.*): to convey that we

מֻזְהָרִים מִזֶּה בָּאֻמּוֹת, שֶׁאִם הָיָה אֶחָד מִן הָאֻמּוֹת קָדֵשׁ, וַאֲפִלּוּ בֵּינֵינוּ, לֹא הֻזְהַרְנוּ עָלָיו, לְפִי שֶׁלֹּא הֻזְהַרְנוּ בַּאֲחֵרִים זוּלָתֵנוּ אֶלָּא בְּעִנְיַן עֲבוֹדָה זָרָה בִּלְבָד.

וְאַל יִקְשֶׁה עָלֶיךָ, אִם־כֵּן מֵאֵי זֶה מִקְרָא נִלְמַד לָאו לְנַשֵּׂא שִׁפְחָה אִם לֹא נֹאמַר כְּדִבְרֵי הַמְתַרְגֵּם? וְשֶׁמָּא תֹאמַר מִדִּכְתִיב: לֹא תִתְחַתֵּן בָּם, זֶה אֵינוֹ שֶׁהֲרֵי מְפֹרָשׁ בַּגְּמָרָא דִּלְשִׁבְעָה עֲמָמִין הוּא דְּאָתָא, וַעֲלֵיהֶם הוּא דִּכְתִיב; וְדַוְקָא בְּגֵרוּתָן, דְּאִלּוּ בְּגֵיּוּתָן לָא שַׁיָּךְ בְּהוּ לְשׁוֹן חִתּוּן, וּכְמוֹ שֶׁנִּכְתֹּב בְּעֶזְרַת הַשֵּׁם בִּמְקוֹמוֹ בְּסֵדֶר וָאֶתְחַנַּן [סי׳ תכ״ז].

אֲבָל אֶפְשָׁר לוֹמַר שֶׁנִּלְמַד אִסּוּר לְשִׁפְחָה בִּכְלַל אִסּוּר כָּל הָאֻמּוֹת שֶׁאֵינָן יִשְׂרְאֵלִים, שֶׁאָסוּר לְהִדַּבֵּק בָּהֶן, וּכְמוֹ שֶׁדָּרְשׁוּ עֲלֵיהֶם חֲכָמִים: מִדִּכְתִיב ״כִּי יָסִיר אֶת בִּנְךָ מֵאַחֲרַי״, לְרַבּוֹת כָּל הַמְּסִירִים; וּכְמוֹ־כֵן שִׁפְחָה כְּנַעֲנִית, מִכֵּיוָן שֶׁאֵינָהּ יִשְׂרְאֵלִית גְּמוּרָה, בִּכְלַל מְסִירִין הִיא, שֶׁהֲרֵי קְצָת מִצְוֹת יֵשׁ שֶׁהִיא אֵינָהּ חַיֶּבֶת בָּהֶן, וְהֵן אוֹתָן שֶׁכָּתוּב בָּהֶן בְּפֵרוּשׁ בַּפָּרָשָׁה ״דַּבֵּר אֶל בְּנֵי יִשְׂרָאֵל״, לְמַעוֹטֵי כָּל שֶׁאֵינוֹ מִבְּנֵי־יִשְׂרָאֵל, כְּמוֹ שֶׁמְּפֹרָשׁ בַּגְּמָרָא בְּמִקְצָת מְקוֹמוֹת, וּבִכְלַל מְסִירִין הוּא בְּכָךְ.

נִמְצָא לְפִי דְבָרֵינוּ כִּי פֵרוּשׁ הַמְתַרְגֵּם אֱמֶת, כִּי יֵשׁ בַּשִּׁפְחָה לָאו, אֶלָּא שֶׁאָנוּ לְמֵדִים אוֹתוֹ מִמָּקוֹם אַחֵר. וְהָרַמְבָּ״ן זִכְרוֹנוֹ לִבְרָכָה יַחְשֹׁב לָאו דְּ״לֹא יִהְיֶה קָדֵשׁ״ לְבַל נַנִּיחַ בֵּינֵינוּ אִישׁ מְזֻמָּן לִזְנוּת כְּדֶרֶךְ הַיִּשְׁמְעֵאלִים, כְּמוֹ שֶׁאָמַרְנוּ; וְלָרַמְבָּ״ם זִכְרוֹנוֹ לִבְרָכָה אֵין לוֹ בָּזֶה לָאו, וְלָכֵן כָּתַב כִּי לֹא בָא הַפָּסוּק רַק לְחִזּוּק אַזְהָרָה שֶׁלֹּא לָבוֹא עַל הַזְּכָרִים, כְּמוֹ שֶׁכָּתַבְנוּ.

וְזֶה לְשׁוֹנוֹ שֶׁכָּתַב בְּזֶה הָעִנְיָן: וְזֶהוּ הַדַּעַת הָאֲמִתִּית שֶׁזֶּה הַלָּאו נִכְפַּל לְחִזּוּק,

48. Explained in §121.

§208 1. I.e. some, but not all: as our author notes in the sixth paragraph, if all the sons are given, the prescribed punishment is not imposed. (This paragraph is based on ShM negative precept §7.)

2. A euphemism for their idol.

3. So Ramban, commentary, Leviticus 18:21.

4. TJ Sanhedrin vii 10.

5. Rashi, TB Sanhedrin 64b, s.v. *sh'raga*; MT *hilchoth 'avodath kochavim* vi 3, and ShM negative precept §7.

6. Commentary, Leviticus 18:21.

7. Ramban, commentary, Leviticus 20:5.

8. Explained in §26.

9. I.e. it is not a particular idol, thus worshipped, but a way of adoration toward any idol.

10. So TB Sanhedrin 64b.

11. Literally, commentators, authors of Talmudic commentaries.

are not adjured about this in regard to the nations; if someone of the nations should be a male prostitute, even among us, we are not cautioned about him. For we were not enjoined about others, apart from ourselves, except in regard to idol-worship alone.

Now, let this not be a difficulty in your eyes: In that case, from which verse will we learn an injunction against marrying a [heathen] slave-woman, if we will not accept the teaching of Onkelos?[5] Perhaps you would say, because it is written, *neither shall you make marriage with them* (Deuteronomy 7:3)?—this cannot be: for it is explained in the Talmud that this is stated in regard to the seven nations;[6] about them was it written, and specifically in the event of their conversion to Judaism. For if they remain heathen, the term "marriage" is not applicable to them, as we will write, with the Eternal Lord's help, in its proper place in *sidrah va'eth-ḥanan* (§427).

It may be said, however, that we can learn the prohibition on a slave-woman from the general ban on all peoples that are not Israelites, it being forbidden to form any bonds with them—as the Sages deduced about them:[7] Since it is written, *For he will turn away your son from following Me* (Deuteronomy 7:4), that enlarges the prohibition to include all who would mislead them. Hence a Canaanite slave-woman is included too: as she is not fully an Israelite woman, she is yet included among those who would mislead us. For you see, there are some precepts which she is not obligated to observe: i.e. those for which it is written explicitly, *Speak to the Israelites*—to exclude anyone who is not of the Israelites—as it is explained in the Talmud in a few places. Hence, because of this, she is included among those who would mislead.

Thus we can conclude, according to our words, that the explanation of Onkelos contains truth: there is an injunction about a heathen slave-woman; only, we derive it from another place. On the other hand, Ramban of blessed memory reckons the negative precept, *neither shall there be a* kadésh (Deuteronomy 23:18), to denote that we should not allow among us any man available for immorality, in the way of the Ishmaelites, as we mentioned. For Rambam of blessed memory, though, there is no negative precept for that; and he therefore wrote that the verse was given only to reinforce the admonition not to have carnal connection with males, as we have written.

Now, these are his words, which he wrote on this subject:[1] This is the true exposition—that this prohibition [of a *kadésh*] was repeated to reinforce it, and not that it should be an admonition to

לֹא שֶׁיִּהְיֶה אַזְהָרָה לַנִּשְׁכָּב, שֶׁמֵּאָמְרוֹ "לֹא תִשְׁכַּב" נִלְמַד אַזְהָרָה לַשּׁוֹכֵב וְנִשְׁכָּב. וּבִגְמָרָא סַנְהֶדְרִין נִתְבָּאֵר שֶׁרַבִּי יִשְׁמָעֵאל הוּא שֶׁיָּשִׂים "לֹא יִהְיֶה קָדֵשׁ" אַזְהָרָה לַנִּשְׁכָּב, וּלְדַעְתּוֹ הַבָּא עַל הַזָּכוּר וְהֵבִיא זָכוּר עָלָיו בִּידִיעָה אַחַת חַיָּב שְׁתַּיִם, וְרַבִּי עֲקִיבָא אוֹמֵר אֵינוֹ צָרִיךְ; הֲרֵי הוּא אוֹמֵר "וְאֶת זָכָר לֹא תִשְׁכַּב מִשְׁכְּבֵי אִשָּׁה", קְרֵי בֵּיהּ לֹא תִשָּׁכֵב; וּלְפִיכָךְ הַבָּא עַל הַזָּכוּר וְהֵבִיא זָכוּר עָלָיו בִּידִיעָה אַחַת אֶצְלוֹ, אֵינוֹ חַיָּב אֶלָּא אַחַת, וְאָמְרוּ בַּטַּעַם הַהוּא: לֹא תִשְׁכַּב וְלֹא תִשָּׁכֵב חֲדָא הִיא. עַד כָּאן.

מִשָּׁרְשֵׁי הַמִּצְוָה, לְפִי שֶׁהַשֵּׁם בָּרוּךְ הוּא חָפֵץ בְּיִשּׁוּב עוֹלָמוֹ אֲשֶׁר בָּרָא, וְלָכֵן יְצַוֵּם לְבַל יַשְׁחִיתוּ זַרְעָם בְּמִשְׁכְּבֵי הַזְּכָרִים; כִּי הוּא בֶּאֱמֶת הַשְׁחָתָה, שֶׁאֵין בַּדָּבָר תּוֹעֶלֶת פְּרִי וְלֹא מִצְוַת עוֹנָה, מִלְּבַד שֶׁעִנְיָן אוֹתוֹ טִנּוּף נִמְאָס וּמְכֹעָר הוּא מְאֹד בְּעֵינֵי כָּל בַּעַל שֵׂכֶל; וְהָאִישׁ שֶׁנִּבְרָא לַעֲבֹד בּוֹרְאוֹ לֹא רָאוּי לְהִתְנַוֵּל בְּמַעֲשִׂים מְכֹעָרִים כָּאֵלּוּ. וּמִזֶּה הַשֹּׁרֶשׁ אָמְרוּ זִכְרוֹנָם לִבְרָכָה שֶׁאָסוּר לְהַשִּׂיא אִשָּׁה לְקָטָן, דִּכְעֵין זְנוּת הוּא; וְכֵן שֶׁלֹּא יִשָּׂא אָדָם זְקֵנָה וַעֲקָרָה שֶׁאֵינָהּ רְאוּיָה לֵילֵד.

מִדִּינֵי הַמִּצְוָה, מַה שֶּׁאָמְרוּ זִכְרוֹנָם לִבְרָכָה שֶׁהַבָּא עַל הַזָּכוּר אוֹ הֵבִיא זָכוּר עָלָיו, אִם שְׁנֵיהֶם גְּדוֹלִים נִסְקָלִין; וְאִם הָיָה הָאֶחָד גָּדוֹל וְהָאֶחָד קָטָן עַד תֵּשַׁע שָׁנִים וְיוֹם אֶחָד, שְׁנֵיהֶם פְּטוּרִין מִדְּאוֹרַיְתָא, וּמַכִּין הַגָּדוֹל מַכַּת מַרְדּוּת מִדְּרַבָּנָן; וְאִם הָיָה הָאֶחָד קָטָן שֶׁלֹּא הִגִּיעַ לִכְלַל שְׁלֹשׁ־עֶשְׂרֵה שָׁנָה וְיוֹם אֶחָד, אֲבָל מִכָּל־מָקוֹם הוּא מִתֵּשַׁע שָׁנִים וְיוֹם אֶחָד וּלְמַעְלָה, הַגָּדוֹל נִסְקָל בֵּין שֶׁבָּא עָלָיו אוֹ הֱבִיאוֹ עַל עַצְמוֹ, וְהַקָּטָן פָּטוּר מִדְּאוֹרַיְתָא וּמַכִּין אוֹתוֹ מִדְּרַבָּנָן.

12. *Ibid.* 64a.
13. Explained in §121.

§209 1. ShM negative precept §350.
2. Even though they observe most precepts which are binding on a Jewish woman; see §207, note 6.
3. Literally, with the *Targum*—i.e. with the Aramaic translation of Onkelos.
4. Ramban, commentary, Deuteronomy 23:18.
5. Literally, if we will not say as the words of the translator; see note 3.
6. That occupied Canaan, whom the Israelites were commanded to extirpate; TB Kiddushin 68b, 'Avodah Zarah 36b.
7. TB Kiddushin 68b.
8. Since both prohibitions are derived from one verse.
9. So the oldest manuscript: *tinnuf*; in the subsequent manuscripts and all printed editions it was changed (probably inadvertently) to *tiruf*, "something daft."
10. TB Sanhedrin 76b.
11. Derived from TB Yevamoth 68b.
12. TB Sanhedrin 54a.
13. See §24, note 14.

the passive participant. For from Scripture's words, *you shall not lie carnally*, we learn an injunction for both the active and the passive participant. In the Talmud tractate *Sanhedrin* (54b) it is explained that it is R. Ishmael who would understand the verse, *neither shall there be a* kadésh, as an injunction to the passive participant. To his mind, if one lies carnally with a male and has a male lie carnally with him in one [state of un]awareness, he incurs two penalties. However, R. 'Akiva says: This is not necessary; here Scripture says, *with a male* lo tishkav, *you shall not lie carnally, as with a woman*; read it as *lo tishachav*, in the passive tense—you shall not have a male lie carnally with you. Therefore if one thus lies with a male and has a male lie with him in one deliberate act, he incurs no more than one penalty.[8] And they said in elucidation of this: *lo tishkav* and *lo tishachav* are but one injunction. Thus far his words.

At the root of the precept lies the reason that the Eternal Lord, blessed is He, desires the settlement of the world He created. Therefore He commanded us that human seed should not be destroyed by carnal relations with males: for this is indeed destruction, since there can be no fruitful benefit of offspring from it, nor the fulfillment of the religious duty of conjugal rights [due one's wife]—this apart from the fact that the nature of this filthy business[9] is very repulsive and loathsome in the eyes of every intelligent human being. It is [simply] not fitting that a man, created to serve his Maker, should become perverted by these ugly deeds. And for this root reason, our Sages of blessed memory said[10] it is forbidden to marry a woman to a small boy, for it is akin to immorality. So too should a man not marry an old or a sterile woman, who is not fit (able) to bear a child.[11]

Among the laws of the precept, there is what the Sages of blessed memory taught:[12] that if someone lies carnally with a male or has a male lie carnally with him, if both are adults they are to be stoned to death. If one was an adult and one a child, until nine years and a day, both are free of penalty by the law of the Torah,[12] but the adult is whipped with lashes for disobedience, by decree of the Sages.[13] If one of them was a minor, not having reached the age of thirteen years and a day, but he was, however, nine years and a day or more, the adult is to be put to death by stoning, whether he lay carnally with the boy or had the boy thus lie with him; and the boy is free of penalty by the law of the Torah, but he is given a whipping by decree of the Sages.[14]

וְאֶחָד הַבָּא עַל הַזָּכוּר אוֹ הַבָּא עַל אַנְדְּרוֹגִינוֹס דֶּרֶךְ זַכְרוּת חַיָּב; אֲבָל דֶּרֶךְ נַקְבוּתוֹ פָּטוּר מִדְּאוֹרַיְתָא וּמַכִּין אוֹתוֹ מִדְּרַבָּנָן; הַטּוּמְטוּם סָפֵק יֵשׁ בּוֹ, וּלְפִיכָךְ אָסוּר מִדְּרַבָּנָן; וְאַנְדְּרוֹגִינוֹס מֻתָּר לִשָּׂא אִשָּׁה; וּמִפְּנֵי חֲשַׁשׁ מִשְׁכַּב זָכוּר אָסְרוּ זִכְרוֹנָם לִבְרָכָה שֶׁלֹּא לִמְסֹר תִּינוֹק יִשְׂרָאֵל לְגוֹי לְלַמְּדוֹ סֵפֶר אוֹ אֻמָּנוּת, מִפְּנֵי שֶׁכֻּלָּן חֲשׁוּדִין עַל מִשְׁכַּב זָכוּר; וְיֶתֶר פְּרָטֶיהָ, בְּסוֹף הַסֵּדֶר כָּתוּב מְקוֹמָן.

וְנוֹהֵג אִסּוּר זֶה בְּכָל מָקוֹם וּבְכָל זְמָן. וְעוֹבֵר עָלָיו, מִכֵּיוָן שֶׁהֶעֱרָה, כְּלוֹמַר שֶׁהִכְנִיס רֹאשׁ הָעֲטָרָה בִּלְבַד, חַיָּב סְקִילָה, כְּמוֹ שֶׁאָמַרְנוּ; וְאִם אֵין עֵדִים וְהַתְרָאָה חַיָּב כָּרֵת בְּמֵזִיד; בְּשׁוֹגֵג חַיָּב לְהָבִיא חַטָּאת.

וְזֹאת מִן הָעֲרָיוֹת שֶׁנִּצְטַוּוּ עָלֶיהָ כָּל בְּנֵי־הָעוֹלָם בִּכְלָל, בֵּין יִשְׂרָאֵל אוֹ כָּל שְׁאָר הָאֻמּוֹת. וְכָתַב הָרַמְבָּ״ם זִכְרוֹנוֹ לִבְרָכָה שֶׁנִּרְאָה בְּעֵינָיו כִּי אֲפִלּוּ עֲבָדִים כְּנַעֲנִיִּים יֶשְׁנָן בִּכְלַל אִסּוּר זֶה שֶׁל זָכוּר, וְנֶהֱרָגִין עָלָיו. אַף־עַל־פִּי שֶׁאֵינָן בִּכְלַל אִסּוּר עֲרָיוֹת שֶׁל קֻרְבָה, שֶׁהֵן מֻתָּרִין אֲפִלּוּ בְּאִמָּם וַאֲחוֹתָם, לְפִי שֶׁהֵם יָצְאוּ מִכְּלַל גּוֹיִים וְלִכְלַל יִשְׂרָאֵל לֹא בָאוּ, אַף־עַל־פִּי־כֵן אִסּוּר זָכוּר, וְכֵן אִסּוּר בְּהֵמָה, שָׁוֶה בְּכָל אָדָם.

[שֶׁלֹּא לִשְׁכַּב עִם הַבְּהֵמוֹת]

רי שֶׁלֹּא לִשְׁכַּב עִם הַבְּהֵמוֹת, בֵּין שֶׁבָּא הָאִישׁ עַל הַבְּהֵמָה אוֹ שֶׁהֵבִיא בְּהֵמָה עָלָיו, הַכֹּל בִּכְלָל, וּבִכְלַל ״בְּהֵמָה״ חַיָּה גַּם־כֵּן — שֶׁנֶּאֱמַר: וּבְכָל בְּהֵמָה לֹא תִתֵּן שְׁכָבְתְּךָ.

מִשָּׁרְשֵׁי הַמִּצְוָה, שֶׁהַשֵּׁם בָּרוּךְ הוּא חָפֵץ שֶׁיִּהְיוּ כָּל הַמִּינִין שֶׁבָּרָא בְּעוֹלָמוֹ עוֹשִׂין פֵּרוֹת לְמִינֵיהֶן, וּכְמוֹ שֶׁבָּא בַכָּתוּב בִּתְחִלַּת הַבְּרִיאָה, שֶׁכָּתוּב בְּכָל מִין וָמִין

14. Similarly MT *hilchoth g'névah* i 10.
15. TB Yevamoth 83b; MT *hilchoth 'issuré bi'ah* i 15.
16. So TB Ḥagigah 4a, etc.
17. Following a rule of MT *hilchoth tum'ath méth* ix 12.
18. TB Yevamoth 81a.
19. TB 'Avodah Zarah 15b.
20. MT *hilchoth 'issuré bi'ah* xiv 18.
21. Since they are owned by Jews, they can become obligated to observe the same precepts as a Jewish woman, if their owner has them undergo ritual immersion; and upon being freed they can become proselytes by another ritual immersion.
22. As they become Israelite to a certain extent (see note 21), their previous family ties are rendered null and void.
23. TB Sanhedrin 58b.

§210 1. So TB Sanhedrin 54b.
2. So TB Ḥullin 71a.
3. E.g. Genesis 1:11, 21, 24.

Whether a person lay carnally with a male or with a hermaphrodite participating as a male, he is equally guilty; but if the latter participated as a female, he is free of guilt by the Torah's law, but receives punishment by decree of the Sages.[15] A *tumtum* is one whose gender is in doubt;[16] he is therefore forbidden by the ruling of the Sages.[17] A hermaphrodite, though, is permitted to marry a woman.[18] On account of a suspicion of homosexuality, the Sages of blessed memory forbade leaving a Jewish child with a heathen to teach him the art of reading or a craft: for they are all suspect about homosexuality.[19] As to the rest of its details, their location is written at the end of the *sidrah* (§211).

This prohibition is in force everywhere, at every time. If someone violates it, once he begins the carnal intimacy, i.e. he intromits the corona alone, he is punishable by a death sentence of stoning, as we stated. If, however, there were no witnesses and a warning, he incurs *karéth* [Divine severance of existence] if it was willful; and if it was inadvertent, he is duty-bound to bring a *ḥattath* (sin-offering).

This is one of the forbidden kinds of relationship about which all mankind generally was commanded, whether Israelites or any other peoples. And Rambam of blessed memory wrote[20] that as he saw it, even Canaanite (heathen) slaves[21] are included under this ban on the male, and they are to be put to death for it. Even though they are not included under the ban on forbidden consanguineous relations, as they are permitted to marry even their mothers and sisters[22]—since they left the category of heathen and did not enter the category of Israelite as yet[23]—nevertheless, the prohibition about a male, and so too the ban on an animal (§210), is the same for all people.

[THE PROHIBITION OF CARNAL RELATIONS WITH ANIMALS]

210 not to have forbidden relations with animals: whether a man lies carnally with a beast or has a beast lie carnally with him, all is included [under the prohibition];[1] and in the general category of "beast" the wild animal is equally included.[2] For it is stated, *And you shall not lie carnally with any beast* (Leviticus 18:23).

At the root of the precept lies the reason that the Eternal Lord, blessed is He, desires that all the species He created in His world should "bear fruit" (offspring) of their kind, as we find in Scripture, at the start of creation, that it is written about every species, *after its kind.*[3] And

"לְמִינֵהוּ". וּמֵהְיוֹת חֶפְצוֹ בָּרוּךְ הוּא בָּזֶה לֹא תִמָּצֵא הַבְּרָכָה וְהַגְּדֻלָּה בְּמַה שֶּׁהוּא בְּהֶפֶךְ, כְּמוֹ שֶׁיָּדוּעַ לָנוּ בִּפְרָדוֹת, שֶׁבָּאוֹת מִתַּעֲרֹבֶת שְׁנֵי מִינִין, שֶׁאֵינָן פָּרוֹת וְרָבוֹת; וְכֵן כָּל אִילָן הַמֻּרְכָּב מִשְּׁנֵי מִינֵי אִילָנוֹת לֹא יִצְלַח לַעֲשׂוֹת פְּרִי כָּמוֹהוּ; וְכָל־שֶׁכֵּן בְּמִין הָאָדָם, שֶׁהוּא מֻבְחַר כָּל הַמִּינִים, שֶׁאֵין רָאוּי שֶׁיִּתְעָרֵב בְּמִין הַבְּהֵמָה, הַפָּחוּת וְהַגָּרוּעַ.

מִדִּינֵי הַמִּצְוָה, מַה שֶּׁפֵּרְשׁוּ זִכְרוֹנָם לִבְרָכָה שֶׁאֵין חִלּוּק בָּזֶה בֵּין בְּהֵמָה גְדוֹלָה לִקְטַנָּה, שֶׁנֶּאֱמַר: וּבְכָל בְּהֵמָה, כְּלוֹמַר אֲפִלּוּ בְּיוֹם לֵידָתָהּ; וְאֵין חִלּוּק בֵּין הַבָּא עָלֶיהָ כְּדַרְכָּהּ אוֹ שֶׁלֹּא כְדַרְכָּהּ, בְּכָל עִנְיָן, מִכֵּיוָן שֶׁהֶעֱרָה בָהּ כְּלוֹמַר כְּשֶׁהִכְנִיס רֹאשׁ הָעֲטָרָה אוֹ הֶעֱרַת הַבְּהֵמָה בוֹ, שְׁנֵיהֶם נִסְקָלִים, הוּא וְהִיא, אִם הוּא גָדוֹל, כְּלוֹמַר שֶׁהִגִּיעַ לִכְלַל עֳנָשִׁין, וְהוּא מֵזִיד; אֲבָל בְּשׁוֹגֵג אֵין הַבְּהֵמָה נִסְקֶלֶת; וְאִם יֵשׁ לוֹ מִתֵּשַׁע שָׁנִים וְיוֹם אֶחָד וָמַעְלָה, הַבְּהֵמָה נִסְקֶלֶת עַל יָדוֹ וְהוּא פָּטוּר עַד שֶׁיַּגִּיעַ לִכְלַל עֳנָשִׁין; וּמִכָּל־מָקוֹם רָאוּי לְיַסְּרוֹ; וְאִם הוּא פָּחוּת מִתֵּשַׁע שָׁנִים וְיוֹם אֶחָד, אֲפִלּוּ הַבְּהֵמָה אֵינָהּ נִסְקֶלֶת עַל יָדוֹ; וְיֶתֶר פְּרָטֶיהָ, בְּסוֹף הַסֵּדֶר נִכְתַּב מְקוֹמָן בְּעֶזְרַת הַשֵּׁם.

וְנוֹהֵג אִסּוּר זֶה בְּכָל מָקוֹם וּבְכָל זְמַן. וְעוֹבֵר עָלֶיהָ בְּמֵזִיד וְיֵשׁ עֵדִים וְהַתְרָאָה, נִסְקָל, כְּמוֹ שֶׁאָמַרְנוּ; וְאִם אֵין עֵדִים, בְּכָרֵת; בְּשׁוֹגֵג חַיָּב לְהָבִיא חַטָּאת קְבוּעָה בִּזְמַן הַבַּיִת.

[שֶׁלֹּא תִשְׁכַּבְנָה הַנָּשִׁים עִם הַבְּהֵמוֹת]

ריא שֶׁלֹּא תִשְׁכַּבְנָה הַנָּשִׁים עִם הַבְּהֵמוֹת, שֶׁנֶּאֱמַר: וְאִשָּׁה לֹא תַעֲמֹד לִפְנֵי בְהֵמָה לְרִבְעָהּ. וְכָתַב הָרַמְבַּ"ם זִכְרוֹנוֹ לִבְרָכָה שֶׁזּוֹ מִצְוָה בִּפְנֵי עַצְמָהּ בְּחֶשְׁבּוֹן הַמִּצְווֹת וְאֵינָהּ נִכְנֶסֶת בִּכְלַל הַמִּצְוָה שֶׁלְּפָנֶיהָ, לְפִי שֶׁאִסּוּר הַזָּכָר לָבוֹא עַל

4. Donkey and horse.
5. TB Sanhedrin 55a.
6. Based on *ibid.* 55b.
7. I.e. if he acted willfully; then there is the same reason for stoning the beast as in the case of an adult: that people should not say, "This is the creature with which so-and-so came to grief" (see § 211, eighth paragraph); *ibid.*
8. See § 209, note 14.
9. Explained in § 121.

§211 1. ShM negative precept § 349.

since this constitutes His desire (blessed is He), no blessing or aspect of greatness will be found in anything that is the opposite of it—as we know of mules, which come from the union of two species,[4] and they cannot bear offspring. So too, any tree that is produced by grafting two species of trees together, will not succeed in producing fruit of its own kind. Then all the more certainly is it true about the human species, the most chosen one of all the species, that it is not proper for it to be joined with an animal species, which is inferior and deficient.

Among the laws of the precept, there is what the Sages of blessed memory explained:[1] that in this regard there is no difference [in law] between an old and a young animal; for it is stated, *with any beast*—in other words, even on the day it is born. And there is no difference in this regard whether one had natural connection with it or unnatural connection, in any way whatever:[5] Once he began the relationship with it, i.e. intromitted the corona, or had the animal do so, both are to be stoned to death, he and it, if he is an adult, which means if he reached the age for punishments,[5] and he acted willfully; but if it was done unwittingly, the beast is not to be stoned to death.[6] Yet, if he is nine years and a day old or more, the beast is to be stoned to death because of him,[7] while he is free of penalty until he reaches the age for punishment. Nevertheless, it is fitting to chastise him.[8] If he was younger than nine years and a day, then even the stoning of the animal is not done on his account.[1] As to the rest of its laws, at the end of the *sidrah* (§211) we will write their location, with the Eternal Lord's help.

This prohibition is in force in every place, at every time. If a person transgressed it willfully and there were witnesses and a warning, he should be stoned to death, as we stated. If there were no witnesses, it is punishable by *karéth* [Divine severance of existence]. If it was done unwittingly, he is obligated to bring a standard unvarying *ḥattath* (sin-offering)[9] when the Temple is in existence.

[THE PROHIBITION ON CARNAL INTIMACY BY A WOMAN WITH AN ANIMAL]

211 that women should not lie carnally with animals: for it is stated, *neither shall any woman stand before a beast to have it lie with her* (Leviticus 18:23). Rambam of blessed memory wrote[1] that this is a separate precept in the reckoning of the precepts, and is not included under the precept before it—because the ban on a man not to lie

הַבְּהֵמָה וְאִסּוּר הָאִשָּׁה שֶׁלֹּא תָבִיא הַבְּהֵמָה עָלֶיהָ, שְׁנֵי אִסּוּרִין חֲלוּקִין הֵן, וְלוּלֵי הַלָּאו שֶׁבָּא עֲלֵיהֶן בְּפֵרוּשׁ לֹא הָיוּ נִלְמָדִין זֶה מִזֶּה. וְהֵבִיא רְאָיָה מִמַּה שֶּׁאָמְרוּ זִכְרוֹנָם לִבְרָכָה בְּפֶרֶק רִאשׁוֹן מִכְּרֵתוֹת: שְׁלֹשִׁים וָשֵׁשׁ כְּרֵתוֹת יֵשׁ בַּתּוֹרָה, וּמָנוּ אוֹתָן, וּמָנוּ בִכְלָלָן הַבָּא עַל הַבְּהֵמָה לְאֶחָד וְהָאִשָּׁה הַמְּבִיאָה הַבְּהֵמָה עַל עַצְמָהּ לְאַחֵר, עִם הֱיוֹתָם מוֹנִים שָׁם כְּלָלֵי הָעִנְיָנִים.

שֹׁרֶשׁ מִצְוָה זוֹ עִם שֶׁלְּפָנֶיהָ בִּכְלָל.

מִדִּינֵי הַמִּצְוָה, מַה שֶּׁאָמְרוּ זִכְרוֹנָם לִבְרָכָה שֶׁאִשָּׁה גְדוֹלָה, כְּלוֹמַר שֶׁהִגִּיעָה לִכְלַל עֳנָשִׁין, שֶׁהִיא בַּת י״ב שָׁנָה וְיוֹם אֶחָד, שֶׁהֵבִיאָה בְּהֵמָה עָלֶיהָ, בֵּין גְּדוֹלָה בֵּין קְטַנָּה — כֵּיוָן שֶׁהֶעֱרָת בָּהּ, בֵּין כְּדַרְכָּהּ בֵּין שֶׁלֹּא כְדַרְכָּהּ, שְׁתֵּיהֶן נִסְקָלוֹת, הִיא וְהַבְּהֵמָה; וְאִם הָאִשָּׁה קְטַנָּה, כְּלוֹמַר פְּחוּתָה מִי״ב שָׁנָה וְיוֹם אֶחָד, הַבְּהֵמָה נִסְקֶלֶת וְהִיא פְּטוּרָה, וְרָאוּי לְיַסְּרָהּ; וְאִם הִיא פְּחוּתָה מִשָּׁלֹשׁ שָׁנִים וְיוֹם אֶחָד, אֲפִלּוּ הַבְּהֵמָה אֵינָהּ נִסְקֶלֶת עַל יָדָהּ; וְיֶתֶר פְּרָטֶיהָ, עִם פְּרָטֵי הָעֲרָיוֹת הַכְּתוּבִים בְּסֵדֶר זֶה, בֵּין עִנְיַן הָאִסּוּר שֶׁבָּהֶן וְחִלּוּקֵיהֶן בֵּין חִלּוּקֵי מִשְׁפְּטֵי הָעוֹבְרִים, הַכֹּל בְּמַסֶּכֶת סַנְהֶדְרִין וּבְמַסֶּכֶת כְּרֵתוֹת וּבִמְקוֹמוֹת מִן יְבָמוֹת וּכְתֻבּוֹת וְקִדּוּשִׁין.

וְכָתַב הָרַמְבַּ״ם זִכְרוֹנוֹ לִבְרָכָה שֶׁאֵלֶּה הָעֲרָיוֹת שֶׁכָּתַבְנוּ בָהֶן שֶׁהֵן בְּכָרֵת, בָּא עֲלֵיהֶן הַכָּרֵת בִּלְשׁוֹן הַתּוֹרָה מְבֹאָר, וּכְמוֹ שֶׁאָמַר הַכָּתוּב אַחַר מִנְיָנָם: כִּי כָּל אֲשֶׁר יַעֲשֶׂה מִכֹּל הַתּוֹעֵבוֹת הָאֵלֶּה וְנִכְרְתוּ הַנְּפָשׁוֹת הָעֹשֹׂת; וּכְמוֹ־כֵן כָּל אֲשֶׁר כָּתַבְנוּ בָהֶן שֶׁהָעוֹבֵר עֲלֵיהֶן חַיָּב מִיתַת בֵּית־דִּין, הוּא כְּמוֹ־כֵן לְשׁוֹן הַתּוֹרָה. אָמְנָם הִתְחַלֵּף הַמִּיתָה וְאָמַרְנוּ בִקְצָתָן סְקִילָה וּבִקְצָתָן חֶנֶק וּבִקְצָתָן שְׂרֵפָה, יֵשׁ מֵהֶן מִן הַכָּתוּב וְיֵשׁ מֵהֶן בַּקַּבָּלָה.

וְכָל הָעֲרָיוֹת כֻּלָּן שֶׁהָיָה אֶחָד גָּדוֹל וְאֶחָד קָטָן, הַגָּדוֹל חַיָּב וְהַקָּטָן פָּטוּר, כְּמוֹ

2. As Rambam declares in his commentary on the Mishnah, K'rithoth i 1.
3. TB Sanhedrin 55a.
4. TB Sanhedrin 55b.
5. See §209, note 14.
6. ShM negative precept §352.

carnally with an animal and the ban on a woman not to have an animal lie carnally with her, are two different prohibitions, and if explicit injunctions were not given for them, one could not be learned from the other. He brought proof from what the Sages of blessed memory taught in the first chapter of the Talmud tractate *K'rithoth* (2a): There are thirty-six transgressions in the Torah punishable by *karéth* [Divine severance of existence]—and they then listed them, including among them one who lies carnally with an animal as one transgression, and a woman who has an animal lie thus with her as another, despite the fact that they list there [only] the general categories.[2]

The root reason for this precept [was given] together with the one before it.

Among the laws of the precept, there is what the Sages of blessed memory taught:[3] if a grown girl; i.e. who has reached the age for punishment, which is twelve years and a day, made an animal, whether old or young, lie carnally with her, once it began intimacy with her, whether in a natural or unnatural way, the two of them are to be stoned to death—both she and the beast. If the girl was a child, i.e. younger than twelve years and a day, the animal is to be stoned, and she is free of penalty;[4] but it is proper to chastise her.[5] If she was younger than three years and a day, not even the beast is stoned on her account.[4] The rest of its details, along with details of all forbidden conjugal relationships written in this *sidrah*, both concerning their prohibition and their differences, as well as differences in the sentences for transgressors, are all in the Talmud tractates *Sanhedrin* and *K'rithoth*, and in certain places in *Yevamoth*, *K'thuboth* and *Kiddushin*.

Now, Rambam of blessed memory wrote[6] that for these forbidden conjugal relationships about which we noted that they are punishable by *karéth* [Divine severance of existence], the penalty of *karéth* is expressed clearly in the language of the Writ: as Scripture states after listing them, *For whoever shall do any of these abominations, the souls that do them shall be cut off* (Leviticus 18:29). Similarly, in all cases where we wrote that whoever transgresses them deserves death by sentence of the *beth din*, it is likewise the instruction of the Torah. However, the death sentence varies, and so we mentioned stoning for some, strangulation for others, and burning for still others. Some of these are [known] from Scripture, and some from the Oral Tradition.

In all these forbidden conjugal relationships, if one was grown and the other was a child, the grown one is guilty and the child is free

שֶׁאָמַרְנוּ לְמַעְלָה; וְכֵן אִם הָיוּ שְׁנֵיהֶם גְּדוֹלִים וְהָאֶחָד יָשֵׁן, הַיָּשֵׁן פָּטוּר, אַף־עַל־פִּי שֶׁאֶפְשָׁר שֶׁנֶּהֱנָה קְצָת בְּעוֹדוֹ יָשֵׁן.

וּבְכָל הָעֲרָיוֹת, וְכֵן בְּכָל שְׁאָר הָעֲבֵרוֹת שֶׁיָּבוֹא עֲלֵיהֶם חִיּוּב בֵּית־דִּין, צָרִיךְ שֶׁיִּהְיֶה שָׁם שְׁנֵי עֵדִים כְּשֵׁרִים אוֹ יוֹתֵר מַתְרִין בָּעוֹבֵר, וְרוֹאִין אוֹתוֹ בְּעֵינֵיהֶם עוֹבֵר עַל הָעֲבֵרָה. וּמִכָּל־מָקוֹם בְּעִנְיַן אִסּוּר הָעֲרָיוֹת הוֹרוּנוּ חֲכָמִים שֶׁאֵין צֹרֶךְ שֶׁיִּרְאוּ הָעֵדִים עִנְיַן הַנִּאוּף לְגַמְרֵי, כְּלוֹמַר שֶׁיִּרְאוּ אֶת הַמַּעֲשֶׂה הָרַע כְּמִכְחוֹל שֶׁבִּשְׁפוֹפֶרֶת, אֶלָּא מִכֵּיוָן שֶׁיִּרְאוּ אוֹתָם כִּמְנָאֲפִים, כְּלוֹמַר זֶה בָּזֶה כְּדֶרֶךְ כָּל הַבּוֹעֲלִין, הֲרֵי אֵלּוּ נֶהֱרָגִין בִּרְאִיָּה זוֹ, וְאֵין אוֹמְרִים שֶׁמָּא לֹא הֶעֱרָה, מִפְּנֵי שֶׁחֶזְקַת צוּרָה זוֹ שֶׁהֶעֱרָה.

וְעוֹד אָמְרוּ זִכְרוֹנָם לִבְרָכָה בָּעִנְיָן גַּם־כֵּן שֶׁכָּל מִי שֶׁהֻחְזַק בִּשְׁאֵר־בָּשָׂר, נֶהֱרָג עַל פִּי הַחֲזָקָה, אַף־עַל־פִּי שֶׁאֵין רְאָיָה בְרוּרָה עַל הַקֻּרְבָה אֶלָּא חֲזָקָה לְבָד, שֶׁבְּנֵי־אָדָם אוֹמְרִים: פְּלוֹנִי בֶּן פְּלוֹנִית הוּא, אוֹ אֲחִי פְּלָנִיתָא, אוֹ אָבִיהָ, וּמַלְקִין וְשׂוֹרְפִין וְסוֹקְלִין וְחוֹנְקִין עַל זוֹ הַחֲזָקָה.

וְנוֹהֵג אִסּוּר זֶה בְּכָל מָקוֹם וּבְכָל זְמָן. וְהָעוֹבֶרֶת עָלָיו וְהֵבִיאָה בְהֵמָה עָלֶיהָ חַיֶּבֶת סְקִילָה כְּמוֹ שֶׁאָמַרְנוּ, וְאִם אֵין עֵדִים וְהַתְרָאָה הִיא בְכָרֵת, וּבְשׁוֹגֵג חַיֶּבֶת לְהָבִיא חַטָּאת קְבוּעָה. וּכְבָר אָמַרְנוּ שֶׁבְּכָל שׁוֹגֵג אֵין הַבְּהֵמָה נִסְקֶלֶת; וְאַף־עַל־פִּי שֶׁאָמְרוּ זִכְרוֹנָם לִבְרָכָה בְּטַעַם סְקִילַת הַבְּהֵמָה, כְּדֵי שֶׁלֹּא יֹאמְרוּ בְנֵי־אָדָם: זוֹ הִיא שֶׁנִּכְשַׁל בָּהּ פְּלוֹנִי — זֶה לֹא נֶאֱמַר אֶלָּא בְּמֵזִיד, כִּי הוּא הַכִּשָּׁלוֹן הַגָּדוֹל, אֲבָל שׁוֹגֵג קְצָת אֹנֶס יֵשׁ בּוֹ.

נִמְצָא לְפִי דְבָרֵינוּ שֶׁאֵין אִסּוּר עַל הַגּוֹיִים מִשּׁוּם עֶרְוָה אֶלָּא אֵם וְאֵשֶׁת אָב

7. TB K'rithoth 11a.

8. TB Sanhedrin 40a, Makkoth 6b (this may have been meant as a general rather than a precise statement: according to MT *hilchoth sanhedrin* xii 2, the warning need not be given by two worthy, acceptable witnesses, but rather by anyone).

9. TB Sanhedrin 37a.

10. TB Makkoth 7a.

11. A Talmudic euphemism for the ultimate intimacy; *ibid.*

12. MT *hilchoth 'issuré bi'ah* i 19.

13. TB Kiddushin 30a.

14. MT *ibid.* 20. (Thus if a strange family moves into a neighborhood and lets it be known how its members are related to one another, and they then act and behave accordingly, we consider it established that they are actually so related.)

15. Explained in § 121.

of penalty,[7] as we stated above. So too, if both were grown, but one was sleeping [at the time], the one who slept is free of penalty,[7] even though it is possible that he had some slight pleasure while asleep.

In all instances of forbidden conjugal relationships, and so with all transgressions which deserve a sentence by the *beth din*, it is required that two or more worthy, acceptable witnesses should be there, warning the transgressor,[8] then seeing him with their own eyes committing the sin.[9] However, in regard to forbidden conjugal relations, the Sages instructed us[10] that it is not necessary for the witnesses to see the act of immorality in entirety—in other words, that they should see the evil deed, "like a brush in a tube of eye-paint";[11] rather, once they see them acting like adulterers, i.e. one with another in the way of all who have conjugal relations, they are to be put to death on the strength of this sight. We do not say, "Perhaps he did not effect connection," because the assumption from this posture is that he did.[12]

Our Sages of blessed memory said further in this regard[13] that if anyone has become firmly assumed to be the close relative of another, he may be put to death on the basis of the presumption, even though there is no clear proof about the family relationship, but only the established assumption—i.e. people say, "So-and-so is that woman's son," or "the brother of that woman," or "her father." Whiplashes, or death by burning, stoning or strangulation, may be given on the strength of such a presumption.[14]

This prohibition is in effect everywhere, at every time. If a woman transgressed it and made an animal lie carnally with her, she would be liable to death by stoning, as we said. If there were no witnesses or no warning, she will be punished by *karéth* [Divine severance of existence]. And if the act was unwitting, she is obligated to bring a standard unvarying *ḥattath* (sin-offering).[15] We have stated previously that in every instance of unintentional transgression, the animal is not stoned to death. Even though the Sages of blessed memory said about the reason for stoning the animal that it is in order that people should not say, "This is the one with which that man came to grief"—that was said for none but a case of deliberate wrongdoing, because then it is a major misfortune [of enormous sin]; but if it happened unwittingly, there is some element of accident in it.

We conclude, then, according to our words, that for heathens there is a prohibition of forbidden conjugal relations only in regard to the mother (§190), the father's wife (§191), a sister from one mother

וְאָחוֹת מֵאֵם וְאֵשֶׁת אִישׁ, כְּמוֹ שֶׁכָּתַבְנוּ בְּסֵדֶר וַיִּשְׁמַע יִתְרוֹ, וְזָכוּר וּבְהֵמָה; וְהָעֲבָדִים אֵינָם בִּכְלַל אִסּוּר עֲרָיוֹת שֶׁל קָרְבָה, וּמֻתָּרִין אֲפִלּוּ בְּאִמָּם וַאֲחוֹתָם, וּכְמוֹ שֶׁכָּתַבְנוּ לְמַעְלָה, לְפִי שֶׁכְּבָר יָצְאוּ מִכְּלַל גּוֹיִים וְלִכְלַל יִשְׂרָאֵל לֹא בָאוּ.

וְעוֹד אָמְרוּ זִכְרוֹנָם לִבְרָכָה בְּטַעַם זֶה שֶׁהָעֶבֶד אֵין לוֹ חַיִס, כְּלוֹמַר שֶׁהֲרֵי הוּא כִּבְהֵמָה לְעִנְיָן זֶה; וְהַכָּתוּב הַמּוֹרֶה עַל זֶה מִדִּכְתִיב: שְׁבוּ לָכֶם פֹּה עִם הַחֲמוֹר, וְדָרְשׁוּ זִכְרוֹנָם לִבְרָכָה: עַם הַדּוֹמֶה לַחֲמוֹר, וְהֵם הָיוּ עֲבָדִים שֶׁל אַבְרָהָם אָבִינוּ. וּמִכָּל־מָקוֹם בְּאִסּוּר זָכוּר וּבְהֵמָה הֵן כְּדַעַת הָרַמְבָּ״ם זִכְרוֹנוֹ לִבְרָכָה, וְטַעַם נָכוֹן הוּא, דְּלָא שַׁיָּךְ לוֹמַר בָּזֶה אֵין לוֹ חַיִס. וַאֲסוּרִין גַּם־כֵּן מִלָּבוֹא עַל אֵשֶׁת אִישׁ שֶׁל יִשְׂרָאֵל, דְּלָא שַׁיָּךְ הָכָא גַּם־כֵּן אֵין לוֹ חַיִס.

וְכֵן הֵם אֲסוּרִין עִם הַנִּדָּה, וַאֲפִלּוּ שִׁפְחָה, שֶׁחַיָּבִין הֵן בְּכָל עֳנָשִׁין שֶׁבַּתּוֹרָה. וּבְפֵרוּשׁ דָּרְשׁוּ זִכְרוֹנָם לִבְרָכָה: ״וְאִשָּׁה כִּי תִהְיֶה זָבָה״, בֵּין יִשְׂרְאֵלִית בֵּין שִׁפְחָה בֵּין גִּיּוֹרֶת וּמְשֻׁחְרֶרֶת.

וְאָמְרוּ זִכְרוֹנָם לִבְרָכָה שֶׁאִם נִתְגַּיֵּר אֶחָד מִן הָאֻמּוֹת, וְכֵן עֶבֶד שֶׁנִּשְׁתַּחְרֵר, הֲרֵי הֵן כְּקָטָן שֶׁנּוֹלָד, וְכָל שְׁאֵר־בָּשָׂר שֶׁהָיָה לָהֶן מִתְּחִלָּה בְּגַיּוּת אוֹ בְעַבְדוּת אֵינָן שְׁאֵר־בָּשָׂר לָהֶן כְּלָל, וּמֻתָּר לָהֶן לִשָּׂא אוֹתָם אֲפִלּוּ הֵן אִמָּם אוֹ אֲחוֹתָם, זֶהוּ מִדִּין תּוֹרָה; אֲבָל חֲכָמִים אָסְרוּ הַדָּבָר כְּדֵי שֶׁלֹּא יֹאמְרוּ שֶׁבָּא מִקְּדֻשָּׁה חֲמוּרָה לִקְדֻשָּׁה קַלָּה, וְתִקְּנוּ הַדָּבָר כֵּן שֶׁאִם הָיָה נָשׂוּי כְּשֶׁהוּא גּוֹי אוֹ עֶבֶד לְאִמּוֹ אוֹ לַאֲחוֹתוֹ, מַפְרִישִׁין אוֹתָן, לְפִי שֶׁאֵלּוּ הָיוּ אֲסוּרוֹת אֲפִלּוּ בְגַיּוּת; אֲבָל אִם הָיָה נָשׂוּי לִשְׁאָר עֲרָיוֹת וְנִתְגַּיְּרוּ הוּא וְהֵן, אֵין מַפְרִישִׁין אוֹתָן, לְפִי שֶׁאֵין כָּאן חֲשָׁשׁ שֶׁיֹּאמְרוּ וְכוּלֵי, שֶׁהֲרֵי שְׁאָר הָעֲרָיוֹת מֻתָּרוֹת הָיוּ בְּגַיּוּת.

16. So TB Sanhedrin 58b; see §209, note 21 (this refers to heathen slaves owned by Jews).

17. TB Yevamoth 62a.

18. I.e. the slaves in the verse who were told to "sit with the donkey."

19. MT *hilchoth 'issuré bi'ah* xiv 18.

20. When she is thus impure.

21. So TB Ḥagigah 4a, etc.

22. Sifra on the verse that follows (*m'tzora, zavim, parashah* 5, 1).

23. TB Yevamoth 22a, etc. and 97b.

24. I.e. what was forbidden him as a heathen is permitted him as a Jew; TB Yevamoth 22a ("sister" in this paragraph means one from the same mother; see three paragraphs above).

(§192), another's wife (as we wrote in *sidrah yithro*—§35), a male (§209), and a beast. Slaves are not included under the ban on forbidden consanguineous relations, and are permitted even their mothers and sisters, as we wrote above (§209): because they already left the category of the heathen and did not yet enter the category of Israelites.[16]

Our Sages of blessed memory taught further regarding this theme,[17] that a heathen slave has no recognized family relations; in other words, he is as an animal in this respect. Scripture indicates this with the verse, *sit you here* 'im, *with, the donkey* (Genesis 22:5), which our Sages interpreted[17] as *'am*, a people, that resembles the donkey; and they[18] were the servants owned by our father Abraham. Nevertheless, they are subject to the prohibition on a male and a beast, in the view of Rambam of blessed memory;[19] and this is a point well taken, because it is not relevant to argue in regard to this that "he has no recognized family relations." They are forbidden as well to be conjugally intimate with a married woman, because here too it is irrelevant that "he has no recognized family relations."

They are equally forbidden to be intimate with a woman ritually unclean from the menses, and even with a slave-woman,[20] because they are subject to all the penalties in the Torah.[21] Indeed, our Sages explicitly interpreted,[22] *And when a woman has a discharge* (Leviticus 15:19)—whether she is an Israelite, a slave, a proselyte, or a freed slave.

Then too, our Sages of blessed memory taught[23] that if someone of the nations was converted to Judaism, and so a slave who was set free, they are like a newborn child: and every consanguineous relative that they had originally, while a heathen or during servitude, is no longer a relation of theirs at all. Hence they are allowed to marry them, even if they are their mother or sister—this by the law of the Torah. However, the Sages banned the matter, so that it should not be said, "He went from a greater state of holiness to a lighter state."[24] Thus they made the regulation that if a person was married, while a heathen or a slave, to his mother or sister, he is separated [from her], since these were forbidden [to him] even in the heathen period. But if he was married to any other consanguineous relation, and both he and she were converted to Judaism, they are not [forcibly] separated, since there is no fear here that people will say, "They went from a greater state of holiness to a lighter state," since other consanguineous relations were permitted him while in the heathen state.

For this reason the Sages of blessed memory placed a ban on a

וּמִן הַטַּעַם הַזֶּה לֹא גָּזְרוּ זִכְרוֹנָם לִבְרָכָה בַּגֵּר אֶלָּא בִּשְׁאֵר הָאֵם וְלֹא בִשְׁאֵר הָאָב; וּלְפִיכָךְ אָמְרוּ זִכְרוֹנָם לִבְרָכָה שֶׁגֵּר מֻתָּר לִשָּׂא בִתּוֹ שֶׁנִּתְגַּיְּרָה, וְכֵן אֵשֶׁת אָחִיו מֵאָבִיו אֲבָל לֹא מֵאִמּוֹ, וְכֵן מֻתָּר בְּאֵשֶׁת בְּנוֹ. וּמֻתָּר לוֹ לִשָּׂא שְׁתֵּי אֲחָיוֹת מִן הָאָב אֲבָל לֹא מִן הָאֵם, וְכֵן הַשְּׁנִיּוֹת כֻּלָּן לֹא גָזְרוּ עֲלֵיהֶן בְּגֵרִים.

וְהָעֲבָדִים שֶׁנִּשְׁתַּחְרְרוּ הֲרֵי הֵן כְּגֵרִים וְכָל מַה שֶּׁמֻּתָּר לָהֶן מֻתָּר לָהֶן, וְהוּא הַדִּין בְּאִסּוּר.

25. TB Sanhedrin 58b, Yevamoth 97b (MT *hilchoth 'issuré bi'ah* xiv 13). The reason for all the laws in this paragraph is that such relations were not forbidden to the heathen according to the Torah; by Torah law a heathen has consanguineous kinship only with and through his mother (four paragraphs above; TB Yevamoth 98a); hence the objection stated in note 24 cannot be raised here. The Sages, however, forbade a convert to marry any woman who would be forbidden to an ordinary Jew because of kinship through a common mother, even if such a woman would have been permitted to the convert in his heathen state. Hence (see below) the ban on marrying two sisters from one mother.

26. Who are forbidden to a Jew by the decree of the Sages.

convert only in regard to a consanguineous relation of the mother, but not such a relation of the father. And therefore they (of blessed memory) ruled[25] that a convert is permitted to marry his daughter who has converted to Judaism, and so too a wife of his brother on the father's side, but not on the mother's side. So is he permitted to take his son's wife; and he is allowed to marry two sisters from one father, but not two sisters from one mother. Similarly, the Sages imposed no ban on "secondary ones"[26] for converts.

Slaves who were set free are like converts [under the law]. Whatever is permitted these is permitted those; and the same rule holds for what is forbidden.